AMERICA a Portrait in History

Prentice-Hall, Inc., Englewood Cliffs, New Jersey

AMERICA
a Portrait in History

DAVID BURNER
State University of New York at Stony Brook

ROBERT D. MARCUS
State University of New York at Stony Brook

EMILY S. ROSENBERG
Honors Program, Central Michigan University

Library of Congress Cataloging in Publication Data

BURNER, DAVID
America: a portrait in history.

Includes bibliographical references.
1. United States—History. I. Marcus, Robert D.,
joint author. II. Rosenberg, Emily S., joint author. III. Title.
E178.1.B92 1974   973   73–14875
ISBN 0–13–024166–0

76325

AMERICA: A PORTRAIT IN HISTORY by Burner, Marcus, and Rosenberg

Cover: Childe Hassam, *Flag Day. Copyright by White House Historical Association*

PRENTICE-HALL INTERNATIONAL, INC., *London*
PRENTICE-HALL OF AUSTRALIA, PTY. LTD., *Sydney*
PRENTICE-HALL OF CANADA LTD., *Toronto*
PRENTICE-HALL OF INDIA PRIVATE LIMITED, *New Delhi*
PRENTICE-HALL OF JAPAN, INC., *Tokyo*

to

William Arthur and Beatrice Bird Burner

Leonard Roger and Dorothy Zimmerman Marcus

Albert Arthur and Helen Griggs Schlaht

contents

PREFACE

As the history of the United States lengthens and its influence spreads, textbooks that introduce students to the subject keep getting shorter. This is less of a paradox than it seems. Teachers of American history have never deliberately beguiled their students into the comfortable illusion that any one book could summarize the nation's complex past. Most students, however, after a few months of handling a thousand-page, double-column, four-pound book, which posed every question he or she found on the examinations, easily drifted into the security-blanket conception of the textbook. Introductory courses in other disciplines with more conceptual structure, such as the sciences, where a textbook actually could communicate nearly everything a first-year student had to know, reinforced this impression. And often the backgrounds of any historical interpretations they encountered—the documents, the key scholarly articles—proved not easily accessible to students, driving both instructors and their classes back to the all-important textbook.

Clearly all this has changed. The instructor can put paperbacks into his students' hands and major collections of reprinted documents and monographs into his college or university library. He also can draw on imaginative collections of documents and of historical interpretations packaged for student use. Even beyond that, modern methods of photoduplication make it possible to reproduce the most arcane materials out of an instructor's own research if he thinks it will strike a chord of student interest. In short, there are now a few feet of smooth path into the tangled thicket of inquiry into the past—enough to encourage students to begin the journey. The task of a modern textbook is to facilitate that journey— not to convince students that they have already reached their destination.

There are many reasons to make this journey. Americans are a historically minded people. All over the country they invest money and energy in preserving the remains of a rapidly vanishing past. They designate buildings historic landmarks, restore old villages, collect "Americana." More important, in every national crisis arguments hinge on which precedent offers the best guide to present policy. Statesmen debate interpretations of the Constitution, a document nearly two hundred years old. Few people have ever believed more firmly in the moot doctrine that history has direct lessons to teach the present.

This, however, is not the principal justification for studying the history of the United States. Historical study benefits us less as a guide to politics than as a goad to imagination. More than any other subject, history extends our vision of American life. With eyes fixed only on the present, we become slaves to our era. With our gaze ranging more widely through time, we develop a sense of the multiple possibilities of experience and of our institutions. History, paradoxically, sharpens our vision of the present by stripping away its inevitability, by suggesting all the possibilities for making a different life. To the present-bound American, automobiles are the mode of transportation, television the media for communication, ballpoint pens the way to write, Norman Mailer the reigning literary giant, Richard Nixon the only President we have. The past is larger than this, crowded with people, and styles, and ideas. The hard journey through it returns the traveller to a present he did not fully see before his trip.

America: A Portrait in History aims to meet the needs of the present generation of students and teachers. Its title, we hope, describes it with precision. This history of the American past attempts to project images that will linger in students' minds. The biographies that begin each chapter introduce people from the past who did things that most students thought typical only of the present: a political balladeer of the 1930s, an eighteenth-century agitator and iconoclast, a gay and proud poet of the nineteenth century, a famous gangster of the 1920s. The social portraits that end each chapter offer glimpses of how people lived in other generations and how they responded to technological innovation. We present society responding to the introduction of the horse, to industrialization, to the radio; "modern" decadence is right there in the high society of the 1890s; life styles that seem current indeed emerged in the era before World War I; propaganda and manipulation of ideas deeply affected people's lives in revolutionary America.

A record, included in the book, offers the angry denunciations of Tom Paine's *Common Sense;* the experience of slavery as narrated by ex-slave Frederick Douglass; the poignant demands of a black woman, Sojourner Truth, at the Women's Rights Convention at Seneca Falls, New York, in 1848; the smug assurance of steel magnate and philanthropist Andrew Carnegie; William Jennings Bryan's "Cross of Gold" speech at the 1896 Democratic National Convention; Charlotte Gillman's "Are Women Human Beings?"; Franklin D. Roosevelt's First Inaugural; Martin Luther King's "I Have a Dream"; and José Gutiérrez on the dreams of his own Chicano ethnic group.

The illustrations offer an unusually active vision of Americans doing things with force and energy. Most of all, the text aims at telling the story of past Americans with clarity and, we hope, in a way that will transmit to students some of the excitement that the authors have found in their own study of American history.

acknowLeDGements

Indispensable help in the composition of this book has come to us from Norman L. Rosenberg of Central Michigan University. We also wish to thank for capable assistance Terry Cooney, James Moore, Steve Stowe, Susan Strasser, Timothy Patterson, and Marian Wilson; our able typists have been Marian Wilson, Patricia Flannery, and Barbara Engels.

We acknowledge with appreciation the comments and suggestions made by colleagues who read parts of this manuscript: Professor Robert Alther, Richland College; Charles Clayton, Southwest Texas State University; Professor Paul H. Conover, Miami-Dade Junior College; Dr. Emmie Craddock, Southwest Texas State University; Asst. Professor Lawrence Curry, Jr., University of Houston; Professor Clifford Egan, University of Houston; Professor Richard Farrell, University of Maryland; Professor Eric Foner, City College of CUNY; Professor Eugene D. Genovese, University of Rochester; Professor Don R. Gerlach, University of Akron; Gerald J. Goodwin, University of Houston; Professor Robert Griffith, University of Massachusetts; Professor Kenneth D. Hairgrove, San Antonio College; Professor Keith A. Hinrichsen, Cerritos College; Professor Frank Huffman, University of Houston; Dr. Douglas E. Johnston, San Antonio College; Professor John R. Johnson, Jr., San Jacinto College; Professor Gary B. Nash, University of California; Professor

James Newbill, Yakima Valley College; Professor Hyland Packard, University of Houston; Professor James Poteet, University of Houston; Dr. Morton M. Rosenberg, Ball State University; Professor Joel Silbey, Cornell University; Professor Edward C. Taylor, South Texas College; Professor James A. Wilson, Southwest Texas State University; Dr. Robert E. Zeigler, San Antonio College.

We did not act on every suggestion, and responsibility for the final manuscript, its strengths and its shortcomings, is ours alone.

AMERICA a Portrait in History

1492-1660

one | THE OLD WORLD AND THE NEW

JOHN CABOT

John Cabot, not his fellow Genoese captain Christopher Columbus, commanded the first European ship to reach the shores of North America during the fifteenth century. Yet historians know surprisingly little about the Italian-born explorer who sailed for England. The most ingenious detective work has uncovered no pictures of Cabot, no letters, not even any first-hand account of his voyage to the New World. But his very anonymity makes John Cabot an appropriate symbol of the "Age of Reconnaisance." Cabot was one of the professional explorers who between 1460 and 1660 broadened literate Europeans' knowledge of the world, who charted most of the waters and much of the land surface of this planet.

In many ways John Cabot's enterprise resembled Columbus's first voyage. Cabot also hoped to reach Asia by sailing west. An all-water route to the Indies would reduce the cost of Eastern products, whose prices were inflated by various middlemen along the traditional land-sea route from Asia through the Italian city-states. And ocean voyages to the west revived old dreams of mysterious islands and "lost" kingdoms in the uncharted Atlantic. Few learned people doubted that the earth was round,

3

and neither Cabot nor Columbus had to demonstrate the theoretical possibility of their projects. The greatest peril, most thought, involved the dangers of a long ocean voyage out of sight of land. Like Columbus, Cabot unsuccessfully offered his services to several other countries before coming to England. He eventually found financial support in the seacoast town of Bristol, England's busiest port, and secured formal authorization from King Henry VII.

In May 1497 Cabot sailed from Bristol with two small ships. Dodging ice floes and challenging the fog-covered North Atlantic, he made a remarkably quick journey. He sighted land, probably the coast of Newfoundland, during the last week in June and spent nearly a month exploring American waters. Cabot believed that he had touched an island near Asia, and he returned to inform Henry VII of his achievement. In a display of rare generosity, Henry granted Cabot the princely sum of ten pounds—which the captain promptly spent on bright silk clothes—gave him a small pension, and authorized a second voyage. Where Cabot went on this return trip will never be known. He and four ships were lost at sea in 1498, and for many years England forgot his discoveries.

Voyages such as John Cabot's reflected the new maritime technology, advances gained from diverse sources. Europeans borrowed heavily from Arab sailors and developed improved styles of their own. Shipbuilders began to construct a variety of new vessels: the giant carracks which could travel great distances and transport many tons of cargo; the small caravels, such as Columbus's *Niña,* which dominated the Atlantic coastal trade; and a bewildering array of intermediate-size ships, such as the fabled galleons of Spain and England. Mariners also perfected different styles of sails and varied types of riggings, giving ships added stability and greater maneuverability on the open seas. And when leaving sight of the coast, seamen could use new navigational aids— charts, compasses, and astrolabes—which permitted them to determine their position with some, though not perfect, accuracy.

But exploration remained an uncomfortable, sometimes risky business. Until introduction of hammocks, crew members slept rolled up in blankets on the decks; only officers enjoyed the luxury of bunks. Disease always threatened mariners. Sanitary facilities were primitive, and in heavy seas only the bravest seamen would use the boxes slung over the side of the ship. Instead, the bottom of the vessel quickly filled with all types of refuse, producing foul odors and dangerous germs. During extended voyages food sometimes ran out, and drinking water often became dangerously infected. (On the other hand, lack of good water required substitution of liquor; Spanish seamen received a liter- and-a-half of wine, and Englishmen got almost a gallon of beer per day.) The sea itself also presented dangers. Despite improvements in navigational devices and shipbuilding, a safe passage required great sailing skill, fair winds, calm weather, and good luck. John Cabot's unhappy fate was not unique.

Sebastien Cabot. *Culver Pictures*

B.C.-1660

48,000–9,000 B.C.	Migrations into New World across Bering Strait land bridge
1,000 B.C.	Old Copper Culture in Great Lakes region
500 A.D.	Hopewell Culture in Ohio Valley
1100	Viking explorations
1492	Columbus's first voyage
1494	Treaty of Tordesillas
1497	John Cabot sails to New World
1513	Juan Ponce de León explores Florida
1517	Martin Luther begins Protestant Reformation
1521	Aztec capital (Mexico City) falls to Hernan Cortés
1534	Henry VIII breaks with Roman Catholic Church
1539–42	Hernando de Soto explores Southeast
1540–42	Francisco Vásquez de Coronado explores Southwest
1565	St. Augustine founded
1585	Sir Walter Raleigh founds Roanoke Island settlement
1607	Virginia Company founds Jamestown
1610	Spaniards found Santa Fe
1619	First record of black slaves being brought to British North America (Virginia)
1620	Pilgrims establish Plymouth
1624	Virginia becomes a royal colony
1622–44	War between Virginians and Indians
1630	Puritans found Massachusetts Bay Colony
1632	Charter granted to Cecilius Calvert (Lord Baltimore) to establish Maryland
1636	Roger Williams establishes Rhode Island; Thomas Hooker founds Connecticut
1636–37	Pequot War in New England
1640–60	English Revolution and Commonwealth government

NATIVE AMERICANS

The first migration to America

The first Americans migrated from Asia. Several times between about fifty and eleven thousand years ago a land bridge across what is now the Bering Strait connected Siberia with Alaska, and Asian tribes, perhaps attracted by better hunting grounds or a milder climate, wandered across this broad plain into North America. These migrants—whom Columbus mistakenly termed "Indians"—gradually streamed southward and eventually populated the entire western hemisphere.

Pre-Columbian American history must be pieced together from scattered archeological evidence and woven from ever-changing theories. Archeologists disagree on the exact dates of the crossings, on the number of separate migrations, and on which Asian groups became the progenitors of which American tribes. We can only guess how long it took the population that moved southward through Mesoamerica to reach Cape Horn. Still, some things about these ancient peoples are known. The western hemisphere man of two thousand years ago was a hunter, pursuing now-extinct varieties of bison, horses, or sloths and killing them with spear points shaped from rock. As the Ice Age animals died out, he gradually turned to food gathering. Archeologists find that milling stones began to appear about the same time that fluted spear points dropped out of use. After a few more thousand years, some groups began to make simple pottery, and in the western Great Lakes region people of the so-called Old Copper Culture (which reached its height over three thousand years ago) fashioned tools and other objects from metal. Slowly, primitive agriculture evolved in some areas. Farmers developed some sophisticated horticultural techniques, domesticating squash, corn, sweet potatoes, and other crops unique to the New World.

The cultures and languages of the western hemisphere varied even more widely than those of the eastern hemisphere. By the time Europeans reached the New World, hundreds of tribes dotted what would become the United States; the native population north of present-day Mexico probably totaled one million.

The Aleuts and Eskimos of Alaska were distinct from all other western hemisphere people in genetics, culture, and language. Largely conditioned by their icy, Arctic environment, these tribes lived in hunting societies with simple social and political organizations.

The fishing tribes of the Pacific Northwest differed from most other groups in their extensive use of slaves and in their preoccupation with status and material wealth. The totem poles which often adorned their plank homes attested to their complex social and religious system.

California contained the largest concentration of population north of Mexico, but there was little governmental organization. People lived in extended families, each of which had its own land and customs. The mild climate made existence less arduous than in the North; wild plants, fish, and game provided an adequate food supply.

The tribes of the Southwest, by contrast, developed an organizationally advanced civilization based upon domesticated agriculture. Their religion, stressing conformity, nonviolence, and gentleness, forbade aggressive behavior. Remains from some of their towns, constructed from stone or adobe, still adorn cliffs in the Southwest.

The nomadic life of tribes on the Great Plains has dominated the stereotypes of western lore, but the Indians of the eastern Plains actually lived for centuries in settled agricultural villages. About the time that the white man landed in America, drought forced some of these tribes to abandon their settlements, and mobile hunting cultures became more common throughout the region. The horses which the Spaniards introduced into North America reinforced this way of life. For food, shelter, clothing, and articles of warfare, the Plains Indians increasingly depended upon the huge herds of buffalo.

Complex, urban-agricultural societies, centering around temple mounds, existed throughout the Southeast before the coming of the white man. By the sixteenth century most of the population had abandoned these ceremonial centers and dispersed into smaller settlements, but Europeans did encounter some remnants of the temple-mound culture. The Natchez tribe, a rigidly hierarchical society governed by an absolute ruler known as the Great Sun, occupied the lower Mississippi region. In present-day Georgia and Alabama the Creeks and several other tribes formed a loose confederation.

In the Northeast, native civilization reached its greatest height. Around A.D. 500 in the Ohio Valley a sophisticated mound-building culture (called the Hopewell after the modern owner of a major excavation site) reached its zenith, and the Hopewell's large trading network spread its cultural influence throughout the eastern half of the United States. After the Hopewell declined, the well-known Algonquian and Iroquois groups emerged, the tribes Englishmen first encountered. Constant warfare between these two groups gave rise, about 1570, to the Iroquois's League of Five Nations, probably the largest political entity north of Mexico.

The first inhabitants of America developed crops which suited its soils; they fashioned clothing and homes which fit its resources and climate; they followed religions which gave spiritual meaning to the events of daily life. Most sought to live in harmony with nature, not to dominate or alter it.

Indian-white relations

The white men who explored and settled the strange western continent came from a civilization deeply immersed in spiritual concerns. They analyzed the new environment less as scientists than as Christians, and the race of men inhabiting the New World raised momentous theological questions. Did Indians have human souls? Did they descend from Adam? Were they innocents untainted by the original sin of Adam's fall? Or were they outcasts of God and agents of the Devil? One explorer reported, "We found the people most gentle, loving and faithfull, voide of all guile and treason, and such as live after the manner of the golden age." But another wrote, "They are, I say, savage, haunting the woods, ignorant, lawless and rude...extremely lazy, gluttonous, profane, treacherous, cruel in their revenge, and given up to all kinds of lewdness."

Debates over the nature of New World peoples spread two conflicting images among Europeans—that of the happy, natural man, innately good and completely free, and that of the deceitful savage whose skin color reflected the dark condition of his soul. Both views provided ample justification for dominating native peoples—either to Christianize them and preserve their purity or to restrain them from harming the Christian newcomers. In any event, practical matters soon became more important than theoretical questions. Whites wanted land; Indians occupied it. Years of tragic and uneven conflict resulted.

The first Indian-white contact in what is now the United States came with the northward expansion of the Spanish empire in the early sixteenth century. Tribes in Florida killed the Spanish explorer Juan Ponce de León and repulsed his expedition. In the latter half of the sixteenth century, Spaniards finally brought Florida under control, pacifying and controlling the Indians through Catholic missions. In the South and Southwest, Francisco Vásquez de Coronado's and Hernando de Soto's early explorations revealed that the region contained little wealth, and Spaniards delayed settling the area until 1610, when they established an outpost at Santa Fe. During the seventeenth century Pueblo Indians of this region were put to work and supposedly converted to Christianity. But in 1680, led by an Indian priest called Popé, the Pueblos revived their native religion and rose against their white masters. They killed hundreds of Spaniards and remained independent for twelve years. Finally, plagues, Apache raids, and a regrouped Spanish force doomed the Pueblo movement. Spain once again took Santa Fe and spread its Empire throughout the Southwest.

At about the same time that Spaniards were conquering the southern part of what is now the United States, French explorers were active along the Northeast coast. They established fur-trading connections with Algonquian-speaking tribes and introduced deadly firepower into the Algonquian-Iroquois rivalry. Gradually, French traders pushed down the Saint Lawrence River and into the Great Lakes region, establishing Indian alliances which would later assist them in conflicts with English settlers to the south.

Except for the "lost colony" at Roanoke, Englishmen did not attempt to inhabit North America until the seventeenth century. The earliest settlers at Jamestown, Virginia, initially lived peacefully with the nearby Algonquian-speaking confederacy. Ruled by Powhatan (whose daughter Pocahontas later married one of the colony's most prominent men), the Indians kept the colony alive by trading corn and other foodstuffs. But as the settlers of Jamestown pressed upon Indian lands, relations grew strained. Powhatan died, and in 1622 another chief, perhaps his brother, led a surprise attack against the colony. Settlements were

Columbus. *Culver Pictures*

ravaged; 350 whites were killed. The incident provoked equally fierce retaliation. In a long war, lasting until 1644, Englishmen smashed the Indian confederacy.

In New England the pattern was much the same as in Virginia: peaceful trading gave way to distrust, resentment, and finally war. In 1636 Massachusetts Bay Puritans, with the help of some neighboring tribes, attacked the Pequot Indians and killed hundreds. By the 1660s the English outposts seethed with anti-Indian hostility, and both sides had ample pretext for revenge. The short period of harmony between the two cultures had passed.

Indian-white contacts in the New World favored the whites. From the Indians, Europeans learned how to survive in the wilderness, how to plant corn, squash, and potatoes. Indian guides and trappers helped white settlers advance and prosper. But to the Indian, the coming of the white man brought disaster. Guns and horses revolutionized the

Indian way of life and made intertribal warfare deadlier than ever before. Worse still, huge epidemics of European diseases swept the continent, decimating the native population and weakening their power to defend their homelands.

EARLY EUROPEAN EXPLORATIONS

The Norsemen The first transatlantic voyages to the New World remain shrouded in mystery. Over the years popular writers and scholars have contributed many different theories, and the recent voyages of Thor Heyerdahl's papyrus craft, *Ra II,* did demonstrate that ancient sailors *could* have crossed the Altantic before the Christian era. Both archeological evidence and ancient sagas do reveal the activities of courageous Norsemen who reached North America around the year 1100. Investigating another sailor's story of a bountiful land toward the setting sun, Leif Ericson sailed from Greenland to a place he called Vinland. Leif and his crew wintered there, returning to Greenland the following spring.

Impressed by Leif's tales, several expeditions tried to plant permanent settlements in Vinland. Opposition from native inhabitants, whom the intruders called "skrellings," and the stormy seas of the North Atlantic quickly doomed the Norse colony. Within twenty years of Leif's voyage, Norsemen's contacts with North America ended forever. For centuries the site of Vinland defied precise location—enthusiastic local history buffs have even claimed that Viking explorers reached Minnesota and Okla-

Representation of Columbus's fleet in a storm. *Culver Pictures*

homa—but recent diggings and carbon-14 tests have suggested that the Norse visitors landed on the northern tip of Newfoundland. These findings have failed to satisfy all scholars, and perhaps other remnants of pre-1492 explorations still await archaelogists' tools.

Between the time of the Norse discoveries and the rediscoveries of Columbus, a period of almost four hundred years, no European reached America. Yet stories of such trips—including one by Prince Madoc of Wales and the Zeno brothers from Venice—abounded during the Middle Ages. Medieval sailors constantly described strange islands which supposedly dotted the Atlantic, and some hardy mariners claimed to have reached these shores. But only one recently discovered map, apparently drawn some fifty years before Columbus's explorations, even contained a reference to Vinland. And some scholars have questioned the authenticity as well as the significance of the "Vinland Map."

Europe and a
wider world

Between 1100 and 1450 Europeans did not forget the outside world. Stories of mysterious islands in the Atlantic, particularly a place called "Antilla," beguiled adventurous mariners. The Crusades, successful attempts to drive the "infidel" Turks from the Holy Land, acquainted Europeans with the people and products of the Middle and Far East. During the thirteenth century a few Italian merchants journeyed across Asia to the ancient kingdom of China. The seemingly incredible accounts of one of these visitors, Marco Polo of Venice, enthralled medieval as well as later readers. Marco Polo presented fairly accurate descriptions of Oriental culture, but other writers penned highly fictionalized versions

Prince Henry the Navigator.
Culver Pictures

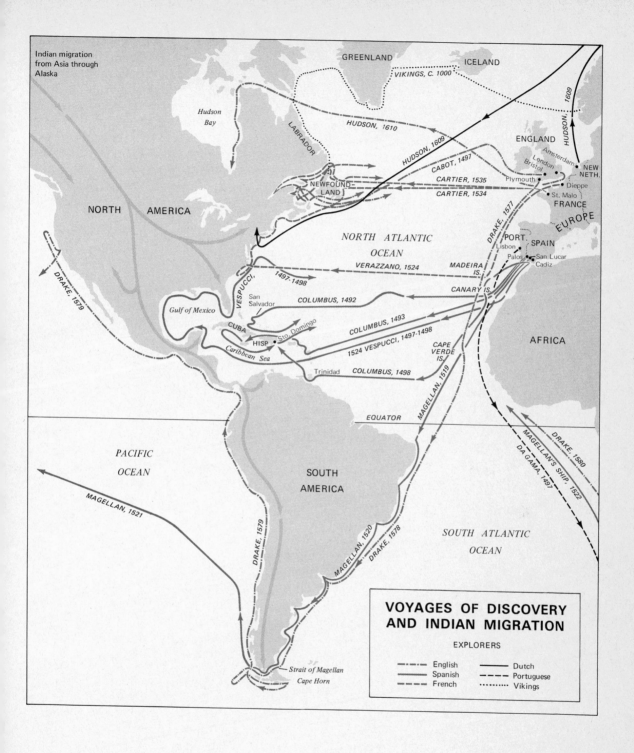

Indian migration from Asia through Alaska

GREENLAND   ICELAND

VIKINGS, C. 1000

HUDSON, 1609

Hudson Bay

HUDSON, 1610

LABRADOR

ENGLAND
Amsterdam
London
Bristol
Plymouth
CABOT, 1497
CARTIER, 1535
Dieppe
CARTIER, 1534
St. Malo
FRANCE
EUROPE

NEW NETH.

HUDSON, 1609

NORTH AMERICA

NEWFOUND-LAND

NORTH ATLANTIC OCEAN

DRAKE, 1577

PORT.
Lisbon
Palos
San Lucar
Cadiz
SPAIN

DRAKE, 1579

VERAZZANO, 1524

MADEIRA IS.

VESPUCCI, 1497-1498

Gulf of Mexico
San Salvador

COLUMBUS, 1492

CANARY IS.

CUBA
HISP.
Sto. Domingo
Caribbean Sea

COLUMBUS, 1493

1524 VESPUCCI, 1497-1498

AFRICA

CAPE VERDE IS.

Trinidad   COLUMBUS, 1498

MAGELLAN, 1519

EQUATOR

MAGELLAN, 1519

PACIFIC OCEAN

SOUTH AMERICA

SOUTH ATLANTIC OCEAN

MAGELLAN, 1521

DRAKE, 1580

MAGELLAN'S SHIP, 1522

DA GAMA, 1497

DRAKE, 1579

MAGELLAN, 1520   DRAKE, 1578

Strait of Magellan
Cape Horn

VOYAGES OF DISCOVERY AND INDIAN MIGRATION

EXPLORERS

—·—·— English	—— Dutch
—— Spanish	——— Portuguese
——— French	········· Vikings

of supposed journeys to strange lands. One notorious and widely read faker, Sir John Mandeville, described all kinds of half-human, half-animal monsters he claimed to have seen during his travels. These accounts, both real and imaginary, touched the curiosity of many Europeans, and the products which passed through the Italian city-states provided tangible evidence of the riches of the mysterious Orient. But during the Middle Ages few Europeans remained long in the outside world; they lacked the resources, technology, or military power to cross the seas or to subdue hostile enemies.

About the middle of the fifteenth century, with Western civilization on the brink of modernity, Europeans began to seek a broader world. Some of this expansionism represented merely a continuation of earlier probings outside Europe. Portugal's Prince Henry the Navigator, who sponsored a series of voyages down the coast of Africa, was a thoroughly medieval person. According to a contemporary chronicler, the prince's objectives included a desire to fulfill the prediction of an astrologer's horoscope and a wish to find the "lost" Christian kingdom of Prester John. But most of the impetus for Europe's outward thrust came from the Renaissance spirit which was slowly spreading over the Continent. Literate Europeans displayed renewed curiosity about the mysteries of the universe; refined maritime technology enabled men to sail with greater ease and safety; more awesome weaponry gave Europeans an overwhelming military advantage over most non-Western peoples; a heightened awareness of the individual and his potential led many men to seek their destiny in far-off lands. And unlike the old feudal realms, the new nation-states could mobilize the great resources which overseas expansion required.

AN AGE OF EUROPEAN EXPANSION: 1460–1660

Between about 1460 and 1660 the nations of Europe—Portugal, Spain, France, Holland, and finally England—began to spread their culture and institutions throughout the world. During this two-hundred-year period, Europeans explored and mapped a good portion of the earth, and they inaugurated several centuries of colonial expansion. The settlement of the Americas began as one phase of this global process.

The European powers unexpectedly encountered the Americas as a roadblock in their search for a westward route to the Orient, but they quickly moved to extend their hegemony over this rich New World. The first travelers were the professional explorers—Columbus, Magellan, Cartier, Verazanno, Frobisher, Coronado, de Soto, and thousands of others—brave and skilled adventurers who reconnoitered the seas and investigated the lands. Driven by a search for personal glory as much as by a desire for wealth, these men made the initial contact with the New

World. They left behind a wealth of charts, maps, notes, and drawings, materials that would assist those who sought to build upon the first discoveries. Some of these later adventurers wanted new territories from which they could extract the wealth, especially the gold and silver, of the indigenous peoples. Religious crusaders, hoping to convert the heathen natives, brought the word of their Christian God (and oftentimes His firepower as well). Other Europeans came to trade, to exchange their goods for the prized possessions of other civilizations.

Particularly in North America, Europeans migrated to establish small colonies, New World "plantations" which would provide permanent homes for persons from the Old World. These first imperial outposts, especially in British North America, hugged the coastlines. Early settlers lived in small, scattered enclaves. They did not consider themselves "Americans" but transplanted Europeans. They generally looked toward the Atlantic and to the mother country for economic support, military assistance, and cultural contacts.

The Iberian nations

A long maritime tradition and Prince Henry's strong support of Atlantic explorations had given Portugal a head start in overseas expansion. After Columbus's first voyage, King John II of Portugal disputed Spain's position in the New World, claiming the Atlantic as his country's special preserve. Eventually a series of papal decrees and the Treaty of Tordesillas (1494) settled the dispute. The two nations agreed that an imaginary line 370 leagues west of the Azores would separate their spheres of control. This "Line of Demarcation" freed Spain from Portuguese intrusion into the Americas—except in Brazil, which further exploration proved to be west of the line—and allowed Portugal to concentrate upon India and the Far East.

Spain, the greatest European power in the sixteenth century, staked out the largest domain in the New World. Employing superior firepower and exploiting divisions within the native population, small bands of Spanish conquistadores toppled the rich Indian empires of Central and South America. In 1521 the Aztec capital, which became Mexico City, fell to Hernan Cortés; several years later one of Cortés's former captains, Pedro de Alvarado, subdued the territory of the Maya; and during the early 1530s Francisco Pizarro claimed the richest prize of all—the Inca Empire of Peru. These soldier-explorers rapidly plundered the native civilizations, fought with one another for power and wealth, and assumed authority over native villages under a medieval institution called the *encomienda*. Technically an *encomienda* did not carry title to the soil or possession of the Indians. In practice, these qualifications were often difficult to perceive, and the royal government soon had to restrict the power of the first generation of *encomenderos*.

After the conquerors came the bureaucrats and the Catholic Church, as the Spanish Crown moved to consolidate and administer the king's New World possessions. Spain created two vice-royalties—New Spain, which encompassed Mexico and Central America, and Peru, which included virtually all of South America—and royal officials subdivided these vast administrative entities into smaller, all-purpose units called *audiencas*. In addition, the Catholic hierarchy dispatched a number of clerical officials to watch over the Church's considerable wealth, spread the gospel among the Indians, and care for the spiritual needs of Roman Catholics. Often criticized as sluggish and corrupt, Spain's lay and clerical bureaucracies somehow worked. The Spanish American Empire remained intact for almost three centuries.

The new realms brought Spain great wealth. The rich silver mines of Potosi and Zacatecas, discovered during the middle of the sixteenth century, produced a steady flow of bullion. In addition to precious metals, Spanish America exported large quantities of tallow, hides, sugar, and dyes. Spain's colonies never attracted large numbers of European immigrants, and much of its colonial wealth rested upon the labor of Indians and black slaves. Unlike the later English colonists, Spanish invaders encountered large sedentary populations which could be exploited as a source of labor. As much as possible, Spaniards retained the pre-Columbian Indian society, and the conquerors tried to take the place of the native ruling elite. Some clerics, particularly Fr. Bartolomé de las Casas, protested Spain's treatment of the native population, and reformers gained some concessions from the Crown. But, ironically, clergymen's complaints also encouraged enslavement of more black Africans as an alternative labor force in Central and South America.

Spanish adventurers also entered the area of the present-day United States. Vainly seeking riches to equal those of Mexico and Peru, Spaniards discovered the Mississippi River, explored the present southwestern United States, and pushed as far north as Oregon and Nebraska. Spain also laid claim to large portions of the Atlantic seaboard, and in 1565 an army expedition built a fortress at St. Augustine on the Florida peninsula, the first permanent settlement in what is now the United States.

France   France was a serious challenger to Spain's power. During the first third of the sixteenth century a series of French expeditions sought both a passage to the Orient and wealth similar to that which Spain had discovered in Central and South America. Some years later French Protestants mounted several private efforts to establish permanent settlements in North America. But tales of golden cities and mountains of precious metals too often lured these Frenchmen away from the more mundane tasks of colony building. Meanwhile Spain remained a jealous rival. In 1565 an army from St. Augustine killed a group of nearly 150 French settlers who had established a small garrison on the South Carolina coast. When Frenchmen returned to North America several decades later, they concentrated upon areas far to the north of Spanish Florida. Private trading companies established outposts in what is now French-speaking Canada; explorers such as la Salle pushed into the center of North America and down the Mississippi River; and eventually the royal government assumed control of the entire area. New France never returned the wealth of Spanish America nor attracted the population of British America, but the French presence did constitute a serious threat to the English colonies to the south.

England

For a variety of reasons England stayed out of North America during most of the sixteenth century. Henry VIII, who succeeded his father in 1508, had many other things on his mind—including, of course, women. The young king showed little interest in the New World, and he quickly returned England to the maelstrom of Continental diplomacy. A series of Anglo-French wars drained his nation's military and economic resources and resulted only in the loss of England's last European territories. And Henry's differences with the Pope over annulment of the king's first marriage not only precipitated a break with the Church of Rome in 1534 but exacerbated religious tensions within England itself. Various groups and powerful clerics struggled over the organization and tenets of the new Church of England. The fierce ecclesiastical conflicts associated with the English Reformation and the dynastic problems which followed Henry's death in 1547 convulsed domestic life for many years. Not until the 1680s, during the second decade of Queen Elizabeth's reign, did England enjoy any real degree of political tranquility.

Throughout much of the sixteenth century, English statesmen struggled to maintain the Spanish alliance, the traditional cornerstone of England's foreign policy. This pro-Spanish policy meant, among other things, that England would respect Spain's position in the New World. Englishmen who were interested in overseas ventures concentrated upon the Middle East and tsarist Russia. But during the last third of the sixteenth century, the golden age of Elizabethan England, the New World became an ever-brighter lure. As England's power increased, its leaders exhibited a heightened sense of national honor and displayd an almost pugnacious desire to gain international glory.

Queen Elizabeth's Protestant advisers proposed a more aggressive policy toward Catholic Spain, and Spanish America offered an inviting target. The steady erosion of Anglo-Spanish relations quickly led to open warfare in the Caribbean. Spain monopolized transatlantic trade during the sixteenth century, and men such as Sir Francis Drake and his cousin Sir John Hawkins grabbed for England's share of this wealth. English interlopers harassed the Spanish fleets, sacked coastal ports, and disrupted normal trade patterns. King Philip of Spain, once a suitor for Elizabeth's hand, fumed and threatened, but the virgin queen refused to discipline her "sea dogs". Although they never broke Spain's commercial

Sir Francis Drake. *Culver Pictures*

stranglehold, these gentlemen-pirates began their nation's involvement in the western hemisphere. England soon established small settlements in the West Indies, British outposts in the midst of Spain's sprawling New World empire.

England also reached into North America. Still hopeful of discovering the Northwest Passage, the ocean shortcut to the riches of Asia, English adventurers pursued the earlier explorations of John Cabot. During the 1570s a number of influential persons, including the queen herself, purchased stock in the Cathay Company, which financed several futile efforts to locate the elusive waterway and to find gold in the northernmost reaches of the Americas. Although Sir Martin Frobisher returned with only several Eskimos and tons of black ore—English alchemists struggled for five years to extract gold from the worthless rock—his expeditions did increase English interest in North America.

COLONIZATION OF VIRGINIA

Despite the failure of the Cathay Company, a small group of expansionists urged greater efforts in the Americas. They suggested development of permanent settlements, New World "plantations" similar to those of Spain and France. American colonies, of course, would provide bases from which English raiders could strike at New Spain, and Sir Francis Drake advanced this idea most vigorously. But others—especially Sir Humphrey Gilbert, one of Queen Elizabeth's most charming courtiers, and two other men, cousins both named Richard Hakluyt—proposed more grandiose schemes. The younger Hakluyt, who spent most of his life compiling information on colonization, contended that American plantations would spread England's Protestant religion, expand the country's shipbuilding industry and naval fleet, decrease its dependence on foreign sources of supplies, provide an outlet for surplus population, and help English explorers discover the Northwest Passage. Hakluyt spoke for increasing numbers of influential Englishmen when he claimed that New World colonies would enhance England's international power and domestic prosperity.

The "lost colony"

With Hakluyt serving as an adviser and propagandist, Sir Humphrey Gilbert, Sir Walter Raleigh (Gilbert's half-brother), and other Protestants from England's West Country launched several abortive projects. After a couple of false starts and problems raising money, Gilbert himself left for the New World in 1583, but after reaching Newfoundland he and two of the expedition's five ships went down during a fierce autumn storm. Raleigh then assumed command, receiving a charter from the queen and naming the area where they finally landed "Virginia." More cautious than Gilbert, Raleigh financed several preliminary expeditions from England before attempting to establish a permanent colony. Finally, in 1587 his group dispatched a party of over a hundred persons, including women and children, beginning a tiny settlement at Roanoke. Outbreak of war between England and Spain—including the famous engagement of the Spanish armada in 1588—prevented an immediate resupply mission, and when a relief party returned three years later they discovered the encampment deserted, the letters "CRO" carved on a tree and the word "CROATOAN" on a doorpost. Where had the colonists gone? Perhaps they abandoned the inhospitable site and sought refuge with the friendly Croatoan Indians. Perhaps the settlers perished at the hands of a more hostile tribe. No one ever found a trace of them, and the fate of the "lost colony" remains a mystery.

America, Land of Plenty—1621 European view. *New York Public Library*

The ventures of Gilbert and Raleigh revealed the practical obstacles to colonization. Despite persistent entreaties and good connections, they failed to convince Queen Elizabeth and her close advisers to open the public purse and extend governmental assistance. As in the Spanish settlements, private investors had to bear the financial costs. The Crown would grant charters and offer encouragement, but it would not provide the cash. In addition to the problem of finances—Gilbert lost a fortune as well as his life—these early efforts demonstrated a number of other difficulties: transporting the large numbers of settlers who were not seamen, finding suitable locations in the New World, achieving harmonious relations with Indian neighbors, and resupplying imperial outposts from England. But England's transatlantic expansion continued, and by the early seventeenth century new projects were underway.

Jamestown   The first English colony in the Americas began not as a political unit but as the private possession of a joint-stock company, a precursor of the modern business corporation, in which investors bought shares and hoped to realize profits from this pooling of capital. In 1606 two groups of capitalist-adventurers secured a charter authorizing them to establish

English plantations in North America. The Plymouth Company immediately sent a small party to Maine, but its tiny settlement quickly collapsed. The better-financed Virginia Company spent more time planning its venture—Richard Hakluyt once again took part—and it landed 144 men near the mouth of the James River in the spring of 1607. The Virginia Company resembled joint-stock companies which operated in Africa and Asia, and investors hoped to duplicate the profits of previous organizations. But these English capitalists never realized their financial dreams; Virginia returned no profits.

If the small Jamestown colony proved to be an economic white elephant for investors, it became a nightmare for many of its earliest inhabitants. Between June 1609 and May 1610 the number of settlers dropped from almost five hundred to about sixty, and the settlement virtually disintegrated during a winter of disease and malnutrition. One survivor claimed that

> *we were constrained to eat dogs, cats, rats, snakes, toadstools, horsehides and what not; one man out of the misery endured, killing his wife powdered her up to eat her, for which he was burned.*

Although conditions were not always this desperate, life in Virginia quickly dispelled the dreams which many immigrants carried to

First day at Jamestown. *Culver Pictures*

the New World. In nearly twenty years of operation the company sent over more than five thousand colonists, but in 1624 the population barely reached twelve hundred.

What were the causes of Virginia's early distresses? Misconceptions about the nature of the enterprise contributed to the colonists' problems. The company's planners hoped that Jamestown would provide a base from which explorers could locate the Northwest Passage, and the company would then dominate the resulting trade. And using the model of Spanish America, they expected to find precious metals. When settlers discovered no gold, the initial plans quickly went awry. Tobacco eventually provided an export, but even this cash crop failed to make the enterprise an immediate success.

The colony also suffered from poor leadership in both England and America. The Virginia Company reorganized itself several times, and there were a number of shakeups in its Virginia command. Under strong leaders such as Captain John Smith and Sir Thomas Dale the colony held together; under less capable direction Virginia fell into economic stagnation and political disorder. And like most Englishmen, Virginians could not live in harmony with neighboring Indian tribes. At first the powerful chief Powhatan and his daughter befriended the newcomers, but relations soon deteriorated. After the Indian attack of 1622, Englishmen retaliated in kind; on one occasion, whites lured a band of peaceful Indians into drinking a toast with poisoned wine.

Virginia's most pressing problem—and one that always proved difficult to solve—involved labor. Dazzled by stories of the New World's great abundance, and encouraged by Spain's exploitation of native populations, the first arrivals did not anticipate that they would have to do much work themselves—except perhaps to count their gold. The first two groups included a high percentage of "gentlemen," a variety of skilled craftsmen, but almost no agricultural laborers. Even a decade after settlement, some Virginians continued to hope that North American Indians would toil for the white man. The company's leaders always had difficulty getting people to work—and this in a colony which stood on the brink of starvation. Perhaps some of this lethargy, which contemporaries attributed to the colonists' poor character, resulted from an inadequate diet. English employers voiced similar complaints about the working habits of their underpaid and underfed laborers. Officials of the Virginia Company tried to meet the labor problem by increasing the incentives to productivity. Over the years, the company established more liberal land grants, encouraged immigration of women, and established a representative assembly, the forerunner of Virginia's famous House of Burgesses.

Although these programs helped alleviate Jamestown's labor problem, the measures created new difficulties for the company. From a largely male business organization Virginia evolved into a small but

The Old Church Tower at Jamestown

increasingly complex society. Men no longer owed their undivided allegiance to the Virginia Company; as husbands, fathers, and land-owners they developed a number of social relationships which often conflicted with their obligations to the company. The colony's directors found it increasingly difficult to get residents to cooperate with each other or to obey their leaders, and in 1624 royal officials decided to terminate the company's charter. Virginia became the first royal colony.

Virginia slowly built strong political and economic institutions. After some years of uncertainty the Crown recognized Virginia's elective assembly, and as the population increased the planter class created effective units of local government. Tobacco eventually gave Virginia a valuable export crop. Ignoring the warnings of many Englishmen, including King James I himself, people consumed more and more of the noxious weed, and Virginians devoted most of their land to its cultivation. Importation of black Africans—the first ones probably arrived in 1619—and

The founding of Maryland Colony. *Culver Pictures*

increased migration of indentured servants provided new sources of labor. Although Virginia faced the problems of a basically one-crop economy, it became one of England's most prosperous New World plantations.

Still, political disorder persisted. The English Revolution of 1640 forced Virginians to choose between the Royalist and parliamentary causes. When most colonists supported King Charles I, the victorious government of Oliver Cromwell sent an expedition to enforce parliamentary control in the "Old Dominion." More important to politics in the later seventeenth century, emergence of a new generation of Virginia-born planters produced fierce struggles for prestige and power among the socioeconomic elite.

MARYLAND

Maryland, Virginia's neighbor to the north, became the first proprietary colony. Maryland was not the possession of a joint-stock company (like Virginia) but the private estate of a single family—the Calverts. Sir George Calvert, Lord Baltimore, hoped to expand his landed wealth and, secondarily, to provide a New World haven for fellow Catholic Englishmen. The Crown also gained from a proprietorship: proprietorships offered another means of establishing North American outposts without the expenditure of government funds.

Fulfilling the plans of his father, Cecilius Calvert secured a charter which gave him all the privileges of a quasi-feudal ruler. During the Middle Ages, for example, the Crown had given sweeping powers to the bishop of the Palatinate of Durham, an area on England's turbulent northern border. Such authority also seemed appropriate in the wilds of North America. The charter of 1632 made Calvert the owner of a vast New World estate and granted him extensive authority. Lord Baltimore owned all the land, determined and collected all rents, issued all legal writs, appointed all administrative officials, confirmed all laws, and supervised defense of the colony. The only significant limitation required the proprietor to make laws "with the advice, assent, and approbation of the freemen of the province", a provision which led Baltimore to create an elective assembly similar to Virginia's House of Burgesses.

Changing conditions slowly altered Lord Baltimore's dreams. The colony never experienced Virginia's early disasters, but Maryland's population remained small, less than six thousand in 1660. Prominent landowners intermittently clashed with the Calvert family over its proprietary privileges, and the assembly became a center of opposition to the proprietor as well as the focal point for power struggles among Maryland's elite. Since Catholics never migrated in large numbers, Protestants soon sought greater influence within the supposedly Catholic plantation. Problems in England also disrupted affairs in Maryland. During the 1640s the English

Civil War, with its spirit of militant Protestantism, put the Calvert family on the defensive. In response to pressures in England and America, Lord Baltimore framed an "Act Concerning Religion" (1649), a document guaranteeing religious toleration to all Christians. And during the 1650s a Protestant faction temporarily ousted the proprietor. Even though Lord Baltimore regained authority in 1660, Maryland never fulfilled George Calvert's early plans.

THE PURITAN MIGRATIONS

Puritanism in Old England

Martin Luther's crusade to reform the Roman Catholic church in the early sixteenth century ended forever the unity and religious consensus of most of medieval Europe. Luther's movement soon became a rival faith, and the questioning of theological dogma brought a proliferation of religious sects.

In England, controversy arising from the Protestant Reformation wracked politics and society for two centuries. In 1534 Henry VIII broke with the Roman Catholic church, but he acted from personal and political, as well as religious, reasons. The new Anglican Church represented a series of compromises between Catholicism and Protestantism. But gradually an opposition group developed; it urged the monarchy to go farther in "purifying" the Church of "Popish" influences. These Puritans, followers of the doctrines of the Swiss theologian John Calvin, believed that people could not achieve salvation through priests, confessions, or even "good works." Accordingly, they asked for an end to excessive ritual, a decrease in the number of sacraments, an abolition of a priesthood which interceded between God and man, and a return to a simpler Christianity based upon an individual's personal relationship to God.

To most Puritans, religion was a matter of preeminent importance; signs of God's "grace" indicated the state of one's soul for eternity. God was omnipotent and had already predestined those who were saved and those who were damned. If a person truly had faith and had undergone the experience of conversion, then he or she could be reasonably sure of being among the elected "saints." But the belief in predestination did not justify moral or religious laxity. Puritans felt a strong commitment to pursue their special "calling" and to do God's work on earth. A pure life did not save one, but it was an indication of salvation.

Devout English Puritans looked with alarm upon the condition of their country. During the early seventeenth century, the Anglican church seemed to lapse more and more into Catholicism, and under James I (1603–1625) and Charles I (1625–1649) the power of the monarchy grew and eclipsed Parliament, where Puritans had strength. Charles appointed

William Laud as archbishop of Canterbury, and this powerful official vigorously suppressed religious and political dissent. Royal tyranny and a Catholic-tinged Anglicanism appeared to go hand in hand; Puritans feared for both their political power and their religion.

The social and economic changes that troubled many Englishmen also disturbed Puritans. Traditional English values—order, stability, respect, exaltation of the common good—seemed lost. The solid family structure and the organic village community appeared to be disintegrating. Population soared; the pace of economic change quickened; prices rose; geographic mobility increased; poverty, vagrance, and crime became more visible. And Puritans worried. Was the widespread dishonesty, immorality, and uncertainty a sign of impending disaster for England?

Migration to
Massachusetts

To some Puritans, migration seemed the only answer; by setting an example, they would try to reform from without the society they had failed to change from within. In 1608 a group of "separatists" fled England for Holland. After a decade of growing discontent with conditions there, however, many decided to sail for America. These "Pilgrims" were Congregationalists, Puritans who believed that individual churches should not be ruled by a church hierarchy and that the "visible" church membership should closely correspond to the "invisible" church of God's elected "saints." Crowded on board the *Mayflower,* the Pilgrims and the other settlers who accompanied them crossed the ocean in sixty-five days. They landed at Plymouth, near Cape Cod, in 1620, outside the jurisdiction of Virginia, the nearest colony, and without authorization to colonize so far north. There they laid out their village in an Indian cornfield.

The Pilgrims took the lead in establishing a new government. They convinced the non-Puritan settlers and servants among them to join in signing the Mayflower Compact, an agreement modeled on a Church covenant. The compact enabled them to create a government based upon mutual consent and, at the same time, insured that the Pilgrims would retain civil control over the entire settlement.

The group was ill prepared for the rugged existence of the New World; they had paltry supplies and possessed little skill in hunting and fishing. Although few people had perished in the trans-Atlantic crossing, over half of the passengers and crew, weakened by the journey, died of scurvy the following winter. Indians, themselves debilitated after two years of epidemics, helped the white settlement adjust and survive. But the relatively homogeneous community at Plymouth remained small. It was eventually engulfed by the expansion of a later Puritan settlement at Boston farther north on Massachusetts Bay.

Like the Pilgrims, the Puritans who founded the Massachusetts

Bay colony in 1630 had been distressed by the policies of the English crown, alarmed over growing immorality in English society, and, in some cases, beset by economic anxiety. But unlike the Pilgrims, Massachusetts Bay's settlers claimed to be establishing a purer version of the Church of England, not separating from it. In 1629 they had obtained a charter to establish the Massachusetts Bay company. Fortunately, the charter, granting the stockholders the authority to govern, did not stipulate that the company had to hold meetings in England. Taking their charter with them, these Puritans sailed to the New World, and their company became a self-governing commonwealth.

In the early Massachusetts Bay colony, the church elders exerted preponderant authority. In theory, only church members could be "freeholders" with the right to vote and only those who gave evidence of "election" were admitted to the church fellowship. Massachusetts was not the totally drab, somber, and repressive society which the word *puritan* connotes today. But it was a strict community: ministers felt personal responsibility to preserve the morality of their flock, and the state of people's souls was of utmost concern to the whole society.

TRANSPLANTED ENGLISHMEN
IN NEW ENGLAND

The founder of the Massachusetts Bay colony, John Winthrop, reflected the anxieties and the sense of mission shared by many of the transplanted Englishmen when he speculated, "who knoweth but that God hath prepared this place for a refuge for many whom he meant to save in the general destruction."

Like Winthrop, other New World Puritans hoped to restore old values just as they sought to purify the Anglican church. They saw themselves not as dissenters or radicals but as perpetuators of traditional morality and stability. Clustering in tightly knit towns, each centered around a church and meetinghouse, they tried to produce a model organic community based upon true Christian living and social order. Laws discouraged any influx of strangers and bolstered the family as the basic unit of society. The structure of houses, the pattern of streets, and the division of land resembled those of a typical English village.

At first, the attempt to create a Godly and orderly society seemed quite successful. Rather than spreading out and accumulating large tracts of land, Puritans turned their backs on the wilderness and sought solace from the strange environment in familiar, cohesive towns. During the early years there seemed to be an upsurge in conversion experiences, and church membership grew. Shiploads of additional settlers arrived, and new Puritan villages enlarged the commonwealth. Puritans dared to hope that their communities were the special objects of God's grace.

Portable footwarmer for church

J. Vanderspriet, *Increase Mather.*
Massachusetts Historical Society

Unorthodoxy and
disunity

The rise of unorthodox beliefs became the Puritan leaders' first trouble-some problem. The Protestant Reformation had always exhibited a tendency toward fragmentation of religious groups. Once lay people began to challenge ecclesiastical structures, to interpret the Bible, and to assess their individual relationships to God, it became difficult to maintain any religious authority. Religion could seem incompatible with an institution dominated by a minister; the individual could himself become a church.

In New England during the 1630s, the tension between minis-terial control and individual interpretation split the religious community. Roger Williams, who migrated to Massachusetts in 1631 and subsequently became the pastor of Salem, charged that the Puritan churches were not taking enough care to exclude the unregenerate from membership. He criticized the Puritan Fathers' imposition of orthodoxy and taught that each person must be allowed the freedom to find God in his own way. His attacks upon the colony's religious practices were disconcerting enough, but Williams also argued that the Massachusetts Bay Company's charter was void because the land belonged to the Indians. In 1635 members of the General Court, the governing body of the colony, banished Williams in an attempt to stop the spread of ideas they considered dangerous to social order and religious discipline.

Williams fled Boston, purchased a tract of land from the Indians, and later obtained a royal charter for his new colony, Rhode Island. He granted complete freedom of conscience in the colony. Although Williams surely did not believe that all religions were equally valid, he abhorred any sort of forced worship. His decision to permit religious freedom was the ultimate culmination of his obsession with religious purity and of a series of separations from possibly unregenerate fellowships. In the end, he could not bear to take communion with anyone but his wife.

Foundation, First House of Burgesses, Jamestown. *Colonial National Historical Park*

A few years after Williams's expulsion, a prominent Bostonian, Anne Hutchinson, provoked another doctrinal crisis. Through a mystical experience, she claimed, God had revealed that she was one of the elect, and she argued that only such direct inner revelations provided sure signs of salvation. Orthodox Puritans also believed in the importance of the mystical conversion experience in which one was suddenly overcome with the knowledge of God's grace, but they also taught that a pure life and good works were fairly reliable outward indications of election. Hutchinson rejected the validity of any such behavioral test (a position called antinomianism), and her influence threatened to undermine the authority of the church. Once again the General Court hurriedly acted to save the colony from dissenters; it banished Anne Hutchinson and a follower.

One of the most prominent Puritan ministers, Thomas Hooker, also split from the Massachusetts Bay colony. Hooker objected to the power, both religious and political, held by the Puritan magistrates. In 1636 he and his flock established the new colony of Connecticut. Their constitution, the Fundamental Orders, allowed even those outside the church to participate in politics.

Seeds of discord Despite doctrinal disagreements, the first generation of New Englanders were filled with a sense of purpose. Most of them thought they had received God's grace and were carrying out His grand design. The majority of the community belonged to the Church, and there was an overlapping of civil and religious functions. But the vision of a model "Citty upon a Hill," a devout, static, and purified society, soon faded. With new people arriving throughout the 1630s there was bound to be contention, even among those who shared the same goals. Settlers came from all over England, and the memories of diverse village ways invariably prompted arguments over how things should be done. What was the common law on a particular point? How should meetings be run? How might the community deal with an errant son or a slothful citizen? And many new people came seeking material rather than spiritual satisfaction; they were not content to forgo personal advancement for the good of the community.

Villages sprawled out; settlers scattered and became less amenable to central control. Boston, the heart of the Massachusetts Bay Colony, grew most rapidly. Soon there were two, then three churches. Occupations became more diverse and status groupings more complex. The unity of the small new settlement shattered.

During the 1640s Massachusetts suffered a severe depression. Ironically, the economic trouble of New World Puritans stemmed largely from the success of their brethren in England. By 1640 the split between the English crown and a variety of opposition groups, including the

Puritans, had become so severe that the king's enemies resorted to revolution. Commanded by Oliver Cromwell and directed by Parliament, the Puritan's traditional stronghold in the English government, the revolutionary forces defeated royal armies and beheaded King Charles I. Cromwell became "Lord Protector" of a "Commonwealth" government which lasted until 1660. With a Puritan ruling in England, the Great Migration into Massachusetts stopped; the influx of English currency, brought by new settlers, ceased to buoy New England's economy. Without a major exportable commodity, the future of the Puritan settlements seemed dim.

But the location of the Massachusetts Bay colony proved to be its economic salvation. Good harbors, especially at Boston, provided the foundation for a thriving commerce. The growth of trade and the development of a shipping industry insured the colony's prosperity. After about 1650, New England began to boom.

The economic reinvigoration of Massachusetts turned out to be a mixed blessing. Wealth turned heads away from the Puritan founders' original purpose and attracted profitseekers who remained outside the religious community. The quickening of economic life seemed to reflect God's favor upon New England, but it also introduced the same flux and vice which had troubled Old England. In addition, election by God surely was not hereditary, and by the 1650s Puritans uneasily noticed

Block Laurens, *Novum Amsterdamum 1650. Courtesy of The New York Historical Society, New York City*

that many of their children were not undergoing the conversion experience which was required for church membership. If the trend continued, Puritans feared the bulk of the population would soon be outside the church.

In 1662 a meeting of Puritan ministers arrived at a solution to the problem of declining church membership. The ministers agreed to baptize the children of church members and to admit them into partial fellowship even though they could not give evidence of grace. To preserve the church's purity, the ministers excluded these "half-way" members from participation in the sacrament of Holy Communion. The Half-Way Covenant did revive lagging church membership, but it also showed that the Puritans' early dreams were yielding to expediency. The colony of Massachusetts, and even the church itself, was no longer a community of "saints."

THE HORSE

Before the sixteenth century, horses were unknown in the western hemisphere. When these strange animals carried the expedition of Hernan Cortés westward into the Aztec heartland, they startled and impressed the native population. Bernal Díaz, a member of the conquering Spanish army, reported that "the Indians thought at that time that the horse and

33

rider were one creature, for they had never seen a horse before." The psychological impact of the beasts was one ingredient in Spain's successful conquest of the great Indian civilizations of America. Realizing their advantage, the conquerors tried to keep the animals out of the hands of unsubdued tribes.

In 1680 the Pueblo revolt near Santa Fe that briefly drove out the Spanish soldiers left herds of horses relatively unprotected. Apache raiders captured many of the animals and spread them northward. During the late seventeenth and early eighteenth centuries, widespread use of horses began to revolutionize the life of the Plains Indians, reinforcing their nomadic existence and becoming prizes of intertribal warfare. Indians became skilled horsemen and grew more efficient at hunting the buffalo upon which their civilization depended.

With the introduction of horses some semiagricultural tribes of the prairies to the east even voluntarily moved westward to become hunters, and this infusion of new people brought the Plains Culture to its height. The portable tepees, the moccasins, the feathered warbonnets, the colorful beadwork, and the buffalo hide drawings—all associated with the Plains Culture—are part of the rich western heritage which is so important in American art and lore. And the horse, a vital part of both the Indian and white way of life, became the very symbol of the cultural clash in the American West.

The huge herds of wild mustangs which once roamed the mountain valleys and cast long shadows upon the Great Plains have gradually dwindled to a few government-protected bands. Once the advance agent of European civilization and a force which transformed the native way of life, the horse itself eventually became the victim of a newer transportation revolution.

THINGS TO THINK ABOUT:
B.C.–1660

Describe the people who inhabited the New World before the arrival of the Europeans. Characterize early Indian-white relations. Harold E. Driver, *Indians of North America* (revised edition 1969) and Alvin M. Josephy, Jr., *The Indian Heritage of America* (1968) provide the best surveys of Indian cultures. C. W. Ceram, *The First American* (1971) is an up-to-date and highly readable popular account of North American archaeology. Wilcomb E. Washburn, *Red Man's Land / White Man's Law*, W. T. Hagan, *American Indians* (1961) and Alden T. Vaughan, *The New England Frontier: Puritans and Indians, 1620–1675* (1965) contain treatments of early interracial contact.

What factors gave an impetus to European exploration and discovery? J. H. Parry's books provide the best starting place. See his *Europe and a Wider World* (1949), *The Spanish Seaborne Empire* (1966), and *The Age of Reconnaissance* (1963). Samuel Eliot Morison's *Admiral of the Ocean Sea* (1942) and *European Discovery of America: The Northern Voyages, 500–1600* (1971) are indispensable. Howard Mumford Jones, *O Strange New World* (1952) is a fascinating and well-written account of European attitudes toward the New World. Charles Gibson, *Spain in America* (1966) is a survey of the Spanish Empire. J. Bartlett Brebner's *The Explorers of North America* (1937) is also useful.

What were the motives behind English colonization? How did the motives vary from colony to colony? Charles M. Andrews, *The Colonial Period of American History* (1934–1938) is a standard account of seventeenth-century colonization. See also Wesley F. Craven, *The Southern Colonies in the Seventeenth Century* (1949); and J. E. Pomfret and F. M. Shumway, *Founding the American Colonies* (1970). Wallace Notestein, *The English People on the Eve of Colonization* (1954); Peter Laslett, *The World We Have Lost* (1965); Carl Bridenbaugh, *Vexed and Troubled Englishmen* (1968); and Michael Walzer, *The Revolution of the Saints* (1965) provide valuable English background.

Why did Puritans emigrate to New England and what kind of society did they hope to create? Trace the early development of New England and evaluate their success. Several studies will illuminate Puritan motivations and aspirations: Alan Simpson, *Puritanism in Old and New England* (1955); Perry Miller, *Errand into the Wilderness* (1956); Edmund S. Morgan, *The Puritan Dilemma: The Story of John Winthrop* (1958); Darrett Rutman, *Winthrop's Boston* (1965) and *American Puritanism* (1970). On dissent in New England see Edmund S. Morgan, *Roger Williams: The Church and the State* (1967); Kai T. Erikson, *Wayward Puritans* (1966); Emery Battis, *Saints and Sectaries* (1962).

1660-1763

TWO | BRITISH America

JONATHAN EDWARDS

"The real life of Jonathan Edwards," writes the great intellectual historian Perry Miller, "was the life of his mind." The greatest theologian that America has produced, Edwards indeed lived a largely inward life, having his first religious experience at the age of five or six, spending long hours training for the ministry, then in his adult life, rising daily at 5 A.M. (4 A.M. in summer) and working about thirteen hours a day in his study. His works, many still unpublished, include about a thousand sermons, several thick volumes of biblical commentary, thousands of pages of "Miscellaneous Observations" (some of them actually long expositions), a number of autobiographical and polemical works, and several lengthy treatises (*The Freedom of the Will* is the most famous) on which his reputation as a theologian largely rests. He also spent about thirty-five of his fifty-five years—he was born in 1703 and died in 1758—meeting the responsibilities of a minister and doing his part in raising a family of eleven children. For relaxation and exercise he chopped wood and rode his horse through the New England woodlands. But even then, if he thought of some new solution to an intellectual puzzle, he would pin a sheet of blank paper to his coat as a reminder. Legends report that he would usually return from his midday ride covered with paper and his wife Sarah would help unpin him.

This quiet and austere man stood at the center of major controversies in the religious history of New England during his own lifetime and for three-quarters of a century after his death. His theology was a gallant effort to preserve the core of Puritanism—its terrifying vision of a wholly omnipotent God saving or damning as He would helpless and sinful men—in the face of a new science stemming from Isaac Newton and John Locke. The newly found confidence in man's ability to understand the world about him had, for many thinkers, removed some of the terror of religion, pushing reason and secular morality to the fore over against the enthusiasm and the anguish of religious emotion. Edwards, as rationalistic as any of his opponents, insisted that these new visions of nature could be fitted to the older vision of the diety, that only through the door of religious experience did a proper understanding of the world of Locke and Newton open to view.

Edwards's theology, apparently so abstract, actually had immediate practical application to people's lives: he became a great champion of the revivals that occurred throughout the colonies—including in his own church in Northampton, Massachusetts—beginning in the 1720s and continuing sporadically into the 1750s. The first Great Awakening in which Edwards participated set a pattern for American religion that has never ceased: the division between revivalistic and nonrevivalistic churches, the emphasis on emotion and "experimental religion," the periodic "harvests" of new converts, the "hellfire and brimstone" sermon to scare the literal hell out of congregations. Edwards's defense of the revivals and his efforts to distinguish between true religious experiences and more secular roots of enthusiasm gave the revivals the intellectual underpinning they needed to become an accepted part of the practice of so many churches.

For another seventy-five years at least Edwards's theology would hold emotional religion in America to the intellectual traditions of Puritanism until, in the early nineteenth century, the emotional and the rational sides of American religion would clearly separate into divisions of style and class that remain familiar down to the present.

1660-1763

1660	Navigation Act
1663	Staple Act
1664	Duke of York seizes New Amsterdam for England
1665	Duke of York transfers Jersey to new proprietors
	Charter granted for Carolina
1669	John Locke's "Fundamental Constitutions" for Carolina
1673	Plantation Duty Act
1675–76	King Phillip's War
1676	Bacon's Rebellion in Virginia
1677	Culpepper's Rebellion in Carolina
1681	William Penn secures a charter for Pennsylvania
1684	Massachusetts Bay Colony's charter revoked
1686–89	Dominion of New England
1688–89	Glorious Revolution in England brings William and Mary to throne
1689–97	War of the League of Augsburg (King William's War)
1689	Leisler's rebellion
1692	Salem witch trials
1699	Wool Act
1702–13	War of the Spanish Succession (Queen Anne's War)
1720s–50s	Great Awakening
1732	Hat Act
	Georgia founded
1733	Molasses Act
1740–48	War of the Austrian Succession (King George's War)
1750	Iron Act
1754	Albany Congress
1754–63	French and Indian War (Seven Years' War)

ENGLISH NORTH AMERICA UNDER THE RESTORATION

In the spring of 1660, more than ten years after his father had perished on Oliver Cromwell's scaffold, Charles II ascended the throne, ending England's stormy Commonwealth period. Some critics charged that Charles seemed to spend more time with mistresses than with affairs of state, but the King was a bright and able man. His reign had important consequences for the plantations in America. By invalidating all existing Commonwealth legislation, the Restoration settlement forced a fresh look at the relationship between England and America. England's business classes hoped for new economic opportunities; Royalist supporters anticipated additional political patronage; and some governmental officials feared these "little Englands" were growing too independent of royal authority.

The navigation system

The new Parliament quickly endorsed the economic policies of the Commonwealth, passing laws that followed the basic outlines of those adopted under Cromwell, with some important refinements. The new Navigation Act of 1660 continued England's monopoly of colonial commerce, restricting all trade to ships built and owned by Englishmen and manned by crews at least three-quarters English. Lawmakers also declared that shippers could export certain "enumerated" products only to England or to another English plantation. The Staple Act of 1663 additionally stipulated that non-English goods bound for America (with a few exceptions such as salt for New England's fisheries) pass through England to be taxed and reloaded onto English vessels. The economic and governmental interests supporting these measures hoped to build a stronger merchant marine at the expense of the Dutch and to establish an integrated imperial economy.

The Navigation and Staple Acts inaugurated a policy later called "mercantilism," a state-controlled economy in which colonies enhanced the prosperity, power, and self-sufficiency of the mother country by providing a source of raw materials and a market for goods. But the term itself only entered common use a hundred years later, and architects of these earlier trade laws possessed no comprehensive mercantile theory. Rather, various economic groups advanced their own interests through favorable legislation, with government officials balancing conflicting demands.

Initially, the Navigation Acts worked little hardship upon the North American colonies. Classifying colonial ships as "English," the measures stimulated the growth of an American maritime industry. And with the exception of tobacco from the Chesapeake area, the original list of enumerated products included only West Indian exports. Economic realities—particularly the availability of credit—dictated that most American exports would go to England anyway, and colonists themselves preferred British products in return. Later, as officials added more restrictions and the colonial economy matured, the Navigation system produced friction within the empire, but these early Restoration measures established regulations accurately reflecting dominant trade patterns.

New York

The Restoration also stimulated a revival of colonization. Faced with constant financial difficulties and a variety of strategic problems, Charles II found land grants an inexpensive means of rewarding royal favorites and an effective way of extending England's domains in the New World. Before the king's death in 1685, several new imperial outposts had sprung up in North America. All began as proprietary colonies, holdings granted

Synagogue at Newport, Rhode Island. *Library of Congress*

as personal estates to a single individual or to a group of English magnates. These powerful allies of the king played key roles in securing charters for new colonies.

In 1664 Charles's brother the duke of York, later King James II, received a broad grant encompassing the Dutch colony of New Netherland. Seizing the opportunity to oust England's hated rival from North America, James quickly dispatched a small expeditionary force. After stopping in Boston to secure additional troops, the fleet's commander sailed into New Amsterdam's inviting harbor and demanded surrender of the settlement. Peter Stuyvesant, New Amsterdam's feisty, one-legged governor, threatened a fight but yielded when citizens refused to follow their unpopular leader. Without a single shot being fired, Peter Minuet's twenty-four-dollar bargain fell to the Englishmen, and they immediately renamed the city and colony New York, in honor of the duke. The new proprietor eased the transition to English rule by guaranteeing Dutch inhabitants fair treatment, tolerating their religion, and recognizing the validity of their inheritance customs. Many old Dutch families continued to dominate New York's society and politics into the eighteenth century, and the city was North America's most cosmopolitan center, containing Dutch, English, French, Swedish, African, and Jewish people. James's goals in New York were primarily political and strategic, rather than economic, and he imposed only a low annual assessment—called a "quitrent" (not a rent but a feudal fee)—on colonial landholders.

New Jersey and Carolina

Financial considerations loomed more important in other proprietary ventures, particularly New Jersey and Carolina. In 1665 the duke of York transferred part of his grant, an area called Jersey, to several Royalist friends. In an effort to lure Puritan settlers from New England, the Jersey proprietors promised religious liberty, a measure of self-government, and sizeable tracts of "free" land. Hoping to develop a profitable estate in the New World, they also imposed a small annual rent on the properties. The New Englanders who migrated southward and the other residents reluctantly paid the required quitrents for a time, but this essentially feudalistic arrangement proved unworkable in a country with abundant land. The colony never fulfilled its owners' financial expectations and, after a series of transactions, split into separate colonies of East and West Jersey. Political complications continued until the government finally remerged them into a single royal colony of New Jersey.

In some ways Carolina's early history paralleled that of New Jersey. Influential Royalists, envisioning a rent-producing estate, secured a charter in 1665 and tried to attract settlers from New England through a variety of economic and political inducements. The largest number of migrants, however, arrived not from New England but from Barbados, and they introduced their sugar plantation economy and slave labor system to the southern part of Carolina. But after five years of little growth, Carolina's future appeared in doubt. Then in 1669 Anthony Ashley Cooper, the earl of Shaftsbury, reorganized the venture. One of the most talented men of his age, Shaftsbury was a gifted writer, resourceful political intriguer, and social visionary. In collaboration with John Locke, a political theorist whose fame ultimately surpassed his patron's, Shaftsbury drafted a new frame of government for the struggling colony.

The "Fundamental Constitutions" was an overly ambitious attempt at social planning. The lengthy and complicated document envisioned a class hierarchy, including a hereditary nobility with peculiarly American titles such as "landgraves" and "caciques." It distributed land and political power according to social status, implementing Shaftsbury's theory that political tranquility derived from a stable socioeconomic order. The generous provisions for large landholders, the proprietor hoped, would also attract wealthy settlers. Few of Shaftsbury's elaborate visions materialized. New World conditions—particularly friction with Indians and the great amount of land—frustrated an experiment geared to static and hierarchical Old World theories. After thirty years and several revisions, Carolina's proprietors scrapped the "Fundamental Constitutions." But Carolina did gradually stabilize as its economy developed. In the south, tobacco and later rice supplanted sugar as cash crops, and Charleston became one of colonial America's leading commercial centers. North Carolina, which lacked an Atlantic harbor, matured more slowly, establishing closer ties to southern Virginia than to the other Carolina plantation.

Pennsylvania and Georgia

Like Carolina, Pennsylvania also began as a combination of idealism and systematic estate planning. The colony's founder, William Penn, belonged to the Society of Friends, a much-persecuted religious group commonly known as Quakers. (When the Society's founder once admonished a hostile magistrate to "tremble at the word of the Lord," the judge derisively called the group "Quakers.") Quakers preached a religion devoid of ceremony and hierarchies: each individual was equal before the Lord and received his faith directly from a divine "Inner Light." Their beliefs, especially the idea of immediate revelation through the "Inner Light," estranged the Friends from more traditional religious groups, and their pacifism and refusal to take oaths angered civil authorities. Penn himself served a short time in jail but, despite his "queer" religious ideas, remained a friend of both Charles II and the duke of York.

In 1680 Penn sought a royal charter for a New World haven for Quakers. Some governmental officials opposed the grant, warning that proprietary colonies were too independent of royal control and ought to be curtailed. But in 1681 the king bowed to Penn's powerful supporters and granted him a large area south of New York. Penn's charter contained several new, specific limitations which reflected the Crown's growing concern with maintaining royal authority in the New World. The proprietor had to respect the Church of England's rights, keep a permanent agent in London, submit all provincial laws to royal scrutiny, allow the king's customs officers into Pennsylvania, and recognize the English government's right to tax the colony.

William Penn planned his colony carefully and in 1682 set sail for America, considering his venture both a "Holy Experiment" for the Quaker faith and an important addition to the Penn family's extensive estates. Displaying a sense of justice and a prudent regard for harmony, he insisted upon purchasing native Americans' lands rather than simply seizing them. The persuasive Quaker also talked the duke of York out of some additional territory along Delaware Bay, an area that later became a separate state. He offered new settlers generous land grants, subject to small quitrents. An extensive publicity campaign throughout Europe, including promotional agents and multilingual pamphlets, touted the glories of the "Holy Experiment." Although Penn failed to attract large numbers of Quakers from the Continent, the first migration from England was comparable to the massive Puritan expedition of 1630. Penn himself wrote the constitution, which guaranteed a variety of individual liberties and offered some degree of popular participation in government. But he retained considerable authority, and the whole system ultimately rested upon the founder's paternalism and the settlers' willingness to follow his direction.

A variety of difficulties kept Penn in England much of the time, and the colony suffered from his absence. Colonists did make a faithful attempt to purchase Indian land, but conflicting ideas about property rights led to numerous misunderstandings. Neither could Pennsylvanians work out land disputes with neighboring Maryland, finally settled by the famous Mason-Dixon line of 1769. Penn hoped that quitrents would "supply me with bread" and would "not be made a reason of rebellion by men in their wits that love their lives and estates," but most settlers refused to pay. Most distressing to Penn, dissident settlers increasingly attacked the great power reserved to the proprietor and his representatives. Antiproprietory elements fought to enlarge the authority of Pennsylvania's assembly, a body Penn conceived as a rubber stamp for his decisions. "For the love of God, me, and the poor country," the exasperated founder once wrote, "be not so governmentish; so noisy and open in your disaffection." Although Pennsylvania eventually prospered, the colony's turbulent early history provided another example of New World conditions frustrating Old World planners.

Most of the proprietary colonies established after 1660, like the earlier ventures, disillusioned their founders. They provided little revenue and became graveyards for a variety of Old World social theories. The last British colony in North America, Georgia (which was not established until 1732), followed the pattern of previous settlements. Serving as a military bulwark against Spanish expansion from Florida, Georgia did secure Britain's claim to the area south of Carolina. But the colony never fulfilled its sponsors' dream of establishing a regenerative haven for British debtors. Georgia's trustees—a group of English philanthropists led by General James Ogelthorpe—staked paupers with land, tools, and supplies; the founders also hoped that prohibitions against rum and black slavery would encourage industrious habits among the new settlers. But relatively few debtors ever arrived, and immigrants from Germany and all parts of the British Isles chaffed under the trustees' restrictions. Finally, in 1752, the Crown assumed direct control of Georgia, and it became a royal colony.

TIME OF TROUBLES

Toward the end of the seventeenth century open conflicts erupted in several colonies in English North America. This "time of troubles," reflecting fundamental tensions in New World society, convinced many English officials of the need for greater royal control over the American domains.

Dissension within the colonies arose out of the unsettled fabric of society and the fragmented nature of politics. In England political control was not only the prerogative but also the responsibility of those gentlemen who possessed social status and substantial wealth. Englishmen naturally sought to transplant this concept of a static social hierarchy to the New World, and during the early years of colonization their attempts generally succeeded, despite the absence of a nobility. The mass of freeholders accepted direction from the most prosperous among them, and these few men comprised a ruling elite. As the struggling plantations matured into more complex provinces, however, New World reality increasingly diverged from the Old World ideal. Although the alluring myths of instant wealth proved inflated, a young man with soaring ambitions could make substantial gains within a relatively short time. But political power rarely matched this rising socioeconomic status. New men seeking positions of political leadership not only found too many others with the same ambition but also discovered firmly entrenched groups, some with ties going back to the first generation. And those in power, unprotected by titles and buffeted by the pressures of a constantly changing society, acutely felt their own insecurity and took their challengers seriously. The resulting rivalry for power produced complicated factional alliances and tumultuous politics. The violence and disruption of the late seventeenth century were less uprisings from below than conflicts between social and economic equals in a fluid society.

Tensions over political control were tied to other potentially explosive issues such as land ownership. If wealth could be gained in a short time, it could also rapidly be lost. And at a time when money and status depended primarily upon landed holdings, easy access to the ultimate source of land—be it the colonial governor, the legislature, or the proprietor—was vital. A man's dream of additional acres or his chance of clearing a disputed title diminished according to his distance from the locus of political power.

Commercial uncertainties also plagued colonial America. By evading regulations or bribing underpaid officials, some colonial merchants began to discover lucrative opportunities outside the legal channels of trade. At the same time, a new element entered the scene: professional royal officials who staked their future upon faithful service to the Crown. They insisted upon rigid adherence to the Navigation laws when the statutes were still relatively new, precedents almost nonexistent, and provisions vague. The seemingly arbitrary actions of customs officials sometimes stirred local resentment, and, by throwing their influence toward one American faction or another, the officials could further disrupt domestic politics. When royal authority lined up on the side of the political "ins," any assault by the "outs" might escalate into an attack upon English authority itself.

Bacon's Rebellion

Bacon's Rebellion in Virginia was the earliest in a series of colonial disruptions which occurred between 1675 and 1700. Differences over Indian policy triggered this violent struggle. In response to warfare on the frontier, Governor William Berkeley, an experienced and once highly popular administrator, advocated a conciliatory stance toward Virginia's native American neighbors, but an opposition faction led by Nathaniel Bacon capitalized on sentiment in favor of a military expedition. The governor's enemies carried additional grievances: an inner circle of Berkeley's friends monopolized offices, Berkeley's colonial government intruded into local affairs, and many disliked the way new land grants were distributed in Virginia's Northern Neck.

In the late spring of 1676 Bacon, a recent arrival in the colony, broke with the governor and began a series of political and military maneuvers which ultimately drove Berkeley from the capital. The Baconites gained control of the colonial government; Virginia's assembly, the House of Burgesses, enacted a series of laws redressing many of their grievances. In response, the governor sought assistance from England, and, worried about disorder in a colony which produced substantial revenues, English officials dispatched an expedition. But before British troops arrived, Bacon's sudden death killed his rebellion. Berkeley quickly reestablished control and embarked upon a ruthless campaign of revenge.

Bacon's Rebellion reflected the growing pains of a new society; it was not a prelude to American independence. Most of Bacon's followers insisted upon their fidelity to the Crown, and Berkeley's rapid reassertion of authority indicated Virginians' fundamental loyalty. Although Bacon's opponents tried to picture his movement as an uprising of the "rabble" and the "rag-tailed," the Baconites represented a group with the same

aura of gentility as the governor and his followers. Bacon himself had been one of Berkeley's close associates, and the other leaders owned substantial property in Virginia. After the Rebellion, Baconite William Drummond, a former governor of northern Carolina, came before Berkeley in a deadly, yet polite, meeting between social equals: "Mr. Drummond, you are welcome. I am more glad to see you than any man in Virginia. . . . You shall be hanged in half an hour," greeted the governor. "As your honor pleases," replied Bacon's lieutenant, and several hours later he was dead. A dissident faction of Virginia's too numerous elite lost out in Bacon's Rebellion.

Dissension in other colonies

Similar, less violent confrontations occurred in other colonies. In Carolina declining tobacco prices, Indian raids, and attempts to enforce trade laws erupted into conflict the year after Bacon's Rebellion. This much more limited incident, Culpepper's Rebellion, followed long-standing factional cleavages between older settlers and more recent arrivals aligned with Carolina's proprietors. Successfully ousting a temporary governor sent from England, the old-line planters established their own government in 1677. The proprietors, anxious to minimize the difficulties before royal authorities stepped in, dropped treason charges against the rebels and acceded to their opponent's regime.

Trouble between proprietary and antiproprietary elements also began in Maryland during the 1670s. In addition to differences over political appointments, trade regulations, and land grants, Maryland seethed with deep-seated antagonisms between the Catholic proprietors, the Calvert family, and the largely Protestant settlers. Dissidents made the assembly the focus of their protests against the Calverts, and the third Lord Baltimore retaliated by reducing the membership and contesting the powers of the lower house. Maryland's politics remained turbulent for a number of years, and open defiance finally developed in 1689 when dissidents rose up against the proprietary regime.

In the Massachusetts Bay Colony events spiraled into a direct challenge to royal authority. A bloody conflict between Indians and whites, King Phillip's War, seriously disrupted New England's society. And before the problems and divisions arising from the war had healed, arrival of a new colonial bureaucrat, Edward Randolph, further aggravated tensions. Randolph launched a vigorous inquiry into Massachusetts's violation of its charter, evasion of trade laws, and defiant attitude toward the royal government. He then returned to England and urged the Lords of Trade to revoke the colony's charter and, if necessary, to enforce royal authority with troops. The Lords of Trade moved cautiously, first asking Massachusetts to explain Randolph's charges. But the reply of the Massachusetts General Court hardly soothed English worries. Claiming that England's laws were "bounded with the four seas, and do not reach America," the court reminded the Lords that Massachusetts sent no representatives to the Parliament which enacted the trade laws. Ultimately the government began legal proceedings to revoke Massachusetts' charter and to take the colony under direct royal rule. The unpopular Randolph also returned to America as a customs collector and immediately prosecuted a number of alleged violations.

Clearly, final decisions were no longer being made in America, and the difficulties in New England, along with disorders elsewhere, prompted royal officials to consider new steps to control their unruly overseas outposts.

TENSIONS WITHIN AN EMPIRE

Even before the controversies in Massachusetts, England had begun to tighten its grip over commerce and government in America. As with the earlier trade laws, British officials followed no master plan, but their reactions to individual problems increased English involvement. The original Navigation laws had contained a significant loophole: by carrying "enumerated" products first to another colony and then to lucrative European markets, merchants could bypass the required stopover and taxation in England. In order to stop this subterfuge of the "broken voyage," the Plantation Duty Act of 1673 imposed a tax at the point of departure. The government also authorized appointment of royal customs officers to collect the duty and to enforce all trade regulations.

In addition to tightening the commercial system, England reinforced its political authority. Following Bacon's Rebellion, the government dispatched almost twelve hundred troops to Virginia, the first such detachment of royal forces ever sent to the colonies. The limitations imposed upon the Pennsylvania proprietorship also reflected the new inclination to reduce the independence of both proprietary and charter colonies. William Penn, the Calverts, and the Carolina proprietors all faced legal challenges to their grants, and in 1684 the Court of Chancery upheld the Lords of Trade and formally revoked Massachusetts Bay's charter.

The Dominion of New England The most ambitious move toward centralized control came in 1686 when England attempted to integrate several colonies—ultimately including New England, New York, and the Jerseys—into one administrative unit, the Dominion of New England. The Dominion's architects hoped to reduce excessive colonial independence and to create a unified military command against the French and Indians to the north. A governor appointed in England and assisted by an advisory Council exercised dominant control, unchecked by any representative assembly. The new governor, Sir Edmund Andros, established his headquarters in Boston and attempted a number of radical changes. Although possessing an impressive set of credentials, Andros rapidly proved a vain and tactless leader. Within hours after arriving in Puritan New England, bringing a retinue "of abject persons fetched from New York," he demanded a place in which to conduct Anglican Church services. He permitted fireworks on the Sabbath, allowed a fencing contest after a midweek religious lecture, and introduced dancing around a maypole onto the Boston Common. Even "gynecandrical" dancing (defined by Increase Mather as "that which is commonly called *Mixt* or Promiscuous Dancing, viz. of Men and Women...together") gained ground, and Puritan divines charged the new Anglican rulers with polluting Massachusetts' religious and moral atmosphere.

Andros did make remarkable progress in strengthening colonial defenses, but he antagonized too many people, particularly in Massachusetts. He packed his Council with outsiders, including the hated Edward Randolph. He also cracked down on New Englanders' most cherished institution, the town meeting, limiting them to a single session per year and shifting some of their duties elsewhere. His new land tax actually lowered rates, but his arbitrary manner of imposing the levy angered many of Massachusetts' independent-minded towns. And Andros's effort

The Smokers' Rebellion. *Culver Pictures*

to sort out New England's tangled land system, by ordering entirely new grants and introducing an annual quitrent, created greater chaos and deeper resentment. Andros faced an impossible task. The young American plantations were far too divided and their politics too factionalized to offer much hope of successfully incorporating existing governments into the Dominion of New England. The Dominion encompassed an area too vast and too diverse to be governed effectively through an entirely new system. The scattered American settlements were simply unprepared for meaningful cooperation, and in the spring of 1689 Andros's regime collapsed. Events associated with England's Glorious Revolution hastened the Dominion's fall.

The Glorious Revolution and its aftermath

In the Glorious Revolution of 1688–89 Britons deposed their second king in less than fifty years. Charles II had always proceeded with caution and stealth, but James II, who succeeded his brother in 1685, inaugurated political and religious policies which alienated large numbers of subjects. James's vigorous assertion of the royal prerogative, contempt for representative institutions, and pro-Catholic measures convinced England's aristocracy to curb his arbitrary rule. When his second wife gave birth to a Catholic heir, who replaced James's Protestant daughter Mary in the succession, influential Englishmen invited Mary and her husband, William of Orange, to come to England. James fled the country, and Parliament offered the throne to William and Mary after they agreed to respect a number of parliamentary rights and privileges.

England's revolution paralleled a series of upheavals in the colonies, some directly related to the overthrow of the Stuart monarch and others merely coincidental to it. Massachusetts learned of English events through fragmentary rumors, and Boston exploded when confirmation of William and Mary's succession came on April 18, 1689. The course of events remains confused, but that day ended with Andros and Randolph in custody, leading Boston merchants in control, and the Dominion of New England in ruins. Throughout New England, prominent citizens pledged their loyalty to the new Protestant monarchs and reestablished their former governments. Further south, New Yorkers also overthrew the Dominion when Jacob Leisler deposed one of Governor Andros's lieutenants. Leisler's Rebellion drew support from several rich merchant families, frozen out of the Dominion's politics, as well as from smaller landowners and New York City artisans. Still another colony, Maryland, experienced major difficulties in 1689; as in New York, influential men outside the proprietors' inner circle spearheaded the revolt against Lord Baltimore's government. A "Protestant Association" overthrew the proprietary regime and established its own interim administration. In the same year, a group of wealthy planters forced northern Carolina's governor, Seth Sothel, to resign and leave the colony. Ironically, he then journeyed to Charles Town, where an opposition faction ousted its own governor and installed Sothel as that colony's chief executive.

By the end of 1690 at least five North American colonies had experienced serious political explosions, and rumblings of discontent persisted elsewhere. What would be the reaction of England's new rulers? They still possessed no master plan for colonial affairs, but a series of new imperial understandings emerged from the chaos of the late seventeenth century.

Despite the parliamentary limitations imposed on the monarchy in 1689, William and his successors remained very much the center of English government. The king conceded none of his own nor his nation's constitutional authority in America. In 1696 England revised and strengthened its commercial regulations. Another Navigation Act, in which the ubiquitous Edward Randolph had his hand, codified earlier laws and established a system of vice-admiralty courts to enforce them. Officials believed that colonial jurors were too lenient and that vice-admiralty courts, which functioned without juries, would offer more vigorous enforcement. Also a new colonial bureaucracy, the Board of Trade, supplanted the ineffective Lords of Trade.

But the king and English officials faced matters more pressing than those in the colonies. Although they upheld the theory of royal supremacy in the colonies, the practice was more one of benign neglect. Allying England with the Netherlands, William immediately took his new subjects into a French war. And since North America became one theater of the ensuing hundred years of Anglo-French conflict, the Crown considered colonial cooperation more vital than governmental experiments. In any event, colonial administrators could hardly even formulate significant changes let alone carry them out. The large number of officers and agencies which dealt with American questions frustrated creation of any comprehensive policy and gave colonial spokesmen a wide field in which to bargain on behalf of American interests. England would not tolerate the kind of open defiance displayed by Massachusetts before the Glorious Revolution, but it still did not attempt to control day-to-day affairs in America.

England came to accept, and to expect, a good deal of colonial self-government. Following the Glorious Revolution, the movement to revoke colonial charters ended. Maryland's and Pennsylvania's charters were suspended for short periods, but only the Jersey proprietors lost their grant entirely. In 1691 even Massachusetts secured a new charter which settled many, though not all, disputes in favor of the Bay Colony. (Massachusetts had to concede royal appointment of its governor even though the assembly retained the power to appoint councillors.) English officials accepted representative institutions as an integral part of colonial political structure, and the elective branch of provincial legislatures gained more and more power. After 1689 England's pressing need for colonial assistance, especially financial aid, during its imperial wars contributed to the invigoration of representative institutions.

The Glorious Revolution became an important symbol for transplanted as well as for native Englishmen. Colonial writers pictured James's ouster as a complete victory for parliamentary monarchy over Stuart pretensions to absolute, divine-right sovereignty. The revolutionary settlement, colonists believed, provided firm guarantees against royal tyranny and served as an important guidepost for establishing their own provincial governments.

COLONIAL GOVERNMENT

Between 1689 and 1763 Americans developed a political system which differed substantially from their English model. One may easily describe colonial America's political institutions; but then as now, formal structures constituted only one part of politics. The colonials' fundamental values, hopes, fears, and informal practices also influenced the operation of government.

The English model Types of government, Americans believed, came in three basic forms: monarchy, rule by one; aristocracy, rule by a few; and democracy, rule by the many. Each had serious weaknesses, and people feared that any one of these "pure" forms would soon "degenerate" into its "corrupted" version: monarchies became absolute tyrannies; aristocratic governments devolved into oligarchic regimes; and democracies degenerated into anarchy or mob rule. All "pure" systems failed because rulers always sought greater power and eventually destroyed individual liberties. But English government seemed to offer a means of checking man's natural passion for aggrandizing power. Following the crises of the seventeenth century, Englishmen had "blended" or "mixed" the three forms into a "balanced" government in which each of the three major elements in English society possessed its own separate institution and provided checks upon the power of one another. The king, of course, supplied the monarchical element; the House of Lords corresponded to the aristocratic form and represented England's titled nobility; the House of Commons provided the democratic element and represented the mass of English freeholders. The revolutionary settlement of 1689 had guaranteed a balanced government and prevented, it was hoped, any repetition of royal despotism.

Despite this precise framework, English politics operated outside its formal theoretical boundaries. The monarchy remained the vital force in the mid-eighteenth century. Through its monopoly over appointments, control over electoral procedures, and other extraconstitutional techniques, the Crown exerted tremendous influence over the House of Lords and, more importantly, over the House of Commons. In alliance with powerful aristocrats, who managed and manipulated the numerous parliamentary factions, the king's government rarely lost a vote in Commons. This informal system, which adjusted most differences between the king and Parliament, clashed with cherished ideas of balanced government. And such violations of constitutional orthodoxy did not go unnoticed. In particular, a small group of political outsiders, the "radical" or "true" Whigs, decried the influence of the king's ministers over Commons and warned that ministerial conspirators were plotting to destroy sacred English liberties. Yet in the hands of skillful political managers, such as Sir Robert Walpole, England's informal arrangements provided long-sought stability, and these radical Whigs remained a small "crackpot" minority.

Colonial institutions

Colonials considered their own institutions replicas of England's governmental structure. The governor was the king's representative in America, possessing, at least in theory, the Crown's power and authority. He defended the royal prerogative, vetoed legislation, summoned and dissolved provincial assemblies, and oversaw enforcement of trade laws. Some governors rose through the ranks of colonial society and politics, but more often the Crown selected an influential courtier or some down-and-out aristocrat who needed to recoup his fortunes. (Like most political offices, a colonial governorship could be a money-making venture.) Almost three-fourths of the governors appointed after 1689 came from noble families, and most attended English universities and colleges. Few men saw the job as part of a permanent administrative career, the average governor serving only about five years. On the whole, colonial governors were intensely political but generally capable public servants.

Colonial theorists compared their provincial Councils to England's House of Lords. Sitting as the upper chamber of the legislature, the Council functioned as a check on the other branch, amending, rejecting, or approving legislative measures. Like the House of Lords, the Council sat, along with the governor, as the highest court in the province and heard appeals from lower judicial bodies. The Council also represented America's untitled aristocracy; usually only the richest, most distinguished men in the colony became councilmen. But as the number of wealthy men with political aspirations increased and vacancies in the upper house grew scarce, the elite also entered the lower chamber and the Council's power and importance declined throughout the eighteenth century. Representing the very top stratum of early American society, the elite of an elite, councilmen tended to be conservative and to support the royal governor and the Crown in constitutional disputes between the colonies and England.

During the eighteenth century the lower house of the legislature, the elective branch, became the most important provincial institution. Called the assembly in most colonies, it was America's equivalent to the House of Commons, and representatives consciously emulated English Members of Parliament. At first merely a consultative body which rubber-stamped decisions of the governor and Council, the assembly gradually assumed greater power. The lower house gained the right to initiate legislation, along with power over financial matters, authority over its own proceedings, and control over the governor's salary. The assembly's rising prestige owed much to the type of men who sat there. Although generally lacking the social status of councilmen, many assemblymen possessed substantial wealth. A recent study of selected legislatures shows that at least 85 percent of the representatives came from the wealthiest 10 percent of colonial society.

Colonial politics After the Glorious Revolution, transplanted Englishmen duplicated the forms of English government, but the reality of political stability eluded them. Although the violent factional clashes of the late seventeenth century subsided, fierce struggles for office still enlivened politics in most colonies. Men who possessed power constantly faced challenges from others, usually their social and economic equals. Although colonials adapted the British institutional structure, the series of informal arrangements which provided stability and moderated factional conflict in Britain did not operate in America. In several fundamental ways, practical politics in America diverged from England's.

Most obviously, the colonial governor, although he possessed the symbols of royal authority, lacked the levers of real power enjoyed by the English Crown. Parliamentary managers, for example, might trade a variety of largely ceremonial positions for support in Commons. But elaborate instructions from England restricted the colonial governor's actions, and a limited amount of political patronage inhibited his ability to deal with disruptive factions in the assembly. The governor simply needed more of these enticements if he was to win over opposition assemblymen. Royal officials in England and local colonial magnates, rather than the provincial governor, controlled most political appointments in America. Some resourceful executives—using their limited patronage, land grants, and lucrative supply contracts—could neutralize opposition for a time, but inevitably the "outs" would outmaneuver the royal representative. In order to win concessions from the governor, some opposition factions blocked the assembly's approval of needed money bills, including provisions for the governor's salary or for defense against the French and Indians.

America's status as a colonized area also intensified political divisions. A large amount of self-government existed, but ultimate authority always resided in Britain. "Outs" appealed over the governor's head to officials and influential supporters in Great Britain, extending political disputes across the Atlantic. Prominent American families retained ties with relatives in England or cultivated new friendships there, using this influence to overturn adverse decisions and to bolster their faction. Similarly, transatlantic business operations solidified relationships between commercial groups on both sides, and English merchants often exerted pressure on behalf of their American associates.

Eighteenth-century America's tremendous population growth and the emergence of a more complex society further disrupted governmental affairs. Population expansion exerted a twofold effect, accelerating those changes which distinguished colonial politics from the English model: more men contested for power, and these political elites confronted a broader-based electorate than in the past. Widespread distribution of property in early America limited the practical effect of landholding restrictions upon the right to vote. Generally 50 to 75 percent of white adult males met the suffrage requirements, and this percentage ran higher in some areas. In addition, vote-hungry officials sometimes ignored the letter of the law; Massachusetts Governor Thomas Hutchinson complained that "anything with the appearance of a man" could cast a ballot in his colony. This potentially sizeable electorate meant that harried "ins" faced a much more difficult task manipulating the political system than their English counterparts and that the expanding group of colonial "outs" could appeal to a wider number of supporters. And the increasingly diversified society multiplied the number of issues which affected citizens' everyday lives. No longer did politics revolve around extremely localized problems, but ambitious politicians could seize upon a number of issues touching provincial and imperial as well as community matters.

New England town government

By the eighteenth century, the disruptions of political factionalism touched even that most cherished American institution, the New England town meeting. Contrary to popular mythology, the town meeting did not begin as a center for vigorous democratic debate and decision making. During the seventeenth century, the wealthiest and most saintly men in the local community filled the key office of selectman, and these officials dominated local affairs. The town meeting offered a place in which the freeholders chose their leaders, usually selected from among the community's elite, and in which the selectmen sought popular confirmation of their own decisions. Participants would never have considered their institution either "democratic" or "undemocratic," at least not in the sense we understand these terms today. The early town meeting reflected the value placed upon consensus; it sprang from local communities' desire to manage affairs in an orderly, cooperative manner.

As society grew more complicated, as more people entered the community, and as new men sought political power, many town meetings became centers for division and contention. The expanding population increased competition for the office of selectman; and with more candidates seeking the position, turnover became more frequent than in the tranquil past. Those who did not become selectmen often turned to the town meeting as an alternative path to power and prestige. Curtailing the selectmen's control over the meeting's agenda and priority of business, rivals used the gathering to focus attention upon themselves and upon the new problems resulting from the diversification of society. These new complexities required more meetings, longer sessions, and considerable expansion in the range of business. The old consensus and conciliatory spirit vanished in many communities, and town meetings became the focus for vigorous debate.

Protest and consensus

Protests in the street also became a form of popular participation in colonial politics. A famous incident occurred in Philadelphia in 1742 when a group of disenfranchised seamen rioted at the polls. Distressed at the Quaker-dominated assembly's refusal to support defense appropriations and annoyed by the elite's arrogant attitude, sailors took out their resentments on Quaker voters. The Philadelphia disturbances evoked some concern among Pennsylvania's gentry, but many colonials remained sanguine about such mass demonstrations, viewing them as an inevitable, sometimes beneficial, part of free government. Popular turbulence, some observors claimed, constituted another check upon political leaders' inevitable tendency to abuse power. A New York writer compared mass protests to "Thunder Bursts which commonly do more Good than Harm." And from the mere existence of sizeable outbursts, argued New Jersey tenants in 1747, it could reasonably be "inferred that...they are wronged and oppressed, or else they would never *rebell agt. the Laws.*" Other Americans felt that mass protest reflected an imbalance in colonial politics which tended to accord too much power to the "democratical" element. They warned of "mobocracy" and lamented the seeming decline of deference and consensus.

Although instability and divisiveness plagued many provinces and localities during the eighteenth century, a spirit of consensus continued to dominate some towns, and some colonies achieved considerable political stability. No colony approached the ideal of a harmonious, balanced governmental system more completely than Virginia. Despite the monopoly of offices by a relatively narrow socioeconomic elite, the mass of colonial men participated in elections. The colonial electorate encompassed about 75 percent of the white adult males, and this proportion approached 95 percent in some areas. Men of "the better sort," who generally began their political careers at the local level, acknowledged that their power ultimately rested upon the approval of the electorate. For the most part, only those who showed talent and dedication moved into positions of greater prestige and responsibility. Virginia's planter elite—the Washingtons, the Lees, the Jeffersons—treated freeholders with respect. These gentlemen-politicians took no vote for granted and spent large sums wining and dining potential supporters. During a hot July election day, George Washington supplied fifty gallons of rum punch, thirty-six gallons of beer, thirty-four gallons of wine, twenty-eight gallons of rum, and two gallons of cider to fewer than four hundred voters. Voting in Virginia was done orally before one's peers, and candidates personally thanked each voter for his support. Of course, such an open process contributed not-so-subtle pressures and often created a band-wagon effect for certain candidates. But, on the whole, the Virginia political system worked well; if disputes were not entirely absent from the colony's politics, those who directed provincial government did possess considerable experience and displayed a rather constant ability to fulfill the expectations of the electorate.

COLONIAL ECONOMY

In the decades after their founding, most colonies developed some type of profitable economic activity and began to change from small, subsistence settlements to more populous and diversified provinces. Seldom specializing in the commodities their founders had intended, the colonies developed their economies less according to grand design than through practical and piecemeal responses to environmental and imperial circumstances.

Development of commercial agriculture

Early settlers in Maryland and Virginia would scarcely have guessed that the minor luxury crop of tobacco would eventually become the cornerstone of the Chesapeake area's prosperity. But the fad of using tobacco suddenly swept England and the Continent, and the product's unique properties made it unlikely that the habit would go out of fashion. Tobacco from these Middle Atlantic states not only satisfied Englishmen but also assisted Britain's balance of trade by providing an important item for reexport to Continental markets.

Likewise, John Winthrop's vision of New England as a godly community isolated from wickedness and popery quickly clashed with the reality of Boston's development as a major commercial center. After some years of economic uncertainty in the mid-seventeenth century, New England finally found profits trading foodstuffs to the West Indies in return for sugar. The British Navigation acts stimulated a native ship-building industry, and capital acquired from commerce and naval construction in turn helped finance lucrative businesses in fishing and export of naval stores. The great merchant families of Boston came to dominate colonial America's carrying trade.

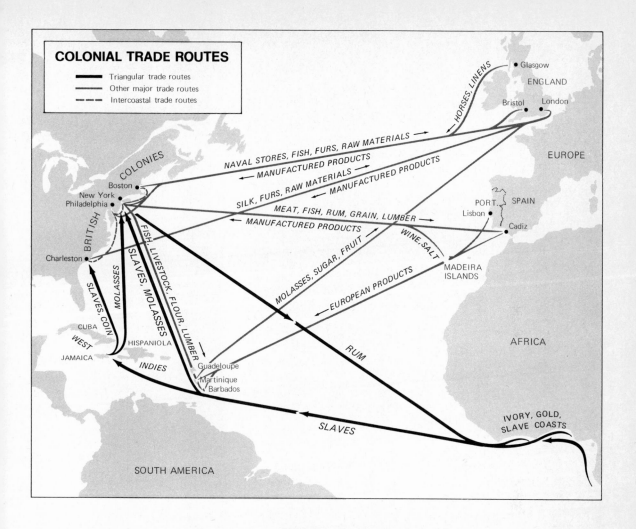

COLONIAL TRADE ROUTES

— Triangular trade routes
— Other major trade routes
- - - Intercoastal trade routes

Glasgow
ENGLAND
Bristol   London
EUROPE

HORSES, LINENS

COLONIES

Boston
New York
Philadelphia

NAVAL STORES, FISH, FURS, RAW MATERIALS
MANUFACTURED PRODUCTS
SILK, FURS, RAW MATERIALS
MANUFACTURED PRODUCTS
MEAT, FISH, RUM, GRAIN, LUMBER
MANUFACTURED PRODUCTS

PORT.   SPAIN
Lisbon
Cadiz

Charleston

BRITISH

SLAVES, MOLASSES

MOLASSES

FISH, LIVESTOCK, FLOUR, LUMBER

MOLASSES, SUGAR, FRUIT

EUROPEAN PRODUCTS

WINE, SALT

MADEIRA
ISLANDS

SLAVES, COIN

CUBA
WEST
JAMAICA
HISPANIOLA
INDIES
Guadeloupe
Martinique
Barbados

RUM

AFRICA

SLAVES

IVORY, GOLD,
SLAVE COASTS

SOUTH AMERICA

Pennsylvania and New York, established somewhat later, surpassed even New England in the production of foodstuffs. The vast flood of non-English immigrants who came to these middle colonies provided the hard-working labor which prosperity in the New World required. After a somewhat longer period of unsuccessful experimentation, the Carolinas also developed cash exports. South Carolina specialized first in rice and then, responding to an English bounty, indigo; and bounties paid for naval stores to supply His Majesty's fleet finally invigorated the long-stagnating North Carolinian economy.

In most colonies city growth accompanied the development of a commercial export economy. At the end of the colonial period less than one out of every ten Americans lived in a city, but urban areas were nonetheless important in the developing social and economic structure.

59

Numb. II.

THE
New-York Weekly JOURNAL.

Containing the freſheſt Advices, Foreign, and Domeſtick.

MUNDAY November 12, 1733.

Mr. *Zenger.*

INcert the following in your next, and you'll oblige your Friend,
CATO.

Mira temporum felicitas ubi ſentiri quæ velis, & quæ ſentias dicere licit.
Tacit.

THE Liberty of the Preſs is a Subject of the greateſt Importance, and in which every Individual is as much concern'd as he is in any other Part of Liberty: therefore it will not be improper to communicate to the Publick the Sentiments of a late excellent Writer upon this Point. ſuch is the Elegance and Perſpicuity of his Writings, ſuch the inimitable Force of his Reaſoning, that it will be difficult to ſay any Thing new that he has not ſaid, or not to ſay that much worſe which he has ſaid.

There are two Sorts of Monarchies, an abſolute and a limited one. In the firſt, the Liberty of the Preſs can never be maintained, it is inconſiſtent with it ; for what abſolute Monarch would ſuffer any Subject to animadvert on his Actions, when it is in his Power to declare the Crime, and to nominate the Puniſhment ? This would make it very dangerous to exerciſe ſuch a Liberty. Beſides the Object againſt which thoſe Pens muſt be directed, is

their Sovereign, the ſole ſupream Magiſtrate ; for there being no Law in thoſe Monarchies, but the Will of the Prince, it makes it neceſſary for his Miniſters to conſult his Pleaſure, before any Thing can be undertaken : He is therefore properly chargeable with the Grievances of his Subjects, and what the Miniſter there acts being in Obedience to the Prince, he ought not to incur the Hatred of the People ; for it would be hard to impute that to him for a Crime, which is the Fruit of his Allegiance, and for refuſing which he might incur the Penalties of Treaſon. Beſides, in an abſolute Monarchy, the Will of the Prince being the Law, a Liberty of the Preſs to complain of Grievances would be complaining againſt the Law, and the Conſtitution, to which they have ſubmitted, or have been obliged to ſubmit; and therefore, in one Senſe, may be ſaid to deſerve Puniſhment, So that under an abſolute Monarchy, I ſay, ſuch a Liberty is inconſiſtent with the Conſtitution, having no proper Subject in Politics, on which it might be exercis'd, and if exercis'd would incur a certain Penalty.

But in a limited Monarchy, as *England* is, our Laws are known, fixed, and eſtabliſhed. They are the ſtreight Rule and ſure Guide to direct the King, the Miniſters, and other his Subjects : And therefore an Offence againſt the Laws is ſuch an Offence againſt the Conſtitution as ought to receive a proper adequate Puniſhment ; the ſevera.
Conſti.

Hub of colonial commerce and home of a powerful merchant elite, Boston ranked first in population and economic activity throughout most of the colonial period, but other cities rose to challenge it—if not to surpass it. New York and Newport flourished after the Restoration of 1660, and Philadelphia and Charleston became large commercial centers around the turn of the eighteenth century. The cities best reflected the diversity— and the inequality—of colonial society: the imposing and roomy homes of the colony's elite; the almshouses which cared for the poor; and the shops where artisans and craftsmen peddled their skills.

A rich belt of commercial farms provided the agricultural surplus shipped out of the seaboard ports. American experience taught the rudiments of an agrarian or physiocratic philosophy—that commerce and wealth derived ultimately from cultivating the land. Jared Eliot, pastor and experimental farmer, expressed a common American belief: "Husbandry is the true Mine from whence are drawn true Riches and real Wealth."

The growth of commercial agriculture depended less upon availability of land—always plentiful in the New World—than upon acquisition of the capital and labor to develop the wilderness. Money was scarce in the colonies, and a planter had to obtain operating cash from British merchants, who generally supplied credit on a year-to-year basis with the cash crop as security. The resulting financial connection between colony and mother country fostered both interdependence and distrust, a mutuality of interests and a potential for discord. In times of hardship, English merchants might lobby in London for legislation favoring their American debtors, but at the same time they threatened the solvency and security of the colonial planter. Many Americans felt that Britain deliberately provided its colonies with an inadequate currency in order to increase dependence upon the mother country.

Labor was an even greater problem than capital. Tenancy, the predominant labor system in Europe, failed dismally in the New World, and neither indentured servants, hired hands, nor large families relieved the shortage of labor. Many colonies competed for settlers by offering tracts of land on reasonable terms; at least in the beginning many people could choose to be small landholders and work for themselves rather than for others. But only white people. Enslaving and importing black Africans became a solution to the labor problem, particularly on southern farms.

Enslavement of Africans   The origins of chattel slavery in the English colonies remain obscure. Blacks probably first came in 1619, but not until the latter part of the century—coinciding with the expansion of tobacco, rice, and indigo cultivation—did their numbers increase enormously. Although statistics on the slave trade are unreliable, Virginia's slave population in 1670 has been estimated at about two thousand. By the end of the century it had grown to six thousand; in the first decade of the eighteenth century it reached over twelve thousand. Mid-century records refer to blacks as "servants for life," and in the following decades chattel slavery emerged as a legal institution associated particularly with skin color. Africans were black, non-Christian, and culturally different; all of these qualities combined to brand them in the white mind as "inferior." Difference, viewed as inferiority, together with the demeaning status of lifetime servitude gradually created the basis for a system of racial slavery. A reinforcing cycle of prejudice and exploitation became the heart of the racial relationship established in colonial America.

The colonial institution of slavery differed greatly from the nineteenth-century stereotype of large work gangs on vast southern plantations. Most slaves lived in the South, but blacks were found throughout the colonies. And few planters owned large tracts of contiguous land. Most farmed a number of small scattered tracts, each with the help of a very few slaves. Many farmers of middling means owned one or perhaps two slaves. These small proprietors worked alongside their chattels and generally treated them well, perhaps mindful of the large capital outlay they represented. Blacks were not always agricultural laborers; some became skilled artisans, providing services which were scarce in a predominantly rural economy.

Self-sufficient farming　　Port cities and commercial farms were the most visible engines of colonial economic development, but the great majority of colonials lived a rural existence which provided little more than the family's keep. True subsistence farms were rare, though, existing primarily in isolated New England hills. Most farms had some outside economic contact. Rivers and streams provided a good transportation network even before the coming of roads, and farmers could barter with or buy from itinerant salesmen and simple country stores. Surplus potatoes or grain would purchase essentials such as salt or gunpowder. The high degree of self-sufficiency was reflected in one South Carolinian farmer's report that "I never spent more than ten dollars a year, which was for salt, nails and the like. Nothing to wear, eat, or drink, was purchased, as my farms provided all."

The large amount of self-produced goods and the frequency of barter make an assessment of the average annual income or the standard of living in colonial America difficult. Still, one can generalize that the typical small-scale American farmer worked hard and lived comfortably, not lacking necessities but enjoying few luxuries. In fact, standards of living depended so directly upon individual labors and skills that Americans developed a strong ethic of individualism and self-reliance. Benjamin

Franklin spoke to this nation of small, independent farmers in his peculiarly American aphorisms: "The Sleeping Fox catches no Poultry. . . . He that lives upon Hope will die fasting. . . . Little Strokes fell great Oaks."

Imperial regulation   The English mercantile system both promoted and retarded the growth and diversification of the colonial economy. The Navigation Acts encouraged colonial shipbuilding, and bounties on commodities such as naval stores, indigo, and pig iron stimulated important exports. Colonial tobacco enjoyed a monopoly in British markets, and British capital financed much of America's economic expansion. New Englanders feared that the Molasses Act of 1733, which placed a high duty upon sugar imported from the French West Indies, might hurt their commerce, dependent upon West Indian trade, but British officials did not enforce the measure strictly. The royal government also shouldered most of the expense for colonial defense.

On the debit side, England's failure to provide an adequate currency for its dependencies hampered economic growth. Most colonies in the eighteenth century began experimenting with paper money, but the lack of a common unit of exchange retarded intercolonial economic ties, and many Americans remained suspicious of their own fluctuating "fiat" money. Moreover, although Great Britain encouraged exploitation of raw materials and cultivation of certain staples, it discouraged American competition with British products. The Wool (1699), Hat (1732), and Iron (1750) acts, which restricted colonial manufacture of these goods, worked little immediate hardship on the immature colonial economy, but they did set limits on future growth.

The notion of imperial specialization—primary products from colonies and manufactured goods from mother country—had a reasonable basis in economic theory. The goal was to create a prosperous and self-sufficient whole, with parts which complemented but did not compete with one another. But colonials increasingly suspected that Parliament's regulatory measures were less the result of beneficent imperial design than the product of intensive lobbying by self-seeking British interest groups. Indeed, after the 1730s most British interests did exert well-organized pressure upon Parliament, and the great acceleration of British industrialization during the 1750s ushered in a true "age of interests" in British politics. North Americans adopted similar tactics, working through paid professional agents or through family or business connections in London, but they felt that their power was poorly organized and generally ineffective. The increased role of pressure groups in the formation of British policy, together with the dynamic growth of the American economy, rendered restrictive economic measures issued from far-off London more and more distasteful to many Americans. Although the imperial system had probably worked to America's net advantage over the century from 1660 to 1760, colonials increasingly dwelt upon its shortcomings rather than upon its strengths.

COLONIAL SOCIETY

Population The words *expansion, growth, flux,* and *diversification* comprise the descriptive vocabulary for the century-and-a-half of English rule. In 1660 British North America consisted of a few isolated agrarian outposts in the midst of native hunting grounds. The colonists, huddled together mainly in Massachusetts and Virginia, totaled less than the attendance at Yankee Stadium for a sunny Saturday's double-header, or one-fifth the size of the Woodstock festival of 1969, or about the population of present-day Boise, Idaho. During the early decades of colonization the lack of great differences among immigrants, the strange environment, and the abundance of land obliterated the social and economic inequalities of the Old World and created a fairly homogeneous society. From meager beginnings, however, the population began to double every twenty-five years, sprawling along the coast and spreading westward toward the Appalachians. A more marked socioeconomic stratification developed, and ethnic differences became more noticeable. By 1760 the colonies contained well over a million inhabitants—rich and poor, white and black, rural and urban, commercial and agricultural, Protestant and Catholic. The population still totaled no more than that of modern Seattle, yet expansion created a complex cultural milieu, a culture distinctly "American."

The population of the colonies grew and diversified rapidly. A great population boom simultaneously occurred in England, but the high birth rate and the influx of Europeans made America's expansion even more startling. In an undeveloped land where labor was scarce and where the years of formal education and childhood were short, children were economic assets. The average fertile marriage in colonial America produced seven children. Patrick Henry, for example, was one of nineteen offspring. Immigration further augmented the population and diversified its ethnic composition. Seventeenth-century settlers came largely from Britain, and they firmly implanted the English language and institutions. But in the eighteenth century other groups began to arrive, some fleeing from war and economic distress, some escaping religious persecution, some landing as servants or slaves. Members of pietistic German religious sects introduced their efficient farming methods into William Penn's Holy Experiment and dominated what was mistermed "Pennsylvania Dutch country." Another numerous immigrant stream, the Scotch-Irish—already the products of one transplantation from Scotland to Northern Ireland—settled the backcountry of Pennsylvania and the Carolinas. The rapid growth of the slave trade introduced yet another major ethnic element. But Africans, unlike other immigrants, could not settle together in cultural enclaves. Controlled by the institution of slavery, they were scattered throughout the colonies. By the time of the American Revolution, half of the population outside New England was non-English, and only New England retained its predominantly British ethnic makeup.

Immigration

Immigrants who freely came to the New World, adapted to its challenges, and lived to praise its bounty left more historical records than those who died, failed, or experienced disappointment. This bias in evidence has made it easy to underestimate the trauma of immigration and the difficulty of moving from a settled society to a wilderness. The shock particularly affected that great number of relatively forgotten men and women who were cajoled into immigration by false propaganda or forced into it by circumstances: Germans lured by exaggerated promises of religious freedom and economic opportunity; redemptioners and indentured servants who pledged to work a certain number of years in return for the cost of passage; British convicts to whom a New World sentence provided an alternative to harsh English justice; and Africans sold into slavery by hostile tribes. To these groups the ordeal of transatlantic crossing sometimes meant death or hardship from which death would have been a welcome reprieve. Packed under deck as human cargo, frequently without adequate sanitary facilities or healthy food, many cursed their fate and longed for home even before seeing American shores. One German traveler reported his shipboard memories: "Smells, fumes, horrors, vomiting, various kinds of sea sickness, fever, dysentery, headaches, heat, constipation, boils, scurvy, cancer, mouthrot"; water which was "very black, thick with dirt, and full of worms"; biscuits full of "red worms and spider's nests"; childbirth in which very few women "escape with their lives; and mother and child, as soon as they have died, are thrown into the water."

Weak, disheartened, and perhaps ill at the end of the crossing, those who came as servants immediately faced even greater hazards. If lucky, they might serve out a four- or five-year indenture as a household servant in a temperate northern colony and then become a small proprietor. If unlucky, as nearly all convicts and many indentured servants were, they could be sent to a southern plantation where the climate and the arduous work threatened to break body and spirit. Unlike black slaves, indentured immigrants were not lifetime investments; having a financial stake only in their short-term health, masters were tempted to drive them beyond their endurance. One authority estimates that only two of every ten indentured servants became a successful farmer, artisan, or overseer. The remaining 80 percent either died during servitude, returned to England, or became propertyless drifters.

Twenty percent of indentured servants eventually attained moderate success, but the hundreds of thousands of African immigrants had virtually no chance of improving their lives. Sold into slavery for profit

AN
Historical ACCOUNT
OF THE
SMALL·POX
INOCULATED
IN
NEW ENGLAND,

Upon all Sorts of Persons, *Whites, Blacks,* and of all Ages and Constitutions.

With some Account of the Nature of the Infection in the NATURAL and INOCULATED Way, and their different Effects on HUMAN BODIES.

With some short DIRECTIONS to the UN-EXPERIENCED in this Method of Practice.

Humbly dedicated to her Royal Highness the Princess of WALES, By *Zabdiel Boylston,* F. R. S.

The Second Edition, Corrected.

LONDON:
Printed for S. CHANDLER, at the Cross-Keys in the Poultry. M. DCC. XXVI.

Re-Printed at BOSTON in N. E. for S. GERRISH in Cornhil, and T. HANCOCK at the Bible and Three Crowns in Annstreet. M. DCC. XXX.

or in exchange for the firepower which Europeans had introduced into the African balance of power, slaves left few written records describing the ordeal of the "middle passage" across the Atlantic or the shock of being enslaved into a hostile and strange culture. But scattered references to attempted suicides and occasional slave mutinies indicate that Africans did not accept their fate passively, and the abounding sadness of their songs—their most powerful legacy of expression—provides insight into their personal tragedies. One white observor of slave ship conditions reported that "it was not in the power of the human imagination to picture to itself a situation more dreadful or disgusting," and he claimed that he lay sick for several months after briefly experiencing the "heat, stench and foul air of the slave quarters." Once in the New World, blacks found none of the mobility, opportunity, political participation, pride of proprietorship, or self-respect for which America was renowned. America proved a hideous prison, and death provided the only escape from life-long degradation.

Mobility   To many white Europeans, however, America did live up to its promise of a new and better life. In the relatively static and stable European social system, people accommodated themselves to the station into which they were born, showing proper deference to those above and displaying expected scorn for those below. Only the most fortunate held land, and this coveted and scarce commodity lay beyond the aspiration of most people. But in the New World social status depended largely upon wealth rather than birth, and land was plentiful. In the American wilderness, socioeconomic position rested partly upon individual effort and tenacity; a landless peasant or a persecuted dissenter could rise above the limits which Old World society imposed. European observers always exalted America's mobility, its abundance of small proprietors, and the absence of restrictive feudal arrangements.

But the hallowed myths of opportunity, freedom, mobility, and rags-to-riches success have been greatly exaggerated. Like foreign observers, too many American historians have focused primarily upon the leaders of society. And the exceptional men who sprang from humble origins, such as Benjamin Franklin, have been elevated into symbols which have come to overshadow the more common reality. It was possible to rise far above one's birth in America, particularly in the seventeenth and early eighteenth centuries, but such success became less and less likely. Population expansion and diversification made colonial society less egalitarian as the relatively undifferentiated agrarian outposts of the mid-seventeenth century grew into the more complex societies of the eighteenth. By the Revolution, America contained a permanently enslaved working class of blacks, a floating group of paupers, a small proletariat of seamen and other hired hands, an urban professional class of artisans and

Ben Franklin. *Culver Pictures*

mechanics, a huge bulk of small landholders, a less numerous group of large-plantation owners, and a powerful merchant elite. As the social spectrum widened and diversified, the range of most people's mobility correspondingly narrowed. White Americans might slip up or down a notch, but less frequently would one move from one end of the scale to the other. Most modern authorities agree that before the Revolution stratification was increasing, mobility was decreasing, and the society was becoming more rigid. New generations of native-born Americans

Women   measured mobility less and less by the criterion of the Old World. Foreigners might still report the New World's openness, but many Americans increasingly experienced its growing rigidity.

Englishmen brought to the colonies their conceptions regarding the proper relationship between man and woman. According to the Puritan leader John Winthrop, a woman's husband "is her lord, and she is subject to him, yet in a way of liberty, not of bondage; and a true wife accounts her subjection her honor and freedom." To the Puritans, the logic did not seem peculiar or anomalous. They could reconcile the apparent opposites of total subjugation and complete freedom, for their religion, particularly the doctrine of predestination, taught that man stood in a similar relationship to God. English common law also placed the woman in a subjugated role, denying a wife any separate identity from her husband. Under the common law, married couples could not enter into legal contracts with each other, for such an action presupposed the wife's distinct identity.

If free white women in colonial America held a subordinate status in the common law, female indentured servants and slaves were doubly oppressed. Indentured women were seldom allowed to marry until their servitude was fulfilled, and most masters reserved the right to lengthen the period of service if the woman became pregnant. Pregnancy supposedly reduced her capacity to work, but in most cases the extension far exceeded the time missed due to childbirth. A poem of the early eighteenth century contains the story of a fictitious indentured servant who, after recalling her happier days and more attractive appearance in England, laments her fate in the New World:

> *In weeding Corn or feeding Swine,*
> *I spend my melancholy Time.*
> *Kidnap'd and Fool'd, I thither fled,*
> *To shun a hated Nuptial Bed,*
> *And to my cost already find,*
> *Worse Plagues than those I left behind.*

Slave women lacked even the minimal rights and promise of eventual freedom which masters accorded to indentured females. Slaveholders frequently encouraged slaves to have children, who then became the property of the master. Most colonies forbade interracial fornication, but enough black women bore mulatto children to make the status of these offspring a pressing legal question. Unlike in most Latin American countries, where masters frequently acknowledged their progeny and mulattoes became a free class, in English America a slave mother's status determined that of her children.

Although the English legal tradition assigned women an inferior place, New World practice apparently raised their status considerably.

Wills reveal that wives could own property, and women occasionally assumed legal responsibility in certain kinds of business endeavors. Colonial records show that couples occasionally contracted with each other, both before or after marriage, regarding the future disposition of their property. Such a procedure diverged from contemporary English custom.

In their day-to-day lives married white women probably felt a good measure of equality and self-esteem because they performed functions every bit as vital to their families' solvency and survival as their husbands' work. The colonial wife did not simply make life comfortable for her family, she made it possible; widowers and widows rapidly remarried, less to have company in old age than to continue the essential division of labor upon which both depended. The woman made clothes, soap, candles, cloth; she milked cows and tended the garden; in busy seasons she worked beside her husband in the fields. Unlike her twentieth-century counterpart, the colonial woman was not primarily a consumer; she was a producer. And few women clamored for sexual equality; if a remote court told her she was unequal, her daily experience contradicted the law.

In fact, the "liberated" woman of the day was not the one who worked equally alongside her husband, but the one who could escape arduous chores and enjoy the more pampered life of the colonial aristocrat. The woman without calluses on her hands and without the swollen legs of a lifetime of standing and bending was the envy of most of her sex. Colonial women viewed farm work and its laborious duties, not their husbands or the courts, as their most constant oppressors. Although their economic importance brought a sense of self-esteem frequently absent in the lives of modern housewives, many women would have welcomed an escape from the drudgery of economic equality.

Childhood and education

In a land where labor was scarce, children also contributed to the economic viability of the family. Unlike their modern counterparts, they were generally an asset to family income rather than a drain on it. Colonial Americans had no concept of "adolescence" and expected children to dress and act like little adults after the age of seven or eight. But if familial responsibilities came early, the opportunities of a wilderness society also provoked tensions within the family, frequently pulling children away from home.

The apparent disruption of family life in the New World was a frequent source of complaint and worry. The president of King's College, Samuel Johnson, bemoaned that "it is obvious that our youth are apace running headlong into all sorts of debauchery and uncontrolled indulgences, which I doubt not is...chiefly owing to the fond indulgence of their parents." Shortly after founding, every colony passed laws demand-

The leopard with the harmless kid laid down
And not one savage beast was seen to frown

The wolf did with the lambkin dwell in peace
His grim carnivorous nature there did cease

The lion with the fatling on did move
A little child was leading them in love;

When the great PENN his famous treaty made
With indian chiefs beneath the Elm-tree's shade.

Edward Hicks, *The Peaceable Kingdom. The Granger Collection*

ing obedience from children, and the potential punishment for disobedience in Massachusetts and Connecticut was nothing less than death. Records do not reveal that any court ever resorted to such extreme punishment. In fact, by permitting a child to present a case in court, such laws guarded against parental abuse at the same time that they sought to curb recalcitrant children. Colonial law reflected the belief that the community, acting through the courts, had an interest in maintaining order within individual families.

In response to fears that the family no longer furnished proper guidance, the general community also increasingly assumed the burden of providing formal education. A famous Massachusetts statute of 1642, which began a trend toward institutionalized education for all members of society, sought to counteract the drift toward social disintegration. The influx of non-English immigrants during the early eighteenth century further strengthened the development of schooling, particularly in Pennsylvania where the British community feared the spread of Germanic language and culture. And as society became more secular, so did education; the inculcation of civic virtue and good citizenship took priority over religious instruction. History became important in a child's studies because, as Benjamin Franklin once explained, "history will also give occasion to expatiate on the advantage of civil orders and constitutions; how men and their properties are protected by joining in societies and establishing government.... Thus may the first principles of sound politics be fixed in the minds of youth." The heavy stress Americans have always placed upon education through formal schools stems, in part, from the colonial search for cohesion and social control in an age of insecurity and uncertainty.

Colonial Americans also founded several institutions of higher education during the colonial period. The founders of Harvard (1636) were primarily interested in training ministers for the Puritan settlements, but the curriculum followed the traditional liberal arts pattern of European universities. Subsequent colleges such as Yale (1701) and Princeton (1746) adopted programs resembling Harvard's; William and Mary (1693) in Virginia was begun under the auspices of an Anglican minister. As increasing numbers of graduates from these schools went into professions other than the ministry, the need for "practical" training grew more apparent. Some of the colleges established in the late colonial period, such as Pennsylvania (1755) and Columbia (1754), introduced courses in agriculture, navigation, and astronomy, in addition to retaining traditional liberal arts subjects found in European universities. Higher education was available to a much wider socioeconomic spectrum in America than in England, and colonial innovations in college curriculum answered the needs of a more egalitarian society.

Folk song and dance

For most American youth, schooling probably seemed less important and certainly less interesting than courtship and marriage. Particularly in the cities, customs changed rapidly, disturbing the older generation, shocking rural visitors, and even surprising foreign observers. A young man described a party he went to in Quaker Philadelphia: "Seven sleighs with two ladies and two men in each, preceded by fiddlers on horseback" rode to a public house where "we danced, sung, and romped and eat and drank, and kicked away care from morning till night, and finished our frolic in two or three side-boxes at the play." In 1755 a British traveler in Virginia reported that "dancing is the chief diversion here," and another was shocked at the widespread dancing of "jigs." Reporting that the dance was borrowed from the slaves, the proper Englishman found it "without method or regularity: a gentleman and lady stand up, and dance about the room, one of them retiring, the other pursuing, then perhaps meeting, in an irregular fantastical manner." Serenading under the window of a favored lady also came into vogue during the late colonial period. Usually the gentlemen first lubricated their throats with strong draughts from a local tavern, yet women reportedly considered the midnight visitation and inevitable disharmony a high compliment.

Like folk songs everywhere, those of colonial America often revolved around courtship, unrequited love affairs, or tragic lovers. American ballads came largely from Britain; "Greensleeves" was one of the most popular and graceful tunes, and it provided the melody for up to eighty different sets of lyrics. The first popular folk song known to be indigenous to the colonies in both words and music also treats a tragic couple, but with considerably less lyricism. Compare the poetic beauty of the English "Greensleeves" ("Alas, my love/ You do me wrong/ To cast me off/ Discourteously...") with the coarser expression of the native song "Springfield Mountain":

> On Springfield Mountain there did dwell
> A lovelie youth I knowed him well. . . .
> He had scarce mowed half round the field
> When a poison serpent bit at his heel. . . .
> They took him home to Mollie dear,
> Which made him feel so verie queer. . . .
> Now Mollie had two ruby lips
> With which the poison she did sip. . . .
> She also had a rotten tooth
> And so the poison killed them both.

The song, describing a true incident in Massachusetts in 1761, spoke with American directness about a distinctly American tragedy.

COLONIAL RELIGION

Decline of organized religion

Most colonial Americans believed in God and defined their place in the universe in terms of a divine order. Yet the vastness of the American wilderness and the preoccupation with sustaining a material existence made organized religious life difficult. One expert estimated that even in pious New England only one out of seven people formally belonged to a church. To the south, the percentage declined to one out of fifteen or twenty. Church membership did expand rapidly during the colonial period, but population grew at an even faster pace, leaving an ever greater percentage of Americans outside the framework of organized religion.

The New World was settled during, and partly as a by-product of, the great religious disputes which wracked Europe in the wake of the

Protestant Reformation, and American religious life reflected the vast range of denominational possibilities. Only Anglicanism in Virginia and Puritanism in New England succeeded in maintaining a semblance of state-enforced unity. But these, the strongest and most established religions, also suffered the greatest proportionate decline in membership and came under increasing challenge from dissenting settlers. Throughout the colonies, religious groups such as Quakers and Baptists flourished, especially during the great non-English immigrations of the eighteenth century.

The widespread indifference to organized religion, in addition to the increasing pluralization of sects, created an atmosphere of toleration which was uniquely American. By the mid-eighteenth century, many colonies had extended full rights of citizenship to members of any faith and the others faced constant agitation to do likewise. The Revolution would confirm this long-term trend toward separation of church and state. Development of religious freedom may seem unarguably beneficent to twentieth-century Americans, but to many colonial observers it reflected an alarming decrease of religious conviction. If one advocated religious liberty, one either doubted the validity of his own belief or was callous enough to allow his countrymen who were wandering astray to go to hell. To many, the disestablishment of religion was an ill omen, a sign that Americans were losing faith and abandoning God.

The rise of rationalism also suggested a decline in religious belief. Reacting against the excessive religiosity associated with the Reformation, Enlightenment thinkers elevated reason and the mind above faith and the soul as tools in the discovery of truth and knowledge. Sir Isaac Newton's enunciation of natural laws governing the universe found widespread acceptance among educated Americans. Unitarianism, a new religion, stressed the importance of reason, questioned the divinity of Christ, and held a mechanistic view of the universe. Unitarianism attracted many colonials, particularly among the cosmopolitan upper classes who accepted Enlightenment ideas.

Even among those who considered themselves members of the more traditional churches, faith seemed to slip away. The vigor, immediacy, and meaning of religious experience gave way to dull exhortation, stylized response, and declining morality. A "deadly formality" smothered church services, and growing numbers of people considered religious routine so tedious that ministers frequently attacked the obvious indifference. Even in New England, Puritan clergy had to condemn manifestations of apathy such as "Sleeping at Sermons."

We may here take notice that the nature of man is wofully corrupted and depraved, else they would not be so apt to sleep when the precious Truths of God are dispensed in his Name, Yea, and men are more apt to sleep then, than at another time. Some woful Creatures, have been so wicked as to profess they have gone to hear Sermons on purpose, that so they might sleep, finding themselves at such times much disposed that way.

The Great Awakening Although formalized religion declined, the longing for mystical experience did not. The general instability, flux, and uncertainty which became prominent toward the end of the seventeenth century and gradually worsened throughout the eighteenth century produced social and psychological tensions throughout the colonies. Unable to understand or to cope with the pace of change, many Americans sought reassurance in faith and in the fixity of religion. They were ready to release pent-up passions in the name of God.

In 1692 the populace of Salem, Massachusetts, experienced a period of religious frenzy when some teenage girls claimed to be the victims of witchcraft. Local Puritan leaders, deeply troubled by the growing indifference to religion, seized upon the incident to root out alleged agents of the devil. Although many participants later regretted their actions, during four months of fanatical "witchhunting" four hundred people were arrested and twenty executed.

Several decades later, the revivals of the Great Awakening brought a more constructive release of tension and outpouring of emotion. Reacting against the sterility and remoteness of established churches, the Awakeners posed a challenge less to doctrinal orthodoxies than to ministerial style. They revived religious enthusiasm, reignited concern over the experience of conversion and the state of one's soul, and aroused a mass outpouring of passion which its participants called the Holy Spirit and its critics called the devil. The movement reflected and, in turn, deepened divisions in society; almost every colony felt its impact.

The Great Awakening began during the 1720s in the middle colonies, where Theodore J. Frelinghuysen and William and Gilbert Tennent developed an emotional style of preaching. The Tennents later established a school to train ministers, many of whom carried the Great Awakening throughout the colonies. In New England the rhetoric of the more famous (but less influential) Jonathan Edwards also stirred rounds of conversions. Edwards disturbed the staid Puritan clergy by his elaborate justifications of emotionalism in religious life. English revivalist George Whitefield's journeys to America in the 1740s climaxed the movement. Whitefield, an early leader of the Methodist movement, toured from Georgia to New England, often holding services in open fields in order to accommodate the largest crowds yet assembled in America. Exhorting his listeners to abandon their wicked and Godless ways, the revivalist produced thousands of conversions. Whitefield claimed that once, while speaking to a group of young women, a "wonderful power" descended on the room, and his listeners "began to cry out and weep most bitterly for the space of half an hour. . . . Five of them seemed affected as those that

Cape Cod church. *Ansel Adams*

are in fits." Throughout the colonies, religion became the prime topic of concern and conversation.

The display of irrationality accompanying revivals alarmed many traditionalists. They charged that the spectacular conversions induced by extravagant rhetoric were false, that only God bestowed grace, and that man could not stimulate redemption. Many conservatives also feared the equalitarian implications of the Great Awakening. The emotional appeal to great masses of people menaced the social order, and the challenge to the established religious hierarchy appeared to threaten authority in general. The resulting divisions between the "New Light" revivalists and their "Old Light" opponents contained social and political as well as religious significance.

During the 1740s the Great Awakening peaked and then quickly subsided. Like an earthquake, it hit briefly but its impact left the social landscape greatly changed. Particularly in New England and New York, it split the previously strong and united religious establishments, dividing the clergy and their congregations into "New Light" and "Old Light" allegiances. Hamlets which had supported one church now often had two feuding factions, and citizens could choose between competing styles of religion. Consensus and homogeneity in Puritan New England vanished forever. Throughout the colonies the Great Awakening shook people's belief in authority from above and perhaps boosted their individuality. It further divided an already disrupted society, contributing to the emerging American pattern of religious toleration, separation of church and state, and a large number of competing denominations.

THE COLONIAL WARS

The rivalries and worldwide wars of the European powers in the eighteenth century spilled over into America. During the seventeenth century, England successfully challenged the supremacy of the Netherlands (in the New World the duke of York captured New Amsterdam) and gradually reduced Dutch power. William and Mary's ascension to the English throne in 1688 (William was a member of the Netherland's royal family) finally allied those two rivals against a new challenger—Louis XIV's France. From 1689 into the nineteenth century, the Anglo-French rivalry dominated world diplomacy, and the early series of wars between the two imperial powers substantially affected the development of the American colonies.

The War of the League of Augsburg (1689–97) and the War of the Spanish Succession (1702–13) were largely confined to Europe. Their New World counterparts, "King William's War" and "Queen Anne's War," took the form of minor border raids between English and French colonists, each employing Indian allies. The struggle took on greater significance in the colonies during the War of the Austrian Succession (1740–48), known in America as "King George's War." This conflict inflated colonials' pride when New England troops captured Louisbourg, the French stronghold which guarded the entrance to the Saint Lawrence River. When Britain returned Louisbourg in the Treaty of Aix-la-Chapelle, many Americans felt bitter, believing their security and sacrifices had been bargained away for remote imperial goals.

The French and Indian War

The next round in the Anglo-French rivalry actually began in America. Following the Treaty of Aix-la-Chapelle, the French began to consolidate their position in the Ohio Valley by building a line of forts. At the same time, Virginia land speculators and Indian traders moved into the region, challenging the French presence. After the French and their Indian allies drove the British colonists out, the British government called a conference in Albany to gain the cooperation of the Iroquois in the struggle against France. In June 1754 seven colonies despatched delegates to frame an alliance with Iroquois chieftains. Benjamin Franklin saw the Albany Congress as an opportunity to promote intercolonial unity, and he proposed creation of a grand council, supported by taxation, which would handle Indian relations, colonial defense, and settlement of western lands. The delegates voted to submit Franklin's "Albany Plan of Union" to the colonial assemblies. But most colonies remained suspicious of any larger authority, particularly one which had the power of taxation. Forging intercolonial unity, which the British crown surely would have prevented in any event, proved as impossible as constructing an alliance with the Iroquois. The Indians refused to support Britain, and Americans continued to allow intercolonial rivalries to interfere with effective defense.

Virginia did not send a representative to Albany but, instead, took direct military action. In 1754 that colony sent twenty-two-year-old George Washington to recapture the Ohio valley. But Washington failed, and Virginians then appealed to England for assistance. The British government responded by organizing an elaborate offensive against the French. General Edward Braddock, who was to deliver the opening blow, met a surprise attack; he was fatally wounded, and his men were routed. The British campaign stalled. In retaliation against England, French and Indian forces began ravaging the entire British colonial frontier, and this "French and Indian War" soon expanded into the Seven Years' War in Europe.

A costly struggle which severely strained Britain's treasury, the Seven Years' War ended in the expulsion of France from North America. In America, the conflict stirred patriotic sentiment. Colonials exulted at the fall of Quebec and Montreal, cheered when the Treaty of Paris gave England control over all of North America east of the Mississippi, and

Printed for John Bowles at the Black Horse in Cornhil.

New England forces landing at Louisbourg. *John Carter Brown Library, Brown University*

erected statues honoring King George III and his war minister William Pitt. At the end of the war in 1763, the British empire had never seemed so strong, united, and secure.

But the long years of struggle against France had, in fact, left cracks in the imperial structure which would soon widen disastrously. While fusing England and her colonies in a common cause, the wars also pointed up glaring differences of interest. Colonials needed British troops for protection but increasingly resented the taxes and other burdens required to support them. Colonial security rested, in part, upon the Royal Navy, yet Americans resisted impressment into its service. Dislike of the British military grew as colonials nurtured the myth that their own civilian militias provided a better fighting force than British regulars. A comparison between colonial success at Louisbourg and Braddock's defeat in the Ohio Valley provided the shred of evidence which made disdain of British efforts plausible, and removal of the French threat after 1763 bestowed the security which made bravado about colonial militiamen less risky. Americans also resented British attempts to halt trade with France and its colonies, and Englishmen felt bitter that the colonials traded with the enemy's merchants at the same time that they expected protection against its armies. The Treaty of Paris, by removing the common Anglo-American enemy, allowed the divergence of imperial interest, which the wars had revealed, to grow even more serious in the years after 1763.

THE COLONIAL EXPERIMENT

Population expansion, ethnic diversity, political instability, and economic growth created an atmosphere of change and uncertainty which brought opportunity to some and bred insecurity for many. Colonial Americans groped for ways to live harmoniously within a pluralistic society, and they moved toward a political tradition which exalted liberty and toleration at the same time that it stressed maintenance of order and social cohesion. The unsettled American existence planted the seeds of a permissive and open society together with those of repression and enforced consensus. When times were good, Americans would look brightly upon the opportunity brought about by rapid change; when times were bad, they would reflect darkly upon the consequences of disorder. Optimistic liberalism and anxious conservatism were equal legacies of the vagaries of colonial development.

There were other paradoxes in the colonial experience, for it meant different things to different people. To successful and adaptable white men who for generations set the tone of our national histories, America was a happy experiment in freedom and individualism. It confirmed man's potential and exemplified his best hopes and dreams. But to others, America was a bitter hoax. A sweet promise turned sour, a utopia turned exile, America was a "land of plenty" where a person could discover he had lost the most important things of life—the relationships and ties to a past which made him feel at home in the universe. To black Africans, the colonies were synonomous with a lifetime of bondage, alienation, and exploitation. The Atlantic crossing was a journey not only beyond a familiar hill, religion, tribe, and family, but beyond the definition of a human being. Finally, to native Americans, the Indian nations, Britain's colonial experiment was merely the opening phase in a nightmare of invasion, conquest, and ultimate defeat. America became the story of an emerging new and powerful civilization, but it was also the bleaker tale of the ravaging and destruction of previous cultures.

MERCANTILISM

Mercantilism in Europe in the sixteenth-eighteenth centuries must be understood in broad terms as an integral part of the transition from feudalism to capitalism in Western society. Although the most articulate practitioner of mercantilist policy was the French Finance Minister Colbert, and the most successful practitioners were the English, mercantilism was not confined to any one country. Although much of mercantilist theory did evolve around the acquisition of gold bullion reserves as a prime object of national policy, it was not simply a monetary program. Mercantilism rather describes a series of strategies employed in various combinations which provided a bridge to the industrial revolution and modern economic development.

The mercantilist system had as its main goal the increase of national economic wealth, measured in gold and achieved through trade. Fundamental to the mercantilist world view was the assumption that the wealth of the world was finite or even fixed, and so gains registered by one country had to come at the expense of another. This assumption meant that international political rivalry was built into the system, expressed in intermittent warfare from the English defeat of the Spanish Armada in 1588 to the conflict between the British and French in the second half of the eighteenth century. The chief vehicle for gaining wealth was foreign trade, in agricultural commodities and increasingly in light manufactured and luxury goods. Each nation aimed at a favorable balance of trade, a net surplus of exports over imports. Domestic producers were protected from foreign competition by tariffs and outright prohibitions against imports of certain goods. The reduction of imports was essential to national self-sufficiency under mercantilism, but there were obvious limitations; England, for example, could hardly supply the needs of its growing textile industry by growing cotton in the British Isles.

The clear alternative to home production was colonial expansion; Britain could get its cotton by controlling India rather than by buying from someone else. Every European nation with the resources to outfit a fleet sent expeditions to "discover" new territory. The Age of Exploration coincided with the Age of Mercantilism. European expansion into the Americas was particularly frenetic, although not always successful. Spain, for example, obtained possession of the rich gold and silver deposits of Central and South America without ever being able to translate that advantage into stable commercial preeminence. The major thrust of American colonial economic activity was in extractive industries—such as mining and lumbering for naval construction—and large scale plantation agriculture achieved typically by the introduction of slavery into the English, French, Spanish, and Portuguese colonies. Colonial expansion produced new resources, new trading patterns, and new markets for home production, and also contributed to world tensions. Conflict over specific areas of the world was only the most obvious result; more fundamental were tensions between the colonies and the home countries and those produced within the European nations themselves.

The administration of mercantilist empires provided benefits for the settlers in the colonies—chiefly markets for their goods and military defense—but only while exacting a price. European nations required their colonies to sell only to the home country, not always obtaining the highest price; shipping had to be done under the home country's flag. Regulation of the colonial economy went deeper, as exemplified by the relationship between England and the North American colonies. In the decades preceding the American Revolution, Britain took a number of steps to hinder the development of American manufactures, prohibiting the export of technology, the emigration of skilled workers, and the establishment of certain factories. Powerful interests among the colonials were at least convinced that British economic regulation was a form of tribute levied on the politically powerless colonies. Historians have differed in their estimates of the cost of mercantilism to the colonies, but it is clear that imperial economic intervention, central to mercantilism, was one source of friction leading to independence movements throughout the Americas.

Within the European nations themselves the very successes of mercantilist practice sped its disintegration. The pursuit of national wealth yielded an accumulation of capital which provided the base for early industrialization; the contribution of domestic and colonial policy in fostering the British textile industry was the prime case in point. International tariffs and duties which had protected infant industry later prevented access to expanded markets. The regulation of prices, wages, and production internally was seen as throttling competition and maximum use of resources. It was not accidental that England produced in Adam Smith the major theorist of free trade and laissez-faire; his *Wealth of Nations* (1776) became the manifesto of the more advanced wing of British industrialists. Smith argued for an end to government regulation at home and for a division of labor internationally; if every nation dropped its trade barriers and specialized in what it produced most cheaply and efficiently, each would improve its long-run position. Expanded economic activity via free trade and unrestricted competition was counterposed to the mercantilist notion of the battle for fixed wealth. This doctrine was particularly suited to England, which had the biggest navy, the largest merchant fleet, and the most advanced industrial sector, and England was the first nation to cast off its mercantilist shackles. Throughout Europe the classic capitalism of the nineteenth century brought the Age of Mercantilism to a close.

THINGS TO THINK ABOUT: 1660–1763

Why did colonization revive after 1660 and why did so many colonies endure a time of troubles in the late seventeenth century? Wesley Frank Craven, *The Colonies in Transition* (1966) and Clarence Ver Steeg, *The Formative Years, 1607–1763* (1963) are general surveys. Several of the selections in James Morton Smith, ed., *Seventeenth-Century America* (1957) and Michael G. Hall et al., eds., *The Glorious Revolution in America* (1964) are useful.

What themes characterize the maturing of colonial society? Max Savelle, *Seeds of Liberty* (1948) is a highly readable synthesis. Kenneth Lockridge, *A New England Town: Dedham, 1630–1730* (1970) and John Demos, *The Little Commonwealth: Family Life in Plymouth Colony* (1970) trace the development of individual towns. Richard Hofstadter, *America in 1750* (1971) and Jackson Turner Main, *Social Structure of Revolutionary America* (1963) contribute to an understanding of colonial society. Winthrop D. Jordan, *White over Black* (1968) is an excellent study of racial attitudes. Perry Miller, *Errand into the Wilderness* (1956), Alan Simpson, *Puritanism in Old and New England* (1955), and William W. Sweet, *Religion in Colonial America* (1942) provide an introduction to religious developments.

How did American politics and government differ from the British model? Bernard Bailyn, *The Origins of American Politics* (1968) is a general discussion. J. R. Pole, *Political Representation in England and the Origins of the American Republic* (1966) and Charles S. Sydnor, *American Revolutionaries in the Making* (1952) are useful specialized studies. Leonard Labaree, *Royal Government in America* (1930) and Jack P. Greene, *The Quest for Power* (1963) point up differences in political structure.

What were the advantages and disadvantages to America of the British imperial system? Lawrence A. Harper, *The English Navigation Laws* (1939) is standard. More recent treatments are Thomas C. Barrow, *Trade and Empire* (1967) and Michael Kammen, *Empire and Interest: The American Colonies and the Politics of Mercantilism* (1969).

1763-1789

three | THE revolutionary generation

THOMAS PAINE

Tom Paine was not quite a founding father. Franklin, Washington, Adams and Jefferson were gentlemen forced into the role of amateur revolutionaries. Paine was a professional revolutionary if he was anything, and he was doubtless no gentleman. They were citizens of their states; Paine was citizen of three countries and lost his citizenship in each. They were all Deists, but only Paine suffered both in his life and in his reputation from being outspoken in his religious beliefs. (Theodore Roosevelt considered Paine "a dirty little atheist.") And invariably we call him Tom Paine, a familiarity we rarely dare with the more august founders.

Yet Paine was a major influence on the American Revolution. His pamphlet *Common Sense* met an overwhelming response in the early days of the war. Published anonymously in January 1776, its revolutionary message reached hundreds of thousands in a nation of but 3 million inhabitants. *Common Sense* was the first American bestseller. Its plea for independence, its direct attack on that "royal brute" King George III, and its plain and vigorous statement of the philosophy of natural rights told Americans everything they had been thinking but not saying. That was Paine's genius: to explain to people in plain language what in fact they were about to do in the age of democratic revolutions. As the distinguished novelist John Dos Passos has written of him: "He had the best nose of any man who ever lived for the political happenings of the moment."

Paine was thirty-seven years old when he arrived in the American colonies. The son of a Quaker corsetmaker, he was born in Thetford, Norfolkshire, in 1737. When he debarked at Philadelphia on November 30, 1774, carried out on a stretcher half dead from typhus, his life to that date had been a story of constant failure. Yet Benjamin Franklin, who had met him in London, was sufficiently impressed to give Paine a letter of introduction to his son-in-law. Paine's career suddenly flowered in the New World; he began writing for a new periodical, *The Pennsylvania Magazine; or, American Monthly Museum,* and rapidly achieved literary eminence. His collaborator on that magazine, Robert Aitken, later described his style of composition:

> He ... was soon seated at the table with the necessary apparatus, which always included a glass, and a decanter of brandy. ... The first glass put him in a train of thinking. ... the second ... illuminated his intellectual system, and when he had swallowed the third glass, he wrote with great rapidity, intelligence and precision, and his ideas appeared to flow faster than he could commit them to paper. What he penned from the inspiration of the brandy, was perfectly fit for the press without any alteration, or correction.

Without doubt he dashed off *Common Sense* in much the same style, sending the first copy from the press to Franklin and signing over his profits to the Continental Army to provide mittens for the troops marching toward Quebec.

Paine lent his extraordinary skills as a propagandist to the patriot cause for the entire war; his *American Crisis* essays appeared at intervals until 1783, and he served as well in a variety of official capacities for the Continental Congress and the state of Pennsylvania. But one revolt scarcely satisfied his firebrand temperament. When the French revolution broke out while he was visiting in Europe, he plunged again into controversy, defending the Revolution and republican ideas in *The Rights of Man* (1791–1792). English authorities detected sedition in the book and arrived to arrest him moments after he had fled to France. The French welcomed him as an international hero of revolution and made him a delegate to the National Convention—no simple matter for a man who spoke no French. And no simple matter for a man who spoke his mind. Paine's courage in arguing against the Jacobins gained him ten months in prison. Only chance spared him from the guillotine, and only the intercession of James Monroe, the American minister to Paris, got him out of prison.

While in prison, Paine began work on *The Age of Reason* (1794–1796), an exposition for the common man of the Deistic religion of the Enlightenment. Although Paine's rationalist belief in a single impersonal god was no different from the religious beliefs of George Washington, Benjamin Franklin, or Thomas Jefferson, his attractive statement of Deism, which became the fountainhead of popular traditions of "free thinking," scandalized the faithful of several countries. Paine had added religious iconoclasm to political radicalism, always a dangerous combination. By the time he returned to the United States in 1802 he was a stranger everywhere—old, attacked, and embittered. He lived out his remaining years—until his death in 1809—fending off attacks by the godly. His neighbors, claiming he was not an American citizen, would not let him vote. At his death, the Quakers would not admit him to their cemetery. And afterwards biographers labored hard to establish the facts about his consumption of alcoholic beverages, considering that they were thereby impeaching his ideas. His best epitaph, perhaps, is the statement made of him by Joel Barlow, the Jeffersonian diplomat and poet: "His own writings are his best life, and these are not read at present."

The *American* CRISIS.

NUMBER I.

By the Author of COMMON SENSE.

THESE are the times that try men's souls: The summer soldier and the sunshine patriot will, in this crisis, shrink from the service of his country; but he that stands it NOW, deserves the love and thanks of man and woman. Tyranny, like hell, is not easily conquered; yet we have this consolation with us, that the harder the conflict, the more glorious the triumph. What we obtain too cheap, we esteem too lightly:---'Tis dearness only that gives every thing its value. Heaven knows how to set a proper price upon its goods; and it would be strange indeed, if so celestial an article as FREEDOM should not be highly rated. Britain, with an army to enforce her tyranny, has declared, that she has a right (*not only to* TAX, but) "*to* " BIND *us* in ALL CASES WHATSOEVER," and if being *bound in that manner* is not slavery, then is there not such a thing as slavery upon earth. Even the expression is impious, for so unlimited a power can belong only to GOD.

WHETHER the Independence of the Continent was declared too soon, or delayed too long, I will not now enter into as an argument; my own simple opinion is, that had it been eight months earlier, it would have been much better. We did not make a proper use of last winter, neither could we, while we were in a dependent state. However, the fault, if it were one, was all our own; we have none to blame but ourselves *. But no great deal is lost yet; all that Howe has been doing for this month past is rather a ravage than a conquest, which the spirit of the Jersies a year ago would have quickly repulsed, and which time and a little resolution will soon recover.

I have as little superstition in me as any man living, but
my

* " The present winter" (meaning the last) " is worth an " age, if rightly employed, but if lost, or neglected, the whole " Continent will partake of the evil; and there is no punish- " ment that man does not deserve, be he who, or what, or " where he will, that may be the means of sacrificing a season " so precious and useful." COMMON SENSE.

1763-1789

1763	Peace of Paris ending Seven Years' War; Pontiac's rebellion
	Proclamation of 1763 closing western lands to white settlement
1764	Carolina "Regulator" movement
	Currency Act
	Sugar Act
1765	Stamp Act and Stamp Act Congress in New York
1766	Stamp Act repealed
	Declaratory Act
1767	Townshend Acts
1770	Townshend Acts repealed
	Boston Massacre
1773	Tea Act
	Boston Tea Party
1774	"Intolerable Acts"
	Quebec Act
	Continental Congress meets at Philadelphia
1775	Battles of Lexington and Concord
	Battle of Bunker Hill
1776	Declaration of Independence
	Howe occupies New York (September)
	American victory at Trenton (December)
1777	Howe occupies Philadelphia (September)
	Saratoga (October)
1778	France enters war against Britain
1779	Spain enters war against Britain
1780	Clinton captures Charlestown
1781	Cornwallis's surrender at Yorktown (October)
1781–89	Articles of Confederation
1783	Treaty of Paris
1785	Land Ordinance of 1785
1786	Virginia's Statute for Religious Liberty; Annapolis convention
1786–87	Shays's Rebellion
1787	Northwest Ordinance
	Constitutional Convention meets in Philadelphia
1787–88	States ratify Constitution

THE REVOLUTIONARY MILIEU

The birth of the American Republic is one of the dramatic events of our history. When did the spirit of revolution begin? Why, after a century-and-a-half of English rule, did provincials reject their mother country? Why did British leaders allow such an explosive situation to develop in the colonies? The direct "causes" of the Revolution remain the subject of great scholarly controversy. Yet one may point to various disruptive tendencies and divisive trends which add up to "a revolutionary milieu," a situation pointing to increased friction between England and her American provinces.

Imperial tensions

By the middle of the eighteenth century America was no longer a series of isolated imperial outposts inhabited by transplanted Englishmen. Americans still patterned their society on the English model but could not quite duplicate the original. They lacked an established church, had no titled aristocracy, and enjoyed a degree of social and political equality unknown in England. And although old hostilities still separated various colonies, newspapers were giving increasing space to stories about inter-colonial events, an indication of growing loyalty and concern with America rather than with the mother country.

As they developed their own economic and political institutions, many Americans became more and more touchy about British "inter-ference." For years the colonies had generally benefited from the British mercantile system; but as the American economy became more commer-

Revolutionary Relics. *Culver Pictures*

cial, certain groups came to resent British actions. Merchants, for example, complained about the inadequate currency system and about British exporters offering goods directly at auction sales rather than through American outlets. Provincial political leaders always sailed a dangerous course between the rocks of British imperial authority and the shoals of colonial rivals ready to denounce excessive deference to British domination. Not that anyone could discover a movement for independence in 1750, or even in 1763. Colonials considered themselves good Englishmen; in fact, they felt they were as good as any other English subjects and not second-class citizens whose rights and liberties could be taken lightly.

Between 1750 and 1763 colonials tangled with London over a variety of issues. The French and Indian War strained relations and left a legacy of mutual bitterness. Regular army officers ridiculed, often unfairly, colonial militiamen's fighting abilities and decried, with more justification, some colonies' stingy defense appropriations. American merchants even sold food to the French and Spanish enemies, reaping huge profits from the illicit trade. In 1754, when General Braddock desperately needed supplies for his ill-fated campaign in the Ohio Valley, at least forty colonial vessels were trading at a single French Canadian port. And other disputes, not directly related to the war, uncovered ominous constitutional challenges to British sovereignty. In Virginia, the assembly and the royal government became embroiled in a complicated legal controversy over the salaries of Anglican clergy. A twenty-three-year-old firebrand, Patrick Henry, lost his case against the English officials, but not before he brazenly argued that the king had violated his compact with the colonies and forfeited "all right to his subjects' obedience." In 1761, a sometimes brilliant, oftentimes irrational Boston lawyer, James Otis, challenged Parliament's power to authorize general search warrants (called "writs of assistance") as a means of uncovering colonial smuggling rings. Otis condemned the writs as "instruments of slavery" and declared that the parliamentary act extending them to America was invalid, a violation of the liberty of Englishmen and the natural rights of man.

Domestic tensions Besides contention with imperial authorities, Americans faced various internal problems, and these domestic tensions created a general atmosphere of discontent which fed the revolutionary fervor once it began. As the colonies grew, geographic, economic, and social distinctions became more apparent, social and economic mobility slowed down, and America's lower class expanded. In as widely diverse places as Dedham or Boston in Massachusetts, New York, and South Carolina, young men more frequently failed to achieve success. And economic dissatisfaction oftentimes carried over into colonial politics, disrupting a political structure already plagued by factional conflict. Friction between residents of the backcountry and inhabitants of more settled areas also arose over defense arrangements along the frontier. In 1764 a group of armed frontiersmen, calling themselves the "Paxton Boys," marched on Philadelphia demanding greater protection from Pennsylvania's Quaker-dominated assembly. In North and South Carolina the coastal elite's lack of concern with frontier needs ultimately provoked vigilante organizations to impose order in the back-country; the antagonism between these "Regulators" and the North Carolina government led to armed conflict.

Religious disputes also wracked American society. The Great Awakening's division between "Old Lights" and "New Lights" persisted and provided one more issue to intrude into the realm of partisan politics. In addition, non-Anglican sects feared that the Church of England was about to establish a separate bishopric for the colonies, a move that would have increased Anglican influence in America. New England Puritans uneasily noticed the remarkable growth of Anglicanism in their section, and suspicious dissenting sects viewed the activities of Anglican-connected groups, such as the Society for the Propagation of the Gospel in Foreign Parts, as dangerous meddling with America's religious freedom.

The imperial crisis which developed after 1763 grew out of a complex mixture of external and internal grievances. No single complaint seems enough to have caused a revolution, but grievances against the crown, together with a variety of domestic discontents, eventually made more and more people feel that they might benefit from an independence movement.

TIGHTENING OF BRITISH CONTROL AFTER 1763

For a number of years English officials had been presenting arguments and plans for closer ties between England and America. Rapid development of America's society and economy coincided with years of virtual self-government, and English leaders discerned a serious absence of centralized control and a growing surliness in their far off provinces. The conclusion of the French and Indian War in 1763 prompted a reassessment of the "American problem" and a decision to restructure Anglo-colonial relations. Although acutely aware of colonial restiveness, British officials nevertheless consistently underestimated America's resentment of tighter British regulation. Their postwar decisions triggered an ever-growing protest movement which ultimately exploded into a war for independence.

England's own government suffered from serious weaknesses in 1763. The king still played a key role, but George III was an inexperienced and often foolish monarch. If the "real" George III did not correspond to the tyrannical despot once painted by superpatriotic American writers, neither did he approach his own ideal of the "patriot king." His deep-seated and perhaps justified animosity toward the great Whig lords who controlled parliamentary factions produced constant instability. Good ministers were hard to find, and during the first decade of his reign George III went through no less than six ministries. Too many English politicians spent their time pursuing patronage and manipulating factions rather than governing the realm. And England's wisest statesman, William Pitt, proved an inept politician, remaining aloof from the Whig managers —"a man standing single," he claimed. Finally, George III turned to George Grenville, an experienced administrator, as chancellor of the exchequer and parliamentary leader. As head of a ministry from 1763 to 1765, Grenville inaugurated a series of measures that widened America's road to revolution.

Events during the French and Indian War (Seven Years' War) encouraged Grenville to restructure the imperial system after France's defeat. The years of warfare in North America highlighted the absence of any unified military or administrative command, and the vast new territories acquired from France posed additional worries. How could Britain guard against future French attack, pacify the Indian nations, protect Englishmen along the fringes of white settlement, and, most importantly, pay for these imperial burdens? The costs of the last French war had doubled England's national debt, and cantankerous British taxpayers wanted no additional levies to support their more lightly taxed colonial brethren. After considering past problems and assessing the postwar situation, Grenville and his colonial advisors introduced a series of new administrative and financial programs for America.

The Grenville measures   Grenville irritated a number of different groups. His ministry's decision to station permanent detachments of British forces in North America immediately raised grumbles about the danger of standing armies, and the Quartering Act (1765), which required colonials to furnish shelter and provisions for the troops, added a related grievance. Even a general Indian uprising inspired by the great chieftain Pontiac failed to convince some Americans of the Redcoats' value. But lingering frontier disorders did contribute to Britain's decision to halt temporarily the surge of white settlers westward. The Proclamation of 1763, which recognized the land rights of Indians and closed the territory between the Appalachians and the Mississippi to whites, antagonized frontiersmen and influential land speculators such as George Washington. The Currency Act of 1764 disturbed other interests, especially debt-ridden tidewater planters and colonial merchants. Extending an earlier edict against making colonial paper money legal tender, the Currency Act threatened to aggravate the acute shortage of hard currency. Although these actions gained Grenville few colonial admirers, they were not the stuff of which revolutions are made. Colonials petitioned Parliament and through their agents in

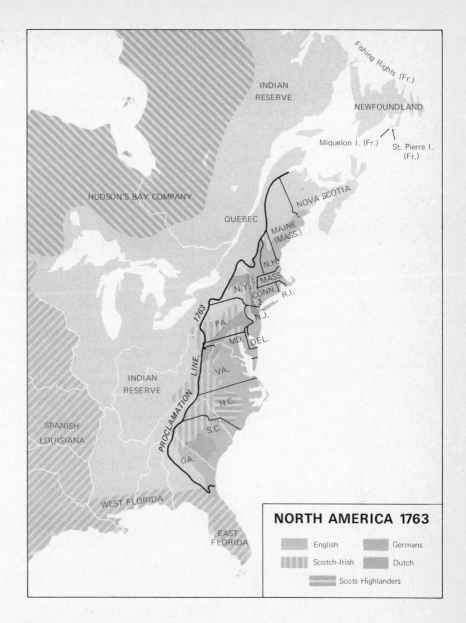

NORTH AMERICA 1763

English	Germans
Scotch-Irish	Dutch
Scots Highlanders	

London sought peaceful redress. But when Grenville touched the vital nerve of taxation, he set off more violent spasms of dissent within the colonies.

English officials believed that colonials could, and should, bear a greater share of Britain's administrative and defense costs in America. Widespread evasion of customs duties and colonial legislators' refusals to vote more funds, Grenville reasoned, demanded new revenue-producing schemes. He discovered, for example, that the British customs service in

North America cost eight thousand pounds a year and returned only about two thousand pounds. He first moved to close loopholes against smugglers and to obtain more revenue from commercial duties. Hoping to curtail widespread bribery of lesser officials who stood in for absentee superiors, the government required all customs officers to reside in the colonies. In another move, unpopular with many Americans, Britain established a new vice-admiralty court at Halifax, in Nova Scotia, and gave it jurisdiction all along the Atlantic coast. Revenue officers could take cases to the admiralty judges in Halifax and avoid bringing alleged smugglers before a jury of their sympathetic potential customers. Finally, the so-called Sugar Act of 1764 (which actually contained a number of new trade restrictions) attempted to revitalize the widely evaded Molasses Act of 1733 by cutting in half the duty on foreign molasses and enforcing the measure more rigorously. Grenville hoped that the lower tax would stimulate sales and provide an independent source for underwriting military costs.

The Sugar Act provoked widespread protest against parliamentary taxation. Political dissidents within colonial legislatures and ambitious opposition figures within town meetings pressed for repeal and vigorously denounced the new British measure. Massachusetts's aristocratic lieutenant governor, Thomas Hutchinson, complained that opposition assemblymen from Boston engaged in "the most injudicious conduct I ever knew the House of Representatives guilty of." Such demagogues, he fumed, "care not for the consequences to the public, provided they can make themselves popular and conspicious." In a number of colonies, legislators and pamphleteers solemnly remonstrated against the tax, citing both economic hardship and grave constitutional problems as arguments for repeal. The New York Assembly went further, issuing a remarkable document paralleling the radical rhetoric of Patrick Henry and James Otis rather than the usual language of legislative protests. Exemption from such "ungranted, involuntary taxes," memorialized the New Yorkers, was not merely a privilege, but "the grand principle of every free state" and "the natural right of mankind." Such sentiments directly challenged Britain's authority to legislate for the Empire, and New York's colonial agent refused to present the petition in London.

The Stamp Act Upon unveiling the Sugar Act, the Grenville ministry had warned colonials that Britain was also considering another tax—a duty for stamps to be affixed to legal and other documents—similar to one used in England. Some colonial remonstrances against the new molasses levy included denunciations of this proposal, but Grenville dismissed them as only ceremonial protests designed for political popularity. English officials, and even many American politicians, believed that the government could collect the proposed stamp tax without much difficulty, and in February

1765 Parliament imposed stamp fees on a wide range of legal documents, newspaper advertisements, playing cards, and even college diplomas. The English government planned to appoint only Americans as stamp agents and to use all the proceeds for colonial expenses. Although the ministry considered the tax itself an extremely light burden (together with the Sugar Act it would cover only one-fourth of Britain's projected expenditures in America), they also regarded it as an important precedent for future taxation in the colonies. And many colonials, realizing the possible implications, unleashed the first substantial resistance to English authority in America.

Predictably, the Stamp Act spawned another round of legal objections. Most colonial lawyers distinguished between Britain's legitimate authority to regulate imperial trade through collection of duties ("external" taxation) and Parliament's illegal imposition of direct revenue taxes within the colonies ("internal" taxation). Others rejected such hairsplitting and denied Britain's authority to levy *any* taxes on its American provinces; only colonial legislatures possessed this power, they argued. In October 1765 nine colonies sent delegates to a Stamp Act Congress in New York. After more than two weeks of debate, the gathering issued twelve carefully phrased resolutions which acknowledged Parliament's legislative authority but rejected its power to levy revenue taxes upon Americans without the consent of colonial legislatures. The Board of Trade regarded the congress, the first such meeting initiated by Americans themselves, as an event carrying a "dangerous tendency."

The unprecedented dissent following announcement of the Stamp Act caught even many Americans by surprise. In commercial centers colonials organized boycotts against the importation of British goods. Opposition politicians and influential citizens encouraged defiance of the law and condemned the political "ins" who faced the anxious prospect of enforcing the unpopular measure. Although ambitious politicians and some members of the upper class encouraged popular protests, they alone did not manufacture or manipulate the spreading discontent. At a time when hard money was scarce, the new revenue measures' requirement of payment in gold or silver struck at more people than merchants or indebted planters.

Mass meetings and street demonstrations circumvented traditional politics. It was a type of dissent which would be seen more frequently in the years to come. Angry laborers, seamen, and struggling artisans, who frequently carried as many grievances against the powerholding elite as against Britain, filled the streets of American cities. Some groups became mobs, attacking symbols of British and colonial authority. Bostonians forced Massachusetts's stamp distributor to resign and ransacked the homes of several prominent citizens. According to Thomas Hutchinson, one "hellish crew fell upon my house with the rage of devils" and spent an entire evening stripping it down to the bare walls and floors.

Charles DeWolf Brownell, *The
Burning of the Gaspee*. *The
Rhode Island Historical Society*

Some opponents of British taxation, calling themselves the "Sons of Liberty," organized more carefully and carried on a wide range of activities against the new laws. These Liberty Boys relied heavily upon newspaper propaganda, but they willingly used force against their British and American opponents. Except in Georgia, such opposition prevented the operation of the Stamp Act, killing Grenville's colonial policy. The violent protest also terrified many solid colonial citizens who began to fear that American dissidents were perhaps as grave a threat as English lawmakers.

When the uproar in America finally reached Britain, circumstances favored redress of colonial grievances. George Grenville no longer served as chief minister, and the marquis of Rockingham's new ministry favored repeal of the stamp duty. Working in concert with the new government, English merchants and manufacturers who sold to America and the colonial agents in London mounted an extensive publicity campaign against the act. Over the vigorous opposition of Grenville and his supporters, who denounced the colonials as "insolent rebels," Parliament repealed the Stamp Act in early 1766. But this was not a total victory for the colonies. A series of parliamentary resolutions condemned both the legislative remonstrances and the protests in the streets. More ominously, Parliament coupled its action on the stamp law with enactment of a Declaratory Act which unequivocally asserted Parliament's power to legislate on *all* colonial matters. British leaders backed down on the immediate source of friction, but by announcing their determination to uphold British sovereignty in America, they also guaranteed future troubles.

The Townshend duties   Many British leaders still wanted colonials to pay a larger share of colonial administrative and military costs, and parliamentary maneuvering over reduction of England's own land tax helped force the American issue. In early 1767, Charles Townshend, chancellor of the exchequer in yet another ministry, unveiled his program. Capitalizing on the frequent distinction between "internal" and "external" taxation, Townshend taxed a wide range of colonial imports including glass, paper, lead, and tea. These duties, he argued, would raise badly needed funds and also impress Parliament's authority to tax upon the disruptive provincials. He further proposed creation of a new American customs service as well as a crackdown on New York's continually defiant Assembly. After Parliament enacted all these potentially explosive measures, the ministry indicated its determination to enforce the trade laws. It appointed several unpopular officials to the new customs board and established the body's headquarters in Boston, the center of opposition to stricter commercial regulation.

Colonial lawyers quickly countered these actions with a new barrage of legal objections, most now totally abandoning the shaky distinction between internal and external taxation. In his celebrated *Letters from a Farmer in Pennsylvania,* John Dickinson claimed that Parliament possessed no authority to impose *any* taxes upon citizens who sent no representatives to that body. Several legislatures drafted formal protests endorsing the "no taxation without representation" principle.

But once again, legal defiance was only a part of Britain's colonial problem. In some areas, enforcement of commercial regulations broke down almost completely. A Boston ship's captain, Daniel Malcom, drew a pistol on two revenue agents searching for illegal wine in his basement. Returning with the sheriff and a search warrant, the agents discovered the captain's house surrounded by a crowd of his friends, and the harried sheriff avoided a direct confrontation only by stalling for time until the search warrant expired. After the disgusted officials departed, Captain Malcom treated his protectors to buckets of smuggled wine. Such cases were not infrequent. Investigating past enforcement, Townshend's customs board discovered only six seizures and one smuggling conviction in all of New England during two-and-one-half years. (Mobs rescued three of the seized ships, and colonial juries acquitted two other defendants.) Initially the new customs officials fared little better, enforcing restrictions only enough to enrage colonial merchants. The same Captain Malcom brought an entire load of illegal wine into Boston on small boats during the night and then boldly sailed his empty ship into port the next day. The vessel's water line clearly revealed his scheme, but enraged customs officers could find no Bostonian who would testify against him. Malcom's friend and fellow smuggler, John Hancock, was less fortunate; the customs board seized his ship the *Liberty* in 1768. But the violent popular reaction forced most of the board's members to flee the city and seek protection from the British navy anchored in the harbor. After long debate and much dissension, colonial merchants all along the coast endorsed another series of nonimportation agreements directed toward repeal of the Townshend duties.

THE GROWING CRISIS

Intellectual origins of the revolution

As the imperial crisis deepened, many Americans increasingly viewed Britain's actions in light of political ideas borrowed from England's Radical Whigs. Half a century earlier, British writers John Trenchard and Thomas Gordon had warned about all rulers' tendency to abuse governmental power and had cautioned citizens to be ever vigilant for encroachments upon their liberties. These opposition pamphleteers even spelled out specific warning signs: undue ministerial influence on Parliament, increasing incursion upon freedom of press, expansion of standing armies, and general political corruption. The revolutionary generation, nurtured on Radical Whig ideology, began to conclude that England's balanced government had fallen and that transatlantic conspirators were plotting the destruction of individual liberties.

"A series of occurrences, many recent events," warned the Boston town meeting in 1770, "afford great reason to believe that a deep-laid and desperate plan of imperial despotism has been laid, and partly executed, for the extinction of all civil liberty...." How else could one explain Britain's actions? Only a Parliament influenced by evil ministers would have enacted the arbitrary stamp tax. The government's persecution of English Radical John Wilkes for criticizing the king and the stamp tax upon colonial newspapers indicated a general assault upon liberty of press. No person familiar with Radical Whig warnings could miss the significance of the British troops which continued to be stationed in the colonies after the Treaty of Paris (1763). "It is absolutely impossible," Trenchard and Gordon had written, "that any Nation which keeps a standing army can long preserve its liberties." Surely Townshend's dispatch of rapacious customs officials to America reflected an effort to extend the ministry's baneful power outside an already victimized England. And evidence of corruption abounded: customs "racketeers" fleecing colonial merchants, Crown favorites holding down multiple offices, and political "ins" freezing out opposition politicians.

Increasingly, colonial publicists expounded these exaggerated views in pamphlets, newspaper articles, and speeches. The Boston *Gazette* warned that when more British troops descended on the city, some Americans would "be pilloried, some whipped, some...lose their ears, and others their heads...." How could people remain passive "till their hands were fast-manacled, and the whole herd of great and little tyrants rush violently on, seeking what they may devour"? Members of opposition factions excoriated the "ins" as part of the conspiracy. John Adams noted that he and other Boston "outs" spent an evening "preparing the next day's newspaper—a curious employment. Cooking up paragraphs, articles, occurrences, etc.—working the political engine." Massachusetts's Governor Francis Bernard and Thomas Hutchinson were forging "chains and manacles," their opponents charged; the "outs" urged people to "strip the serpents of their stings" and reject these "guileless betrayers of their country."

Colonial "ins" denounced such critics as dangerous "demagogues" who threatened constitutional balance by stirring up the passions of "licentious" mobs for their own political gain. Perhaps some colonials were cynical propagandists, fanning popular discontent for political advantage, but others sincerely believed that the "august and once revered fortress of English freedom—the admirable work of ages—the BRITISH CONSTITUTION seems fast tottering into fatal and inevitable ruin." In such an emotionally charged atmosphere even legitimate grievances sometimes transcended the frail confines of reality. Although no vast

Paul Revere, *Boston Massacre. The Metropolitan Museum of Art, gift of Mrs. Russell Sage, 1910*

The Tea Act   ministerial conspiracy ever existed, many Americans began to prepare for a last-ditch defense of their liberties.

At the height of the protests against the Townshend duties, Great Britain retreated one last time. American complaints and economic pressure figured in the decision, but fierce power struggles within England, growing urban radicalism, and the ever-present French threat were probably more potent reasons for the reversal. In 1770 Parliament repealed all the Townshend duties except the tax on tea. King George himself intervened and insisted that the tea duty remain as a demonstration of Britain's constitutional authority to tax its provinces. By 1770 other sore points began to heal. Following a clash between British redcoats and civilians in Boston—the celebrated "Boston Massacre"—the government withdrew royal forces from the city, a move which undercut protests against standing armies. In commercial centers, the boycott against importation of British goods soon collapsed, and merchants resumed their old trading patterns. And even resistance to the new customs board subsided. The troubled imperial waters appeared calm between 1770 and 1773.

But it was the unnatural lull before the approaching storm. Parliament had removed the immediate focus of discontent, British taxation, but most basic sources of discord remained. The colonies and the mother country were still at odds over the fundamental constitutional issue: Parliament's power to legislate for America. Twice Britain had retreated in the face of colonial protest, but each time insisting upon its authority to act in the future. English politics remained confused. A variety of different economic interests bombarded Parliament with special requests for favorable legislation, and the new ministry of Lord North found it difficult to frame a coherent colonial policy. In America, political factionalism persisted. Rival elites and popular leaders stood poised to challenge the control of the colonies' rulers. And perhaps most important, many Americans still harbored suspicions about Britain's ultimate intentions in North America; deepseated fears of a conspiracy against American liberties could not be eradicated in a short time.

Then in 1773 a new British measure rekindled colonial apprehensions and sent opposition groups into action. The "Tea Act" was a seemingly innocent piece of special-interest legislation, designed to assist the nearly bankrupt East India Company. Parliament allowed the company to export tea from England without duty and to sell it directly through its own agents rather than through American merchants. By this governmental assistance, the tottering company could not only make a profit but actually undersell colonials who offered smuggled Dutch tea. England, of course, would collect the tea tax, the last of the Townshend duties still in force. Everyone gained, it seemed, except the colonial merchants cut out of the scheme and the many Americans who saw the act as another sign of British treachery. According to John Adams, Parliament "threw off the mask," so that all alert patriots could see the depths of Britain's determination to tax American subjects.

The Intolerable Acts The East India Company's attempt to land tea in Boston set off a chain of events which every American patriot at one time faithfully committed to memory. Poorly disguised as Indians, a group of Bostonians held their famous tea party in Boston harbor. Exasperated with colonial defiance— "the die is now cast," proclaimed King George, "we must not retreat"— English officials retaliated with measures the colonials called the Intolerable Acts. The Boston Port Act closed Boston harbor until colonials paid for the wet tea leaves; the Massachusetts Government Act transferred the Massachusetts assembly's traditional power to appoint members of the council to the governor; it also limited the powers of the obstreperous town meeting; and armed with a new Quartering Act, the Crown sent redcoats back into Massachusetts's capital. Soon after these measures, the Quebec Act gave the former French province control over a large area west of the Appalachians, land claimed by various American colonies. Angry and fearful, Americans established interprovincial Committees of Correspondence, and in 1774 twelve colonies sent delegates to a Continental Congress in Philadelphia. The Congress formed the "Association" —an agreement which authorized various types of economic pressure

Boston Tea Party. *Culver Pictures*

Horatio Greenough, *George Washington. The Smithsonian Institution*

Detail from John Trumbull, The Declaration of Independence, July 4, 1776. *Yale University Art Gallery. Purchased John Trumbull, 1831*

against Great Britain until colonial grievances were redressed. And American lawyers, such as Thomas Jefferson and James Wilson, went beyond earlier denials of Parliament's authority to tax the colonies and rejected its power to legislate at all in North America. Attempts by British and colonial moderates to settle the grievances failed; both sides prepared for armed conflict. After Paul Revere's ride to warn the countryside, American minutemen and British regulars skirmished at Lexington and Concord in "April of '75." And less than two months later a full-scale clash occurred at Breed's Hill, the fabled battle mistakenly named for Bunker Hill. The second Continental Congress convened and authorized an American army—"for the preservation of our liberties," it claimed, not for independence. But as new peace overtures failed, radical separationists such as the fiery Thomas Paine urged a complete break with the mother country. The tyrannical plot against American liberties had gone so far, radical patriots warned, that colonials had to cut away from England's despotic government and decaying society. Finally in early July 1776 separationists in the Continental Congress pushed through acceptance of a Declaration of Independence, an event confirmed by Jefferson's immortal document of July 4, 1776.

The move toward independence

Independence was by no means inevitable in 1776, nor did most Americans support the decision. John Dickinson's "Liberty Song" ("Come join hand in hand brave Americans all, and rouse your bold hearts at fair liberty's call") provoked a loyalist's outraged reply: "Come shake your dull noodles, ye pumpkins, and bawl, and own that you're mad at fair Liberty's call." Many Americans remained loyal Englishmen, convinced that separation was not only treasonous but unwise. Disunity remained a barrier to any American military or political effort; America's rag-tag bands of irregulars seemed no match for England's military might; and many people believed that any further disruption of established governments might unleash the discontent seething within American society. Throughout the colonies, influential leaders and ordinary citizens opposed the patriot cause, often endangering their property and person. Devotion to the cause of American liberty did not necessarily include toleration for opposition. Patriots suppressed pro-English publications, ransacked loyalists' homes, and drove many Tories to Canada or to England. From the beginning, those supporting independence labored to convince their apathetic and doubting countrymen that the fateful step taken in July 1776 was the correct one.

Jefferson's Declaration of Independence, in one sense, represented an effort to "sell" the patriot movement. Drawing upon familiar ideas—the whole gamut of Radical Whig principles—Jefferson outlined the course of Britain's conspiracy against American liberties. After the more famous statements about man's natural rights and the theoretical justification for revolution, the Declaration concluded with a lengthy

Retreat on Long Island. *Culver Pictures*

catalog of British misdeeds. Jefferson directed his charges against George III; the king, not Parliament, now became the director of the conspiracy. "He has" destroyed representative institutions; "he has" established "a multitude of New Offices...to harass our people, and eat out their substance"; the king has "kept among us, in times of peace, Standing Armies"; and "he has" committed a number of other actions "scarcely paralleled in the most barbarous ages, and totally unworthy of the Head of a civilized nation." There could be only one reaction to such "a long train of abuses": independence from Britain and establishment of a republican society in America.

In declaring independence and embarking upon their experiment with republicanism, patriot leaders hoped to escape the corruptions they saw ravaging Georgian England. The decisions of 1776, however, also carried other implications. Advocates of republicanism believed that they could purify their own nation, establishing more just political, economic, and social institutions. During the years of controversy over imperial policy, many American writers had looked within themselves as well as at Great Britain; increasingly they urged attention to such problems as human slavery, religious toleration, political representation. And in a very important sense, the American Revolution acted as a catalyst for dealing with such concerns. But before devoting their full energies to reconstructing their own society, the revolutionary generation confronted the difficult task of breaking Britain's nearly two-century-long control. Political and social reform depended upon victory on the battlefield.

WAR AND DIPLOMACY

The colonial militia's successes around Boston in the spring of 1775 had contributed to the American myth that British regulars were less effective than the colonials' civilian volunteers. This initial self-confidence and abhorrence of a professional military establishment hampered commanders such as George Washington, who realized that defeating Britain would require not sporadic commitment but disciplined training, assured financing, and interstate cooperation. Throughout the war, General Washington's most difficult obstacles stemmed less from British power than from the apathy, disunion, and civilian tradition of the former colonies. The Continental Congress had no authority to conscript men for military service and could not offer the salaries or equipment to attract great numbers of volunteers. Everything depended upon the state legislatures, but they were jealous of their local autonomy, reluctant to levy taxes, and suspicious of any sort of national power, particularly a professional military. Indifference abounded, and enthusiastic rebels seemed difficult to find when times got hard. Most Americans were farmers with crops to tend and families to feed; they would eagerly volunteer for a brief fight near their homes, but were reluctant to join the army on a long-term basis.

Shortages of men, money, and equipment made conventional warfare impossible. Greatly outnumbered by British forces, Washington's strategy was simply to maintain an army in the field, to avoid decisive defeat, and to engage the British only when surprise might tip the odds in his favor. American commanders compensated for their other deficiencies by superior knowledge of the terrain and experience gained from years of guerrilla-type warfare against Indian enemies. American politicians also sought alliances with Britain's European rivals. They hoped that unyielding persistence, spiced with occasional battlefield successes, would bring France, still seeking revenge for its humiliation in the Seven Years' War, to America's assistance.

In August 1776 Great Britain landed twenty thousand troops on Long Island near Brooklyn in its first major offensive against the rebellious colonials. Washington's army proved no match for the advancing British, and it retreated out of Manhattan and through New Jersey. As it crossed the Delaware River into Pennsylvania, the American army was on the verge of collapse, decimated by casualties and desertions, dispirited by defeat, and with most men nearing the end of their period of enlistment. Washington needed a victory, and he carefully selected the time and the victim. Leading his army through the cold and snow, he attacked the British quarters at Trenton on Christmas day, finding the enemy caught up in holiday celebrations. The Americans took nine hundred prisoners and followed up the triumph with another success at Princeton a few days later. These victories lifted American spirits, generated reenlistments, and perhaps saved the Continental Army from early dissolution.

Throughout the spring of 1777 the British troops continued to move slowly and indecisively, hoping the American effort would die of apathy or show signs of accommodation. Making the fatal mistake of underestimating America's staying power, the British government and its generals did not take Washington's ragged army seriously. Finally British soldiers did occupy Philadelphia, but holding population centers was far easier than controlling the countryside. The Continental Army could always retreat toward the interior, avoiding defeat, prolonging the conflict, and striking back only when success seemed possible. And victory did come. General John Burgoyne, a vain and incompetent British commander marching south from Canada into New York with some seven thousand troops, found himself entrapped by the skillful maneuvers of the American generals Horatio Gates and Benedict Arnold. Too busy with his mistresses to move rapidly and too egotistical to admit the colonial threat, Burgoyne lost several hundred men each time his armies clashed with American troops. Finally on October 17, 1777, Burgoyne surrendered his entire army at Saratoga.

French assistance and victory

Saratoga provided Americans with the spectacular battlefield victory their diplomatic goals required. For a year, France had secretly provided assistance to the rebellious colonies, dispensing goods and finances through a phony trading company headed by French author Pierre Caron de Beaumarchais. France also tried to convince Spain to join in a war against Britain. But Spain, possessing a large American empire of its own, feared recognizing colonial revolutions or allying with rebels, and France had hesitated to embark upon a war alone. After Saratoga, however, Great Britain dispatched a commission to deal with American grievances, and the French government feared that Americans might accept reconciliation. Not wanting to miss the opportunity to splinter Britain's empire, on February 6, 1778, France agreed to a treaty of alliance with America. Both promised to sign no peace treaty with Britain without the other's consent, and France renounced future claims to English territory on the North American continent. About a year later, Spain devised a pretext for entering the war and signed an alliance with France which committed that country, and indirectly its American ally, to recapture Gibraltar from Great Britain.

America's war for independence expanded into another phase of

An Eighteenth-Century Kissinger

the Continental power struggle. As Britain turned its military efforts toward the European conflict, its control of the seas and narrow version of neutral sailing rights increasingly antagonized Continental neutrals. Even England's traditional ally, Holland, eventually joined Russia, Denmark, Sweden, Portugal, Austria, and the two Sicilies in a League of Armed Neutrality against Great Britain. Most European nations neither extended direct military aid to America nor recognized its independence, but the colonial cause clearly benefited from this widening of the war.

109

French assistance brought little immediate relief to American troops. When the French alliance was consummated, Washington's army was at Valley Forge enduring the harshest winter of the war without adequate food or provisions. In the spring, Washington followed British General Clinton from Philadelphia back up to New York, hoping that the French navy would assist him in an attack. But British control of the American coastline remained tight, and the French fleet under French Vice-Admiral the comte d'Estaing turned south to protect the French West Indies. Washington's disappointed forces could only keep a wary eye on Clinton's troops in New York and await the French fleet's return. Meanwhile, Great Britain launched a campaign to take the South, where they believed loyalist sentiment would make victory easier. After capturing Georgia and the important port of Charles Town, South Carolina, British troops under Cornwallis set out toward Virginia. Eventually they reached Yorktown, a coastal settlement which could be reenforced only

The capture of Major Andre (from engraving by A. B. Durand)

by sea. As Cornwallis camped in this vulnerable location, Washington finally received the long-awaited notification that France was detaching part of its West Indian force to help in a campaign on the mainland. Leaving some troops to watch Clinton in New York, Washington dashed to the Chesapeake Bay area in time to coordinate an attack with the French fleet. On October 19, 1781, Cornwallis, who was boxed in by the joint French-American effort, surrendered his entire army.

The treaty of Paris   The setback at Yorktown and its increasingly serious difficulties in Europe convinced Britain to recognize American independence even though it still had undefeated armies in the field. But the French alliance and the instructions of the Continental Congress tied the American envoys in Paris (Benjamin Franklin, John Jay, and John Adams) to France and, indirectly, to the promise of capturing Gibraltar for Spain. The Spanish complication, hints that Britain would offer more generous terms in direct negotiations, and growing evidence that France might sacrifice American interests for other British concessions caused American negotiators to break their orders and violate the terms of the French alliance. They opened direct two-party talks with Britain and negotiated a settlement.

The treaty of Paris (1783) did not satisfy all American desires. Americans who had hoped to secure Canada or to obtain trading privileges with England were disappointed. The treaty left vague the northern boundary with Canada and the southern boundary with Spain; it did not clarify disputed fishing rights; and Britain made no concessions to American commerce, which now lay outside the imperial system. Two other terms of the agreement—Britain's promise to evacuate posts in the Old Northwest and America's recognition of debts owed to British creditors and Loyalists—would cause problems of noncompliance in the postwar period.

But the commissioners did negotiate more favorable terms than American military power alone warranted. They received recognition of independence and a highly favorable western boundary, the Mississippi River. The Anglo-American agreement was presented to France as a *fait accompli*, and England then negotiated settlements with France, Spain, and Holland. The world was again at peace, and America had been the chief beneficiary of European rivalries.

THE INTERNAL REVOLUTION

As the struggle for independence proceeded, Americans became ever more conscious of their place in human history. The patriots of "seventy-six" embarked upon more than the first colonial war for national independence—itself a massive undertaking. They viewed their task as constructing nothing less than a secular version of John Winthrop's "City upon a Hill": a society in the New World which would avoid the miseries of the Old and fulfill the dreams of republican theorists. Almost every other nation had succumbed to some type of despotism, Americans believed, and only in America, with the forms and spirit of republicanism, could true freedom persist. A well-ordered republican society, Americans hoped, would bring the harmony and tranquility so conspicuously absent during the years of imperial turmoil. The revolutionary generation never achieved this ideal of a harmonious society, but their republican revolution did carry a number of significant changes.

Social change   Any upheaval such as the American Revolution inevitably sends shockwaves throughout the entire society. The forced and voluntary exile of British sympathizers eliminated many who were conservative and resistant to change. Exact figures remain elusive, but between fifty and one hundred thousand loyalists fled the country; and, although some returned after the war, many did not. This massive exodus—proportionally larger than the dispersal of Royalists during the French Revolution—created opportunities for ambitious newcomers. Some members of the old elites, political casualties of the revolutionary power struggles, left public life, and new men quickly took their places. The Revolution's effect on economic opportunity is less clear. Obviously, some patriot families reaped substantial profits, but others suffered severe losses from wartime dislocations. Confiscation of Tory property, which states usually auctioned to the highest bidder, provided land for some tenants and small farmers, but most loyalists' holdings went to wealthy farmers or speculators.

The revolutionary movement accelerated certain progressive trends already evident in colonial America. It gave the *coup de grace* to primogeniture and entail—feudal land rules which imposed legal roadblocks to the transfer of titles and the dissolution of large estates. For a number of years landowners had generally been evading these laws, but their formal abolition demonstrated the revolutionary generation's commitment to a more open society and antipathy to feudal trappings inherited from the Old World.

The Revolution also hastened religious changes. Although Massachusetts and Connecticut continued to require taxpayers to support a denomination which the state recognized, most states abandoned the official establishment of religion—the practice by which one sect held a privileged legal position. Some states adopted clauses guaranteeing freedom of religion, and Thomas Jefferson's celebrated Statute for Religious Liberty in Virginia (enacted in 1786) became a model for others to follow. The precise scope of religious liberty remained unsettled—it was certainly more restrictive than in our own day—but the revolutionary generation saw protection of this freedom as a basic requirement for a truly republican society.

The rhetoric of the Revolution was rich in ringing phrases about liberty. Patriots claimed to be not only escaping from English tyranny but extending freedom in their own society. As with much political writing, some of this was self-serving and more than a little hypocritical. (Tories, for example, discovered that freedom did not include the right to oppose the Revolution.) But many members of the revolutionary movement carried a sincere commitment to the ideals of the Declaration of Independence.

Attempts to deal with the enslavement of millions of black people provided a clear example of the patriots' commitment to liberty as well as the practical limits of their idealism. The obvious conflict between Jefferson's assertion that "all men are created equal" and the fact of human bondage spurred a sizeable antislavery movement. In northern states, where blacks labored both as fieldhands and domestic slaves, America's first abolitionists achieved success. Some states such as Vermont and Massachusetts ended the institution outright; others such as Pennsylvania and New York, which included greater numbers of slaveholders, opted for gradual emancipation. In his original version of a code for the United States' territories, Jefferson proposed a total ban on slavery. Although Congress rejected this, they did approve a less sweeping prohibition applying only to the areas of the Old Northwest. But south of Mason and Dixon's line, where the majority of slaves were held, the antislavery cause made little headway. Many southern patriots conceded slavery's immorality and its conflict with revolutionary theory, but they contended that economic considerations and racial tensions made abolition impossible. Slavery, they concluded, was a necessary evil. Some, such as Washington and Jefferson, soothed their consciences by emancipating slaves in their wills, but most continued to endure the contradiction between a Revolution for liberty and the perpetuation of bondage.

Political change   The Revolution did mark an important watershed in the move toward less stringent suffrage requirements for white males. By emphasizing the idea that governments derived their legitimacy from consent of the governed, America's revolutionaries placed a new emphasis upon the right of electing public officials. The day of universal manhood suffrage had not yet arrived, but some states did revise the technical limitations on voting. Property qualifications gradually gave way to taxpaying requirements, and greater popular involvement in government meant that the right to vote took on a new practical importance.

During the revolutionary era, more and more people participated directly in the political process. Extraconstitutional bodies sprang up in many states and began operating as quasi-governmental institutions, sometimes organizing the militia, regulating prices, levying taxes, and promoting commercial activities. In western Massachusetts, for example, a series of extralegal committees and conventions held effective power for a number of years, and even the new state constitution of 1780 did not end attempts by middling farmers to defy the state administration's claim of authority.

Not all popular politicking was extralegal. State legislatures opened their doors to more men from the middling ranks, particularly farmers, and to more representatives from interior and backcountry areas. In most postrevolutionary legislatures, fewer wealthy landowners, merchants, and lawyers held seats than in the prewar legislative bodies. Even the upper houses, once the bastion of society's elite, included more men of moderate circumstances. And Pennsylvania, under the influence of political radicals from Philadelphia and the backcountry, drafted a constitution in 1776 which eliminated the upper house altogether, giving broad power to a popularly elected assembly.

Attention to the suffrage question and increased popular participation reflected the emergence of new ideas about the nature of government and political power. The years of controversy with England's Parliament and king stimulated a reaction against elitist institutions and the politicians associated with them. Radicals, such as Thomas Paine in his popular tract *Common Sense,* condemned the traditional Whig ideal of balanced government. Arguing that a balance between the monarchical, aristocratical, and democratical elements was unnecessary for the maintenance of liberty, Paine bitterly attacked the English Crown and aristocracy as modern remnants of "ancient tyrannies." He claimed that such outmoded ideas and institutions bore no relationship to a republican polity. Paine's democratic ideas, which called for maximizing the political role of the people unchecked by elitist contrivances, horrified the many Americans who believed they had fought a Revolution to preserve balanced government, not to overthrow it. John Adams of Massachusetts, for example, rushed to the defense of the English ideal, urging that only a properly balanced government would provide republican stability.

An assessment The war for independence brought internal turmoil and change, but not social revolution. The struggle never became a clear-cut conflict between rich and poor; people of all economic circumstances lined up on both sides. And neither did the Revolution bring any radical redistribution of wealth. The flight of loyalists and the expropriation of much of their wealth undoubtedly contributed to economic mobility, but the long-term growth of a sizeable impoverished element, already evident by the middle of the eighteenth century, continued after independence. A recent study of Boston reveals that the Revolution had little impact upon the increasingly unequal distribution of wealth and growing social distinctions. And just as ideas about liberty did not bring economic leveling, neither did political trends always fulfill the hopes of radical democrats.

Many patriot "outs," who replaced pro-British "ins," held views about balanced government and social stability very similar to those of their predecessors. Groups of angry yeomen and legislatures containing more middling farmers did not automatically serve the underdog any better than the colonial elites had done. The tangled events of the 1780s revealed some significant internal changes, but the heart of the American Revolution was national independence, not social upheaval.

AMERICA UNDER THE ARTICLES OF CONFEDERATION

Independence failed to solve most old problems and produced a number of new disputes over revolutionary goals. The years of fighting forged no consensus, and during the 1780s Americans found themselves divided, often bitterly, over the nature of their new polity and over the proper composition and conduct of government.

Almost a century ago, a popular historian labeled the years between 1781 and 1789 "The Critical Period." Coloring events according to his great reverence for the Constitution of 1789, John Fiske pictured a country about to disintegrate into chaos: a depressed economy, an inadequate political system, a confederation of jealous states, and a foreign danger of immense proportions. Only the semidivine Founding Fathers and their sacred Constitution saved the day, preserving America as one nation. Even today Fiske's treatment influences scholarly debate, and historians continue to argue the "criticalness" of the "Critical Period." By now much of this controversy has become stale. Although no one would seriously maintain that Fiske's superpatriotic discussion is sound in every respect, attempts to revise his hyperboles cannot erase the great crisis which the revolutionary generation *themselves* felt during the 1780s.

Constitution making in the "critical period"

One of the first tasks facing Americans was the creation of new political institutions to exercise the governmental authority seized from Great Britain. Bitter wrangling accompanied the drafting of the first national constitution, the Articles of Confederation, and the final document represented a triumph for local interests and people who feared an overly centralized government. Reflecting Americans' recent experiences with royal governors and the British Crown, the new central government lacked a chief executive officer. It had no upper legislative chamber and no effective judicial system. Even the single-house legislature lacked several crucial powers, particularly over taxation and regulation of interstate commerce. Individual states wielded great authority. Each state delegation to the Confederation Congress, no matter how numerous its constituency, cast only one vote; important legislative questions required nine yeas, and constitutional changes needed the approval of all thirteen state legislatures.

Immediately after the break with England, states also began writing new constitutions (all except Connecticut and Rhode Island, which retained their colonial charters). Various political and economic interests maneuvered to mold the documents to their advantage, and the precise results differed from state to state. But several common patterns emerged —legacies of Radical Whig theory and of recent colonial experiences. Fears that the executive branch might gain too much influence produced severe restraints upon most postrevolutionary governors. States generally limited a governor to a one-year term and deprived him of veto power over legislative decisions. Constitution framers in New Jersey and North Carolina stripped their executives of all appointive powers, and eight state governors owed their position to the legislature, the most powerful branch of government. Almost every state retained the bicameral system with an elective senate replacing the colonial council as the upper house.

Americans took the job of constitution making seriously. "To form a new Government requires infinite care and unbounded attention," advised George Washington in 1776; "for if the foundation is badly laid, the superstructure must be bad." But despite such warnings and the constitution makers' best efforts, the onrush of problems quickly seemed to threaten the institutional stability of the new nation.

The western problem   The lure of the West—a persistent attraction throughout American history —glowed anew with the birth of the Republic. Woodsmen such as Simon Kenton and Daniel Boone led pioneers westward into Tennessee and "Kaintuck." And to the north and south of the Ohio Valley, other Americans pushed out from the seaboard, seeking their fortunes from the soil. Land was the most available source of quick wealth, and the financial stakes ran high. A secure title required an equally firm hold on the levers of governmental power, and the West became the scene of intricate power struggles involving Indian nations, European governments, local politicians, and speculator-politicians from the eastern seacoast. Such infighting always complicated and oftentimes disrupted both national and state politics. Overlapping state claims to territories beyond the Appalachians had held up ratification of the Articles of Confederation, and the nominal cession of all lands to the national government did not end western difficulties. During the mid-1780s settlers in the Tennessee region set up the state of "Franklin" in a futile effort to organize an independent government and to obtain recognition from the Confederation. Ethan and Levi Allen, heroes of a revolutionary victory at Ticonderoga, dickered with Great Britain over making Vermont, still not a state, a province of Canada. And a lingering dispute between Pennsylvania and Virginia over the Pittsburgh region flared into a brief conflict.

The national government did provide the blueprint for orderly settlement of the West. The Land Ordinance of 1785 laid out the familiar checkerboard, six-mile-square township pattern for the lands of the Old Northwest—roughly the present states of Ohio, Indiana, Illinois, Michigan, and Wisconsin. In an attempt to raise national revenues, it also authorized sale of 640-acre sections at a minimum price of a dollar per acre. Two years later Congress enacted the famous Northwest Ordinance of 1787 which established a procedure for incorporating three to five new states into the Union on an equal basis with the original thirteen. Largely drafted by Thomas Jefferson, the ordinance also guaranteed civil liberties, safeguarded religious freedom, provided public support for education, and abolished slavery in the Northwest territories. Land speculators, who persuaded congressmen to sell over a million acres to the Ohio Company at the bargain price of nine cents an acre, greatly assisted the passage of the long-delayed measure. But despite such chicanery, the Northwest Ordinance was probably the Confederation Congress's most substantial accomplishment; it formed the guidelines by which new lands would be admitted to the Union in the future. The weak central government, however, would have faced great difficulty ever executing the plan. Too many other problems plagued the Confederation during its brief history.

Political and economic weaknesses

At times, central authority seemed virtually nonexistent. Without a chief executive, the Confederation functioned through a series of boards, an arrangement which initially frustrated administrative efficiency. Gradually, a small central bureaucracy with single executives heading most departments took shape, but Congress remained ineffectual. During the first three months of 1785 it lacked a quorum and could pass no legislation at all; and during the last three months of that year and January of 1786, it had a quorum for a total of only ten days. Even when attendance permitted legislation, the Articles severely limited Congress's ability to act. Denied any specific authority over interstate commerce, for example, it proved unable to deal with many economic problems. Repeated attempts to augment the national government's power over commercial affairs failed to clear the hurdles of ratification by the states, where sectional and special-interest groups flexed their political muscles.

Perhaps the most important dilemma—certainly the most complicated one—was money. Winning independence from Britain had left Americans with sizable war debts, including a $40 million national deficit and scattered state obligations. Repayment presented numerous difficulties involving state finances, the solvency and power of the national government, and ultimately the viability of the entire American economy.

Some states began liquidating their obligations through issuance of paper money, a method which frightened creditors who feared rapid depreciation of this "rag money." Debtors, of course, generally favored paper since currency inflation would allow them to pay off notes more easily. In most areas of the country, the shortage of both hard and paper money created a divisive political issue, and conflicting factions fought out the currency question in the separate state legislatures. By 1786 seven states had printed paper money, and this currency proved fairly stable in states such as New York, Pennsylvania, and South Carolina where powerful commercial groups supported it. But other states were less fortunate. Rhode Island, for example, issued so much paper that some merchants, defying a law which imposed fines upon creditors rejecting the bills, closed their doors rather than accept paper currency.

Money was also a problem for the national government, which faced war debts and administrative expenses. Often-heard claims that the Confederation was completely broke are unfounded, but Congress, if not destitute, remained poor. A request for the states to contribute $10 million produced little more than 10 percent of this amount by the end of 1783. Timely loans from Dutch bankers helped keep the government afloat, but efforts to arm the Confederation Congress with the critical taxing power failed. Advocates of a stronger central government, particularly Secretary of Finance Robert Morris, vainly proposed methods to raise revenue: a national poll tax, a land tax, a liquor tax, and finally a tax on imports. Several amendments permitting a duty on imports failed to win the needed approval of every state; the importing areas of Rhode Island and New York provided the major stumbling blocks.

The debt-taxation controversy carried broad political implications. Strong nationalists such as Robert Morris and the young New Yorker Alexander Hamilton wanted the central government to assume all revolutionary obligations as a means of expanding the authority of the Confederation and reducing the independence of the states. A national debt offered the lever to gain the power to tax, and the taxing power would clear the way for a more active and stronger national union.

The unpredictable American economy troubled many businessmen who hoped for greater economic expansion following independence. Although the depression of the 1780s was not a deep one, the country never fully rebounded from the inevitable postwar downturn. Both merchants and commercial farmers felt the lack of an adequate currency system and effective national banks. While exporters suffered from British restrictions against American commerce, domestic manufacturers and merchants could obtain no national protection against the English products that flooded American markets. As before the Revolution, many merchants faced potentially ruinous competition from English firms, which dumped goods at auction sales and avoided American middlemen. Many states adopted economic legislation of their own, but commercial interests wanted more uniform and more vigorous national action. The desire to increase foreign trade, to encourage American commerce and industry, and to erect interstate financial institutions led many American business interests to support the nationalist cause.

Ineffective diplomacy

The revolutionary movement had drawn much of its idealism from the dream of making America the proud beaconlight of republicanism in a world ravaged by tyrannical regimes. But the new nation's first contacts with foreign powers revealed its minor position on the world stage. Many European governments still regarded the former British colonies as faroff provinces, semicivilized and unworthy of much respect. John Adams, America's first minister to England, suffered a series of diplomatic affronts, and his demands for more courteous treatment met only the mocking suggestion that the fractionalized provincials should send thirteen representatives rather than only one. Perhaps most galling to American nationalists was Great Britain's refusal, in violation of the Treaty of Paris, to evacuate its forts in the Old Northwest. Instead, Americans believed that British officers used the outposts to encourage Indian raids against frontier settlements.

Foreigners had good reasons for displaying a lack of confidence in American diplomacy. Several states blatantly violated the Paris treaty by continuing to confiscate Tory property and by blocking repayment of prewar British debts. When Holland, an early and firm supporter of American independence, sent a diplomatic representative in 1783, he had trouble even finding the Confederation government, which was absent from the capital and barricaded in Trenton, New Jersey, against a threatened army revolt. Squabbling congressional factions largely nullified John Jay's attempt to negotiate with Spain over the Mississippi River area, and state interference prevented any national policy toward the Indian nations. Many Americans began to fear that the divided Confederation could never preserve independence nor make America's republican experiment appear credible to a doubting world.

Localism vs. centralism

Toward the end of the 1780s, revelations of the government's weaknesses attracted growing numbers of people to the nationalist cause. Although early efforts to invigorate the Confederation failed, nationalists continued to press for change. But their attempts to form a stronger central government met opposition from localistic interests that feared weakness less than despotism.

On the important issues—particularly taxation and monetary policy—large numbers of Americans continued to favor the localistic control that the nationalists derided. The phrase "consent of the governed" took on a new intensity after the Revolution, as citizens presented their representatives with petitions and instructions and demanded that elective officials accurately mirror their constituents' will on all questions of

Shays's Rebellion. *Culver Pictures*

national and local policy. Such practices—which conflicted with notions about a representative's duty to act according to his own best judgment—reflected a pervasive distrust of political institutions, including elected legislatures, and a general movement for greater popular involvement in government. To people who desired to maximize democratic control, the Articles of Confederation seemed to provide an adequate national structure, and further centralization seemed to pose a threat to political liberty at the state and local levels.

But other Americans feared the growth of popular participation. In many states, turnover among representatives was rapid, and elitist critics complained of inconsistent and ill-advised legislation. A North Carolina jurist and later Supreme Court justice, for example, labeled the state's 1780 laws as "the vilest collection of trash ever formed by a legislative body." State legislatures expanded their activities into almost every area, and constitutionally enfeebled governors and weak judiciaries offered ineffective checks. Increasingly, established interests voiced fears that legislatures were becoming too representative of popular desires, too "democratical." Acts setting aside court decisions, revising legal contracts, and making paper money legal tender indicated, to some, the growth of legislative despotism—a tyranny of the popular element and the collapse of balanced government.

Anxieties about political dissent outside formal institutions accompanied the nationalists' fears of legislative dominance. The revolutionary practice of popular protest—what eighteenth-century constitutionalists called "the people out of doors"—continued into the 1780s. But men of power and influence began to view such activities with great alarm; many who had considered popular protests acceptable under British rule regarded them intolerable in a republican polity where citizens had peaceful access to the ballot boxes. "Mobs are a reproach to Free Government," argued a writer in 1783; they originated "not in Oppression, but in Licentiousness." To some, Massachusetts provided the most frightening example of the "people out of doors." In 1787 a group of western farmers, under the nominal leadership of one Daniel Shays, openly defied the state government. Protesting excessive taxes, the high cost of judicial services, and the generally procreditor monetary policies, the "Shaysites" forcibly closed courts in several counties. When confronted with a superior force, largely financed by private subscriptions from wealthy Bostonians, the rebels disbanded after a short but deadly skirmish.

Shays's Rebellion seemed to indicate that the Articles of Confederation could not provide political stability any more than they provided an effective foreign or economic policy. And by 1787 enough influential people had been converted to the nationalist cause to make drastic measures seem possible. Strengthening the Articles had proved hopeless because local interest groups and state legislatures blocked amendments; the nationalists therefore turned to the expedient of convoking a constitutional convention.

THE CONSTITUTION

The Constitutional Convention

The nationalist forces pursued their cause with renewed zeal after the middle of the decade, and the Constitutional Convention of 1787 culminated their efforts. The year before, a convention to discuss interstate commercial relations had been held at Annapolis, Maryland. Attendance disappointed advocates of stronger national institutions—delegates from only five states arrived in time for the session—but the meeting concluded with a call for another gathering the following spring in Philadelphia. In early 1787 the Confederation Congress adopted a resolution supporting this venture and urging states to select delegates.

In mid-May 1787 heavy spring rains left the Philadelphia area mired in a sea of mud, and on the day the convention was to begin only a few delegates were even in town. Slowed by the hardships of eighteenth-century travel, delegates trickled into Philadelphia during the next several weeks. Rhode Island never sent a delegation, but by the end of the month the convention had a quorum. Retreating behind closed doors in Pennsylvania's State House, delegates quickly selected the revolutionary hero, George Washington, as presiding officer. Secret sessions, the normal procedure for that time, freed representatives from direct public pressure but also obscured much of the inner maneuvering from later historians. The convention's official records contain little substantive information, although a young Virginia delegate fortunately left copious notes on the proceedings. Throughout the muggy Philadelphia summer, James Madison faithfully recorded the debates, summarizing important speeches and noting various proposals for creating a new government.

The convention included many of the country's leading figures. The fifty-five-year-old Washington, still every inch a military hero, lent his commanding presence but played little part in the lengthy sessions. Although he also offered little of substance, Benjamin Franklin brought the prestige of the young nation's most distinguished elder statesman to the Pennsylvania delegation. Pennsylvania also sent Robert Morris, a financial wheeler-dealer who would wind up in a debtor's prison; James Wilson, one of the republic's greatest legal scholars and a future Supreme Court justice; and tough, cynical, one-legged Gouverneur Morris, a man of national interests who actually lived in New York. The Empire State sent the strong nationalist Alexander Hamilton; but suspicious George Clinton, the state's cagy political boss, dispatched two of his own supporters to outvote Hamilton in New York's three-man delegation. With the already legendary Washington in the chairman's post, James Madison dominated the strong Virginia delegation. Five-foot-four and barely one hundred pounds, Madison proved a vigorous champion of a stronger national union and a keen student of political systems both ancient and modern. Although less well known by later generations, Roger Sherman of Connecticut and John Rutledge of South Carolina were among the most skillful political horse traders of their time, and they played key roles in the convention's bargaining.

Drafting of the Constitution

Technically authorized only to revise the Articles of Confederation, delegates went beyond this limited mandate. The ultranationalists immediately seized the initiative when Governor Edmund Randolph presented the so-called Virginia Plan, an entirely new framework prepared largely by Madison. It called for abandoning the confederated structure of the Articles in favor of a substantially strengthened central government. The precise details of the Virginia Plan proved unacceptable to most delegates, but it put supporters of less sweeping changes on the defensive. After several days of vigorous debate, delegates rejected a counterproposal, the Paterson or New Jersey Plan, which offered changes within the general confederation framework. The nationalists had succeeded in setting the terms of future debate.

Through the miserably hot summer, delegates endured protracted wrangling, most of it coming over the nature of the two-house legislature and the powers of the new chief executive. In mid-July the hot spell suddenly broke, and with the cool weather came several parliamentary breakthroughs. The celebrated "Connecticut Compromise" resolved the stalemate over the structure of the legislature. The House of Representatives was to be chosen by popular vote and apportioned according to population; but each state legislature would select two members of the Senate, a system which gave smaller states equal representation with larger ones in the upper chamber. Many delegates also hoped that the stiffer requirements for senators and indirect elections through state legislatures would give the Senate a "higher tone" than the more "democratical" House. The question of the presidency dragged on longer, but delegates finally reached general agreement on the length of the chief executive's term, the extent of his powers, and the manner of his selection. The oddly designed electoral college under which the president was elected by "electors" rather than by popular vote, really satisfied no one, but it did provide a means of postponing the issue for several years. Washington was the obvious choice for the office as long as he wanted it, and many believed that no other person would ever receive a majority in the electoral college, and so the House of Representatives, as a matter of course, would make the final decision every four years.

Following agreement on the legislative and executive branches, delegates worked on other provisions of the new constitution, granting additional authority to the new central government and in some cases restricting the powers of the states. A committee of detail, dominated by Gouverneur Morris, polished the language and, in several instances, probably strengthened the nationalistic tenor of the document. Ultimately,

Ralph Earl, *Mrs. Alexander Hamilton. Museum of the City of New York*

thirty-nine members of the convention signed the document, and its supporters began planning their campaign to get it ratified by specially chosen state conventions.

The ratification struggle   No one easy formula explains the complicated nature of either the drafting or the ratification of the Constitution. The most obvious explanation still remains the most satisfactory: groups and individuals who saw the nation's and their own best interests served by a stronger union favored the new document; those who disliked or feared greater central power stood in opposition. Many persons saw the Constitution as a necessary compromise, an imperfect product which represented at least a partial fulfillment of their desires.

John Trumbull, *Alexander Hamilton. Yale University Art Gallery*

A variety of people saw benefits to be gained from the new governmental framework. To those fearful that radical, "democratical" elements might overwhelm the state governments, the Constitution seemed to offer a national bulwark against upheavals from below. Many of the delegates to the convention had expressed dissatisfaction with the excess of democracy during the 1780s and opposed erecting a central government which would be too dependent upon popular "whim." An upper house chosen by the state legislatures and a president selected by an electoral college reflected many of the framers' desire to check or subject to "successive filtration" the selection of national officers. The new document provided for national regulation of interstate commerce, satisfying commercial interests and ambitious businessmen who felt state efforts had proved inadequate during the Confederation era. Specific prohibitions upon state interference with contractual obligations and upon state issuance of paper money appealed to people who feared that popularly dominated legislatures might override the rights and interests of propertied elements. A general clause giving the national Congress power to levy taxes remedied one of the crucial defects of the Articles of Confederation. And the authority to create a national system of courts meant that the new central government would possess a more adequate means of enforcing its actions upon individual citizens.

Proponents of the document, nationalists who misleadingly termed themselves the "federalists," generally outmaneuvered the "antifederalists," the critics of the Constitution. (The "federalists" who favored the Constitution should generally be distinguished from the Federalist party of the 1790s.) A number of states, especially smaller and weaker ones which had suffered during the Confederate period, ratified rather quickly. A stronger national union promised greater military protection for isolated Georgians, tax relief for hard-pressed New Jerseyites, and a variety of attractions for residents of tiny Delaware. By early 1788, six states approved the charter drafted at Philadelphia.

But in states where ratification was not such an automatic decision, newspapers quickly filled with charges and countercharges, political theorizing on a high level, and demagoguery of the basest sort. Pamphleteers wielded their best prose, and orators unleashed their choicest rhetoric. The fate of America's republican experiment, almost all the participants agreed, rested in the balance.

Faced with a federalist bandwagon, antifederalists mobilized their resources. Appealing to many Americans' fear of power vested in a distant government and playing upon localistic interests, critics cataloged a multitude of defects. The Constitution was too "aristocratical," too "monarchical," dangerous to individual liberties, and a threat to the power and independence of the states. Many opponents of the proposed charter concentrated upon the absence of any bill of rights.

Antifederalists struck familiar and loud political notes, but feder-

Amos Doolittle, *A Display of the United States of America to the Patrons of Arts and Sciences. . . .* The John Carter Brown Library, Brown University

alists proved to be better organized and more resourceful political artists. Supporters of the Constitution emphasized the positive benefits of a more powerful national union: stronger defense against foreign and domestic foes, greater stability, and economic prosperity. Federalists soon conceded the need for a separate bill of rights, specifying certain individual liberties, and promised to enact suitable amendments after the basic framework gained acceptance. Adopting the rhetoric of their opponents, they claimed that the entire document was an expression of the popular will, flowing directly from the sovereign people. "The proposed Government," proclaimed John Jay, "is to be the government of the people—all its officers are to be their officers, and to exercise no rights but such as the people commit to them." Federalists contended that the Constitution created a popularly based, perfectly blended government; by separating, checking, and carefully distributing governmental power, it ensured a republican government powerful enough to solve the nation's pressing needs, yet limited enough to pose no serious threat to public liberty. Seeking a government which would check leveling tendencies, these practical politicians of the "better sort" found themselves wedded to popular, even "democratical," rhetoric.

Ultimately, the federalists' arguments, the positive attractions of the new Constitution, and the influential array of Americans supporting ratification, particularly General Washington, carried the day in the key states of New York and Virginia. By November 1789, all states, save ever-recalcitrant Rhode Island, ratified. Federalists could congratulate themselves on a substantial accomplishment. America's commitment to republicanism, many persons believed, had been rescued from the perils of the 1780s: geographical fragmentation, social disintegration, economic decay, and political radicalism.

The living Constitution

Most federalists argued that the Constitution provided a government of only limited and enumerated powers. But, as antifederalists quickly pointed out, the document did outline a much stronger central government than had existed under the Articles of Confederation. The new Constitution gave Congress important new powers, created an independent executive branch, authorized a federal judicial system, and placed new limitations upon the states.

Under the provisions of Article I, Congress gained several crucial powers. Most importantly, it could levy taxes "for the Common Defence and general Welfare" and regulate foreign and interstate commerce. After 1789 nationalists continually cited the "general welfare" and commerce clauses as constitutional justifications for extending the national government's role in economic affairs and later in social problems. Congress also obtained authority to coin and borrow money, to declare war and organize military forces, and to make "all Laws which shall be necessary and proper for carrying into Execution" its enumerated powers.

Establishment of a strong executive department further increased the importance of the national government. Future chief executives would determine the exact scope of presidential powers, but the Constitution itself gave the president independent status, broad appointment powers, a veto over congressional legislation, initiative in foreign affairs, and authority as commander in chief of the armed forces.

The Constitution also authorized a national judicial structure, a system for enforcing federal laws. The Founding Fathers established a Supreme Court with original jurisdiction and with the power to hear appeals from lower courts with "such Exceptions, and under such Regulations as the Congress shall make." The Constitution itself did not provide for a system of lesser federal courts but left this task to Congress. In 1789 the first Congress passed a Judiciary Act which set up a federal court system, defined procedures for appeals through the federal courts, and extended the right of appeal to include certain cases from state courts.

Finally, the Constitution contained several specific limitations upon the states: they could not make treaties with foreign nations, coin money, levy import or export duties, or pass laws "impairing the Obligation of Contracts" (apparently a move to prohibit bills favoring debtor interests).

As events would demonstrate, the Constitution left many points unclear. Most of the ambiguities and omissions were deliberate. The men at Philadelphia appreciated popular opposition to substantial innovation and wisely realized that no piece of paper could answer all the constitutional questions which would face a nation. The Constitution, for example, drew no precise dividing line between national and state authority. Although Article VI clearly stated that the Constitution, federal laws, and treaties should be "the Supreme Law of the Land," the document did not specify the manner in which the national government should enforce this "supremacy clause." In clashes between national and state authority, who would settle the dispute? The Constitution made no provision for judicial review, the doctrine that the United States Supreme Court should be the final arbiter of the constitutionality of congressional and state legislation. This doctrine evolved slowly through the decisions of the Supreme Court itself. But the Constitution did provide a starting point, a working paper, which would allow rulers and ruled to shape policies and institutions for the future.

Throughout the nineteenth and early twentieth centuries most Americans exalted the Constitution as a semireligious document. If not carved on tablets of stone, it nevertheless represented a set of laws which the illustrious Founding Fathers had brought down from the mount. In 1913 a member of the New York bar eulogized the Constitution in these terms:

> *Our great and sacred Constitution, serene and inviolable, stretches its beneficent powers over our land...like the outstretched arm of God*

*himself. . . . O Marvellous Constitution! Magic Parchment! Transform-
ing World! Maker, Monitor, Guardian of Mankind!*

Perhaps even federalists would have blushed at such hyperboles; but
they considered the work of the Philadelphia convention very important.
To most federalists the frame of government offered another opportunity
to establish republican political institutions in the New World. The Constitution represented another phase in America's republican revolution.

PROPAGANDA AND
THE AMERICAN REVOLUTION

The reasons for separation from England given in the Declaration of
Independence could not capture the flavor of two decades of political
propaganda in the colonies. Tom Paine's *Common Sense,* the most
widely circulated and best remembered example, was only the tip of the
iceberg. The colonists, especially those in the more densely populated
Atlantic seaboard, actively debated and discussed political principles and
practice with a fervor unfamiliar to modern Americans. Literacy was
widespread by eighteenth century standards, and a wide variety of newspapers and tracts circulated through a large segment of the population.
Political tracts arguing for or against British policy, for or against independence or revolution, were cheap and plentiful, setting forth every
imaginable political, philosophical, and religious perspective on current
situations. Debate was not restricted to the wealthy and highly educated,
but was common to all classes; in the '60s and '70s, the colonies were
a model of a politicized society. The importance of conscious propaganda
in shaping the support for the break with England is difficult to over-
estimate.

While the Tory view was skillfully argued and readily available,
opposition to Britain produced a richer and more significant body of agita-
tional literature. Colonial polemicists drew heavily and directly on the
radical Whig tradition of English dissent. Great attention was paid to the
writings of Trenchard and Gordon, spokesmen for the Whig opposition to
the Crown in the early eighteenth century. In the *Independent Whig* and
Cato's Letters, Trenchard and Gordon had articulated a conspiracy theory
of the abuse of power by the monarch. Political power, in their view,
was ultimately based on force and compulsion, and possessors of power
were inevitably aggressive and expansionist, conspiring to subjugate the
rest of society. The English constitution, mixing elements of monarchy,
aristocracy, and democracy, was the best safeguard of liberty available,
but even it was constantly in danger of being reduced to some form of
despotism. The colonists assimilated this line of reasoning, and when
they began to perceive British policy as increasingly oppressive, it was
often explicable only as a seizure of power by a cabal of would-be oli-

"Spirit of '76"

garchs. The apparent daily validation of the Whig analysis gave force to the ideology of revolution.

The saturation of the colonies with the radical Whig analysis contributed to revolutionary sentiment, but also unleashed an impulse of social egalitarianism to match the broad social base of its proponents. The radical defense of citizens liberties against the tyranny of Britain could also be used as a demand for the abolition of slavery, for direct democracy rather than republicanism, for social revolution rather than simply national independence. Such implications were taken up by certain religious denominations, like the Quakers, by small farmers in many places, and particularly by the small but growing numbers of urban workingmen. The Sons of Liberty, from an early point giving activist expression to revolutionary politics, often had merchants or lawyers as leaders, with artisans and mechanics furnishing the muscle. Merchant seamen, occupying a central position in a mercantile economy, figured among the most ardent revolutionists. The egalitarian implications of revolutionary rhetoric continued to have currency after the revolution, establishing the basis for a critique of American society by the abolitionists and other reformers in the nineteenth century.

Like any modern revolution, the American Revolution was of necessity a managed affair. Tory opponents, accepting like the Whigs certain conventions of political argument, maintained that sentiment for independence was the result of a conspiracy of deranged firebrands, and the charge contained at least a kernel of truth. Overcoming the parochialism of thirteen separate colonies, unifying a population spread out over a large geographical area, and building the morale required to pursue a protracted war against the reigning military power of the era were problems which could not simply be dealt with spontaneously. The Committees of Correspondence, the Sons of Liberty, and the hundreds of independent pamphleteers and newspaper publishers gave a necessary coherence to diffuse grievances. While it would be mistaken to see the development and promotion of revolutionary ideology as the principal cause of the Revolution—as the Tories did and some historians since have done—organized and conscious propaganda work in the colonies was an essential ingredient in turning opposition into revolution.

THINGS TO THINK ABOUT:
1763–1789

What issues divided the colonists from England ? Why did some Americans move toward independence ? Why did other Americans remain loyal in 1766 ? The following general accounts suggest different perspectives: Merrill Jensen, *The Founding of a Nation* (1968); Edmund S. Morgan, *The Birth of the Republic, 1763–1789* (1956); Bernhard Knollenberg, *Origin of the American Revolution* (1960); Lawrence Henry Gipson, *The Coming of the Revolution* (1954); and Esmond Wright, *Fabric of*

Freedom, 1763–1800 (1961). Bernard Bailyn, *The Ideological Origins of the American Revolution* (1967) is an important work. Jack M. Sosin, *Agents and Merchants: British Colonial Policy and the Origins of the American Revolution, 1763–1775* (1965) and Michael G. Kammen, *A Rope of Sand: The Colonial Agents, British Politics, and the American Revolution* (1968) offer conflicting views. Patricia U. Bonomi, *Politics and Society in Colonial New York* (1972) and Pauline Maier, *From Resistance to Revolution: Colonial Radicals and the Development of American Opposition to Britain, 1765–1776* (1972) discuss internal developments.

What were the results of the Revolution? Why were the 1780s considered a "critical period" in American history? A general assessment which has been criticized over the years is J. Franklin Jameson, *The American Revolution Considered as a Social Movement* (1926). Two books by Merrill Jensen present a provocative view of the 1780s: *The Articles of Confederation* (1940) and *The New Nation* (1950). See also Jackson Turner Main, *The Upper House in Revolutionary America, 1763–1788* (1967); Gordon S. Wood, *The Creation of the American Republic, 1776–1787* (1969); and Forrest McDonald, *E Pluribus Unum: The Formation of the American Republic, 1776–1790* (1965). R. R. Palmer, *The Age of the Democratic Revolution: A Political History of Europe and America, 1760–1800* (2 vols., 1959 and 1964) is an excellent comparative study.

What political, economic, and social forces help explain the movement for a new constitution? In addition to the books cited in the previous question, see Jackson Turner Main, *The Antifederalists: Critics of the Constitution* (1961); Robert E. Brown, *Charles Beard and the Constitution* (1956); Forrest McDonald, *We, The People: The Economic Origins of the Constitution* (1958); and Robert Allen Rutland, *Ordeal of the Constitution* (1965). Cecelia M. Kenyon, *The Antifederalists* (1964) is a valuable documentary collection.

1789-1816

FOUR | THE new nation

ELI WHITNEY:
THE TINKER AS THINKER

Most Americans of the revolutionary era followed Thomas Jefferson in viewing their new country as an essentially agrarian society. But a few, such as Alexander Hamilton and Tench Coxe, visualized a nation enriched and transformed by the rapid growth of manufacturing. Two nearly insurmountable obstacles stood in the path of such a future: America lacked both capital and a supply of cheap labor. Capital required European investment in American enterprises, something possible only if the new nation could discover a major export corp. The labor supply could never match what European rivals had available, but machinery might be an answer to this problem. To solve one of these economic riddles would be enough to assure a man immortality. That one man would essentially solve both strains belief. Yet Eli Whitney, nimble son of a three-hundred-pound Massachusetts farmer, removed the last barrier to making King Cotton the nation's steady export crop and then perfected the "uniformity system" of interchangeable machine parts that made the modern factory system possible. As one of Whitney's biographers has remarked:

It is scarcely asserting too much to say that the two aspects of Whitney's pioneering work at the opening of the century met in conflict on the battlefields of the Civil War.

Eli Whitney, born in Westborough, Massachusetts, on December 8, 1765, liked neither schoolwork nor farmwork, but he loved to putter about the workshop where his father made the farm's tools and furniture. Whitney early showed a happy blend of entrepreneurial and mechanical skills. Working out of his father's simple shop, he established a thriving business in nail making during the Revolution. And when reconversion to peacetime pursuits ruined the nail business, he switched to hatpins and fared equally well. But unlike the other tinkerers who dotted the Massachusetts countryside, Eli recognized the limits of puttering and resolved to gain a college education. By the time he graduated from Yale, Whitney was nearly twenty-eight years old and had no plans beyond a vague inclination to read law. Almost by accident, he headed south seeking a position as a tutor that never quite materialized. Wholly by chance he met the widow of Revolutionary War hero Nathaniel Greene, apparently fell in love with her, and settled (with what exact effects the records discreetly do not tell) as a more or less permanent guest on her substantial but decaying plantation.

One day toward the end of 1792 some guests broached the standard topic that southern gentlemen discussed then : the sorry economic plight of their region. They lamented the failure of anyone to suggest a workable way to make use of the short staple upland cotton that grew as a weed in the fields and as a cultivated plant, for its pretty white flower, in southern ladies' gardens. English factories, revolutionized by a series of technological improvements in the eighteenth century, hungered for cotton, but the prickly green seeds in short staple cotton—the only kind hardy enough to grow away from the seacoasts—made it uneconomical to produce : a slave, hands bloodied from the seeds, could clean but one pound of cotton in a day. Mrs. Greene, proud of her northern boarder, was sure that the ingenious Mr. Whitney could "do anything," and, eager to please his hostess, he tried. Ten days later he had tinkered up a little model "gin" (short for "engine"). Within six months a working gin, capable of producing fifty pounds of clean cotton a day, sat locked in Mrs. Greene's basement. By the next growing season the American Cotton Kingdom had begun to grow, and southern planters hurried to forget that they had ever discussed the abolition of slavery.

Although Whitney gained a patent on the cotton gin, he discovered that it was impossible to make money out of owning rights to so simple and so badly needed a machine. The gin was too easy to duplicate and suits for infringement were too hard to win. Whitney tried and even won some small victories, but he soon realized that his fortune would never come from his most significant invention; he quickly turned his clever hands to the most advanced area of technology in almost any age—weaponry. With the patronage provided by contracts with the federal government and some of the states, he set about creating tools and machinery that would enable him to make all the parts of guns so accurately that they could be "as much like each other as the successive impressions of a copper-plate engraving." Whitney succeeded after eight years in creating the prototype of the modern factory. His gun factory at Mill Rock just outside of New Haven, Connecticut, reduced the complex processes of weaponry to a series of simple operations, each performed on a different machine. Well before his death in 1825 Whitney had found the financial success that had eluded him in his work on the cotton gin.

Whitney was devoted to technology and, perhaps, to little else. He never expressed a political opinion and said nothing about slavery, the institution whose life he prolonged for three generations. He contributed to a local church and occasionally attended, but to the sorrow of his pious relatives he took no interest at all in the state of his soul. Perhaps he was Mrs. Greene's lover, but we do not know. It was not until after her death, when Whitney was in his fifties, that he finally married and had a family. His faith in technology survived all else. Dying of an enlarged prostate gland—an untreatable condition in those days—he waded through all the best medical literature of the age, then designed a catheter for self-treatment which may well have prolonged his life an extra two years—years largely devoted to providing for the future of his beloved Mill Rock ordnance factory.

1789-1816

1788	George Washington elected president
1789	French Revolution
	Tariff Act; Tonnage Act; Federal Judiciary Act
1791	Congress charters Bank of the United States
1792	George Washington reelected president
	Eli Whitney invents cotton gin
1793	Outbreak of war between France and Britain
	President Washington proclaims neutrality
1794	Jay's Treaty with England
	"Whiskey Rebellion"
	Battle of Fallen Timbers—General Anthony Wayne defeats Indians
1795	Pinckney's Treaty with Spain
1796	John Adams (Federalist) defeats Thomas Jefferson (Democratic-Republican)
	Washington's Farewell Address
1797	XYZ Affair
1798	Alien and Sedition Acts
	Virginia and Kentucky Resolutions
1798–1800	Quasi-war with France
1800	Convention of 1800 with France
	Thomas Jefferson (Democratic-Republican) defeats John Adams (Federalist)
1801	Judiciary Act (repealed in 1802)
1801–05	Midnight Appointees
	Barbary Wars
1803	*Marbury* v. *Madison*
	Louisiana Purchase
1803–06	Lewis and Clark Expedition
1804	Impeachment proceedings against Justice Samuel Chase
	Thomas Jefferson (Democratic-Republican) defeats Charles C. Pinckney (Federalist)
	Aaron Burr kills Alexander Hamilton in a duel
1807	*Chesapeake-Leopard* affair
	Embargo Act
1808	James Madison (Democratic-Republican) defeats Charles C. Pinckney (Federalist)
1809	Non-Intercourse Act
1810	Macon's Bill No. 2
1811	General William Henry Harrison defeats Tecumseh near Tippecanoe River
1812	James Madison (Democratic-Republican) defeats DeWitt Clinton (Federalist)
1812–15	War of 1812 against England
1815	Hartford Convention
	Treaty of Ghent

THE FOUNDATIONS OF A
NEW NATION

The search for national identity: a republican style

The leaders of the new nation believed in their country's uniqueness—a republican innocent in a world of decadent monarchies—and they attempted to develop a style and national symbols appropriate to America's special role. The classical republican heritage of Greece and Rome provided a constant source of inspiration and imitation. Writers often urged Americans themselves to recapture the virtue, simplicity, and self-sacrifice of the ancient republics. And the nation's institutions also looked toward the classical past. The names "president," "Congress," and "Senate" derived from Latin roots, and the first American decimal coinage, designed by Thomas Jefferson, followed Roman rather than British precedents. The figure of "Liberty" appeared in classical dress, a kind of republican goddess who guaranteed the soundness of the new currency. American architects revived neoclassical motifs; the capitol building in the new republican center of Washington exemplified this style.

But Americans also sought to emphasize their own special virtues and simplicity. Noah Webster, for example, proposed a new American spelling, one which would reform the irregularities and imperfections of English usage. Webster urged dropping "all superfluous or silent" letters: *bread* would become *bred; head* would be spelled *hed;* and your *friend* would be your *frend.* He further suggested "substitution of a character that has a certain definite sound for one that is more vague and indeterminate." Instead of *mean, grief, daughter,* or *rough,* Webster wanted *meen, greef, dawter,* or *ruff.* A corrected orthography would produce a more uniform language which "would remove prejudice, and conciliate mutual affection and respect" in different sections and among persons of different social ranks. It would also "make a difference between the English orthography and the American, . . . an object of vast political consequence." Webster's ambitious reforms may have been impractical, but real changes did creep into American spelling. British words such as *centre, enquire,* and *honour* were Americanized.

Establishment of the national government also illustrated the search for an American identity. The president's title provoked a controversy. The Senate suggested something that would underline the importance of the position: "His Highness, the President of the United States of America, and Protector of the Liberties of the Same." But others denounced such pretensions, and George Washington demurred on his own preference, "His Mightiness, the President of the United States." The simple appellation "Mister President" gradually became accepted usage. When Washington took the oath of office he suggested the majesty of his new position by wearing expensive European silk stockings and by carrying a dress sword; but his plain worsted suit, made in Hartford, Connecticut, expressed American nationalism and republican simplicity.

139

Washington and his successor John Adams generally displayed cold formality toward strangers, and critics accused both presidents of monarchical pretensions. On the other hand, lanky Thomas Jefferson, with his simple clothes and cotton knee stockings (a trimming which seemed barbaric to the more aristocratic members of the Federalist party), epitomized the democratic statesman. Jefferson used manners and dress as political assets, charming backcountry congressmen with his "down home" farming talk and his informality—worn-out slippers, faded breeches, and nearly threadbare waistcoat. Displaying his admiration for the egalitarian philosophy of the French Revolution, he outraged Federalists by opening his inaugural address with the greeting "Citizens." Jefferson, at least in many of his manners, launched the "president as Everyman" theme, a role perfected by Andrew Jackson and followed by most later presidents.

But foreigners often found the republican style of American life and politics crude and disgusting. One asked:

> But how could I love a land
> Where the mob is monarch really,
> Where there are no King-pins, and
> People chew and spit so freely?

Establishment of the capital city

One of the national government's most urgent needs was a permanent home. "Where will Congress find a resting place?" asked the New York *Advertiser* in 1798. "Every place they have taken to reside in has been made too hot to hold them; either the enemy would not let them stay, or people made a clamour because they were too far north or too far south, and obliged them to remove." Indeed, since 1774 the national Congress had resembled an eighteenth-century road show rather than a stable governmental institution, residing first in Philadelphia, then in Baltimore, Lancaster, York, Philadelphia again, Princeton, Annapolis, Trenton, and New York. No matter that a variety of real problems forced such itinerancy; the dignity and credibility of the new administration demanded a national capital site.

After a good deal of discussion and the inevitable political deals (Alexander Hamilton agreed to support a capital site near Virginia in return for Jefferson's support of a part of his economic program), Congress selected the present site on the Potomac River for the federal district. But lot hunting was just the first step. Throughout the first two decades under the Constitution, the District of Columbia struggled to become a showplace for republicanism. Land sales went slowly; at the first auction in 1791 the government unloaded only thirty-five of its ten thousand lots. At a later auction, President Washington himself purchased four lots, but even this gesture failed to send prospective purchasers rushing to become his neighbors. Parsimonious congressmen had hoped to use land sales to finance construction of the federal city, and the low demand forced them to appropriate more public funds. The slow pace of construction paralleled the sluggish land sales. When Jefferson's administration arrived in 1800, officials found the Capitol barely finished, the White House half-finished, and the Supreme Court building only an architect's dream. Boggy land, lack of skilled workmen, and inhospitable weather retarded construction on some projects and halted it completely on others. What passed for roads proved impassable during rains, and much of the area remained encased in woods and bogs. Legend tells of a group of congressmen who, returning from a dinner party, spent the entire night searching for Capitol Hill amidst the gullies and swamps. And once people arrived at their destination, things did not always go smoothly. Part of the Senate chamber's ceiling collapsed in 1803, narrowly missing the vice-president; the White House grounds remained littered with the remnants of construction work; and a visitor in 1806 warned that on a dark night "instead of finding your way to the house, you may, perchance, fall into a pit, or stumble over a heap of rubbish."

Conceived as a glorious symbol on the scale of ancient Athens or Rome, the federal city more accurately reflected the republic's struggle to find a sense of national unity and purpose. Popular political culture hampered efforts to establish any imposing physical presence for the new national government. The disorganized and semi-isolated Washington community provided a symbolic, yet tangible, affirmation of the central government's distance from most of its citizens.

The beginnings of a national economy

Establishment of a firm economic base was another prerequisite for national growth. During the colonial period there were several different "American" economies, each tied more to England than to each other. After 1763, however, colonials began to recognize an increasing mutuality of economic interest among themselves, and the long war for independence provided additional impetus to a national economic pattern. The British blockade of the American seacoast cut off the supply of many imported articles, stimulating domestic manufacturing. Rapid growth occurred in the production of items such as nails, tools, firearms, paper, cloth, and iron. Iron manufacture, the basis of an industrial economy, flourished in Pennsylvania and gave the Middle Atlantic states a new industrial importance.

Independence removed imperial regulations, officially liberating American commerce. American merchants opened new avenues of trade with France and Holland and ventured into the Far East and Latin America. Nonetheless, Americans remained primarily reliant upon trade with their former mother country. The Revolution's greatest contributions to economic growth were perhaps the least tangible: promotion of nationalism and intercolonial unity, bringing together prominent men from throughout the colonies, encouragement of a grand vision of America's greatness and destiny, and transference of economic sovereignty from Britain to America.

The war's temporary impetus to domestic manufacturing, the possibilities of wider commercial contacts, and the growth of nationalism were not enough to create a suddenly prosperous and well-balanced economy. In fact, the postwar depression indicated that independence might have done more to dampen than to encourage prosperity. Cornwallis's campaign in Virginia had disrupted the tobacco fields which provided the bulk of American exports, and wartime needs had increased domestic use of previously exported iron ore. Yet America's import needs did not decline as fast as its capacity to export, and the new country's uncertain fiscal state inhibited foreign investment. Consequently, America's balance of trade deteriorated sharply. A severe shortage of currency, related to the unfavorable trade balance, grew worse when the paper money issued to finance the war was withdrawn and not replaced by any other circulating medium. The weak political structure of the Articles of Confederation was only a partial cause of the postwar depression, but it did provide a convenient scapegoat. Those who advocated stronger central power, the architects of the Constitution, had urged formation of a new government which could promote foreign trade, stimulate domestic manufacturing as a substitute for importation, and remedy the currency problem.

The Constitution created the foundations for a national market and for the emergence of public credit, two prime requisites of growth. Under the new government, states could not erect barriers against the products or population from other states. Congress had the powers to establish a national currency, adopt uniform bankruptcy laws, establish post offices, and grant copyrights and patents. All of these provisions promoted unified growth within the country and prevented splintering and compartmentalization of the nation's economy. Through its authority to regulate the currency and to tax, the central government also possessed the means of discharging its foreign and domestic debts. This restoration of public credit was important to future development; it fostered confidence, stability, and investment in the new national economy. Just as the Constitution provided a framework for a stable political system, it also laid the foundations for an expanding national economy.

A new diplomacy   In its concentration upon nation building, the United States could not turn its back on world affairs. Just as the imperial wars had affected our colonial development and European rivalries had assisted the winning of independence, so relations with European powers continued to condition our national existence. But there was little precedent for the direction of foreign affairs. Colonial America's foreign relations had been handled by

W. J. Aylward, *U. S. S. Constitution. Courtesy New York Graphic Society*

Great Britain; during the Revolution, military expediency had guided our course; and the Articles of Confederation were too weak for effective formulation or execution of international objectives. In 1789 Thomas Jefferson became the first secretary of state, and he helped establish guidelines for America's foreign relations.

The broad goals of American diplomacy established during the nation's early years stemmed partly from the colonial past and partly from the world situation at the time. Like its mother country, America was a trading nation; its prosperity depended upon finding markets for agricultural goods and upon its ability to import what it needed on favorable terms. Its economy had developed in the context of the British mercantile system. And while Americans had chafed at British restrictions, their prosperity was inextricably woven into the pattern of English trade. As colonies, Americans had sought the advantages of imperial membership without the burdens of British restrictions; as an independent nation they continued to seek the same by advocating free trade. Born into a world of restrictive trading spheres, America's peace and prosperity depended upon its ability to open up closed mercantile systems. Freedom of the seas and equality of commercial treatment became recurring themes of American diplomacy—through the War of 1812, Woodrow Wilson's Fourteen Points, and the cold war.

Americans' belief in free trade comprised part of a broader sense of world mission. Americans no longer shared John Winthrop's earlier vision of a pure religious commonwealth which would set an example for the corrupt Old World, but they still held a similar, though secularized, view of themselves as harbingers of a new political form—republicanism. Distrusting the Old World of courtly intrigue and economic regulation, they offered in its place the revolutionary doctrine of liberty, encompassing both open political participation at home and free commercial intercourse abroad. They sought to avoid any corrupting political connection with Europe and to become a "beacon of liberty," setting a path for other nations to follow. Always fearful that participation in European dynastic quarrels would compromise their independence or their commerce, Americans adopted as cornerstones of their foreign policy neutrality, political isolation, and avoidance of entangling alliances.

Political nonentanglement, free trade, and republicanism distinguished American foreign policy from that of Europe, but the style of its diplomacy was even more unusual and revolutionary. Displaying an aversion to courtly procedure, partly from embarrassed ignorance and partly from a search for republican simplicity, Americans both shocked and fascinated European diplomats. Silas Deane, an American envoy to Paris during the Revolutionary War, wrote that "Parade and Pomp have no charms in the eyes of a patriot," and even the cosmopolitan John Adams lectured Frenchmen that "the dignity of North America does not consist in diplomatic ceremonials or any of the subtleties of etiquette;

Cornhusking could be an occasion for socializing. *Harper's Weekly*

it consists solely in reason, justice, truth, the rights of mankind..." Amid the wigs and lace of European courts, Benjamin Franklin personified the virtuous, uncorrupted republican "wearing my thin grey straight hair that peeps out under my only coiffure, a fine fur cap, which comes down to my forehead almost to my spectacles." In warm Parisian summers, Franklin flaunted his fur hat, the symbol of a less civilized and presumably more innocent society, and he chuckled about "how this must appear among the powdered heads of Paris." After adoption of the Constitution, Americans did try to enhance the dignity of their new government by employing more ceremony and following more carefully the etiquette of the day, but foreigners were still startled by the coarseness of American speech, dress, and habits. Like later revolutionaries throughout the world, Americans initially took pride in simplicity and austerity. Benjamin Franklin looked as incongruous in the parlors of Europe as Fidel Castro, visiting the White House in his full beard and military fatigues, seemed to the outraged President Eisenhower nearly two centuries later. One American observed that his country "has not many charms for the dissipated and voluptuous part of mankind, but very many indeed for the rational sober minded and discreet." Plain dress and simple manner provided symbols for egalitarianism; they were part of the republican style.

Organization of the first two-party system

During the 1790s Americans had their first experience with a national two-party system. The Constitution of 1789, by creating a stronger central government, transferred many political disputes to the national level, but it set down few ground rules for deciding specific issues. Certainly the Founding Fathers did not anticipate a system in which organized parties struggled for control of the government. But the issues of the 1790s created such deep divisions that Americans formed political parties to mobilize broader support for their views.

There could be only one choice for the nation's first president—George Washington. And the "father of his country" won reelection to a second term in 1792. But unanimity gradually disappeared. Washington's first cabinet included both Alexander Hamilton and Thomas Jefferson, and the president often sought advice from his fellow Virginian James Madison. Yet within a few years, Hamilton and Jefferson became the focal points for an intense party controversy, and Madison, partially in response to Hamilton's economic proposals, played a key role in organizing opposition to the policies of Washington and Hamilton. Hamilton established a progovernment newspaper, under the editorship of the vitriolic John Fenno, to argue the administration's case, and Jefferson later encouraged the poet-journalist Philip Freneau to start an anti-Hamiltonian paper. The two editors traded slanderous literary broadsides, and their more illustrious backers, writing under pseudonyms, soon joined the fray.

This division within Washington's cabinet culminated in the resignations of Jefferson and then Hamilton, but their retirements did not interrupt the formation of two antagonistic national factions, Hamilton's "Federalists" and Jefferson's "Democratic-Republicans." By 1794 a definite opposition group, looking to Jefferson for inspiration but directed largely by Madison and a shadowy political operator named John Beckley, confronted the Washington administration. And at the same time that factions were forming in Congress, national issues brought state groups into the national political picture. In New York, for example, the powerful state faction headed by Governor George Clinton became part of the Jeffersonian movement. Although many issues precipitated party development, partisan differences focused upon two vital concerns: foreign alignment and national economic priorities.

THE DEBATE OVER FOREIGN ALIGNMENT

The ambiguities of the revolutionary settlement and the years of indecisive diplomacy under the Articles of Confederation created a number of foreign problems for the new government. When George Washington took the oath of office, England still occupied several forts in the Old Northwest which Britain had ceded to the United States in the Treaty of Paris. Britain justified its continuing presence by claiming that America had first violated the treaty by refusing to pay prewar debts and failing to honor the claims of loyalists. Americans also wanted Britain to lift restrictions on American trade with the West Indies and British North America. Spain continued to present problems in the South and West, banning American shipping from the Mississippi and claiming the Yazoo River as Florida's northern boundary, a line which the Americans did not recognize. Relations with France were fairly good, but after the revolutionary overthrow of the monarchy and the outbreak of war in Europe, the terms and responsibilities of the Franco-American alliance of 1778 remained unclear.

Francophiles vs. Anglophiles

Some Americans, particularly Secretary of State Thomas Jefferson, viewed the French Revolution of 1789 as an elaboration of their own revolutionary ideals and saw the new French republic as a natural ally which could balance British influence. Admirers of the French Enlightenment, grateful for French aid in the struggle for independence, generally uninvolved in commerce with Great Britain, and perhaps interested in expansion into Canada, the Jeffersonians cheered the progress of France's Revolution and tried to minimize its excesses. When France declared war on Great Britain in the spring of 1793, these Americans donned tricolor emblems and urged moral, if not material, support for France.

But America was still a cultural appendage of Britain, and Anglo-American ties proved stronger than the bitterness which had accompanied the war for independence and more lasting than the infatuation with France. Family connections spanned the ocean, and even many native-born Americans spoke of England as "home." The Revolution only temporarily disrupted economic connections, and, at the end of the struggle, trade and finance began to slip back into their prewar pattern. English mills depended largely upon American cotton; one-fourth of all British exports came into the American market; and large institutions such as Baring Brothers specialized in and lobbied on behalf of American trade. Britain received over half of America's total exports and supplied over four-fifths of its imports. Business interests in both countries favored keeping America within an informal trading empire even though it had successfully seceded from the formal one. And after the outbreak of the French Revolution, many political conservatives became anxious to reach an accommodation with Britain and to abrogate the French alliance. They felt closer to the British system of balanced government and saw France as an example of liberty degenerating into licentiousness and anarchy. Fearing the growth of radical Jacobin Clubs in America, some urged President Washington to declare neutrality in the struggle between England and France, an action which would tacitly terminate the French alliance.

During Washington's second term, which coincided with the outbreak of war between France and Britain in 1793, United States policy became unmistakably pro-British. Following the advice of Alexander Hamilton, the president issued a neutrality proclamation. And although British measures against American shipping—which violated the American definition of neutral rights—threatened to provoke acrimony, Britain's timely restraint prevented development of serious disputes. The administration became increasingly anti-French due to the blatantly partisan activities of the new French minister to the United States, Edmond Genêt. Genêt spent his time propagandizing, recruiting for France, and organizing privateers to operate against Britain from American ports. Even James Madison, a leading Francophile, branded Genêt's behavior as that of a "madman," and Washington finally requested the minister's recall. Long out of sympathy with the pro-British drift of policy and embarrassed by Genêt's tactless behavior, Jefferson subsequently resigned from Washington's cabinet. Jefferson's departure left Hamilton and John Adams, both Anglophiles attuned to commercial interests, as the president's principal advisers.

Jay's treaty   As relations with France deteriorated, the Anglo-American detente reached its height. Men who wanted to soothe irritants between England and America dominated both governments, and President Washington dispatched to London a skilled diplomat, John Jay, with instructions to settle disputes over neutral rights and imperial restrictions. Great Britain would not even discuss the American proposition that "free ships made free goods" in time of war and refused to change its own definition of neutral rights, which made American ships carrying contraband subject to seizure. But rather than break off negotiations because of this impasse over neutral rights, Jay went on to reach settlements on other matters. Fearing the outbreak of hostilities on the Anglo-American frontier, Britain agreed to withdraw from the Northwest posts; it opened the East Indian trade to Americans; and it lifted some minor restrictions on trade with the West Indies. To negotiate other outstanding disputes, Jay and British Foreign Secretary Lord Grenville agreed to establish joint commissions to discuss the northeastern boundary problem and to settle prerevolutionary debts still owed by Americans. The final treaty did not fulfill Jay's instructions and greatly disappointed many Americans, including the president. But it did achieve all that a weak country could reasonably have expected, and settling small matters surely was wiser than settling none at all. Above all, Jay's Treaty preserved good relations with Britain, providing the new nation with a few more years of security in which to establish its government without involvement in foreign wars.

But Jay's Treaty split the country. It further polarized pro-British Federalists and pro-French Republicans, the two factions which had been forming throughout Washington's administration. The division reflected more than simple foreign policy preferences; in the heated battle over the ratification of Jay's Treaty each faction sought an international alignment which advanced its own sociopolitical philosophy and its economic self-interest. The Jeffersonian faction interpreted the Federalists' aversion to republican France as a sign of dangerous monarchical tendencies, and they charged Jay with sacrificing the national interest in favor of those commercial groups which wanted accommodation with Britain. When Thomas Pinckney a year later secured spectacular concessions from Spain, including right of navigation on the Mississippi and recognition of America's western and southern boundary claims, Republicans drew unfair analogies between Jay's and Pinckney's treaties to substantiate their charges that Jay's pro-British terms bordered on treason. The Hamiltonian or Federalist faction charged these critics were blind to the best interests of the country, disloyal to the policies of the national government, and supporters of a radical "mobocracy." The Senate ratified Jay's Treaty, but only after acrimonious debate which helped coalesce America's first system of political parties.

By the time Washington left office in 1796, factional disputes had reached such heights that the outgoing president feared for the future of his country. In his Farewell Address, inspired by Hamilton, Washington articulated his distrust of political factions (meaning, of course, the Jeffersonians) and of entangling alliances (meaning the one with France).

The Farewell Address, which is still read annually in Congress on Washington's birthday, was not intended as timeless or universal advice from the Father of His Country. It was, rather, a partisan spokesman's response to the particular political climate after Jay's Treaty.

THE DEBATE OVER ECONOMIC PRIORITIES

Hamiltonianism vs. Jeffersonianism

Basic differences over economic priorities also influenced the pattern of alignments during the 1790s. The Constitution provided only the institutional framework for a national economy; it did not sketch details nor execute changes. Responsibility for implementing a new economic program and for promoting growth fell upon Washington's secretary of the treasury, Alexander Hamilton. Hamilton's economic plans aimed at ensuring that America's most wealthy and powerful groups had a stake in the success of the new government. Appealing for support among the common people as the Jeffersonians did, Hamilton believed, would only create disorder and misguided policy. Jabbing at the Jeffersonians and the egalitarian philosophy spread by the French Revolution, Hamilton wrote that "the voice of the people has been said to be the voice of God; and however generally this maxim has been quoted and believed, it is not true in fact. The people are turbulent and changing; they seldom judge or determine right." Hamilton sought direction and support from the "rich and well-born," while the Jeffersonians mobilized those groups, both rich and poor, who felt victimized by Federalist measures.

Hamilton's financial program also rested upon the premise that commerce and manufacturing were the keys to economic prosperity. He believed that "an extension of commerce and manufactures, the rapid growth of our cities and towns, would lead to the consequent prosperity of agriculture, and the advancement of the farming interest." Industry would provide the farmer with a home market for his products, lessen his reliance upon foreign buyers and world prices, and supply him with implements at a lower cost than imported tools. Hamilton's theories, which reflected his admiration for England's mercantile economy, ran counter to the agrarian beliefs of the Jeffersonians. Strongly influenced by French physiocratic thought, Jeffersonians believed that a country's true wealth sprang from the land and its products. And the majority of Americans, being farmers, agreed that agricultural profits provided the only sound basis for industrial and commercial growth.

Jeffersonians were consequently interested in promoting westward expansion and in dispersing population away from cities and on to new farming lands; Hamiltonians conversely believed that westward settlement would diminish the "active" wealth of the country. Pointing out that new settlements furnished little surplus yet consumed many products made by the labor of others, Hamilton argued that expansion of the agricultural frontier diminished capital accumulation, drained off a needed supply of labor, and retarded the entire economy.

Both Hamiltonians and their Jeffersonian critics desired a prosperity balanced among agricultural, commercial, and manufacturing sectors, but they differed over which sector held the key to general growth and which should consequently be accorded the government's attention. Throughout the 1790s Hamilton's view of national priorities prevailed; after Jefferson's election in 1800, agriculture and westward expansion would receive greater consideration.

Hamilton's economic program

The Federalist financial program, emphasizing the country's manufacturing and mercantile sectors, provided the stability and coherent planning which revolutionary governments frequently lack. If Hamilton was an elitist, he was also a nationalist with an understanding of economics and a shrewd appreciation of political dynamics.

The first Federalist measure, the Tariff Act of 1789, aimed at the "encouragement and protection of manufactures" and the collection of revenue. It placed import duties primarily upon the types of articles manufactured in America, such as carriages, gunpowder, paint, and paper, but also provided some protection for native agricultural commodities such as hemp, indigo, and cotton. Although the rates now seem extremely low compared to the prohibitive scales of later American tariffs, this first act did establish the precedent of protectionism. America, the advocate of free trade and open ports abroad, embraced restrictionism as its own national policy.

Another Federalist measure offered assistance to American shipping interests. Placing high duties on foreign-built and foreign-owned ships entering American ports, the Tonnage Act of 1789 gave Americans a virtual monopoly over their fisheries and coastal trade. From 1790 to 1808 responding to the favorable position of neutral trade during the European wars, the United States doubled its shipping capacity. By the latter date, United States ships carried 92 percent of the country's total trade and conducted business throughout the world.

The Revolutionary War had left America's finances in disarray and confusion, and the new government's most pressing economic problems involved untangling the war debts, establishing good credit, and erecting a stable currency system. Both state and national governments had issued a variety of securities to finance the war, and before 1791 speculators had purchased these bonds at greatly reduced prices. Some states had mustered the financial resources to liquidate their bonds; others had ignored the obligations. To cut through the tangle of bond issues and creditors' claims, in 1790 Hamilton proposed a simple solution: the national government would fund the entire public debt, paying the full value of the national securities to their current holders and assuming the payment of all state obligations. Hamilton insisted that paying off the debt in full would restore the nation's credit. He also had a political purpose—to give bondholders a stake in the continuation of the new government. Funding the debt with a uniform system of paper notes would also expand the currency supply and provide a uniform national medium of exchange. Internal taxes, particularly a tax on liquor distilling, would finance retirement of the securities.

Hamilton's program of assuming state obligations and funding the entire debt passed Congress and did help rejuvenate the Union's financial situation. But it also provoked heated controversy. Opponents of the measures, Jeffersonians such as James Madison, pointed out that funding at face value bestowed unreasonable profits upon speculators who had bought the paper from the original holders at a fraction of face value. Madison argued that the original purchasers should be reimbursed, but he could suggest no practical method of tracing back each security transaction. Hamilton's opponents also pointed out that assumption penalized those states which had worked to pay off their debts and rewarded those which had done nothing for their creditors.

Agrarian spokesmen were particularly bitter at the way Hamilton's

John Vanderlyn's portrait of Robert Fulton—steamboat entrepreneur. *Collection of Randall J. LeBoeuf, Jr.*

program was to be financed. In western Pennsylvania, farmers raising products used in making liquor charged that they were being taxed to reward a class of wealthy speculators, and in 1794 some resisted the levy. Rioting broke out, and mobs tarred and feathered some revenue agents. Hamilton labelled the protests an "insurrection." Convincing President Washington to dispatch 15,000 militiamen to quell the disorder, Hamilton used this "Whiskey Rebellion" to demonstrate the central government's new power.

To ensure that the value of governmental securities would remain on a par with gold and silver and provide an adequate and stable currency, Hamilton proposed creation of a national bank. The bank's stock was subscribed both by the national government, to lend the institution authority and prestige, and by private citizens, to give the wealthy a stake in the country's financial stability. The proposal initially met opposition from followers of Jefferson. Advocating a strict, or narrow, interpretation of the Constitution, they questioned the national government's authority to charter such a bank and warned against Federalists' broad construction of the Constitution. But the banking measure passed. The new bank helped ease the currency problem and handled the government's money safely and efficiently.

Hamilton's financial programs enlarged the wealth of those already affluent. And because the measures' effects were regressive—that is, they tended to shift the distribution of income in favor of the rich at the expense of the poor—Hamilton was attacked by his own contemporaries and by many later historians more concerned with social justice. Concentration of wealth, however, did provide the domestic capital accumulation needed for long-term economic growth. By the time the Federalists left office, the infusion of new, reliable paper money had rejuvenated the economy; prices and business activity had begun a healthy rise; and America's credit rating abroad was excellent, a condition which would have seemed impossible a few years earlier.

ECONOMIC GROWTH

During the 1790s the United States developed the basis for sound economic growth, balanced between manufacturing, commerce, and agriculture. Economic change was still very slow, but it did begin to transform the country, creating new opportunities and altering the nature of the labor force.

Commerce and industry Hamilton's special constituency, the manufacturing-mercantile elite, made substantial advances under the new government. They developed a thriving merchant fleet which traded in ports throughout the globe; American shipbuilding techniques and shipboard conditions were among the best in the world. The period has been called the Golden Age of America's merchant marine.

Industry continued to consist mainly of small-scale, self-employed handicraftsmen: blacksmiths, tailors, coopers, carpenters, weavers, wheelwrights. But larger enterprises signalled the dawn of industrialization. There were iron foundries, glass factories, shipyards, and distilleries; mills turned out lumber, flour, cloth, paper, and gunpowder; mines and quarries testified to the growing demand for raw materials for manufacturing and construction. From this beginning, industrialism in the United States would gradually accelerate throughout the nineteenth century.

The growth of industry and commerce brought changes in the labor force. Development of factories and merchant marine increased the number of hired wage earners, a small class throughout much of the colonial period. In addition, new textile mills brought women and children into the salaried work force for the first time. Women had traditionally produced yarn and cloth in their households, and it seemed natural for mills to employ them in the same capacity. Textile work was tedious, with its regimentation, repetitious tasks, and long hours, but it did broaden the definition of a woman's role to include employment outside the home. In one sense, salaried work opened new choices for women, rendering them less dependent upon family and marriage. In another sense, it only made some of them doubly oppressed: first as women with an inferior status in custom and law, and second as members of a powerless working class.

The birth of "king cotton"

The most significant economic developments during the 1790s came in the all-important agricultural sector. Colonial America's favorable balance of trade had been based largely upon the great staple export commodities: rice, indigo, and tobacco. Independence freed planters from selling only to Great Britain, but it also deprived them of the bounties and favored treatment they had enjoyed under the imperial system. Thrown into turmoil by the southern campaigns of the Revolutionary War and later afflicted by adverse market conditions, these commodities never recovered their prerevolutionary stature. Throughout the 1790s rice growing declined, indigo cultivation collapsed entirely, and tobacco prices plummeted. Poverty threatened southern agriculture, and the decline of reliable cash crops endangered the country's balance of trade. Paralleling the decline of traditional exports, however, was the rise of a new staple that would have a great impact on the nation's long-term development: cotton.

Before the invention of the cotton gin in the early 1790s, cotton could be grown only on small, labor-intensive farms. But the new machine enabled production to expand over large areas, and technological advances in the British textile industry boosted England's demand for cot-

The cotton gin. *Library of Congress*

ton. England's textile mills, the basis of its prosperity, imported over half of their cotton from the United States. In the twenty-five years between 1791 and 1816 annual raw cotton production rose from 4,000 bales to 260,000 bales; cotton would become America's preeminent cash crop, the source of its prosperity and the generator of its future economic growth.

The expansion of cotton farming in the South caused a spectacular change in labor patterns. The institution of slavery had grown little during the first two decades after independence. Many revolutionary leaders realized the contradition of bondage in a country which claimed to be the freest of any on earth; others feared racial mixture and wanted be keep the New World pure from supposedly inferior Africans. In addition, the export crops requiring slave labor were on the decline. But introduction of the cotton gin and the subsequent expansion of cotton cultivation greatly increased the demand for slaves. There may be doubts

155

about whether slavery would have died of its own accord had cotton not swept southern agriculture, but the new crop certainly did revitalize the institution and make it seem economically essential to the country's prosperity.

During the early years under the Constitution, the United States began to develop a national economy in which regional specialization contributed to the success of the whole. Export agriculture and the profits from America's merchant marine brought revenue into the new country, while the growth of manufacturing lessened America's dependence upon foreign markets and trade.

PARTISAN DIVISIONS WIDEN

Fear of "factions" Each faction distrusted the programs and motives of the other. During the first disputes between Hamilton and Jefferson, the latter advised President Washington that more than merely "speculative differences" divided the secretaries of treasury and state. Hamilton's program, Jefferson warned, "flowed from principles adverse to liberty, and was calculated to undermine and demolish the republic. . . ." Jeffersonian writers commonly referred to Federalists as "crypto-monarchists" who were plotting to undermine the Revolution and to reestablish monarchy in America. Even Washington himself became the target of vicious remarks; in Virginia his opponents toasted "a speedy death to President Washington." A group of New Yorkers burned John Jay in effigy and threw stones at Alexander Hamilton.

Federalists' distrust of Jeffersonians was no less. Many Federalists equated Jeffersonians with traitorous radicals who wanted to bring about mob rule and make American streets run red with Federalist blood. Following the Whiskey Rebellion of 1794, Federalists, including President Washington, bitterly criticized the Democratic-Republican societies (political clubs associated with the Jeffersonian movement) for inciting resistance to the government. The societies and their publications were accused of spreading "wicked, false and seditious" misrepresentations "with the seditious intention of slandering the measures of the government and its administrators." Such "licentious" criticism, Federalists charged, endangered the safety of the Republic. They believed that dissent meant disloyalty to the nation, and one Federalist newspaper proclaimed, "He that is not for us, is against us."

Political observers often noted, privately as well as publicly, the frenzied, sometimes hysterical, political atmosphere. "Warm debates [and] high political passions," Jefferson wrote a friend, were nothing new, but "public men no longer seemed to separate political and personal differences. Men who have been intimate all their lives, cross the streets to avoid meeting, and turn their heads another way, lest they should be obliged to touch their hats."

The political tensions of the 1790s reflected, in part, the legacy of revolutionary America's political culture, particularly the tendency to see an embattled republic surrounded by foreign foes and infested with domestic dangers. The histories of previous republics revealed a familiar theme of disintegration because of foreign wars, domestic political disputes, and internal decay. Might not the difficulties of the 1790s, some Americans wondered, indicate that their own republic was about to suffer the same unhappy fate as ancient Greece and Rome?

The growing political divisions seemed to confirm fears that the republic was endangered. Acceptance of the legitimacy of political parties came slowly; the fact of political organization preceded general acceptance of the idea of a two-party system. Only a few men believed that political parties could perform valuable functions in a free republic: formulating alternative policies, presenting them to the electorate, and implementing programs supported by a majority of citizens. Instead, partisan organizations appeared to be dangerous instruments of selfish men which impeded, rather than advanced, expression of the general will. To most Americans of the 1790s, factions were symptomatic of a disease within the body politic; they reflected acrimony and disintegration. Even the ambitious men engaged in creating the electoral machines which we would call "parties" believed that parties were, at best, necessary evils. "If I could not go to heaven but with a party," Thomas Jefferson once said, "I would not go there at all."

The election of 1796   The factional cleavages which had developed within each state and within Congress, particularly over the issues of economic and foreign policy, came to a head in the election of 1796. Washington's decision to retire to Mount Vernon rather than to seek a third term created the first real contest for the presidency. In 1796 the Federalists offered Vice-President John Adams, and Thomas Jefferson ran with the organized support of the Democratic-Republican faction. While Adams and Jefferson remained quietly above the battle—it was still considered bad taste for a candidate to electioneer actively—their supporters circulated newspapers and pamphlets explaining the issues to prospective voters. Jeffersonians charged that "JOHN ADAMS is an avowed MONARCHIST;" Federalists condemned Jefferson as a radical who would revolutionize society.

The results of the election revealed that the parties were fairly evenly matched. Adams won with 71 electoral votes, but Jefferson received 68. A switch of two votes from one candidate to the other would have reversed the outcome. The balloting also showed the strength of regional loyalties: the candidate from Massachusetts swept New England; the Virginian attracted southern states and Pennsylvania. Although Adams won the contest, some Federalist electors failed to support his running mate, Thomas Pinckney, and Jefferson became vice-president. (Under the original provisions of the Constitution, the candidate who finished second in the electoral college voting became vice-president.) Federalists continued to control the presidency, but Jefferson's new office gave him a prominent position from which to launch his next try for president in 1800. And, as the balloting for Pinckney revealed, the Federalist party was split. Many Federalists, including members of Adams cabinet, looked to Alexander Hamilton rather than to the president for leadership and direction.

XYZ affair and the
quasi-war with France

Under Washington's successor, John Adams, political factionalism and foreign problems grew even worse. Jay's Treaty, together with French seizures of American ships bound for London, brought the United States and France to the brink of war. In 1797 the new president named a three-man commission (Charles Cotesworth Pinckney, John Marshall, Elbridge Gerry) to negotiate the difficulties and, at the same time, urged Congress to strengthen the nation's defenses. Jeffersonians charged that Adam's commissioners were too pro-British and that the military measures were aimed less against France than against domestic dissenters. But Jeffersonian complaints faded when news reached America that three French envoys (unnamed, but designated X, Y, and Z) had demanded a bribe as the price of opening the talks. When Adams lay the records of this indignity before Congress, there was an anti-French uproar. Congress formally repudiated the French alliance, suspended commerce, and authorized American ships to seize French armed vessels. The Atlantic Ocean became the scene of an undeclared naval war between the United States and France.

Federalists encouraged a rising tide of war fervor. One Federalist spokesman penned a new chorus to the patriotic ditty "Yankee Doodle":

> *Yankee Doodle, mind the tune,*
> *Yankee Doodle dandy,*
> *If Frenchmen come with naked bum,*
> *We'll spank 'em hard and handy.*

Under the guise of patriotism and national honor, some Federalists tried to muzzle criticism of the government and organized vigilance committees to watch the activities of Republican politicians and publishers. Mobs assaulted Jeffersonian editors and sacked offices of Republican journals. One summer evening twelve hundred young men marched to the president's home in Philadelphia offering to serve in a war against France, and Adams, a sword at his side, met them in full military uniform. Mrs. Adams encouraged people to wear black cockades, ribbons such as American soldiers had worn during the Revolution, and one afternoon in the yard of the State House in Philadelphia a scuffle broke out between wearers of the black cockade and Republicans adorned with the red or tricolor cockades which symbolized France. The cavalry finally restored order, but the president, alarmed at the "terrorism," had arms brought from the War Office to his house through back alleyways. Rumors swept the South that French revolutionary ideas were encouraging slave uprisings on the pattern of the recent revolt in the French colony of Santo Domingo. And the people of Charleston, believing a French invasion was imminent, declared a state of emergency and raised money to erect defenses.

The Alien and Sedition acts In 1798 the Federalist majority rammed though Congress a series of measures which reflected their fear that the nation was in peril and their belief that the troubles stemmed from the "radical" Jeffersonian faction.

John Singleton Copley, Study for the portrait of John Adams. *The Metropolitan Museum of Art. Purchase, 1960. Harris Brisbane Dick Fund*

Claiming that immigrants from France and Ireland were carriers of radicalism (and one source of Jeffersonian political support), Federalists passed three laws designed to counteract the danger from foreigners. The Alien acts increased the prenaturalization period from five to fourteen years, empowered the president to expel aliens whom he considered dangerous, and authorized him to deport alien enemies during wartime or to impose restraints upon their freedom if they remained in the United States. Congress also passed a sedition law which, among its other provisions, made it a crime to publish seditious libels—any "false, scandalous and malicious" writings against the government, the Congress, or the president. Although designed to blunt the barbs of Jeffersonian writers against the Adams administration, the Sedition Act did incorporate several guarantees which actually liberalized the law of seditious libel: allowing defendants to plead truth as a defense and permitting a jury rather than a judge to determine whether or not the writer's publications were libelous. Still, blatantly partisan judges and Federalist jurors quickly showed Jeffersonian writers the difference between libertarian rules and their practical application.

The Virginia and Kentucky resolutions

The obviously partisan tenor of the Alien and Sedition acts did not escape the Jeffersonians. They let loose a torrent of criticism, and some immediately ran afoul of the Sedition Act. Condemning the act and the subsequent prosecutions as violations of Americans' sacred right of free expression, some Jeffersonian lawyers argued for an almost unlimited constitutional right of political discussion, a proposition which only confirmed Federalists' fears about Jeffersonian radicalism. Although the debates over the Sedition Act were inconclusive (the act automatically expired in 1801 and the Supreme Court did not determine its constitutionality), the law provoked the first full-scale examination of the limits of a free press in America.

Jefferson and his primary collaborator, James Madison, drafted legislative denunciations of the Alien and Sedition acts and helped push them through the Kentucky and Virginia legislatures in 1798. The two Virginians concentrated upon the supposed threat to the reserved rights of the states, arguing that the Constitution had created a confederation of sovereign states which retained the power to determine, either together or singly (the two resolutions differed on this point), when the national government had exceeded the limits of its authority. After going through several theoretical metamorphoses, the so-called states' rights or compact theory enunciated in these famous resolutions became the standard constitutional position of groups who found themselves outvoted at the national level. Jefferson and Madison, however, probably never intended the resolutions as justifications for nullification of national laws or for secession. The vague language of the Virginia and Kentucky resolutions served an obviously political purpose: identifying the Jeffersonians as sympathetic to many Americans' fear of a distant central government.

John Adams chooses peace

As tensions mounted at home and the nation conducted an undeclared "quasi-war" against France on the seas, President Adams began to reconsider his anti-French policy. Led by Hamilton, the so-called High Federalists urged greater military preparation and conformity at home. But Adams increasingly suspected what the Jeffersonians already fervently believed—that High Federalists were more concerned about suppressing domestic opposition than foreign foes. The president deplored England's growing violations against neutral commerce and noted France's conciliatory gestures following America's violent reaction to the "XYZ affair." Hoping to prevent outright war, Adams sent new negotiators to France. Dealing now with Napoleon Bonaparte, who wanted to avoid conflict in the New World and concentrate upon Europe, the Americans signed a convention on September 30, 1800, which preserved the peace. France accepted the American principle that "free ships made free goods" and voided the alliance of 1778 that had troubled Franco-American diplomacy. Hamilton and his followers were furious at what they considered the president's desertion from Federalist ranks, and, although Adams ran for a second term, the divisions among the Federalists and the reconciliation with France opened the way for a Jeffersonian-Republican victory in 1800.

PARTISAN POLITICS UNDER JEFFERSON

The election of 1800

By 1800, Federalists had largely thrown away their chances for victory. Any hope of muzzling the opposition press through piecemeal libel prosecutions was doomed to failure in a country as large as the United States, and the several dozen cases only rebounded against the Federalists themselves. Federalists also proved unable to maintain party unity. The "High Federalists," who lionized Hamilton, recoiled from President Adams for his decision to settle the undeclared naval war with France, and "Honest John" Adams, a firm believer in the ideal of balanced government, had no taste for the aristocratic pretensions of the Hamiltonians. Finally, too many Federalists proved reluctant to engage in the grubby political tasks of organizing and campaigning. Politics, they believed, was the avocation of gentlemen who should not have to stoop to the tactics of their demagogic opponents. Capitalizing on Federalists' disadvantages, the Jeffersonians ran an aggressive campaign, and the ticket of Jefferson and Aaron Burr outpolled the Federalist candidates Adams and C. C. Pinckney. The Democratic-Republicans scored a narrow yet clear-cut triumph, capturing the presidency and control of both houses of Congress.

161

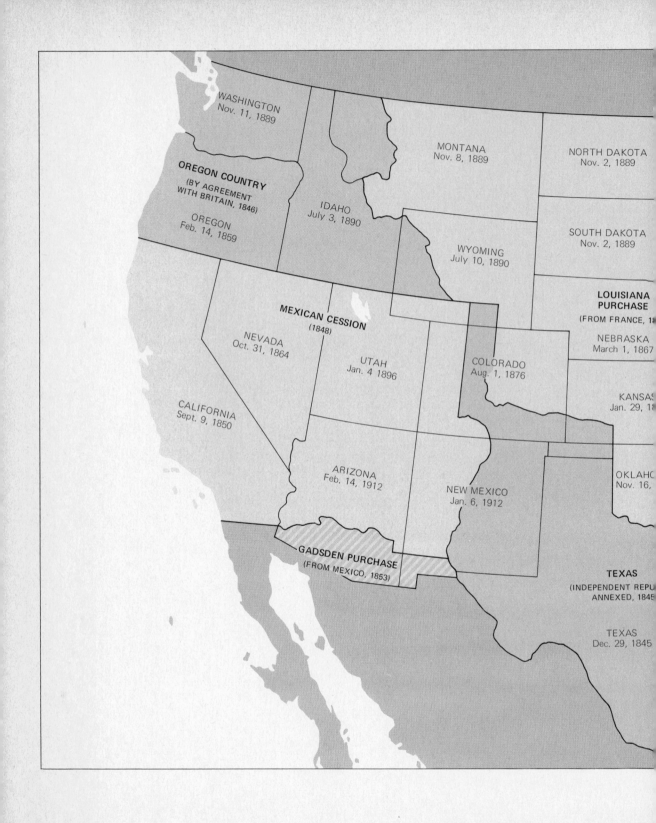

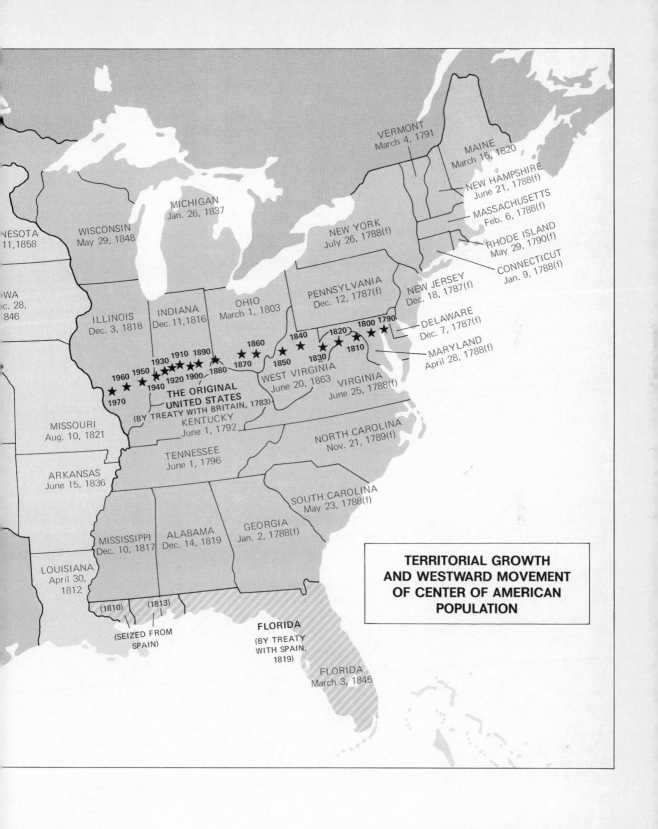

MICHIGAN
Jan. 26, 1837

WISCONSIN
May 29, 1848

NESOTA
11, 1858

VERMONT
March 4, 1791

MAINE
March 15, 1820

NEW HAMPSHIRE
June 21, 1788(f)

MASSACHUSETTS
Feb. 6, 1788(f)

RHODE ISLAND
May 29, 1790(f)

CONNECTICUT
Jan. 9, 1788(f)

NEW YORK
July 26, 1788(f)

NEW JERSEY
Dec. 18, 1787(f)

PENNSYLVANIA
Dec. 12, 1787(f)

DELAWARE
Dec. 7, 1787(f)

MARYLAND
April 28, 1788(f)

WA
c. 28,
846

IOWA

ILLINOIS
Dec. 3, 1818

INDIANA
Dec. 11, 1816

OHIO
March 1, 1803

1800 1790
1820
1840
1860
1870
1850
1830
1810

1910 1890
1930
1960 1950
1920 1900
1940
1880
1970

THE ORIGINAL
UNITED STATES
(BY TREATY WITH BRITAIN, 1783)

WEST VIRGINIA
June 20, 1863

VIRGINIA
June 25, 1788(f)

MISSOURI
Aug. 10, 1821

KENTUCKY
June 1, 1792

NORTH CAROLINA
Nov. 21, 1789(f)

ARKANSAS
June 15, 1836

TENNESSEE
June 1, 1796

SOUTH CAROLINA
May 23, 1788(f)

MISSISSIPPI
Dec. 10, 1817

ALABAMA
Dec. 14, 1819

GEORGIA
Jan. 2, 1788(f)

LOUISIANA
April 30,
1812

(1810)   (1813)

(SEIZED FROM
SPAIN)

FLORIDA
(BY TREATY
WITH SPAIN,
1819)

FLORIDA
March 3, 1845

TERRITORIAL GROWTH
AND WESTWARD MOVEMENT
OF CENTER OF AMERICAN
POPULATION

Following the election, partisan tensions continued because of the uncertainty over which Jeffersonian candidate would actually become president. The electoral rules of 1800, which were subsequently altered by the Twelfth Amendment, took no account of party tickets for president and vice-president. Because no Democratic-Republican elector thought to omit a vote for Aaron Burr, the New Yorker received the same number of electoral votes as Jefferson, and the final decision fell upon the House of Representatives. Federalists began maneuvering, hoping to elect Burr rather than Jefferson, and Burr seemed willing to make a deal. But after intense political bargaining, the details of which may never fully be known, enough Federalists finally abstained from voting to give Jefferson the necessary margin.

Many Americans felt that a great crisis had passed in 1800. Control of the national government had passed from the Federalists to the Jeffersonians; and the transition had been peaceful. Democratic-Republicans claimed a great victory for the survival of republican government and sang the praises of "Jefferson and Liberty," a campaign song which expressed the political passions of the 1790s:

> The gloomy night before us flies,
> The reign of terror now is o'er,
> No gags, inquisitors, or spies,
> The hordes of harpies are no more.
> Rejoice, Columbia's sons, rejoice,
> To tyrants never bend the knee,
> Join with heart and soul and voice,
> For Jefferson and liberty.

The Judiciary Act of 1801 and the midnight appointees

Before surrendering control of the national government, Federalists had tried to guarantee a stake in national policy making by insuring their domination of the national judiciary. Adams's best-known move was the appointment of John Marshall, a moderate Federalist who had opposed the Alien and Sedition laws, as chief justice of the United States. But the famous jurist, whom Adams selected out of desperation after several other Federalists had rejected the position, was only one of many late-term judicial selections. The Federalist-sponsored Judiciary Act of 1801 reduced the Supreme Court's membership by one, thereby preventing Jefferson from filling the first vacancy on the High Bench, and created a system of district courts. Although the act did provide necessary reforms —for example, it relieved aged Supreme Court justices from the onerous burden of riding across the country to sit on lesser federal courts—the act's supporters saw it as a means of creating additional positions for deserving Federalists and of denying Jeffersonians immediate control of the courts. The new Judiciary Act, together with another bill providing for the District of Columbia, authorized President Adams to appoint nineteen new judges and a large number of marshalls, district attorneys, justices of the peace, and other legal officials.

During his last months as chief executive, Adams rushed over two hundred appointments to the Senate for approval. (Although two hundred is hardly a striking number in the day of giant governmental bureaucracies, at the turn of the nineteenth century the entire federal "bureaucracy" numbered little more than two thousand persons.) Jefferson complained that Adams was making appointments until "9 o'clock of the night, at 12 o'clock of which he was to go out of office." Other Democratic-Republicans charged that the president's acting secretary of state, none other than Chief Justice–designate John Marshall, was still signing appointment papers at the stroke of midnight. Adams's "midnight appointees" became a prominent political issue, and Jefferson refused to honor some of these selections. In making his own appointments, the new president decided that he would select only Jeffersonians until at least half of the federal officeholders were of his own party.

Impeachment of Samuel Chase

But some Jeffersonians could not wait for normal attrition to clear the decks of Federalists. In 1802 Democratic-Republicans repealed the Judiciary Act of 1801, a step backward in terms of judicial efficiency but a political move which eliminated the new Federalist judgeships and returned the Supreme Court to six judges. Impeachment of a few rabid Federalists promised an even more forceful remedy, and the Jeffersonians' first target was an easy one. District court Judge John Pickering suffered from alcoholism and severe mental problems. Even many Federalists conceded Pickering's incompetency, and the Senate removed him from his high judicial office. Democratic-Republicans then turned on Associate Supreme Court Justice Samuel Chase, with the strong hint that Chief Justice Marshall might be their next victim.

Chase, a prominent Maryland Federalist who had signed the Declaration of Independence, had displayed obvious partisanship during several infamous trials under the Sedition Act. And after Jefferson's victory of 1800, Chase abandoned even the pretense of impartiality, using the federal bench to harangue jurors on the evils of Jeffersonianism. Chase's conduct represented bad political judgment; it probably violated legal ethics; but did it satisfy the Constitution's requirement for impeachment? According to the Constitution, justices could be removed only for "high crimes and misdemeanors," transgressions which did not seem to include being an outspoken Federalist. After a spectacular impeachment trial in which attorneys for Justice Chase completely outmaneuvered the Jeffersonian prosecutors, the Senate voted to acquit the justice. This decision, at a time of intensely partisan passions, created a powerful precedent against using the impeachment power as just another weapon of political warfare. And perhaps Justice Chase's close call led other judges to temper (or at least to conceal more carefully) their political preferences while on the bench.

The Senate vote saved Chase and provided a bulwark for judicial independence, but politics still enveloped the Supreme Court. In several other important cases, Chief Justice Marshall and President Jefferson cautiously sparred over the limits of their respective offices. The two men were distant cousins, and both employed their casual manners as political assets. But their points of similarity only intensified their dislike for one another.

Marbury v. Madison

In the case of *Marbury v. Madison* (1803), their most dramatic clash, Marshall scored an impressive political-judicial triumph. Beginning as a minor dispute over Jefferson's failure to honor one of Adams's (and Marshall's) "midnight appointments," the case became a test of will between the two astute politicians. Employing sometimes questionable logic, Marshall wrote a masterful opinion. He first ruled that Marbury, an obscure Federalist office seeker, had a right to his position as a justice of

Life mask of Thomas Jefferson

the peace and that Jefferson's refusal to confer it represented an unlawful presidential action. Had Marshall stopped here, he would have been on record as asking the Democratic-Republicans to produce Marbury's commission, which Jefferson would have naturally refused to do. Such a move would have been a sharp rebuff to a Federalist-dominated Supreme Court, an institution still struggling for recognition as a coequal branch of the government. But Marshall proved too good a politician to put himself, and the Supreme Court, in such a vulnerable position. After lecturing his cousin on the president's responsibilities, Marshall then ruled that the Supreme Court had no power to require Jefferson to confer Marbury's appointment. Why? Because the portion of the Judiciary Act of 1789 under which Marbury had brought his case to the Supreme Court was unconstitutional. Therefore, after considering the merits of the case, Marshall concluded that the Court had no authority to hear the dispute in the first place. And the Chief Justice's last point—the assertion that the Supreme Court was the final arbiter of the meaning of the Constitution—provided an important precedent for judicial review of the acts of Congress and the president.

The battle over the Court ended in victory for advocates of an independent judiciary. Marshall's carefully structured opinion in the *Marbury* case avoided a showdown with President Jefferson, and the acquital of Chase prevented a possible campaign against other Federalist justices. Although the Court did not declare another act of Congress unconstitutional until 1857 (the ill-fated *Dred Scott* decision), the Supreme Court slowly emerged as a major part of the national governmental structure. Under the leadership of Chief Justice Marshall, the justices increased their role in shaping national priorities, particularly in the area of economic policy. And in their own appointments to the Supreme Court, Jefferson and his Democratic-Republican successors—James Madison and James Monroe—generally selected moderate lawyers who favored an effective national court system. In almost every state a similar pattern developed: supporters of strong judiciaries, both Federalists and Jeffersonians, blunted the attacks of radicals who wished to reduce the power of the judicial branch within the American political structure. During this formative era, both federal and state judges began to develop an impressive body of American legal precedents.

Revival of the Federalist party

At first glance, the Jeffersonian party dominates political events between 1800 and 1815. Only Jefferson and his close friend James Madison occupied the new, still-ramshackle White House during these years. Democratic-Republicans entered Congress in steadily increasing numbers, and the Jeffersonian tide even swept over the political shores of Federalist New England. The Jeffersonian party became so successful, in fact, that it could survive some bitter internal squabbling in New York and Pennsylvania without surrendering political initiative to the Federalists.

But all Federalists did not suddenly give up and slip away after the defeat of 1800. The soothing words of Jefferson's inaugural address—"We are all Republicans, we are all Federalists"—failed to lull many Federalists into submission. Only eight electoral votes had separated John Adams from a second term, and they took this as a hopeful sign. Jeffersonian lies and slanders, they believed, had temporarily fooled voters, but such political delusions would, hopefully, prove only temporary. Although the election of 1800 provided a political catharsis after the frenzy of the 1790s, partisan passions quickly reheated, and the two parties clashed with renewed fervor.

Federalism—the once-proud banner identified with Washington, Adams, and Hamilton—was in trouble but not dead. Stung by charges of aristocratical ideas and spurred on by younger members of the party, Federalists gradually adopted much of the organization, style, and even the rhetoric of their Jeffersonian rivals. Although they never created a viable national structure, Federalists did establish state and local organizations, controlled from above but with all the fanfare of popular participation. Local meetings and conventions brought together Federalist supporters, framed resolutions, and nominated candidates. In 1812, sixty leading Federalists from eleven states held a closed-door meeting in New York to discuss their presidential candidate. Delegates made no formal nomination, but this gathering constituted a primitive version of our present national nominating conventions. Federalists also formed over two hundred local "Washington Benevolent Societies." Ostensibly charitable groups named after the revolutionary hero and first president, these groups, again dominated by a few leading party men, served as valuable adjuncts to the Federalist electoral organization.

Federalists accompanied their new organizational structure with a more popular style of campaigning. Abandoning their elitist stance of the 1790s, they held mass meetings, parades, barbecues, and election rallies. Convinced that Jeffersonians had lied and slandered Federalists out of national office, party leaders established a small network of partisan newspapers. Along with Jeffersonian papers, these four-page sheets helped make citizens more aware of partisan issues, even if the vituperation and distortions did little to clarify alternative positions. Some Federalists even engaged in stump speaking, direct political appeals which older Federalists had long equated with cynical demagoguery. And on election days, party workers provided information, ballots, and transportation to the polls.

Federalists adopted some of the vocabulary of popular politics, claiming that they represented the true will of the people. Some charged that Jeffersonians were nothing but a group of aristocratic Virginia planters who masqueraded as friends of the people and would sell out American republicanism to help Napoleonic France. A few Federalists even made appeals to various minority groups, particularly Irish and

Unique three-story chapel
at Hamilton College in
Clinton, New York

Jewish voters who had occasionally been targets of Federalist hostility during the 1790s. Federalists also became fervent supporters of personal liberties, especially freedom of the press, and pictured the Jeffersonians as opponents of individual freedom. Propagandists howled in unison when New York Republicans prosecuted a Federalist editor for libeling President Jefferson and then refused to allow him to offer any evidence of the truth of his charges, which the Federalists' Sedition Act allowed as a defense.

All these electoral techniques revived the Federalist party and ushered in a brief period of vigorous political competition. With both parties actively seeking greater popular support, more voters went to the polls. Electoral politics became an important part of men's lives (this was still long before the day of women's suffrage). Even tipplers distinguished taverns according to whether they were Jeffersonian or Federalist pubs. The rebirth of the Federalist party gave American voters new experience with the formality, if not the reality, of popular government. Most Federalists did not abandon deeply held convictions that only the "best men" should hold political office, but they decided that it was better to camouflage elitist pretensions and compete directly for votes.

Despite their refurbished image, Federalists never discovered the magical issue that would return them to national power. The Jeffersonian ideal of a limited national government satisfied many Americans—small farmers who disliked expensive governmental "frills," striving businessmen who distrusted governmental favors to established interests, and all those who never forgot the Federalists' "reign of terror" during the 1790s. The Jeffersonians cut taxes and kept the national government small; the Federalists seemed able to offer no attractive alternative. The party lost ground in the congressional elections of 1802, and Democratic-Republicans also made solid gains in important state elections, moving out from their southern strongholds into the Middle Atlantic states and even into some New England states. The 1804 presidential election proved a rout. President Jefferson received one hundred sixty-two electoral votes while his Federalist opponent C. C. Pinckney garnered only fourteen (nine from Connecticut, three from little Delaware, and two of Maryland's votes). The year 1804 proved unfavorable for Federalists in another way. Aaron Burr, disinherited and distrusted by the Jeffersonians, killed Alexander Hamilton in a fateful duel at Weekhawken, New Jersey. Hamilton's death removed one of the Federalist's key inspirations, a man who provoked strong hatreds but who possessed great political and legal talents.

THE LURE OF THE WEST

Jefferson and the West   A British diplomat described Jefferson as "a tall man, with a very red freckled face, and gray neglected hair, ... his appearance being very much like that of a tall, large-boned farmer." The well-traveled, highly educated Virginia aristocrat would have liked the description. One of the most cosmopolitan men of his time, Jefferson nonetheless reserved his greatest admiration for the farmers who comprised the bulk of America's population. "Those who labor in the earth are the chosen people of God," Jefferson wrote, "in whose breast He has made his peculiar deposit for substantial wisdom and genuine virtue." In envisioning the great future of America, Jefferson faced westward rather than to the east; he looked to the richness of the soil rather than to the burgeoning cities. In fact, like the many agrarian spokesmen who have followed in his tradition, he distrusted urban areas, believing that concentrations of population spawned corruption and disorder, conditions which were inimical to the growth of republican government.

Jefferson looked to the West to provide room for a growing agrarian population and foresaw the day when Americans would expand to the Pacific coast. But unlike later exponents of "manifest destiny," Jefferson did not view expansionism as annexation or as the accumulation of far-flung territory. America's mission was not an imperial one. He hoped that the West coast would one day contain "free and independent Americans, unconnected with us but by the ties of blood and interest, and employing like us the rights of self-government." America was to be a fount of population, and its government would provide "a standing

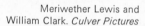

Meriwether Lewis and William Clark. *Culver Pictures*

monument and example." Jefferson believed that only small republics were viable and that great distances might destroy representative government. His concern for the West came not from expectations of territorial aggrandizement but from his desire to assure security for America's western borders and to develop trade routes for a westwardly expanding population.

Jefferson's interest in the West predated his presidency. While in Paris during the 1780s, Jefferson dreamed of sending explorers to the Pacific coast and developing a northwest passage to the Orient. By the middle of his first term, rumors of extensive British and Spanish operations in the West and his own scientific curiosity produced a plan to reconnoiter the unknown country. In 1803 he asked Congress to appropriate funds for an expedition to the Northwest, and he instructed its leaders, Meriwether Lewis and William Clark, to explore the Missouri River and its tributaries to the Pacific Ocean, seeking "the most direct & practicable communication across this continent, for the purposes of commerce." Although the Lewis and Clark expedition, after proceeding across the Rocky Mountains and down the Columbia River valley to the sea, reported no easy water route to the Pacific, their journey did stimulate interest in interior fur trade. It also whetted the appetites of a future generation of expansionists who became determined to wrest the Northwest from Britain.

The Louisiana purchase The Louis and Clark expedition reflected Jefferson's interest in a remote continental commerce and a distant destiny, but his most immediate problem involved a nearer and more essential waterway, the Mississippi. In an age without trucking, railroads, or canals, natural river systems provided the highways of contact between interior areas and the rest of the world. Commercial agriculture, which had long hugged the accessible coastal plain, could not move westward into less crowded territory unless the Mississippi water system was open to American use. An outlet to the sea at New Orleans was essential to Jefferson's dream of an agrarian nation with a dispersed population.

In the Pinckney Treaty of 1795, Spain had granted Americans access to the Mississippi and to the port at New Orleans. And, although some Americans were uneasy about Spanish presence to the south and west, Spain's power was declining and it posed little aggressive threat. In 1802, however, Americans learned that Spain had ceded the large territory of Louisiana to France; Napoleon Bonaparte envisioned a sprawling New World empire centering around the rich island of Santo Domingo and extending onto the North American continent. The strategic threat of such a powerful neighbor controlling the vital Mississippi chilled even the pro-French Jeffersonians, who began to develop a rationale for America's own possession of the former Spanish territory. "God and

Albert Bierstadt, *Valley of the Yosemite. Courtesy Museum of Fine Arts, Boston*

nature have destined New Orleans and the Floridas to belong to this great and rising empire," exclaimed one American who expressed the growing belief that Americans possessed a natural title to these lands. Initially bolstered by a defensive rationale, the desire to achieve security by controlling contiguous territories would gradually develop into a vigorous doctrine of aggressive expansionism.

Early in 1803 Jefferson sent James Monroe to Paris to assist the American minister to France, Robert Livingston, in negotiating the purchase of New Orleans and Florida. But unknown to the Americans, Bonaparte's plans had recently changed. America was to become the beneficiary of one of the greatest real estate bargains in history. The black slave population of Santo Domingo, under the leadership of Toussaint L'Ouverture, turned the slogans of revolutionary France against their masters and declared the island independent of white colonial rule. After unsuccessful attempts to quell the rebellion, Bonaparte decided to scrap his New World empire and concentrate on European conquests. Anticipating early hostilities with England, Napoleon needed cash. He also wanted to avoid fighting. Confiding to advisors his fear that England

173

would quickly seize French Louisiana when war broke out, he concluded that the Americans "ask of me only one town in Louisiana, but I already consider the colony as entirely lost; and it appears to me that in the hands of this growing Power it will be more useful to policy, and even to the commerce of France than if I should attempt to keep it." On April 11 French Minister Talleyrand surprised Livingston by offering to sell the whole of Louisiana, and the American diplomats shortly agreed, without authorization, to pay $15 million for the huge area between the Mississippi and the Rocky Mountains. From a simple attempt to preserve western commercial outlets, the Jefferson administration, almost by chance, launched the nation on a course of continental expansion.

The Louisiana Purchase encountered loud protests in America, particularly among Federalists. The Constitution contained no provision for acquisition of new territory, and Federalists, reversing the broad constitutional position they had argued for economic issues, now embraced "strict constructionism." Behind the Federalists' new constitutional position lay partisan concerns about the national power balance. Representing the mercantile-manufacturing interests located primarily in the more settled Northeast, Federalists feared a new expanse of land. One anti-expansionist representative argued that "the vast and unmanageable extent which the accession of Lousiana will give to the United States, the consequent dispersion of our population; and the destruction of that balance which it is so important to maintain between the Eastern and Western States, threatens, at no very distant day, the subversion of our Union." But Jeffersonians, not wanting to waste time with a constitutional amendment, now argued for a broad constitutional interpretation and for ratification of the treaty with France. Over Federalists' objections, the Senate did approve the treaty, and in 1804 Jefferson won reelection by an overwhelming electoral majority.

The sale of Lousiana served both America and France well, but the native Indian nations of the West proved the losers. In 1786 Jefferson had written that "not a foot of land will ever be taken from the Indians without their own consent," and the Louisiana Treaty guaranteed existing Indian rights. But by his second inaugural address, Jefferson was speaking about America's mission to "civilize" Lousiana's native inhabitants and to settle them as farmers onto smaller tracts of land. Jefferson never directly confronted the problem of Indian rights and Indian-white relations in the new lands, for during his presidency the expansion of whites into the Louisiana Territory had not really begun. But his successors would find the clash of cultures one of the most troublesome legacies of the purchase and would discover that Jefferson had already sketched a justification for Indian removal.

Thomas Jefferson was not a jingoistic expansionist. Nonetheless, his beliefs and the actions of his administration contributed to the developing spirit later termed "manifest destiny." In response to the French threat, Americans began to develop justifications for expansionism based upon natural rights and national security. Likewise, the Jeffersonian emphasis on farmers as divinely ordained carriers of the nation's destiny contributed to the later argument that Americans had more right to own western lands than did hunting-based Indian societies. In addition, acquisition of Louisiana began a pattern in which sectional and political rivals viewed territorial expansion as a method of enlarging their power within the Union. The issue of domestic political balance helped propel a course of empire which eventually led to the disruption of the Union.

FOREIGN PROBLEMS UNDER THE REPUBLICANS

The Barbary wars

When the Adams administration boosted military expenditures in the wake of the XYZ affair, Jeffersonians cried out that militarism would subvert republican government. Accordingly, Jefferson reversed the Federalist policy when he became president. Relying upon America's physical isolation to provide security from foreign threats, the third president drastically cut military appropriations.

But chieftains of the Barbary Coast of North Africa soon taught Jefferson that a nation depending upon transoceanic commerce needed a navy. For years Barbary Coast states had demanded tribute from commercial vessels in the Mediterranean, and in the 1790s the American government had signed treaties buying protection for its trade in the area. But in 1801, with American tribute payments in arrears, the leader of Algeria seized a ship and the pasha of Tripoli raised his demands. Jefferson quickly dispatched a naval force to the Mediterranean. The consequent "war" against the Barbary corsairs saved the navy from reduction; naval expenditures nearly doubled between 1802 and 1806. After four years of fighting, frequent changes of command and tactics, and an increase in tariff duties to finance the costly venture, the United States finally signed a peace treaty with Tripoli. The terms were better than the pasha had granted to any other power, but the Americans, still agreeing to pay a sizeable bribe, had not really won their point. The Mediterranean campaigns hardly enhanced the navy's glory, but the war did stimulate creation of a military academy at West Point and provided experience for America's naval officer corps.

Anglo-American commercial conflict

Concern for American commerce on the high seas continued to dominate Jefferson's second term. Although renewal of war between Britain and France in 1803 initially allowed Americans to make huge profits as neutral traders, the economic measures adopted by the warring nations increasingly impinged upon American commerce. French decrees enforcing Napoleon's "Continental system" of economic blockade against England were matched by British orders in council sharply restricting trade with France. American captains found it impossible to trade with either side without violating the laws of the other.

Britain, the greater naval power, enforced its decrees more effectively than France, and grievances against British seizures of American ships mounted. Britain forbade trade in a wide list of contraband items, declared that ports not open in peace could not be opened in war (a measure directed against the newly opened trade with the French West Indies), and declared illegal the "broken voyage" (a subterfuge by which goods originating in French colonies would be shipped to France through neutral American ports). Upholding a definition of neutral rights which Americans had developed during the Revolution, Jefferson insisted that "free ships make free goods," that Britain's definition of contraband was too broad, and that trade with French colonies and the "broken voyage" were legal.

Added to the technical disputes over neutral rights was the more emotional issue of impressment. The Royal Navy, enforcing a broad definition of British citizenship, seized sailors from American vessels, claimed they were British citizens, and impressed them into naval service. Certainly many Englishmen did try to escape the notorious hardships of their navy by taking well-paying employment on American vessels, but the high-handed manner with which British officials dragooned men off United States ships angered Americans. In 1807, when the British *Leopard,* searching for deserters, attacked the American warship *Chesapeake,* killing and wounding many men, tempers in the United States rose. Impressment increasingly became a symbol of disrespect for America's national honor and hard-won independence.

Although Jefferson felt a duty to uphold American rights, he hesitated to embark upon an expensive military buildup. Instead, he decided to employ economic coercion. Both Britain and France, Jefferson reasoned, depended upon America's carrying trade and would be substantially hurt without it. In 1807 Congress enacted Jefferson's Embargo Act which prohibited American ships from leaving for any foreign port. Although designed to protect commercial rights, the measure rebounded against American export trade. The wharves of the northeastern ports lay empty, and producers of agricultural exports suffered as well. Nationalistic outcries against Great Britain changed to loud laments over disappearing prosperity and to vociferous attacks against the Republican administration.

James Madison's measures

Federalists felt an upsurge in political support, especially in the Northeast, and charged Jefferson with ruining the country. Poet William Cullen Bryant, in an anti-Jeffersonian satire, demanded "Go, wretch! Resign the Presidential chair." All Federalists hoped to turn the country's economic

John Quidor, *Rip Van Winkle at Nicholas Vedder's Tavern.*
Museum of Fine Arts, Boston. M. & M. Karolik Collection

Pie Plate. *Philadelphia Museum of Art: Given by John T. Morris*

Thomas Rossiter and Louis Mignot, *Washington and Lafayette at Mt. Vernon.*
The Metropolitan Museum of Art, Bequest of William Nelson, 1905

William Sidney Mount, *The Power of Music*. The Century Association

woes into electoral gains in the election of 1808. But the Federalist presidential nominee, Charles Cotesworth Pinckney, could not compete against Jefferson's handpicked successor and scion of the Revolutionary generation, James Madison. Federalists gained strength in the Northeast and in Congress, but Republican policies prevailed in the White House.

James Madison continued his predecessor's policy of economic coercion, with some changes designed to limit the impact upon America's economy. Just before leaving office Jefferson had terminated the unpopular embargo and substituted a "Non-Intercourse Act" which reopened American trade with all nations except England and France. Virtually impossible to enforce due to the difficulty of ascertaining a ship's real destination, Congress replaced the Non-Intercourse Act with Macon's Bill No. 2 in 1810. The new bill, another variation of the Jeffersonian tactic of economic pressure, authorized commerce with both belligerents but cleverly stipulated that, if either country repealed its objectionable measures, the United States would close its ports to the other. Seizing his chance, Napoleon promptly issued a vague promise to make amends, and Madison invoked nonimportation against Britain. By the time Britain agreed to withdraw its regulations, Congress had already declared war.

Western antagonism toward Britain

More than a desire to defend neutral rights propelled America's headlong rush into war against the world's greatest power. For a variety of reasons, westerners lent active support to the prowar movement. For one, they frequently blamed their own economic distress, resulting from the commercial depression, upon British assaults against American shipping. In addition, western spokesmen looked longingly at Canada, viewing it as a vulnerable target which could be retained or bargained back to England in return for concessions on neutral rights and Indian relations. Most important, many believed that Britain was helping native tribes resist the western movement of white settlers. In 1794 General Anthony Wayne defeated Indians in the Ohio territory at Fallen Timbers, but frontier problems did not end. About 1806 a Shawnee leader, Tecumseh, and his half-brother, the Prophet, began to confederate tribes in the Old Northwest to fight white expansion and to prevent other chiefs from signing over any more land. Whites near the frontier feared Tecumseh's militant rhetoric and growing strength. Ignoring their own provocative behavior toward the tribes, they charged Britain with inciting the Indians, even though British officers probably did little more than donate occasional food supplies. In 1811, Governor William Henry Harrison, charged with dispersing the Indian confederation, defeated Tecumseh's forces at Prophet's Town near the Tippecanoe River in Indiana. The Battle of Tippecanoe, celebrated as a triumph over an Anglo-Indian conspiracy, encouraged war fever and land hunger throughout the West.

Garneray's *Battle of Lake Erie.*
Courtesy Chicago Historical
Society

THE WAR OF 1812

Articulating all of the various grievances against Britain, a group of young nationalists coalesced in the Twelfth Congress elected in 1810. These "war hawks," men such as Henry Clay and John C. Calhoun, provided the leadership for a prowar movement aimed at gaining recognition for maritime rights, restoring the country's prosperity, vindicating national honor, preserving worldwide respect for republican government, eradicating the Anglo-Indian problem, and creating expansionist possibilities in Canada or in Florida.

America goes to war

Expecting almost everything from the war, Americans were ready to sacrifice almost nothing. At heart, Americans feared a large military more than they cheered a war, and as the struggle grew difficult it became increasingly unpopular. The entire spectacle of America self-righteously challenging the world's greatest power became semifarcical. Commercial depression strained the national treasury, based upon tariff revenues, and Congress's refusal to recharter the national bank made financing of the war even more difficult. One congressman bemoaned that the "honor of the Country is gone, & the Government is paralized." The Congress which declared war on England adjourned without appropriating funds to increase the size of the navy; America launched a war with a naval force totalling sixteen vessels. But after a few false starts, the small navy at least performed credibly. Less could be said for the army. Only one of the seven major-generals had battlefield experience, and there was no system for supplying troops. Major-General William Hull softened up Canadians for an invasion by proclaiming that he was offering them "the invaluable blessings of civil, political, and religious liberty." He promised emancipation "from tyranny and oppression," but what Hull termed emancipation, Canadians called invasion. The General's forces proved as ineffective as his words. If Tecumseh had not been allied with Britain before the war, he worked with them now, and at Detroit Hull was forced to surrender. The Canadian campaign ended almost as soon as it had begun; the American war effort stalled.

Americans not only failed to execute a successful offensive but even seemed unable to organize a defense. The commander in charge of protecting the nation's capital was so sure that British troops would not attack Washington that he failed to undertake even the simple precautions of roadblocks or trenches. And in 1814 when the British did begin an advance toward the newly built city, they marched for five days and twenty-one miles into Maryland through thickly wooded forest without encountering so much as a rifle shot or a felled tree. Finally, outside of Washington an American army made a brief stand, but the best opportunities for slowing the British columns had passed. Redcoated troops marched into the city as night fell, and the American president and cabinet, fleeing westward into the hills, saw the sky above Washington lighten and flicker. British commanders had set the Capitol, the White House, and the other governmental buildings ablaze.

Federalist opposition and the Hartford convention Federalist candidates reaped the benefits of popular bitterness against "Mr. Madison's War." The Embargo and Non-Intercourse Acts, which required embarrassing extensions of national power by the party of limited government, had allowed Federalists to embrace the cause of minimal government and turn it against the Jeffersonians. And when hostilities finally broke out in 1812, Federalism gained still more, especially in New England. In the congressional elections of 1814 the Jeffersonians were routed.

New England Federalists took their most fateful step when they began to play upon sectional emotions. Capitalizing on the War of 1812's unpopularity in the region, especially among economically distressed farmers in the Connecticut River valley, some Federalists moved toward a strong states' rights stand. They adopted statements similar to the ones used by the Jeffersonians in 1798, and a few extremists ultimately flirted with talk of disunion and secession. In late 1814 Federalist leaders met at Hartford, Connecticut, to consider ways to "reform" the national union. Rejecting any idea of secession, delegates framed a series of constitutional amendments: limiting federal officeholders to native-born citizens; requiring a two-thirds vote of Congress for a declaration of war, for the admission of new states, or for the enactment of commercial regulations; and restricting the president to a single term. The Hartford Convention also proposed elimination of the three-fifths clause, the constitutional provision which allowed southern states to count three-fifths of their black population in determining representation in the House of Representatives.

The Hartford Convention represented a familiar political tactic—an effort by a dissatisfied and outvoted minority to protect its interests through constitutional change—but the movement ended in complete disaster. Those connected with the Hartford Convention were denounced as traitors, and the Federalist party itself bore the same stigma. Anti-British feeling still ran strong in the young nation, and the Federalists had always suffered from identification with English influences. Federalists, Jeffersonians charged, had always been monarchists and Tories. The Hartford Convention, which met between December 15, 1814, and January 15, 1815, coincided with two overshadowing events: the Peace of Ghent, which ended the War of 1812, and the Battle of New Orleans, which produced an outpouring of patriotic breast beating and made the convention seem the work of foolish or traitorous malcontents. New England Federalists quickly dropped their crusade for constitutional change, but the taint of disloyalty proved too strong. The Federalists continued as a force in local and state politics after 1815, but the party was dead as a national institution. The Federalists' antiwar stance had proved popular in the short run but politically fatal in the end.

Americans won few victories in the War of 1812, but the British government had learned in the revolutionary struggle that Americans needed only to protract the conflict, not to win it. The burning of Washington, D.C. was Britain's last spectacular success. The subsequent British siege of Fort McHenry failed, the bombardment producing only Francis Scott Key's lyrics to "The Star Spangled Banner," the song adopted much later as America's national anthem. The war effort was unpopular in the former colonies, especially in New England where some Federalists considered secession, but it was doubly disliked in Britain. Although some English conservatives applauded the opportunity to rid the world of the Jeffersonians and their supposedly dangerous doctrines, most Englishmen doubted if such gains were worth the costs of continued commercial disruption and increased taxation. As in 1783, British officials finally decided American friendship was more valuable than holding out for harsh peace terms. On Christmas eve of 1814, after a few months of negotiations at Ghent in Belgium, American and British representatives agreed to cease hostilities on the basis of *status quo ante bellum.* The treaty left unsettled the issues over which the nations had fought—British spoliations of American commerce, fishing rights, impressment, definitions of neutral rights and duties, uncertain boundaries, and Indian relations. These disputes would occupy diplomats in the future.

RELATIONS WITH THE INDIAN NATIONS

United States relations with the Indian nations have received far less attention than diplomacy with Europe, a bias which reflects white Americans' belief that continental expansion was a "manifest destiny." Yet conquest and empire building, often based upon deception, broken promises, and blood, were the products of conscious policy and planning, not the random results of a blameless inevitability. White Americans did not spread across an empty continent, nor did they tame savages who happened to occupy territory belonging to the United States; rather, by treaty or war, they took land which belonged to other nations and killed or removed the previous occupants.

The problem of land rights Land ownership was the central dilemma of Indian-white relations. Colonial precedent and the subsequent policies of the American government recognized Indian land rights and treated tribes as independent nations. The national government interpreted territorial gains from foreign powers, such as the Lousiana Purchase, as acquisition of a paramount right to purchase Indian lands in the area if the natives were willing to sell, not as automatic possession. Under the law, only the national government could make a treaty with an Indian nation for the purchase of territory. Washington's secretary of war enunciated federal policy: "The Indians being the prior occupants, possess the right of the soil. It cannot be taken from them unless by their free consent, or by the right of conquest in case of a just war." Such a policy, deriving from Anglo-American concepts regarding private property, ignored the realities of Indian communal ownership and unbounded hunting grounds. It opened the way for federal commissioners, conspiring with white settlers and land speculators, to convince chiefs to relinquish titles to tribal land over which they had no valid personal jurisdiction. But, although abuse was widespread, at least the government ostensibly insisted upon a legal transfer of title.

Most frontiersmen, on the other hand, felt little guilt over taking Indian land illegally. "By the law of nations," one western governor wrote, "it is agreed that no people shall be entitled to more land than they can cultivate." The words stemmed directly from the natural-law, agrarian philosophies of Benjamin Franklin and Thomas Jefferson. Treaties with the Indians did not have to be respected, wrote another western governor, because such agreements "were expedients by which ignorant, intractable, and savage people were induced without bloodshed to yield up what civilized peoples had a right to possess by...command of the Creator."

Throughout the early national period, two conflicting views of Indian rights uneasily coexisted in the United States: the courts and the national government recognized Indian titles and frequently tried to keep peace on the frontier by preventing squatting, illegal seizure, or fraudulent alienation of Indian lands; settlers ignored the courts, evaded attempts at law enforcement, pressed their local governments to carry out an anti-Indian policy, and convinced themselves that they had a superior right to the land. The white nation's conduct was based upon these contradictions between law and practice, between theory and prejudice.

The War of 1812 on the frontier

Obtaining Indian titles through a "just war" satisfied both the national courts and the settlers. The War of 1812 was waged as much against Indian nations along the frontier as against Great Britain. In fact, to many westerners, the proud Shawnee Tecumseh, with his plan for a strong Indian confederation, seemed a more immediate threat than the king of England. And in battle, Tecumseh's warriors proved themselves more skilled than their red-coated allies; they fought to save their native lands, not to subdue a distant country. Tecumseh explained that his goal was "for all the red men to unite in claiming a common and equal right in the land.... No groups among us have a right to sell, even to one another, much less to strangers who want all and will not do with less." Recovering from his defeat at Tippecanoe (1811), Tecumseh joined British troops in halting the American army at Detroit in 1812. And the Creek nation to the south, influenced by Tecumseh's powerful oratory and spectacular successes, also took up the battle. More ruthless than the Shawnee chief, the Creeks terrorized whites on the Spanish-American frontier. But United States troops finally defeated the Indian nations, killing Tecumseh at the Thames and crushing the Creeks at Horseshoe Bend. If the settlement with England in the Treaty of Ghent was indecisive, the results on the frontier were not. The Indian nations were shattered. And although Indians had participated in much of the fighting, their British allies abandoned them and they were not parties to the Treaty of Ghent. After 1815 the United States government signed separate peace agreements with individual tribes. The defeat of the Shawnee and Creek in the War of 1812 began the federal government's policy of clearing new western lands for white settlement.

RESURGENT NATIONALISM

The War of 1812 and the inconclusive Peace of Ghent are minor footnotes to European histories of the Napoleonic struggles. But they helped provide symbols of national identity which still loom large in Americans' nationalistic heritage. The young nation fought both Indians and Europeans, and these two enemies helped to define white Americans' image of themselves. On the western frontier, Americans saw themselves as heralds of progress and carriers of civilization. They drove back the "savages" and introduced agriculture, common law, and Anglo-Saxon institutions. But when compared to Englishmen, Americans viewed themselves as robust children of the wilderness, unspoiled by the over-sophisticated refinements of the Old World. Victory over the Indians and Andrew Jackson's spectacular triumph over the superior British force in the battle of New Orleans—which ironically occurred after American delegates had signed the peace treaty—turned an unpopular conflict into a cherished symbol of national honor. Rugged frontiersmen with long rifles, it seemed, could vanquish all comers; America stood at an optimum peak somewhere between the valleys of barbarism and over-civilization.

American nationalists puffed a potentially disastrous war into a struggle of epic proportions. "The Hunters of Kentucky," a song embellishing the battle of New Orleans and glorifying the victorious general— Andrew Jackson—became popular throughout the country.

> We are a hardy, freeborn race, each man to fear a stranger,
> Whate'er the game, we join in chase, despising toil and danger
> And if a daring foe annoys, whate'er his strength and forces,
> We'll show him that Kentucky boys are "alligator horses."

MONTICELLO

Thomas Jefferson's country estate, Monticello, illustrates its master's inventiveness as well as America's response to a new environment. Jefferson began building his "little mountain" home near Charlottesville

Jefferson's Monticello

in 1768 on land which his father had owned. The site overlooks the Blue Ridge Mountains in the west and the Virginia plains to the east, vistas which had intrigued Jefferson since childhood. Unable to find a competent architect in the colonies, the resourceful Virginian studied a few books, drew his own plans, and supervised most of its forty-one years of construction. Although he combined currently popular styles—laid out as an Italian villa, Monticello also has a Greek portico, a Roman dome, and colonial detail—Jefferson relied principally upon Andrea Palladio, the architect who had created the "Georgian" style in England. Taken together, Monticello's diverse design did much to launch the "classical revival" which swept the United States during the early nineteenth century.

If stylish, the thirty-five-room manor did not lack substance. Jefferson's originality focused upon graceful use, not just symmetrical display. Most colonial estates grouped carriage house, kitchen, stable, laundry, and smokehouse in separate buildings removed from the main house. For convenience and efficiency, Jefferson moved these functional areas indoors, connected to the living quarters. He built them under terraces which flank Monticello on either side and open away from the inside. This innovation was soon copied throughout the South. Between the two basements, this Enlightenment figure constructed separate storage rooms for wine, beer, hard cider, and rum.

Even more than its architecture, Monticello is noted for its gadgetry. A pair of glass doors between the main hall and a drawing room open simultaneously when only one is pushed—Jefferson had installed a series of gears under the floor, much like a modern bicycle-pedal system. The planter-architect set European "alcove beds" into the walls throughout the house, but added an ingenious variation in his own suite: one side of the bed opens onto his study, the other side onto his bedroom. Apparently frustrated by its perverse obscurity, Jefferson connected the weathervane on the roof of Monticello to a dial on the ceiling of the portico so he could read the wind without going outside.

Style, contraptions, and even its history mark Monticello as uniquely American. In 1781 a platoon of British soldiers led by Captain McLeod raided the house in hopes of capturing its owner, then governor of Virginia; Jefferson narrowly escaped down the mountainside. After a life of political and diplomatic service to the nation, he retired from the presidency in 1809 and returned to the just-completed house. Despite spiraling financial debts, aggravated by the costs of Monticello's upkeep, Jefferson was able to live in the house until his death on July 4, 1826, thanks to loans from friends. The plantation itself never profited its owner, partly because the man who believed that "all men are created equal" could never come to terms with, or even exploit, the slavery that supported his intellectual life amid the quiet splendors of the mansion. On the centenary of Jefferson's burial at Monticello, the house became a national shrine and has since been completely restored and furnished with original pieces.

THINGS TO THINK ABOUT:
1789–1816

How do you explain the troubled political atmosphere of the 1790s? What domestic problems faced the new nation? What foreign dangers did it confront? John C. Miller, *The Federalist Era 1789–1801* (1960) is a general survey. Richard Buel, Jr., *Securing the Revolution: Ideology in American Politics, 1789–1815* (1972) is more interpretive. Marcus Cunliffe's *George Washington: Man and Monument* (1958) is an interesting book. Politics are discussed in Joseph Charles, *The Origins of the American Party System* (1956); William Nisbet Chambers, *Political Parties in a New Nation: The American Experience 1776–1809* (1963); and Richard Hofstadter, *The Idea of a Party System: The Rise of Legitimate Opposition in the United States, 1780–1840* (1969). Foreign affairs are treated in Alexander De Conde, *The Quasi-War: The Politics & Diplomacy of the Undeclared War with France, 1797–1801* (1966); and Felix Gilbert, *To the Farewell Address: Ideas of Early American Foreign Policy* (1961).

Why did the Federalist party fail? What trends contributed to the Jeffersonian successes? Stephen G. Kurtz, *The Presidency of John Adams* (1957) and Manning J. Dauer, *The Adams Federalists* (1953) are standard accounts. James Morton Smith, *Freedom's Fetters: The Alien & Sedition Laws & American Civil Liberties* (1956) and Leonard W. Levy, *Legacy of Suppression* (1960) present conflicting interpretations of the Sedition Law. David H. Fischer, *The Revolution of American Conservatism: The Federalist Party in the Era of Jeffersonian Democracy* (1965) is an important study. Marshall Smelser, *The Democratic Republic 1801–1815* is a general interpretation of the Jeffersonian Era. Patrick C. T. White, *A Nation on Trial: America and the War of 1812* (1965) and Harry Coles, *The War of 1812* (1965) are short summaries.

What problems did the new nation face in 1815? What gains had been achieved since independence? James Sterling Young, *The Washington Community, 1800–1828* (1966) and Richard E. Ellis, *The Jeffersonian Crisis: Courts and Politics in the Young Republic* (1971) are important monographs which also provide broad interpretations of this period. Seymour M. Lipset, *The First New Nation* (1963) is an attempt at comparative history. Curtis P. Nettels, *The Emergence of a National Economy, 1775–1815* (1962) and Russel B. Nye, *The Cultural Life of the New Nation* (1960) are standard accounts. Reginald Horsman, *Expansion and American Indian Policy, 1783–1812* (1967) and Francis Paul Prucha, *American Indian Policy in the Formative Years* (1962) are helpful.

1816-1840

FIVE | AMERICA IN MOTION

ANDREW JACKSON

Andrew Jackson evoked both fierce loyalties and strong hatreds; to some he was "Old Hickory," to others "King Andrew." A poor boy made good, a South Carolina frontiersman turned Tennessee aristocrat, at the time of his election the sixty-one-year-old Jackson had been a lawyer and a judge, a highly successful land speculator, an army general, and a fabled Indian fighter. He adorned his plantation-mansion, the Hermitage, with hand-paintad wallpaper, filled it with fine art works, and operated it with the labor of over a hundred black slaves. Behind him lay a number of successful duels—from one he carried a piece of lead near his heart—and a reputation as a gambling man who liked fast horses and expensive wines. Jackson's political opponents tried to play up his deficiencies, but a number of more popular, widely accepted images surrounded Jackson.

The literature, slogans, and campaign songs of Jackson's supporters evoked powerful symbols, images which seemed to satisfy many Americans' search for a stable national identity. Jackson often appeared as the sturdy yeoman farmer, breaking the ground with his sacred plow and filling out America's God-ordained agrarian paradise. Unburdened by too much "book learnin' " or overly sophisticated notions,

Jackson relied upon common sense and good old American practicality. Jackson also appeared to represent the perfect compromise between the wild savagery of the American wilderness and the decadent culture of Europe. Had he not shown his superiority over both the uncivilized Indians and the overcivilized Englishmen? Through his "superior" virtue and intelligence, Jackson the Indian fighter had vanquished the Creeks and Seminoles, and he had supposedly employed his frontier spirit and fighting techniques to outwit the British General Packenham at the Battle of New Orleans. Neither the Old nor the New World could defeat the conquering hero, nature's nobleman. In an age of romanticism, at a time of disturbing commercial and industrial changes, and in an era of great internal mobility, the nostalgic symbols surrounding Jackson appealed to many Americans, reassuring them of the validity of old ways.

In his struggle against the second Bank of the United States, Jackson invoked all these images. Jackson long opposed the national bank as a dangerous, antirepublican institution, and when Congress granted it a second twenty-year charter in 1832, Old Hickory vetoed the bill. Jackson's message, carefully calculated for its political appeal, read like the scenario for a morality play. The bank—an evil, corrupt, and artifically created "monster"—threatened to destroy opportunity for the "real people"—the thrifty, hard-working, and God-fearing people whose "success depends upon their own industry and economy" rather than upon special governmental privileges. By killing the bank, with its complicated financial dealings and fluctuating paper credits, Jackson could return the nation to the simple and stable ways of the early republic.

But if Jackson's veto message suggested the Jeffersonian past, his vigorous use of presidential authority presaged the more active chief executives of the future. The old soldier argued that only the president, not the Congress and certainly not the Supreme Court, owed his office to the votes of the entire nation. The president stood as the chief representative of the sovereign people, a position which made him the repository of the popular will and the best interpreter of the Constitution. And throughout the war over the national bank, Jackson demonstrated political skills appropriate to his exalted vision of the presidency. Using his prestige, wielding his patronage, and sometimes feigning his celebrated rages, he completely outflanked the pro–national bank forces. Congress failed to override the veto, and Jackson won a second term in the elections of 1832. Throughout his years as president, but particularly during the "Bank War," Jackson transferred his own man-of-the-people image to the office itself. The president became the symbol of "everyman," and the contest for the White House became the key to American politics.

1816-1840

1816	James Monroe (Democratic-Republican) defeats Rufus King (Federalist) Charter of national bank Tariff of 1816
1817	Rush-Bagot agreement limits naval armaments on Great Lakes Government orders Ohio Indians to sell lands and move west
1818	Andrew Jackson seizes Pensacola Convention with Great Britain
1819	Adams-Onís treaty with Spain *McCulloch* v. *Maryland* Economic panic
1820	James Monroe (Democratic-Republican) defeats John Quincy Adams
1820–21	Missouri Compromise
1823	Monroe Doctrine
1824	John Quincy Adams defeats Andrew Jackson, William H. Crawford, and Henry Clay. No candidate receives a majority and House of Representatives decides the contest
1825	Opening of Erie Canal "New Harmony" started
1826	Panama Conference
1828	Tariff of 1828 Andrew Jackson (Democrat) defeats John Quincy Adams (National Republican)
1829	John C. Calhoun's *South Carolina Exposition and Protest*
1830	Indian removal act
1831	Garrison's *The Liberator* begun Nat Turner leads slave rebellion
1832	Jackson vetoes recharter of national bank Andrew Jackson (Democrat) defeats Henry Clay (National Republican) and William Wirt (Free-Mason) Black Hawk War Tariff of 1832 ; South Carolina nullifies tariffs of 1828 and 1832 John C. Calhoun resigns as Vice-President
1833	Force Act Compromise tariff of 1833
1835–38	Seminole War
1836	Martin Van Buren (Democrat) defeats William Henry Harrison, Hugh L. White, Daniel Webster, and W. P. Magnum (Whigs) Specie circular Texan independence movement: battles of the Alamo and San Jacinto
1837	"Gag rule" on antislavery petitions
1837–39	Economic panic
1840	William Henry Harrison (Whig) defeats Martin Van Buren (Democrat) Brook Farm established

ONE PARTY POLITICS, 1816–1824

National politics during the "Era of Good Feelings"

Disintegration of the Federalist party removed much of the drama and excitement from national politics. James Monroe, the nation's fifth president (1817–25), was the last and least distinguished member of the "Virginia dynasty" of Jefferson, Madison, and Monroe. Lacking the heroic stature of Washington, the charm of Jefferson, and the intellectual sophistication of Madison, Monroe brought few striking qualities to the chief executive's office. Perhaps most important, he failed to project any dynamic sense of purpose or national identity. The revolutionary era had passed, and new concerns associated with a faster-moving commercial society faced the country. Stodgy old James Monroe seemed an anachronism; even his style of dress suggested an earlier, more placid age. On formal occasions the president often appeared in a well-faded uniform from the Revolutionary War, and he regularly wore the silk stockings, knee-length pantaloons, and white-topped boots of an age already passed. But at a time when national party competition had disappeared and the presidency itself had lost some of its earlier glamour, Monroe seemed an adequate president. He won an easy victory over several rivals in 1816, and he captured a second term in 1820, winning all but one of the votes in the electoral college.

In the absence of competing national parties, politics centered on personalities. John Quincy Adams from Massachusetts, son of the nation's second president, projected great intellectual depth and moral commitment. He performed capably as Monroe's secretary of state, inspiring the famous doctrine which bore the president's name. John C. Calhoun, the brilliant constitutional theoretician from South Carolina, served as secretary of war. Monroe had initially offered Calhoun's post to Kentucky's Henry Clay, but Clay considered only the State Department, the traditional stepping-stone to the White House, worthy of his considerable talents. He stayed in the House of Representatives, hoping to use the speakership as an alternative route to the presidency. And perhaps the most charismatic of all these politicians, William Crawford of Georgia, remained as secretary of treasury. A man with an impressive physical appearance and a winning personality, Crawford also proved a cagy political operator. A favorite of southerners, Crawford cast himself as the true disciple of Thomas Jefferson, a crusader for frugal and limited government.

With three of these leading personalities in Monroe's own cabinet and the fourth looking on from Capitol Hill, Washington became the scene of extremely bitter factional in-fighting. Cabinet officers avoided speaking to one another and sometimes deliberately tried to undermine each other's power and prestige. Rivalry carried over into Washington's social life, then as now one of the primary means of cultivating political favor. Only "Calhoun men" would be welcome at Calhoun's fashionable parties, and only "Crawford men" attended functions at the Georgian's house.

For the most part, however, these power struggles remained confined to Washington itself. The national government exerted only a limited impact upon most people's lives, and many citizens displayed little interest in national politics. The Jeffersonian ideal of limited government predominated, both in the minds of most citizens and in the actions of their representatives in Washington. The brief surge of nationalistic legislation after the War of 1812——the rechartering of the national bank, the passage of a mildly protective tariff, and a movement for federally financed internal improvements—quickly faded. Several days before he left office in March of 1817, President Madison vetoed a bill providing federal funds for a variety of transportation projects. Monroe pursued a

Charles Bird King, *John Calhoun.*
Courtesy of National Portrait
Gallery, Smithsonian Institution

cautious policy on federal aid, suggesting a constitutional amendment to overcome legal pitfalls and vetoing a congressional measure providing money for the Cumberland Road, a national turnpike.

The Missouri question

During the "Era of Good Feelings" the problem of slavery continued to confront America, but even the complicated debates over slavery in Missouri failed to excite the nation or to inflame popular passions. Had the issue led to war, one historian has suggested, the battle would have been fought on the floor of Congress with a puzzled nation looking on.

Particularly in Virginia, the cradle of enlightened Jeffersonian republicanism, gentleman planters had long debated the moral, political, and financial dimensions of slavery. But these discussions remained in the comfortable world of theory and speculation; serious thought of general emancipation stopped at the seemingly insoluble questions of economics and "race mixing." Not until 1819 did the slavery issue first disrupt national politics.

In 1819 statehood for Missouri threatened to disrupt the equal balance between free and slave states, and some northerners opposed Missouri's application. A representative from New York, James Tallmadge, Jr., proposed that Congress prohibit further introduction of slaves into Missouri and insist on gradual emancipation. This move took politicians by surprise and set off vigorous debate in Congress. Speakers ranged over a variety of moral, political, and constitutional arguments. Some even charged that the whole furor looked like a political conspiracy to divide northern and southern Jeffersonians and to revive the Federalist party. Finally, compromisers led by Henry Clay of Kentucky adjusted the difficulties. The famous Missouri Compromise of 1820 included acceptance of Missouri as a slave state, admission of Maine as a free state, and establishment of a "free soil" line for the lands of the Louisiana Purchase. Barring slavery from all areas north of the line 36°30′, except Missouri, Congress carried out the tacit principle of sectional equality.

Some people, reflecting upon the Missouri question, saw it as an ominous sign, a harbinger of more serious problems to come. Southern advocates of limited government, the "Old Republican" faction, considered the episode even more frightening. Allowing Congress to prohibit slavery in even a portion of the Louisiana Purchase, they argued, represented a dangerous concession of power. And since the Missouri struggle seemed to indicate that southerners might not always dominate the government in Washington, they should work to keep slavery and race, the South's own concerns, out of national politics. The Missouri question revealed the tensions hidden just beneath the surface of national life.

State and local politics

The most significant political developments during the "Era of Good Feelings" occurred at the state and local levels. Here, government played a more important role in people's lives; both issues and personalities seemed more immediate than in national affairs. Out of the struggles for office within the various states came a broadening of the suffrage and new ideas about the nature and organization of politics.

American lawmakers gradually liberalized laws restricting the right to vote. The widespread distribution of property in America and the practice of ignoring the letter of the law had always helped to soften landholding requirements, but the mere existence of suffrage restrictions created a political issue. In addition, the commercial revolution and consequent growth of cities meant that an ever-increasing number of men would never own enough land to meet traditional suffrage requirements. In order to appeal to this group, ambitious politicians, supported by wealthy urban interests, championed the cause of suffrage extension. The traditional Whig argument that only property owners possessed the "virtue" and the necessary "stake in society" required of intelligent electors fell before the combined logic of demographic changes, economic self-interest, and political advantage. Most states abandoned property-holding restrictions in favor of small taxpaying requirements or unrestricted suffrage for white, adult males.

The state political conflicts, which played an important role in the movement for suffrage extension, brought other changes. Politicians continued to experiment with the campaign techniques and the forms of organization begun during the era of the first national party system. Although the Federalist party lingered as an influence in New England and in Maryland, politics in most states revolved around factions rather than coherent parties. In New York, however, opponents of the powerful Clinton faction began to champion the necessity of organized parties. Martin Van Buren and other members of the so-called "Albany Regency" claimed that their organization differed radically from the personal clique headed by the Clinton family. Rather than something to be feared and, if possible, suppressed, a political party—popularly organized, responsive to the desires of its loyal members, and devoted to principles rather than personalities—provided the key to democratic government. Only through parties (and especially their own), argued members of the "Regency," could Americans achieve effective representative government.

The election of 1824   Expansion of the *potential* electorate, wider use of popular campaign techniques, and new ideas of the legitimacy of parties produced no immediate upsurge of interest in national politics. Voter turnout remained low, less than the number of voters who came out in earlier national and state contests. The presidential election of 1824 reflected the lack of interest and the confusion in national politics.

The 1824 presidential election produced no winner. Despite a choice of four factional candidates, few voters seemed to care; only about one-quarter of the potential electorate bothered to vote. Henry Clay, Speaker of the House and proponent of the "American system," favoring

John Singleton Copley,
John Quincy Adams. Courtesy,
Museum of Fine Arts, Boston

a national bank, a protective tariff, and internal improvements at federal expense, ran fourth. William H. Crawford, Monroe's choice, who had recently suffered a serious illness, received only a few more electoral votes than Clay. The top two runners were Andrew Jackson with ninety-nine electoral votes and John Quincy Adams with eighty-four. Jackson won a plurality, but since no candidate obtained a majority of the electoral votes, the House of Representatives had to make the final decision. After some complicated maneuvering—historians may never unravel all the details— representatives bypassed Jackson and selected Adams. One of Adams's first acts as president was to name as secretary of state, Henry Clay, the fourth-place finisher who had swung his votes to Adams. The Secretary of State had traditionally been heir-apparent to the president, and many people suspected some kind of backroom deal between Adams and Clay.

The charge of a "corrupt bargain" gave Adams's presidency

(1825–29) an inauspicious start, and Adams proved to be one of America's least successful presidents. He proposed federal support for all types of internal improvements, a national university, and assistance to the sciences. But congressmen ignored his program and rejected such a vigorous assertion of federal power. Only two years after taking office the president admitted, "with uncontrollable dejection of spirits," that "my career is closed."

Perhaps cautious congressmen had good reason for forgetting Adams's suggestions. When members of the Fourteenth Congress raised their salaries from six dollars per day to fifteen hundred dollars per year, voters reacted with anger. Almost two-thirds of the members of this "extravagant" Congress did not return to Washington for the next session. To most Americans, the national government remained a distant abstraction, something to be forgotten unless its officials raised taxes or tried to interfere in local concerns.

Throughout Adams's term, opposition groups, particularly in the South and East, began to rally around Andrew Jackson. Once a factional leader within the party of Jefferson, Madison, and Monroe, Jackson now became the nucleus for a new party—the Democrats. The Adams presidency closed the era of one-party politics.

RELATIONS WITH SPANISH AMERICA, 1816–1824

Acquisition of Florida

"Nature has decreed the union of Florida with the United States," declared a governor of Lousiana. This theme of geographical predestination sounded familiar to Americans. It had resounded in debates over the Louisiana Purchase, and acquisition of that vast territory made possession of Florida seem even more inevitable. In 1810 the Madison administration encouraged West Florida to revolt against Spain and join the United States. Then, during the War of 1812, American forces seized the Spanish garrison at Mobile. By 1815 Spain retained only East Florida, a large finger of territory which attracted American adventurers and expansionists. In 1818 General Andrew Jackson crossed into Spanish territory to attack the Seminole tribe and remnants of the defeated Creek nation. But Jackson did not stop with the Indians; he also seized the Spanish settlement of Pensacola. President Monroe subsequently repudiated Jackson's territorial grab, but Secretary of State John Quincy Adams supported the general's brazen action and issued a virtual ultimatum to the Spanish minister, Luis de Onís: Spain must either control the Indian menace "at once" or cede East Florida to the United States. The Spanish government realized that Americans' growing power and land hunger made possession of Florida difficult, and it conceded Adams's terms. In the Adams-Onís Treaty (1819) Spain transferred East Florida to the United States and yielded its claim upon Oregon. In return, the United

The Monroe Doctrine

States assumed $5 million in private claims against Spain and accepted a boundary (the 42nd parallel) which left Spain in uncontested possession of Texas.

Spain's problems in its other New World colonies influenced the decision to cede Florida to the United States. After Napoleon had placed his brother Joseph on the Spanish throne, many Spanish colonies pledged their loyalty to the deposed king, Ferdinand VII, and declared independence from the French-controlled regime. In 1814 Ferdinand returned to Madrid, but colonial ties had disintegrated beyond repair. Throughout Latin America the initially loyalist movements became full-fledged struggles for independence.

The United States was ambivalent in its response to the Spanish-American revolts. Secretary of State Adams doubted the capacity of the former Spanish colonies to govern themselves and did not want the issue of United States recognition to interfere with a favorable settlement of the Florida question. Others, especially Henry Clay, believed that Spanish Americans were striving to form republics on the North American model and that the United States had a duty to provide at least moral support. Clay was flattered that, according to him, "they adopt our principles, copy our institutions, and, in many instances, employ the very language of our revolutionary papers." Following ratification of the Adams-Onís Treaty, the United States finally did become the first country to recognize, in 1822, the Provinces of the Rio de la Plata (Argentina), Colombia, Chile, Peru, and Mexico. But Secretary of State Adams did not consider recognition an expression of faith in Latin America; it was a warning that Americans opposed further European colonization in the New World. In the next year, President Monroe issued a manifesto elaborating upon the principles of noncolonization and noninterference.

The background to the Monroe Doctrine lay in the complexities of European diplomacy. The conservative reaction that descended upon Europe after Napoleon's defeat raised the possibility of renewed colonization in the New World. Great Britain and the United States both feared that France and Spain might make a joint effort to collect or regather New World possessions or that Spain might transfer its remaining territories to the more powerful France. For Englishmen, the continued independence of Latin America and a "no-transfer" principle involved both power balances and economic expediency. British manufacturers and exporters did not want Latin American markets again to disappear behind the walls of Spanish mercantilism. Accordingly, British Foreign Minister George Canning invited the United States to issue a joint statement with his government supporting the independence of Spain's former colonies, enunciating the principle of "no-transfer," and renouncing any territorial ambitions (a promise that would preclude any further expansion by the United States).

Canning's proposal sparked little interest in Washington. Monroe and Adams did not want to tie United States diplomacy so closely to Britain. But Canning's suggestion, in addition to Russia's claim to much of Oregon, did prompt Monroe to announce his own policy concerning the Western Hemisphere. The president's message, inspired by John Quincy Adams's continentalism and distrust of Europe, was directed at the status of Latin America and at Russian and British claims in the Pacific Northwest. It set forth the principles of no-transfer, freezing the existent colonies (such as Cuba) in the hands of their present owners, and of noncolonization and nonintervention, closing the hemisphere to any further European imperial designs. Monroe drew a clear distinction between the Old World and the New World. Picturing the Western

Joel T. Hart, *Henry Clay.*
Corcoran Gallery of Art

Hemisphere as republican and pure and Europe as reactionary and corrupt, he concluded that neither should interfere in the affairs of the other. After Monroe's pronouncement, the United States learned that Britain had obtained France's promise not to assist Spain in recovering its colonies. It was this Polignac Memorandum and the power of the British navy, rather than the Monroe Doctrine, which guaranteed the security of the Latin American independence movements.

The Monroe Doctrine was a pretentious document which the United States had no power to enforce. It was met with contempt and ridicule in Europe, and the numerous interventions in Latin America after 1823 revealed that it provided little protection against European incursions. In terms of immediate impact, Monroe's statement meant little. Reflecting aspiration more than reality, it sprang from a sense of mission rather than a knowledge of power. It weighed heavier in the national ego than in the international balance. In a few years Americans largely forgot Monroe's Doctrine as they forgot Monroe himself.

Relatively unimportant in 1823, the Monroe Doctrine eventually dominated United States–Latin American relations. As American power grew, the doctrine's principles hardened into dogma. In the United States it gradually became less of a defensive warning against European encroachment and more an offensive justification for creation of a United States sphere of influence. In Latin America, where the doctrine had received some initial praise, its aggressive implications soon made it an ominous warning. The United States expanded across North America, taking Texas, parts of Mexico, and threatening Cuba and the Caribbean; the southern republics began to suspect that the United States opposed European meddling only to advance its own hegemony in the hemisphere. Latin Americans uneasily pointed out that the doctrine did not foreclose United States imperialism and was issued without the consultation or consent of the very territories it purported to protect. Throughout the nineteenth century, the embrace which promised security grew suspiciously tight.

The Panama conference Although the heart of the Monroe Doctrine was nationalism, not Pan-Americanism, it did contribute to the idea of creating a protective league of New World republics. Simón Bolívar, the great liberator of much of Spanish America, had proposed an inter-American congress excluding the United States, but after Monroe's speech Bolívar's advisers convinced him to invite the North American republic. The conference was to be held in Panama in 1826. John Quincy Adams, now president, and his secretary of state Henry Clay agreed that the congress could be useful: it might increase commerce, endorse the United States' definition of neutral rights, and establish the United States as an example to the younger nations.

Adams nominated several envoys and sent their names to Congress for confirmation.

In Congress unexpected opposition arose. The stormy debates over participation in the Panama Conference reflected the beginnings of a new opposition party and suggested how seriously Americans had taken President Washington's warning against foreign entanglement. Sectional divisions, already revealed in the conflict over statehood for Missouri, also added to the controversy; many southerners feared that the conference would discuss touchy issues such as slave trade and recognition of the black, ex-slave republic of Haiti. The dissension over the Panama Conference culminated in a nonfatal duel between Secretary of State Clay and Senator John Randolph of Virginia, but the Senate, not the field of honor, held the fate of this diplomatic question. The debate lasted so long that, although the Senate did finally confirm Adams's envoys, the delegates arrived too late to participate in the conference. The United States treasured nonentanglement more than Pan-Americanism, and interest in inter-American conferences languished for half a century.

THE ECONOMY, 1816–1824

The Anglo-American connection

After 1815 restoration of good relations between the United States and Great Britain opened the way for increased British investment and a strengthening of trade ties. During the early nineteenth century, the Anglo–American connection became so strong that the American war for independence, if placed purely in an economic context, paled in significance. The way in which the American and British economies came to complement each other indicated the good judgment of the British statesmen who had advocated conciliation at Paris and at Ghent to preserve America in an informal economic empire.

After 1815 British financiers and businessmen participated in every dynamic sector of the United States economy; the pattern of English involvement paralleled the role British capital played in its own colonies and in Latin America. Too small to produce sufficient raw materials, Britain sought to develop foreign sources of prime commodities and to create markets for its exports. In particular, Great Britain wanted cotton for its expanding textile industry, and British capital helped finance the westward expansion of the Old South's cotton culture. Trade between the two countries boomed, doubling between 1830 and 1836. After 1830 the United States also became the prime recipient of British foreign investment. Railroad, canal, and bank bonds found ready purchasers in London, and the credit of the national bank of the United States was closely tied to the worldwide financial operations of British banking houses such as Baring Brothers. As America's balance of trade became ever more reliant upon cotton exports and upon continued

British credit, its dependence upon the health of Britain's economy, especially its textile industry, proportionately increased.

This link between America's growth and British capital had some beneficial consequences. Partly because influential interest groups on both sides of the Atlantic had a stake in cooperation, numerous diplomatic questions were settled peacefully. In 1815 America and Great Britain signed a trade convention; the Rush–Bagot agreement of 1817 limited naval armaments on the Great Lakes; and a convention in 1818 dealt with disputes over fisheries, extended the previous trade agreement, fixed the United States northern boundary at the 49th parallel, and established joint occupation of the Oregon Territory. Mercantile restrictions on trade with the British West Indies continued to rankle Americans, and United States tariffs provoked grumbles among British merchants, but these were only minor irritants. In addition, the Anglo–American economic tie contributed to United States development. Britain's cotton purchases generated prosperity throughout the entire American economy, eventually even reinvigorating the manufacturing sector, which had been hurt by British competition after the War of 1812. British capital helped finance many of the high-risk projects which American capitalists were too poor or too cautious to back. America's inland transit system, particularly railroads, benefited from British plungers, who sometimes suffered great financial loss on American bonds.

But the British connection also had drawbacks. Britain's economic trouble quickly spread to the United States whenever Britishers called in their loans. National or state economic planners were ill equipped to cope with depressions arising out of international economic problems. And America's growing reliance upon one major export commodity, cotton, increasingly tied its prosperity to prices set in foreign markets. The economic specialization and interdependence of Britain and America may have been efficient in international terms, but the recurring economic "panics" of the pre–Civil War period revealed that America possessed only limited control over its own prosperity. If the strong British connection helped develop the American economy, it also helped make it vulnerable and unstable.

The panic of 1819   The end of the War of 1812 brought both depression and prosperity to the United States. At the end of the war, English manufacturers opened their warehouses, releasing surpluses accumulated during the years of suspended trade. Flooding the American market at low cost, British exporters proved too competitive for many of America's infant industries. Even the higher tariff of 1816, passed in the upsurge of nationalism which followed the war, failed to curb the inflow of British products. New England's commerce remained healthy, but the area's manufacturing was hit so hard that the whole region complained of depression and out-migration.

The much larger agricultural sector of the economy, however, benefited from the end of the war. Crop failures in Europe produced a high foreign demand for primary products, and cotton prices in particular shot up. The defeat of several Indian nations during the War of 1812 opened new western territories and encouraged land speculation. Land values soared; credit expanded unrealistically; farmers cultivated ever-larger amounts of acreage.

In 1816 Congress chartered a new national bank (the charter for Hamilton's first Bank of the United States had expired in 1811), and in the Supreme Court decision *McCulloch* v. *Maryland* (1819), Chief Justice Marshall upheld the bank's constitutionality. Handing down an opinion which had great consequences, Marshall wrote that the national government had broad authority to carry out legitimate constitutional ends—the doctrine of implied power—and that states could not hamstring federal programs such as the national bank. But the new national bank provided neither a sufficiently elastic national currency nor effective controls over state banks. The land boom, which rested partly upon circulation of unsound paper money continued unabated, as a variety of local bank notes became available throughout the backcountry. The free-wheeling, high-risk, and high-profit atmosphere fascinated speculators and adventurers just as it bewildered many ordinary farmers.

In 1819 the bubble of agricultural prosperity burst. The price of cotton on the world market dropped precipitously, and land values plummeted faster than they had climbed. The national bank, incompetently managed and with inadequate specie reserves, called in loans to meet its obligations. The bank's actions merely quickened the recessionary spiral. Local banks also struggled to reduce outstanding loans and to retire issues of paper money. Demanding payment from people who expected a renewal of credit, bankers found themselves owning mortgaged land, stores, and hotels. And to those who faced foreclosure or were the victims of unreliable paper money, the very weakness of the banking system made it seem excessively strong. Depression spread throughout the country, and unemployment rose.

Economic uncertainty bred discontent and frustration. To some, it held the gambler's possibility of windfall riches, narrowly missed; it spawned a group of ambitious "men-on-the make" who were jealous of those at the top and determined to join or replace them. To others, the economic cycle revealed not the opportunities but the hazards of banks, paper money, and speculation; it encouraged a longing for a mythical past in which economic and moral stability reigned over a garden of small farmers, bestowing rewards upon the thrifty and hardships upon the profligate. The panic of 1819 seemed to be a divine punishment upon a nation too caught up in material pursuits, but it hit unequally and without regard for individual morality. Jackson's Democratic party, coalescing throughout the 1820s, played upon memories of the panic of 1819, capitalizing on a "common man," underdog image which both appealed to the hopes and played on the fears of the disparate groups which felt that the economic system did not serve their interests.

DEVELOPMENT OF THE SECOND PARTY SYSTEM, 1824–1840

Between 1824 and 1840 politicians created a second national party system. This new two-party system rested, in large part, upon long-term developments: the removal of suffrage restrictions; the move in most states toward popular election of presidential electors (rather than election by state legislatures); and the growing acceptance of the legitimacy of party organizations. In addition to these legal and constitutional trends, the election of 1824 produced the type of charismatic figure who could capture the public's imagination and infuse new glamour into national politics. Andrew Jackson—general, Indian fighter, and master politician—dominated the political stage. In alliance with a highly skilled political manager, Martin Van Buren of New York, Jackson created a new political force, the Democratic party, and forced his opponents into establishing an anti-Jackson organization, the Whig party.

The election of 1828   Almost immediately after the House of Representatives selected John Quincy Adams over Jackson in 1824, the Tennessean began his second crusade for the presidency. Reacting to the defeat with characteristic outrage, Jackson charged that Adams and Henry Clay had stolen the election through a "corrupt bargain." Clay, "the Judas of the West," had received "his thirty pieces of silver" in the form of the secretary of state's job. Jackson proved a popular candidate, and Van Buren created the necessary organization to boost "Old Hickory" into the White House. Lining up influential state leaders, particularly in the South, Van Buren carefully pieced together a network of alliances and set up a string of pro-Jackson newspapers across the country. Jackson's congressional supporters faithfully opposed almost every one of President Adams's programs, and Van Buren helped push through the Tariff of 1828, a measure designed to appeal to protectionist interests in key northern states. Meanwhile, Jackson took only the vaguest public stands on issues, particularly the tariff, relying upon his personal appeal and Van Buren's politicking to carry the election.

After an unbelievably dirty campaign—in a nation with a tradition of nasty campaigns—Jackson won the election of 1828. No charge seemed too base. Digging up a long settled mix-up over Jackson's wife's divorce from her first husband, Adams's men charged Jackson with wife stealing and adultery. In other accounts, Jackson appeared as the murderer of twelve men, the son of a prostitute, an illiterate backwoodsman, and a rum-soaked gambler. Jacksonian papers replied in kind. Adams was a pompous aristocrat, a squanderer of public funds, and a corrupt ally of the even more corrupt "Harry" Clay. A Pennsylvania paper falsely charged that the president's wife was born out of wedlock. Small wonder that Adams, following the lead of his father but defying other outgoing presidential examples, refused to attend Jackson's inauguration.

More than twice as many voters cast ballots in 1828 as in 1824, but turnouts, with only a few exceptions, still failed to match the totals of earlier state and national elections. To a large degree, the new Jacksonian party rested upon a southern, proslavery base. Jackson rolled up huge popular and electoral majorities throughout the South, a reflection of his sectional appeal, his own status as a slaveholder, and his supposed affinity for the Jeffersonian doctrine of limited national authority. He carried enough crucial Middle Atlantic states and areas in the West to outweigh Adams's solid grip on New England's votes. For the next eight years (1829–1837) President Andrew Jackson dominated national political life.

Emergence of the Whigs   Jackson's political success produced growing opposition. Initially, "King Andrew's" opponents lacked cohesion, and political alliances were unsettled. The Anti-Masonic party, a group emphasizing enmity toward the order of Free Masons, gained strong support in New England, New York, and Pennsylvania. Offering a political vehicle for ambitious young politicians—William Seward, Horace Greeley, and Millard Fillmore began their careers in the party—the Anti-Masons strongly opposed Jackson. In 1831 the Anti-Masonic party held the first national nominating convention, a gathering similar to the religious revivals familiar to many party supporters. Nominating William Wirt, a former member of the Masons, the party gained only seven electoral votes in the 1832 presidential balloting and failed to establish firm national roots. The equally short-lived National Republican party also opposed the Jacksonian coalition, and ran Henry Clay for president in 1832. By 1834 the new Whig party fused the National Republican party, Anti-Masonic party, and other anti-Jackson groups into a second broad political coalition.

Creation of the Whig party and renewal of the contest for the presidency brought two-party competition to almost every state in the Union. Two-party systems first emerged in New England and in the Middle Atlantic states. The selection of Martin Van Buren as Jackson's successor on the 1836 Democratic ticket catalyzed anti-Jacksonian sentiment in the South and the West and encouraged formation of Whig organizations in those regions. Although Whigs embraced new electoral techniques more slowly than Jacksonians, the anti-Jacksonian forces finally adopted their opponents' tactics. Both parties relied upon conventions to provide a sense of popular participation, rallies and parades to entertain their supporters, and carefully managed newspapers to send out the party "line." In 1836 Van Buren defeated several Whig candidates, sectional favorites such as Daniel Webster of New England. Yet better Whig organization and popular identification of Van Buren with the panic of 1837 spelled the "Little Magician's" political doom in 1840. A Whig campaign ditty from the 1840 campaign expressed the sentiments of his enemies:

> *Who never did a noble deed?*
> *Who of the people took no heed?*
> *Who is the worst of tyrant's breed?*
> *Van Buren!*

The Whig's own "Log-Cabin and Hard Cider" campaign of 1840 demonstrated their mastery of Jacksonian techniques, and their own country boy–turned–soldier, General William Henry Harrison of Indiana, defeated Van Buren by a sizeable margin.

The election of 1840 clearly demonstrated that the second national party system had come of age. The "log-cabin and hard cider" campaign inaugurated a series of hard fought contests between Democrats and Whigs. The old fears associated with the first party system disappeared, and the vast majority of Americans now accepted the legitimacy of two-party competition as an article of democratic faith. In most national, state, and even local elections the two parties ran candidates and mounted free-swinging campaigns. Strategists organized their parties like political armies. Leading national politicians operated from Congress or the White House; state and local leaders provided the lesser "officers" throughout the nation; and the mass of white adult males constituted the loyal political "soldiers" in the field. On election days, the "generals" skillfully maneuvered their "troops" to the polling places and planned strategies for winning the political battle. Turnouts were uniformly high, and voters, Democrats more than Whigs, exhibited a great degree of party loyalty. Straight party voting generally characterized Jacksonian elections. The vigorous two-party competition, which developed in most areas of the nation, helped to bridge the gulf between the "common man" and the central government in Washington. After the development of the second party system, national affairs never seemed as distant as they had appeared to many people during the "Era of Good Feelings."

Whigs vs. Democrats:
sources of support

Andrew Jackson identified the Democratic party with the popular causes of hard money and antimonopoly. To many people, the national bank symbolized unstable paper currency and special governmental favors to a privileged few. By opposing recharter of the Bank and by adopting a

George Caleb Bingham, *The County Election. The St. Louis Art Museum*

hard money policy (pp. 221-222), the Democrats gained the support of farmers who feared paper money, urban workers who favored hard currency, and small businessmen who opposed monopolistic privileges to established business interests. The Democratic party's strong proslavery stand attracted voters in the slave states, and Jackson's appeal as the hero of the Battle of New Orleans proved a political asset in many areas of the South and West. Democrats also reached out to immigrants, especially to Irish and German Catholics, and brought them into the Democratic coalition.

Much of the Democratic program and rhetoric suggested a neo-Jeffersonian philosophy that government, especially at the national level, should limit the range of its activities; on the other hand, Whigs generally championed the cause of an active, expansive central government. Leading Whig politicians, men such as Henry Clay from Kentucky and Daniel Webster from Massachusetts, advocated an activist policy. Clay favored federal aid to canals, railroads, and turnpikes; he urged creation of a strong central bank which could help to stabilize currency and promote economic expansion; and he urged high protective tariffs which would safeguard infant American industries against foreign competition. Whigs also envisioned the active promotion of moral reforms. The crusades against evils such as alcohol and slavery held great appeal for many Whigs. And, of course, the party also gained support from people who disliked the Jacksonians' programs and the Democratic constituency. Whig voters, for example, tended to be hostile to Irish and German Catholics and to other immigrant groups that were coming into the United States.

WESTWARD MOVEMENT

Indian removal   During the War of 1812, Andrew Jackson had led a successful campaign against the Creek Indians in the Southeast. After the war, he continued his career as Indian fighter, pressing into the Spanish territory of East Florida to engage the Seminoles, who had been joined by remnants of the Creek nation. In 1819 when Spain ceded East Florida to the United States, the Seminoles were forced westward and their rich lands opened to whites.

On the northern frontier the government also took steps to expand the territory available for white settlement. In 1817 the federal government ordered tribes in Ohio to sell their lands and migrate farther west. In the following years many Indian nations, recognizing the futility of resistance, signed over their territories and left their homes. White settlers gradually spilled westward, and within five years after the War of 1812 five new western states joined the Union.

Although disunited and demoralized by defeat, not all Indians

American School, *The End of the Hunt. National Gallery of Art,
Gift of Edgar William and Bernice Chrysler Garbisch*

Thomas Eakins, *The Fairman Rogers Four-in-Hand.*
Philadelphia Museum of Art: Given by William Alexander Dick

Thomas Eakins, *Arcadia. The Metropolitan Museum of Art,*
Bequest of Miss Adelaide Milton de Groot (1876-1967), 1967

Winslow Homer, *Skating on Union Pond. The J. Clarence Davies Collection,
Museum of the City of New York*

peacefully acquiesced to the march westward after 1817. The Cherokee in Georgia claimed their legal rights as a sovereign nation and refused to sell their lands. In response the Georgia legislature ignored treaties which the Cherokee had concluded with the federal government and, arguing that the Indians were subject to state jurisdiction, required them to give up their territory. The issue went to the Supreme Court, where Chief Justice John Marshall ruled against Georgia and upheld the traditional position of the federal government—that state legislatures could not abolish land rights guaranteed by federal treaties. Marshall's decision caused a furor, and westerners appealed to President Jackson not to execute it. Ex–Indian fighter and shrewd western politician, Jackson complied. Flaunting the judicial process by supporting Georgia, he attacked Marshall's decision and asked Congress to set aside a western region into which the Indians could be moved. Congress acceded to Jackson's request.

Following Jackson's repudiation of legal precedent, the government began forceably removing Choctaw, Creek, and Cherokee from their homes in the Old Southwest. The Seminole nation, already driven from their lands in Florida, were also ordered to march westward once again. But many Seminoles refused, and a young chief, Osceola, resumed warfare with the white man. Osceola's band disrupted the frontier for three years, but this Seminole War (1835–38) also ended in failure for the Indian people.

Resistance to forced migration also developed in Illinois, where portions of the Sauk and Fox tribes, led by Black Hawk, refused to leave their rich ancestral lands. Black Hawk initially hoped that, if his people remained peaceful, they would be permitted to keep their farming communities and live alongside the incoming whites. But incessant military pressure from frontier garrisons forced Black Hawk into war. It was a one-sided fight. Twice the Indian leader attempted to surrender peacefully but met only intensified warfare from whites. In the final battle of the Black Hawk War, the Bad Axe Massacre, United States troops killed all but 150 of the original thousand Indian men, women, and children. To Indians, this incident, one of the bloodiest in Indian-white history, indicated that the alternative to removal was extermination, and further attempts at resistance faltered in face of this white ruthlessness.

Jackson's political opposition denounced the barbarities of removal and warned against the states' rights implications of the president's decision to support Georgia's defiance of the Supreme Court. But most of the nation approved Jackson's Indian policy. Forced migration, which continued throughout the 1830s, represented a victory for frontier land hunger over long-standing legal precedent. By the end of the decade, westerners were pouring into the tier of states extending from the Great Lakes to the Gulf of Mexico.

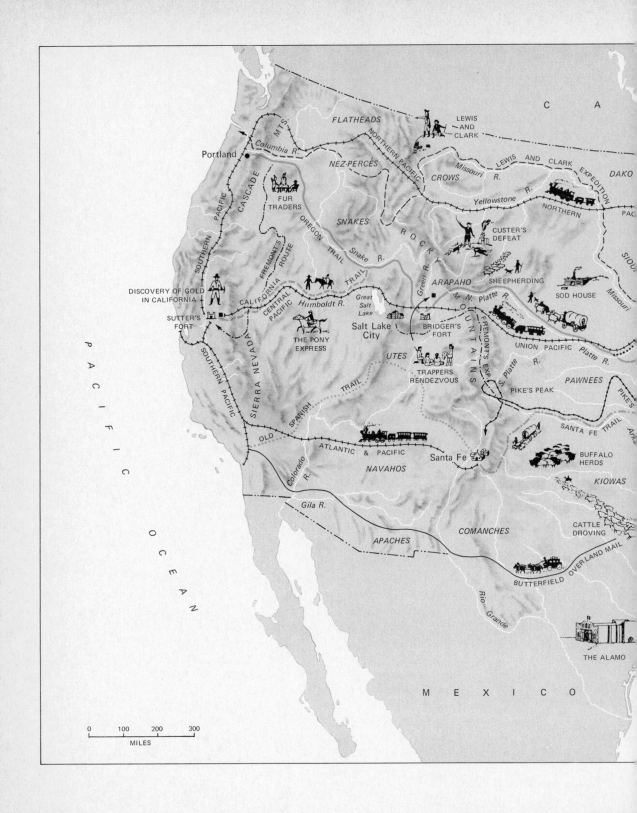

C A

Portland

Columbia R.

FLATHEADS

LEWIS
AND
CLARK

NORTHERN PACIFIC

NEZ-PERCES

CROWS

LEWIS AND CLARK EXPEDITION

DAKO

Missouri R.

Yellowstone R.

NORTHERN

PAC

SNAKES

Snake R.

CASCADE MTS.

OREGON TRAIL

FREMONT'S ROUTE

TRAIL

CUSTER'S
DEFEAT

ROCKY

SHEEPHERDING

SIOU

SOD HOUSE

Missouri

SOUTHERN PACIFIC

FUR
TRADERS

DISCOVERY OF GOLD
IN CALIFORNIA

SUTTER'S
FORT

CENTRAL
PACIFIC

CALIFORNIA

Humboldt R.

Green R.

ARAPAHO

Great
Salt
Lake

N. Platte R.

MOUNTAINS

UNION PACIFIC

Platte R.

THE PONY
EXPRESS

Salt Lake
City

BRIDGER'S
FORT

FREMONT'S EXP.

SIERRA NEVADA

UTES

TRAPPERS
RENDEZVOUS

S. Platte
R.

PAWNEES

PIKE'S

PIKE'S PEAK

SOUTHERN PACIFIC

SPANISH TRAIL

OLD

Colorado R.

ATLANTIC & PACIFIC

Santa Fe

SANTA FE TRAIL

Ark

BUFFALO
HERDS

Gila R.

NAVAHOS

KIOWAS

PACIFIC

COMANCHES

CATTLE
DROVING

APACHES

OVERLAND MAIL

BUTTERFIELD

Rio Grande

THE ALAMO

O C E A N

M E X I C O

0   100   200   300

MILES

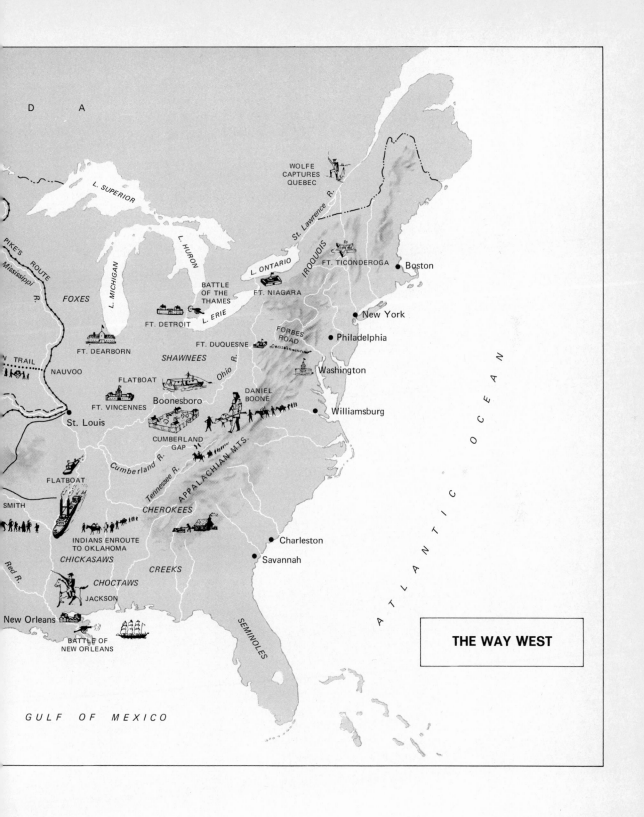

THE WAY WEST

Jackson's policy of Indian removal, a forerunner of the reservation concept, sprang from a variety of motives. Jackson had achieved national fame as an Indian fighter during the War of 1812, and his long campaigns on the southern frontier led him to think of Indians as a threat to national security. Although Indian hostility stemmed largely from grievances against encroaching whites, Americans found it easier to rationalize Indian attacks as products of foreign conspiracy. And Indian nations did frequently ally with America's foes—France in the colonial period, then England and Spain. To Jackson, Indians were "the enemy," and having encountered them primarily on the battlefield, he saw them as basically savage and brutal. They stood in the way of progress and civilization; they had to be removed. Opening Indian lands to white developers also squared with Jackson's political ambitions. His policy reflected the wishes of his western constituency, especially speculators and farmers; it made him a hero to the (white) common man who wanted cheap land. Yet, like most conquerers, Jackson believed that his actions were also in the best interests of his victims. He saw Indian removal as a humanitarian alternative to continued conflict with white frontiersmen—clashes which might eventually destroy the Indians entirely. Strategic security, advancement of "civilization," political expediency, and a paternalistic benevolence all came together in Jackson's policy.

By the mid-1840s, the Indian nations had been pushed beyond the bounds of white settlement, and the national government promised to protect their permanent rights in the new area. But such pledges had existed before and would echo in treaties afterwards. They meant little. The United States government was moved by the desires of its citizens, and its citizens were moving inexorably westward.

The secession of northern Mexico

In their search for new western lands, some Americans looked toward the huge expanse of northern Mexico—called Texas. Westerners had denounced the Adams-Onís Treaty that relinquished American claims to Texas (1819), and many, such as Thomas Hart Benton, helped form the new Democratic party. But renunciation of Texas seemed to trouble politicians more than pioneers, who began settling Texas under agreements with the Mexican government. During the first few years after independence from Spain, Mexico encouraged immigration in order to develop its sparse northern areas and, in accordance with contemporary racial theory, to balance the country's preponderant Indian population with whites. In 1821 Stephen Austin, assuming a patent granted to his father, began to invite Americans to settle along the Brazos River, and other American-owned land developments followed Austin's pattern. Thousands of pioneers, many of them slaveowners, became residents of Coahuila, the northeastern province of Mexico.

Gradually the Mexican government became uneasy. Mexico's original design of populating the North with many nationalities was unsuccessful, and the area quickly became a cultural extension of the United States. Mexican law forbade slavery and required the Roman Catholic faith; American immigrants openly flaunted both requirements. Many Americans boldly proclaimed their desire to annex Texas, and after Jackson's election in 1828 the Democratic party press began steadily drumming the expansionist theme. Jackson instructed his minister in Mexico to purchase land west of the Nueces River. When Mexico ignored his overtures, he launched various intrigues to dismember northern Mexico.

After 1830 the Mexico government attempted to bring Texas under tighter control. It prohibited further colonization from "adjacent" foreign countries, ordered military occupation, and attempted to strengthen economic ties between central and northern Mexico. Texans responded by petitioning the Mexican government for separation from Coahuila and reorganization as a new province with a constitution patterned after that of Massachusetts. But Mexican authorities feared that separation from Coahuila would only lead to secession from Mexico and refused the Texans' request. Texas was not the only unruly province in Mexico; throughout the country regional leaders vied for power with authorities in Mexico City. And when the strong military commander Santa Anna came to power, he decided to suppress all disruptive tendencies. He abolished the federalist Mexican Constitution of 1824, instituting a strong centralist government with no state legislatures. Santa Anna then suspended civilian government in potentially troublesome areas and reasserted control over provincial customs houses. Finally, in 1835 he ordered an army northward to enforce the new decrees and to assert the authority of the central government.

As the army approached, Texans began to organize a resistance. At first they claimed to be fighting only to restore the principles of Mexico's old 1824 Constitution. But when Mexican forces overwhelmed the Alamo mission in San Antonio, killing all 187 defenders, Texans rallied behind the cause of independence. In March 1836, Sam Houston was named commander in chief of their military force.

By most accounts, Houston was a physical "giant" (six feet, two inches), a flamboyant dresser, a pursuer of women, and a convincing speaker. He had served under Jackson in the Creek War of 1813, and Jackson subsequently used his influence to gain Houston an appointment as federal subagent for Cherokees in 1817. The following year Houston resigned his post in an effort to attend law school, but the experience led to politics rather than to the bench. In 1823 and again in 1825 he was elected to Congress, where he became an early supporter of Jackson's efforts to win the presidency. In 1827 he was elected governor of Ten-

RAFFLE

Mr. Joseph Jennings respectfully informs his friends and the public that, at the request of many acquaintances, he has been induced to purchase from Mr. Osborne, of Missouri, the celebrated

DARK BAY HORSE, "STAR,"

Aged five years, square trotter and warranted sound; with a new light Trotting Buggy and Harness; also, the dark, stout

MULATTO GIRL, "SARAH,"

Aged about twenty years, general house servant, valued at *nine hundred dollars*, and guaranteed, and

Will be Raffled for

At 4 o'clock P. M., February first, at the selection hotel of the subscribers. The above is as represented, and those persons who may wish to engage in the usual practice of raffling, will, I assure them, be perfectly satisfied with their destiny in this affair.

The whole is valued at its just worth, fifteen hundred dollars; fifteen hundred

CHANCES AT ONE DOLLAR EACH.

The Raffle will be conducted by gentlemen selected by the interested subscribers present. Five nights will be allowed to complete the Raffle. BOTH OF THE ABOVE DESCRIBED CAN BE SEEN AT MY STORE, No. 78 Common St., second door from Camp, at from 9 o'clock A. M. to 2 P. M.

Highest throw to take the first choice; the lowest throw the remaining prize, and the fortunate winners will pay twenty dollars each for the refreshments furnished on the occasion.

N. B. No chances recognized unless paid for previous to the commencement.

JOSEPH JENNINGS.

nessee. But after his brief marriage collapsed in 1829, Houston quit as governor and moved west to Texas. There he lived with an Indian woman and was formally adopted into the Cherokee tribe.

In Texas Houston soon became involved in anti-Mexican agitation. And less than two months after being appointed commander of the American "militia," Houston led his troops to a decisive victory against Santa Anna near the San Jacinto River.

Mexican armies were never able to regain control of Texas. Although the Mexican government did not recognize Texan independence, after April 1836 Texas was in fact self-governing. Sam Houston became the first president, and following a prudent delay of ten months, the Jackson administration extended recognition to the new Lone Star Republic.

Texas gained independence from Mexico, but many Americans and Texans favored its annexation to the United States. The new Texas Constitution permitted slavery, and southerners hoped to widen their political base by bringing in new slave areas. But the foreboding debates over Missouri had presaged trouble, and both Whigs and Democrats were reluctant to revive the slavery question, fearing it might splinter their parties along sectional lines. Texas, the product of excessive regionalism and Civil War in Mexico, would soon contribute to these same disruptive phenomena in the United States.

NATIONALISM VS. SECTIONALISM

The specter of racial conflict

Throughout the antebellum years, southerners increasingly feared racial upheaval. The ever-expanding volume of antislavery literature convinced some southerners that outside agitators were stirring up trouble within the South. David Walker, a free black man who had migrated from the South to Boston, called for militant resistance in a fiery *Appeal to the Colored Citizens of the World* (1830). And William Lloyd Garrison's much more restrained newspaper, *The Liberator* (begun in 1831), also alarmed fearful whites, stirring visions of massive slave revolts. In 1822 South Carolina officials uncovered an alleged plot for a slave uprising in Charleston led by a charismatic free black man, Denmark Vesey. Defectors within the movement revealed the plot, and Charleston officials aborted it. Other South Carolinians suggested, as have some historians, that overly fearful whites exaggerated the Vesey affair out of all proportion, but officials hanged thirty-five alleged plotters and sent many other blacks out of the state.

An even more disturbing incident occurred in Virginia in 1831, when Nat Turner led the bloodiest slave revolt in United States history. Nat Turner, like Denmark Vesey, possessed great personal magnetism and oratorical powers. A Baptist preacher, Turner believed that a divine wish guided his struggle to liberate fellow blacks. "I saw white spirits and black spirits engaged in battle, and the sun was darkened—and thunder rolled in the heavens, and blood flowed in streams." Turner's supporters murdered almost sixty whites before state and federal troops, with savage swiftness, crushed the two-day uprising. Militiamen and soldiers massacred more than a hundred slaves, some of them unconnected with the rebellion, and officials later hanged about twenty more slaves and free blacks, including Nat Turner himself.

*Shoring up
southern unity*

Alongside their fears, many white southerners carried a sense of guilt over this institution so obviously in conflict with the ideals of a progressive republican society. But after about 1830 southerners increasingly suppressed these doubts and began to develop a new proslavery argument. Previously, most supporters of slavery defended it as a "necessary evil," and Senator William Smith's often-quoted assertion that slavery was a "positive good" stood almost alone in southern rhetoric. Following Nat Turner's uprising and the emergence of a more militant abolitionist movement in the North—events which were linked together in the minds of many southerners—the "positive good" argument became more popular. Beverly Tucker, a member of an illustrious Virginia family which had

In Full Stride (artist unknown). *Philadelphia Museum of Art, photograph by A. J. Wyatt*

traditionally apologized for slavery, urged southern writers to defend the institution and "to convince our own people" of slavery's benefit to the South and to the entire nation. Sanctioned by the Bible and the laws of nature, slavery provided a harmonious solution to the South's racial dilemma and offered beneficent tutelage to the "happy" but "inferior" blacks. Thomas Dew, a professor at William and Mary College, even suggested that slavery upgraded the status of the black woman. "She ceases to be a mere 'beast of burden' [and becomes] the cheering and animating center of the family circle."

Southerners also took more concrete steps to shore up sectional unity. Legislatures enacted tougher slave codes and laws curtailing the liberties of free blacks. Stressing the fact that Denmark Vesey and Nat Turner were literate, restrictionists pushed through stricter prohibitions against teaching blacks to read. Although black people bore the brunt of the restrictions, the repression ultimately touched whites as well. Slave-state legislators forbade publication or distribution of antislavery materials, and public pressure silenced other critics of slavery. Several prominent university professors left the South, and others suppressed their doubts about the morality and legitimacy of the "peculiar institution." The entire southern population moved toward at least an outward consensus on the question of slavery. Dissent from proslavery orthodoxy became rare in the Old South after 1830.

Southerners also sought to stifle criticism from outside the region. In July 1835 a mob of South Carolina fire-eaters seized antislavery materials from the post office and burned them at a huge public bonfire in Charleston. After the Carolina book burning, proslavery officials within Andrew Jackson's administration allowed southerners to censor the mails and to stop the flow of antislavery materials into the South. In 1836 a group of southern politicians, some of whom sought to embarrass presidential candidate Martin Van Buren, urged the House of Representatives not to accept any petition advocating abolition of slavery in the District of Columbia. Traditionally, Congress had accepted such petitions and then immediately rejected the request, but antipetition forces feared that any admission of Congress's authority over slavery in the District would set a dangerous precedent. Following angry debates, the House accepted a modified "gag" rule: Congress would receive petitions but automatically table them without formal consideration.

Abolitionists never enjoyed much public support, even in the North, and during the 1830s antiabolitionist mobs harrassed writers and speakers. A Boston mob dragged William Lloyd Garrison through the streets with a rope around his neck; in 1838 a hostile crowd killed an Illinois abolitionist, Elijah Lovejoy. But such violence in the free states, coupled with suppression of criticism within the South, allowed the antislavery movement to broaden its appeal. Repressive tactics, though seemingly successful, eventually worked against slaveholding interests.

Branding proslavery interests as a threat to the freedoms of all Americans, white and black, antislavery publicists incorporated the civil liberties issue into their crusade. And the book burnings, censorship of mails, and moves to restrict the right of petition provided antisouthern writers with abundant copy. In seeking to safeguard their sectional interests, proslavery activists overreacted and only further isolated themselves.

Controversy over nullification of federal law

The most extreme overreaction was South Carolina's ill-fated attempt to nullify the tariffs of 1828 and 1832. South Carolina suffered all of the general southern problems, only more so. In addition to concern over antislavery literature and fears of slave uprisings, South Carolina's tidewater planters faced severe economic difficulties. The tariffs seemed to epitomize South Carolina's dilemma. The import duties raised the price of goods and reflected the state's subservient economic position; extension of national power in the form of a tariff created another precedent that antislavery leaders might one day apply to the "peculiar institution." After several years of agitation in South Carolina and in Washington, a group led by John C. Calhoun, who subsequently resigned the vice-presidency, succeeded in getting the state to declare the federal tariffs null and void in South Carolina (November 1832). In his *South Carolina Exposition and Protest,* Calhoun claimed that state nullification of unconstitutional federal laws provided the only means to protect the South's minority interest and the only way to preserve the Union itself. If the South lacked the power to strike down illegal legislation, secession would be the only recourse.

President Jackson quickly moved to nullify nullification. Although a proponent of limited government and a strong supporter of slavery, Jackson firmly believed in the supremacy of the national government. He denounced nullification as treasonous and reportedly threatened to have Calhoun hanged. Granting Jackson's request for power to meet the crisis with force, Congress gave the president authority to use the military to execute federal laws in South Carolina. At the same time, Congress passed a new tariff which established a timetable for lowering duties over the next ten years. Jackson's strong stand doomed nullification, and the compromise tariff allowed South Carolina radicals to retreat with some grace. A state convention repealed their nullification of the tariff, but perpetuated Calhounite theory by nullifying Congress's "Force Act." Jackson ignored this meaningless gesture, permitting the nullifiers their hollow victory.

Between 1815 and 1840 forces of nationalism remained stronger than disunionist tendencies. Events of 1832–33 indicated that South Carolina's fire-eaters stood alone, and the nullifiers found themselves isolated in their own section. No person was more aware of the lack of southern unity or of the dangers which lay ahead than John C. Calhoun.

Slater's Mill, Pawtucket, Rhode Island. *The Rhode Island Historical Society*

Henry Clay caricatured Calhoun as "tall, careworn, with furrowed brow, haggard and intensely gazing, looking as if he were dissecting the last abstraction which sprang from the metaphysician's brain, and muttering to himself in half-uttered tones, 'This is indeed a real crisis.'" After the nullification controversy, Calhoun became the symbol of the Slave South, and the graying, stone-faced leader struggled to create a sense of regional identity. Greater sectional tensions lay ahead.

ECONOMIC CHANGE DURING THE JACKSONIAN ERA

Boom   After the panic of 1819, revival of the demand for cotton once again helped restore prosperity, and agricultural expansion together with Indian removal pushed the cotton frontier westward. As the plantation economy grew, so did the need for slave labor. Prices for fieldhands rose sharply, but, rather than making slavery less economical, higher prices merely increased southern planters' stake in the system. With so much capital invested in slaves, perpetuation of slavery became more and more important to the solvency of plantation owners and, indirectly, to the nation as a whole.

Prosperity in agricultural exports helped revive industrial growth. Cotton textile mills once more sprang up throughout New England, New York, and Pennsylvania; the iron industry, production of tools and machines, and processing plants of various kinds again prospered. The factory system slowly replaced household manufacture as a source of boots, shoes, woven cloth, and hats. Interchangeable parts, the technological advance which eventually revolutionized American industry, began in the manufacture of small firearms. And American goods began to compete successfully with British products. A large and prosperous national market gave new incentives to production; inventors adapted machines to replace scarce labor wherever possible; and abundant water power provided a ready source of energy. Improvements in transportation and the tariffs of 1816, 1824, and 1828 also contributed to growth. Although the cost of labor was high in comparison to Europe, workers remained largely unorganized and presented industrialists with few demands. The one limited attempt at unionization, the National Trades Union, collapsed when unemployment and depression again hit the economy in 1837.

By the mid-thirties a new peak of prosperity and speculative frenzy had been reached. Government land sales soared; British investment rose; inflation steadily mounted. Moreover, the demise of the central banking system left the government with no effective means of regulating money and credit.

The bank war The struggle between President Jackson and the president of the Bank of the United States, Nicholas Biddle, was one of the most dramatic episodes of Jackson's presidency. Jackson and many of his followers had opposed the national bank ever since the panic of 1819. Even though during the 1820s, under Biddle's leadership, the bank had pursued more responsible policies, Biddle had antagonized many politicians and some state banking interests. His aristocratic manner and unrestrained use of the bank as a powerful economic regulator made Biddle a perfect target for the Jacksonian party.

The bank's charter was to expire in 1836, and Biddle feared that Jackson would block its renewal. On the advice of Henry Clay and Daniel Webster, who believed that Jackson would not veto the bank's recharter on the eve of an election, Biddle decided to ask Congress to recharter the bank four years early, in 1832. But his political calculations were wrong. Jackson vetoed the bill and issued a flamboyant verbal attack upon the "monster" bank.

In his veto message and throughout the campaign of 1832, Jackson invoked memories of the panic of 1819 and pictured the bank as a symbol of centralism, despotic power, and special interest. Posing as a crusader for the common man and old-time values, he easily defeated his opponent, Henry Clay, and took his election as a mandate to continue his war against Biddle and the bank. During his second term the president deposited no more government funds in the national bank, depositing the money in "pet" banks around the country. Biddle's bank was dead even before its charter formally expired in 1836.

The panics of 1837 and 1839

Jackson's slaying of the "monster bank" pleased Democrats, particularly those associated with local "pet" banks, but it did little to bring the inflated economy under control or to encourage confidence among foreign investors. British investors, fearful of America's deteriorating balance of trade and apprehensive about their own credit position, began to call in overseas obligations. Americans frantically sought hard currency to meet their debts, but specie was in short supply. Banks were unable to redeem their paper money, and people holding deteriorating notes from unsound banks found themselves caught in a financial squeeze. Panic spread across the country.

The Locofocos, a powerful splinter group from the Democratic party in New York, demanded that Jackson return the country to "sound" hard money, and many farmers echoed the Locofocos' claim that there was something sinister and immoral about paper currency. Like these hard-money advocates, the president also attacked the symptom of eco-

Thomas Sully, *Nicholas Biddle.*
The Historical Society of Pennsylvania

nomic distress rather than its cause. He issued a Specie Circular requiring that purchasers pay hard money for all land bought from the government. A few years earlier, such a measure might have benefited the economy by curtailing the wild speculation and inflation, but by 1836 it accelerated contraction of the currency and made further land purchases more difficult. Land values, a barometer of and contributor to the earlier inflation, now both reflected and accelerated the economic downturn.

By May, 1837, almost all banks had suspended specie payments; their irredeemable notes were worthless. As economic distress in both England and America grew, the British textile industry began to waiver and the price of cotton fell. Depression settled upon the country, and, after a brief improvement in 1838, grew even worse in 1839.

The Jacksonian age and the business cycle

The economy of the early nineteenth century was marked by an increase of foreign investment, growing reliance upon one export crop, expansion of transportation systems and industries, optimistic and sometimes careless speculation, and uneven banking practices. The result was a cyclical pattern of boom and bust, of rapid inflation followed by severe currency contraction. To today's analyst, the Jacksonian economy reveals the dangers of excessive reliance upon foreign investment and a single major export. The Jacksonian business cycles also illustrate the need for a flexible national banking system working to control inflation and counteract depression.

But few Americans understood the forces at work in their unstable economy; fewer still had the knowledge to master them. Americans of the early nineteenth century sought to explain economic instability in terms of less complicated scapegoats: "powerful" banks, unsound money, foreign conspiracies, unscrupulous aristocrats. Economic uncertainty intensified social and political tensions within the country. Class differences seemed more apparent, and condemnations of "special privilege" were met with dire warnings about giving power to the ignorant masses. Sectional rivalry grew, as westerners blamed eastern capitalists for their problems and easterners blamed irresponsible western speculators; and all sections, particularly the South, grew jealous of the political power of the others. Politics became more rancorous, and an array of social reformers began advocating moral solutions for the turbulence of the age. The Jacksonian era was a time of fluidity and change, and the economic cycles both mirrored and contributed to this milieu.

GOVERNMENT AND THE ECONOMY

Promotion of transportation systems

An English visitor to America complained that "the only distinction—the only means of raising himself above his fellows left to the American—is wealth; consequently, the acquisition of wealth has become the great

The Erie Canal. *Culver Pictures*

spring of action." The avid pursuit of riches undoubtedly contributed to a quickening of national economic growth during the Jacksonian age. America had its full share of speculators, inventors, and entrepreneurs, and these ambitious men laid the basis for a dynamic capitalist economy. But private capital and individual initiative were only two ingredients in America's development. Governmental policy, particularly on the state and local level, also assisted growth.

The promotional activities of state and local governments centered upon improving transportation. A good transportation network would attract manufacturers, commercial farmers, and settlers; it would lower the cost of goods and boost the volume of available products. Throughout the Jacksonian era, Americans sought prosperity for their state or town by building toll roads, canals, and railroads.

Before the War of 1812, the country was bound together principally by poorly maintained country roads. Bumpy, overgrown, and frequently impassable, such roads hindered the growth of interregional trade and communication. As early as 1808 Albert Gallatin had submitted a plan for federal financing of such internal improvements, and for decades congressmen such as Henry Clay worked for similar schemes. But although a succession of presidents did approve small grants to assist a few specific projects, all consistently opposed federal funding of any comprehensive network of roads. The only major federal undertaking was the National Road which stretched from Cumberland, Maryland, through the heart of the country to Columbus, Ohio, and finally to Vandalia, Illinois. In the absence of federal initiative, the states assumed the burden of road construction. States contributed large grants or, in some cases, owned the roads directly. Within a few decades after 1815, states poured millions of tax dollars into highways; New York and Pennsylvania led the nation in total mileage. On only a few roads, however, did profits measure up to expectations. Maintenance costs exceeded toll revenues, and many companies went bankrupt and allowed their roads to slip into disrepair. The mania to build turnpikes subsided quickly, and Americans turned to a potentially cheaper and more lucrative means of transit—the canal.

The spectacular success of the Erie Canal set off the frenzy of canal building. Pushed through the New York legislature in 1817 by DeWitt Clinton's powerful political machine, the bill to finance a canal linking Albany, on the Hudson, with Buffalo, on Lake Erie, seemed a great gamble. No canal in the United States had ever been profitable, and a waterway of such magnitude presented enormous technical difficulties as well as an unparalleled expenditure of public funds. But, upon completion of each section, toll revenues poured back into the state treasury, and the critics fell silent. After it opened in 1825 the canal soon became so crowded that it had to be widened.

The Erie's phenomenal success and the development of the steamboat stimulated ambitious schemes and countless surveys throughout the country. But the huge capitalization required to dig a canal made governmental participation or ownership imperative. As with turnpikes, the federal government provided only limited assistance in the form of land grants or small subscriptions of stock. States and localities assumed most of the financial burden and throughout the 1830s incurred rapidly mounting debts. By 1840 Americans had built enough canal mileage that, if laid in a straight line, it could have connected the Atlantic and Pacific oceans at the widest transcontinental breadth. Some stretches were profitable and beneficial, but many more were costly failures. Once touted as a means of filling state treasuries, canals soon proved a terrible drain, and after the financial panics of 1837 and 1839 states undertook few new projects.

The disappointing return on turnpikes and canals did not extinguish the fever to improve the nation's transportation system. Throughout the rest of the century, Americans energetically crisscrossed the country with the wood and steel of railroad lines. Construction of a few small tramways began in the 1820s, and in 1828 the first major railroad, the Baltimore and Ohio, was chartered. Many early railroads ran only short distances, designed as feeders into the major waterway and canal systems, but major eastern cities which had inadequate water connections with the hinterland began to promote longer lines. By 1840 the nation's total railroad mileage equaled that of the canals, and many lines successfully competed with canal companies for business.

As with the other means of transportation, public funds encouraged railway construction. The national government financed surveys and, between 1830 and 1843, lowered tariff duties on iron. State legislatures, again taking the lead in public assistance, granted tax exemptions, required newly chartered banks to subscribe to railroad stock, extended large grants, and sometimes operated the lines directly. But outright state ownership of railroads was never as great as it was of canals, and the empty treasuries of most states stalled new projects. Still, grants and other incentives from states and localities, added to the foreign investment which American railroads attracted, did provide sufficient impetus to private companies. In the 1840s and 1850s, railroad building boomed and overshadowed all other forms of transportation.

The federal government and the economy

State and local governments played the predominant role in stimulating economic growth, but the policies of the federal government were also important. Despite the failure of Henry Clay's comprehensive plan for national development (called the American System)—a protective tariff, national bank, and federally financed internal improvements paid for with proceeds from the sale of public lands—national government still played some role in development. Congress passed protective tariffs, which provided some shield for America's infant industries. A free immigration policy augmented the labor force. Jacksonians promoted western development by keeping down the price of public lands, and Indian removal increased the amount of saleable land in the public domain. Whigs considered Jackson's destruction of the national bank an attack on orderly economic growth, but Jackson viewed the action as a blow against monopoly. Democrats insisted that their policy curtailed the power of a conservative elite who favored the status quo, feared open competition, and desired the kind of statism and legislative privilege found in Europe. They claimed that Jacksonian economic policies created opportunities for greater numbers of people and provided an atmosphere for unrestricted development. The national government of the Jacksonian age did not play the extensive role in determining economic decisions that it does today. But its general policies were designed to remove impediments in the way of economic growth, and it helped set the basis for America's liberal, capitalist economy.

RELIGIOUS MOVEMENTS AND SOCIAL FERMENT

During the first half of the nineteenth century, a variety of religious movements appeared and flourished in the United States. Feeding on the excitement of revival meetings, many of these enthusiasms demanded a literal interpretation of the Bible, including a belief in the second coming of Christ and the establishment of God's kingdom on earth. Amid a population anticipating the literal fulfillment of prophecies, prophets and interpreters aroused much interest, and reported mystical experiences achieved great reknown. Western New York—often called the "burned-over district" because it had been seared so many times by the fires of religious enthusiasm—provided an incubator for many infant movements. Converts came from a larger field stretching from northern New England through New York to the states of the Ohio Valley. In all their diversity and passion, these movements represented the extremes of rural evangelical Protestantism.

Spiritualism Attempts at contact with the spirit world have occurred in many places at many times, but the spiritualism of mid-nineteenth century America is notable for its vigor and wide appeal. Some saw it as another science to be linked with chemistry, mesmerism, and the like in probing the ultimate mysteries of death and immortality. But for most the spectacular nature of spirit contacts probably held far more interest.

In early 1848 a strange presence supposedly entered the lives of Maggie and Katie Fox of Hydesville, New York. Wherever the young girls were, peculiar rappings sounded to the consternation of their superstitious mother. The intrigued Mrs. Fox and her pleased daughters presently worked out a system of communication with the presumably other-worldly source of the rappings; soon the neighbors flocked to observe this mysterious conversation. With an older widowed sister acting as manager, the Fox girls began to hold exhibitions—at the insistence of the spirits, of course—and quickly developed into professional mediums charging fees.

With the wide publicity given the Fox sisters, mediums rapidly appeared all over the country, and spiritualist circles developed in nearly every town and village. Mediums and managers refined their techniques as they went along; the Foxes' managing sister, for instance, discovered that total darkness could produce many more manifestations of the spirits' presence. Table moving, spirit writing, and cold ghostly hands led a chain of developments that within a few years produced all the phenomenological paraphernalia familiar to twentieth-century spiritualists. The spiritualist excitement, though seeming only silly to many, filled for thousands of people a real need to know more about a world beyond death. Even when the Fox sisters some years later admitted that their whole career had been a great fraud (the original rappings had been produced by the joints of their toes), many spiritualists remained undeterred.

William Miller   Another New Yorker became the most important American exponent of the view that Christ's second coming was imminent. William Miller, a hardworking farmer of old New England stock, became caught up in a revival shortly after the War of 1812 and spent the rest of his life pondering religious questions. Believing in Biblical literalism, he studied for years the prophecy of Christ's reappearance and filled his free time with careful and intricate calculations of the exact date men could expect His return. The unassuming Miller was slow to reveal his eventual conviction that the Second Advent would occur *about* the year 1843, but a sense of responsibility and inquiries from neighbors encouraged him to publically announce his discovery in 1832. Slowly, then more quickly as the dread year 1843 approached, Miller made crowds of converts with his quiet but deeply sincere and frightening sermons. Ministerial disciples with a knack for publicity soon spread Miller's views over a wide area. As the excitement and tension climbed ever higher, followers demanded a definite date for the world's end. Miller himself was hesitant to attempt a specific prediction, believing faith to be the central element of his creed. His disciples, however, were less cautious. As 1843—the Last Year—passed, March of 1844 came to be accepted as the crucial month. When nothing occurred an old and ill William Miller humbly admitted his mistake, saying he had done his best. But the lesser chieftains of the movement were not ready to quit. Millerite leaders chose October 22, 1844 as the new date for the Advent, later talking Miller into accepting it. Excitement rose higher than before as extensive preparations were made to enter the kingdom. The faithful prepared white ascension robes and neglected nearly all secular business after the first of October. On the night of October 21, Millerite groups gathered on hilltops to meet together the new world, their faith evident in the lack of provision for eating or sleeping. As the night and the next day and then the next night passed, children and old people suffered greatly. Horrible thunderstorms suggested that the end was near. As time continued a few Millerites committed suicide, and there were several cases of insanity. This last great disappointment effectively ended the Millerite movement.

Shakers   Some of the fervent young religious movements of the early 1800s encouraged believers to join together in exclusive communities of the faith-

Winslow Homer, *The Morning Bell. Yale University Art Gallery*

ful. Each member gave up much of his free will and a varying amount of his property to further divine unity and the blessed prosperity of the whole community. Though individual members might be ever so humble, these societies tended to appear exclusive and arrogant to outsiders. This stance, added to the friction between communist and individualist values, often brought resistance and even persecution from the larger society, usually proportionate to the aggressiveness of the innovating sect.

The Shaker Society, characterized by quiet, well-ordered villages, had little trouble with outsiders. Only when Shaker leaders went proselytizing and began competing with revivalists for converts did they encounter significant opposition. The Shakers—who received their name from a unique sacred dance in which they shook sin from the body through the fingertips—had come to America with the arrival of Ann Lee and a few followers in 1774. Mother Ann's life represented to the Shakers a spiritual expression of divine truth, a continuation of Christ's work, this time deriving from the feminine side of God's personality. The Shakers were millennialists and also spiritualists, since Mother Ann received inspiration through trance and revelation. To familiar pietistic dogmas and Biblical literalism, they added absolute celibacy as a religious requirement. Since the millennium was near, propagation was unnecessary; continence would increase the purity of the believers. At the height of their success in the 1830s, about six thousand Shakers inhabited some twenty settlements in seven states. In their villages the Shakers developed labor-saving devices, clean-lined furniture, and occasionally beautiful, highly functional buildings which remain patterns for modern designers. Some Shaker communities lasted into the twentieth century, but since members could not reproduce, Shakerism gradually died as the belief in an imminent millennium waned.

Mormons The most important of the new religions which rose in western New York was Mormonism. A farm boy of poor and unpromising background, Joseph Smith created this religion in the 1820s after claiming to have seen visions and to have discovered in the ground gold plates containing ancient writing. These plates, when translated by Smith, became the *Book of Mormon* which paralleled certain parts of the *Old Testament* and included the supposed history of an Israelite tribe as well as multiple contemporary references. Many questions have been raised concerning the character of Smith and the existence of gold tablets, but whatever irregularities were involved in Mormonism's founding they are far less significant than its growth and survival as a vital religion. Smith and his disciples clearly tapped important reservoirs of religious feeling.

Smith helped found an Ohio Mormon Community in 1831 while another was begun in Missouri. Friction between the exclusivist, expansionist Mormons and their neighbors forced the abandonment of both settlements by 1839 when Smith founded Nauvoo, Illinois, on the Mississippi. By 1844 Nauvoo boasted the largest population in the state with 15,000 people, But again the Mormons were in trouble locally. Smith's secret authorization of polygamy for top officers of the church produced difficulties not only with outraged neighbors but with dissident Mormons inside Nauvoo. Mormon leaders, moreover, envisioned Nauvoo as a semi-independent territory within the United States and seemed to encourage vague notions of a Mormon empire in the Northwest. When local "gentiles" and the state militia beseiged Nauvoo, Smith was arrested and later murdered by a mob. Under Brigham Young, their new leader, the Mormons in 1847 marched toward the West, finally settling in what is now Utah. Through long, difficult, and carefully planned work, they prospered as a centrally controlled religious, political, and economic entity. The Mormon Church remains today a powerful force in Utah and a thriving religion in many areas of the country.

Communitarianism

"The whole question of effecting a social reform may be reduced to the establishment of one Association, which will serve as a model for, and induce the rapid establishment of others," wrote Albert Brisbane, an American exponent of the utopian socialism of Frenchman Charles Fourier. Americans like Brisbane believed that small communitarian groups, isolated from society, could develop social principles which would spread to and purify the whole nation. More than fifty such experiments sprang up in nineteenth-century America, some drawing inspiration from religious teachings, others from the European utopians such as Fourier or Robert Dale Owen. Most lasted only a brief time; all eventually failed. But these communities eloquently reflected a belief in human perfectability. They were short-lived monuments to a faith that America could become a society of harmonious and happy individuals sharing cooperatively with one another.

Robert Dale Owen, the famous British theorist who inspired so many American utopians, organized his own communal experiment at New Harmony, Indiana. Owen believed that the American West provided the unformed and egalitarian climate which a new social system required, and in 1825 he collected a disparate group of followers. He hoped to transform them into a prosperous, hard-working, and self-governing community. But Owen discovered it "was premature to unite a number of strangers" to operate "for their common interest, and live together as a common family." Quarrels and internal dissatisfaction beset the project, and Owen finally gave up, concluding that America could not develop a successful communism because cheap land and high wages fostered excessive individualism and discouraged cooperative action.

Brook Farm, begun during the 1840s near Boston, gained special fame because of its illustrious membership, mostly New England intel-

Asher Durand, *Kindred Spirits*. New York Public Library

Charles Grandison Finney, evangelist. *Courtesy Oberlin College*

lectuals such as George Ripley (its founder), Nathaniel Hawthorne, and Charles A. Dana. Combining transcendentalist beliefs with the utopian blueprint of Fourier, Brook Farm's inhabitants tried to enrich their lives by balancing intellectual and manual labor. "The economical failure was almost a foregone conclusion," one observer reported, "but there were never such witty potato-patches.... The weeds were scratched out of the ground to the music of Tennyson and Browning." Residents at Brook Farm ran a highly successful experimental school which attracted children of New England's intellectual elite, but economic problems and a series of natural disasters forced abandonment of the farm after a few years.

The most successful community in terms of profit and longevity settled at Oneida in upstate New York. Organized by John Humphrey Noyes, an exponent of a religious creed called perfectionism, settlers at Oneida turned to industry, rather than agriculture, as an economic base. The community prospered from manufacturing steel traps, sewing silk, and fashioning silver utensils. But Oneida's social life was even more unusual than its economic base. Trying to minimize competition and to foster a communal spirit, Noyes forbade marriage or "special love." Instead, the group practiced "complex marriage," a system in which each member was theoretically married to every other. Although the widely misunderstood practice horrified nearby residents, sexual behavior at Oneida was highly regulated and was always based upon mutual consent. Oneida's women enjoyed far more equality than those on the "outside." In nineteenth-century America, respectable women were expected to disdain sexual relations, to concentrate upon household and child-rearing tasks, and to wear the confining fashions of the day. Occupational equality did not exist, and the marriage contract still gave women an inferior legal status. At Oneida, however, women had sexual equality, were substantially freed from "kitchen slavery," wore trousers, and cropped their hair. Children became the entire community's responsibility, and women worked alongside men in the fields and factories. Sharing work and profits, the Oneida community practiced a simple and successful socialism until the 1880s when pressure from outside critics forced them to abandon "complex marriage" and break into families. Oneida's factories subsequently became joint-stock companies, subscribed by the individual families which had made up the community.

The impulse for reform While a few social visionaries tried to perfect small communities as patterns for the whole society, others worked within society to cure specific ills. During the Jacksonian era, societies formed to distribute Bibles, encourage Sunday schools, improve prisons, provide care for the needy and insane, improve and expand education, promote temperance, end warfare, gain equal rights for women, return American blacks to Africa, and abolish slavery.

The sources of reform were diverse. Personal experience and self-interest affected reformers such as the women's rights activists Angelina and Sarah Grimké and the black abolitionist Frederick Douglass. Others, especially those associated with the Bible Society and the American Tract Society, came from an upper-class, Calvinist elite; they considered themselves the moral stewards of the nation. They feared that unless they inculcated the mass of people with proper values, social disorder would grow worse. "The gospel is the most economical police on earth," said a leader of the Home Missionary Society. The great revivalist Charles G. Finney and the religious enthusiasm of the 1830s inspired crusaders such as the antislavery activist Theodore Dwight Weld to campaign against immorality. And the prevalent belief in moral perfectionism sharpened the conviction of many reformers. Abolitionist editor William Lloyd Garrison, for example, became so obsessed with moral purity that he burned a copy of the Constitution, thereby symbolically dissociating himself from a nation contaminated by the evil of slavery.

The various reform efforts produced mixed results. Although Bible and Sunday school movements generated countless propaganda tracts, donations dried up during the depression of the late 1830s. Dorothea Dix's crusade to build asylums for the insane met with some success, but most states continued to confine the mentally ill in almshouses. Prison reform also came slowly; most states did abolish imprisonment for debt and some ended public executions and capital punishment. Solitary confinement replaced the lash in some prisons, and many institutions began to adopt the "Auburn system" of individual cells.

Education also underwent some slow changes. Although compulsory-attendance laws did not come for many years, states gradually offered schooling for those who desired it. Acceptance of Horace Mann's "progressive" ideas somewhat eased the harsh discipline and boredom of many classrooms; coeducation gained some adherents; and many academies and colleges added practical courses to their classical curricula. A group of western colleges followed a new concept: combining manual and intellectual training. Founded by radical reformers, these schools, such as Oberlin in Ohio, became centers of educational experimentation and antislavery activism.

The temperance crusade was, in the short run at least, one of the more successful reforms. Although temperance advocates who used moral appeals made little impact, those who shifted to political action scored significant victories. In 1851 Maine passed America's first statewide prohibitionist statute, and in the years before the Civil War, many states followed Maine's lead and prohibited or restricted the sale of alcoholic beverages.

The American Peace Society also gained momentum throughout the antebellum period. The Mexican War may have revealed the society's weakness in affecting national policy, but the war's unpopularity augmented the movement's membership. As sectional tensions rose over the slavery issue, however, peace advocates frequently decided that slavery was a greater moral evil than war, and the peace movement collapsed as the South seceded from the Union.

The women's rights movement, fighting a society that permitted wife beating "with a reasonable instrument," probably created as much notoriety as change. Lucy Stone, an antislavery and women's rights activist who retained her maiden name after marriage, refused to pay taxes because she was not represented in the government; scores of "radical" women began to wear the less constricting "Bloomer" costume; Susan B. Anthony helped a woman kidnap her child from her husband's custody (men had prior legal rights to their children). Such activities alienated most Americans, and even many sympathetic males abandoned women's rights when it threatened to divide the antislavery movement. Led by Lucretia Mott, Elizabeth Cady Stanton, and Susan B. Anthony, women held conventions (the most famous met at Seneca Falls, New

York, in 1848) and brought their concerns before the public. But despite their energy and intelligence, fundamental changes in attitudes, occupational choice, legal status, and political participation remained elusive.

The antislavery movement gradually overshadowed and subsumed all other reforms. Crusaders against slavery, although initially small in number, contributed to the growing sectional division and accomplished their objective of freeing blacks only after a long and bitter war.

Reform during the antebellum period was complex and various. Some crusaders sought to purify society through example; others took direct action to correct specific problems. Some were radical, wanting to introduce new mores into American life; others were conservative, striving to save or restore older values. Many believed that social reform could come only through individual moral regeneration; a few sought to better the individual by first improving conditions in society. Reformers frequently disagreed on goals and method, but they also shared many feelings: frustration at the disorder in society, apprehension about the loss of consensus and community, fear of declining morality. They held a faith that America's unsettled society could still be redirected onto a proper, moral path. The restlessness pervading American life produced both a fear of the country's present plight and a hope that right-thinking individuals could create a better world.

THE AMERICAN ROMANTICS

The world was watching America after the Revolution; Europeans were particularly curious about what the new democracy would produce in the way of new institutions and new forms of culture. Accounts of trips to America were tremendously popular in Europe. Some of them, like Frances Trollope's *Domestic Manners of the Americans* (1832), expressed disdain for crude American customs. Others exhibited intense optimism. Alexis de Tocqueville, who visited America in 1831–32 and whose *Democracy in America* (1832) is the best known of these accounts, was on the optimistic side—but his opinions were mixed. Americans had no native literature, he wrote, since most American writers composed literary works which were really English in substance and in form. A truly American, democratic literature, he predicted, would lack "order, regularity, science, and art...Style will frequently be fantastic, incorrect, overburdened, and loose, almost always vehement and bold. Authors will aim at rapidity of execution more than at perfection of detail.... there will be more wit than erudition, more imagination than profundity; and literary performances will bear marks of an untutored and rude vigor of thought, frequently of great variety and singular fecundity."

But even while Tocqueville wrote, a generation of writers was appearing in America who had never been British subjects; it proved successful at establishing a literature which was new—American—in both substance and form, and at the same time good enough to establish for them a European reputation. Foremost among these early figures were Washington Irving (1783–1859), James Fenimore Cooper (1789–1851), and Edgar Allan Poe (1809–1849).

Poe's work is probably the most difficult for modern readers to evaluate because it is easy to dismiss as simple tales of horror or jingle-like verse. But the "jingles" contain his best qualities; "The Bells," one of his best-known poems, is an example of Poe as a literary craftsman concerned with essential qualities of diction and language. This concern with general principles of writing occupies high intellectual ground today. At the same time Poe regarded the universe as a work of art to be grasped aesthetically and as a whole. Only the poet, Poe argued, could glimpse the harmony at the center of things and bring mortals closer to it. This aesthetic credo, combined with Poe's alcoholism and the protagonists of his horror tales, created what one critic has called the poet as his own mythic figure, the artist as outcast or outsider.

James Fenimore Cooper's work is now often thought of as children's literature, especially his *Leatherstocking Tales*, a series of novels which began with *The Pioneers* (1823), ended with *The Deerslayer* (1841), and included his most famous novel, *The Last of the Mohicans* (1826). These are novels of adventure, describing the boundary between two cultures, one civilized and one wild. In part Cooper used this boundary, and the relationship between Indians and white men, to create a distinctly American past for the new American art to draw upon; the Indian wars provided him with the material for novels which could really be American in substance. His concern was not with Indians in general, but with the final stages of their culture, their interaction with "civilization." At the same time, Cooper's themes are similar to a major theme in American literature—the conflict between corruption and innocence, sophistication and naivete, aesthetics and morality—which reappeared as Europe vs. America in the later works of Hawthorne, Henry James, F. Scott Fitzgerald, and Ernest Hemingway.

Like Cooper's writing, Washington Irving's novels and stories used the theme of the boundary between two cultures. He is best remembered for his rich use of local color; his stories explore the picturesque geography and culture of the area he knew best, upstate New York. But this old-fashioned local color is juxtaposed with the new civilization. "Rip Van Winkle," his most famous short story, demonstrates his (and Rip's) ambivalence towards the rejection of the past involved in political and social revolution. And he described the town in "The Legend of Sleepy Hollow" with undisguised rejection of the newer, bustling American life: "I mention this peaceful spot with all possible laud; for it is in such little retired Dutch valleys...that population, manners, and customs remain fixed; while the great torrent of migration and improvement, which is making such incessant changes in other parts of this restless country, sweeps by them unobserved."

FRONTIER REVIVALISM

Religion on the American frontier ranged from colorful revival meetings to more prosaic Methodist and Baptist proselytizing. The more extreme "enthusiasms" which periodically swept the country peaked during the 1830s and early 1840s when the great evangelist Charles G. Finney harangued the sinful in the backwoods of New York and Ohio. Emphasizing individual religion—the congregation would often pray for a particular person—Finney preached that social usefulness, not salvation of the soul, was the proper object for the Christian. Some prayer meetings abandoned rationality and even decorum as participants occasionally broke into paroxysms of emotion, throwing themselves upon the ground, barking like dogs, screaming fitfully.

But isolated radicalism and tent-meeting revivalism had a much less permanent impact upon western religion than did more conventional Protestantism. John Wesley, the founder of Methodism in England, argued that the form of church government was secondary, a tenet which provided Methodists with a unique capacity to adapt their religious organization to changing conditions. Methodist doctrine centered upon freedom of the will and individual responsibility, thus deepening the affinity between Wesley's theology and America's frontier. Even before 1800, Methodist

George Inness, *The Lackawanna Valley. National Gallery of Art*

circuit riders, or traveling preachers, had become standard characters in the western panorama, as stereotyped as the pioneer or land speculator. Poorly clad and usually atop a mangy horse, these itinerants brought religion, news, and companionship to scattered settlers and, at the same time, spread Methodism throughout the Middle West. The more sedentary Baptists could never quite match the ubiquity of Wesley's lieutenants.

Francis Asbury transplanted the ideal of an itinerant ministry to America and became the nation's first, and most influential, circuit rider. He arrived in New York City in 1771 and, unlike his colleagues, traveled around the countryside preaching wherever he could find an audience. Asbury established the principle that circuit riders should rely upon hospitable settlers, instead of a salary, for food and shelter, although later the Church provided about a hundred dollars annually for clothes and horses. The itinerant's strenuous, transient life meant that he was seldom married. Circuit riders were often as rowdy as the frontier they rode: the famous Peter Cartwright, for example, regularly beat up outsiders who disturbed his meetings.

Because early Methodists lacked a university to train their ministers, Asbury's example of apprenticeship quickly substituted for academic training. Although the Church eventually insisted that its preachers read certain books, most circuit riders graduated only from "Bush College," on-the-job training with other men. Largely because of this, fewer than one-third of the itinerants became ordained ministers. Circuit-rider organization also adapted to the frontier. In each of six regions, annual conferences heard reports, admitted new preachers, and assigned new circuits. As pioneers filled in the countryside, the formerly immense circuits (some were several hundred miles long) contracted, and preaching became more frequent. Halfway through the nineteenth century, when the midwestern frontier closed, the circuit rider disappeared into the settled life of regular parishes. The itinerants had served Wesley well: by 1844 the Methodists had become the largest Protestant denomination in America, with slightly over a million members.

THINGS TO THINK ABOUT:
1816–1840

How did America's political culture change between 1815 and 1840? Why has this political era been called the age of the common man? General political accounts include George Dangerfield, *The Awakening of American Nationalism, 1815–1828* (1965); Glyndon Van Duesen, *The Jacksonian Era* (1963); Richard P. McCormick, *The Second American Party System* (1966); and Robert V. Remini, *The Election of Andrew Jackson* (1963). The following more specialized studies are also very useful: Marvin Meyers, *The Jacksonian Persuasion* (1957); John William Ward, *Andrew Jackson: Symbol for an Age* (1955); Lee Benson, *The*

Concept of Jacksonian Democracy: New York as a Test Case (1961); and Richard Hofstadter, *The Idea of a Party System* (1969).

How did the tempo of American life quicken in the years between 1815 and 1840? What social changes occurred during these years? What economic changes? How did these changes affect different parts of the expanding nation? On economic changes see Stuart Bruchey, *The Roots of American Economic Growth* (1965), Douglas C. North *Growth and Welfare in the American Past: A New Economic History* (1966), and Peter Temin, *The Jacksonian Economy* (1967). The banking issue is treated in Bray Hammond, *Banks and Politics in America* (1967) and James R. Sharp, *The Jacksonians versus the Banks* (1970). Southern society may be understood through the following works: Clement Eaton, *The Growth of Southern Civilization* (1961); William R. Taylor, *Cavalier and Yankee* (1961); William Freehling, *Prelude to Civil War* (1966); Anne Firor Scott, *The Southern Lady: From Pedestal to Politics* (1970); and W. J. Cash, *The Mind of the South* (1940). Older accounts of slavery are listed in the next chapter; Ann J. Lane, ed., *The Debate over Slavery* (1971) contains a number of revisionist essays. For other aspects of American development see Richard C. Wade, *The Urban Frontier* (1959); Ray A. Billington, *Westward Expansion* (1967), Douglas T. Miller, *Jacksonian Aristocracy* (1967); and Stephen Thernstrom, *Poverty and Progress* (1964). Interesting summaries of social developments may be found in Edward Pessen, *Jacksonian America* (1969).

How do you explain many Americans' sudden concern for social reform during this era? Alice Felt Tyler, *Freedom's Ferment* (1944) and C. S. Griffin, *The Ferment of Reform* (1967) are general surveys which present different interpretations. Specialized studies include Whitney R. Gross, *The Burned-Over District* (1950); Timothy L. Smith, *Revivalism and Social Reform* (1957); Bernard A. Weisberger, *They Gathered at the River* (1958); and David J. Rothman, *The Discovery of the Asylum* (1971). Titles listed in the following chapter are also relevant, particularly those on abolitionism. On the opposition to abolitionists, see Leonard L. Richards, *"Gentlemen of Property and Standing"* (1971).

1840-1860

SIX | IMPENDING CRISIS

HARRIET BEECHER STOWE

Harriet Beecher was an "odd" child, according to her brother Henry. When she was fifteen years old (in 1826) she had already read much of her father's theological library. For her part, Mrs. Stowe later recalled with fondness her "non-resistant" childhood in Massachusetts and Cincinnatti and her intense admiration for her "God-like" father. As a young woman Harriet was gentle and retiring. Like many young ladies of her class, she attended a seminary school where she endeavored to become gracious and uncomplaining. Her young womanhood included not only periods of neurotic self-doubt, but also times of dramatic religious experience.

Her father, Lyman Beecher, was appointed president of Lane Theological Seminary in 1832. Here Harriet met a young teacher, Calvin Stowe, whom she married four years later. Stowe encouraged his wife's first writings for literary magazines, and she supported him during his long encounter with troubling hallucinations and intellectual inertia. The Stowes had five children in the first seven years of their marriage, and Mrs. Stowe's writing was steeped in the need for self-sacrifice and other-worldly aspiration.

In 1850, Bowdoin College offered Calvin Stowe a professorship,

241

and the Stowes moved there in the spring of the year. Mrs. Stowe had long admired women writers who were "leaders and prophetesses," and within a few months of her arrival in Maine she began to turn her moral attention to matters of a worldly nature. American black slavery arrested her with "an icy hand" after a chance reading of a southern slave-dealing newspaper. Mrs. Stowe began a considerable research into the institution of chattel labor, reading southern defenses of slavery as well as the virulent attacks on it by Theodore Weld, Lydia Child, and Frederick Douglass.

The Fugitive Slave Law of 1850 precipitated her creative energy, and she wrote *Uncle Tom's Cabin* in serial form in 1852 for the *National Era.* Mrs. Stowe later described the novel as having been "dictated" to her from a source outside of herself. The novel's power was overwhelming. Mrs. Stowe was an international celebrity in a time when few writers were acclaimed as equals with men of politics and business. Her horror at her country's acquiescence in what she saw as a prime evil was both shared and denied. One measure of the novel's power was its generation of imitations. More than fifty novels with slavery as their essence appeared after 1852, thirty of which were intent on showing the institution as beneficial. None of these, however, seem to match *Uncle Tom's Cabin* in its force as a "novel of redemption." And whatever its sentimentality, the novel is a powerful record of human agony and paradox, in which Tom is less a psychological reality than an archetype of freedom.

Mrs. Stowe wrote twenty more major books after *Uncle Tom's Cabin,* most notable of which are *Oldtown Folks* (1869) and *Poganuc People* (1878). Both of these latter novels view New England life and, like *Uncle Tom's Cabin,* have much to do with woman's role in nineteenth-century family life. Mrs. Stowe retired to Florida in the late 1880s.

1840-1860

1837	*Caroline* incident
1838	Aroostook War
1840	World Antislavery Convention
1841	Inauguration and death of William Henry Harrison John Tyler becomes president
1842	Webster-Ashburton Treaty *Prigg* v. *Pennsylvania*
1844	James K. Polk (Democrat) defeats Henry Clay (Whig) and James Birney (Liberty)
1845	Annexation of Texas by joint resolution of Congress Slidell mission to Mexico
1846	Oregon boundary settled at 49th parallel Wilmot Proviso forbidding slavery in Mexican cession fails to pass
1846–47	Mexican War
1848	Treaty of Guadalupe Hidalgo Zachary Taylor (Whig) defeats Lewis Cass (Democrat) and Martin Van Buren (Free-Soil)
1849	California Gold Rush
1850	Emerson's *Representative Men* Hawthorne's *The Scarlet Letter* Compromise of 1850 President Taylor dies, Millard Fillmore becomes president
1851	Melville's *Moby Dick* Stowe's *Uncle Tom's Cabin*
1852	Franklin Pierce (Democrat) defeats Winfield Scott (Whig)
1854	Thoreau's *Walden* Kansas-Nebraska Act
1855	Whitman's *Leaves of Grass* "Bleeding Kansas"
1856	James Buchanan (Democrat) defeats John C. Fremont (Republican) and Millard Fillmore (Know-Nothing)
1857	*Dred Scott* v. *Sanford* Lecompton Constitution
1858	Lincoln-Douglas debates
1859	John Brown's raid
1860	Abraham Lincoln (Republican) defeats John C. Breckinridge (Southern Democrat), Stephen A. Douglas (Democrat), and John Bell (Constitutional Union)

A SOCIETY IN TRANSITION

Between 1850 and 1855, American literature saw a great burst of crea-
tivity, with the publication of Ralph Waldo Emerson's *Representative*
Men (1850), Nathaniel Hawthorne's *The Scarlet Letter* (1850) and *The*
House of Seven Gables (1851), Herman Melville's *Moby Dick* (1851),
Bartleby the Scrivener (1853), and *Benito Cereno* (1855), Henry David
Thoreau's *Walden* (1854), and Walt Whitman's *Leaves of Grass* (1855).
All but Whitman had published major works previously, but none was
especially popular. Whitman, for example, published *Leaves of Grass* at
his own expense, and Thoreau lost money on the publication of *Walden.*
Hawthorne and Melville, especially, supported themselves by writing
short works for popular magazines and gift books, and their popularity
was then eclipsed by that of lesser writers who are now forgotten.

The religious philosophy of Unitarianism provided the background
for what has been called the "American Renaissance." The "party platform"
of Unitarianism was a sermon by William Ellery Channing, "Unitarian
Christianity," delivered in Baltimore in 1819. Drawing on a new kind of
biblical interpretation, maintaining that the biblical revelations of God
were refracted through human language and history, Channing outlined
doctrines "which distinguish us from other Christians." The first was the
unity of God, as distinct from the doctrine of the Trinity. Equally important was the moral perfection of God, whose goodness, justice, mercy,
and concern for human beings contrasted with the Calvinistic doctrines
of depravity, election, and eternal damnation. Channing further defined
true holiness—love to God, love to Christ, and benevolence towards one's
fellow men. Unitarianism thus contained the notion of perfectionism, the
doctrine that man must be perfected on earth, and Unitarians therefore
were among the most active members of nineteenth-century movements
for social reform. Channing's ethical teaching was compressed into his
statement, "The adoration of goodness—this is religion."

Through Ralph Waldo Emerson, another Unitarian minister, literary romanticism in America took a philosophic turn and influenced the
leading writers of the mid-nineteenth century. In his essay *Nature* (1836),
Emerson pleaded for an original relationship with the universe, one that
transcended restricting forms of logic. Hence the term transcendentalist
came to be applied to the group of New England intellectuals of which
Emerson was the central figure. Through the simple manifestations of
nature, Emerson believed, man could perceive spirit; the universe, to the
receptive mind, could become a living thing, much like a living plant or
animal.

Henry David Thoreau made Emerson's ideas more understandable
in *Walden* (1854), an account of a two year stay at Walden pond in
Massachusetts. In this and other writings, Thoreau achieved insight into

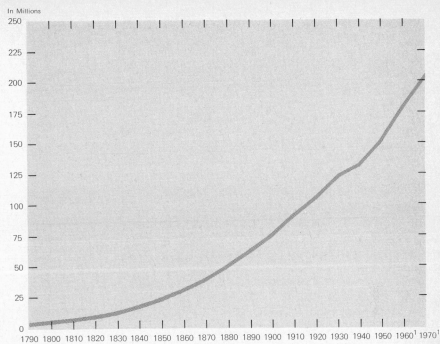

In Millions

Population of the United
States, 1790–1970

1790 1800 1810 1820 1830 1840 1850 1860 1870 1880 1890 1900 1910 1920 1930 1940 1950 1960[1] 1970[1]

[1] Includes Alaska and Hawaii

the spiritual world through metaphors derived from nature. Each individual thing in nature he found a symbol of the order and beauty of the whole. The book itself develops as an organic thing, changing from within; the building of a shack, or the reconstructing of a personality, follow the seasons as the narrative is condensed into a year for literary purposes.

Herman Melville's *Moby Dick* (1851), the finest novel of the century, is one of the most complex expressions of these themes, displaying deep levels of ambiguity and meaning in studying the misfortunes of existence. Captain Ahab, deprived of his leg and his sexuality by the great white whale, goes to sea in search of freedom and knowledge. At one moment the reader suspects that man's accommodation to the universe simply shapes his whole concept of it. The malevolence or benevolence he sees is merely a projection of his own feelings. Then Ahab quarrels with God in his boundless rhetoric: "All visible objects are but as pasteboard masks. . . . To me the white whale is that wall, shoved near to me. Sometimes I think there's naught beyond. I see in him outrageous strength with an inscrutable malice sinewing it. That inscrutable thing is chiefly what I hate."

Walt Whitman was in many ways the fulfillment of the Emersonian

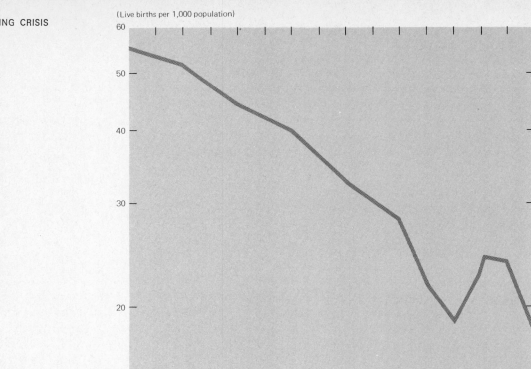

(Live births per 1,000 population)

Birth Rate, 1820–1970

Source: Statistical Abstract of U.S., 1971.

tradition. Whitman was a new kind of artist: the differences between literature and life were to him only a language experiment. Art was not oblique to life; it *was* life in the sense in which he referred to his collection of poems, *Leaves of Grass* (1855)—"who touches this book touches a man." (A woman once wrote to Whitman suggesting that they might conceive a child on a mountaintop; Whitman wrote on the letter, "Insane Asylum," whereupon his secretary asked if he had ever read his own work.)

A dedicated romantic, Whitman believed that the source of great poetry is the common and humble; at its best his poetry is soft and delicate. Typically, he chose for the title of his collection the smallest, most universal sign of nature's fertility. The technical sources of his work were in oratory, Italian music, and the sounds of nature. Oratory stresses the full beauty of the spoken word, and Whitman's rhythms are based on the parallel sentence structure so familiar to the orator. From Italian music he took the swellings and fallings off, the crescendos and diminuendos, the verbal equivalents of "easily written loose-fingered chords." Finally, Whitman believed poetic rhythm an organic response to centers of experience, the sounds of wind, pulsations of the body, and, reflecting his basic passivity, the "billowy drowse of the sea, of the elastic air...It effuses my flesh in eddies and drifts it in lacy jags."

For Nathaniel Hawthorne, nature was more a symbol than a source, and his stories contain numerous powerful examples of its symbolic use. Hawthorne's work takes its flavor from historical sources more than natural ones, and rests on the dramatic analysis of complex human interactions; he called his chosen form the "psychological romance." But his characters—they are never heroes or heroines—do not simply interact with each other; they are also bound to and affected by deeper forces. These take the form of ancestral curses (as in *The House of the Seven Gables*) or Satan-like characters, but they represent the forces of innate depravity and original sin from "whose visitations, in some shape or other, no deeply thinking mind is always and wholly free," as Hawthorne wrote to Melville. Clearly Hawthorne inherited more from his Puritan ancestors, one of whom was a judge at the Salem witch trials, than the historical settings and details which he used in his writing.

Like other writers of the American Renaissance, Hawthorne took an interest in the social and political world. Whitman wrote political poetry—most notably "When Lilacs Last in Dooryards Bloomed" and "Oh Captain, My Captain," two poems about Abraham Lincoln. Thoreau went to jail for refusing to pay taxes in support of the Mexican War, and produced the famous essay on "Civil Disobedience" which became the philosophical basis for Mahatma Gandhi's mass movement in India. But Hawthorne was involved in more conventional politics; he wrote a campaign biography of Franklin Pierce, who had been his classmate at Bowdoin College, and held several political appointments, including the United States consulship in Liverpool, England and, earlier, the position in the Salem Custom-house which provided him with the material for the introductory essay to *The Scarlet Letter*. Furthermore, he saw himself as a critic of the Transcendentalist social and political positions which came out of the intellectual community at Concord, and the Transcendentalist journal, the *Dial*.

Hawthorne's longest and best-known criticism of social reformers is found in *The Blithedale Romance*. The community of Blithedale is modeled upon Brook Farm, an actual experimental community with close ties to the Transcendental movement, and the place where Hawthorne spent eight months in 1841. Besides a critique of Brook Farm and its social reformers, Hawthorne included in *The Blithedale Romance* a portrait of a woman named Zenobia, who is both the expression of the dark and high-spirited female character found in much of Hawthorne's work and, critics agree, a character modeled upon Margaret Fuller, a dominant member of the Transcendentalist circle. Editor of the *Dial* and a close friend of Emerson's, Fuller's influence was strongest in her personal and intellectual interactions, rather than in her writing. She was a feminist, but died too early to be part of the women's rights movement;

her contributions were instead philosophical (through her book *Woman in the Nineteenth Century*) and through personal interaction (she held a series of "Conversations" for the women of Boston in 1839).

Immigration   Fleeing from political turmoil or economic distress in their homelands, over 4 million immigrants entered the United States during the 1840s and 1850s. Some made their way west, turning Minnesota into a "little Scandinavia" and dotting Milwaukee with German-style breweries and taverns. But trapped by poverty or afraid to leave the more secure circle of fellow countrymen, most swelled the slums of coastal cities. Like immigrants in other periods, the predominately Irish and German new-

W. S. Mount, *Eel Spearing at Setauket. Reproduced through courtesy New York State Historical Association, Cooperstown*

comers of the mid-nineteenth century encountered discrimination and deprivation rather than instant success. One authority has estimated that one-third died within three years; the hardship of the voyage and the disappointments after landing proved too much. Immigrants who naively expected to find goodness and ready opportunity were easy victims of fraud. Quick-buck artists descended upon each incoming ship, taking newcomers' cash or possessions in exchange for misleading promises of transportation, lodging, or employment. The exploitation and robbery of immigrants became a national scandal; in 1854 the Commissioners of Immigration estimated that over the past decade swindlers had taken $2.5 million from immigrants who landed at New York.

The influx of immigrants further disrupted an already unstable social fabric. These strangers became targets of virulent prejudice. During the 1850s the widespread anti-immigrant feeling gave birth to a nativist and anti-Catholic political party—the Know-Nothings—and employers often refused to hire Irish and German laborers because of their supposed taste for whiskey and beer. One Irishmen set his complaint to music.

I'm a decent boy just landed from the town of Ballyfad,
I want a situation, and I want it very bad,
I have seen employment advertised, "tis just the thing," says I,
But the dirty Spalpeen ended with "No Irish need apply."

Urban problems Cities were ill equipped to deal with this massive influx of new people, and the prior inhabitants blamed the disruption upon the moral character of the immigrants. These charges were unfair. Many newcomers came from rural America, and the very growth of urban centers created new problems such as sanitation and traffic congestion. As urban charity rolls and crime statistics mounted, alarm spread among established Americans; they began to search for new methods of maintaining social control. Temperance crusaders, capitalizing on the identification between liquor and foreigners, zealously advocated prohibitionist measures as a means of Americanizing newcomers. A variety of recently redeemed drunkards visited the immigrant wards, sensationally describing or vividly displaying the results of excessive tippling and eliciting pledges of abstinence from their listeners.

But Americans did not depend upon moral suasion alone. Discovering that they could no longer cope with disorder, crime, drunkenness, or simple congestion on an individual basis, leading citizens created the first police forces. In the past, a city dweller largely protected his own person and property; in a smaller, slower-moving city, disorderly behavior might be tolerated. With growth of a faster-paced, interdependent society, offenses such as drunkenness became more serious matters. As criminals became more sophisticated and the rewards of lawlessness became more tempting, citizens demanded an active, professional police force. Instead

Railroad suspension bridge near Niagara Falls. *Library of Congress*

of waiting for private citizens to come to them with complaints, policemen were supposed to seek out lawbreakers and prevent crimes. The precise functions and procedures of police work developed slowly, but by mid-century full-time law-enforcement agencies were a permanent part of urban life.

Westward movement

Throughout the first half of the nineteenth century Americans rushed westward. Promise of greater opportunity just over the next western hill seemed to glow even brighter than at other times in our history. In addition to the eternal quest for new lands—territory for the gluttonous appetite of King Cotton and other agricultural staples—the lure of precious metals began to fire peoples' imaginations. Discovery of gold in California in 1848 lured prospectors, plungers, and prostitutes to squalid gold rush towns and to larger hellholes such as San Francisco's "Barbary Coast." But there were also opportunities for more reputable entrepreneurs; Levi Strauss, for example, made a fortune selling sturdy, riveted jeans to hard-working miners. By mid-century, the United States extended its power from Atlantic to Pacific, pushing aside Indian nations and conquering half the territory of its Mexican neighbor. A Democratic journalist called this fulfilling our "manifest destiny."

Conditions in more settled areas forced some settlers westward. High birth rates meant that parents could not partition the family farm into enough homesteads, and they watched their offspring strike out for new lands. Relatively few went past the 80th meridian or on to California, but more and more people settled in the great Middle West. New Englanders, for example, streamed into western New York and northern Pennsylvania before pressing on to northern Ohio, Indiana, and Illinois and southern Michigan. Americans' cavalier attitude toward their environment also forced successive younger generations toward the Pacific. When so much new land seemed available, many farmers resisted adoption of scientific soil-saving techniques. Better to mine your holdings as intensively as possible, leave them exhausted, and seek new areas to exploit. Every section of the country experienced some soil exhaustion, but none as much as the South, where first tobacco and then cotton robbed the ground of vital nutrients. Cotton planters, southern versions of the fabled pioneer, expanded into the rich lands of Alabama and Mississippi and later edged into Arkansas and Texas.

Both the national government and energetic westerners encouraged the westward migration. Washington provided military forces to roll back the Indians and then sold off the territories to the white man. Federal land policies favored rapid disposal of the national domain. Some provisions—setting the minimum purchase at only eighty acres and allowing squatters first chance—favored smaller settlers. But large speculators discovered innumerable ways of obtaining sizeable tracts, and they, too, favored rapid settlement. Successful promoters rarely embraced large, self-contained areas; instead, they scattered their holdings in order to attract buyers to homesteads near other settlers. Many smaller farmers, with spare cash or good credit, became speculators themselves, adding a section here or there and hoping to sell at a profit when newcomers arrived.

The American spirit of boosterism, so often identified with the "Babbitts" of the 1920s, pervaded this age as well. Western businessmen touted the glories of their locale, and western newspaper editors filled their columns with promotional material. Such propaganda and booster spirit contributed not only to settlement of farms but to the growth of thriving commercial centers, such as Chicago, Cincinnati, and St. Louis. The pace of growth in many places outstripped the imagination of even the most optimistic boosters and fueled their desire for further expansion. Rural speculators and urban promoters engaged in spirited competition to attract newcomers to their areas.

THE PRESIDENCY OF JOHN TYLER

Tensions along the northern border

The rush into new lands created a series of problems with neighboring nations. Throughout the 1830s, tensions mounted along the northern frontier from Maine to Oregon, and violent clashes between Americans and British North Americans (Canadians) flared wherever the boundary line was unclear. Americans' sympathy and clandestine aid to an unsuccessful independence movement in eastern Canada further provoked Canadian authorities. In 1837 Canadians sneaked across the border and burned an American ship, the *Caroline,* which rebels had chartered to transport supplies. One American died. Tempers rose throughout the northern frontier, and the ugly incident showed the fragility of Anglo-American friendship.

War fever and northern land hunger seemed once again to be rolling the nation into war with Britain. In 1838 the State of Maine sent a posse into the Aroostook River region, a disputed lumberjacking area between Maine and New Brunswick. Canadians called up troops; Maine summoned its militia and asked for federal support. Congress authorized the president to sign up fifty thousand volunteers and approved a $10-million war credit. The "Aroostook War" threatened to become a full-scale Anglo-American conflict. The problem of escalating border violence fell upon a new administration.

A political maverick

The rollicking "hard cider" campaign of 1840 swept William Henry Harrison and the Whigs into office. On March 4 the hero of Tippecanoe was inaugurated; on April 4 he was dead. For the first time in the nation's history, the vice-president took over the presidential powers. John Quincy Adams, darkly forecasting trouble for the Whig party under Vice-President John Tyler's leadership, wrote in his diary: "This day was in every sense gloomy—rain the whole day."

John Tyler of Virginia was a political accident. Once a supporter of Andrew Jackson, Tyler (who had fifteen children—the most of any United States president) was placed on the Whig ticket in an attempt to attract southern states' righters. His views on crucial issues of the day —internal improvements at federal expense, national bank, and protective tariff—differed from the traditional Whig program of Henry Clay. And Tyler rapidly displayed his independence from the Whig mainstream, vetoing national banking legislation which Clay had adroitly maneuvered through Congress. In September 1841, all of Tyler's cabinet members resigned except Secretary of State Daniel Webster, and the Virginian became a president without a party.

The Webster-Ashburton treaty and the annexation of Texas

If a lack of loyal supporters handicapped the Tyler administration, it also gave it a broad freedom of action. Having nothing to lose, Tyler could take bold stands which the leaders of the national parties, carefully attempting to balance sectional interests, could not risk. Tyler the maverick reopened expansionism as a national political issue. The four years of his administration were devoted to foreign affairs with neighboring countries to the north and south.

Disputes over the Canadian boundary presented the most urgent problem, and Secretary of State Webster was determined to avoid war with England. Meetings between Webster and a British emissary, Lord Ashburton, produced an agreement splitting the disputed land in Maine and adjusting the boundary near Lake Champlain and between Lake Superior and Lake of the Woods. Secretly, Webster organized a propaganda campaign in Maine to prepare citizens there to accept his compromise, and the Webster-Ashburton Treaty became very popular despite Webster's territorial concessions. Pleased that he had preserved peace with England, Webster also resigned from Tyler's cabinet, which was, by this time, filled with ex-Democrats.

Webster's successor as secretary of state was John C. Calhoun. Like Tyler, Calhoun had a devotion to states' rights, believed that the federal government had no right to bar slavery from the territories, and favored expansion into the Southwest to give the South greater power within the Union. Calhoun and Tyler revived the issue of Texas. They submitted a treaty of annexation to the Senate, arguing that the United States should take Texas before British influence became too strong there. But many senators of both parties charged that Calhoun had invented the British "plot" for his own sectional interests, and the treaty failed to attract the necessary two-thirds vote. Tyler and Calhoun were undeterred.

Just before he left office, the president obtained a joint resolution (which required only a majority vote) from both houses of Congress annexing Texas to the Union. Mexico promptly broke off relations with the United States.

JAMES K. POLK AND AMERICAN EXPANSIONISM

Tyler had brought the issue of expansionism to the center stage of American politics. And in 1844 the Democrats passed over Martin Van Buren, their most prominent leader, to nominate an avowed expansionist, James K. Polk. To preserve sectional harmony within the party, Democrats wrote a platform promising both admission of Texas (to please southerners) and acquisition of Oregon (to please northerners). Henry Clay, the Whig nominee, could not counteract the growing popularity of "manifest destiny," and Polk, former Speaker of the House and Governor of Tennessee, became president.

The Oregon settlement

Throughout the campaign, Polk promised to assert American control over all of the Oregon Territory, which the United States and Britain had jointly occupied since 1818. Once in office, however, Polk began to search for a compromise with Britain, preferably at the 49th parallel. The British minister in Washington at first rejected such a boundary, which would place the Columbia River wholly in American hands. But the British government, beset by domestic problems and aware of the great number of Americans settling north of the Columbia, finally decided that the territory was not worth the risk of war. Britain accepted the 49th parallel (all of Vancouver Island remained British), and Polk put the settlement before Congress. In June 1846 the Senate ratified the division of Oregon. Although some Democrats angrily charged Polk with going back on his pledge to acquire "all of Oregon or none," most senators recognized that the recent declaration of war against Mexico made settlement of the Oregon question imperative.

The coming of war with Mexico

When the United States annexed Texas, it inherited a dispute over the southern boundary. Texans claimed that their republic stretched as far south as the Rio Grande River; Mexicans, while refusing to recognize Texan independence at all, claimed that the boundary of the province was the more northerly Nueces River. The national government could have avoided difficulties with Mexico by simply accepting the Nueces line, but expansionists pressed Polk to uphold the Texan claim. Late in 1845, Polk sent John Slidell to Mexico to negotiate a settlement. Polk was not prepared to compromise on the boundary, but he did offer to assume payment of American claims against the Mexican government in return for Mexican acquiescence. He also authorized Slidell to purchase

The Alamo. *Culver Pictures*

New Mexico and California. When two successive Mexican governments refused to receive Slidell on the grounds that his appointment as a minister had never been approved by Congress, Polk decided to use more forceful tactics.

On the president's order, General Zachary Taylor moved fifteen hundred troops out of Corpus Christi on the Nueces into the disputed territory. And as Taylor's army levied its cannon upon the Mexican port of Matamoros, American naval units blockaded Matamoros and approached Vera Cruz. In Washington, President Polk began composing a war message to Congress. On the evening of May 9, 1846, Polk received word of a "provocation" which could spice his request for a declaration of war. Mexican forces had crossed the Rio Grande and "shed American blood on the American soil." Polk quickly revised his address and presented it to Congress.

The Senate and the House both voted overwhelmingly for war, but the conflict stirred a storm of opposition, especially in the North. Anti-slavery spokesmen charged that the president had provoked war to gain new slave territories. Many pointed out that Polk's so-called American

255

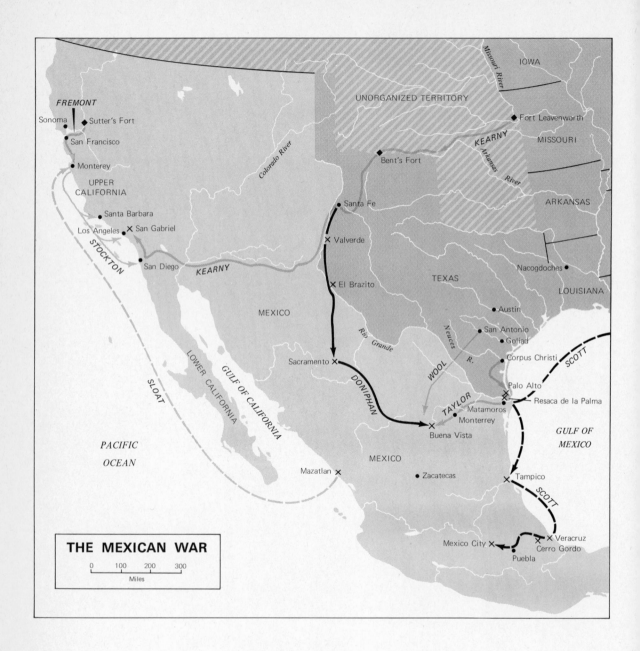

THE MEXICAN WAR

0   100   200   300
Miles

soil was actually disputed territory which United States troops had no right to occupy. The American Peace Society grew in membership, and Henry David Thoreau went to jail rather than pay taxes to support the war. One Whig congressman, who had once been a neighbor of the president in Tennessee, accused Polk of "an artful perversion of the truth . . .to make the people 'believe a lie.'"

Expansionists considered the war's opponents unpatriotic; to them the president's war message brought dreams of acquiring New Mexico, or California, or even all of Mexico. "War At Last," proclaimed the headline of the *Indiana State Sentinel.* Some people speculated that the United States could collect an indemnity from defeated Mexico in land instead of cash; others hoped that Mexican provinces would welcome United States troops and voluntarily ask to add their star to the American flag. James Russell Lowell, a Whig satirist, wrote that "our Destiny higher an' higher kep' mountin'" as our troops marched deeper into Mexico.

The Mexican war   Invading American forces found a nation which was embroiled in civil turmoil. Mexico, like its northern neighbor, was plagued with sectional disunity. Vacillating between attempts to create a strong central government and localistic desires to preserve provincial autonomy, Mexico sought the same political goal which also eluded the United States—a cohesive federalism. In the midst of such tensions, during the 1830s Mexico had fought off a French invasion and unsuccessfully tried to prevent the secession of the part of Coahuila province called Texas. These national crises left the nation even more fragmented; political instability mounted as various groups vied for control of the central government. The protracted political and economic instability made Mexico an easy military target. Compared to the United States army, Mexican troops were ill equipped, and its government was bankrupt from the long years of maintaining armies in the field.

United States military campaigns met with few defeats. On the northern front, General Taylor took Matamoros and Monterrey (in Mexico). Polk then ordered half of Taylor's army to follow General Winfield Scott in an attack on Vera Cruz. (Polk may have been genuinely dissatisfied with Taylor's performance or may have wanted to curtail the growing popularity of the Whig general.) With only half an army, Taylor still defeated the Mexican General Santa Anna at Buena Vista and Cerro Gordo. "Old Rough and Ready" then started toward Mexico City. In the meantime, General Scott's army landed on the eastern coast near Vera Cruz. A participant of the campaign described the day:

> We had an excellent opportunity of witnessing the landing of the first party—an interesting spectacle, as we fully expected they would receive a warm reception from the Mexicans. . . . The scene was certainly exciting and imposing: the military bands of different regiments

stationed on the decks of the steamers, transports, and men-of-war, played the national airs of "Yankee Doodle," "Hail Columbia," and the "Star Spangled Banner."

Scott's army then closed in on the Mexican capital, and after a few days of guerrilla resistance Mexico City surrendered.

From the beginning of the conflict, it was clear that the American goal was not just settlement of a boundary dispute but conquest of western territory. Before the war, Polk had secretly instructed an envoy to California that "if the people [of California] should desire to unite their destiny with ours, they would be received as brethren." When the war began, some Americans had already declared the independence of the "Bear Flag Republic" of northern California, and during the war Colonel Stephen Kearney took New Mexico and California in the name of the United States. Acquisition of these far-flung provinces, never under effective control of Mexico City, had long been the dream of expansionists who viewed the Pacific ports of California as a gateway to trade with the Orient.

The treaty of Guadalupe Hidalgo

With large portions of the country in enemy hands and the capital city occupied, a new Mexican government began seeking a peace settlement. Polk had previously dispatched Nicholas P. Trist as a negotiator, and although in late 1847 Polk recalled Trist to Washington, the emissary ignored the president's instructions and signed the Treaty of Guadalupe Hidalgo. The treaty granted the United States the Rio Grande boundary, New Mexico, and California in return for a payment of $15 million and the assumption of American citizens' claims against the Mexican government. The terms were not exactly what Polk had wanted, and he was furious at Trist for disobeying his orders. But the president was reluctant to reopen negotiations and submitted the agreement to the Senate. Withstanding pressure from some expansionists to use the opportunity to take all of Mexico, the Senate ratified the treaty and formally ended the war with Mexico. It was a victory for the United States, but one which reopened the explosive issue of the extension of slavery.

THE OLD SOUTH

A "white man's country"

The antebellum South presented a study in diversity. Many areas of the Upper South and tidewater regions faced severe economic decay. Years of intensive agriculture exhausted the soil, making commercial farming less profitable than in the newly settled portions of the cotton states. The 1850s were boom times for Mississippi and Alabama. But in many parts of the Appalachians, the mountain highlanders lived as their people had for years. Hardy outdoorsmen, the mountaineers displayed the fiercest brand of independence. And although the South lacked the great urban areas of the North, cities such as Richmond, Charleston, New Orleans, and Baltimore dotted the periphery. The South also failed to match the North's industrial output, but southerners did try to encourage industrialization during the 1850s.

Contrary to the beliefs of most northerners, especially Republican writers of the 1850s, the South was not a land inhabited solely by rich planters, impoverished "white trash," and enslaved blacks. Most southern whites lived on small farms not unlike those north of the Mason-Dixon line. Strongly independent and jealous of their right to be left alone, these yeomen approximated Jefferson's notion of the ideal citizen. They played an active role in local government and came to resent northern charges that they were simply tools of the planter "oligarchy." Throughout much of the South, society was just emerging from the frontier stage. The *code duello* remained part of genteel culture, and the "plain folk" often settled differences in equally violent, if less sophisticated, ways.

Despite the large middling class, the white plantation culture did seem to dominate southern society. Large plantations contained most of the South's vested wealth—in land and black slaves—and produced the bulk of its cash crop—cotton. The life of a plantation grandee represented the ideal to which most white southerners aspired before the Civil War. But plantation life was not all mint juleps, fancy balls, and lavish clothes. A plantation owner was a hard-working businessman with field work to supervise, workers to oversee, and books to balance. And his wife seldom conformed to the southern belle stereotype. Managing a large household required energy and intelligence, as well as graceful manners.

In some ways, the Old South resembled other sections of the country, but in one crucial way it was unique: the peculiar institution of chattel slavery distinguished it from the rest of the nation. Not only did the institution shape the South's economic relationships, but it provided a system of racial control. Even whites who held no slaves—the vast majority of southern society—had a vested interest in perpetuation of the institution. U. B. Phillips, a historian who was born in the South, summarized white people's attitude toward race and slavery in a famous article, "The Central Theme of Southern History." This theme, Phillips wrote, was the determination that the South should remain a "white man's country."

Slavery and black life   Southern slavery was no more homogeneous than the South itself. Slaves toiled on large plantations and worked on small farms; they rode as cowboys on the Texas frontier and sweated in front of blast furnaces; they lifted heavy cotton bales as deckhands and performed the intricate tasks of skilled craftsmen; they suffered in dark coal mines and served drinks on luxurious plantation verandas; they lived throughout the rural South and settled in urban areas as well. And black women were not simply child bearers, house servants, or mistresses of white owners. They too performed a variety of roles. In short, slavery was a flexible economic institution which could be adapted to enterprises other than cotton production. Black people were not ignorant, childlike fieldhands who were suited for no other task than picking cotton.

Most slaves in the Old South did work on plantations, and their labor helped to make cotton king. Almost half the black slaves belonged to planters who owned thirty or more bondsmen. Many of these toiled in the newer states of the Old Southwest. Here the work was harder and the conditions more brutal than in the more settled areas. Even the slave codes were harsher in the states of the Deep South. Many masters provided primitive living conditions, minimal clothing, and barely adequate food. Other owners, of course, were more generous, but few slaveholders lived up to the paternalistic image which has become part of the legend of the Old South.

Enslaved blacks faced the constant task of adjusting to the conditions of bondage. Outright resistance was suicidal, as the fate of Nat Turner's followers and of individual rebels clearly demonstrated. Similarly, escape to northern free soil was extremely difficult. Contrary to the legend of the underground railroad, only a few fugitive slaves ever reached the promised land to the north.

Instead of confronting their masters directly, blacks developed various stratagems of accommodation and subtle resistance. Under the pressure of slavery, a few may have become the docile "Sambos" which nineteenth-century apologists and some later historians have described. But many merely assumed the role of a childlike innocent. They became particularly adept at malingering, breaking tools, or deliberately fouling up a job, clever and oftentimes effective ways of attacking the system. A considerate owner, however, might receive greater loyalty and better performance.

Considering the hardships of slave life, blacks did remarkably well in preserving their identity and creating a unique culture. The black family, for example, may have been a more cohesive unit than historians and sociologists once believed. If plantation records contain instances of families being broken up, these same sources reveal many cases in which families remained intact, oftentimes over several generations. And even when spouses or children were sent to other areas, black people retained a great sense of family. After emancipation, thousands of blacks wandered across the South in search of relatives and loved ones.

The vast treasure of folklore demonstrates the extent to which slaves retained a sense of black identity. Slaves blended African and New World materials into their own culture. Black spirituals reveal the sorrows of slave life and refute the legend of contented "darkies" singing happily in the fields. As Frederick Douglass wrote, "Every tone was a testimony

Madewood Plantation, Louisiana. *Brown Brothers*

against slavery.... Slaves sing most when they are most unhappy. The songs of the slave represent the sorrows of his heart." Spirituals spoke not of freedom in the realm of heaven but of liberty on this earth. One song, ostensibly about the biblical Samson, expressed the wish that "if I had my way, I'd tear this building down." Similarly, field hollers and shouts, rather than indicating contentment, served a definite purpose in the slave's own society. These work songs provided the coordination and timing which were essential to men working under close and difficult conditions. They also helped combat the boredom of mindless field labor.

The brutality of chattel slavery and its obvious conflict with the ideals of American democracy may have bothered many southerners. But after the turbulent 1830s, articulate dissent from the dominant proslavery argument became rare in the Old South. Criticism of the peculiar institution came from the North.

THE ANTISLAVERY MOVEMENT

Colonization and gradualism vs. immediatism

The antislavery crusade had deep roots. Many Americans were embarrassed over the existence of chattel slavery in a republican land, in a nation which espoused the egalitarian rhetoric of the Declaration of Independence. Following the American Revolution a number of states abolished slavery, and opponents of the institution hoped that emancipation would gradually spread to other areas of the country as well. A number of important American leaders—Henry Clay and John Marshall, for example—supported the movement to colonize slaves and free blacks in Africa, a solution which would eliminate both slavery and racial problems.

Although many Americans, especially northerners, opposed the institution of slavery, most rejected immediate efforts to eradicate it in the South—a course which raised serious constitutional, economic, and emotional issues. Most antislaveryites believed that eradication of the "peculiar institution" could come only after a gradual process; they avoided any radical or immediate action.

But during the 1830s a small noisy band of activists began to call for the total and immediate abolition of slavery in the United States. To these crusaders slavery was both a national and an individual sin. They believed that right-thinking people should work to eradicate human bondage from society immediately; Americans could not wait for time or divine providence to solve the problem. Abolitionists such as William Lloyd Garrison considered African colonization and gradual emancipation dead-end courses. Large-scale transplantation of blacks outside the United States raised serious practical obstacles and grave moral difficulties. And southerners' militant opposition to gradual emancipation indicated that the antislavery movement could lose little by adopting a more

Patent medicine

A chair for an insane person

*The abolitionist crusade
in the 1830s*

radical stance. The victory of the British abolitionist movement in the early 1830s gave renewed hope to advocates of immediatism of the United States.

Abolitionism became one of the most prominent of the reform movements which emerged during the 1830s. Many abolitionists believed in the doctrine of "perfectionism." Perfectionists such as John Humphrey Noyes, who led the Oneida community, argued that all men, through an act of individual will, could cleanse themselves of sin and live in harmony with divine law. When enough individuals embraced God's way, the larger society could be purged of evils such as slavery. Believers in this romantic religious faith claimed that reform was not a political but an ethical question. By using the techniques of moral suasion—appealing to Americans' consciences rather than employing legal coercion—they hoped to end slavery in America.

Perfectionist beliefs led William Lloyd Garrison to abolitionism. He first embraced gradualism in the 1820s and worked with the famed Quaker abolitionist Benjamin Lundy before establishing his own newspaper, the *Liberator*. In unequivocal, bombastic language, Garrison preached the cause of immediate abolition with no compensation for slaveholders. "I *will* be harsh as truth, and as uncompromising as justice. ...I will not equivocate—I will not excuse—I will not retreat a single inch—AND I WILL BE HEARD." Many northerners dismissed him as a fanatic, and a Boston mob roughed him up in 1835; few subscribers rushed to purchase the *Liberator,* and for many years free blacks bought most of the copies. But newspapers throughout the country reprinted Garrison's fiery columns, and slaveholders cursed his name. The Massachusetts editor came to symbolize the abolitionist cause.

Abolitionism had leaders other than Garrison and gained adherents outside New England. Some of Garrison's contemporaries and a few later historians considered Theodore Dwight Weld an even more important figure. Like Garrison, Weld entered the movement because of intense religious convictions about the evils of slavery. After being converted by the famous evangelist Charles G. Finney, Weld devoted his life to the cause of moral reform. While a student at Cincinnati's Lane Theological Seminary in 1834, Weld organized debate on the slavery question. After eighteen days of discussion, students endorsed immediatism and rejected colonization. The next fall Weld and about forty others left Lane to attend Oberlin Institute in nearby Elyria, Ohio. Securing funds from two prominent New York City reformers, Arthur and Lewis Tappen, the Lane militants made Oberlin a center of abolitionist activity. Weld employed the techniques and rhetoric of the religious revival and converted many middle westerners to abolitionism; he and his followers

Henry Ward Beecher, the abolitionist preacher, in wood. *Abby Aldrich Rockefeller Folk Art Collection, Williamsburg*

spread their message throughout western New York, western Pennsylvania, and the Old Northwest. Weld also joined with his wife, Angelina, and her sister, Sarah Grimké, to write *Slavery as It Is*. A compilation of southern newspaper accounts which described the cruelties of slavery, the popular tract offered documentary evidence to support the abolitionists' moral outrage.

Abolitionists tried to organize one broad institution—the American Antislavery Society. Garrison, Weld, the Tappen brothers, and the Grimké sisters all belonged to the organization which claimed as many as five hundred local chapters. The national society supported a drive to seek, "in a constitutional way," congressional abolition of slavery in the District of Columbia and prohibition of the interstate slave trade. Abolitionists bombarded congressmen with petitions and memorials on various antislavery issues. Largely directed by Theodore Dwight Weld, the petition campaign attracted wider popular support after southern congressmen tried to "gag" the petitioners by automatically tabling their memorials. Former President John Quincy Adams, then a congressman from Massachusetts, led the battle for the right of petition, and "Old Man Eloquent," though never an advocate of immediatism, lent greater respectability to the movement. American abolitionists also sought closer ties with British reformers, and in 1840 many attended the World Antislavery Convention in London.

Divisions in the movement: 1840

By 1840 the American Antislavery Society faced deep internal divisions. A variety of issues splintered the movement: doctrinal conflict among various religious denominations, personality clashes, and disputes over incorporation of other moral reforms into the abolitionist cause. The major irritants involved women's rights and the question of political action versus moral suasion.

When Garrison's New England Antislavery Society voted to accept women on equal terms with men, several important male leaders promptly resigned. At the London World Antislavery Convention of 1840 female abolitionists found themselves segregated in the gallery, prompting Garrison and other sympathetic men to join them there. Most Garrisonians stoutly supported the women's cause, and female participation in the abolition movement gave a substantial boost to the campaign for women's rights. But many male antislavery activists charged that feminism would only sidetrack and dilute the crusade for black people's rights.

The dilemma of political involvement proved to be an even more divisive issue. By 1840 some antislaveryites considered moral suasion a failure; they had not even touched slavery in the South and had attracted few followers in the free states. The "log cabin and hard cider" campaign of 1840 symbolized Americans' fascination with politics, and many antislavery activists could not resist the lure of the political game. Over the strident objections of Garrison and other devout moral suasionists, political abolitionists formed the Liberty party. They selected James G. Birney, a slaveholder turned abolitionist, as their presidential candidate and framed a platform which called for abolition of slavery throughout the United States. Lost in the hubbub of the Whig-Democratic battle between Van Buren and Harrison, the Liberty party attracted little attention and less than eight thousand votes. Birney, in London for the World Antislavery Convention, was not even in the country. In the next presidential contest Birney did considerably better, winning almost sixty-five thousand votes, but the political abolitionists still hardly threatened the two dominant parties.

The tactics of nonviolent abolitionism

Some moral suasionists, such as Lewis Tappen, ultimately became political abolitionists, but others remained true to the original program. Garrison and his followers consistently opposed the Liberty party experiment, arguing that political involvement forced compromises of fundamental principles and inhibited freedom to agitate on the slavery issue. And any political effort seemed hopeless until individuals recognized the immorality of human bondage. Rejecting all types of coercive measures and retaining his romantic faith in the cause of perfectionism, Garrison even refused to vote.

But abolitionists were not simply romantic idealists. Many were hardheaded radicals who recognized the need for nonviolent agitation. They tried, unsuccessfully, to organize a boycott of slave-produced products; they worked to force churches into antislavery stands; a few helped slaves escape from bondage on the fabled "underground railroad" (more of a legend than a reality); many more assisted black fugitives who had fled on their own; and a very few, such as Henry David Thoreau, refused to pay taxes to support the Mexican War which he felt would extend slave territories. Abolitionists also recognized the propaganda value of some types of political agitation, particularly the appeal for state personal-liberty laws. These statutes defied federal law by providing procedural safeguards for persons accused of being fugitive slaves. Some even approached state interposition against the national government. Although they offered little real protection to blacks, the drive for personal-liberty laws did help dramatize the fugitive slave issue and connected antislavery with the cause of individual liberty.

Public appearances by fugitive slaves also brought home the fact of slavery to northern whites. Blacks made a dramatic impact when they told stories of life in the South, and many, including the famed abolitionist Frederick Douglass, spoke at antislavery meetings. Initially the protégé of white abolitionists, the highly intelligent Douglass quickly asserted his independence. His autobiography, a poignant account of slave life, sold numerous copies. Later Douglass edited his own newspaper, consistently urging militant action to bring about the abolition of slavery in the United States.

THE DEVELOPMENT OF SECTIONAL PARTIES

Free-soil and political sectionalism

The Mexican War widened the antislavery movement and gave it new vitality in the North. Acquisition of vast territories by the Treaty of Guadalupe Hidalgo raised the prospect of slavery's expansion into the West. Northerners who showed little concern about enslavement of black people in the South saw the spread of the "peculiar institution" as a cause for great alarm. Slavery once again became a national political issue. In 1846 David Wilmot, a Pennsylvania Democrat, introduced a bill in Congress which would have barred slavery from the area acquired from Mexico. The Wilmot Proviso passed the House of Representatives several times, but slave-state senators blocked it in the upper chamber. Wilmot's proposal marked a new turn in the antislavery crusade—the fight to make the western territories "free soil."

Unlike abolitionism, free-soil was purely a political movement. During the 1840s, many members of the Liberty party worked to shift their party's emphasis away from abolitionism toward an antislavery stance with broader appeal. In particular, Salmon P. Chase of Ohio—who later became a prominent Republican senator, member of Lincoln's cabinet, and chief justice of the United States—began to formulate a new program for the Liberty party. Chase accepted the dominant legal view that the Constitution protected slavery in the South, but he argued that the national government, without touching slavery in the southern states, should attack the institution wherever else it existed or might expand. This meant a ban against any new slave states, abolition of slavery in the District of Columbia, repeal of national fugitive slave laws, and prohibition of slavery in the territories. Chase's effort failed to revitalize the Liberty party, but his proposals formed the basis of the free-soil movement after 1848.

The election of 1848

In 1848 the Free-Soil party challenged the two major parties. The new coalition incorporated several factions: Liberty party men, including Chase; free-soil Democrats such as David Wilmot; "Barnburner" Democrats who opposed the party's nominee for president; and antislavery or "conscience Whigs" such as Charles Sumner of Massachusetts. More than ten thousand delegates traveled to Buffalo, New York, for the party's first convention, and most of them assembled under a huge tent to hear speeches from the movement's most illustrious orators. The revivalist atmosphere did not carry over into the nearby church, where hardheaded politicians chose former President Martin Van Buren, hardly an antislavery zealot, to head the party's ticket. Van Buren did pledge support for basic antislavery demands, and Salmon P. Chase authored a strong free-soil platform.

Despite the Free-Soilers' enthusiasm, the election of 1848 provided no clear national referendum on the slavery issue. The major parties carefully obscured the territorial question and offered two candidates who could not excite even their closest supporters. Rotund, old Lewis Cass, the Democratic nominee, had held his first national office under Jefferson. By 1848 his opponents ridiculed his slow manner—a young Illinois Whig, Abraham Lincoln, once compared Cass to an ox—and decried his lack of imagination. The Whigs did little better, drafting General Zachary Taylor. A veteran of more than forty years in the military, Taylor possessed no other governmental experience of any kind. Even his brother admitted that "Old Rough and Ready" seldom bothered to vote and lacked familiarity with political questions. But the party needed a winner, and the White House always seemed to elude the most prominent Whigs, Henry Clay and Daniel Webster. Taylor was nominated on the fourth ballot. In the election the Whig candidate outpolled his two rivals. Van Buren ran a very distant third, but Taylor's margin over Cass was very thin, each man carrying fifteen states. Had the Whigs lost either New York or Pennsylvania, Lewis Cass rather than Taylor would have faced the sectional storm which gathered around Washington between 1848 and 1850. Not since the troubled times before the Missouri Compromise had political leaders faced such agonizing choices involving the future of slavery in the United States.

The growing crisis The most complicated and, in the long run, the most explosive problem involved the status of slavery in the lands seized from Mexico. Southerners such as John C. Calhoun argued that the national government, being the agent of the sovereign states, had a clear constitutional duty to protect slaveholders' property in the territories, the common possessions of all the states. They bitterly rejected Free-Soilers' claims that Congress possessed the authority to prohibit slavery in these areas. Between these irreconcilable extremes lay several compromise positions. Some politicians, including outgoing President James K. Polk, believed that Congress could exercise independent jurisdiction over slavery in the territories and that it should simply extend the old Missouri Compromise line of 36°30' to the Pacific. Others, such as Senator Stephen A. Douglas of Illinois and Lewis Cass, contended that Congress and the slave states should leave the whole question to the persons who established territorial governments. This expedient of "popular sovereignty" allowed the democratic process to operate and permitted Congress to avoid a decision. And a few politicians suggested that the entire matter, which required intricate legal hairsplitting, should go to the final arbiter of the Constitution—the Supreme Court.

The territorial dilemma taxed even the wisest politicians' ingenuity, but there were other problems as well. Discovery of gold at Sutter's mill sent "Forty-niners" rushing to the West Coast, and in 1850 California sought admission to the Union as a free state. Many southerners regarded this possibility, which would tip the sectional balance against the South, as an ominous sign. The South, they argued, must find new slave territories or it would become a political minority. Other slave-state spokesmen revived complaints about the Fugitive Slave Act of 1793, a law which gave individual states primary responsibility to assist in the recovery of runaways. When the Supreme Court ruled that states need not enforce the federal act (*Prigg* v. *Pennsylvania*, 1842), several northern states adopted laws which prohibited their officers from aiding slave claimants. Southern representatives decried these measures and demanded a national system of enforcement. In addition to the problems of California and fugitive slaves, congressmen also confronted disputes over the boundaries of Texas, the status of Texas's prestatehood debts, and the abolition of the slave trade in the District of Columbia.

Congress debated these questions in an emotionally charged atmosphere. Political feelings ran so high in the Thirtieth Congress that the House required seventeen days and sixty-three ballots before its members could agree upon a Speaker. Northern and southern representatives sometimes allowed sectional distrust to flare into open hostility. When little Henry Foote of Mississippi persisted in taunting Thomas Hart Benton, the hulking Missourian charged toward his frightened tormentor. Foote backed away, holding off Benton with a cocked revolver. "Let the assassin fire," thundered Benton: "A pistol has been brought here to assassinate me." Most representatives armed themselves with pistols or knives, and cooler heads narrowly averted several violent confrontations. Outside Congress, southern extremists called a slave-state convention to meet in Nashville. Several members of the South Carolina delegation to the Nashville Convention openly urged secession if Congress failed to meet slave-state demands.

The old order passes

The nation's aging statesmen failed to break the impasse in 1850. Henry Clay, returning to the Senate after an absence of five years, attempted to put together a compromise package. He proposed admission of California as a free state, creation of territorial governments in New Mexico and Utah without any reference to slavery, abolition of the slave trade but not the institution in the District of Columbia, reduction of Texas's territorial claims in New Mexico, federal assumption of Texas's prestatehood debts, and a tougher Fugitive Slave Law. But Clay's omnibus bill stalled;

unlike as in 1820, the "Great Compromiser" could not harmonize sectional differences. President Taylor, among others, strongly opposed Clay's plan.

The remaining members of the great triumverate, John C. Calhoun and Daniel Webster, fared no better than Clay. Calhoun, so weak that he could not read his climactic speech, implored northerners to stop heaping abuse upon the South and to concede southern requests for sectional parity. Three days after Calhoun's address, venerable Daniel Webster replied with his "Seventh of March Speech" ("Mr. President, I wish to speak to-day, not as a Massachusetts man, nor as a northern man, but as an American"). As usual, "Godlike Daniel" enthralled the galleries with his slow, measured delivery. A female admirer once remarked that "nobody was so wise as Webster looked," an observation that prompted a witty senator to reply, "not even Webster himself." On this occasion Webster gave one of his finest performances, arguing that the law of nature would exclude slavery from New Mexico and that Congress need not worry about the matter. But Webster's speech changed few, if any, votes in favor of compromise. Within the month, Calhoun, long a symbol of southern ideals, succumbed to tuberculosis. Congress remained deadlocked until late summer. The House chamber became, in the words of one representative, "a mammoth cave, in which men might speak in all parts, and be understood in none."

The compromise of 1850

Fate, economic self-interest, and a young senator from Illinois ultimately resolved the deadlock. In July 1850, President Taylor suddenly died, a tragedy which fortuitously removed one obstacle to compromise. His successor, Millard Fillmore of New York, a practical politician with much experience, supported congressional efforts at accommodation. Meanwhile, a powerful lobby of Texas bondholders who held depreciated securities pushed for acceptance of Clay's proposals, including federal assumption of Texas's debt. Senator Stephen A. Douglas broke down the omnibus package into separate measures, skillfully maneuvering them through Congress. Douglas succeeded where his elders had failed. In early September, Congress passed the final part, the new Fugitive Slave Act, and the "Compromise of 1850" became the law of the land.

In retrospect, it is clear that the Compromise of 1850 did not settle the basic sectional problems. Congress accepted neither free soil nor southerners' demands for federal protection of slavery in the territories. Adopting the expedient of popular sovereignty, Congress left the question to the people in New Mexico. The new Fugitive Slave Law also proved to be divisive. Abolitionists and northern blacks denounced it as a cynical concession to slave hunters and a threat to civil liberties. The law contained no procedural safeguards, and it allowed federal slave commissioners higher fees when they found in favor of slaveholders and against alleged fugitives. Critics charged that slave catchers would use the act to enslave free blacks as well as to recover fugitive slaves. Some blacks immediately fled to Canada; others determined to resist the act. Free blacks in Boston rescued an alleged fugitive, Shadrach, from a slave commissioner's hearing room, and during an attempted apprehension at Christiana, Pennsylvania, a slave claimant was killed. Pledging their opposition to the law, leading abolitionists in Boston formed a vigilance committee which tried to frustrate operation of the act. "No slave hunting in the Old Bay State" remained a popular slogan throughout the 1850s. Although never as controversial as the territorial question, the new Fugitive Law intensified sectional differences.

Congressional action on the Compromise of 1850 also reflected the growing sectional strains within the major parties; the shrine of party loyalty was losing its sanctity. The stability of the two-party system had always depended upon avoidance of controversial sectional issues, but by mid-century both Whigs and Democrats found that they could no longer dodge such questions. In 1850 the territorial problem divided the Senate into not two but four political groups: northern Whigs who supported free soil; southern Democrats who insisted upon making at least part of the West into slave territory; northern Democrats who supported popular sovereignty; and southern Whigs who endorsed the northern Democratic position.

THE GATHERING STORM

An uneasy calm For several years the Compromise of 1850 did soothe sectional tensions; most Americans seemed to want it to work. The Nashville Convention adjourned with moderates outvoting secessionist delegates. Throughout the slave states, pro-Unionist sentiment dominated, and people failed to rally around the banner of "southern rights." Most northerners also accepted the basic outlines of the settlement. Even resistance to the fugitive law was matched by numerous examples of slaves being returned to the South. The new President Millard Fillmore and most northern leaders vowed that the national government would enforce the law.

The presidential election of 1852 demonstrated the strong pro-compromise spirit. Both party platforms warmly endorsed the decisions of 1850, and the two candidates espoused the same position. Whigs bypassed the aging Webster and the incumbent Fillmore in favor of another military man in the tradition of Harrison and Taylor—General Winfield Scott. "Old Fuss and Feathers" carried an impressive war record, but his electoral chances suffered from his close ties with antislavery Whigs. Despite the general's public support for the Compromise and the defection of radical free-soilers from his camp into a third party, Scott still seemed too dangerous for many southerners.

Sidewheelers on the Ohio River.
*The Public Library of Cincinnati
and Hamilton County*

The Democratic candidate, Franklin Pierce of New Hampshire, lacked Scott's liabilities. A handsome, affable nonentity, he too had served as a general in the Mexican conflict. When the leading contenders knocked each other off at the convention, the darkhorse Pierce captured the nomination on the forty-ninth ballot. A relative unknown, Pierce appeared to be everything to virtually every faction within the party. After a particularly dirty campaign—stories of Pierce's undoubted fondness for alcohol and Scott's alleged dishonesty abounded—the Democrats won a smashing victory, carrying all but four states. "The Whig Party seems almost annihilated," wrote one prominent party leader; "There may be no political future for us," another accurately prophesied. Scott enjoyed the unenviable distinction of being the last nominee to carry the Whig's once-proud banner.

Pierce's triumph was a disaster—both for "Poor Pierce" (as he came to be called) and for the nation. Shortly before entering office, his only son died in a railroad accident, an event which deeply saddened the new president and sent the first lady into a deep mental depression. On several occasions she held seances in the White House, hoping to communicate with her deceased son. In addition, Pierce himself suffered from persistent bad health, and he found Washington's humid summers particularly uncomfortable. Political discomforts also plagued the chief executive. The popular choice of too many factions, Pierce ended up with a squabbling cabinet drawn from all shades of Democratic opinion. Beset with these personal and partisan difficulties, Pierce also soon confronted a revival of sectional strife. The truce of 1850 proved to be short-lived.

The Kansas-Nebraska act

As in 1850, it was the problem of slavery's expansion which struck the sectional sparks. In January 1854 Stephen Douglas, chairman of the Senate's Committee on Territories, reported out the fateful Kansas-Nebraska Bill. As finally amended, it provided for organization of the vast Nebraska Territory, part of the old Louisiana Purchase, into separate areas of Kansas and Nebraska. More important, the bill abrogated the Missouri Compromise, which prohibited slavery north of 36°30′, and substituted Douglas's pet doctrine of popular sovereignty in both territories. If approved, the Kansas-Nebraska Bill would permit slaveholders to carry their "peculiar institution" north of the free-soil line of 1820, a proposition which Douglas himself predicted would "raise a hell of a storm." Although Douglas recognized the problems the bill raised, he tragically underestimated how violent his "hell of a storm" would become.

What prompted Douglas, principal architect of the Compromise of 1850, to reopen the sectional conflict? This issue remains a puzzling historical problem. Douglas was a long-time supporter of western expansion, and organization of the Nebraska country promised to speed up settlement and perhaps hasten construction of the long-delayed transcontinental railroad. Whatever Douglas's own motives, he activated other political forces. Reviving the argument that slaveholders possessed the constitutional right to carry their property anywhere in the territories, most southern Democrats quickly endorsed the Kansas-Nebraska measure. Repeal of the Missouri Compromise and passage of the Kansas-Nebraska Bill became points of sectional honor for many southerners. And at a hastily called meeting with Douglas, President Pierce also approved the bill. Confirming his contemporaries' judgment that he was a "doughface"—a northern politician with southern sympathies—Pierce made acceptance of Douglas's measure a test of loyalty to the national Democratic administration.

The Kansas-Nebraska Bill reopened the great debate over the future of slavery. Free-soilers denounced repeal of the Missouri Compromise as a violation of a solemn constitutional trust, as a triumph of slavery over freedom, and as a conspiracy of slaveholders and their allies against republican government. A rapacious "slave power," they charged, threatened the liberties of all Americans, north as well as south, white as well as black. The area of freedom had shrunk; the area of bondage was now expanding. Douglas vigorously defended his bill, arguing that his

William Mason : Engine #25. *Courtesy Baltimore and Ohio Railroad*

formula expressed the very essence of American democracy. Ridiculing suggestions that slavery would spread throughout the sprawling Nebraska Territory, he claimed that in "that climate" it was "worse than folly to think of its being a slave-holding country." Much of the debate degenerated into sectional name calling and personal attacks. Southerners frequently challenged northern representatives' sincerity about the racial question. Did opponents of the bill want blacks to come northward, asked South Carolina's Pierce Butler: "No, Sir; they would resist them with the bayonet."

Northern Democrats and southern Whigs, torn between party and sectional loyalties, faced an agonizing choice. Just before midnight on May 22, 1854, the House of Representatives joined the Senate in approving the bill. The close final vote, 113–100, illustrated the sectional cleavages: only nine slave-state congressmen, seven of them Whigs, opposed the measure; every northern Whig voted nay; and fifty-six northern Democrats broke party ranks to cast negative ballots. The party disarray in Congress quickly spread to the rest of the nation's politics.

Political realignment

A major political reshuffling followed enactment of the Kansas-Nebraska Bill. The Whig party quickly disintegrated, a victim not only of the territorial question but also of divisive cultural issues such as attitudes toward prohibition and the recent wave of immigration. The two-party system came apart during the 1850s; as many voters and leaders looked for new political homes, partisan alignments became extremely fluid. In Pittsburgh, for example, an "anti-Nebraska" coalition, controlled by former Whigs, briefly challenged the Democrats. And in Pittsburgh as elsewhere, the American or "Know-Nothing" party suddenly became a major force. Riding the crest of antiforeign and anti-Catholic sentiments and projecting an image of moral and political reform, the Know-Nothings did well in New England, Pennsylvania, and the Ohio Valley. After the elections of 1854, they could claim forty-three seats in the House of Representatives. Know-Nothings also gained power within several states. In Massachusetts they elected a governor and captured both houses of the legislature in 1855. The American party quickly faded, but another new party, the Republican, proved to be more successful. Republicans controlled the national House of Representatives in 1854 and swept to victory in many northern states.

The Republicans quickly became a major party. Initially capitalizing upon the "anti-Nebraska" furor, the new party provided a banner for all free-soilers. Republican organizers stressed their party's opposition to the extension of slavery. Borrowing earlier free-soil rhetoric, Republican orators championed the idea that an aggressive "slave power" was conspiring to make slavery a national rather than a local institution.

Northern citizens, Republicans argued, must stand firm against the spread of slavery and defeat the "slave power's" nefarious conspiracy.

"Bleeding Kansas" Conflicts over extension of slavery continually disrupted national politics after 1854. In Kansas, the Kansas-Nebraska Act touched off a bitter power struggle between pro- and antislavery forces. The territory became the first sectional battleground, and neither side paid much attention to the niceties of the democratic process. During the spring elections of 1855, so-called border ruffians crossed from Missouri to help vote in proslavery interests, but free-soilers formed a rival territorial government at Topeka. President Pierce gave his blessing to the proslavery administration.

Violence soon replaced political warfare. After a prosouthern band ravaged the antislavery town of Lawrence, an antislavery zealot named John Brown murdered five proslavery settlers in revenge. Although the disorder probably reflected the inevitable disorganization in any new territory, "Bleeding Kansas" soon entered the national political maelstrom. The struggle on the Great Plains became the center of an ever-widening sectional whirlpool. In May 1856 South Carolina Congressman Preston Brooks attacked Charles Sumner, beating him to the Senate floor with a birch cane. "Bully" Brooks's assault kept Sumner out of the Senate for several years, turned the Massachusetts senator into an antislavery martyr, and made Brooks a hero to many southerners. Brooks told his brother that "The fragments of the stick are begged for as *sacred* relicts [sic]."

James Buchanan and the election of 1856 The Brooks-Sumner affair reflected the political emotionalism associated with "Bleeding Kansas" and the territorial issue. Trying to cool passions and avoid further controversy, Democrats resurrected an old party workhorse, James Buchanan of Pennsylvania, for the presidential campaign of 1856. During the Kansas embroglio, Buchanan had been safely out of the country, serving as ambassador to Great Britain, and the sixty-six-year-old bachelor seemed to be a "safe" candidate. The Republicans also bypassed more prominent free-soilers in favor of the military hero and explorer John C. Fremont. Although a supporter of nonextension, Fremont's other political views remained vague. Fremont was an avowedly sectional candidate and the Republicans a purely northern party. The Know-Nothings tried to frame a national platform which would straddle the territorial issue. When a nonextension proposal failed, northerners such as Senator Henry Wilson of Massachusetts bolted the Know-Nothing convention and began their political pilgrimage to the Republican party. The remaining delegates selected former President Millard Fillmore as the Know-Nothing's standard bearer. In November Buchanan won the presidential contest, but the Republican party showed surprising strength. Fremont came within four hundred thousand votes of Buchanan's total and carried eleven northern states.

Buchanan, aged and in poor health, immediately faced serious problems. If the vexing free-soil controversy were not enough, a sharp recession hit the nation in 1857. This downturn underscored the importance of several unsettled economic questions. Renewed agitation over internal improvements, national banking legislation, and protective tariffs highlighted party differences. Appealing to former Whigs within their ranks, the Republicans supported a federally financed internal improvements program, a national banking act, and higher tariff schedules. In addition, the new party endorsed a homestead act which would provide free land for western settlers.

The Dred Scott decision

Despite problems with the economy, Buchanan gave greatest attention to the territorial question. The president initially hoped that a decision in a case brought before the Supreme Court in 1856 might remove the issue from partisan politics. Not only Buchanan but a number of other parties maneuvered to obtain a decision from the High Court favorable to their interests. The case, *Dred Scott* v. *Sandford,* ostensibly involved the freedom of a black man who claimed that his brief residence on the free soil of Illinois and Minnesota Territory had emancipated him from bondage. From the outset, however, Dred Scott's status was secondary. The real issue concerned Congress's authority to prohibit slavery in the national territories. The Court could have dismissed Scott's claim on technical grounds. But Buchanan, working through Justice Robert C. Grier, pressed for a broader decision; several southern justices wanted to use the case to support the proextension argument; and two northern justices countered with the free-soil position. When a decision was reached in 1857, each justice issued his own opinion, provoking abundant confusion and providing ample political ammunition for almost every position.

Chief Justice Roger Taney mustered five votes for his majority opinion. Taney, a Maryland Democrat, ruled that black people were not citizens and thus were not entitled to sue in federal courts. The Founding Fathers, he argued, regarded blacks as "being of an inferior order, . . . altogether unfit to associate with the white race, . . . so far inferior . . . that they had no rights the white man was bound to respect." The chief justice went on 'to declare that the Missouri Compromise violated the due-process clause of the Fifth Amendment. Any prohibition against slavery in the territories deprived slaveholders of the right to take their "property" into the area. The Missouri Compromise of 1820, which barred slavery north of 36°30', was unconstitutional. And by the same reasoning, the Republican position of free soil had no legal standing.

Two free-state justices, John McLean of Ohio and Benjamin R. Curtis of Massachusetts, rejected Taney's views, and many northerners joined in denouncing the chief justice's opinion. Conceived as a means of resolving the territorial question, the *Dred Scott* decision only intensified the sectional controversy.

The Lecompton constitution and Kansas

Like his predecessor Franklin Pierce, Buchanan aligned his administration with the South. Hoping to gain admission of Kansas as a slave state, the president endorsed a constitution drafted by prosouthern representatives at Lecompton, Kansas. Free-soilers had boycotted this convention, but they later turned out in large numbers to reject the constitution in a popular referendum. Despite this clear result, a product of the principle of popular sovereignty, Buchanan decided to force the Lecompton constitution through Congress.

The Lecompton constitution provoked Stephen Douglas and other Democratic supporters of popular sovereignty into an open break with the Buchanan administration and southern representatives. Some anti-Lecompton Democrats entered the Republican party, and a few Republican leaders began to hope that Douglas might become their nominee for president in 1860. Finally in 1858 a compromise solution, the English Bill, postponed the Kansas issue by authorizing yet another referendum, but the Democrats' intraparty wounds never really healed. The resulting split divided the Democrats, setting the stage for a complete rupture at their 1860 national convention.

The Lincoln-Douglas debates

As the Democratic party fragmented, the Republicans gained new strength. The 1858 elections demonstrated their appeal throughout the North, and the senatorial contest in Illinois uncovered a new party leader. A lanky former Whig named Abraham Lincoln stumped the state, debating the incumbent, Stephen A. Douglas. Both men agreed that expansion of slavery into the western territories was unacceptable to free-state interests. Slavery constituted a moral evil of such dimensions, Lincoln argued, that the nation must take a firm stand against its expansion. The "Little Giant," who at five feet, four inches provided a striking visual contrast to the towering Lincoln, reiterated his previous positions: popular sovereignty represented the only truly democratic solution to the problem, and the law of nature, in any event, made slavery an impossibility in the West. Unlike Lincoln, Douglas refused to consider the morality or immorality of slavery; he saw the problem as one of practical politics. On this point the Lincoln-Douglas debates highlighted an important difference between free soil and popular sovereignty.

The contestants also raised the issue of the *Dred Scott* case. Lincoln demanded that Douglas explain the effect of the *Dred Scott*

An early daguerroeotype of Lincoln. *Library of Congress*

decision—which held in favor of slavery's constitutional right to expand into the territories—on the doctrine of popular sovereignty. Caught in a political whipsaw, Douglas declared that people in a territory could still, in effect, bar slavery. They could refuse to enact the "local police regulations" which protected slaveholders' property. Without such territorial laws, the institution would not exist. Douglas's answer satisfied his constituents in Illinois, but it created further problems with southern Democrats who had already damned him for his stand against the Lecompton constitution. Although he returned to the Senate from Illinois in 1858, he faced stern slave-state opposition in his quest for the White House. And the debates elevated Lincoln to the role of leading dark horse for the Republican nomination. He and other prominent Republicans continued to advocate reversal of the *Dred Scott* decision and to praise the glories of free soil.

John Brown and Harper's Ferry

While politicians debated and planned for 1860, a determined old man plotted a more radical course. John Brown left Kansas, seeking to carry out his crusade against slavery in another part of the nation. Believing his was a divine mission, Brown secured financial assistance and oblique encouragement from several prominent abolitionists, including Frederick Douglass. Brown did not reveal his entire plan, and his supporters did not inquire too deeply. What emerged from John Brown's tortured soul was a fantastic, bizarre scheme to overturn slavery in the South itself. He hoped to provoke a slave uprising, arm black guerrillas, and create a black state in the hills of Virginia. In October 1859 he and eighteen followers seized the federal arsenal at Harper's Ferry, Virginia. As with everything else he had ever tried, this bold move failed. The black revolt never materialized. Instead a detachment of marines under Robert E. Lee beseiged Brown and forced him to surrender. Quickly tried and convicted of treason by a Virginia court, Brown and six coconspirators died on the gallows.

Brown's execution was a harbinger of the impending crisis. Cautious persons throughout the nation decried his actions, but others saw him as a symbol of a larger, more fundamental controversy. Many southerners pointed to Brown's act as a tangible sign of northern fanaticism. Displaying the lances which Brown had hoped to distribute to rebelling slaves, southern speechmakers raised the dreaded spector of racial warfare, the vision which had haunted so many southerners since the 1830s. The South had to unite, many people argued; it had to meet northern aggression with united resistance. And secessionists claimed that the incident at Harper's Ferry demonstrated that only through separation from the North could the South achieve security. At the same time, many northerners saw John Brown as the symbol of their supposed commitment to freedom and the South's attachment to slavery. Having faced death with courage and dignity—he stood for eight minutes on the gallows before the hangman threw the lever—Brown became a martyr to a noble cause. Longfellow, Emerson, and William Cullen Bryant penned laudatory verses; for a short time Brown's grave became an antislavery shrine; and during the Civil War soldiers went into battle singing:

> *John Brown's body lies a-mouldering in the grave....*
> *He's gone to be a soldier in the army of the Lord,*
> *His soul goes marching on.*

The election of 1860

The election of 1860, which like John Brown's raid both mirrored and intensified the divisive forces loose in the nation, demonstrated that the country was now divided along sectional lines.

In trying to select a candidate and frame a platform the Democratic party split into two antagonistic groups. At their April convention in Charleston, S.C., delegates immediately clashed over the territorial question. Southern extremists issued an ultimatum: the party must positively endorse the view that the national government should protect slavery in the territories. When delegates approved a vague plank supporting the principle of popular sovereignty, most southerners bolted the convention. Party leaders adjourned the session and called another meeting for Baltimore in June. This second gathering finally nominated Stephen Douglas for president and reaffirmed the earlier position on slavery in

John Brown, fanatic in a righteous cause

the territories. Once again southern representatives walked out. They and others who gathered independently in Richmond, Virginia, selected John C. Breckinridge as their presidential nominee and adopted a strong proextension platform.

Encouraged by the rupture of Democrats, the Republicans sought a winning ticket for 1860. Bypassing the controversial antislavery Senator William Seward of New York, the Republican convention nominated Abraham Lincoln of Illinois. Lincoln offered good antislavery credentials, possessed a strong following within the party, had relatively few political enemies, and lacked Seward's radical reputation. A person of strong principles, Lincoln was still a shrewd politician. The former railsplitter-turned-frontier lawyer also perfectly fit the popular image of the self-made man. The Republican platform reflected Lincoln's moderate image. It pledged support for free soil, a higher tariff, federally financed internal improvements, and a homestead bill. Republicans hoped to add to the eleven northern states which they had carried in 1856.

The Republicans' strategy and organization paid off in 1860, but the campaign seemed to reflect a martial spirit which was rising throughout the nation. Republicans organized groups of young men—the "Wide Awakes"—who paraded in paramilitary regalia, brandishing flaming torches, to the accompaniment of brass bands. Southerners formed similar organizations, and paramilitary groups paraded through the larger towns of the Old South. Hoping to dampen this sectional fervor and knowing that he could never win, Douglas traveled to all parts of the country. The "Little Giant" drove himself to the point of exhaustion, speaking several times a day. A fourth political organization, the Constitutional Union party, also preached the cause of national unity, but its candidate carried only three states. Although Lincoln gained little more than 40 percent of the popular vote, he easily captured a majority in the electoral college. He carried every free state except New Jersey, but he won only a handful of votes in the South. Despite their protests to contrary, the Republicans were a sectional party which espoused a pronorthern, antisouthern ideology.

REPUBLICAN IDEOLOGY

Free soil, white soil Republicans brought home the importance of slavery to northerners. Slavery was not merely some peculiar economic institution which regulated the conditions of labor between blacks and whites in the South. Rather it was, Republicans contended, a way of life, a social and economic system which accounted for the fundamental differences between the North and the South. And northern citizens should recognize, Republicans declared, that their party stood against the "slave power's" conspiracy to spread this baneful institution throughout the country.

The Republicans' attack upon slavery and the "slave power" always

Signing of treaty between United States and Japan, 1857. *Culver Pictures*

emphasized the principle of free soil. They further pointed out that "free soil" meant "white soil"—that prohibition of the spread of slavery into the territories also provided a barrier against migration of black people into the West. Arguing that the Democrats proposed to "flood Kansas and the other Territories with Negro slaves," Republicans claimed that "we are the only white man's party in the country." During his debates with Douglas, Lincoln made clear his belief in the inferiority of blacks and his opposition to granting them social equality. Many Republicans, including Lincoln, continued to believe that colonization of blacks outside the United States offered the ideal solution to the nation's racial problem. Many Republican voters disliked the "peculiar institution" and despised black people as well; for them fear of slavery's extension and contempt for the enslaved went hand in hand.

Not every Republican, of course, expressed racist ideas, and many displayed racial attitudes which were far more enlightened than the views of most Americans. But few openly espoused the cause of black equality. Henry Wilson, senator from Massachusetts, reflected the ambivalence of many Republicans when he asked white America to "educate, if we can, these poor colored children, and enable them, as far as possible, to improve their condition in life." Confronted with Democratic taunts about the "black abolitionist" Republicans, most free-soilers encouraged the idea that the Republican party was truly the "white man's party."

Slavery, free labor, and the nation's future

The Republican party's attachment to free soil also sprang from their free-labor ideology and their critique of southern society. Courting northern whites under their slogan of "free labor," Republicans posed as champions of social and economic opportunity for free, white workers. They argued that the independent "middling" person, no matter what his occupation, constituted the backbone of American society. "Under every form of government having the benefits of civilization," said a New York Republican, "there is a middle class, neither rich nor poor, in which is concentrated the chief enterprise of the country." Republicans emphasized the importance of the agricultural West in a society of free labor. They declared that their proposed homestead law would promote rapid settlement of the West, provide a safety valve for dissatisfied and unemployed eastern laborers, and encourage the type of virtuous citizenship which had characterized the early republic. "The middling classes who till the soil, and work it with their own hands," claimed a Pennsylvania Republican, "are the main support of every free government." Since the days of Jackson the Democratic party had trumpeted such ideas, but Republicans claimed that the Democrats' alliance with the southern "slave oligarchy" demonstrated the hypocrisy of their slogans. The curse of slavery, Republicans argued, should not be allowed to destroy free labor elsewhere.

Republicans contrasted a dynamic, fluid, middle-class North with what they claimed to be a static, structured, elite-dominated South. Speaking in Michigan in 1860, William Seward declared that the South offered only "exhausted soils, sickly states, and fretful and discontented people." The slave states, Republicans charged, lacked the virtuous, independent citizenry of the North. "Great wealth or hopeless poverty," claimed a New Yorker, "is the settled condition" of the South. Although such statements grossly distorted reality, they circulated widely in the North.

The West always held a special significance in Republican's free labor ideology. It was the land of opportunity, the area in which the whole nation might find a new spirit of republicanism. The Republican party pledged to protect this territory for free labor and free government. The "slave power's" designs upon the broad plains had to be defeated; once slavery took root, it would be very difficult to remove. In the West, Republicans argued, the basic conflict between southern and northern society was joined. In 1858 William Seward proclaimed; "It is an irrepressible conflict between opposing and enduring forces, and it means that the United States must and will, sooner or later, become either entirely a slave-holding nation, or entirely a free-labor nation."

In 1860, Republicans argued, the nation stood at an important crossroad in its march toward freedom and progress. In Republicans' view of history, the Founding Fathers had recognized the evil of slavery but tolerated it for political reasons. The Republicans of 1860 were also willing to declare that they would not touch the institution where it existed. They would even fulfill the fugitive slave clause of the Constitution, although many wanted the Fugitive Slave Law of 1850 modified to protect the liberties of free blacks. But Republicans remained firmly opposed to slavery's expansion. As they looked at the world around them, Republicans saw that enlightened nations had all rejected slavery, progressing toward a higher plateau of civilization. The United States, the beacon light of republican government, could not lag behind. If a free-soil line were not drawn, plots to extend slavery's domains would always convulse the nation. Acceptance of the principle of free soil, most Republicans concluded, provided the vital first step toward the eventual destruction of the institution of human bondage in the United States. In 1860 Carl Schurz, a prominent Republican reformer, asked southerners to "stop and consider where you are and in what day you live. . . . You stand against a hopeful world, alone against a great century, fighting your hopeless fight. . . against the onward march of civilization."

INDUSTRY AND TECHNOLOGY

Before the Civil War, much of America's manufacturing was done not in large factories and by great corporations but in relatively small individual establishments or partnerships which employed an average of about ten workers each. Widely scattered and located near sources of raw materials, these small plants primarily served local markets. Some economic theorists envisioned a continuation of the largely decentralized economy based in towns and small cities. Henry C. Carey, a prominent economist of the 1850s, expressed distrust of an economic system in which producer and consumer lived far apart. To Carey, the nearer a farmer lived to "the hatter, the shoemaker, and the tailor, the maker of ploughs and harrows, the less will be the loss in labor in exchanging his wheat for their commodities." But at the very time Carey wrote, growth of the factory system, the emergence of the corporation, and development of a national economy were steadily eroding old ways.

The growth of machine technology provides a good example of the complex, interrelated nature of industrial growth in the late antebellum years. Before the wave of immigration in the 1840s, the shortage of labor had encouraged capitalists to mechanize their operations. After 1840 businessmen in New England and in the Middle Atlantic states, mobilizing the capital which was more abundant in these areas, continued to expand their large manufacturing enterprises. The increased dependence upon mechanization created a whole new industry of machine making. Before 1840, most manufacturers fashioned their machines in their own shops; after that date, specialized operations began turning out machines and machine tools. Machine technology was transferable: technical discoveries made in one industry could be adopted to a wide variety of others. New techniques spread rapidly. This phenomenon of "technical convergence" enabled American manufacturers to improve the production of items such as firearms, sewing machines, and bicycles—products seemingly unrelated in nature and use but closely related in technology.

THINGS TO THINK ABOUT:
1840–1860

What changes were occurring in the United States at mid-century? Economic changes are described in Stuart Bruchey, *The Roots of American Economic Growth, 1607–1861* (1965), Douglass C. North, *The Economic Growth of the United States, 1790–1860* (1961), and George R. Taylor, *The Transportation Revolution, 1815–1860* (1951). Oscar Handlin's *Boston Immigrants* (1959) is very readable. Roger Lane, *Policing the City: Boston, 1822–1855* (1967) treats an important topic. The following books provide different views of the Old South and slavery: Eugene D. Genovese, *The Political Economy of Slavery* (1965); U. B. Phillips, *Life and Labor in the Old South* (1929); Kenneth M. Stampp, *The Peculiar Institution: Slavery in the Ante-Bellum South* (1956); Stanley Elkins, *Slavery: A Problem in American Institutional and Intellectual Life* (1959); and Richard C. Wade, *Slavery in the Cities* (1964). Thomas D. Clark, *Frontier America* (1969) and Henry Nash Smith, *Virgin Land* (1950) analyze myth and reality about the West.

What were the differences between abolitionism and free soil? Why did the abolition movement fail to attract large numbers of supporters? Why did the free-soil crusade gain more and more adherents? Gerald Sorin, *Slavery, A New Perspective* (1972), Louis Filler, *The Crusade Against Slavery, 1830–1860* (1960), and Martin Duberman, ed., *The Antislavery Vanguard* (1964) contain general treatments. David Brion Davis, *The Problem of Slavery in Western Culture* (1966) is an intellectual history. Carleton Mabee, *Black Freedom* (1970) discusses nonviolent tactics. John L. Thomas's *The Liberator* (1963) is a critical biography of William Lloyd Garrison. Benjamin Quarles, *Black Abolitionists* (1969) treats a long-neglected subject. Racial prejudice is described in Leon F. Litwack, *North of Slavery: The Negro in the Free States, 1790–1860* (1961); George Frederickson's *The Black Image in the White Mind: The Debate on Afro-American Character and Destiny, 1817–1914* (1971) is more analytical. Two important political figures are discussed by Richard Sewell, *John P. Hale and the Politics of Abolition* (1965) and James B. Stewart, *Joshua R. Giddings and the Tactics of Radical Politics* (1969).

How did the Mexican War reopen the sectional controversy?
Frederick Merk discusses the origins of expansion in *Manifest Destiny and Mission in American History* (1963) and *Fruits of Propaganda in the Tyler Administration* (1971). Two recent studies of the war itself are Otis A. Singletary, *The Mexican War* (1960); and Seymour V. Conner and Odie B. Faulk, *North America Divided: The Mexican War, 1846–1848* (1971). Chaplain W. Morrison, *Democratic Politics and Sectionalism: The Wilmot Proviso Controversy* (1967) and Holman Hamilton, *Prologue to Conflict: The Crisis and Compromise of 1850* (1964) discuss the political outcome.

What were the issues which severed the Union in the 1850s?
The slavery question is treated, along with the racial dilemma, in Allan Nevins, *Ordeal of the Union* (2 vols, 1947) and *The Emergence of Lincoln* (2 vols., 1950), James A. Rawley, *Race and Politics: "Bleeding Kansas" and the Coming of the Civil War* (1969), and Roy F. Nichols, *Disruption of American Democracy* (1948). Eric Foner, *Free Soil, Free Labor, Free Men: The Ideology of the Republican Party before the Civil War* (1970) is an excellent study. Michael F. Holt, *Forging a Majority: The Formation of the Republican Party in Pittsburgh* (1969) and Frederick C. Luebke, ed., *Ethnic Voters and the Election of Lincoln* (1971) discuss factors other than slavery and antislavery. The southern response may be traced in Avery O. Craven, *The Growth of Southern Nationalism, 1848–1861* (1953), David M. Potter, *The South and the Sectional Conflict* (1968), and Stephen A. Channing, *Crisis of Fear: Secession in South Carolina* (1970).

Thomas Cole, *View of the Falls of Munda. Museum of Art, Rhode Island School of Design,*
Jesse Metcalf Fund

1860-1876
seven | war and peace

WALT WHITMAN

Sensual, mystic, egoist, nationalist—all suggest the insistent celebration of life that characterized Walt Whitman. His poetry revels in the paradoxes of the new, expansive country. Closeness to nature, egalitarian assertiveness, a spirited, almost innocent humanity set apart both the nineteenth-century poet and nineteenth-century America. Yet if Whitman were child of his environment, his poetry became the father of a distinctively American literary tradition.

Whitman's life, apart from his writing, was almost commonplace. Born in 1819 in a small farming village near Huntington, Long Island, his family moved to Brooklyn four years later. Walt attended school intermittently until he was twelve years old, when he became a printer's apprentice. For the next twenty years Whitman's journalism career flourished—he became editor of the Brooklyn *Eagle*—only to founder when his ardent free soil sentiments angered Democratic publishers all over New York City. Although he joined his father in the real estate business, during the 1850s he concentrated more and more on poetry. In 1855 Whitman published *Leaves of Grass*, the first of nine versions of the only volume of poetry he wrote. Despite enthusiastic praise from Ralph Waldo Emerson—"I greet you at the beginning of a great career"—Whitman never became popular in the

United States, though toward the end of his life he was well-known in England. During the Civil War, too old to fight, he went to Washington as a government clerk and stayed there until 1873, when a paralytic stroke permanently destroyed his health. He lived with his brother George, in Camden, New Jersey, until his death in 1892.

Despite Whitman's sedentary life, his poetry proclaims the American spirit. Understanding the compelling magnetism of the western frontier, Whitman reveled in its naturalness, its freedoms. His best-known though hardly most original poem, "Pioneers! O Pioneers!" catches the exhiliration when old fetters fall away:

> All the past we leave behind
> We debouch upon a newer mightier world, varied world,
> Fresh and strong the world we seize. . . .

America's newness led Whitman in two directions, one toward democracy and individualism, the other toward mysticism. Noted for his unique ability to catch the sounds of workingmen or "the blab of the pave," Whitman glorified the individual, particularly his inherent goodness. This egalitarian element slowly receded as the poet more and more focused upon man's relationship to the universe. In "Passage to India" he wrote:

> Nature and Man shall be disjoined and diffused no more,
> The true son of God shall absolutely fuse them.

As Whitman contemplated eternity, the unity of existence—"I believe a leaf of grass is no less than the journey-work of the stars"—a confident mysticism soon pervaded his work. His realistic style shifted toward one more of collage, of symbols piled upon each other to create intuitive response. Content, too, changed. The final version of Whitman's longest poem, "Song of Myself," propels the reader among obscure complexities, shadows of substance and feeling:

> Do I contradict myself?
> Very well then. . . . I contradict myself.
> I am large. . . . I contain multitudes.

From it all emerges a sense of man's ultimate meaning—his sexuality, purposefulness, life itself—integrated, identified, even in a way sublimated into some timeless cosmos, a "wheel'd universe" before which the soul can "stand cool and composed."

1860 - 1876

1860	Abraham Lincoln elected president
1860–61	Secession of Southern States and formation of the Confederacy
1861	Firing on Fort Sumter, April 12
1862	Homestead Act and Morrill Land-Grant Act
1863	Emancipation Proclamation, January 1 Battle of Gettysburg and Lincoln's Gettysburg Address
1864	The Wade-Davis Bill, congressional blueprint for reconstruction Lincoln reelected
1865	Lee's surrender at Appomattox Courthouse, April 9 Assassination of Lincoln, April 14 Andrew Johnson's Reconstruction Proclamation 13th Amendment in effect, December 13
1866	14th Amendment passed; ratification complete 1868
1867–68	Reconstruction Acts
1868	U.S. Grant elected president
1869	First transcontinental railroad completed 15th Amendment passed; ratification 1870
1872	Crédit Mobilier scandal Grant reelected
1877	Rutherford B. Hayes declared president after disputed election Last federal troops widthdrawn from the South

THE DREADED ENCOUNTER

Secession and the failure of compromise

Even before Abraham Lincoln began his long journey from Springfield to Washington, seven states of the Lower South had left the Union. Seventy-year-old James Buchanan sadly watched them go, hoping that time and a new administration might reunite the nation. The Democratic president proclaimed secession illegal and declared the Union "perpetual." After bringing several strong Union Democrats into a reorganized cabinet, he also refused southern demands to surrender several military installations, including Fort Sumter in Charleston harbor. But Buchanan qualified this nationalism with the claim that the central government possessed no authority to coerce wayward states back into the "perpetual" Union. And even if the Constitution allowed the power of coercion, he feared that a forceful response would set off the larger conflict he wished to avoid. Long considered prosouthern, the aging president believed that abolitionists' fanaticism and the free-soil Republicans' menacing statements had pushed the South into a corner. In time, Buchanan hoped, northern extremists might temper their stands and permit some new compromisers to solve the difficulties as in 1820 and 1850.

But the "compromise of 1860" never came. A number of individuals and groups did seek some peaceful means of restoring the Union. A House "Committee of Thirty-Three" and a Senate "Committee of Thirteen" discussed various compromises; and a conference of elder statesmen, chaired by former President John Tyler, gathered in Washington in early 1861. Neither this Washington Peace Convention nor the congressional committees could resolve the crucial issue: the matter of slavery in the territories. The most widely discussed compromise proposal, championed by Senator John J. Crittenden of Kentucky, called for extension of the Missouri Compromise line to the Pacific and for adoption of an irrevocable constitutional amendment which guaranteed protection of slavery wherever it existed. These and other "peace" proposals were futile. The extremist fire-eaters, then dominating politics in the cotton states, probably would have rejected the Missouri Compromise solution; more important, Lincoln and the Republican party rejected any concession on the territorial issue. "Free soil" had been one of the party's founding principles, not an electoral slogan which Republicans would concede

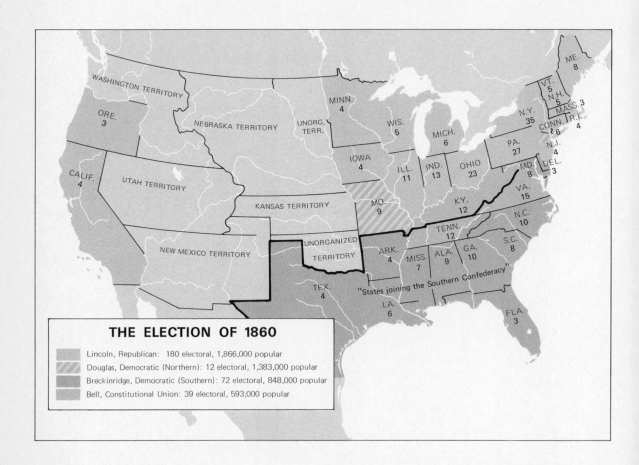

THE ELECTION OF 1860

Lincoln, Republican: 180 electoral, 1,866,000 popular
Douglas, Democratic (Northern): 12 electoral, 1,383,000 popular
Breckinridge, Democratic (Southern): 72 electoral, 848,000 popular
Bell, Constitutional Union: 39 electoral, 593,000 popular

to secessionists. Any agreement which permitted slavery to expand south of 36°30′, Lincoln believed, would only encourage the slave powers' designs upon Mexico and Latin America. The nation had to take a firm stand against slavery's expansion.

Although Lincoln and the Republicans rejected any compromise on the free-soil question, they did not consider their stand a necessary commitment to war. Throughout the secession crisis, many Republicans still believed in the possibility of a peaceful solution to sectional differences. Secession seemed an impermanent aberration, not a permanent fact of national politics. But Republicans differed on how to achieve reconciliation. Immediately after slipping into Washington to avoid a rumored assassination plot, Lincoln began conferences with leading Republicans, especially William Seward of New York. Many Republicans considered the New Yorker the party's real leader, and, as secretary of state, Seward probably expected to dominate the less-experienced man from Illinois. Seward did persuade Lincoln to delete from his inaugural address a statement which proclaimed an intent to "reclaim" Union property already seized by the secessionists. But Lincoln quickly proved to be his own man.

The problem of the forts

After taking the oath of office, Lincoln announced his position. Facing a raw March wind and reading in his high-pitched voice, the president assured the South that Republicans harbored no designs upon slavery in the slave-holding states. They would favor a constitutional amendment to protect slavery and would enforce the Fugitive Slave Law. But he made no concession of free soil, severely condemned secession as "anarchy," and pledged to "hold, occupy and possess" all Union property within the Confederate zone.

The most immediate problem was Confederate pressure upon federal facilities and military installations, especially Fort Sumter in South Carolina and Fort Pickens in Florida. Sumter, an important symbol of Union authority within the Lower South, provided the first test of Lincoln's policy and leadership. Sumter's commander faced an acute shortage of supplies, and Buchanan's earlier attempt to restock the fort with an unarmed merchant vessel had met successful resistance from Confederate harbor batteries. Faced with a decision on Sumter and several other forts, Lincoln carefully polled cabinet members and other important leaders. During these deliberations, Seward lost much of the president's respect by suggesting that the administration might provoke a war with European powers to unite the country against a common enemy. After great soul-searching, Lincoln took the calculated risk of sending a relief squadron to Fort Sumter. On April 4, 1861 he publicly announced the dispatch of several vessels.

Did Lincoln lure the South into firing the first shot? Persistent charges that he deliberately maneuvered the South into the aggressor's role are unfair. No longer confident of peace as he had once been, Lincoln certainly realized that his actions raised at least the *probability* of setting off hostilities. But Lincoln still believed that there was a *possibility* that the resupply mission might reach Sumter without a fight. The new Confederate government, however, believed it could not permit a successful relief expedition and decided to take the fort immediately. On April 13, a bloodless bombardment forced surrender of the garrison and began the most bloody conflict in American history.

Upon hearing news of Sumter's surrender, Lincoln acted swiftly. Without waiting for Congress to reconvene, he issued an executive proclamation calling for seventy-five thousand volunteers to put down "combinations too powerful to be suppressed by the ordinary course of judicial proceedings." When Congress reassembled on July 4, 1861, it legitimized this and several other quasi-military decisions, but from the beginning the president displayed strong executive initiative.

And the war came Since Confederate guns had resolved the issue of the forts, the status of the slaveholding states of the Upper South became the president's next dilemma. When he took the oath of office, eight of the fifteen slave states remained outside the Confederacy, and the president now struggled to keep as many as possible in the Union. In all of these states Unionist sentiment existed, but the Sumter incident forced immediate decisions. Virginia, Arkansas, Tennessee, and North Carolina quickly opted for secession. From seven the Confederacy had become eleven.

The sectional tug-of-war then shifted to the border states; through a variety of stratagems the administration worked to prevent the four remaining slave states from leaving the Union. After anti-Union mobs attacked federal troops and cut the critical rail line between Baltimore and Washington, Lincoln sent a detachment of troops into Maryland. Although Kentucky boldly defied the president's call for volunteers by declaring its "neutrality," Lincoln played a more cautious game there. He considered Kentucky—ironically, both his birthplace and that of the Confederacy's Jefferson Davis—the key area. "I hope to have God on my side," Lincoln reportedly said, "but I must have Kentucky." He refrained from sending troops to the Blue Grass State immediately, preferring to dispatch a shipment of "Lincoln Rifles" to Unionists in the western part of the state and to wait. In the end, the president's policies succeeded: Kentucky, Maryland, Delaware, and Missouri remained in the Union. In addition, western Virginia broke off from the rest of the state and entered the Union as West Virginia in 1863. The war had come, but the new president surprised his critics and boldly took command.

ANOTHER NEW NATION

Confederate government

The founders of the Confederacy claimed to be preserving traditional liberties and a settled way of life from the assaults of a hostile central government. The election of Lincoln and the "Black Republicans," argued secessionists, demonstrated the corruption of the American electorate and reflected the South's minority status; in such a situation, southerners must not innocently await the greater oppression which would surely follow. Only through separation could white southerners control their own destiny and enjoy the benefits, as they understood them, of republican government. Secessionists were not rejecting the American experiment; they believed that they were preserving it in its true, original form. They could leave the Union proclaiming that the North had trampled upon the Constitution, abandoning the cause of limited government and menacing the property rights of slaveholders. The Confederacy represented a revolution to conserve traditional values, not to change them.

The Confederate constitution demonstrated secessionists' basic agreement with American institutions. The delegates who assembled at Montgomery, Alabama, in February 1861 were generally moderate rather than fire-eating secessionists, and they selected Howell Cobb, a respected Georgian, as president of the constitutional convention. The constitution, largely drafted by Alexander Stephens of Georgia, followed the general outlines of the federal Constitution of 1787. In a few instances the southern constitution departed from the Union document: in the incorporation of a bill of rights into the constitution itself, in a six-year term for the president, and in a specific-item veto for the chief executive. It differed most radically from the original, of course, in providing specific guarantees for slavery. And unlike the Constitution of 1787, the Confederate document contained the word "slave" rather than some euphemism such as "persons bound to labor or service."

After accepting the constitution, delegates selected Jefferson Davis of Mississippi as provisional president. Davis had left Kentucky for Mississippi at an early age, attended West Point, served with some distinction in the Mexican War, and married into a wealthy planter family. Probably the best-known southern politician since Calhoun, Davis served as a United States senator and as Franklin Pierce's secretary of war during the 1850s. Acutely aware of the great burdens which secession thrust upon him, Davis labored hard—probably too hard—to make the Confederacy a success. He proved reluctant to delegate power and spent too much time on small details. One of his cabinet officers complained that the president had a tendency "to slide away from the chief points to episodical questions" and that cabinet meetings "would exhaust four or five hours without determining anything." Davis clashed with a number of prominent southern officials, especially Vice-President Alexander

Fort Sumter, South Carolina—the
beginning of the War between
the States. *Harper's Weekly,
April 1861*

Stephens, Calhoun's heir as the region's expert in tortured constitutional metaphysics. Although basically shy and reserved, Davis did provide a symbol of integrity and purpose which, at least initially, compared more than favorably with the awkward and inexperienced Lincoln.

Problems of the
Confederacy

The Confederacy could easily adopt or perhaps even improve upon America's governmental institutions; translating form into reality proved more difficult. Traditional southern fears of centralized authority and old-fashioned obstructionism frustrated Davis's administration. Governor Joseph Brown of Georgia, for example, consistently denounced outside interference in his state's affairs, even when such "meddling" involved crucial military arrangements. A few state courts issued writs of *habeas corpus* to release men who were attempting to evade the Confederacy's unpopular draft law. And in the hills of North Carolina and Georgia, "moonshiners" strongly resisted the efforts of Confederate officials seeking copper coils from homemade stills.

The absence of organized political parties also hindered the Confederate government. Lacking the lever of party loyalty—the Confederacy never developed a two party system—Davis found it more difficult than Lincoln to control his cabinet. Davis went through no less than six secretaries of war, five attorneys general, and four secretaries of state. Unlike Lincoln, Davis possessed no party machinery with which to fight obstructive state leaders, and he simply had to suffer the opposition and abuse from independent state chieftains such as Brown and Robert Toombs in Georgia. Finally, the lack of party organization impeded efforts to inform and mobilize the Confederate electorate. Lacking the party hoopla which had surrounded Jacksonian politics, Confederate elections apparently generated little excitement and failed to stimulate voter interest.

But in the end, the absence of available resources and lack of time to develop alternatives, not poor leadership or unshaped institutions, doomed the Confederacy. A sectional balance sheet clearly reveals the Confederacy's desperate situation: only one-fifth of the nation's manufacturing, less than half of the population, an acute shortage of hard coin and bullion. The South's chaotic railroad system consisted of mostly short lines, eleven different track gauges, and too little rolling stock. Largely devoted to agriculture, the Confederacy lacked the technology and skilled labor to undertake rapid industrial expansion. Richmond was the only significant industrial center, and the Confederate government soon left tiny Montgomery for Virginia.

The Confederacy's leaders worked hard to overcome these economic handicaps. After initially relying upon supplies from Europe, Josiah Gorgas, chief of ordnance for the Confederate states, built up a series of arsenals throughout the South. Both the administration in

Richmond and state governments tried to encourage development of enterprises such as textile mills, mining operations, shoe factories, and ironworks. But the South never approached the North's industrial output, and war destroyed most of the gains. Unfortunately for the "lost cause," the industrial spurt came too late and produced too little. Lack of materials forced some Confederate manufacturers to resort to bizarre expedients—such as using lard as a lubricant and cloth soaked in linseed oil for machine belts.

The Confederacy always faced serious money problems. Neither taxes nor loans provided enough revenue to run the war or to meet other pressing needs. The central government finally resorted to "tithing-in-kind," requiring farmers to pay the government one-tenth of their output of wheat, corn, peas, beans, and other crops. Officials also resorted to the printing press, issuing vast quantities of paper money. This unstable paper (which was not legal tender) quickly drove all other currency out of circulation, and merchants resorted to various expedients to compensate for the lack of small coins. Counterfeiters enjoyed a thriving trade. The Confederacy's harried treasurer, struggling to run his own presses fast enough, even suggested a plan by which the government would take in bogus bills, affix a "valid" stamp, and reissue them as legitimate currency. The currency problem undercut public confidence in the Richmond government and produced dangerous inflation. The price of flour in Richmond more than doubled between 1860 and 1862; soap went from ten cents to a dollar a pound; and coffee shot up from fifty cents to twenty dollars per four pounds. And although it was no comfort to Virginians, coffee was even more expensive in Texas at seven dollars per pound.

Southern society at war   Within a few years food shortages plagued many areas of the agrarian South. Cities, urban magnets which attracted ever-greater numbers of poor farmers seeking work and war refugees seeking protection, faced the most severe problems. In April 1863 some Richmond women, led by one of their number brandishing a six-shooter and a bowie knife, started a bread riot which escalated into a scramble for any type of food from anywhere. Richmond's City Hospital, for example, lost over three hundred pounds of beef during the looting. Only the intervention of Virginia's governor, a detachment of troops, and Jefferson Davis himself calmed the mob and stopped the pillaging. Richmond's experience was not unique; similar uprisings beset Atlanta, Macon, and Mobile, where marchers demanded "Bread or Peace." As always, the poor suffered most, but the wealthy also discovered that money could not always secure the amenities of cultured living. Southerners began substituting water for whiskey, and "cold-water parties" became the fad—even in fashionable old Charleston. One Carolina host judged his Christmas party a great success and concluded that the cold-water punch "answered admirably.

We danced until 2 o'clock. There were plenty of young ladies in town."

The war disrupted more than the drinking habits of Charleston's socialites; the conflict produced some significant social adjustments for women. Many plantation ladies began to work as nurses for the wounded or to run plantations in their husbands' absence. A few served the cause as spies and smugglers. And many women from the growing urban slums and impoverished rural areas labored, far less gloriously but just as effectively, in the new factories and ammunition plants. With the disruption of normal family life among soldiers, women also found the "world's oldest profession" a profitable enterprise.

Secession changed the ways in which whites exploited black labor, but the totality of the conflict also demonstrated black people's crucial place in southern society. On some plantations, where the white males had donned the gray, black slave "drivers" assumed greater responsibilities. In order to free more whites for military service, manufacturers used greater numbers of black laborers; in one Alabama factory black people provided more than three-quarters of the work force. In Virginia, which had more highly diversified and developed industries than most other slave states, black workers performed almost every service imaginable. Blacks labored on defense structures, unloaded ships, performed skilled crafts, and tended to wounded whites in overcrowded hospital facilities. The army used blacks as labor troops, and in the last

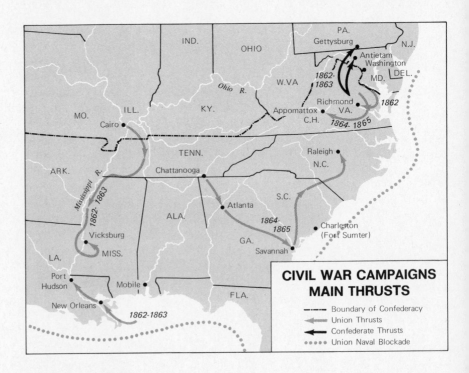

CIVIL WAR CAMPAIGNS
MAIN THRUSTS

----- Boundary of Confederacy
⬅ Union Thrusts
← Confederate Thrusts
••••• Union Naval Blockade

desperate days of the conflict the Confederate Congress authorized recruitment of slaves and free blacks to serve in the armed forces. Some black units were formed, but the war ended before they joined the regular Confederate armies. Although blacks never joined "Johnny Reb" in the front lines, they did play a significant role in the struggle for southern independence. Many others, seeing the opportunity to escape bondage, fled to the northern lines.

The war's effect on race relations is hard to measure. Some historians have suggested that the war produced gradual changes in the slave system which would have "reformed it to death." The war itself informally loosened the chains of slavery, and some state legislatures did enact laws extending the civil and legal rights of black persons. But the fearful reaction to President Lincoln's Emancipation Proclamation and the tragic history of Reconstruction suggest that white southerners were still committed to maintaining their area as a "white man's country."

THE CIVIL WAR

The war in perspective Writers have undoubtedly devoted more words to the American Civil War than to any other conflict in human history. The war coincided with significant improvements in journalism, particularly more effective use of the telegraph and greater reliance upon "on-the-spot" reporters. The press bombarded the public with accounts of the war's progress. In some instances battle plans or other classified information fell into the hands of scoop-hungry journalists who passed the news along to eager readers. And there was always the inevitable second-guessing of wartime strategy and tactics. In addition, more serious writers churned out endless pages of what one critic has called "patriotic gore." Lee's final surrender at Appomattox hardly interrupted these analyses, which reached epidemic proportions during the centennial observances of the 1960s.

Much of the writing concentrates upon the leading military heroes. Robert E. Lee, the quiet Virginian who turned down command of the Union armies to serve his beloved state, still dominates the literature. Scion of a distinguished Virginia family, Lee struggled against heavy odds to defend his native land and to keep his army in the field. And no account of the war can omit Thomas J. Jackson, a devoutly religious man who left Virginia Military Academy to become Lee's trusted "right hand." When "Stonewall" Jackson fell at Chancellorsville, a victim of his own troops' misdirected fire, the Confederacy lost their most skillful tactician, a general who consistently befuddled Union commanders with his lightning moves. In older accounts of the campaigns, Confederate leaders generally came off better than their Yankee counterparts, but recent writers have restored much of the luster to hard-drinking, tough Ulysses S. Grant. Lacking the dignified charm and fine breeding of Lee, Grant proved to be a skillful planner. Gaining President Lincoln's confidence in the less-publicized western campaigns, Grant later exploited the Union's superior resources to force Lee's surrender in the East. Generally the villain in magnolia-scented accounts, fierce William T. Sherman did lay waste a sixty-mile strip in Georgia, but he also was a resourceful field commander, outmaneuvering Confederate forces protecting Atlanta and the Deep South. Each of these men and almost every other important general has at least one sympathetic biographer and an equal number of detractors. But fighting under these near-legendary figures were many anonymous "Johnny Rebs" and "Billy Yanks," men who gave their lives and health for causes which many probably never really understood.

The Civil War, often called the first "modern" war, took a frightful toll in human lives. Submarines, ironclad ships, and torpedoes made their first appearance. More important to the average soldier, new designs in firepower also changed land warfare. Whereas the old smoothbore musket was a hit-or-miss type of weapon, the new rifles propelled a much more accurate, much deadlier missile. Although rifled cannons were not so much in evidence as infantry rifles, the old smoothbore cannons fired murderous cannisters filled with lead slugs, producing the same effect as gigantic sawed-off shotguns. Commanders adjusted slowly to these and other types of new military technology. Close formations and straightforward charges too often proved suicidal to the men in the ranks. Even in our age of B-52s, rockets, and "smart" bombs, Civil War casualty figures seem staggering. During a single day of fighting at Antietam, the North lost over twelve thousand men and the South about an equal number. And other battles which lasted two or three days proved proportionately bloody.

Even if a soldier were not killed at once, his chances for survival were not good. Camps offered only the most primitive sanitary facilities, and smallpox, dysentery, and typhoid could prove as fatal as the new weaponry. That conditions were not worse owes much to philanthropic organizations—such as Clara Barton's and the U.S. Sanitary Commission—which were organized to improve the life of the ordinary Union soldier. Because of the lack of money, conditions in the southern ranks were worse and relief efforts less extensive. Little could have been done to improve medical facilities in any case; doctors simply had not yet unraveled all the mysteries of treating infections nor discovered the need for sterilizing surgical instruments. Ambulance facilities were also primitive, and when a wounded soldier reached a medical tent he was often left in the hands of a tired surgeon working under extremely difficult conditions. Perhaps the most unfortunate men of all were those who rotted away in barbaric prison camps. Although commanders probably never carried on deliberate extermination policies, the fatality rate from disease and malnutrition reached three thousand per month in the stockade at

W. Homer, *The Army of the Potomac—A Sharp-Shooter on Picket Duty.*
Library of Congress

The 52nd Illinois Regiment, called the Lincoln'
Regiment, parades through Elgin. *Illinois
State Historical Library*

Andersonville, Georgia. And Union prison camps were better only by comparison; nearly as many Confederates died in Union installations as Yankees perished in southern camps. Writing of the centennial "celebrations," Robert Penn Warren suggested that a day of national mourning would be a more appropriate memorial.

The course of battle For most participants, the war's first battle, Bull Run (Manassas), killed the initial burst of war enthusiasm. Although "Old Fuss and Feathers" Winfield Scott was too infirm to command troops, this hero of the Mexican War joined others in warning against an ill-prepared Union advance into Virginia. But war is propelled by political as much as by military considerations; believing that the Union cause needed a quick victory, Lincoln ordered General McDowell to move on Richmond. Fashionable Washingtonians followed in their carriages, hoping to enjoy the action. Considering their lack of preparation, troops from both sides fought bravely, but General Thomas Jackson's forces held like a "stonewall," and the South had its first victory. Caught in the jam of onlookers, servants, and carriages, Union troops became confused; a fairly orderly retreat turned into a rout. Union forces had entered battle amid cries of "On to Richmond" and poems such as:

> A hundred thousand Northmen
>   In glittering war array
> Shout, "Onward now to Richmond!
>   We'll brook no more delay;
> Why give the traitors time and means
>   To fortify the way
> With stolen guns, in ambuscades?
>   Oh! Answer us, we pray."

After Bull Run, Confederates gleefully sang:

> Yankee Doodle, near Bull Run,
>   Met his Adversary,
> First he thought the fight he'd won,
>   Fact proved quite contrary
> Panic-struck he fled, with speed
>   Of lightning glib with unction,
> Of slippery grease, in full stampede
>   From famed Manassas Junction.

Neither side could rejoice for long; the war became a sobering and brutal business, four long years of suffering and bloodshed.

The overall Confederate strategy seemed clear: to stave off defeat until foreign powers extended recognition and assistance or until time forced the Union to recognize southern independence. Southern armies, however, could not remain totally defensive, waiting for the fumbling Union giant to find its strength; whenever possible, Confederate forces assumed the offensive to keep the larger Union armies off balance and to hurt morale in the free states. This strategy of an "offensive defense" was similar to the one employed by General Washington during the American Revolution, but the Confederacy did not always carry it off. Too often gray-clad troops were chewed up in inconclusive engagements with larger Union armies.

Gradually, Union strategists devised a plan of their own. After the initial stabs at Richmond, Union armies attacked on a broad front, in the western areas of the Confederacy as well as into Virginia. Following Grant's promotion to general commander, he and Lincoln followed a strategy of keeping maximum pressure on the Confederate armies. Their aim was less to conquer territory than to grind down southern manpower with the Union war machine.

War weariness and victory

By 1863 war weariness became apparent in both the North and South. Jefferson Davis faced continual sniping from his political opposition, and, for a time, Lincoln feared that he might not defeat Democratic presidential candidate General George B. McClellan in 1864. Running under the "Union" rather than the Republican party label, Lincoln capitalized upon nationalist sentiment and, in an effort to attract wider support, selected Andrew Johnson, a war Democrat from Tennessee, as a running mate. These political moves and union battlefield victories contributed to the president's reelection. Lincoln eventually outpolled McClellan by a wide margin, but his early electoral problems revealed the depths of popular frustration over the war.

Although the supply of army volunteers never dried up (partly because the Union offered a sizeable bounty to enlistees), both sides resorted to the first forced drafts in American history. Neither southerners nor northerners appreciated the innovation, but the Union law, which permitted draftees to buy their way out of the service, proved particularly unpopular. Antidraft riots broke out in New York City in 1863, forcing the government to send in federal troops. In the Confederacy, troop morale suffered because of the continual tardiness of paychecks.

In the end, the Union proved too strong for the outproduced, outgunned, and outmanned Confederacy. Initially Lee's forces did well in the Virginia campaigns, but in the bloody one-day Battle of Antietam (September 17, 1862) a larger Union army stopped a Confederate thrust northward. Antietam was an important turning point: it convinced England to postpone recognition of the Confederacy and encouraged President Lincoln to issue his Emancipation Proclamation. Despite the more publicized eastern campaigns, however, Union armies achieved their first great successes in the West. Here they employed their naval superiority

U. S. Grant: a better general than Robert E. Lee? *UPI*

in the Gulf of Mexico and along the Mississippi. With the surrender of Vicksburg on July 4, 1863, the Union gained control of the Mississippi River and split the Confederacy in half. At almost the same hour, another Union army threw back Lee's forces at a small college town in Pennsylvania—Gettysburg. Lee had hoped that his Pennsylvania campaign would compensate for the expected defeats in the West, but the Confederacy's deepest penetration into Union territory ended in disaster. Lee's troops suffered heavy casualties, and the defeat killed any chance of British recognition. Hard fighting lay ahead, and the Union strategy involved considerable time and manpower. But by April 1865 Lee's army had dwindled to twenty-five thousand ragged, tired, and hungry soldiers. Shortly after the dramatic meeting between Lee and Grant at Appomatox Court House, the other large Confederate army surrendered to General Sherman in North Carolina. The war was over. Southern legends of the "lost cause" began to take shape.

Black Yankees As the war dragged on, the Union began to use black troops against the South. Initially the Lincoln administration refused black volunteers; they feared that the appearance of black Yankees on the battlefield might suggest that the war had purposes in addition to restoration of the Union. Some northern officials also doubted the black man's fighting ability and feared racial friction within the military. But black leaders and white abolitionists continued to press the issue, hoping that military service would strengthen the case for emancipation and national protection of black peoples' liberties. Black abolitionist Frederick Douglass complained that blacks "were good enough to help win American independence, but they are not good enough to help preserve that independence against treason and rebellion." Eventually, northern war weariness and pressure from abolitionists led to acceptance of blacks in 1862. By the end of the war, almost one hundred eighty thousand blacks served in the army—about 10 percent of the total enlistees—and nearly fifty thousand—or about 25 percent—sailed with the navy.

Black soldiers faced even greater hardships than their white counterparts. Despite overwhelming evidence to the contrary, some commanders never altered their prejudices against blacks and relegated them to labor battalions. Because of discriminatory promotion policies, few blacks attained the rank of sergeant or gained officers' commissions. And throughout most of the conflict, the War Department even discriminated at the pay line: black privates received three dollars a month less than whites. Southerners also singled out black Yankees. Some Confederate commanders announced a policy of killing even those black soldiers, who surrendered, or of forcing them into slavery. Such action only encouraged blacks to fight harder. After observing two black regiments, General N. P. Banks reported that "whatever doubt may have existed heretofore

Sailors on the deck of the U. S. S. Monitor, James River, Va., July 9, 1862. *J. F. Gibson, photographer. Library of Congress*

as to the efficiency of organizations of this character, the history of this day proves conclusively to those who were in a condition to observe the conduct of these regiments, that the Government will find in this class of troops effective supporters and defenders."

POLITICS AND POLICY
IN THE NORTH

Economic legislation   The War for the Union dominated northern attention between 1861 and 1865, but it did not prevent politicians from dealing with other questions. Some of Congress's legislation advanced broader goals, especially encouragement of commerce and industry. The voluntary exodus of slave-state representatives removed some agrarian opponents of aid to business and, more important, reduced the number of sectional interests which Congress had to balance. The result, however, was not a simple victory for northeastern businessmen over agricultural representatives. Instead, a number of conflicting interest groups—occupational as well as sectional—lobbied in the wartime Congresses. Congressmen ultimately enacted a series of laws directed at the needs of the manufacturing and commercial sectors as well as at the dreams of agriculturalists.

Congress faced long-standing disputes over tariffs and national banking legislation. In the Morrill Tariff of 1861, passed shortly before Lincoln took office, Congress raised duties to 1846 levels. And during later sessions protectionists secured additional levies which boosted rates higher than they had ever been before. Congress also revised the country's banking structure. Ever since Andrew Jackson slew the "Monster"—the second Bank of the United States—the country had lacked a central banking system. The National Banking Acts of 1863 and 1864 created a series of national institutions which were to invest one-third of their capital in federal bonds. The banks could then issue paper money—national bank notes—in amounts up to 90 percent of the market value of these securities. In order to discourage the circulation of state bank notes, Congress later imposed a 10 percent tax on the issues of all institutions which did not join the national banking system. The new measures provided a more stable, national currency.

The wartime Congresses also extended federal aid for internal improvements. Competing sectional and commercial groups scuttled proposals to improve the Illinois Ship Canal and to construct a new waterway from Lake Michigan to the Mississippi River, but Congress did approve the long-delayed transcontinental railway. Plans called for the new road to run across the middle of the country from Omaha to Utah and then on to California. In addition to removing slave-state congressmen who desired a southern route, the war gave the project the justification of military necessity. In a series of acts during the 1860s, Congress granted private railroad developers 30 million acres of public land and extended generous loans. Once the sectional obstacles were eliminated, most representatives approved the railway proposal, a measure in line with the nineteenth-century policy, extending to this day, of using government to promote transportation projects.

The national government also offered assistance for other economic purposes. The Homestead Act, similar to a bill vetoed by President Buchanan in 1860, fulfilled Jeffersonians' vision of a continent of independent yeoman farmers. Under the 1862 act, settlers could file a claim to 160 acres of public land, live on this quarter-section for five years, and then receive title upon payment of a small fee. Republican congressmen, especially those from the Middle West, considered the Homestead Act a vital piece of party legislation.

The Morrill Land Grant Act of 1862 secured broader geographical support. In return for federal land grants, states would finance colleges devoted to education in agriculture, engineering, and military science (the forerunner of present day ROTC programs). Sometimes considered a western-oriented measure because of its agricultural features, the Morrill Act actually drew significant support from eastern representatives who believed that their most populated states would gain the most from the land grants.

When the war came, some critics expressed fears about the strength of the national government. The extension of authority during the war, whether viewed as a return to the Hamiltonian vision of national power or as a new assertion of federal supremacy, represented a substantial victory for those interest groups who sought to expand the power of the central government over the economy.

Lincoln and civil liberties

The Civil War raised grave constitutional problems involving the powers of the national government versus the rights of individuals. In 1860 federal courts possessed few guidelines for civil liberties cases, particularly for those involving the limits of dissent. To many lawyers, the infamous Sedition Act of 1798 always stood as a stark symbol of governmental repression. But the Supreme Court had never determined its constitutionality, and many legal authorities considered the Sedition Law perfectly valid. Although American Indians, Mexicans, and fugitive black slaves felt the brunt of federal coercion, during the first five decades of the nineteenth century legal disputes between the federal government and individual white citizens were rare. Requiring the extension of federal power, the Civil War forced development of some clearer standards in civil liberties cases.

Although faced with widespread criticism of the war and its conduct, Lincoln sought no new sedition law and mounted no systematic drive against protesters. A lawyer himself, Lincoln always agonized over civil liberties questions; more important, he wished to avoid political

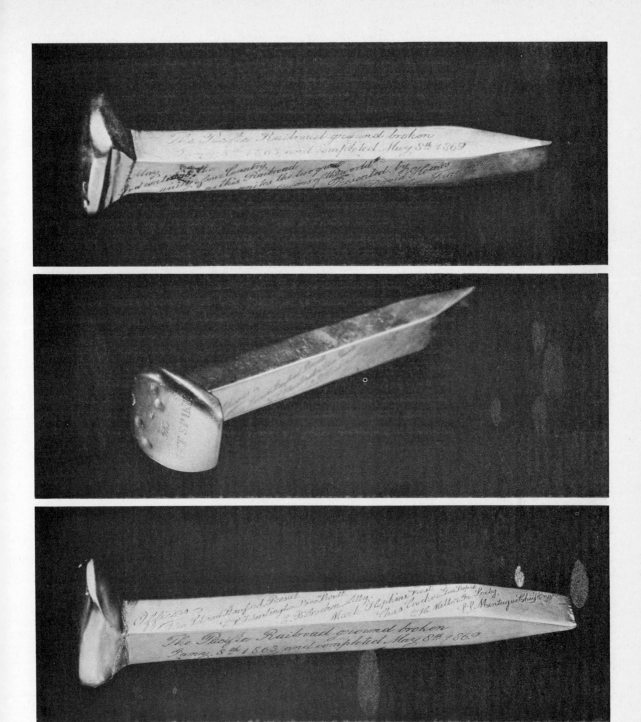

The Golden Spike commemorates the completion of the first transcontinental railroad.
Courtesy Union Pacific Corporation

and constitutional embroglios. Spectacular legal prosecutions, he believed, would only rebound against his administration. And even if he had wanted to conduct a reign of terror against dissenters, he lacked the prerequisites. There was no extensive federal apparatus to investigate and prosecute critics, and the Lincoln administration did not enjoy enough popular support to risk the backlash against such a crusade.

But Lincoln did not permit dissent to go unchecked. Instead of instituting judicial proceedings, the president suspended the writ of *habeas corpus* (a court order requiring authorities to bring a prisoner before a judge), and he ordered the State Department to arrest individuals under his executive power. Such procedures, which bypassed the courts and ignored congressional authority over *habeas corpus,* produced numerous protests. Despite the criticism, in the fall of 1862 Lincoln issued a general proclamation which declared that anyone discouraging enlistments, resisting conscription, or committing any disloyal act was subject to martial law and trial in military tribunals. The War Department enforced Lincoln's proclamation and arrested at least thirteen thousand persons, most of whom the government never brought to trial.

The most notorious example of military justice involved an outspoken Ohio politician, Clement Vallandigham. One of a noisy group of self-styled "Peace Democrats" (called "Copperheads" by Republicans and prowar Democrats), Vallandigham denounced the conflict as more than a mere military struggle to save the Union. Speaking for many midwestern Democrats, he claimed that the war endangered civil liberties, the traditional Democratic doctrine of limited government, and the interests of agriculture. As a congressman from 1860 to 1863, Vallandigham trumpeted all these themes and also stoutly opposed moves toward emancipation of blacks. "We are in the throes of a revolution," he argued, "and I cannot see what the issue is yet, but I dread the worst." Vallandigham's platform became "the Constitution as it is, the Union as it was." Defeated for reelection in 1862, he escalated his attacks, and in 1863 General Ambrose Burnside (most famous for giving side-whiskers their name) arrested the fiery Ohioan for his criticism of the war.

Burnside's ill-advised action permitted Vallandigham to play the role he long coveted—martyrdom—and gave Lincoln what he did not want—a hero for the antiwar movement. A military commission convicted Valladigham and confined him to prison for the duration of the war. Protests quickly developed across the country forcing Lincoln to find a way of blunting the Vallandigham issue. Using his executive power once again, Lincoln changed the sentence to banishment to the Confederacy, but even this failed to eliminate his determined adversary. Fleeing the South for Canada, Vallandigham ultimately returned to Dayton and renewed his verbal assaults on the Lincoln administration and the war. The president now wisely ignored him. The United States Supreme Court refused even to hear the Ohioan's claim that his arrest and trial were unconstitutional. Adroitly ducking the issue, the Court ruled that it possessed no jurisdiction over the proceedings of military commissions (*ex parte Vallandigham*, 1864.)

After the war was safely over, however, the High Court rejected the methods employed by Lincoln. In *ex parte Milligan* (1866), the justices ruled that martial law and military trials for civilians "can never exist where the civil courts are open, and in the proper and unobstructed exercise of their jurisdiction." Written by one of Lincoln's closest political associates, David Davis of Illinois, the *Milligan* decision represented belated vindication for persons such as Clement Vallandigham and provided some firmer legal protection for the right of dissent.

How should one judge Lincoln's record on civil liberties? Most constitutional experts have argued that the law courts must sometimes balance individual freedoms against the needs of the entire community. Lincoln himself believed that the chief executive should use his powers to protect the nation in times of serious peril. He also claimed that his moves were not "vindictive" but "preventive"; they were undertaken "not so much for what has been done, as for what probably would be done." But some libertarians have claimed that balancing individual freedoms and societal "needs" inevitably dilutes personal liberties. Lincoln's actions presaged more serious violations of individual freedoms during World Wars I and II. And if the Great Emancipator did not adopt the sweeping measures of Woodrow Wilson and Franklin Roosevelt, it may have only been because he lacked the means of coercion and the popular support these later wartime presidents enjoyed. Any final assessment of Lincoln's record largely depends upon how one weighs the sometimes conflicting values of personal liberty and public safety.

THE CIVIL WAR
AND THE RACE QUESTION

The war and racial justice

The North first envisioned the war as one to save the Union. Lincoln maintained that the nation was indivisible and that "no State, upon its own mere motion, can lawfully get out of the Union." Soon after hostilities began, Congress adopted a resolution which announced the limited purpose of the northern war effort: it was "not waged...in any spirit of oppression or for....overthrowing or interfering with the rights or established institutions of those states." This statement committed the government only to an effort "to defend and maintain the supremacy of the Constitution." In short, the administration's task was to put down the illegal insurrection without abolishing slavery or affecting the status of black people.

As the conflict dragged on, however, the question of war goals became more complicated. A small group of Republicans championed the theory that the seceding states had committed constitutional "suicide" and reverted to territorial status. They were not still members of the indivisible Union, as Lincoln maintained. Such constitutional arguments were not mere hairsplitting; if the secessionist areas were territories, then Congress could exercise greater authority in "reconstructing" them after the war. Some Republicans envisioned not only emancipation but legal, political, and economic gains for the former slaves. Other congressional Republicans supported more moderate goals, and some conservatives joined Democrats in opposing any change in the South's pattern of race relations. Alignments shifted according to precise issues, but gradually a small, ill-defined group of "radical" Republicans emerged as the champion of abolishing slavery and protecting the rights of black people.

Wartime pressures and events pushed northern racial policies in a libertarian direction. To be sure, white racism remained strong—New York City's antidraft rioters lynched several blacks and burned an Afro-American orphanage in 1863—but abolitionists and black civil rights leaders achieved some successes during the war. The national government made a number of symbolic gestures which repudiated the racist position of the Supreme Court in the *Dred Scott* decision. For the first time, blacks sat in the congressional visitors' gallery, attended lectures at the Smithsonian Museum, and marched in a presidential parade. More important, Congress repealed an 1825 law which prohibited blacks from carrying the mail, abolished slavery in the territories, enacted a plan of compensated emancipation for the District of Columbia, and ended the ban against black witnesses testifying in federal courts. And some states, under pressure from the civil rights forces, passed statutes desegregating public transportation facilities and repealed other discriminatory laws. Black people still did not enjoy all the rights and privileges of whites, but some progress toward racial justice occurred during the Civil War.

The crusade for emancipation

White abolitionists and black leaders pressed for emancipation. President Lincoln resisted these entreaties, fearing that any early move would alienate Unionists within the slave states. Early in the war, the president modified General John C. Fremont's order freeing all slaves in Missouri. By 1862 Lincoln altered his views somewhat; he asked Congress to grant federal funds to any state which would adopt a program of gradual emancipation. Although Congress failed to act on this suggestion, the Second Confiscation Act (1862) declared that all slaves of rebel masters would be free as soon as they came within the Union army's lines. Appeals from abolitionist groups and Congress's piecemeal attacks on slavery provided two reasons for Lincoln to issue his Emancipation Proclamation; concern that European nations might recognize the Confederacy

Antietam. *Alexander Gardner, photographer*

Draft riots in New York City.
Culver Pictures

also influenced the president's decision. "I cannot imagine that any European power would dare recognize and aid the Southern Confederacy," he wrote, "if it became clear that the Confederacy stands for slavery and the Union for freedom."

In September 1862, following the Union victory at Antietam, Lincoln issued a preliminary Emancipation Proclamation. Frequently misunderstood as a primarily humanitarian gesture, the preliminary proclamation and the final one which followed were actually conservative, highly political documents. The president's action applied only to areas of the Confederacy still in rebellion on January 1, 1863; it exempted the border states and all parts of the South which were then in Union hands. Secretary of State Seward reportedly observed that the administration emancipated slaves "where we cannot reach them" and held them "in bondage where we can set them free." Employing no ringing phrases on behalf of human liberty, Lincoln justified qualified emancipation as "a fit and necessary war measure for suppressing the rebellion." Lincoln further suggested that Congress should provide a system of gradual, compensated emancipation under state control. The president's actions were limited—in many respects the Emancipation Proclamation added little to the Second Confiscation Act—but they were not without significance. Most northern blacks applauded the president, viewing his moves as important first steps toward total emancipation. Following announcement of the preliminary Emancipation Proclamation, army recruiters began enrolling black volunteers, long a goal of Afro-American leaders. And in January 1865 Congress, with the support of the president, submitted the Thirteenth Amendment—outlawing slavery throughout the nation—to the states for ratification.

THE PROBLEM OF RECONSTRUCTION

Lincoln, Congress, and Reconstruction

Emancipation did not end the problems involved in restoring the Union; it made them more difficult. Lincoln originally hoped for a speedy end to the war and a rapid resumption of antebellum political ties. Although events on the battlefield made these goals impossible, the president continued to advocate a flexible, moderate approach to postwar Reconstruction. Lincoln had never been an abolitionist or a supporter of the broad libertarian goals of some antislavery Republicans. He always approached racial issues cautiously. Even after supporting emancipation, he hoped that the process would be gradual and largely under the direction of state officials in the former slave areas. Colonization of blacks outside the United States, he thought, was the ideal solution to America's racial problems. And Lincoln was always a cagey politician. He had spent most of his political life in the now-defunct Whig party, and he undoubtedly

Lincoln in the White House.
Culver Pictures

wished to shape moderate policies which would attract former Whigs in both the North and the South.

In late 1863 Lincoln outlined a formal plan for Confederate areas coming under Union control. He offered a relatively easy Reconstruction for whites and minimal changes for blacks. Under his "10 percent plan," whenever a total of white voters equal to one-tenth of those who had voted in 1860 took an oath of future loyalty to the Union and its laws, they could form a new state government. Before the war ended, Lincoln recognized "10 percent" governments in Arkansas, Tennessee, and Louisiana, and he organized Unionist regimes in other areas of the South. But Congress refused to admit representatives from these states, and their electoral votes were not counted in the presidential contest of 1864. Lincoln agreed that Congress should play some role in the Reconstruction process, but he always sought to maximize presidential leadership and minimize congressional participation.

Abolitionists, black leaders, and radical Republicans urged congressmen to demand more fundamental changes in the South, particularly firm guarantees for the civil and political rights of blacks. The radicals did not control Congress, but even moderates supported a more thoroughgoing program than the president's 10 percent plan. The Wade-Davis Bill of 1864 required 50 percent of white adult males to take loyalty oaths before southerners could form new state governments; furthermore, before persons could vote for delegates to state constitutional conventions, they would have to take "ironclad" oaths, swearing that they had never supported the secessionist cause. Despite pressure for guaranteeing suffrage to blacks in the South, Congress, like the president, limited the vote to whites. But Lincoln saw the Wade-Davis Bill (which unlike his own plan would not be operative until after the war) as too harsh and as a challenge to presidential leadership. To the surprise of many Republicans, he pocket-vetoed the bill.

Lincoln and many members of his party in Congress differed over the details of Reconstruction, but it would be inaccurate to picture him as seriously at odds with more than a few radicals. Lincoln and congressional Republicans agreed on a number of fundamental issues: the necessity for Republican party unity; the need for the national government's participation in the Reconstruction process, and the requirement of some minimal guarantees for the rights of newly freed slaves. And on the crucial suffrage question, Lincoln seemed to offer some hope of compromise with even the radicals. Shortly before his death, the president endorsed at least qualified suffrage for "very intelligent" blacks and former black soldiers in the Union army. Throughout the war, Lincoln and Republican congressional leaders worked out policy on a number of issues, and Lincoln's whole political career revealed that he knew the value of flexibility. The tragic events at Ford's Theatre, however, removed

Lincoln from the scene and brought to the White House an unknown political factor: Andrew Johnson of Tennessee.

The first
President Johnson

Andrew Johnson puzzled his contemporaries, and historians have done little better explaining this complicated man. Rising to prominence as a Jacksonian Democrat, Johnson received the second spot on the 1864 ticket because of his strong pro-Union views. He himself was an intended target of the plot which struck down the president, but Johnson's rum-soaked would-be assassin lost his courage. Thrust into power at a crucial point in the nation's history, Johnson was a politician without a party, a former slaveowner presiding over emancipation, and a racist confronting strong pressures to extend civil rights to black Americans. Johnson sometimes seemed all too aware of his humble origins and his limited qualifications for high office. But like any president succeeding a fallen leader, he enjoyed initial goodwill, even from many radical Republicans. The break with Congress, which would lead to his impeachment, came gradually and was largely Johnson's own doing.

Johnson's failure owed mainly to his inability to appreciate the mood of most congressmen and the majority of northern voters. He wanted a lenient "restoration" process, and he hoped to carry it out quickly and present Congress with a *fait accompli*. Such a course was obviously bound to alienate congressional Republicans, particularly when it turned out that the so-called Johnson government in the South contained a number of former Confederate leaders and adopted laws placing blacks in a position of quasi slavery. These "black codes" restricted the rights of blacks in a number of ways, but the most ominous sections required them to work and provided stiff penalties for unemployment or lack of a permanent residence. The Civil War had deeply touched many northerners, and the gray tinge of the "restored" governments and the black codes seemed to indicate that southerners remained rebels at heart. Northerners began to insist that the South acknowledge defeat, and changing the status of blacks seemed an appropriate sign. In addition, growing numbers of Republicans demanded that emancipation mean something more than slavery under a different name. Congress created the Freedmen's Bureau, a federal agency designed to provide economic and social assistance to blacks, and passed the Civil Rights Act of 1866, a measure which conferred citizenship on the freedmen and guaranteed a number of their civil and political rights. When Johnson vetoed both of these measures—actions which Congress overrode—he separated himself from Republican moderates and from many northern voters. Eventually in March 1868 Johnson's congressional enemies initiated impeachment proceedings, charging the President with "high crimes and misdemeanors in office." The legal case against Johnson was weak, but political passions ran high. Johnson escaped by only one vote.

Why did Johnson misread the situation? Historians have proposed numerous explanations. Johnson the political outsider failed to understand congressional politics and isolated himself from the Republican majority. Raised in the states' rights tradition of Andrew Jackson, Johnson perhaps truly believed that Congress possessed no constitutional power to pass the Freedmen's Bill and the Civil Rights Act; certainly he relied upon constitutional limitations in justifying his vetoes. Johnson, an insecure man with little formal education, may have felt inadequate and outclassed in the presence of the southern belles and plantation gentlemen who argued their cases at the White House. And his own racism could have blinded him to many northerners' desires to protect the civil and political rights of former slaves. The president appeared to feel that an antiblack stance would prove politically advantageous, appealing to his natural Democratic constituency as well as to conservative and moderate Republicans. Whatever Johnson's motives, his miscalculations ended presidential influence over Reconstruction; the initiative passed to Congress, and "Radical Reconstruction" began.

Radical Reconstruction

For over a century, writers have examined Radical Reconstruction. Even writers whose views differ widely have generally agreed that the years between 1867 and 1876 were a tragic period, an agonizing story of prejudice, politics, and unfulfilled promises.

The earliest critics of Reconstruction condemned it as a cynical and brutal rape of southern society. Political opportunism and hatred of the South, it was claimed, motivated the radical Republicans' policies: military rule under the four Reconstruction Acts (1867 and 1868); black suffrage; and violation of the spirit, if not the letter, of the Constitution. Prosouthern accounts stressed the corruption of Reconstruction regimes, the unruliness of former slaves, the greed of northern "carpetbaggers," and the treachery of southern "scalawags." Reconstruction was a dark epoch, a perversion of America's liberal tradition. In this view, the lifting of radical rule by the white "redeemers" represented a return to constitutional government and to proper racial relations in the South.

Although the exaggerated legends of Radical Reconstruction persisted, during the 1930s interpreters began to see other motives. These writers claimed that the radical Republicans really represented northeastern business interests, greedy capitalists who feared that a speedily reconstructed South might regain its political power and overturn northern businessmen's control of the national government. Idealistic rhetoric and moral platitudes, it was implied, masked the sordid economic motives of the business-dominated Republican party: exploitation of the South and advancement of industrial over agrarian interests. Reconstruction was a tragedy because it solidified predatory capitalists' hold upon American government.

More recently, a new generation, writing during the civil rights struggles of the 1950s and 1960s, has viewed Reconstruction as another phase in black Americans' search for justice. To these authors, radical Republicanism represented the last burst of abolitionist idealism; the radicals tried to provide national protection for the rights of the freedmen and to extend some measure of social and economic assistance. Not particularly vindictive and not the tools of a capitalist conspiracy, congressional Republicans, moderates as well as radicals, undertook their actions only after they realized the extent of southern intransigence and presidential obstructionism. And their measures were not unusually severe, particularly when compared to the postwar policies of other victorious nations. The national government committed only a small number of troops to military Reconstruction, and the entire process lasted only a few years in most states of the former Confederacy. From this perspective, the tragedy of Reconstruction came not from its harshness but from its relative mildness. Northern efforts brought few dramatic changes in the status of black people; Reconstruction only temporarily interrupted white supremacy in the South.

THE RECONSTRUCTED UNION

Reconstruction and the South

Reconstruction did represent an attempt to achieve a degree of racial equality for blacks. Two important additions to the Constitution, the Fourteenth and Fifteenth Amendments, laid the basis for greater federal protection of civil and political liberties. The Fourteenth Amendment offered a definition of national citizenship which included black people; it prohibited states from denying any person "life, liberty, or property without due process of law"; and it warned that no state could "deny to any person within its jurisdiction the equal protection of the laws." Although during the late nineteenth and early twentieth centuries the Supreme Court used the Fourteenth Amendment to shield business corporations from state regulation, there is little evidence to suggest a business conspiracy behind the amendment. Its framers saw it as a constitutional bulwark not only for newly freed blacks but for all citizens; it was intended to be "Everyman's Constitution." The required number of states ratified the Fourteenth Amendment in 1868.

Two years later the Fifteenth Amendment declared that a citizen's right to vote "shall not be denied or abridged...on account of race, color, or previous condition of servitude." Applying to blacks in the North as well as to former slaves in the South, the amendment had nationwide political implications. Some northern supporters of the amendment may have been concerned with protecting crucial black votes in key districts, but others risked a white backlash to guarantee suffrage to the black man.

In the South, Reconstruction governments drafted new constitu-

Charles Sumner. *Brown Brothers*

tions and reestablished civilian rule. In many respects, the postwar constitutions significantly improved upon antebellum documents. Delegates in most states provided for universal public education and authorized numerous public aid projects. After much debate, constitutional conventions finally brought universal male suffrage to the South. Despite their own inexperience and the hostility of many supporters of the old order, constitution makers, both black and white, framed documents which served most southern states for over a generation.

Contrary to postwar propaganda and historical legend, ignorant and corrupt blacks under the thumb of evil whites did not dominate Reconstruction governments. Blacks occupied some state and numerous local offices, but they never controlled any southern state. And black officials were not particularly dishonest or incompetent. Undoubtedly corruption existed, but the chicanery of Reconstruction governments must be measured against the records of white southern administrations before and against the sorry reputation of many northern governments during this era. On the whole, Reconstruction governments made substantial progress toward postwar recovery. They improved roads, encouraged railway construction, promoted investment, and established the South's first public school systems. Much of the so-called extravagance of Reconstruction legislators merely represented expenditures for needed, sometimes long-delayed, public projects.

During the Reconstruction years, the national government provided limited assistance for the freedmen in the South. Over the veto of President Johnson, congressional Republicans created the Freedmen's Bureau, an agency to coordinate relief activities and to ease the difficult transition from slavery to freedom. The bureau found employment opportunities, supervised labor contracts, and tried to safeguard black peoples' legal and political rights. But although the bureau's contemporary critics generally indicted it for doing too much to assist blacks, many later historians have noted the agency's ambivalent record. Many well-meaning officials were overly paternalistic; others displayed outright prejudice toward black people; some encouraged blacks to enter into coercive sharecropping contracts; most did too little to enlarge opportunities for the former slaves.

The Freedmen's Bureau provided some help, but the national government never made a full-scale commitment to black advancement. A few radicals, notably Thaddeus Stevens of Pennsylvania, advocated confiscation of some plantations and redistribution of the land to the former slaves. But most congressmen and northern citizens recoiled in horror at expropriation and extensive federal aid. Freedmen's hopes of obtaining "forty acres and a mule" quickly faded.

Private philanthropic and religious groups also tried to uplift the freedmen. Black people themselves played significant roles in some of these aid societies, but they lacked the financial resources of white organizations. Various sectarian groups, especially the Congregational Church, sent both money and representatives to the South. Church-related educational institutions gave many black children their first opportunity to learn to read and write. Blacks quickly took advantage of the new schools, and many teachers commented upon the enthusiasm of the former slaves. Church groups helped establish black colleges and industrial schools, and the Freedmen's Bureau extended some financial assistance to missionary schools, including Howard University in Washington, D.C.

The end of Reconstruction

American reform movements have generally ended in failure or achieved only partial success; the first crusade for racial justice followed this unhappy pattern. The idealism and commitment initially associated with congressional Reconstruction gradually faded into opportunism and indifference. Congress failed to renew the Freedmen's Bureau in 1869; white terrorist organizations, such as the Ku Klux Klan, intimidated blacks in the South; southern whites who had once accepted Reconstruction governments began to withdraw their support; and increasing numbers of northern citizens lost interest in the whole Reconstruction process. To be sure, Reconstruction did not collapse overnight. During the early 1870s Congress passed several Force Acts aimed at the KKK and other night-riding bands. And the Republican administration of Ulysses S. Grant mustered sufficient manpower to put the first Klan out of business by the end of 1871. In 1875 Congress approved a Civil Rights Act which guaranteed equal rights in public places and forbade exclusion of blacks from jury duty. (In 1883 the Supreme Court declared the act unconstitutional.) As late as 1876 a few federal troops remained in South Carolina, Florida, and Louisiana. But the zeal for reform had largely vanished, and the Republican party, once the catalyst for social change, became less a force for racial justice and more a bulwark for the status quo.

Republicans faced a renewed challenge from the Democratic party as well as divisions within their own ranks. In 1868 General Grant, who captured the Republican presidential nomination without much opposition, won a comfortable victory over his Democratic rival, Horatio Seymour of New York. But the strength of the Democrats, traditionally the antiblack party, slowly revived. While Republicans waved the "bloody shirt," denouncing Democrats as traitors to the Union, their opponents concentrated on the race issue, indicting Republicans for their problack policies. "I say that we are not of the same race; we are so different that we ought not to compose one political community," announced a prominent Indiana Democrat: "I say...this is a white man's Government, made by the white man for the white man." Some Republicans also began to question their party's southern strategy, and intraparty dissatisfaction diluted Republican enthusiasm for Reconstruction. In 1872 Grant easily turned back a challenge from a coalition of Democrats and "Liberal Republicans," who offered newspaper editor Horace Greeley, a well-known reformer, as their candidate. But in 1874, beset by the political and financial scandals of the Grant regime, the party surrendered control of the House of Representatives to the Democrats and nearly lost its majority in the Senate.

Faced with serious political problems, the Grant administration began to back away from an active Reconstruction policy. In contrast to its earlier action against the KKK, it offered little federal resistance to a new southern offensive against blacks—the "Mississippi plan." As described by a Mississippi editor, the plan was simple: "Carry the election peaceably if we can, forcibly if we must." White Democrats armed themselves, formed paramilitary units, disrupted Republican meetings, and terrorized blacks. Between 1874 and 1876 the strategy spread, and a series of "race riots" swept across the South. In reality most of these were simply pogroms against blacks, part of white redeemers' efforts to break the radicals' control and end the crusade for black equality. The national government generally failed to oppose the Mississippi plan. When Mississippi's last radical governor appealed to Grant's attorney general for protection of black voters in 1875, he received a negative reply. The attorney general curtly informed the governor that northern citizens were "tired of these annual autumnal outbreaks in the South."

Reconstruction ended in the aftermath of the bizarre presidential election of 1876. Ohio Republican Rutherford B. Hayes and New York Democrat Samuel J. Tilden were both conservative gentlemen and experienced governors of large states. Both stood for honesty in government, civil service reform, sound money, and both planned to withdraw federal troops from the South. The range of disagreement between them was slight indeed. Yet the November election began one of the more tense episodes in American political history.

On election night grave robbers broke into the tomb of Abraham Lincoln and attempted to steal his corpse, lending a tone to what followed. Tilden distanced Hayes in the popular vote and apparently in the electoral college as well. But irregularities in three southern states threw nineteen electoral votes in doubt, leading the Republicans to contest the outcome. The Democrats countered with a challenge to one Republican electoral vote in Oregon (all that Tilden needed for victory), and the election quickly escalated into a major constitutional crisis. Angry Democrats threatened a renewed Civil War. Sinister men plotted to assassinate officials involved in the electoral imbroglio—one in Louisiana was shot and wounded. A Democratic editor went to jail for an editorial which invited Hayes's assassination if he were made president.

Scanthus Smith, *Monitor and the Merrimac. Art Collection of The Union League of Philadelphia*

After a long winter of threats, maneuvers, and negotiations, southern Democrats abandoned Tilden when Hayes agreed to remove the last federal troops, to grant patronage and recognition to white southerners, and to support economic legislation for the region. This compromise of 1877 was a major step in the reconciliation of the two recently warring sections, and in the North's abandonment of southern blacks. It signaled the formal end of Radical Reconstruction.

THE MERRIMAC AND THE MONITOR

If the Civil War accelerated America's economic and social growth, nowhere was the quickened pace more apparent than in military technology. On land, change was largely one of degree: larger armies fought longer battles which required more and more organization and materiel. At sea, however, strategic necessity produced a revolutionary departure from earlier techniques. The confrontation between the ironclads *Merrimac* and *Monitor* in 1862 symbolically ended the era of wooden frigates and began the modern age of armored battleships.

After initial skirmishes on land had demonstrated that the war would not end quickly, the North embarked upon a double strategy: naval blockade and an indirect assault upon Lee's armies in northern Virginia. The Union navy soon sealed off the Confederacy's major ports, but southern engineers working in the naval yards at Norfolk threatened to undo not only the blockade but also General McClellan's methodically slow advance up the peninsula between the York and James rivers. The Confederates had raised and rebuilt the Union frigate *Merrimac*, which federal sailors scuttled shortly before Virginia had seceded. Lacking both time and the necessary facilities for conventional repairs, the engineers simply covered the hull with armor plates, put ten cannon behind this iron wall, and mounted a ram on the prow. Though scarcely maneuverable and totally unseaworthy, the proto-battleship had one great advantage: wooden ships could not sink it, even at close range, because their cannon could not penetrate its metal hull.

On March 8, 1862, the ship, rechristened *Virginia*, led a Confederate flotilla against a squadron of federal ships stationed in Hampton Roads, the strait between the James River—and thus on McClellan's flank—and the Chesapeake Bay. Unprepared, the Union navy quickly lost two frigates and the steamer *Minnesota* to the invincible, unconventional craft. Washington's leaders panicked at the news, while the *Merrimac*'s victory provoked jubilant hopes throughout the South that ironclads might destroy the blockade and perhaps even launch an attack on New York or Philadelphia.

Both reactions proved premature. Technology, particularly war-spurred ideas, cannot be hidden from eager patriots elsewhere. As early as October 1861, a Union engineer, John Ericsson, had already begun to build an armored vessel, the *Monitor*. In contrast to southern improvisation, Ericsson had designed his ship from the outset to be an ironclad. Often called "the cheese-box on a raft," the *Monitor* had two cannon mounted in a revolving turret on a deck barely above water level, sophisticated innovations which made it less vulnerable and more maneuverable than its counterpart. The navy towed the just-completed ship into Hampton Roads in time to confront the *Merrimac* when it returned on March 9. All day the two ships battled, their armor defenses vastly superior to their guns. Both unbeatable, the struggle ended in a tactical draw. In a larger sense, however, the Union had triumphed, if only because the stalemate assured the blockade, although the *Merrimac* temporarily slowed Mc-Clellan's peninsular campaign. By early May 1862, the United States Navy had recaptured Norfolk; with the Merrimac now without its base of supply and requiring too much water to escape up the James River, the Confederates sank their ship on May 9. Although not decisive to the course of the Civil War (except in a negative sense), the *Monitor-Merrimac* clash foreshadowed the modern age of naval warfare and soon set off an armaments race among European seapowers.

THINGS TO THINK ABOUT: 1860–1876

What were the conflicting issues during the secession crisis? See David M. Potter, *Lincoln and His Party in the Secession Crisis* (rev. ed., 1962); Kenneth M. Stampp, *And the War Came* (1950); Richard N. Current, *Lincoln and the First Shot* (1962); and Stephen Channing, *Crisis of Fear* (1970).

What advantages did the North have during the war? What handicaps did the South labor under? How did the war affect society in both sections? See David Donald, ed., *Why the North Won the Civil War* (1960); Bruce Catton, *Centennial History of the Civil War* (3 vols., 1961–65); F. Vandiver, *Their Tattered Flags* (1970); Emory M. Thomas, *The Confederacy as a Revolutionary Experience* (1971); and Allan Nevins, *The War for the Union* (3 vols., 1959–70). Two books by Bell I. Wiley treat the life of ordinary soldiers: *The Life of Johnny Reb* (1943) and *The Life of Billy Yank* (1952). George M. Frederickson treats intellectual developments in the North in *The Inner Civil War* (1965). The role of black people is discussed in Benjamin Quarles, *The Negro in the Civil War* (1953) and James M. McPherson, *The Negro's Civil War* (1965). The struggle for emancipation is discussed in James M. McPherson, *The Struggle for Equality* (1962) and John Hope Franklin, *The Emancipation Proclamation* (1963).

Why did black Americans fail to achieve real equality during the era of Reconstruction? What changes did the war make in race relations? General accounts include: Kenneth M. Stampp, *The Era of Reconstruction* (1965); William R. Brock, *An American Crisis* (1963); John Hope Franklin, *Reconstruction After the Civil War* (1961); Rembert W. Patrick, *The Reconstruction of the Nation* (1969); and W. E. B. DuBois' classic account, *Black Reconstruction in America, 1860–1880* (1935). Excellent specialized studies are Eric L. McKitrick, *Andrew Johnson and Reconstruction* (1960); John H. and LaWanda Cox, *Politics, Principle, and Prejudice, 1865–1866* (1963); Joel Williamson, *After Slavery. The Negro in South Carolina During Reconstruction, 1861–1877* (1965); and Robert Cruden, *The Negro in Reconstruction* (1969). Another excellent monograph is Willie Lee Rose's *Rehearsal for Reconstruction* (1964). C. Vann Woodward's *Reunion and Reaction* (1951) explains the process by which Reconstruction was liquidated.

Rutherford B. Hayes: Winner in
the electoral college.
Culver Pictures

Samuel J. Tilden: Winner of the
popular vote. *Culver Pictures*

1876-1890

EIGHT | an aGe OF COnFiDenCe

CHIEF JOSEPH

The Nez Percé of the far Northwest contradicted almost every stereotype of the Indian. Ensconced in the narrow valleys between the Cascade and Bitterroot mountains (lands now parts of Idaho, Washington, and Oregon), they apparently never attacked settlers before their great war with the whites in 1877. They had aided Lewis and Clark in 1805. In 1831 they sent a delegation to St. Louis to discover the source of the white man's "medicine." The Nez Percé welcomed outsiders and were quick to learn from and trade with them. They even survived a gold rush into their lands in the sixties, remaining at peace despite numerous outrages by the miners. Nonetheless, friction sharpened in the 1860s as cattle ranchers eyed lands on which Indian horses grazed. In 1863 the federal government negotiated a treaty to delimit Indian land titles, but a group of braves, loosely led by Old Joseph, the father of a more famous Joseph, rejected it. Turning away from the Christianity they had learned from missionaries, they began a peaceful but determined resistance to the white man's designs on their ancestral lands. "My son," Old Joseph whispered as he lay dying, "you are the chief. . . . You must stop your ears whenever you are asked to sign a treaty selling your home. . . . This country holds your father's body. Never sell the bones of your father and your mother."

339

Chief Joseph was ever true to this stern injunction. Although he struggled to avoid conflict, his people's fate was all too typical: rapacious settlers pressing for land, unfeeling Indian agents, bungling in governmental departments, an unsympathetic general, a forced and hurried evacuation of their lands, and finally young braves driven to fury and terrible violence. Once at war, Joseph and his tribe enacted one of the great feats of military prowess and human endurance (for this army traveled with its women and children, its sick and aged.) A United States Army ROTC instruction manual describes Joseph's achievement: "In 11 weeks, he had moved his tribe 1600 miles, engaged 10 separate U.S. commands in 13 battles and skirmishes, and in nearly every instance had either defeated them or fought them to a stand-still." Joseph and fewer than two hundred braves withstood an army. The effort, of course, was doomed to failure, and with its failure, the Nez Percé would no longer exist as an independent people. Chief Joseph surrendered on October 5, 1877. His memorable speech gave all the reasons:

> I am tired of fighting. Our chiefs are killed. Looking Glass is dead. The old men are all killed. It is the young men who say yes or no. He who led the young men is dead. It is cold and we have no blankets. The little children are freezing to death. My people, some of them, have run away to the hills and have no blankets, no food; no one knows where they are, perhaps freezing to death. I want time to look for my children and see how many of them I can find. Maybe I shall find them among the dead. Hear me, my chiefs, I am tired; my heart is sick and sad. From where the sun now stands, I will fight no more forever.

The Nez Percé's fighting days were over.

For all his fame as a guerrilla leader, Chief Joseph was essentially a diplomat. When the United States government immediately reneged on the terms under which he had surrendered, shipping the tribe to Indian Territory (the present state of Oklahoma), Joseph began a careful and patient campaign to return his people to their mountain home. While he never succeeded in regaining his beloved Wallowa Valley—Old Joseph's gravesite—after five years of direct interviews with the president, the secretary of the interior, and numerous congressmen, and by enlisting the editorial support of several eastern journals, he did get his dispirited and rapidly decreasing tribe back to the mountains where they could thrive again. In his new home in western Washington, Joseph became an Indian elder statesman, a national symbol of courage and freedom. He returned to the Wallowa Valley but once, in 1900, an old man. There he found only the consolation that a settler—a man with, as he said, "a spirit too rare among his kind"—had enclosed and cared for his father's grave.

1876-1890

1876	Disputed Election, November 7; December 6 Rutherford B. Hayes (Republican) elected president; defeats Samuel J. Tilden
1877	Chief Joseph surrenders *Munn v. Illinois*
1879	Henry George, *Progress and Poverty*
1880	James A. Garfield (Republican) elected president; defeats Winfield S. Hancock
1881	Helen Hunt Jackson, *A Century of Dishonor* Garfield is assassinated; Chester A. Arthur becomes president
1882	Chinese Exclusion Act
1883	Pendleton Civil Service Act
1884	Grover Cleveland (Democrat) elected president; defeats James G. Blaine
1885	Josiah Strong, *Our Country*
1886	Henry W. Grady, "The New South" Haymarket Massacre, May 4 AF of L organized
1887	Interstate Commerce Act Dawes Severalty Act Edward Bellamy, *Looking Backward, 2000–1887*
1888	Benjamin Harrison (Republican) elected president; defeats Cleveland
1890	Sherman Antitrust Act Sherman Silver Purchase Act

THE DEPRESSION OF THE 1870s

Americans glimpsed a threatening future in the long depression of the 1870s. The collapse of Jay Cooke & Co., the nation's best-known banking house, on September 18, 1873, marked the beginning of six lean years. At first it had seemed unreal: when a newsboy shouted the headline *"All About the Failure of Jay Cooke"* a policeman promptly arrested him for incitement to riot. No one could believe that Jay Cooke, who had sold bonds for the Union during the Civil War, who had befriended presidents and supported churches, could be bankrupt. But soon the dismal economic reality sank in: the orgy of railroad building in the sixties and early seventies which had spanned the continent and doubled the nation's tracks was over for a while. Europe, with its own financial troubles, would not invest large sums in America to build railroads before settlement and commerce caught up with mileage already constructed. The expansion of heavy industry ground to a halt and depression settled over the land.

Working people suffered most from the unstable economy. When groups of unemployed workers called for a public works program to provide jobs, their negotiators met only scorn and their meetings were brutally suppressed. Seven thousand laborers jammed a New York City park to demonstrate in 1874 and the police moved in. "It was the most glorious sight I ever saw," exulted the commissioner, "the way the police broke and drove the crowd. Their order was perfect as they charged with their clubs uplifted." Samuel Gompers, future leader of the American Federation of Labor, remembered how he had "barely saved [his] head from being cracked by jumping down a cellarway." Labor violence peaked in the great railroad strikes of 1877. Workers took control of Pittsburgh until President Hayes called in the United States army. Dozens of men died; millions in property was destroyed; leading journals dreamed nightmares of social revolution.

Other kinds of disorder—some new, some long familiar—disturbed the American dream of progress. Roving gangs of young toughs in San Francisco gave the language a new word: "hoodlum." Their New York counterparts were "street rats": the Baxter Street Dudes, the Little Dead Rabbits, the Hudson Dusters. The Daybreak Boys, thieving from the piers at dawn, were all under twelve years old. The New York Society for the Reformation of Juvenile Delinquents reported their business "largely on the increase."

On the West Coast, rioting unemployed workmen shouting "The Chinese must go!" burned dozens of buildings in San Francisco's Chinatown and for months afterward no Chinese could walk the streets in safety. The outbreak came after twenty-five years of anti-Chinese propaganda in California. Chinese immigrants, at first welcomed as a source of cheap labor, soon were despised for undercutting American workmen and for being strange and "un-American" in their ways. California law invalidated their testimony in courts, barred them from public employment, and forbade them from intermarrying with whites. Segregated schools became common, as did informal vigilante groups keeping them out of the gold fields and other favored kinds of work. California's campaign against the "coolies" received national endorsement in 1882 when Congress, in the Chinese Exclusion Act, made the Chinese the first national group forbidden entry into the country.

The return of confidence Yet the mood of 1877 was short-lived. Americans had peered into the abyss and drawn back. After all the threats of renewed civil war, a compromise solved the election dispute between Hayes and Tilden, and the North forgot about the atrocities that persisted in the South. The two parties emerged untarnished from the electoral conflict with the renewed loyalty of millions of Americans who voted more consistently and followed their parties more faithfully than at any other time in our history.

Late in the decade the economy swung upward. The middle class had sustained but the slightest economic damage from the long depression; although it was a slow time for heavy industry and fresh long-term investment, commerce nevertheless paced briskly as prices dropped sharply to induce sales. As a result, real income—the amount people can buy with the money they receive—rose spectacularly in the depression decade. Despite wage cuts and unemployment, even factory workers gained in purchasing power. As the seventies ended, the nation—its farthest reaches being settled, immigrants pouring onto its shores, its cities growing, and its influence gaining in the markets of the world—looked confidently ahead. Americans envisioned a future that would be, if not pure gold, at least gilded by the prospect of economic advance. Fastening on the title of a popular novel by Mark Twain and Charles Dudley Warner published in 1873, they accepted the name "The Gilded Age" for the generation of industrialization and expansion that followed the Civil War.

THE WILD WEST

By the late nineteenth century the West was settling into the familiar checkerboard of farms and range. But this last frontier also contained the "Wild West" of ten-gallon heroes and villains famous in story, song, and advertisement. Legends grew about the mining frontier, the cattle towns, and the Indian wars. From the late forties into the eighties, the

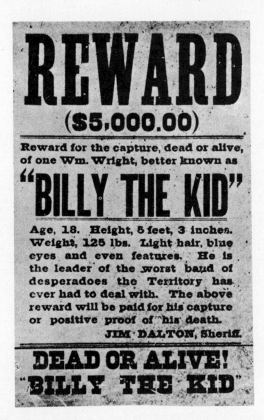

REWARD
($5,000.00)
Reward for the capture, dead or alive, of one Wm. Wright, better known as
"BILLY THE KID"
Age, 18. Height, 5 feet, 3 inches. Weight, 125 lbs. Light hair, blue eyes and even features. He is the leader of the worst band of desperadoes the Territory has ever had to deal with. The above reward will be paid for his capture or positive proof of his death.
JIM DALTON, Sheriff.
DEAD OR ALIVE!
"BILLY THE KID"

L. A. Huffman's portrait of Red Panther, Cheyenne Scout. *The Huffman Pictures, Coffrin's Old West Gallery, Miles City, Montana*

Robert Lindneux, *Trail of Tears.*
Courtesy Woolaroc Museum
Bartlesville, Oklahoma

West experienced one mining boom after another: California in '49, then Pike's Peak and Virginia City, Oro Fine Creek, Helena, Leadville, the Black Hills, Virginia City again, Leadville again, and so it went. In the same era the cowboys brought millions of cattle to the railroads for shipment to eastern markets. First they came on "long drives" from Texas up the famous trails—the Chisholm, the Goodnight-Loving, the Western, and the Shawnee—then from open-range ranches farther north where a few watering places on the dry grasslands allowed free grazing over miles of government-owned land. And always there were the Indians: driven west, herded into reservations, coerced into treaties and then betrayed, attacked, and defeated. The Wild West was a scene of exploitation and violence, one whose largeness of scale gave it a mythical and poetic dimension.

Behind the tales lurked many paradoxes. Mining gold and silver had glamour for nineteenth-century Americans—fanatics for bright, hard, heavy, "real" currency, and distrustful of the new instruments of credit. But the work was little different from mining coal or iron ore. For all the grizzly and venturesome prospectors, large eastern-financed corporations —with cumbersome equipment, lots of capital, railroads, and a labor supply—underwrote the extractions and reaped the rewards.

The cowboy is a glamorous figure, the image of the historic American: strong, silent, masculine, independent, rude but honorable, the conqueror of nature and the lesser breeds. In reality, it was a dirty, rough, lonely, and ill-paid job for men who because of character or background had rejected their society or been rejected by it. Large numbers of them —perhaps 25 percent—were black. When time and distance transformed cowboys into national folk heroes, the black cowpunchers disappeared from view until the 1960s.

Soldiers and Indians

And the Indian wars—source for a thousand films with interchangeable red targets falling before the white man's guns—also differed from their appearance in legend. When white men pushed west of the Mississippi they met perhaps a quarter-million Indians on the plains and in the mountains—Sioux, Blackfeet, Crow, Cheyenne, Arapaho, Apache, Comanche, Osage, and Pawnee, as well as Nez Percé, Ute and Shoshone in the mountain valleys. Government policy traditionally treated these tribes, somewhat contradictorily, as independent nations capable of negotiating treaties with the United States and as wards of the Great White Father in Washington. Old promises of a frontier dividing Indians and settlers gave way in the sixties to the realities of tribes herded onto reservations. And the fiction of tribal independence disappeared as settlers found old treaties standing in their way.

By the seventies the Plains Indians were reaching the end of their independent existence. Most of the tribes were nomadic, traveling with the massive herds of buffalo, or bison, which provided them with food as well as supplies for their teepees, blankets, and clothing. Encroachments on the land would have taken their final toll in any case, but the wanton slaughter of buffalo for food, sport, or hides virtually extinguished them as a species in scarcely ten years after the Civil War and doomed the Indian civilization dependent on hunting them.

Neither side was ever wholly guiltless in the events that led to racial war. The white settlers and soldiers, however, whose overwhelming strength allowed them considerable freedom of choice, were virtually always the aggressor. The Indians responded to the white advance in many ways, but none led to any but a disastrous outcome. Most bowed to superior force and accepted the reservations provided for them, but some made high tragedy of the pursuit of freedom. Bands of Sioux, for example, skirmished for years to remain on their hunting grounds. In 1876 the army sought to drive the last renegades onto reservations. Colonel George A. Custer was one of several officers giving chase to Chief Crazy Horse and his braves. Just before the two armies met, the Sioux medicine man, Sitting Bull, had a vision during the Sun Dance ceremonies of white soldiers falling into the Indian camp upside down. His vision became prophecy when Custer led his small force of 250 men to their death in a head-on encounter with thousands of braves at the Little Big Horn in Montana Territory. Tribes who resisted, like the Nez Percé or Sioux, fared neither better nor worse than those who did not. Only after the Indians could no longer fight did some of them, like Chief Joseph, begin to appear as noble remnants rather than dangerous savages.

Destruction of the Indians' potential to resist led to a general softening of tensions between them and the whites. A number of books —Helen Hunt Jackson's *A Century of Dishonor* was the most famous— presented their case. The net result was the Dawes Severalty Act of 1887, which attempted to end tribal life by turning the Indians into independent farmers. The act contained about equal portions of ignorance and good will, and its results were disastrous. The century of dishonor gave way to a half-century of Indian cultural disintegration. Presidents Hoover and Roosevelt reversed the policy once again to encourage tribalism, but the Indian civilization had suffered an irremediable blow.

AGRICULTURE AND INDUSTRY

Farming was still the nation's leading industry. Its growth continued to finance America's startling industrial expansion. Farm products accounted for about three-quarters of American exports. Acreage increased enormously as the farming frontier filled out the continental United States. Specialization, new machinery and scientific techniques, and improved transportation raised the yield of these expanding farmlands. Burgeoning cities and industry here and abroad created a growing market for this bounteous production. The early eighties were boom times. Prices for farm commodities remained high, land values climbed steeply, and huge wheat-growing "bonanza farms" used giant combines to make fabled profits.

Yet this expansion exceeded market conditions. Improved transportation opened new and competitive foreign farmlands even more rapidly than it created fresh markets. And the innovative techniques meant heavier capital investment than the relatively primitive credit system could provide, raising interest rates to painful levels. Farm tenancy rose throughout the country as did such onerous mechanisms for financing farms as crop liens and sharecropping, especially in the South. By the mid-eighties the ever-larger crops forced farm prices down, making fixed charges like mortgages a progressively larger burden. Still, optimism survived until 1887, when a severe drought in the Kansas

Sitting Bull. *Culver Pictures*

Villa of Brule, Sioux Indian encampment. *Library of Congress*

wheatfields ushered in a lengthy period of reduced rainfall across the Great Plains. A precipitous drop in land values foreshadowed a general depression in agriculture that would trouble American farmers for more than a decade.

Economic attitudes   In little more than a generation, America changed from an agricultural nation to the industrial giant of the world. Families moved westward, population grew, buildings climbed upward, cities spread outward. The world Americans entered so rapidly—of whirring machinery, sprawling cities, exotic new neighbors—seemed a vast juggernaut which no man controlled. Even businessmen, who seemed more attuned to industry than anyone else, did not fully understand it, but the promised benefits were too vast to reject.

348

Americans pursued economic growth with single-minded devotion. To explain the causes of this growth is to talk about the entire society. The Victorian lady, for example, tied tightly into her corset, bedecked with countless petticoats and an elaborate gown which swept the earth before her, might be confined to a narrow domestic circle by custom, and almost to her couch by the rigidity of her clothing. Yet in consuming 116 yards of material (her grandmother used but twenty-six and her flapper granddaughter got by with only half that and a little rouge), she was creating not only a market for textiles but also an inducement for her husband to labor from dawn to dusk. And labor he did. "I cannot be idle," one representative businessman wrote in his diary; "to me, idleness is the most terrible punishment."

Government as well, responding to this urge, dedicated itself not so much to laissez-faire as to what one writer has called "entrepreneurial liberty": the opening of opportunity to men of business. Subsidies to railroads, a freewheeling national banking system, a generous land policy, protective tariffs, and an endless array of state and local legislation and judicial decisions cleared the way for industry and thwarted the hopes of such opponents as the fledgling labor movement.

Population　A rapidly growing population provided the basis for economic growth. Here was labor, markets for goods, warrants for a larger future to fire the enthusiasm of investors and the daring of entrepreneurs. Immigration provided a goodly part of the increase: 2½ million immigrants in the seventies, 5 million in the eighties, 25 million in the whole period from the Civil War to World War I. Yet the domestic population increase exceeded the European influx as a source of manpower: native-born groups more than doubled between the end of the Civil War and the close of the century. Rural folk, still a majority of the nation, maintained high birth rates and sent a flood of young men into the cities seeking excitement and opportunity and often finding instead a place in the swelling armies of labor. While urban birth rates declined throughout the period, life expectancy increased. Investment in such public health facilities as improved water supply and sewers paid striking social dividends. A growing, healthier, better-educated, and more skillful labor force was, according to the most sophisticated modern calculations, the main multiplier of economic growth in the period, exceeding the importance of either capital investment or invention.

Investment capital　"Confidence" is the businessman's magic word. Where it exists money appears, and when it vanishes so does capital. Nineteenth-century Americans took money terribly seriously just because capital was both scarce and skittish. The willingness to invest in land, transportation, and industry required either something near a certainty of substantial profit or strong hopes for fabulous riches. The network of world communications was not what it would become in the twentieth century. A German or English investor required special inducements to send his money to America where he could scarcely follow its progress. Even an investor in an eastern city might find difficulty in checking on an enterprise in the West. Thus the confusion and irregularity of American economic expansion becomes understandable. A "boom" psychology, bonanza profits, subsidies to guarantee investments or insure profits—all had a certain cockeyed logic in coaxing some $3 billion out of foreign investors during the Nineteenth Century.

In almost every way, this capital base for industrialism came from the land. It is easy to forget that nineteenth-century men—like all men before them—thought of wealth largely as land. The growth of a vast agricultural kingdom and great mineral resources constituted the nation's fundamental material capital. Spreading agriculture provided food, population surpluses to support growing cities, markets for manufactured goods, and over three-fourths of our foreign exchange. From this came European tools, goods, and capital. Agriculture directly supported the great initial burst of industrial activity in America, the building of a vast railroad network to carry farm products. Railroads, mining,

Growth of the American economy since 1870

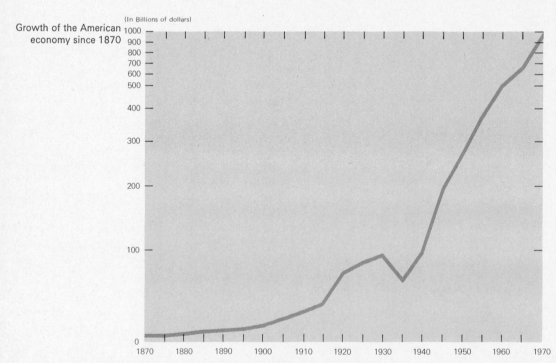

(In Billions of dollars)

Figures for years 1870 to 1960 are averages of the annual GNP for 5 year periods.
Figures for 1960 to 1970 represent total amount GNP for that year only.

and land absorbed the bulk of foreign investment, and all of these depended on the riches of the soil and the population spreading over it. No wonder that farmers late in the century could not understand their failure to profit from industrialization. In the words of a favorite farm protest song:

> *When the farmer comes to town,*
> *With his wagon broken down,*
> *O, the farmer is the man who feeds them all!*
> *If you'll only look and see,*
> *I think you will agree*
> *That the farmer is the man who feeds them all.*

Refrain:

> *The farmer is the man,*
> *The farmer is the man,*
> *Buys on credit till the fall;*
> *Then they take him by the hand,*
> *And they lead him to the land,*
> *And the merchant is the man who gets it all.*

"MAINE TO CALIFORNIA"

Railroads and American business life

"The generation," wrote Henry Adams, "...was mortgaged to the railroads." Between the 1830s, when the American railroad network began, and the mid-nineties, when it was more or less complete, over one hundred sixty-six thousand miles of track crisscrossed the land, creating national markets and shaping the economy for generations.

The railroads grew in phenomenal spurts of construction: 28,000 miles in the sixties and early seventies, 73,000 in the boom times of the eighties, another 20,000 during the nineties. Independent short lines rapidly consolidated into giant unified systems: the Pennsylvania, the Erie, the New York Central, and the Baltimore and Ohio in the East, the Southern and the Atlantic Coast Line to the South, the Illinois Central, the Chicago and Northwestern, the Missouri Pacific, and the Chicago, Burlington and Quincy in the Middle West. Even more spectacular to the railroad-conscious men of the Gilded Age were the five transcontinental roads pushed through between 1869 and 1893. Four of these, the Union Pacific-Central Pacific system, the Southern Pacific, the Atchison, Topeka and Santa Fe, and the Northern Pacific, profited from generous federal, state, and even local subsidies. Only James J. Hill's Great Northern line, the last to be completed, came solely from private funds. Americans took transcendent pride in the transcontinentals, considering them as much their own property as the property of bankers and railroadmen.

James J. Hill's achievement was the Great Northern Railroad. *Minnesota Historical Society*

Contemporary financial machinery could scarcely cope with investments of this magnitude. In an economy where an industrial facility like an up-to-date oil refinery cost fifty thousand dollars, railroads worth tens of millions were already common. A double-barreled attack coaxed investment in this wholly new kind of enterprise. Promoters offered investors bonds with assured interest, sometimes directly or indirectly guaranteed by government subsidies, and common stock as well. The bonds assured an equity in their investment in almost any circumstances; the stock offered the chance of huge profits if all went well. The result, of course, was heavily overcapitalized railroads, loaded down with large interest payments and "watered" stock far in excess of a road's potential.

Normal profits could not service such debts. Railroads avoided bankruptcy by creating the illusion of prosperity: the railroad promoter sold not just railroads, but expectations. The best way to keep up such expectations was through rapid expansion and high dividends. Railroads raced for new markets, building parallel to each other and stealing each others' freight business by general rate cuts or special rebates to large customers. At the same time they exploited the markets they monopolized by charging high rates. Often builders skimped on construction costs to meet their debts and pay their dividends and milked capital out of their

N. H. Trotter, *Held Up. The Smithsonian Institution*

John D. Rockefeller: industrial
statesman or robber baron?
Brown Brothers

lines by organizing separate construction companies—so that, for instance, Jay Gould the railroad president could overpay Jay Gould the railroad builder with his investors' money. The process built a lot of railroads, but at the cost of financial chaos, periodic depression when the boom psychology collapsed, and the growing insecurity of virtually every segment of society. Railroads became a symbol of industrial disruption, attractive at first—Whitman wrote of the locomotive's "fierce-throated beauty"—but finally feared and hated.

Whose railroads?   The railroads moved steadily toward completing a national market. The entire country exulted when technical improvements such as the air brake, automatic signaling devices, telegraphic communications, the Pullman sleeping cars, magnificent iron and steel bridges, standard track gauges, and uniform time zones brought closer an effective transportation and communications network. But the tightening financial organization and the railroads' obvious power over government frightened the public. Competition gave way, first to informal trusts and then to holding companies setting rates and parceling out markets. "Competition don't work well in the transportation business," said one railroadman. Large shippers had competing railroads at their mercy: John D. Rockefeller not only received secret discounts on his oil shipments, he even forced railroads to "rebate" to him part of what they charged his rivals. And the little men, if they were not served by more than one railroad, paid for it all.

Attempts to control the railroads began in the Middle West. The National Grange of the Patrons of Husbandry, founded in 1867 to provide social life for farm families, turned to politics after the depression began. In the early seventies, Granger-dominated legislatures in Illinois, Iowa, Minnesota, and Wisconsin passed laws establishing state commissions with powers to regulate railroads, grain elevators, and warehouses. The Supreme Court in the so-called "Granger Cases" upheld this legislation in 1877. But the railroads fought a dogged legal battle against the state commissions and finally in the Wabash case (1886), the Court, now with several new justices, threw out state regulation of interstate lines. By that time, numerous shippers and even some railroadmen tired of cutthroat competition had joined the farmers in a drive for national regulation. Congress responded in 1887 with the Interstate Commerce Act. This law forbade some discriminatory practices and followed the precedent of the Granger laws in establishing a commission to police the railroads. The Interstate Commerce Commission, hampered by adverse court decisions, failed to exercise serious control over the railroads for nearly a generation. Its precise legal powers would only emerge after numerous court cases and further legislation in the twentieth century. Nevertheless, it provided an important precedent for a number of independent regulatory agencies which, still fraught with controversy, persist into the present.

A national economy   Where railroads led, industry followed. Each major industry took a similar route toward national markets, technical improvements, and increased central control. And all saw vast production at lower prices. The steel industry grew out of a single technological advance: the Bessemer process for turning brittle iron into harder, more flexible steel by blowing air through molten iron to burn out its impurities. The oil industry arose suddenly in the sixties as scientists and entrepreneurs discovered the possibilities of oil as an illuminant and lubricant. The Re-frigerated railroad car, the growth of city populations, and a large cattle-range industry on the Great Plains transformed meat packing from a local butcher's trade to a centralized national industry. The same process occurred in numerous other fields: electricity, textiles, shoes, liquor, agricultural machinery, prepared foods. All were helped by revolutions in communication: the typewriter, the large-scale use of the telegraph, the telephone, cash register, adding machine, electric light, electric engine, linotype machine. On this technological base, astute men created new means of centralizing decision making, processing information, controlling far-flung operations, monitoring prices and products. From it rose a typical modern class—the white-collar worker; a characteristic modern form of organization—the bureaucracy; and a characteristic modern hero (and villain)—the great industrialist. Of the three, the first two were the most important, but the "captain of industry" caught the imagination of contemporaries and of historians.

Heroes of business   American society had always admired businessmen, but never more so than in the period between the Civil War and the Great Crash of 1929. The dramatic spread of railroad and manufacturing with its inevitable effect on day-to-day life was a running advertisement for the captain of industry. The great railroadmen, manufacturers, and bankers became national heroes, their names famous everywhere, their stories inspirations for young men. The public held its breath as Cornelius Vanderbilt and Jay Gould battled for control of the Erie Railroad; as California's "big four"—Leland Stanford, Charles Crocker, Collis P. Huntington, and Mark Hopkins—pushed the Central Pacific east in competition with the Union Pacific moving west. John D. Rockefeller's piety and financier Jim Fiske's extravagant ways both aroused wonder. The great meat packers, Philip Armour, Gustavus Swift, Nelson Morris, and Michael Cudahy became literally household words, their names staring forth from the shelves at every American housewife. Similarly, the word "cigarette" would immediately suggest the name of James B. Duke; mention of copper brought the Guggenheims to mind; J. P. Morgan was virtually a synonym for banking;

Pennsylvania oil fields. *Culver Pictures*

Andrew Carnegie for steel; Henry O. Havemeyer for the sugar industry. None of this was literally true: it was never that easy to monopolize a huge industry. But these men's careers, with their titanic struggles for control of great companies, seemed apt symbols of the growth and concentration that the era experienced.

America harbored as well an antibusiness tradition, attacking economic man for his materialism, business leadership for its undemocratic character, and commercial ethics for their cautious avoidance of the "strenuous life." A few reformers delivered this message to the Gilded Age public, but the extollers of business like Andrew Carnegie, who identified enterprise with "Triumphant Democracy," drowned them out. Late-nineteenth-century America squared the ideas of business leadership and of democracy by viewing industrialists as common men risen from the ranks. Horatio Alger, Jr., in numerous popular success novels, sublimated an explicit sexual interest in boys into a legend of how young newspaper sellers rose to become important businessmen. Serious analysts assumed that great men came from poor rural families. This myth, reborn anew each generation, generalizes the atypical experiences of a few to a whole social class. Statistical studies have repeatedly shown that most people climb to dominant positions in the American economy from

357

a start relatively high up, with "advantages" of education, connections, good marriages, and the like. For every Andrew Carnegie who started from poverty there were about six who began with status, and in each succeeding generation still fewer rose from the masses to the elite.

The achievement The successful businessmen of the nineteenth century were not inventors or technicians. They organized men, commandeered resources and capital, drove down production costs, and put the pieces together in a national market. They took risks, expecting both high profits for reinvestment and reduced risks in their future operations. Representative men like Andrew Carnegie and John D. Rockefeller dealt in basic commodities —steel and oil—and devoted their energies to producing them cheaply and selling them widely. This required larger plants, more reliable transportation, and beating competitors to markets—mostly by lowering prices. Sometimes the age demanded more sinister methods: deliberately setting off price wars, cutting off supplies and transportation, intimidating suppliers and customers. None of these businessmen was responsible for the kind of technological improvement that we associate with Henry Ford. Their efforts, however, allowed their customers to buy, for example, the same oil sent through similar pipelines and railroad cars and marketed by the same means in the same containers all over the country. Multiplied through numerous industries, these advantages created the framework of a national economy, facilitating the mobility of millions of Americans from place to place and the expansion of hundreds of secondary industries.

Most of all, the great industrialists offered a semblance of form and control to an otherwise incomprehensible development in human history. They were the heroes of an age desperately searching for order. For the small measure of it they could bring amid the threatening excitement of industrial growth, they were most handsomely rewarded.

LABOR

Unorganized workers The great strikes of 1877 forced middle-class Americans into sudden awareness of the discontented workers in their midst. While factory life was far from new in the seventies, the idea of a permanent and essentially separate industrial working class was both novel and difficult to accept. America's image of itself made no provision for this: a land of opportunity could not have a class without room for advancement. Workers themselves hesitated to view their status as unchanging—and who could blame them. Many had but recently left the farm or Europe in an effort to improve their circumstances. Yet fluctuations in the economy made the laborer's lot insecure, while new, high-speed machinery made work increasingly tiresome, nerve-wracking, dangerous, and personally unrewarding. Tangible evidence of this decline in the status of labor seemed present as women and children performed more and more of the functions that once required a man's strength and skill.

This alienation of the worker grew despite nearly full employment and wages which, thanks to shrinking prices, brought a better standard of living throughout the eighties. The industrial labor force had expanded rapidly: from under a million in 1860 to over 3 million in 1890. But workers felt control over their lives slipping from them, thought they got too little of the gains of industrialism, and found themselves baffled by their own middle-class aspirations as the possibility of living up to them seemed to recede with each passing year.

Deep fault lines ran through the working class. White laborers rarely accepted blacks. Native-born workers resented new arrivals from Europe (and even more so Asians) and consistently championed restrictive immigration policies. Skilled workers generally held aloof from unskilled. Workers who lived in small industrial towns might be an accepted part of a community, identifying with the interests of other local people, but residence patterns in large cities separated factory workers from the middle class. Loyalty to political party frequently collided with commitment to a labor union. Bigoted foremen and craft unions often kept an informal monopoly on the best jobs. "That job is not a hunky's job," one ambitious immigrant heard, "and you can't have it." No wonder that labor spoke with no single voice, but instead drifted with the winds of opinion on "the labor question," clinging to shibboleths of individualism and dreams of a middle-class future while toying with collectivist utopias and political nostrums. Workingmen said little, even when asked, and labor leaders blew an uncertain trumpet. They were not alone in their confusion about the implications of the onrushing industrial system. Neither businessmen nor the government officials and academic experts who began collecting statistics in this era showed much insight into the world of the factory. Labor leaders simply paid more harshly for their uncertainties, since their constituency bore the brunt of industrialism.

The Knights of Labor   Labor organization remained local and largely confined to a few skilled crafts such as printing and cigarmaking until the prosperous years of the late '60s and early '70s stirred workers to organize. About three hundred thousand joined unions, but hard times after an unsuccessful attempt at forming a labor party decimated their ranks. A second upsurge came in the 1880s with returning prosperity and an unprecedented number of strikes, most local and many quite informal. A remarkable national organization, the Noble Order of the Knights of Labor, was the beneficiary—not the instigator—of this new labor militancy.

The Knights defy any standard classification. Founded as a secret society in 1869, they were partly a fraternal organization, partly a political reform agency, and partly a federation of unions. Ten years later, under the leadership of Terence V. Powderly, they threw off their secrecy, dropped their fraternal rituals, and came out for the eight-hour day. The organization began to grow: from less than ten thousand members in 1879, it rose to forty-two thousand in 1882. Then in mid-decade the economy weathered a brief downturn. This dip, which scarcely affected the middle class, aroused an unprecedented militancy among working-men. Workers flocked to the Knights' banner: one hundred ten thousand in 1885, over seven hundred thousand a year later. More men struck than ever before—first to avoid wage cuts during the depression, then to gain increases or shorter hours. A nationwide movement for the eight-hour day did in fact force a small decline in the average workday.

The Knights offered workers little that was immediate or tangible. Opposed to strikes, craft unionism, and even collective bargaining, the movement's main appeal was its utopian promise of a brotherhood of labor. Nor was this mere rhetoric. Sixty thousand black workers flocked to its banner. Women joined. So did unskilled laborers. Yet skilled workers came too. Despite the Knights' ideology, which looked toward cooperative ventures to turn workers into middle-class Americans, it expressed the solidarity of workers quite as vividly as it expressed their confusion about their role in society. Utopian, decentralized, and probably as democratic as any organization in American history, it floated forth on a sea of optimism.

Haymarket! This inchoate militancy built toward a tragic climax. At a demonstration in Chicago's Haymarket Square, as a few anarchists harangued an apathetic crowd of workmen, 180 policemen charged, some man unknown to history threw a dynamite bomb, and the police opened fire on the crowd. Seven people died and dozens were injured. The episode resulted from hysteria building up over labor activity, and the bombing led to yet further hysteria: a court found eight anarchists, none ever linked to the actual bombing, guilty, and four of them were hanged. The labor move-ment—which had no part at all in the terrible Haymarket affair—was the great loser. The "spirit of 1886" of labor optimism and militancy dis-appeared in an instant, and the Knights went into a decline almost as precipitous as their rise.

The collapse of the Knights of Labor in the aftermath of the Haymarket Riot perhaps symbolized the darkening mood of the late eighties better than any other single event. Workingmen and the forces of middle-class humanitarianism would remain apart for a half-century of industrial organization, while the hardheaded, successful, and con-servative American Federation of Labor advanced the interests of a thin segment of skilled workers, rejecting any larger role in the organization of industrial society.

CITIES

*"How Ya' Gonna Keep
'Em Down on the Farm
after They've Seen
Broadway?"*

Popular ballads crooned "Carry Me Back to Ole Virginny" and sighed to be "Down By the Old Mill Stream." Churchmen and reformers denounced the city as a hotbed of vice and crime. Rural politicians artfully drew boundaries and apportioned legislatures to control its power. Yet the streams of humanity flooding the urban centers was larger even than the western migration; millions of Americas joined millions of European immigrants in the emerging cities. And the products of the city, both its goods and its culture, washed back across the land, wiping out folk cultures and creating an urban mentality which made the city the natural goal of young men and women everywhere.

The cities grew enormously. In the decade of the eighties Chicago doubled in population; St. Paul, Minneapolis, Kansas City, and Denver nearly tripled. American cities were unlike most others in the world's history. The religious, strategic, and governmental forces behind urbanization in much of the world were weak in America. Our cities were organized almost exclusively on commercial principles. They lacked the public vistas of palace, church, plaza. Instead we carved them into gridlike patterns and then sliced them into standard lots of about twenty-five by one hundred feet to maximize real estate profits. Most services were left to private enterprise. For a time, people—their eyes still on the rural past—simply failed to realize their needs. Garbage disposal is no problem in the country and health care is easily enough left to the individual. So too with food supply, transportation, even fire prevention. Children reared outside cities need few special provisions. Even most of the mentally ill can be cared for at home. The city environment changed all this. Health care was everyone's concern when epidemic threatened. Water supply and sewage were early recognized as the indispensible urban public services. Other urban needs such as transportation and food could yield profits and with minor controls stayed in private hands.

The nineteenth-century city was a most uncomfortable place. Contemporary accounts dwell on filth, stench, disease, and fear of the poor rootless denizens of the slums. No one could miss the traffic in vice, the lack of "wholesome recreation," the narrow, mean lives of overcrowded residents, the endemic animosity and violence between the various races and nationalities of the city.

One solution to urban problems was technical: new inventions could make life more comfortable. Cities encouraged inventions, both because they offered large markets and because they had available the technical knowledge and skills that a creative mind might combine into a practical device. Inventors, typically, were city people, and their neighbors eagerly adopted whatever was new. Electric lights, the electric

361

trolley, subways and elevated railroads, the telephone—all were developed and nearly instantly applied en masse to the cities' problems. And all made fortunes for those who controlled them. New York City streets in the late nineteenth century were dark with wires and pipes. Every citizen had to thread his way through poorly understood electrical installations, and murderous industrial machinery. The American rate of industrial accidents rose to the highest of any nation in the world. Yet people flocked into cities, accepting new devices and delighting in each novelty though it slay them. They thoroughly learned the lesson of technological solutions to social problems: Americans began to think it their peculiar genius.

"Yankee Ingenuity" became a cliché and men like Thomas Alva Edison national idols. Edison, the "Wizard of Menlo Park" (site of his New Jersey research laboratory), was an apt symbol: after his day, technological innovation would become more expensive, impersonal, corporate. Last of the great tinkerers, Edison was also the nation's first director of a research laboratory devoted to invention.

This attitude, even if it could extend too far, rested on hard accomplishment. Ingenious and massive engineering solved municipal water and sewage problems. The crucial problem of internal transportation gave way dramatically late in the eighties with the introduction of the electrically powered trolley. This multiplied enormously the area available to city workers, relieving housing problems by initiating the suburban exodus that has continued to the present. Further aid came from the new steel-girder construction and the elevator. Cities could now build both up and out. As a consequence, the range of people who could afford adequate housing dipped deep down into the lower middle class. Older center-city areas continued to decay, but the more skilled workers could at least begin to hope for access to decent quarters outside the factory districts. While poor laborers bounced about from slum to slum or from city to city looking for jobs, a narrow stratum of workers— printers, construction workers, and the like—might, with the help of working wives and children, buy a small house in the closeby suburbs, pay into a burial society, and save a few dollars in a savings bank. This small elite of labor formed the core of organized workers, especially in the American Federation of Labor, while the shifting masses beneath them remained too transient for either organization or political power.

City civics   The cities were arenas of suspicion and mistrust rather than integrated communities. Civic consciousness remained weak among people who moved often or were new to the city. The philosophy of social Darwinism, which held that society evolved as a vast organism with no rational control, suited the urban scene well. In the Gilded Age it was essentially the philosophy of the city. The battles of nature, red in tooth and claw,

"Let Us Prey." *Culver Pictures*

seemed to be duplicated in the counting rooms and on the pavement. Men in despair of controlling their environment took refuge in such fatalism.

The problem of the city was on every tongue and in almost every book. Reform-minded Americans saw it as a political failure. Churchmen and women's groups considered the city a moral disaster area. Social scientists and novelists viewed it as the home of emerging class distinctions, of extremes of wealth and poverty which they could not square with the ideals they understood. Especially, they saw that normal commercial ethics met their nemesis in the city. Everywhere the supplying of urban services—public or private—carried the stigma of corruption, much as railroad building had done. Electric lights, trolleys, telephones, and subways did not lend themselves to various and competing efforts: they simply worked better as single enterprises. Monopolies, called franchises, became the standard means of providing for these services. This public sale of economic opportunity inevitably trailed bribery and theft in its wake. And outright public expenditures worked no better: a squat little County Court House cost the New York City taxpayers $13 million, about $9 million of it going into the pockets of city "boss" William Marcy Tweed and his friends.

The city machine   The politics of the city symbolized all that was new and uncomfortable about this strange and novel environment, and people automatically thought the worst. Traditional methods constantly failed to provide services, and new procedures inevitably outraged moral sensibilities formed in a simpler world. Most outrageous of all, according to reformers, were the political machines, informal organizations of lower-class voters held together by jobs, favors, and bargains. They, rather than the official organs of government, seemed to run the cities. Reformers condemned these "rings" for turning elections into a bargaining for favors instead of a test of opinions. They saw these organizations as a bar to efficiency and to the improvement of public services, as pirates taking their levy on the public. Naturally, they blamed them for the many and obvious ills of city life.

This attack was not wholly false. Corruption was rife and the expectation of it made taxpayers unwilling to invest public funds in needed municipal services. On the other hand, the political machines performed useful services in adjusting the new immigrants and the new arrivals from the countryside to city ways. They helped the bewildered new city dwellers pick their way through the hazards of urban life, finding them jobs, getting them out of legal tangles, and giving them some scrap of pride in the fragile neighborhood communities they managed to create. Stressing ethnic identity, the machine politicians ratified the preference of the first generation for retaining the religion and something of the culture of their forefathers. And it introduced them to an interest-group politics in some ways more modern and serviceable than the official civic ideals of Yankee reformers.

Yet the machines were products of the urban evils from which the immigrant and everyone else suffered, and they offered no way out. Public health services could benefit the poor more than having the block captain occasionally pay for a doctor's services. Welfare agencies could give more help than the basket of coal or the Thanksgiving turkey that might come from the boss. The machines offered the cities no future, and their reformer enemies, so arrogant and wrong in the short run with their condescension toward immigrants and their condemnation of "favors," were surely right in the end. Eventually—for good or ill—rational and bureaucratic methods would replace the clan loyalties and political favors of the machine.

Toward urban America

The Gilded Age kept its balance by condemning the city while moving to it en masse. A society that is moving away from the city in the present should not uncritically accept that age's negative portrait of urban life. Cities held (and hold) enormous advantages. Life in all its variety, and culture from the entire world, came only through cities. Magazines, the publishing industry, artists, educational innovations, symphonies, museums—all were part of the excitement of cities. City people did new things, creating their own culture and draining the countryside of creative talent.

And anyone who looked carefully could find glimmerings of a new sense of urban community. A startling array of associations—clubs, settlements, religious and secular self-help and study organizations—gave shape to people's lives. Middle-class ladies struggled to help their poorer neighbors. Newspapers replaced gossip over the back fence, keeping people in touch with their new world. Spectator sports, especially baseball, gave city people a focus for their new pride in being New Yorkers or Chicagoans or Clevelanders.

Women in the cities

Women especially found new freedoms in the cities. The movement for women's rights gained ground principally among urban women, who could much more easily congregate and engage in public activity than their rural cousins. The two major woman's rights associations, Susan B. Anthony's National Woman Suffrage Association and Lucy Stone's American Woman Suffrage Association, centered in New York and Boston respectively. Women formed associations to better society, to alleviate the lot of the poor, to fight for temperance or against prostitution. In the new settlement houses, many women found fresh outlets for their energies and new ways of living. Modeled after English examples, these houses, set in the midst of immigrant slums, provided contact

The first Ku Klux Klan. *Culver Pictures*

between members of the respectable middle class and the poor. There the immigrants learned "American" standards and found help with their day-to-day problems. The people—mostly women—of the settlement houses found new careers in social work. Many of the great women of twentieth-century America—Jane Addams, Eleanor Roosevelt, Frances Perkins—discovered their public vocations in this special form of post-graduate education.

These efforts in the late nineteenth century provided invaluable experience for the more vital women's movement of the progressive era. The largest gains—except for those made in the women-scarce far western states—came principally in the cities. Here, paraphrasing what Frederick Jackson Turner has written of the American frontier, was the other place where the cake of custom was broken and where newness and innovation was the rule. The Gilded Age was still uncomfortable with the city. In a few years some literate Americans would finally put their minds where their feet—and their hearts—had carried them, and see the cities not just as a problem, but also as the hope of America.

The New South

In 1886 Henry W. Grady, a leading southern newspaper editor, addressed a New York mercantile audience on "The New South." This oration, which made him a national figure and a regional hero, refuted the traditional antebellum image point by point and pictured a New South with factories instead of plantations, business in place of politics, economy rather than luxury; a region with an effective, inexpensive, and docile labor force, not the shiftless "Sambo" that Northerners envisioned. Part boast, part promise to northern investors, this assertion rested on a substantial economic recovery in the late seventies and early eighties from the acute devastation of the Civil War. The South built more miles of railroad in the eighties than in all its previous history. Birmingham, Alabama, an exhausted cornfield at the beginning of the seventies, was well on its way to leadership in American production of pig iron. A "cotton mill crusade" to "bring the factories to the fields" swept the South as investment in this industry became virtually a civic mission. Production of raw materials and crude industrial goods—turpentine, lumber, iron, coal, cotton yarn, cottonseed oil, fertilizer, and tobacco products—all grew impressively. And by the late seventies southern agriculture had regained ground lost in the war time and postwar disorders: in the next years cotton, sugar, and tobacco production forged ahead of the pre-war crop size. All this offered substance for Grady's vision of a New South "less splendid on the surface, but stronger at the core [with] a hundred farms for every plantation, fifty homes for every palace; and a diversified industry that meets the complex need of this complex age."

The 1880 census had revealed a vast increase in the number of southern farms, which Americans gratefully accepted as proof of the death of the old plantations. Americans did not notice or want to notice that the demise of the plantation system was as mythical as the glories with which they now invested its past. For on closer examination, the "fifty homes" that replaced the "palace" were the miserable cabins of ex-slaves, and the "hundred farms" did not belong to the poor tenants who worked them under an onerous system of share-cropping which reduced its victims to peonage but a shade above the slavery of old. Desperate for credit—always a necessity for farmers—the ex-slaves had to mortgage their future crops for supplies. This placed them in bondage to the storekeepers who furnished them with food, tools, and seed. In a capital-scarce economy the storekeeper himself paid high interest rates, and he more than passed them on to his credit customers, who, being in his debt, could not go elsewhere for goods.

The system was vicious: many farmers ended the year in debt, necessitating the same arrangement for the next year—and at worse terms. In addition, the merchant, to make sure he got paid, demanded the cropper devote every possible acre to the "cash crop," cotton. Even more than before the war, the South suffered from a one-crop economy. These credit conditions, added to the chronically depressed cotton prices of the late nineteenth century, made the farm protest of the nineties more extreme in the South than in any other part of the nation.

For all the "New South" rhetoric, the area had scarcely begun to industrialize. The South remained overwhelmingly rural, and despite the undeniable economic progress of the eighties, it was by far the poorest part of the country. The growth that did occur profited northern capital more than the South. The most lucrative southern industries, such as lumbering and mining, were largely in northern hands. Discriminatory freight rates encouraged the production of raw materials or crudely processed goods and discouraged the more profitable manufacture of finished products. Industrialism brought little in the way of increased markets to southern farmers, nor did the jobs it created significantly improve the life of poor southerners, black or white. In fact, the great inducement to bring capital to the South was shockingly low wages. Southern promoters boasted of the "family wage," requiring full-time labor of entire families for survival. Profits from such manufactures averaged 22 percent of investment in a typical year, with well-managed firms earning as high as 75 percent annually. And this was white man's work—or more strictly, white folks' work, since two-thirds of the operatives were women and children. Cotton mills were off-limits to blacks.

Blacks Black Americans were the poorest people in a poor land. For a half-century after emancipation they remained largely in the South and on the land—land that they did not own. They worked for wages, or on shares, or as tenants. Some moved into the towns; many migrated from the southern Atlantic states toward richer bottomlands in Alabama, Mississippi, Louisiana, and Texas. But only a few found opportunity.

Frederick Douglass wrote a fascinating autobiography about his rise from slavery.
Blanche K. Bruce, Frederick Douglass, Hiram R. Revels. *Culver Pictures*

America's first black members of
Congress. *Culver Pictures*

Sharecropping, harsh labor-contract laws, and imprisonment for minor crimes—which meant working under the most deplorable conditions as convict labor leased to the large coal, lumber, or railroad-building corporations—left most blacks in conditions only slightly improved from slavery. The political promise of Reconstruction had given way to cruel disappointment. The federal government's support for their civil rights had vanished with the abandonment of Reconstruction and the Supreme Court's refusal to sustain civil rights legislation.

Yet the picture was not wholly bleak. Small but vital gains created the institutions and the men and women on which black hopes for the future would rest. A few black farmers became landowners in the prosperous early eighties; some urban blacks rose into a precarious middle class of storekeepers, caterers, sleeping-car porters, and skilled craftsmen. A more solid stratum of leaders grew out of the schools and churches. Education offered the best hope. Supported first by the Freedmen's Bureau, then by northern philanthropists, industrial education in particular allowed blacks to progress with the least opposition and often with the positive support of white Americans, northern and southern. The industrial-education movement grew throughout the seventies and eighties, well before Booker T. Washington gave it national publicity and leadership—and long before its limitations became clear to thoughtful black leaders. In the eighties, with vocational-training schools like Hampton and Tuskegee blossoming, it seemed a major ground for optimism.

The industrial-education movement formed part of many black leaders' general strategy of coalition with prosperous whites, which had replaced the old and obviously exhausted radical alliance of Reconstruction. Booker T. Washington, the talented, wily, and energetic president of Tuskegee Institute, rose from slavery to dominance of black political life preaching a doctrine of industrial training, black self-improvement, accommodation to white prejudices, and cooperation with southern Democrats and northern Republicans. This conservative strategy brought philanthropic support for black education, federal patronage and behind-the-scenes power (Washington held tight rein over both), and some leverage in southern politics.

Blacks continued to vote in fairly large numbers in the eighties, to hold minor offices as well as a few seats in Congress, and to receive some share of the limited services that poverty-stricken southern governments offered. One result of this was a measure of integration, especially for middle-class blacks. This strategy also restricted violence against poorer blacks by providing powerful and respected political allies. Conservative southern Democratic leaders like L. Q. C. Lamar in Mississippi and Wade Hampton in South Carolina worked to maintain decency toward blacks and a limited but real political role for them. This was without doubt political exploitation, a strategy to divide the lower classes racially the better to rule them, and it condescended to blacks, who were herded to the polls to vote as instructed. Yet it ended most of the slaughters of the mid-seventies and was mildness itself compared to the horrors that would come in the nineties in the organized system of intimidation, segregation, and disenfranchisement known as Jim Crow. Black leaders knew that they had made a retreat after Reconstruction; they would soon learn to their horror that it had turned into a rout. Like all strategies for black-white cooperation in American history, this one was a makeshift, bore some fruit for several years, raised high hopes, and ended in violent disappointment.

RESPONSES TO INDUSTRIALISM

The Gilded Age was a bewildering time: the political system ignored many obvious needs and with few exceptions the era's social thought was either confused or evasive. Most Americans fronted the world with a personal Christian faith that said little about social problems. These were often left to the "laws" of political economy, which assured progress only if men avoided too much collective effort to direct change. Analogies drawn from science buttressed these beliefs. Some used Charles Darwin's picture of nature—a struggle for existence in which the fittest survived—to support the classical economists' views of society, although most businessmen simply considered themselves as the Christian stewards of society's wealth. Most reformers looked for ways to solve specific problems within the laissez-faire framework: increase credit through some scheme for greenback or silver currency, or upgrade government through civil service reform, or raise wages through producer cooperatives or private bargaining between workers and employers.

Henry George, a California journalist, explored more profoundly the ills of industrial society. In 1879, his *Progress and Poverty* asked why poverty endured amid vastly increased wealth. Reflecting on his experience of western land booms, George noted that where men gathered to work, the value of land rose. One man's labor turned into his neighbor's "unearned increment" in the form of increasing land prices and rent, making landlords wealthy and workers poor. A "single tax" on land, expropriating this profit earned from other men's efforts, would remove all other tax burdens while preventing the growth of damaging social classes—millionaires and paupers. George's analysis, which tied the new and elusive industrial wealth to land—a familiar form of property—offered an easier way to understand changes in American life than did the more orthodox economics of the period. Two million people bought his books in a quarter-century, and his theory, spread by hundreds of Single Tax Clubs, influenced a generation of reformers.

Everywhere one looked men were building pieces of a new institutional structure with strengthened capacities to attack social problems. The vigorously growing Protestant churches soon responded to the new age. A "social gospel" movement, heralded by Josiah Strong's best-selling polemic *Our Country* (1885), sought to return the churches to the social role they had exercised in the heroic antislavery days. A humanitarian impulse, sparked by religious enthusiasms, turned hundreds and soon thousands of men and women to active engagement in an early war on urban poverty. In this era, charity began its transformation into organized philanthropy: what began as sentimental pathos toward the "deserving poor" (with its accompanying vicious hostility toward the "depraved classes") began to turn into the empirical study of poverty and the profession of social work. Despite misunderstanding, condescension, and formidable ethnic barriers, middle-class Americans opened settlement houses in poor neighborhoods and began making contact with the victims of industrial society.

Education   Men who might despair of answers to the economic and political questions of the age turned to education. Booker T. Washington was anything but isolated in his belief that only the right kind of education could solve major social problems. The public school became an object of nearly mystical faith: it would Americanize the immigrant, urbanize the farmboy, tame the radical, and make the worker temperate and industrious while teaching him basic skills. These dreams, mixing spiritual uplift, industrial education, and social control, were beyond any institution's capacities. But in the last thirty years of the century, school enrolments increased over 250 percent and illiteracy rates dropped by half. Kindergartens and public high school systems were among the innovations beginning to spread in the period. And above them towered the new universities, moments of an age of cultural growth.

This concern for learning did not end with the school-aged population: adult education mixed artfully with entertainment in the chatauqua summer schools and traveling lecturers; public libraries blossomed under the patronage of Andrew Carnegie and others; popular newspapers and magazines found audiences among the millions of Americans with elementary educations. Joseph Pulitzer, publisher of the St. Louis *Post-Dispatch* and the New York *World,* showed how a "people's newspaper," as he called it, could be built on bold headlines, pictures, sensations, comics, sports stories, first-rate political and financial reporting, and crusading exposures of corruption. This was the age of the reporter: people wanted "the news," not editorial opinion. Newspapers were the city equivalent of the small town's back-fence gossip: everything a little racier than in reality. With news of events came news of new products: behind the newspaper and magazine revolution was the rise of advertising—another institution shaping the emerging society.

Culture—high and low   A new popular culture—one critic dubbed it the "chromo-civilization"—dominates our image of the late nineteenth century: the "yellow press," dime novels, McGuffey readers, chautauqua, humor magazines like *Frank*

Leslie's Jolly Joker, Horatio Alger novels, houses built in grotesque imitation of medieval fortresses with turrets and curlicues and cast-iron deer on the lawn, immigrants with heavy accents, and rich men and women draping their overweight bodies with every kind of ostentatious display.

This picture is not false—only one-sided. It was a time of cultural growth as well. The Gilded Age got its name from Mark Twain's book of that title. And while contemporaries thought of Twain primarily as a humorist and the author of children's books, Ernest Hemingway cited *Huckleberry Finn* as the one great American novel. Twentieth-century critics rejected the age's writing as anemic and "genteel" and only later discovered that Henry James was our major novelist and William Dean Howells a central figure in American literary history.

All three of these major writers illustrate the complexity of the early industrial age. Twain denounced business morals but sought the society of tycoons. He played at being a funnyman—an eccentric dressed in a white suit—while pillorying the shallow sensationalism of the newspapers. His contemporary Henry James wrote dozens of carefully crafted novels and stories pitting American innocence against European corruption and rapacity. Yet he found the decadent Continent a far more comfortable home than his native land. And Howells, editor, critic, and novelist, maintained his position atop the pantheon of genteel American letters while calling for an end to laissez-faire capitalism in *A Traveller from Altruria* (1894) and publicly denouncing the hanging of the Haymarket martyrs.

Thorstein Veblen in *The Theory of the Leisure Class* (1899) burlesqued the American plutocracy's "conspicuous consumption" of every "honoric" commodity, such as the masterpieces of European culture. New American millionaires did at times buy paintings by the yard along with titled husbands for their daughters—in both cases ignorant of the product they were receiving. Nevertheless, many a collector who began by wasting huge sums on worthless paintings eventually acquired expert guidance and purchased the art treasures now on view in the great American museums. And this same age produced several important American painters: Thomas Eakins and Winslow Homer, realists largely free from the sterile conventions of nineteenth-century academic art; Albert Pinkham Ryder, whose eerie canvases were intensely romantic yet wholly unsentimental; and the expatriates, James A. McNeill Whistler and Mary Cassatt, whose absorption in European art styles would eventually influence post-World War I art in this country.

POLITICAL LIFE

The Gilded Age enjoyed its public life. Politics played a larger, if not a more important, part in American life than ever before or since. A greater proportion of eligible voters went to the polls, and more voted according to party preference than at any other time in our history.

Chautauqua meetings drew thousands of culture-hungry Americans. *Brown Brothers*

Before the age of mass spectator sports and mass media, politics provided entertainment, information, and social life. More important, in a period of rapid change and disintegration of old communities, it offered a familiar cast of friends and enemies. It addressed immediate loyalties rather than larger national perspectives.

Throughout most of the country, local politics held an intense popular interest. Contests usually pitted ethnic and cultural groups against one another. If the old Americans were Republicans, the new immigrants would be Democrats; in western states, the stream of northern immigrants carried their Republicanism with them and southern settlers their loyalty to the Democrats. Virtually the whole flow of information about public affairs came through the channel of party: newspapers were party organs; social clubs, like the Union League Clubs growing out of the war, had party labels attached to them; even the run of daily conversation in the barber shop, saloon, or grocery came from the same source, for no self-respecting Republican would have his beard trimmed in a "rebel" Democratic barbershop any more than a Democrat would trade with a "Black Republican." Politics was one way of establishing identity, a substitute for community. Just as a present-day American might identify himself by length of hair, width of tie, or model of car, so men of that day (in most states women could not vote) used political loyalties as a means of saying who they were.

National issues   National politics, far removed from this fierce localism, was pallid by comparison. The main issues of style and culture that divided ethnic groups on the local level had no clear expression in national affairs, for the federal government had not yet entered everyday American life as it would in the twentieth century. Little of importance rested on the resolution of the principal national issues. The problem of civil rights for the freedman had turned into stale recrimination even before the collapse of Radical Reconstruction. Republican promises to protect blacks' voting rights in the South and to aid their education with federal funds failed because Republicans cared more about tariff and currency policy while Democrats, fiercely racist, deeply opposed any federal intervention in the South. The parties spoke differently about tariff protection, with Republicans favoring the highest rates, but when it came to legislation, serious efforts at reforming the tariff vanished into a set of particular interests. The tariff indeed was, as one Democratic candidate had asserted, "a local issue," affecting different areas and industries in different ways. On the currency question (see pp. 389–391), neither party could unite sufficiently to enact a consistent program. Some economists think that the resulting instability in financial arrangements itself hampered the economy. Finally, the question of civil service affected only a limited number of people, and here positive accomplishment proved possible. Nonetheless, the Pendleton Act of 1883, which initiated the merit system for some federal employees, had to await the dramatic assassination of President James A. Garfield by a crazed political office seeker before becoming a law.

Dead center

The Gilded Age is the classic case of "dead-center" politics. When people are not sure where they are going they may either gamble on strange directions or, more often, they will simply cling to the familiar and see that nothing very much is allowed to change. In the confident eighties, this latter approach dominated. The parties remained poised in an amazingly even balance: presidential elections were close, party divisions in Congress narrow, and most of the time no party controlled all branches of government at once. With parties so closely balanced, innovation became a risk. In any case it was unnecessary. Even the "out" party felt no need for new appeals, since the old ones were probably good enough to win the next election. Nor did the parties need strong leaders to woo the electorate. Better to take someone safe and available. And so we have the men who dominated Gilded Age politics: respectable, able, even dedicated, but faceless—our forgotten presidents, Hayes (1877–1881), James A. Garfield (1881), Chester A. Arthur (1881–1885), Grover Cleveland (1885–1889), Benjamin Harrison (1889–1893). Only the one Democratic president of the era, Grover Cleveland, lives in party tradition, and most of his historical importance comes from the events of his second troubled administration in the nineties. Thomas Wolfe, a major American novelist of the 1930s, looked in amused wonder at his father's passionate devotion to such heroes. This was the age of the "four lost men":

> For who was Garfield, martyred man, and who had seen him in the streets of life? Who could believe his footfalls ever sounded on a lonely pavement? Who had heard the casual and familiar tones of Chester Arthur? And where was Harrison? Where was Hayes? Which had the whiskers, which the burnsides: which was which? Were they not lost?

Yes, they were: lost when pressing problems in the late eighties and the nineties made their kind of politics suddenly an anachronism.

Toward a new age

In the late eighties the serious problems of industrialism surfaced again as they had in 1877. The uprising of labor shattered the age's complacent attitudes. Henry George, the celebrated reformer, provoked national attention when he ran for mayor of New York City in 1886 as the candidate of a new Labor party. Against the opposition of Republicans, Democrats, and the Catholic Church, and probably losing thousands of votes in the Tammany-controlled electoral count, he nonetheless received a recorded vote of nearly seventy thousand—almost one-third of the total. In the same year (and in spite of the Haymarket bombing) a labor party in Chicago succeeded in electing several state legislators and judges and came within a whisker of electing a congressman. Men talked of a new Labor party in the near future, perhaps with Henry George as its presidential candidate. These hopes would not be realized, but the assumption behind them—that old political loyalties were at last weakening and new ones might soon emerge—proved true.

Farmers became as restless as workers. The Southern Alliance, a farmers' organization, suddenly in 1886 began to mushroom much as the Knights of Labor had done. Soon after, with the collapse of the agricultural land boom in Kansas and the onset of drought and farm depression, a Northern Alliance began a similar, if less spectacular growth. In the 1890s these two groups would merge into the People's party, or Populists, the greatest agrarian radical movement in American history.

Popular interest in reform ideas quickened in the late eighties and early nineties. The great upheaval of labor in 1886 inspired Edward Bellamy, an unsuccessful lawyer, editor, and author who had brooded for years over society's injustices, to write *Looking Backward: 2000–1887*, a utopian fantasy describing an ideal society set safely in the future. Bellamy dubbed its socialist economy "Nationalism," made its citizens staunchly religious, and blessed them with peace, justice, and a charming array of gadgets. The book sold a half-million copies within a few years, inspired fifty other authors to publish utopian romances, and gave rise to 165 Nationalist Clubs. Dozens of organizations promoted the book. The Theosophists endorsed it. So did the Women's Christian Temperance Union and the Grangers; it influenced the populists and various forms of American socialism. *Looking Backward* expressed the vague and unconscious socialism of the heart for which millions of respectable Americans yearned, a society transfigured by grace—not by class conflict or social revolution.

Fresh hopes jostled against old fears. The churches, no longer complacent, worried about the "social problem." Reform had widened its vision while conservatives prepared to defend the society which industry had created. Public debate turned to great abstractions: the "trust question," the "labor question," the "immigrant question," the "currency question." The confident eighties rapidly slid into the anxious nineties.

CAPTAINS OF EDUCATION

While men like Andrew Carnegie and John D. Rockefeller built the country's basic industries, other men nearly as famous in their time built the great universities. The transformation they wrought in higher education was almost as great as what the captains of industry did in steel and oil. Earlier in the nineteenth century American colleges had been ministerial preserves for their faculty and administrators and gentlemen's clubs for their students. Most instructors dished out a routine classical curriculum, emphasizing recitation and rote memory. All this began to change after the Civil War. The Morrill Act of 1862 offered a public subsidy for the state schools. Wealthy industrialists made the founding or extension of private universities a fashionable philanthropy. The founding of Johns Hopkins in 1876 and the reforming of Harvard under President Charles W. Eliot, beginning in 1869, were major examples of the new university. The emphasis was on science and research. Instead of a fixed classical curriculum, Eliot's elective system allowed students to follow their own interests and faculties to offer instruction in their own wide ranging fields of inquiry.

The clerical hold on education broke: Harvard abolished compulsory chapel in 1886, and large secular universities—Wisconsin, Michigan, MIT, Cornell, Johns Hopkins, Harvard, and Columbia—began to dominate educational philosophy. Faculty were better trained (many in German universities), better paid, and more independent. They soon gathered together in professional organizations to protect and extend their newfound status and to enforce professional standards in their field. Thus the American Historical Association was founded in 1884, the American Economic Association in 1885; the psychologists organized in 1892, and the sociologists in 1905. In many cases they were creating a public role for their expertise that would eventually take them beyond the reaches of the university into government, industry, and organized philanthropy. They were a new class, the organized intelligentsia, whose influence would soon be noticed in the progessive era.

The important academic statesmen of the period—Daniel Coit Gilman of Johns Hopkins, Eliot of Harvard, James B. Angell of Michigan, and William Rainey Harper of the University of Chicago (which began in the nineties with a large bequest from John D. Rockefeller)—were among the most clearsighted men of the age. They brought together organized scientific knowledge, traditional culture, the patronage of industry, and the children of successful Americans. Their aim was to create the rudiments of an elite, disciplined, cultured, yet up-to-date and scientific-minded leadership for an essentially leaderless and confused society. Eliot, who made his social goals particularly explicit, argued that universities "should exert a unifying social influence." They should draw students from a large area (he instituted entrance examinations in fifty cities to undo Harvard's inbreeding of students from father to son). This would enable Harvard to rise above "political discussions and divisions" and become "a school of public spirit, . . . patriotic in the best sense." In an age with a largely sterile official politics, this was a more sensible and in the long run more influential politics. It would soon be the age of the expert.

THINGS TO THINK ABOUT:
1876–1890

How could the ambitions of white American settlers and the needs of Indians both have been met in the nineteenth century? On the western movement see first Frederick Jackson Turner's classic essay "The Significance of the Frontier in American History" (a paper originally delivered in 1893), in Turner, *The Frontier in American History* (many current editions); Ray Allen Billington's comprehensive *Westward Expansion* (1967); and specificially on the Plains area, Walter Prescott Webb, *The Great Plains* (1931). For the history of the West seen from an Indian point of view, read Dee Brown, *Bury My Heart at Wounded Knee* (1971).

How did industrialism affect American life? Robert H. Wiebe, *The Search for Order, 1877–1920* (1967), Samuel P. Hays, *The Response to Industrialism, 1885–1914* (1957), and John A. Garraty, *The New Commonwealth, 1877–1890* (1968) are important attempts to describe the impact of industrialism. Thomas C. Cochran and William Miller, *The Age of Enterprise* (1942), remains a useful introduction to economic history.

What kind of men became "Captains of industry"? William Miller, *Men in Business* (1952) studies the backgrounds of successful businessmen; Edward C. Kirkland, *Dream and Thought in the Business Community, 1860–1900* (1956) studies their attitudes; Sigmund Diamond. *The Reputation of the American Businessman* (1955) studies what people thought about them. Matthew Josephson, *The Robber Barons* (1934) gives a hostile view of their activities. Allen Nevins, *Study in Power: John D. Rockfeller* (2 vols., 1953) is more sympathetic. John G. Cawelti, *Apostles of the Self-Made Man* (1965) deals with the myths surrounding this subject.

How did workers respond to industrialism, and how did American society respond to the workers in their midst? Philip Taft, *Organized Labor in the United States* (1964) is a convenient summary. For studies of particular strikes, see Robert V. Bruce, *1877: Year of Violence* (1959); Henry David, *The History of the Haymarket Affair* (1936); and Donald L. McMurry, *The Great Burlington Strike of 1888* (1956).

Why did Americans consider the governance of cities their greatest civic failure? On urbanization see Arthur M. Schlesinger, *The Rise of the City, 1878–1898* (1933) and Constance M. Green, *The Rise of Urban America* (1965). On city government see Alexander B. Callow, Jr., *The Tweed Ring* (1965) and Seymour Mandelbaum, *Boss Tweed's New York* (1965) as well as Zane L. Miller's *Boss Cox's Cincinnati* (1967). Richard Sennett's *Families Against the City* (1969) is an interesting analysis of urban tensions. For an overview of immigrants in the cities see Oscar Haudlin's graphic *The Uprooted* (1951).

After Reconstruction ended, did the South revert to its old prewar patterns or was it a "New South" as Henry Grady said? Two books by C.

Vann Woodward, *Origins of the New South, 1877–1913* (1951) and *The Strange Career of Jim Crow* (2nd revised edition, 1966) are indispensable. W. J. Cash, *The Mind of the South* (1941) has heavily influenced our view of all the South's history.

How did blacks respond to the end of Reconstruction? August Meier, *Negro Thought in America, 1885–1915* (1963) carefully analyzes the debates among black leaders. Rayford W. Logan, *The Negro in American Life and Thought: The Nadir, 1887–1901* (1954) examines opinions in the press. George B. Tindall, *South Carolina Negroes, 1877–1900* (1952) and Vernon Lane Wharton, *The Negro in Mississippi, 1865–1890* (1961) are superior state studies. Louis R. Harlan, *Booker T. Washington, The Making of a Black Leader, 1865–1901* (1972) is the first volume of a major biography. Students should read Washington's own *Up From Slavery*, originally published in 1901 (numerous editions).

How did Americans understand the changes their society was undergoing? Were they equipped to deal with it? Eric Goldman, *Rendezvous with Destiny* (1952), Richard Hofstadter, *Social Darwinism in American Thought* (1940), and Sidney Fine, *Laissez-Faire and the General-Welfare State* (1956) all deal with the emergence of reform ideas. George A. Barker, *Henry George* (1955) is a thorough study, as is Arthur E. Morgan, *Edward Bellamy* (1944). Henry F. May, *The Protestant Churches and Industrial America* (1949) describes the religious response.

What was all the tumult and shouting about in Gilded Age politics? Matthew Josephson, *The Politicos, 1865–1896* (1938) is readable and acerbic; H. Wayne Morgan, *From Hayes to McKinley* (1969) is readable and admiring of its subject. Allan Nevins, *Grover Cleveland* (1932) is an excellent biography. Ari Hoogenboom, *Outlawing the Spoils* (1961) deals with one of the era's successes, civil service reform. Woodrow Wilson's contemporary account, *Congressional Government* (1885), remains worth reading as does James Bryce, *The American Commonwealth*, originally published in 1888 (several editions).

1890-1900

nine | THE anxious nineties

JACOB S. COXEY

"Coxey's army is no longer a joke," wrote a Washington newspaper as the Commonwealth of Christ marched over the Pennsylvania mountains. "The growth and progress of this horde of desperate characters are most serious matters for Washington to contemplate." The Secret Service feared that Coxey's band of unemployed workmen marching on the District of Columbia might raid the United States Treasury; "No vault could withstand a determined man with drill and nitroglycerine," wrote a Secret Service agent. "And what could an army of one hundred thousand desperate and determined men do?"

      The depression of the mid-nineties was a blockbuster. Most of the nation's railroads went into bankruptcy; banks closed by the hundreds, businesses by the tens of thousands; millions of workers lost their jobs. Thousands of workers, especially in the Far West, banded together into so-called armies of the unemployed to seek work, commandeer free rides on trains to move toward employment, even to keep from starvation by pooling what they could beg. Jacob S. Coxey's inspiration was to transform these aimless unfortunates into a "petition with boots on."

      Coxey was a successful businessman, a pillar of the community of Massillon, Ohio. In rimless glasses and a well-cut business suit, this forty-year-old man of medium height and build, brown hair, small mustache, and

383

earnest but undramatic speech hardly seemed a terrifying figure. Nonetheless, "J. S. Coxey's Good Roads Association of the United States and Commonweal of Christ," better known as Coxey's Army, dominated the newspapers for weeks during 1894, forcing prosperous readers, as one journalist noted, to listen to "the inarticulate clamor for work for the workless" angrily buzzing across the nation.

Coxey offered his followers a program: "Good Roads and the Non-Interest Bearing Bonds." Both would have authorized the secretary of the treasury to issue legal tender notes (Coxey's answer to the currency question). Under the Good Roads Bill, the federal government would use the notes to hire workmen at a dollar and fifty cents per eight-hour day. Under the Bonds Bill, local and state governments could deposit special bonds in the treasury in return for legal tender notes which they would use in the same way to employ men on municipal improvement projects. Something like this plan, condemned as madness in the nineties, would become government policy in the next great depression of the 1930s. Coxey illustrated the sincerity of his belief in this panacea by christening his son Legal Tender Coxey and bringing him and his mother on the great march from Massillon to Washington, D.C.

Coxey laid the groundwork for his enterprise with some care. He secured the cooperation of leading Populists and of numerous labor groups. He also spent two thousand dollars advertising the venture until the press itself descended to provide unlimited free publicity. Although most of the marchers were genuinely unemployed workmen, the charlatans and publicity seekers of the age did not pass up this opportunity. One, in fact, was at Coxey's right hand: Carl Browne, known familiarly as "Old Greasy" for his presumed hostility to bathwater. Huge, bearded, and unkempt, Browne was always dressed in a Wild West constume, complete with Mexican silver half-dollars for buttons. Soon to join them was a man quickly dubbed "the great unknown." A born leader who rapidly gained an important place in the army, he refused to reveal his identity, giving reporters a running story with which to flummox their readers. He was "Captain Livingstone, late of the British army" by one account; "Jensen, a Swede employed by the Pinkerton detective agency" according to another. A women—the wife of the Great Unknown?—swarthed in heavy veils would appear and disappear. Then there was Cyclone Kirtland, the Pittsburgh astrologer; Honore Jaxon, half-breed Indian dressed in feathers and hired by the Chicago *Times* to make the march eating nothing but oatmeal; and snappily dressed Douglas McCallum, author of "Dogs and Fleas, by one of the Dogs."

The newspapers had a field day. Browne converted Coxey to Theosophy, a religious fad of the day. According to Browne, Coxey and he were, respectively, the "Cerebrum" and the "Cerebellum" of Christ. Their soul power would automatically convert Congress to their religious, economic, and political beliefs. The artistic Browne painted a banner for the army with a picture of the Saviour looking suspiciously like Browne himself and the motto "Peace on Earth, Good Will to Men. He Hath Risen, but Death to Interest on Bonds."

The march was full of strange happenings. Browne fought the Unknown who separated from Coxey and formed his own little army after at last identifying himself as the man who had made and sold "the great Kickapoo Indian Blood Medicine" at the recent Chicago World's Fair. Coxey and his associates put up at good hotels every night while the men slept on straw. He even went off periodically to confer with Populist leaders, attend to his sand business, or sell a few of his horses. Coxey's daughter by an earlier marriage ran away from home to join her father in Washington and led the hosts as the "Goddess of Peace" dressed in white with flowing blonde hair on a prancing stallion. In Washington only twelve hundred others converged with Coxey's group of a mere five hundred, and instead of Congress enacting his program under the irresistible pressure of soul force, police arrested Coxey and Browne for stepping "upon certain plants, shrubs, and turf then and there being and growing" on the Capitol grounds—in short, for disobeying a Keep Off the Grass sign.

Contemporaries scarcely knew what to make of the Coxey episode. Most newspapers held it up to ridicule. Congress shrugged it off, although not without angry speeches from Populists who objected to the treatment Coxey had received. Yet tens of thousands lining the streets through which the ragged army tramped had shown sympathy with its aims. "The Coxey-ites," wrote a perceptive English journalist who observed them, "ridiculed by the classes, have the sympathy of the masses." Coxey and the other industrial armies roaming the West and seeking to join him had made some points difficult to ignore: that men, unemployed, even destitute, could nonetheless display their power by means outside the ordinary channels of politics; that new pressures on American institutions could no longer be ignored; and that the operation of the economy, even a private economy, was no private matter.

Then there were other points that almost no one got. The age of media politics had arrived. Coxey's real achievement was in forcing the newspapers to do his work for him. The charlatanism, the comedies, the sensations had performed a function: while publicizing the trivial, the newspapers had carried the serious message of want and need as well. Eventually, the nation would learn that media exposure, the manufacture of events, even the soul force that Carl Browne espoused could have serious political meaning. Coxey's march was a beginning for an important strain in twentieth-century public life. And Coxey never changed: in 1928, shortly before his death, he was still good copy, as he again urged a march of the unemployed on Washington. Few took such unemployment seriously in 1928, but they would soon see their error. Before long, men would be marching again, and for much the same reasons that Coxey had led his Commonwealers.

1890-1900

1892	Populist Party nominates General James Baird Weaver for president
	Cleveland again elected president; defeats Harrison and Weaver
1893	Repeal of Sherman Silver Purchase Act
1894	Coxey's Army
	Pullman strike
1895	Venezuela Boundary Dispute
1896	William Jennings Bryan delivers "Cross of Gold" speech to Democratic Convention and later is endorsed by Populist Party
	William McKinley (Republican) elected president; defeats Bryan
1898	Sinking of the *Maine* in Havana harbor
	Spanish-American War, 20 April—10 December
	Plessy v. Ferguson
1899	Thorstein Veblen, *The Theory of the Leisure Class*
1900	Gold Standard Act
	Foraker Act
	McKinley reelected president; defeats Bryan

BILLION-DOLLAR POLITICS

American politics during the Gilded Age had seemed singularly incapable of confronting the problems created by rapid industrialization. But even the most hidebound leaders began to sense the rising discontent and tried to respond. Grover Cleveland's State of the Union message in 1887 was a novel call to action. The only such message ever devoted to a single topic, it demanded reductions in the tariff in order to end a troublesome government surplus, to lower the price of such necessities as textiles, sugar, and coffee, and—so he asserted—to strike a blow at the "trusts." Cleveland succeeded in defining the terms of debate both in Congress and in the presidential campaign of 1888. He failed, however, either to push tariff reduction through the Republican-controlled Senate or to gain reelection (although he topped his Republican rival, Benjamin Harrison, in the popular vote).

The Republicans now controlled the White House and both houses of Congress. Party leaders, sensing the voters' new restlessness, eagerly sought to do something positive. Harrison, a conscientious Presbyterian elder, must have liked the biblical text about casting one's bread upon the water; he had Congress spend most of the surplus on an improved navy, a subsidy to the American merchant marine, coastal defenses, and improved rivers and harbors. Nor did this ex–Civil War general forget his old army comrades. "It is no time now," he intoned, "to use an apothecary's scale to weigh the rewards of the men who saved the country." In four years he doubled the number of pensioners. This busy Congress also passed the McKinley Tariff, which lowered revenues by raising rates to prohibitive levels; cut excise taxes on tobacco and alcohol; and passed two important pieces of legislation bearing the name of the long-time Republican senatorial expert on economic questions, John Sherman of Ohio–the Sherman Antitrust Act and the Sherman Silver Purchase Act.

New directions

This Congress, the first one to appropriate more than a billion dollars ("This is a billion-dollar country" was House Speaker Thomas B. Reed's bland explanation), was a confusing signpost pointing down many criss-crossing roads. Speaker Reed had autocratically modernized procedures in the House of Representatives in order to push through this large legislative program. The problem of a treasury surplus that had plagued the nation since the late sixties disappeared, replaced in 1894 by the problem of a deficit in the national accounts. The McKinley Tariff established a national economic policy that encouraged the growth of manufacturing establishments by protecting them from foreign competition, while the Sherman Antitrust Act discouraged their growth by holding them liable to prosecution for limiting competition. Businessmen did not appear upset. The large investment in things nautical, which built on efforts that had begun earnestly in the eighties, shaped modern American naval power and offered a potent inducement for overseas expansion.

Prophetic in another way was the failure of two bills that had been on the Republican agenda for a generation. One provided federal funds for education and the other national control of elections. Aimed at defending or augmenting the rights of blacks, both lost in the shuffle of Republican economic legislation. Henceforth, the Republicans would protect business, not blacks, while Democratic governments in the South were free at last to institute one of the world's harsher racial regimes.

The Sherman Silver Purchase Act touched on the deepest confusions of all. Republican congressmen voted solidly for it, yet almost no one liked the bill. Sherman himself was "ready to repeal it" the day it became law, but feared worse in its stead. People always feared something worse on the "currency question," the great conundrum of the age, endlessly dull and technical yet endlessly debated—perhaps the key to some great door to prosperity and equality. James A. Garfield recorded in his diary the sad story of Mr. David Batcheller Mellish, a New York congressman who "devoted himself almost exclusively to the study of the currency, became fully entangled with the theories of the subject and became insane," dying in an asylum.

Money and banking

Money and banking had ever been potent issues in American politics because the nation had always lacked a satisfactory banking system. Hamilton and Jefferson divided over the Bank of the United States and the issues of funding the national debt. Andrew Jackson found his enemy in the second Bank of the United States. The Civil War saw a new banking system that tied banknotes to government bonds, and the federal government printed hundreds of millions of "greenback" dollars. In the postwar era, then, money was a genuinely complicated subject: by the time of the Sherman Act, the government had issued nine different kinds of currency. In addition, banknotes circulated backed by government bond holdings. Somewhere in this tangle, most people believed, was the source of the economy's ills: the periodic panics and depressions and especially the steadily declining prices, so painful to farmers.

In the sixties and seventies, those who wished to halt the decline in prices and the shrinking of the money supply had rallied to the standard of the greenbacks, the money issued during the war. Conservatives responded with an attempt to contract the currency by removing from circulation this fiat money, backed only by the government's word. The issue ended in a compromise, with $300 million in greenbacks retained, but given gold backing. This assured their value, and few were ever turned in for coin.

The "Crime of '73" Farmers and manufacturers who wanted more money in circulation next turned to silver. Gold and silver had been the joint standard of currency throughout national history, but silver, long overpriced in comparison to gold, had not circulated as coin for years. People would not spend as currency silver dollars worth about $1.03 for their metallic content. In the early seventies, the situation threatened to change as great silver-mining deposits in the West began to pay out their treasure. Financiers and their representatives in Congress, worried over the inflationary possibilities of this new source of currency inserted into a coinage act in 1873 a clause removing the silver dollar from the list of official coins. Most inflationists unthinkingly let through this apparently minor amendment. Soon, silver flooded the market and its price dropped to a level where coining it paid. At that point, its newfound political friends, realizing that it was no longer a legal monetary standard, cried foul. The Currency Act of 1873 became the "Crime of '73," part of a vast conspiracy against the people by politicians like John Sherman, bondholders, bankers, and sinister English and Jewish agents of international finance.

There was a germ of truth in these exaggerated charges. Men had knowingly demonetized silver, and while they had not conspired in the dark of night, neither had they shared their expert knowledge of the silver market with others in Congress. This act had clearly profited those who held government bonds and long-term debts—eastern bankers and rentiers and their western allies. And these people were, just as the silverites claimed, closely tied to international financiers and foreign governments. They were part of a worldwide economy whose reliance on gold currency caused prices to decline steadily, benefitting creditors and hurting debtors.

The advanced commercial nations, led by Great Britain, had already eliminated silver from their currency, creating a system of international finances based on gold that assured uniformity of price levels throughout most of the world. This expedited international markets in agricultural staples, simplified the commercial activities of England's merchants, and provided a uniform standard which gave investors some assurance about their foreign holdings. American industry built on a capital base of European investment, and payment on that investment was expected to be in gold. Naturally, in a world undergoing fabled economic expansion but whose gold supply increased slowly, the stock of gold never kept up with this economic activity. In terms of gold, prices of other goods throughout the world constantly declined.

While the linking of a gold standard and declining prices was not just the imaginings of conspiracy-minded farmers, the stories, endlessly repeated in the West, of bags of gold and secret agents with vaguely Jewish names corrupting the American Congress came straight from overheated imaginations. John Sherman did not need to be bought;

European objets d'art grace the Fifth Avenue home of John Jacob Astor. *Brown Brothers*

men like him simply saw America's economic future in maintaining the flow of gold from overseas. In this he could scarcely be called incorrect. Nor was he deceived about its implications, although he dared express them only in private:

> Undoubtedly [he wrote] the tendency of all civilizations is to make the rich richer and the poor poorer. . . . Labor becomes more abundant and cheaper, property increases and the fortunate few enjoy the greater share of the blessings of life. He would be a wise man who could change this course of civilization, and a very bold one to try to do it.

Silver legislation The outraged cries of silver men in the seventies brought yet another compromise, the Bland-Allison Act of 1878. This committed the government to purchasing at least $2 million worth of silver per month to be made into coins. Much of it never went into circulation, and the act had little effect on the currency supply. Yet the compromise survived until 1890, when a shift in the balance of power in the Senate lent new force to the desires of silver miners and inflation-minded farmers.

The entrance of six western states into the Union created a "silver bloc" which forced passage of the Sherman Silver Purchase Act. The silver senators wanted still more than the 4.5 million ounces of silver that the new law required the government to purchase each month. They argued for the free coinage of whatever silver anyone brought to the mint. Conservatives wanted far less, fearing that this unsettling of the government's finances would disturb trade and bring on depression. The Sherman Act was an unstable compromise. It survived only until 1893 when Grover Cleveland fronted down the silverites to repeal it, splitting his party in the process.

Later generations have generally looked down on the "rusty dogmas, piecemeal expedients, idealistic cure-all nostrums and political jockeying" that went into the currency question. Yet this effort at public education deserves respect, however limited its results. A reasonable modern parallel would be the issue of nuclear-arms limitations. Everyone agrees that the fate of the world hangs on this question. Most people understand that it is an elaborate, technical issue of strategies and diplomacy, although a few believe that there are simple and immediate unilateral solutions. Up to this point the parallel is quite exact. The great divergence comes in the political uses of the issue: disarmament has never been the issue of a presidential election or the subject of sustained and intense public debate in Congress and the press. Generally it has been left to experts and soldiers, with some academic experts kibbitzing from the sidelines. The great currency debate was a monument to nineteenth-century democracy: strident and sometimes uninformed, but usually public and often at a high level. Even the cries of conspiracy bespoke the common assumption that this was everyone's business, a belief that has too rarely applied to public issues in the twentieth century.

AGRICULTURAL DISCONTENT

The agrarian ideal
Most of the soldiers in the Revolutionary and Civil wars were farmers; so were most of the men behind our national heroes—Jefferson, Jackson, Lincoln, and Grant. This was as it should be according to nineteenth-century thought: democracy rested on a sturdy and independent yeomanry, men close to the soil, capable of running their own affairs. Politicians and journalists extolled the virtues of agricultural pursuits. The growth of cities confirmed these assumptions: cities were sores on the body politic, corrupt enemies of democracy. The nation showed its feelings by granting rural areas a disproportionate number of seats in state legislatures. Farmers could be secure knowing that their representatives sat squarely on the fulcrums of power.

Yet progressively through the post–Civil War period, farmers learned to fear that someone else had his hand on the levers. The theoretical power of "the people"—which farmers took to be themselves—had ceased to be the real force directing their lives. Farmers in the new or underdeveloped areas—Illinois and Iowa in the 1870s, Kansas, Nebraska, and the Dakotas in the late eighties and nineties, and many parts of the southern backcountry—experienced this most directly. Burdensome mortgages threatened their land, declining agricultural prices suddenly made their crops less valuable, and profit margins shrank as freight rates took a larger share of their crop prices (despite a more or less steady decline in the rates themselves). The farmers' political strength, as well, somehow evaporated as it flowed from the local courthouse to the state legislature to the halls of Congress.

Agrarian protest
Sporadic protest movements suddenly turned into an angry political revival in the late eighties as drought in the West, sagging prices for cotton and wheat, and tighter money turned frustration into fury. Farm groups, previously concerned with local matters like cooperative purchasing, rounding up stray cattle, or dealing with horse thieves, turned to politics in the 1890 elections.

In the West the revival took the form of third parties and agricultural alliances; in the South it was mainly such alliances struggling to capture the Democratic party. Everywhere three-party politics created odd coalitions or "fusions," so that when the outcome became known it was still hard to tell just how much the alliances had won. Contemporaries usually credited them with victory. By that standard eight southern legislatures plus Kansas and Nebraska were in alliance hands, three senators and forty-four congressmen receptive to their wishes were on their way to the capital, and they had done well enough in two other northern states to hold the balance of power. Such a showing was more than encouraging, it was intoxicating. Alliance leaders immediately began making overtures to representatives of labor, hoping to create a new national party to replace one of the old ones, much as the Republicans had displaced the Whigs in the 1850s.

The populists   In February 1892 a meeting of eight hundred farm leaders, reformers, and a few labor leaders organized the People's party, quickly to become known as the Populists. They called for a national convention to meet in Omaha on July 4, and there, besides nominating a presidential ticket, adopted the most farreaching party platform in American political history. An elaborate preamble offered an apocalyptical vision of a nation "brought to the verge of moral, political, and material ruin" by a conspiracy of greedy private interests. The new People's party would do what neither the Republicans nor the Democrats had even done: expand the power of government "as rapidly and as far as the good sense of an intelligent people and the teachings of experience shall justify, to the end that oppression, injustice, and poverty shall eventually cease in this land." In this pledge lies much of the history of twentieth-century American politics, at least the history of its aspiration and rhetoric: the new century's liberalism would be in large part a scramble by people very different from the Populists to meet some of the Populists' demands without major disruptions of the social order.

Populism and   The more concrete aims of the Populist platform also influenced the
twentieth-century   future: their call for a graduated income tax, a postal savings system,
reform   some form of government financing of farm credit, the direct election of senators, the enforcement of laws against importing labor by contract, and steps toward achieving the eight-hour day for industrial workers. All these eventually came to pass. The Populists' general objective of using government control of the money supply to improve business and agricultural conditions became financial orthodoxy, although their particular nostrum—the free and unlimited coinage of silver at a ratio of sixteen to one with gold—never got a trial for that purpose. But none of these accomplishments came under the leadership of Populists; and some items on their list never became law—the public ownership of railroads and of telephone and telegraph companies, the prohibition of alien land ownership or the one-term presidency. Those parts of the Populist platform that were finally enacted bore the mark of the corporate and urban world which put them through and have, perhaps, ended being very different from anything the Populists envisioned. For the Populists, leaders as well as followers, were, as the founder of the party in Oklahoma said,

"ordinary folk," not the "better classes," and what people do for themselves is by that fact different from what their betters do for them.

The Populists, who could get but 8 percent of the presidential vote in 1892 and then merged with a renovated Democratic party in 1896, succeeded principally in frightening the other parties and injecting new notes into political argument. They commanded hard support only in a few rural areas; the older, more settled regions rejected their apparently radical appeal. The expansion of government under more conservative auspices over the next half-century reflected their program rather than their ideas, which were deeply embedded in the nineteenth century. They sought, perhaps paradoxically, to use government to return initiative to individuals and the local community. For example, their "subtreasury plan" would have provided government financial instruments and warehousing to make farmers their own bankers, able to use their own nonperishable stored produce to generate their own credit. The Populists also believed in government by party, not by experts, and in revivalistic public debate heavy with moral overtones. They sought to impose their view of righteousness on others, not by sly manipulation but by open debate and exhortation. In this sense, they may well have been out of place in an increasingly heterogeneous nation. They were somewhere between the old image of the farmer as "the people" and the new realities; soon the farmer would pass into a minority of the population and have to advance as a special-interest group, as greedy as all the rest. The Populists resisted this, eternally to their credit. What became of their dreams in the twentieth century would have seemed as tarnished to them as their silver standard does to us, a discounting of idealism at—perhaps—sixteen to one.

THE SECOND CLEVELAND PRESIDENCY

The election of 1892 offered few surprises and, outside the strongly Populist areas, even less excitement. President Harrison stood on the record of the billion-dollar Congress, former President Cleveland on his performance in the White House from 1885 to 1889. Except for the Democrat Cleveland's promise of modest tariff reform, the two men had the same credentials: a proven capacity to run the nation's business in sound, conservative, if unimaginative fashion. When Cleveland and his party gained a clear-cut victory, few solid citizens anticipated serious change. Even strongly Republican and protection-minded businessmen might echo Andrew Carnegie's estimate of Cleveland as "a pretty good fellow." The previous year, at the height of the national currency debate, Cleveland had delighted bankers with a public letter denouncing free silver as "a reckless and dangerous experiment." Many thought his moderate views on tariff reform and his remarks against the growth of trusts would allay discontent without upsetting anyone's interest: "People will now think the Protected Manfrs. are attended to and quit agitating," commented Carnegie on the election outcome.

      Yet Cleveland raised very different hopes as well. Heady words like "liberal" and "reform" had already attached themselves to his first administration: reforms of civil service, the tariff, pensions, Indian policy, trusts, railroads. He had found support in 1892 from men with ideas very different from the cautious businessmen who financed his presidential campaign. Populist leaders quietly backed him in exchange for Democratic endorsement of their local candidates. Henry George campaigned actively for Cleveland, as did Eugene V. Debs, then a Terre Haute labor leader and soon to be America's leading socialist. Cleveland, despite his contemporary reputation for bluntness, had in fact maintained a delicate political balance over the years. He was confident that it would continue in his second administration.

The depression of the nineties

He proved wrong: economic depression led his party to disaster. Only weeks after he took office a stock market panic ushered in major collapse. Statistics show that the depression of the seventies was sharper and the Great Depression of the 1930s longer and more costly, but in the human terms that matter this was the worst depression in American history. It came after large parts of the population were locked in cities and before generations of effort at social welfare had softened the blow that fell on the urban poor during a depression. And like the next great depression, it landed hard upon farmers, who had already suffered years of bad times. In the depression's deepest trough, the winter of 1893–94, more than 2½ million men walked the streets and rode the rails seeking work. Charities and a few local governments offered scant aid. But contemporary beliefs about the damaging effects on character of relief, even when given in exchange for work on public projects, stymied any large-scale assistance. Government officials and publicists as well as reformers and welfare workers repeated Cleveland's famous statement during his first administration that "though the people support the Government the Government should not support the people." Meanwhile people died from cold and hunger. Many survived through the largesse of saloonkeepers connected with the political machines. "Hinky Dink" Kenna, one of the more corrupt of the "gray wolves" on Chicago's Board of Aldermen, in a single week fed eight thousand destitute men in his First Ward saloon. When one of his employees demanded a nickel from an unfortunate with too much appetite, Hinky Dink promptly fired the offending bartender. Few people forget such things on election day.

Silver repeal

Grover Cleveland's solution to the problems of depression was rather more theoretical than this. He, like so many of his contemporaries, saw

Toilers of the Sea, Albert Pinkham Ryder. *The Metropolitan Museum of Art, George A. Hearn Fund, 1915*

the answer in the currency question. The problem was to restore the confidence—that most mysterious quantity—of businessmen, and the issue that worried businessmen most was clearly silver. Forthright action in favor of gold would, Cleveland and his advisors believed, loosen the paralysis that had fallen upon American industry, offering the only permanent relief for the unemployed.

Cleveland proceeded with a presidential vigor unparalleled since Lincoln's wartime leadership. Fresh from a dramatic, secret, and life-endangering operation aboard a friend's yacht in which a cancer on the roof of his mouth was removed, he called a special session of Congress. He then staked his entire political capital on forcing through repeal of the Sherman Silver Purchase Act over the objections of a large part of his own party. Had the economy then swung upward, he would have earned an overwhelming triumph. Instead it sagged to its nadir and Cleveland was left with popular hatred, a divided party, and a long term as president stretching before him lacking all support in Congress: "Think of it!," Cleveland lamented: "Not a man in the Senate with whom I can be on terms of absolute confidence."

Grover Cleveland versus his party

As late as 1892 only Cleveland had seemed capable of holding together the disparate elements making up the Democratic party: the conservative bankers and merchants, the low-tariff railroadmen, the southern business leaders along with the urban immigrants and workmen and the thousands of poor and middling Democratic farmers in the South and West. After 1893 the party crumbled at his every touch. As the depression shrank tax receipts and treasury balances, Cleveland had to go to Wall Street, virtually hat in hand, to float the bonds that would save the United States government from bankruptcy. An undersecretary of the treasury wrote in distress (and of course in secret) of the "curious spectacle of the U.S. finances being controlled by a committee, of which J. P. Morgan is Chairman, and the majority of whom are Hebrews, while the Secretary of the Treasury sits, practically powerless in his office." Cleveland's western and southern enemies understandably thought the worst. "When Judas betrayed Christ," one-eyed Ben Tillman told the angry farmers he led in South Carolina, "his heart was not blacker than this scoundrel, Cleveland, in deceiving the Democracy."

Nor could Cleveland gain any lost ground by turning to other issues. He failed to control Congress's efforts at tariff reduction and got five months of party-destroying argument in the Senate and a bad bill in the bargain. The main provision of the Wilson-Gorman Tariff palatable to his western and southern enemies, a small tax on large incomes, died almost instantly at the unsympathetic hands of the Supreme Court. This in fact climaxed a series of unpopular decisions protecting manufacturers from the new antitrust law and holding labor unions and their leaders

Edward Steichen, *J. P. Morgan,* 1903—"I'm not in Wall Street for my health." *Collection, The Museum of Modern Art, New York. Gift of the photographer*

liable to penalties under vague and comprehensive "blanket" injunctions against cooperative activities—including, of course, strikes.

1894: Crisis year　Class antagonism far beyond anything seen before in America surfaced in 1894. Coxey's Army was a symptom of deep conflict. The great Pullman strike, arriving on the heels of numerous labor disturbances, looked to many like the long-awaited social revolution. Eugene V. Debs, the brilliant and energetic leader of the American Railway Union, led a massive boycott against the Pullman Palace Car Company of Pullman, Illinois; the railroad owners retaliated by stopping all trains into Chicago, and with the help of a compliant judge, an eager United States attorney general, and an obstinate president, fearing disorder and insistent on moving the mails through Chicago, succeeded in getting federal troops to break the strike. Grover Cleveland had added another clutch of enemies, including Governor John Peter Altgeld of Illinois, who engaged in public recriminations with Cleveland for sending federal troops in the absence of any request from the state. Public opinion supported the president, but Altgeld would have his revenge two years later in leading Cleveland's enemies at the Democratic National Convention.

The congressional elections of 1894, coming at the trough of the depression, gave a clear reading of society's tensions. The administration suffered the greatest political defeat in American history. From a commanding 218 representatives in the House, the Democrats shrank to 105, giving the Republicans a majority of 140. The Populists gained another four hundred thousand votes, but their geographical base of support had shrunk rather than increased and their larger totals came mostly from fusion arrangements. The older parties were stealing their issues and some of their support. For all the discontent in the land, the Republicans, not any radical group, had profited from the distress of the decade. But the results also illustrated the popularity of the silver issue. Democrats, trapped by Cleveland's currency policy and the tariff fiasco, did not elect a single congressman anywhere between Ohio and California. After 1894 it appeared that the Democrats were already split on the currency question and that western Republicans were pushing toward a disruption in their party. The 1896 election would be the most important in decades.

THE ELECTION OF 1896

The results of 1894 set the political tone for 1896. The dominant note was Republican confidence. Men began actively to seek the nomination as soon as the congressional results came in, and by early 1896 the contest had largely ended. William McKinley of Ohio, identified with high tariffs and with a fuzzy record on currency, popular with workingmen and a solid favorite in the Middle West, easily outdistanced the other candidates. The party met in St. Louis in June to nominate him, placating his eastern rivals with a firm declaration in the platform to maintain the "existing gold standard." A small bolt of western silver Republicans bothered the Republican leadership not at all. McKinley's hometown band mockingly played "Silver Threads Among the Gold" as the leader of the Republican silver forces, Senator Henry M. Teller of Colorado, delivered as emotion-laden speech of farewell to the party he had helped found forty years before. Mark Hanna, McKinley's campaign manager, happily shouted "Go! Go!" A correspondent for the Omaha *World-Herald* scrambling over the reporters' desks to view the scene more closely was equally excited: ex-Congressman William Jennings Bryan of Nebraska had worked for a moment like this all of the past three years.

Enter
William Jennings Bryan

The Democratic convention, meeting in Chicago in July, was the most dramatic national party conclave until the same party met in the same city seventy-two years later. Administration Democrats put up a hard fight for gold, but three years of intense debate and organization and the obvious political need to repudiate the unpopular Cleveland gave the silver forces a huge majority. Bryan's brilliant speech defending the silverite's platform gave them a candidate as well.

Thirty-six years old and with a national political experience of only two terms in Congress, the young Nebraskan seemed an unlikely presidential candidate. But he had labored assiduously to combine the silver forces—Democratic, Populist, and Republican—and was a true representative, even an embodiment, of western small-town and rural culture, a genuine man of the people. Most of all, he was a great orator in an age that valued oratory above most else. Generations of western schoolchildren would later declaim his famous convention speech. His cry of defiance against the eastern world of banks and merchants and railroadmen: "We beg no longer; we entreat no more; we petition no more; We defy them!" rung across the prairies for generations. His stately conclusion—"You shall not press down upon the brow of labor this crown of thorns, you shall not crucify mankind upon a cross of gold" —although widely denounced by his enemies in 1896 as blasphemous (especially since he accompanied it with the appropriate gesture of pressing his hands against his brow), remains a permanent part of the folklore of American politics.

The convention, badly in need of a viable silver candidate, accepted him on the fifth ballot the next afternoon. The Populists, meeting afterward, had no real choice but to accept him as their candidate as well: he had maintained excellent relations with their leaders and stood for their most popular if not for the full range of their goals. If they had refused and he had come anywhere near election, they would have been considered betrayers of the cause.

The peerless leader. *Library of Congress*

Bryan's platform   Bryan launched the first modern barnstorming campaign, covering eighteen thousand miles, making six hundred speeches, and reaching perhaps 5 million people. He talked mostly about silver, not because he was a fanatic but because this was the only issue that held together his supporters and because the other major issue, the tariff, could only cost him votes by reminding voters of his party's failure to win reform. Also, he recognized that silver, whatever the technical virtues or demerits it had as a monetary standard, had come to symbolize economic reform. Bryan advocated a federal income tax, wanted to limit severely the note-issuing role of private banks, opposed the kind of injunctions that had been issued during the Pullman strike, and was devoted to tariff reform. He argued that until silver won there was "no other reform that can be accomplished." Opponents who sensed that there were more reforms to come if Bryan became president were surely correct.

On the other hand, Bryan's Populist followers who thought he would do less than they wished were correct as well. Bryan was the first national exemplar of a new kind of liberalism that would soon be called progressivism—devoted to active reform of existing economic institutions without, however, destroying or fundamentally altering them. Silver, because it lacked appeal to workingmen who saw that inflation would hurt their standard of living, was an unfortunate issue on which to argue the need for reform. But it was the only possible issue at that point in time, and Bryan gave it the best defense he could. He fought for a reform movement that would both meet modern needs and preserve intact the agrarian world of his childhood—a gallant, impossible program.

Bryan versus McKinley

Aside from Bryan, the Democrats had practically nothing else. Many Democratic organizations in the East and Midwest abandoned him. When they did not openly support the opposition, they backed a "gold Democrat" ticket fielded to draw votes away from Bryan. Worse yet, every major business interest except a few silver-mine owners turned against the Democrats. Where previously most contributions came from individual businessmen and were more or less evenly divided between the parties, suddenly, with no Democratic directors objecting, corporations could support the Republicans straight out of their treasuries. Businessmen sooned gained confidence in the Republican manager, Marcus Alonzo Hanna, a Cleveland millionaire industrialist turned politician. There were virtually no bars to what they could give. Hanna raised several million dollars to blanket the nation with 250 million pieces of campaign literature and paid speakers to orate for McKinley and newspapers to support him. A scrawled note from Hanna would move hundreds of the party faithful over the rails to Canton, where McKinley, flanked by his aging mother and invalid wife, could deliver set little speeches for national distribution through the newspapers. At Hanna's word, banks threatened to foreclose mortgages or deny credit if McKinley were not elected. Hanna became an instant legend.

"Dollar Mark" the great "national boss" blended as much legend with the tamer reality as his adversary, the "boy orator of the Platte." (The Platte River in Nebraska was rumored to be six inches deep and six miles wide at the mouth.) Hanna had performed a function much like other businessmen in the Republican party in the past. But he had performed it somewhat better and in more fortunate circumstances. He was an apt symbol of the marriage of business and politics which the

Republican party consummated in 1896. It would be a lasting arrangement. For the next generation, Republicans would be the numerical majority in the nation, and leaders of large-scale business and finance would dominate party councils. Hanna was the Gilded Age's appointment with the twentieth century. Americans, as Henry Adams recognized, had declared themselves "once for all, in favor of the capitalistic system with all its necessary machinery."

The outcome The electoral outcome was obvious by early fall. McKinley collected 271 electoral votes, Bryan only 176. A higher proportion of eligible voters turned out than in any other national election before or since. Bryan, who lost by half a million votes, nevertheless had a higher popular-vote total than any candidate prior to that year. Cries of foul play rent the air, and there is no question that they reflected a reality: economic coercion was rampant and corruption common. But the charge that the Republicans won only by these tactics is untrue, for subsequent elections repeated the results of 1896. The election of 1896 was the decision not merely of a moment but of a generation. Henceforth, until the next great swing of the political wheel in the 1930s, Republican majorities, high tariffs, and sound money would be the rule. The last, ironically, proved least important of all. Late in the decade the economy—and prices—began to swing upward in a long economic spiral that would endure until 1929. And suddenly currency was abundant—not from silver, but from the gold that angry farmers had so despised. A new way of extracting the metal from low-grade ores, the cyanide process, together with fresh discoveries in Australia, Alaska, and South Africa at last made gold an adequate base for the international monetary system. The silverites had essentially been correct about the inadequacy of the world's gold stock in the early nineties to meet economic needs. Bryan, one might say, had won his point by losing his issue. The next reform movement, progressivism, would consist of urban as well as rural people, and they would worry about inflation, not falling prices. And Bryan would be there, having lost what he immediately called "The First Battle" but fighting on.

THE ISOLATED EMPIRE

The United States had always been an imperial nation, gathering new territories, settling new lands, brushing aside those who stood in its path. Through most of the nineteenth century Americans purchased, fought for, or took from the willing hands of settlers a western empire carved largely from the old Spanish conquests.

The Civil War added a new dimension to American expansion, for the conflict created not only a larger and more ambitious central

The Gulf Stream, Winslow Homer. *The Metropolitan Museum of Art, Wolfe Fund, 1906*

government, but a powerful navy as well. William H. Seward, the aggressive secretary of state during Reconstruction, actively sought overseas expansion. In addition to purchasing Alaska—on the continent but separated from the rest of American territory—Seward seized the unclaimed Midway Islands far out in the Pacific and tried to buy Denmark's possessions in the West Indies. Both Denmark and the islands' inhabitants were willing, but the United States Senate was not.

President Grant had similar ambitions and they met a comparable fate. With Cuba in revolt against Spain after 1868, he looked longingly for an American role in the West Indies, but Secretary of State Hamilton Fish thought it unwise. Grant especially wanted to annex Santo Domingo, but even the most heavy-handed presidential pressure could not overcome the Senate's opposition. A treaty that would have gained us a naval station in Pago Pago foundered on the same shoal. Despite a healthy measure of ambition for overseas expansion, the weight of American thinking was still against foreign adventures. As if to remove temptation, Congress allowed the Civil War navy to decay to a point where the English wit Oscar Wilde called it the chief romantic ruin that America could offer the tourist.

Mulberry Street, lower East Side
New York City. *Library of Congress*

The American people before the nineties based their rejection of an overseas empire on arguments which by this time had the force of tradition. The Founding Fathers, especially Washington and Jefferson, had told them to look resolutely westward both to advance their interests and preserve their freedoms. American institutions could accommodate a vast continental empire divided into new sovereign states with populations similar in race and culture to the older areas. But the Constitution would not tolerate rule over foreign populations, men with strange tongues and political habits unsuited to American liberties. This would mean an enlarged federal government, standing armies, corps of diplomats, and sinister alliances with the corrupt nations of Europe. And in the "uncivilized" world expansion presented fresh racial dilemmas, a major objection to the Santo Domingan adventure. Who needed this, when in the West opportunity beckoned and to the east the Atlantic Ocean provided security without armies, navies, or alliances?

Voices for expansion

This traditional rationale for isolation remained a bulwark against most foreign adventure until the nineties, but fresh events, needs, and ambitions chipped away at it. By the end of the century, we were the foremost industrial power. Adventurous souls saw that this offered opportunities for glory on the world's stage; practical ones sensed, especially during depressions, the need for world markets; religious leaders discovered a moral duty to spread American institutions and Christian missions. New intellectual currents, especially social Darwinism, emphasized the conflict of races and cultures in the world and with it the need to compete for markets and power. The theories of Captain Alfred T. Mahan, asserting that naval power determines the course of history, powerfully influenced leaders of opinion in government, the military, and to a lesser extent businessmen.

Islands in the Pacific

Foreign policy, however, is more the result of specific events than of grand theories, and events everywhere were sucking America into the vortex of world affairs. Fresh experience reversed the old aphorism: the flag followed trade. For example, American merchant ships in the Pacific had long made stopovers in Hawaii and Samoa. A few countrymen, seeing opportunities there, settled, creating economic involvements and attracting missionaries. Transcontinental railroads in the United States and the advance of steam transport across the Pacific increased their economic importance. With the European nations hungrily gobbling up the unclaimed areas of the world, settlers looked to the American government for security, while American administrators eyed sites for naval stations such as Pearl Harbor in Hawaii. Once European penetration of these areas began, American prestige was at stake, and private adventures became diplomatic, even military concerns.

In Samoa conflicting German, English, and American interests in the South Pacific archipelago produced a decade of intrigue leading to a naval confrontation in 1889. Fortunately, a hurricane dispersed fleets, and a conference created a tripartite protectorate over the islands. The arrangement, abandoned ten years later, marked a turn in American policy from its traditional isolationism.

Hawaii

Hawaii blossomed into a far more important outpost of the American economy. Missionaries there advertised the islands' economic possibilities in the religious press, attracting settlers who organized the native sugar industry. A reciprocity treaty in 1875 admitted their produce duty-free, booming the Hawaiian economy and tying it tightly to that of the American mainland. The American navy moved into Pearl Harbor, gaining treaty rights to this great natural basin in 1887.

Then in the nineties disaster struck. The McKinley Tariff removed the duty on sugar, wiping out the Hawaiian advantage in the American market. A year later political trouble followed hard on the economic problems. A new monarch ascended the throne of this American-run but nominally Polynesian kingdom. Queen Liliuokalani, a genuine nationalist, was determined to return power to the natives, now threatened not only by American domination but also by competition from tens of thousands of Chinese, Japanese, and Portuguese imported to work on the sugar plantations. Early in 1893 she proclaimed a new constitution eliminating the white-controlled legislature. The new regime survived but three days. American planters, with the aid of an enthusiastic United States minister and a detachment of sailors and marines placed to threaten the Royal Palace, staged a bloodless coup d'etat. They raised the Stars and Stripes and declared Hawaii an American protectorate.

The successful revolutionists raced to Washington and within two weeks had signed a treaty of annexation with the eager State Department. Still they had not been fast enough. With the Harrison regime about to end, the Senate delayed and the new secretary of state withdrew the treaty. Cleveland investigated, objected to the skullduggery of the planters and the minister, and tried to reinstate the queen. The Americans, firmly in control, would have none of it and finally forced Cleveland to recognize their government. Once the Republicans returned to power, they annexed Hawaii (1898) by joint resolution of the two houses of Congress, avoiding a treaty fight in the Senate.

Latin America

Latin America lacked the available native territories that dotted the Pacific, but American interests there were at least as great. Americans saw economic possibilities and hungered for a canal across Central America linking their Atlantic and Pacific maritime interests. Secretary of State

James G. Blaine, who served in the brief Garfield administration and then for most of Harrison's, looked for ways to assert American leadership in the hemisphere. He organized a Pan-American Conference in 1889, and sought unsuccessfully for trade and arbitration agreements. A minor incident in Valparaiso which angered President Harrison almost led to open conflict between the United States and Chile in 1891. Americans seemed anxious for a chance to flex their muscles.

The Venezuela boundary dispute

They got their chance in 1895. Cleveland, his popularity at a low point, seized on an old dispute between Great Britain and Venezuela over the latter's border with British Guiana. Championing the cause of small nations, he demanded that England submit to American wishes and, gratuitously, proclaimed that the United States was "practically sovereign on this continent." England at first ignored the American threats, but when Cleveland persisted in his belligerent posture and received enthusiastic popular support in the press and in Congress, the British government reconsidered its course. They were threatened by a rising Germany and faced incipient revolt in South Africa. To add the United States, with its huge potential strength, to the list of enemies was, said the British colonial secretary, "an absurdity as well as a crime." The English agreed to arbitration, winning most of the disputed territory that way. The result, paradoxically, was a marked improvement in Anglo-American relations. Having been to the brink, the two nations, recognizing their economic and diplomatic need for each other, embarked on their course of close friendship in the twentieth century.

THE CUBAN REVOLUTION

Americans had coveted Cuba for most of the nineteenth century, and only northern fears of new slave states prevented its annexation before the Civil War. Along with Puerto Rico, Cuba comprised all that remained of the once-great Spanish Empire in the New World. Revolution broke out there in 1868 and continued for a decade. During those years Americans watched the brutal conflict raging close to their shores, and in at least one instance our government cautiously declined an excuse for intervention.

Much had changed when the rebels renewed the conflict in 1895. The second Cuban Revolution was a shocker. The rebels deliberately laid waste the island, burning crops in order to push out their rulers and, by damaging American interests, to force the United States to intervene. The Spanish, under a new commander, Valeriano Weyler, adopted a policy of herding the population into camps to separate them from the rebels. In a world not yet accustomed to concentration camps, the results—about two hundred thousand dead of starvation and epidemic—horrified millions.

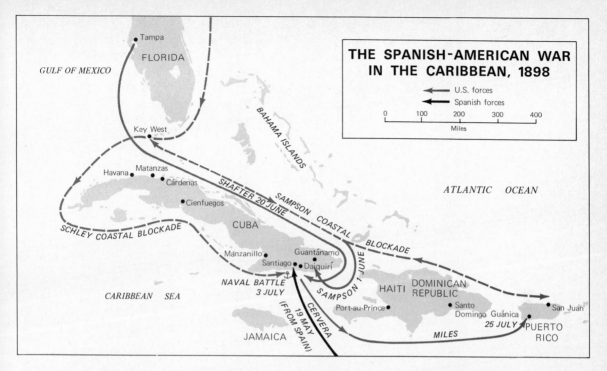

THE SPANISH-AMERICAN WAR
IN THE CARIBBEAN, 1898

←—— U.S. forces
←—— Spanish forces

0   100   200   300   400
Miles

GULF OF MEXICO

Tampa
FLORIDA

Key West

Havana Matanzas
Cárdenas
Cienfuegos

BAHAMA ISLANDS

ATLANTIC   OCEAN

SHAFTER 20 JUNE
SAMPSON COASTAL BLOCKADE
SCHLEY COASTAL BLOCKADE

CUBA

Manzanillo Guantánamo
Santiago Daiquirí
NAVAL BATTLE
3 JULY

SAMPSON 1 JUNE

CERVERA
19 MAY
(FROM SPAIN)

CARIBBEAN   SEA

HAITI DOMINICAN
REPUBLIC
Port-au-Prince Santo
Domingo Guánica
25 JULY

JAMAICA

MILES

San Juan

PUERTO
RICO

The yellow press A new journalism spread these atrocities throughout the country. Two rival New York papers, Joseph Pulitzer's *World* and William Randolph Hearst's *Journal,* made dashing reporters and sensational articles a national craze. When news was lacking, they were not above creating it. Spanish policy was just made for these "yellow press" tactics: heart-rending scenes for reporters to present, shocking sights for artists to capture, outrages for editors to exaggerate. Spanish soldiers got the full treatment: they were murderers, torturers, sex fiends. Expansionist-minded political leaders, anti-Catholic clergymen, and Cuban propagandists vouched for the truth of these stories. The public, which had already demonstrated its jingoistic mood in the Venezuela incident, absorbed these stories for three years with ever-rising demands that something be done.

Steps toward war McKinley, who genuinely sympathized with Cuba's agony, was scarcely the man to resist these pressures. A popular joke went: "Why is McKinley's mind like a bed?" "Because it has to be made up for him every time he wants to use it." Still, businessmen, just recovering from their own agony during the long depression, objected to fresh upsets that might damage the economy, and many leaders of opinion repeated the traditional arguments against entanglement. McKinley moved cautiously. A strong but carefully worded protest brought a softening of Spanish policy, and with the rebels weakening during 1897, chances of war diminished.

409

Then two dramatic events in February 1898 shoved Americans toward conflict. One was the De Lôme letter—the private thoughts of Dupuy de Lôme, Spanish minister in Washington, written to a friend, stolen, and purchased by William Randolph Hearst. In this note, the minister had contemptuously expressed the current opinion of McKinley: that he was "weak and a bidder for the admiration of the crowd." De Lôme resigned as soon as the letter appeared, but the American public was furious and the wavering McKinley edged one step closer to war.

In the midst of this furor, the American battleship *Maine*, sent to Havana to protect American lives and property, exploded in Havana harbor, killing 264 men on board. The newspapers instantly blamed Spain: "Remember the *Maine*! To hell with Spain!" became the cry.

Destruction of the U. S. Battleship Maine. *Culver Pictures*

$50,000 REWARD.—WHO DESTROYED THE MAINE?—$50,000 REWARD.

EDITION FOR GREATER NEW YORK

The Journal will give $50,000 for information, furnished to it exclusively, that will convict the person or persons who sank the Maine.

NEW YORK JOURNAL
AND ADVERTISER.

The Journal will give $50,000 for information, furnished to it exclusively, that will convict the person or persons who sank the Maine.

NO. 5,572. Copyright, 1898, by W. R. Hearst.—NEW YORK, THURSDAY, FEBRUARY 17, 1898.—16 PAGES. PRICE ONE CENT in Greater New York, Elsewhere TWO CENTS.

DESTRUCTION OF THE WAR SHIP MAINE WAS THE WORK OF AN ENEMY.

$50,000!

$50,000 REWARD!
For the Detection of the Perpetrator of the Maine Outrage!

The New York Journal hereby offers a reward of $50,000 CASH for information FURNISHED TO IT EXCLUSIVELY, which shall lead to the detection and conviction of the person, persons or government criminally responsible for the explosion which resulted in the destruction, at Havana, of the United States war ship Maine and the loss of 258 lives of American sailors.

The $50,000 CASH offered for the above information is on deposit with Wells, Fargo & Co.

No one is barred, be he the humble but misguided seaman acting out a few miserable dollars by acting as a spy, or the attache of a government secret service, plotting, by any devilish means, to revenge fancied insults or cripple menacing countries.

This offer has been cabled to Europe and will be made public in every capital of the Continent and in London this morning.

The Journal believes that any man who can be bought to commit murder can also be bought to betray his comrades. FOR THE PERPETRATOR OF THIS OUTRAGE HAD ACCOMPLICES.

W. R. HEARST.

Assistant Secretary Roosevelt Convinced the Explosion of the War Ship Was Not an Accident.

The Journal Offers $50,000 Reward for the Conviction of the Criminals Who Sent 258 American Sailors to Their Death. Naval Officers Unanimous That the Ship Was Destroyed on Purpose.

$50,000!

$50,000 REWARD!
For the Detection of the Perpetrator of the Maine Outrage!

The New York Journal hereby offers a reward of $50,000 CASH for information FURNISHED TO IT EXCLUSIVELY, which shall lead to the detection and conviction of the person, persons or government criminally responsible for the explosion which resulted in the destruction, at Havana, of the United States war ship Maine and the loss of 258 lives of American sailors.

The $50,000 CASH offered for the above information is on deposit with Wells, Fargo & Co.

No one is barred, be he the humble but misguided seaman acting out a few miserable dollars by acting as a spy, or the attache of a government secret service, plotting, by any devilish means, to revenge fancied insults or cripple menacing countries.

This offer has been cabled to Europe and will be made public in every capital of the Continent and in London this morning.

The Journal believes that any man who can be bought to commit murder can also be bought to betray his comrades. FOR THE PERPETRATOR OF THIS OUTRAGE HAD ACCOMPLICES.

W. R. HEARST.

POWDER MAGAZINE

NAVAL OFFICERS THINK THE MAINE WAS DESTROYED BY A SPANISH MINE.

George Eugene Bryson, the Journal's special correspondent at Havana, cables that it is the secret opinion of many Spaniards in the Cuban capital that the Maine was destroyed and 258 of her men killed by means of a submarine mine, or fixed torpedo. This is the opinion of several American naval authorities. The Spaniards, it is believed, arranged to have the Maine anchored over one of the harbor mines. Wires connected the mine with a powder magazine, and it is thought the explosion was caused by sending an electric current through the wire. If this can be proven, the brutal nature of the Spaniards will be shown by the fact that they waited to spring the mine until after all the men had retired for the night. The Maltese cross in the picture shows where the mine may have been fired.

Hidden Mine or a Sunken Torpedo Believed to Have Been the Weapon Used Against the American Man-of-War---Officers and Men Tell Thrilling Stories of Being Blown Into the Air Amid a Mass of Shattered Steel and Exploding Shells---Survivors Brought to Key West Scout the Idea of Accident---Spanish Officials Protest Too Much---Our Cabinet Orders a Searching Inquiry---Journal Sends Divers to Havana to Report Upon the Condition of the Wreck.

Was the Vessel Anchored Over a Mine?

BY CAPTAIN E. L. ZALINSKI, U. S. A.

(Captain Zalinski is the inventor of the famous dynamite gun, which would be the principal factor in our coast defence in case of war.)

Assistant Secretary of the Navy Theodore Roosevelt says he is convinced that the destruction of the Maine in Havana Harbor was not an accident. The Journal offers a reward of $50,000 for exclusive evidence that will convict the person, persons or Government criminally responsible for the destruction of the American battle ship and the death of 258 of its crew.

The suspicion that the Maine was deliberately blown up grows stronger every hour. Not a single fact to the contrary has been produced.

Captain Sigsbee, of the Maine, and Consul-General Lee both urge that public opinion be suspended until they have completed their investigation. They are taking the course of tactful men who are convinced that there has been treachery.

Washington reports very late that Captain Sigsbee had feared some such event as a hidden mine. The English cipher code was used all day yesterday by the naval officers in cabling instead of the usual American code.

William Randolph Hearst reports the calamity in his *New York Journal, February 17, 1898*

Actually only the Cuban rebels stood to gain from the atrocity, but no proof has ever come to light about who planted the mine that exploded the ship's powder magazines.

Hopes for peace sank with the *Maine.* Still, American policymakers managed to pave the road to war with blunders. The administration made a set of demands—an armistice, American mediation, and an immediate end to the concentration camps. Spain agreed. In fact, it agreed to everything but Cuban independence. McKinley ended up in the ridiculous position of requesting a declaration of war against Spain in the same message in which he informed Congress that the enemy had capitulated to every American demand. The president had not in fact, made the needs of the moment sufficiently clear: without independence, the Cubans would not cease fighting, nor would the American jingos be satisfied. McKinley could control neither the rebels nor his own Congress. The war resolution contained the Teller Amendment, promising "to leave the government and control of the Island to its people." The nation had pledged a war against the Spanish Empire, not an adventure in American imperialism.

War in the Philippines The conflict, fortunately for our poorly equipped army, was fought largely at sea. Assistant Secretary of the Navy Theodore Roosevelt had already sent a secret order to Commodore George Dewey, commander of the Asiatic squadron, to prepare an attack on the Spanish fleet at Manila in the Philippines. Once word of the declaration reached the Orient, Dewey steamed toward Manila. On May 1 his modern fleet sailed against the decrepit Spanish ships under Admiral Montojo. Dewey made the remark "You may fire when ready, Gridley" that so entranced his compatriots; and seven hours later the Spanish fleet was no more. Not a single American died in the battle. Dewey asked for troops, and on August 13 a combined force of Americans and Philippine nationalists under the leadership of Emilio Aguinaldo captured Manila. America, fighting for Cuban freedom, had gained a Pacific empire, one they would soon regret having.

War in Cuba In Cuba the end came even more quickly. The Atlantic Squadron blockaded the island, holding the Spanish fleet in Santiago harbor. A ragtag American army of a few regulars and many thousand volunteers, with few supplies and itchy woolen uniforms for the tropical heat, gathered at Tampa, Florida. Seventeen thousand men, including Lieutenant Colonel Theodore Roosevelt and his pickup regiment of "Rough Riders," invaded Cuba in June. On July 1, with Roosevelt's men and some black troops leading the way, the army stormed up San Juan Hill, making Teddy a national hero and persuading the Spanish that San-

The World.

1,011,068 PER WEEK-DAY APRIL AVERAGE. GAIN in One Year - - - 338,748

"Circulation Books Open to All."

1,011,068 PER WEEK-DAY APRIL AVERAGE. GAIN in Three Years - - - 461,205

"Circulation Books Open to All."

VOL. XXXVIII. NO. 13,410. PRICE **FIVE** CENTS.

NEW YORK, SUNDAY, MAY 8, 1898.

PRICE **FIVE** CENTS.

DEWEY'S MARVELLOUS NAVAL ACHIEVEMENT—— THE WORLD'S SPLENDID NEWS VICTORY.

Spanish killed and disabled, 618— one-third their fighting force. Americans killed, none.

American Flag now flying over Spain's two greatest forts in the Philippines.

Eleven Spanish Ships Destroyed, 300 Spaniards Killed Outright; No American Ships Disabled, No American Sailors Killed; Only Six Injured———Capt. Mahan, the Pre-Eminent Strategist, to The World: "Commodore Dewey Has Fought the Greatest Naval Battle on Record"———All Spanish Forts Destroyed; Dewey Now Has Manila at His Mercy.

AMERICAN SHIPS, CONSTANTLY IN MOTION, FOUGHT AT RANGE OF ABOUT ONE MILE; THE SPANISH TORPEDO BOATS WERE SUNK AS THEY ADVANCED TO STRIKE.

By The World's War Correspondent, E. W. Harden, who was on the United States Gunboat McCulloch throughout the Battle.

(*Copyright, 1898, by the Press Publishing Company, New York.*)   (*Special Cable Despatch to The World.*)

HONG KONG, May 7.—At daybreak on Sunday morning, May 1, Commodore Dewey's Asiatic squadron, six fighting ships, the Olympia, Baltimore, Boston, Concord, Raleigh and Petrel, annihilated the Spanish fleet of the Philippines.

Dewey captured the naval arsenal and the forts at Cavite, Manila Bay.

ELEVEN SPANISH WARSHIPS DESTROYED.

Dewey's fleet sunk seven cruisers, four gunboats and two transports, and captured one transport, several tugs and a small steamer. Among the cruisers and gunboats sunk were the flagship Reina Maria Cristina, Castilla, Velasco, Don Juan de Austria, the Isla de Cuba, General Lezo, Marquez del Duero, Mindanao and Ulloa.

The Spaniards lost three hundred killed. Four hundred of them were wounded.

The Governor-General of the Philippines officially reported that the Spanish squadron lost in killed and disabled six hundred and eighteen—about one-third of their fighting force.

Not one American was killed, although the battle was hard fought and lasted three and a half hours.

The American gunners and American guns were infinitely better than the Spanish.

War in the Philippines. *The World, May 8, 1898*

tiago was lost. This was an error, since the army, Rough Riders and all, was too ridden with dysentery to advance, and the navy (remembering the *Maine*) feared to engage the enemy in the heavily mined harbor. Nevertheless, the brave Spanish Admiral Pascual Cervera, acting on orders, sailed his antique fleet out of the harbor to the complete destruction he anticipated. With an American army occupying Puerto Rico and the Spanish army trapped without transport, the Spanish commander surrendered on July 16. Spain sued for peace and the armistice took effect on August 12. John Hay, soon to be Secretary of State, voiced the American mood when he remarked that it had been a "Splendid Little War."

THE NEW EMPIRE

The war had been quick and relatively painless. Fewer than five hundred men died in combat, and the war did not damage the economy as businessmen had feared. The divisions in American society, so visible in

413

Cornelius Vanderbilt. *Library of Congress*

mid-decade, seemed to vanish in an orgy of nationalism. Americans fell in love with the idea of empire. Popular opinion was all in favor of holding the "Phillipines" (as Americans misspelled them at first); businessmen, changing their minds, now saw the islands as a route to increased Asian trade. Missionaries and humanitarians saw new fields for their labors.

The
anti-imperialists

An influential group of citizens, however, sensed that the realities of empire might be less pleasant than the glow produced by patches of American yellow on the world map set against the English pink and the French green. These anti-imperialists were a mixed lot. Ex-Presidents Harrison and Cleveland opposed annexing overseas territory, as did William Jennings Bryan. Many prominent Democrats wanted no part of the Philippines, but neither did such respected Republicans as Speaker Reed and John Sherman. College presidents, intellectuals, writers, and reformers, as well as some labor leaders, joined the antiimperialist crusade.

These opponents of imperialism argued that holding colonies went against the Constitution and that governing foreign territories without their consent violated American ideals. But less benevolent motives intruded as well. Southern Democrats frankly wanted no more dark-skinned Americans. Samuel Gompers, too, feared an influx of "Negritos" willing to work at low wages. Few of these anti-imperialists opposed American economic penetration abroad. They simply thought that taking colonies was the wrong way to proceed, and this argument, rejected at first, would eventually prevail.

The peace treaty

In 1898 McKinley saw that most Americans favored holding the islands. Public opinion would not tolerate returning them to Spain and feared their falling into the hands of another power. The American peace commissioners bought the Philippines for $20 million from an unwilling but helpless Spain. In addition, Spain granted Cuban independence, assumed Cuba's debt, and ceded Puerto Rico and the island of Guam in the Pacific. With the annexation of Hawaii coming in the same year, we were indeed an empire.

Still, there was the Senate, always a more difficult adversary for McKinley than the Spanish. Anticolonial feeling and Democratic manipulations almost defeated the treaty, but McKinley found support from an unexpected quarter. Bryan, opposed to annexing the islands but thinking to make anti-imperialism his theme for 1900, did not urge his Senate followers to oppose ratification. Even so, the treaty barely won the needed two-thirds. Bryan then proceeded to obscure the issue during the campaign by polishing up the free-silver question once again. The contest did not become the referendum on empire which Bryan had promised,

Keppler's "The Bosses of the
Senate." *Library of Congress*

PUCK.

THIS IS A SENATE of THE MONOPOLISTS and BY THE MONOPOLISTS and FOR THE MONOPOLISTS!

ENTRANCE FOR MONOPOLISTS

STANDARD OIL TRUST.

COPPER TRUST.

STEEL BEAM TRUST.

NAIL TRUST.

PLOUGH STEEL TRUST

J. Keppler.

BOSSES OF THE SENATE.

but his overwhelming defeat nevertheless destroyed anti-imperialism as a national issue. McKinley won a second term with the ardent imperialist and war hero Theodore Roosevelt as his vice-president.

Governing an empire

The course of empire moved smoothly for Americans everywhere but in the Philippines. In Cuba enlightened military rule stamped out yellow fever, built schools, and modernized the economy and public administration. Under limitations imposed by the Platt Amendment, which gave the United States veto power over its diplomacy and a naval base at Guantanamo Bay, Cuba resumed internal independence in 1902. For the moment, and in fact for decades, it became essentially an American satellite.

Puerto Rico accepted American rule with equanimity. In 1900 Congress by the Foraker Act established a civil government, denied Puerto Ricans American citizenship (they finally got it in 1917), and fixed some tariffs on their exports to the mainland. A challenge to the tariff provisions on the grounds that Puerto Rico was part of the United States lost in the Supreme Court. This case, *Downes* v. *Bidwell* (1901), was one of the so-called insular cases in which the Court, through the most involuted logic, ruled that the Constitution followed the flag only as closely as Congress allowed. Within rather broad limits, we could do what we would with the new possessions.

The Philippine insurrection

The Philippines, source of the most serious domestic arguments, also proved the most difficult area to govern. Until the Spanish defeat American commanders in the area had encouraged the independence movement under Aguinaldo. When the Fillipinos realized that they were changing masters, not gaining independence, large-scale revolt broke out, giving Americans their first taste of putting down a nationalist rebellion. This war was neither little nor splendid. It took three years and forty-three hundred American lives; it required, ironically, American use of concentration camps—better equipped versions of what we had condemned in Cuba—and was marked by atrocities on both sides. As the war petered out, a commission headed by William Howard Taft, then an Ohio judge, worked with great success to improve relations with the Filipinos. Taft, showing both genuine sympathy and delicate tact, succeeded in getting natives to join in a new political beginning. Military rule gave way in 1901 to a civilian government with Taft as appointed governor.

The open door

The Philippines taught an important lesson. Even Theodore Roosevelt, who more than any other man had been responsible for the events leading to our acquisition of this Pacific archipelago, soon wanted to drop the burden of rule. Americans began to see the merits of a more informal empire, thinking to gain the profits and the strategic values of other lands without the responsibilities of owning and running them. This new, noncolonial imperialism achieved its best statement and first important triumph in the "Open Door" notes which Secretary of State John Hay sent to the major powers in 1899 and 1900.

The United States, suddenly a Pacific power, faced an immediate need for a policy in the area. China, like the Spanish empire, had collapsed before a new and aggressive naval power during the brief Sino-Japanese war of 1894–95. European powers, fearing that Japan would acquire all China's commerce, rushed forward to carve out their own pieces of the tottering empire. This left Secretary Hay in a dilemma. Anti-imperialist sentiment at home made it impossible for America to join the feast or even to combine with a willing Great Britain to put a stop to it. But American businessmen demanded the State Department do something to prevent their being shut out of a potentially lucrative market.

Hay found the answer in a clever bit of diplomacy. He sent a circular letter to all the powers asking them to respect the trading rights of others and not to impose discriminatory duties within their spheres of influence, but rather to allow Chinese officials to continue collecting the Chinese tariffs. This was something like an invitation not to sin: too vigorous an assent suggested that one had erred and was mending his ways, but to reject the note was a confession of guilt. Consequently, most of the replies were ambiguous. Nevertheless, Hay announced in 1900 that the powers had all "accepted" his proposals. Again, who could contradict him? Hay had bought diplomatic advantage on the cheap: Japan, Russia, France, Germany, and Great Britain did not carve up all China only because they feared falling into war with each other in the process. Meanwhile, Hay took credit for saving China. A nationalist uprising, the "Boxer Rebellion" which broke out in China the next year, gave Hay the chance to reinforce this impression. Worried that the occurrence might serve as an excuse for further dismembering China, he issued another round of notes which went even a step further in their promise to maintain Chinese sovereignty.

The "Open Door" notes were a sensation in the United States. Henry Adams wrote that "Hay put Europe aside and set the Washington Government at the head of civilization." This was an exaggeration. We were not a power in Asia, and the China market remained more a mirage than an economic reality. The door to China had opened but a crack.

The "Open Door" notes did however, throw wide the gates for an American president to make his entrance onto the world stage unhampered by arguments over imperialism. The notes provided a legal and moral formula for asserting American interests in the absence of military force. Hay knew that no nation was prepared to upset the balance of force in China. When the day came that some power—Japan, for example

—felt strong enough to do so, then the United States would have to put a heavy shoulder to keep that door open. And no one, not even Hay's bellicose friend Theodore Roosevelt, believed that the American public was ready for that. Hay had made us an Asian interest without being an Asian power. The dangers and confusions inherent in this policy reverberated through the twentieth century and are not yet stilled.

THE BRADLEY MARTIN BALL

Not everyone went hungry or felt anxious in the nineties. Wealthy Americans remembered the "Gay" nineties. The gayest event of all was the Bradley Martin Ball. This unparalleled extravaganza took place at the Waldorf Hotel in New York on the night of February 10, 1897, after weeks of preparation by New York society and of anticipation in newspapers all over the country. Eight hundred socialites spent about four hundred thousand dollars imitating kings and queens in what newspapers described (in banner headlines) as "the most splendid private entertainment ever given in this country." The *New York Times* Sunday magazine devoted its first seven pages to photographs of the assembled "royalty." At the ball guests actually referred to the leaders of the "quadrille d'honneur," Mrs. Cornelia Sherman Bradley Martin and John J. Astor, as "Queen" and "King."

Mrs. Bradley Martin, daughter of a New York banker and wife of a wealthy lawyer, conceived this "crowning glory of the social life of New York of this century." One winter morning while reading in the newspapers of how the poor were suffering from the depression, she decided to cheer people up and "give an impetus to trade" with a costume ball. Requiring her guests to dress in accurately rendered court costume from the "most lavish periods of history," Mrs. Bradley Martin quickly precipitated a massive contest in ostentation: preparations for the hall alone cost one hundred twenty-five thousand dollars, and Mrs. Bradley Martin's Mary Queen of Scots costume—black velvet and white satin with a jewelled stomacher and a ruby necklace—made its intended impression. However, some observers were more struck with Mrs. Astor's uncanny ability to find places on her dark blue velvet gown for two hundred thousand dollars' worth of diamonds. The banker August Belmont was clearly the most gallantly dressed man in a ten thousand dollar suit of gold-inlaid steel armor. The newspapers reported the price of everything. The real losers were the fifty women who dressed as Marie Antoinette: "It was painful to contemplate," reported one society editor, "the future of all these young women who were to lose their heads." But they like everyone else at the ball could lose their sorrows amid the twenty-eight courses—including "Sorbet fin de siècle"—at the midnight champagne supper.

The ball was both a triumph and a disaster. "It may not be surpassed in another hundred years," oozed one society reporter: "It was a gorgeous, superb, and wonderful spectacle." Yet a prominent Episcopal rector had warned that such an occasion in a time of depression and social tension was "ill-advised." He proved correct. Newspapers condemned the Bradley Martins for their extravagance. Clergymen preached sermons against them. College debating societies resolved their iniquity. The New York assessor wreaked a more practical vengeance by doubling their taxes. The Bradley Martins surrendered their hopes of becoming the royalty of New York society, permanently retreating to England. In a final and characteristic gesture, they gave a farewell dinner for eighty-six intimate friends. The newspapers faithfully reported that it cost $116.28 a plate.

The Bradley Martin Ball ended neither social extravagance nor its fascination for the public. But "society" began to fear the whip of the press, especially when journalists combined reports of such orgies of big spending with muckraking accounts of the business practices that had created these fortunes. Eight years later, the dandy James Hazen Hyde had to flee the country after spending two hundred thousand dollars on a masked ball. He should have known better: daddy's company, Equitable Life, was under heavy political attack in 1905. Nor did public opinion respond any more favorably to Harry Lehr's "dog dinner," at which his friends' dogs dined on paté. Rich people began to learn that what titillated the public did not necessarily win its approval. Since "society" has learned that lesson, Americans have found it far less interesting.

Mrs. Bradley Martin

THINGS TO THINK ABOUT:
1890 - 1900

Why did the public find the currency question so exciting? On the political background of the issue see Irwin Unger, *The Greenback Era* (1964), Walter T. K. Nugent, *Money and American Society* (1968), and Allen Weinstein, *Prelude To Populism* (1970). For the economic backgrounds see Milton Friedman and Anna J. Schwartz, *A Monetary History of the United States* (1970). The flavor of debate is best caught in William H. Harvey, *Coin's Financial School* (1895), available in modern editions.

What place did populism have in the American reform tradition? John D. Hicks, *The Populist Revolt* (1931) is still the best general account. Richard Hofstadter, *The Age of Reform* (1955) poses important questions about populism. Norman Pollack, *The Populist Response to Industrial America* (1962), Walter Nugent, *The Tolerant Populists* (1963), and C. Vann Woodward, "The Populist Heritage and the Intellectual," *American Scholar* 59 (1959) : 55–72 (frequently reprinted) try to answer Hofstadter's questions. But read the populists themselves in George B. Tindall, ed., *A Populist Reader* (1966).

Were Grover Cleveland's actions in his second term an indication of courage, cunning, or stupidity? Allan Nevins *Grover Cleveland* (1932) is a sympathetic account. Horace S. Merrill, *Bourbon Leader: Grover Cleveland* (1957) votes against Cleveland as does J. Rogers Hollingsworth, *The Whirligig of Politics* (1963). Geoffrey Blodgett, *The Gentle Reformers* (1966) portrays with great insight one group of Cleveland's supporters. Francis B. Simkin, *Pitchfork Ben Tillman* (1944) describes one of Cleveland's enemies.

Why after a generation of "Dead-center" politics did the Republicans emerge as the dominant party in 1894? Three important studies examine in detail voting patterns in the nineties: Paul Kleppner, *The Cross of Culture* (1970), Richard Jensen, *The Winning of the Midwest* (1971), and Samuel T. McSeveney, *The Politics of Depression* (1972). Elmer E. Schattschneider, *The Semi-Sovereign People* (1960) offers a suggestive approach to the meaning of these changes.

What was at issue in the "Battle of the standards" in 1896? Robert Durden, *The Climax of Populism* (1965) analyzes the Populists' stake. Paul W. Glad, *McKinley, Bryan, and the People* (1964) is a graceful and perceptive account of the election. Stanley L. Jones, *The Presidential Election of 1896* (1964) is thorough. For pictures of the major figures, see Paolo E. Coletta, *William Jennings Bryan* (3 vols., 1964–69)—everything you always wanted to know about Bryan; H. Wayne Morgan, *William McKinley and His America* (1963)—a sympathetic biography; C. Vann Woodward, *Tom Watson; Agrarian Rebel* (1938)—brilliant portrait of an important Southern Populist.

How did Americans react to the depression of the 1890s? Donald L. McMurry, *Coxey's Army* (1930) is the standard work on that episode.

Almont Lindsey, *The Pullman Strike* (1942) and Stanley Buder, *Pullman: An Experiment in Industrial Order* (1967) cover the era's greatest upheaval. Charles Hoffman, "The Depression of the Nineties," *Journal of Economic History* 16 (1956) : 137–164 and Samuel Rezneck ,"Unemployment, Unrest, Relief . . . During the Depression of 1893–1897," *Journal of Political Economy* 61 (1953) : 324–45 give some measure of the depression's impact. John Higham, *Strangers in the Land: Patterns of American Nativism, 1860–1925* (1955) and Donald E. Kinzer, *An Episode in Anti-Catholicism* (1964) show some of the less savory reactions. Arnold M. Paul, *Conservative Crisis and the Rule of Law* (1960) superbly analyzes the courts' reactions to the tensions of the nineties. For the Bradley Martin Ball and other pleasures of the "gay nineties" read Dixon Wecter's entertaining work, *The Saga of American Society* (1937).

Why did the United States build an overseas empire at the end of the nineteenth century? David M. Pletcher, *The Awkward Years* (1962) deals with the early eighties. Walter LaFeber presents a tightly reasoned argument for the economic basis of expansion in *The New Empire* (1963) ; Ernest R. May, *American Imperialism: A Speculative Essay* (1968) is suggestive. William A. Williams, *The Tragedy of American Diplomacy* (1959) and George Kennan, *American Diplomacy, 1900–1950* (1951) sharply define two approaches to American foreign policy that have divided diplomatic historians.

Why did the United States go to war with Spain over Cuba? Richard Hofstadter, "Manifest Destiny and the Philippines," in *America in Crisis*, edited by Daniel Aaron (1952) offers an explanation applying social psychology. H. Wayne Morgan, *America's Road to Empire* (1965) and Ernest R. May, *Imperial Democracy* (1961) examine the Cuban crisis. Joseph E. Wisan, *The Cuban Crisis as Reflected in the New York Press* (1934) argues the importance of "yellow journalism." On the war itself see Frank Friedel, *The Splendid Little War* (1958).

Why did the United States keep the Philippines? Leon Wolff, *Little Brown Brother* (1961) describes the Philippine insurrection. Robert L. Beisner, *Twelve Against Empire* (1968) is a well-written account of a number of leading opponents of imperialism. Williams, cited above, is shrewd on the meaning of the argument over imperialism. On the rest of the American Empire see David F. Healy, *The United States in Cuba, 1898–1902* (1963) ; Merz Tate, *The United States and the Hawaiian Kingdom* (1965) ; and Edward Berbusse, *The United States in Puerto Rico, 1898–1900* (1966).

Which was the Open Door policy: Realistic economic diplomacy or pointless idealism? George Kennan's and W. A. Williams's works cited above argue the issues vigorously. See also Thomas J. McCormick, *China Market* (1967), A. Whitney Griswold, *The Far Eastern Policy of the United States* (1938), and Tyler Dennet, *John Hay* (1933).

1900-1918

ten | progressive america

JANE ADDAMS OF THE NINETEENTH WARD

When twenty-nine year old Jane Addams opened Hull House on the corner of Polk and Halsted Streets in Chicago, this settlement house joined the Nineteenth Ward's other institutions—nine churches and 250 saloons—in ministering to the needs of a densely packed neighborhood of Italian, German, Jewish, Bohemian, and French-Canadian immigrants. Jane Addams vividly recorded the scene that greeted her in 1889:

> The streets are inexpressibly dirty, the number of schools inadequate, sanitary legislation unenforced, the street lighting bad, the paving miserable and altogether lacking in the alleys and smaller streets, and the stables foul beyond description. . . . Rear tenements flourish; many houses have no water supply save the faucet in the back yard.

There she provided a social and cultural center for the urban poor, offering them friendship when they wanted it and charity when they needed it, and forcing an unwilling city to provide them with social services such as garbage collection, improved sanitation, and playgrounds.

Her great competitor in service to the ward was one of the saloonkeepers, Johnny Powers, the district's alderman. On election day he drove about tossing nickels to the children and cigars to the men. Whenever one of his constituents died, Johnny was there with flowers and baskets of food —kosher food if the family was Jewish. They called him "The Chief Mourner." And, by Addams's own testimony, "one out of five voters in the Nineteenth Ward held a job dependent on the good will of the alderman," working for the city or for the telephone or streetcar companies that purchased valuable franchises from Powers and his friends. The upright Jane Addams and the thoroughly corrupt Johnny Powers were political enemies, and Powers won all the elections in the ward. Yet the future was on Addams's side. The private charities of Hull House would become the municipal social services of the future, and these welfare services would put men like Johnny largely out of business.

How did the well-bred daughter of a state legislator from a neat village in northern Illinois find herself among the poor of the Nineteenth Ward? Jane Addams inherited a tradition of concern for the downtrodden. Her father, a Quaker, an abolitionist, and a Republican legislator who exchanged letters with Abraham Lincoln, instilled in her a sense of mission and a stern morality. At college in the 1870s she defended "the woman's cause" and showed a gift for public speaking. Representing her school in a statewide oratorical contest, she placed fifth out of ten in a fierce competition: William Jennings Bryan only finished second!

After college, Jane Addams attempted to go to medical school, but her health, never too strong, prevented her. She had a slight curvature of the spine from birth which necessitated four major operations during her lifetime and persuaded her that marriage was not a possibility. Now she was face to face with the problem of finding what she should do in life. For eight years she struggled with "the snare of preparation"—studying, writing, traveling, worrying, and feeling hemmed in by the restrictions of being a "lady." Finally in 1888 she found her answer at Toynbee Hall, London, the pioneer social settlement. She and a friend, Ellen Gates Starr, bravely set forth on a new adventure at Hull House, understanding only their own need to find useful work. But in their big house amid all the little and miserable hovels, they could learn as well the needs of a city.

Hull House was an much an intellectual as a social center. Writers like John Dewey, Henry Demarest Lloyd, and W. E. B. Du Bois came to lecture and argue. Most important of all, Miss Addams and her coworkers studied their own city, writing a steady stream of books and papers mapping the human geography of urban America. A generation of pioneers in social work and dozens of vital precedents for social services emerged from over forty years of work.

From 1915 to the end of her life in 1935, Jane Addams added to her life's mission an ardent opposition to war. She helped found a number of women's groups opposing war, some of which are still active. During and immediately after World War I, she took part in efforts to feed "enemy women and children" and was bitterly attacked for it. The Daughters of the American Revolution expelled her for refusing to support the war effort. But years later, in 1931, she was corecipient of the Nobel Peace Prize. As always Jane Addams, the noblest progressive of them all, flourished in unpopular causes.

Mrs. Blaney, Mrs. Wilmarth, and Miss Addams. *Culver Pictures*

1900-1918

1901	Platt Amendment
	Assassination of McKinley (September 6); Theodore Roosevelt becomes president
1902	Newlands Act
1903	Departments of Commerce and Labor established; Elkins Anti-rebate Act
1904	Roosevelt corollary to Monroe Doctrine
	Roosevelt reelected president; defeats Alton B. Parker
1905	Portsmouth Peace Conference
	Lochner v. *New York*
1906	Hepburn Act
	Pure Food and Drug Act
	Meat Inspection Act
1907	Gentlemen's Agreement with Japan
1908	White House Conservation Conference
	Muller v. *Oregon*
	William Howard Taft (Republican) elected president; defeats Bryan
1910	Mann Elkins Act
1912	Socialists nominate Eugene Debs for president; Progressives nominate Theodore Roosevelt on Bull-Moose Ticket
	Woodrow Wilson (Democrat) elected president; defeats Taft, Roosevelt, and Debs
1913	Sixteenth Amendment, the Income Tax
	Seventeenth Amendment, Popular Election of United States Senators
	Federal Reserve Act
1914	Federal Trade Commission Act
	Clayton Antitrust Act
1915	Sinking of the *Lusitania*, May 7
1916	Adamson Act
	Federal Farm Loan Act
	Wilson reelected president; defeats Charles Evans Hughes
1917	United States enters World War I on April 6
	Espionage Act
	Lever Food and Fuel Control Act
1918	Republicans gain control of Congress, November 5
	Armistice Day, November 11

A SETTING FOR PROGRESSIVISM

The first years of the twentieth century, the "progressive era," recall Teddy Roosevelt and Woodrow Wilson, "trustbusting" and campaigns against corrupt bosses and tainted beef, horseless carriages, Greenwich Village, and the first World Series. Its flavor of high moralism and exuberance comes from a richly various group of reformers. They sought many of the goals that have ever since been identified with reform in this century: regulation of large corporations, rooting out corruption in government, alleviating urban poverty, improving labor conditions, and elimination waste and inefficiency in the use of natural resources. Progressives injected a special urgency into political and intellectual life that marked off their times from the less vivid age of dead-center politics that preceded them.

A new generation   The sharp change in public mood came from a new generation moving onto the national scene. Typically, progressives were young, native-born, Protestant, and college-educated. Most were small businessmen or members of a profession, people with influence in the local community. Many had toyed with advanced ideas and new forms of political action in the late eighties and early nineties. They read Edward Bellamy and Henry George, adopted the message of the social gospel, and engaged in the eternal battle against municipal corruption. But the anxieties of the mid-nineties had driven most into firm support of McKinley against Bryan's apparently dangerous ideas.

These young reformers were not radicals but fiercely patriotic Americans who believed almost literally in the ideals learned in church, from political rostrums, and in college. But these well-established men and women had seen enough to realize the gap between the practices of American industrial life and the principles of morality, honesty, and open opportunity they had been taught. They also saw the comfortable little communities of their childhood, identified with every social virtue, losing their influence and independence to an increasingly national, industrial, and urban-based economic system. Yet they did not reject this new America. The more sophisticated progressives saw in the emerging social sciences and the new social and industrial organizations possible ways to marry the new technology to old moral standards. Few, however, saw any mass audience for reform until the turn of the century, when new conditions suddenly offered them an opportunity.

Prosperity and a new   McKinley, billed in 1896 as the "advance agent of prosperity," proved as
social class   good as his slogan. Returning affluence was an indispensible ingredient in progressivism, a comfortable cushion against the shock of new ideas and social experiments. It made people more tolerant and less defensive. They no longer grasped at the familiar to demonstrate their belief in the soundness of American institutions. Now they possessed the confidence to push toward careful changes. At last they felt ready to take control of the onrushing industrialism of the age.

Inflation, an untoward product of prosperity, helped progressives find an audience. People accustomed to a lifetime of sinking prices reacted with suspicion to the steady inflation which began late in the nineties and continued throughout the progressive era. Today's economists blame the inflation on fresh gold supplies and economic expansion, but contemporaries feared that trusts and labor organizations were ganging up on a helpless and disorganized public to raise prices. This conception of the public as "consumers" was new to the age. It reflected both the new stress in the economy on consumer goods—such as the new automobiles—and the rise of a new social group, the white-collar class of clerks, teachers, salespeople, technicians, and the like. An insignificant fraction of the population a generation before, these 6 million people, by the progressive era, formed about two-thirds of the urban middle class. Remaining close to their rural and small-town roots, they could still find the city's ways shocking. They lacked any economic organization and had to turn directly to politics for expression of their needs. With no traditional place in the political order, they naturally looked with some favor on insurgents. While few themselves became important in politics, they were the progressives' steady voting public.

A disrupted society

Americans saw a society that had always been open and individualistic turning into a world of large organizations. Members of some professions, even when they prospered, began to feel less important in the world or less independent in their lives. Clergymen saw their rich parishioners rise to dominance over them not just economically, but even as social and moral arbiters. Lawyers increasingly sold their services to corporations in order to prosper; earning more, they enjoyed less freedom and felt less important. Small businessmen who once lorded it over their suppliers now purchased their goods from the "barbed wire trust" or the "flour trust" at prices set in some big-city headquarters. If the goods came high, these merchants denounced "monopoly prices"; even if the price was attractive they felt a little smaller than before. They delighted when reformers promised to cut the trusts down to size.

Nor were men and women on the rise content to leave things as they were. College professors, for example, were growing in professional standing and income throughout the period, but as members of increasingly larger institutions, many dominated by wealthy benefactors, they too were ready to do battle. And besides, they dealt in ideas: if they could transform their new reform ideas into action, their status in society would rise with the reform movement. Men and women in the new urban professions such as social work, public administration, and city planning felt the same way. For them reform meant replacing amateur direction (or none at all) with their own expertise: they were reformers by profession.

Progressive women

The progressive movement, like the reform movements that had dotted American life before the Civil War, offered some new opportunities for American women. Social work especially attracted daughters of the

24 GENUINE COLUMBIA P RECORDS AND THE OXFORD JR. TALKING MACHINE ALL COMPLETE

8⁷⁵

YOUR OWN SELECTION OF SUBJECTS

THE NEW OXFORD JR. TALKING MACHINE IS A STRICTLY HIGH CLASS TALKING MACHINE FOR REPRODUCING STANDARD SIZE WAX CYLINDER RECORDS. IT IS A THOROUGHLY WELL MADE MACHINE AND NOT TO BE COMPARED IN ANY WAY WITH THE CHEAP MACHINES THAT HAVE BEEN SO EXTENSIVELY ADVERTISED RECENTLY.

IT IS A HIGH CLASS MACHINE, MADE IN AMERICA, made by expert and experienced workmen in one of the largest and most successful talking machine factories in the world. It is made of good materials throughout, fitted with a high class spring motor, with machine cut gears, everything about it strong and substantial. It is made with patent feed device which holds the reproducer firmly in place as it travels along over the surface of the record. There are cheap talking machines made without feed device, and with such machines the reproducer slips and slides off the surface of the record, but this trouble is entirely prevented in the Oxford Jr. Talking Machine, as the reproducer is held firmly and guided in its course over the surface of the record by the patent feed device, exactly the same as the highest priced machines. This machine is made with heavy, solid and substantial iron base, finished in black enamel, with gold stripe decorations. It is made with standard size tapered mandrel, and will use any standard size of wax cylinder record, Columbia, Edison or any other standard make.

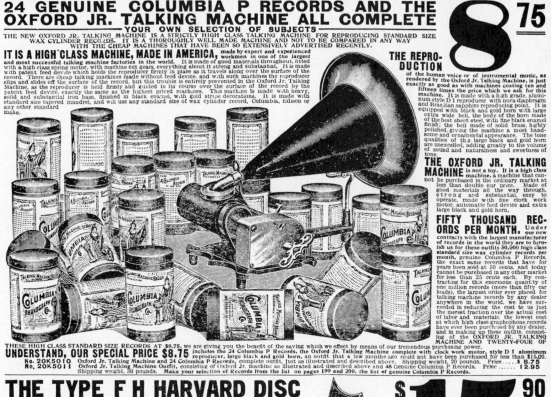

THE REPRODUCTION

of the human voice or of instrumental music, as rendered by the Oxford Jr. Talking Machine, is just exactly as good as with machines costing ten and fifteen times the price which we ask for this machine. It is made with a high grade, aluminum style D 1 reproducer with mica diaphragm and Brazilian sapphire reproducing point. It is equipped with black and gold horn with large extra wide bell, the body of the horn made of the best sheet steel, with fine black enamel finish; the bell made of solid brass, highly polished, giving the machine a most handsome and ornamental appearance. The tone qualities of this large black and gold horn are unexcelled, adding greatly to the volume of sound and naturalness and sweetness of tone.

THE OXFORD JR. TALKING MACHINE is not a toy. It is a high class machine, a machine that cannot be purchased in the ordinary market at less than double our price. Made of good materials all the way through, strong and substantial, easy to operate, made with fine clock work motor, automatic feed device and extra large black and gold horn.

FIFTY THOUSAND RECORDS PER MONTH. Under our new contracts with the largest manufacturer of records in the world they are to furnish us for these outfits 50,000 high class standard size wax cylinder records per month, genuine Columbia P Records, the exact same records that have for years been sold at 50 cents, and today cannot be purchased in any other market for less than 25 cents each. By contracting for this enormous quantity of one million records more than fifty car loads, the largest order ever placed for talking machine records by any dealer anywhere in the world, we have succeeded in reducing the cost to us just the merest fraction over the actual cost of labor and materials, the lowest cost at which high class graphophone records have ever been purchased by any dealer, and in making up these outfits, consisting of the OXFORD JR. TALKING MACHINE AND TWENTY-FOUR OF

THESE HIGH CLASS STANDARD SIZE RECORDS AT $8.75, we are giving you the benefit of the saving which we effect by means of our tremendous purchasing power.

UNDERSTAND, OUR SPECIAL PRICE $8.75 includes the 24 Columbia P Records, the Oxford Jr. Talking Machine complete with clock work motor, style D 1 aluminum reproducer, large black and gold horn, an outfit that a few months ago could not have been purchased for less than $15.00.

No. 20K5010   Oxford Jr. Talking Machine and 24 Columbia P Records, complete outfit, just as illustrated and described above.   Shipping weight, 20 pounds.   Price..... $ 8.75
No. 20K5011   Oxford Jr. Talking Machine Outfit, consisting of Oxford Jr. machine as illustrated and described above and 48 Genuine Columbia P Records.   Price...... 12.95
Shipping weight, 30 pounds.   Make your selection of Records from the list on pages 199 and 200, the list of genuine Columbia P Records.

THE TYPE F H HARVARD DISC TALKING MACHINE

$15⁹⁰

The Large Flower Horn with which this machine is equipped, possesses, to an unusual degree, the magnificent acoustic or tone qualities which are peculiar to the latest type of flower horns. The unusual musical qualities of the flower horn, its ability to reproduce sound more absolutely true to the original music, is due to the peculiar curves and the extra wide flaring bell, which avoids the usual retardation of the sound waves, thereby giving a deep, clear and natural tone to every note.

THIS HORN is made with fine baked on enamel finish, ornamented with gold stripes, and besides the great improvement which it makes in the musical quality of the machine, also contributes greatly to the beautiful appearance of the outfit.

THE MELLOWNESS OF TONE AND REAL MUSICAL QUALITY

of the reproduction, as rendered by the Type F H Harvard Talking Machine, is due partly to the new sound analyzing reproducer with which it is equipped and partly to the special acoustic properties of the flower horn, or rather to the combination of these two features. This reproducer is the latest product of the largest talking machine manufacturer in the world and represents the result of years of constant experiment and improvement. It is called the "sound analyzing" reproducer because of its ability to bring out every tone clearly and with the exact tone quality of the original music. It not only increases the volume of sound, but enriches the quality and reveals tones which with the earlier and less perfect types of reproducers were lost entirely. It is equipped with the automatic needle holder by which the needle is clamped into place and held securely by a spring lever; a slight pressure upon this lever instantly releases the needle, thus avoiding the use of the annoying set screw arrangement used in other reproducers.

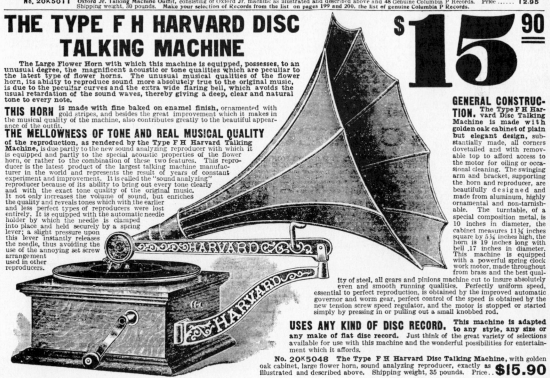

GENERAL CONSTRUCTION.

The Type F H Harvard Disc Talking Machine is made with golden oak cabinet of plain but elegant design, substantially made, all corners dovetailed and with removable top to afford access to the motor for oiling or occasional cleaning. The swinging arm and bracket, supporting the horn and reproducer, are beautifully designed and made from aluminum, highly ornamental and non-tarnishable. The turntable is of special composition metal, is 10 inches in diameter, the cabinet measures 11¾ inches square by 5¾ inches high, the horn is 19 inches long with bell .17 inches in diameter. This machine is equipped with a powerful spring clock work motor, made throughout from brass and the best quality of steel, all gears and pinions machine cut to insure absolutely even and smooth running qualities. Perfectly uniform speed, essential to perfect reproduction, is obtained by the improved automatic governor and worm gear, perfect control of the speed is obtained by the new tension screw speed regulator, and the motor is stopped or started simply by pressing in or pulling out a small knobbed rod.

USES ANY KIND OF DISC RECORD. This machine is adapted to any style, any size or any make of flat disc record. Just think of the great variety of selections available for use with this machine and the wonderful possibilities for entertainment which it affords.

No. 20K5048   The Type F H Harvard Disc Talking Machine, with golden oak cabinet, large flower horn, sound analyzing reproducer, exactly as illustrated and described above.   Shipping weight, 35 pounds.   Price.. **$15.90**

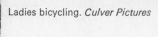
Ladies bicycling. *Culver Pictures*

A Manhattan "El." Courtesy of
*The New York Historical Society,
New York City*

middle class seeking meaningful lives in a world outside the home. Many broke with the constricted Victorian role of household goddess and found careers in the burgeoning settlement houses or in the public schools.

Yet most of the new professional outlets for women conformed to old stereotypes of the woman's "proper" role. Women found most of their opportunities in the "angel of mercy" professions: teaching school, nursing, and social work. These were the areas supposed to require a female's tender touch. They were not the highest-paying posts in the white-collar world.

Women's political activity increased markedly. The National Federation of Women's Clubs, a preserve of genteel culture and dabbling in the arts, turned to serious political and philanthropic activity. The new president of the Federation informed its members in 1904 that "Dante is dead. He has been dead for several centuries, and I think it is time we dropped the study of his *Inferno* and turned our attention to our own." The president of the National Association of Manufacturers warned businessmen to watch out what reform ideas their wives absorbed at the club meetings. Yet his worries may have been unnecessary. The clubwomen pursued sensible and stoutly middle-class reform goals, while the more radical women exhausted their energies in the fight for women's suffrage rather than in broader feminist or social crusades.

THE PROGRESSIVE MIND

A half-century of rapid industrialization and urban growth had produced a special new generation of men and women ready to grab for control of their onrushing society. Delicately poised between the private, individual virtues of an agrarian order and new demands for efficiency and collective efforts, they reflected their dual heritage in their often-conflicting ideas. They determined to uphold pure and absolute moral standards which they feared would otherwise perish on the battlefield of the economy. Yet their greater sophistication in economics, psychology, jurisprudence, and sociology was teaching them to distrust large abstractions and to devise flexible techniques that could monitor progress while insuring social justice. Similarly, they longed to keep open the hallowed avenues of individual opportunity while they recognized the need for organization in every part of the common life and were themselves prolific organizers. Caught between old dreams and new insights, they struggled with evangelical zeal and deep sincerity to achieve what were, in fact, conservative changes in the social order.

A new enlightenment Few men and women active in the progressive movement were original or consistent thinkers—people in the midst of furious activity rarely are— but they gained strength and inspiration from a new "enlightenment" that, like its eighteenth-century predecessor, worshipped at the shrine of science. Men had longed dreamed of a "science of society." By the dawn of this century, thinkers in almost every field thought they saw this dream coming true. The pragmatists—Charles Sanders Peirce, William James, and John Dewey—announced an end to sterile wrangling over ultimate truths. Philosophers needed only to study the way scientists and technicians used concepts in their work. Finding truth in the laboratory, they maintained, was simply a matter of determining what an idea *did*, what difference it made, what effect it had. Physicists did not argue about what "force" really was; they simply traced its effect. The social sciences could do the same. Social engineers could empirically study how things worked—an electoral system or a court or a factory—without worrying whether they had properly defined words like "democracy" or "justice" or "equity."

This pragmatic approach struck sympathetic chords throughout intellectual life. Only recently having achieved separate identity as academic disciplines, the new social sciences rapidly moved on to find roles in the bureaucratic organizations arising about them. Political scientists and economists at institutions like the University of Wisconsin operated as a research bureau for progressive reformers. Sociologists and philosophers became innovators in education and social work. This stress on practical application relieved each field of its formal adherence to its own first principles, tempered grand theorizing, and introduced a refreshing empiricism which both shattered old beliefs within the learned professions and informed Americans about their country. This "revolt against formalism," as it has been called, reached everywhere. The great architectural innovators of the day, for example, liberated themselves from outmoded traditions of design, allowing the functions their buildings would serve to determine the form of their architecture. Louis Sullivan and Frank Lloyd Wright saw a lightness and simplicity in the clean lines of the new bridges and machinery that the heavy masonry edifices about them lacked. In keeping with a practical, scientific age, their work—which they identified with democratic values—replaced forbidding imitations of aristocratic rockpiles with easier, more open buildings.

A new literature Literature as well felt the influence of science. Writers struggled to accommodate the new realistic mentality to their traditions of idealism and romance. Adopting "naturalistic" techniques of piling detail on detail, Frank Norris presented a vast social panorama in *The Octopus* (1901) and *The Pit* (1903). Theodore Dreiser in *Sister Carrie* (1900), *The Financier* (1912), and *The Titan* (1914) portrayed in graceless but effective prose a distinctly modern world. His unsentimental treatment of sexual experience caused a publisher to suppress *Sister Carrie* for a decade. Dreiser's huge, gloomy novels, with their rich and accurate detail, seemed to penetrate as none had done before the mysteries of the multitudinous urban scene.

URBAN PROGRESSIVISM

Progressivism found its first target in the cities. The urban middle class had long been offended at the notion that rich men whose baronial mansions dwarfed their own made common political cause with the urban poor, whose tenements made their cities unhealthy and unsafe. Mismanaged and corrupt government that granted large favors to the rich men building the cities and small favors to the poor, they argued, prevented anyone from controlling the direction of urban growth. Sporadic revolts of the middle class had occasionally brought in temporary reform administrations, but until late in the nineteenth century their achievements were slight. Then in the nineties, reformers, with European models of municipal government before them, experience in managing large business enterprises behind them, and the new social sciences for guidance, boldly attacked the job of reorganizing the cities.

New heroes The first of these urban reformers was Hazen S. Pingree, a wealthy manufacturer who became mayor of Detroit in 1890. Sobered by the depression of the nineties, Pingree moved beyond the old-fashioned reformism of "good government" and "driving the rascals out" to become a champion of social justice and to set a standard of positive municipal achievement. His program included lowering the cost of public utilities, fairer taxation policies, public ownership of some utilities, improvements in lighting, sewers, transit, roads, schools, and parks, and even a measure of poor relief during depression.

Pingree was the first of a series of reform mayors, often flamboyant men, who spread progressivism to a national audience. These included the colorful Samuel M. ("Golden Rule") Jones of Toledo and his successor Brand Whitlock, James D. Phelan of San Francisco, Seth Low of New York, Tom Johnson of Cleveland, and Mark M. Fagan of Jersey City. Amid exciting controversy and with considerable fanfare in the press, these men, aided by various reform groups, dispelled the fatalism that had long surrounded the subject of city government. Not only did they bring some serious reform, they also educated a new generation of urban-minded reformers, men who overcame the typical American bias in favor or rural and small-town life to become the first important group of public figures to embrace the city as (in the words of one of them) the "hope of democracy."

Yet democracy seemed strangely served in many of the municipal reforms. Progressives preferred organizing governments which limited rather than extended the people's control over their officials. In response to a tragic tidal wave, Galveston, Texas, replaced its ineffectual government with a commission of five men who served together as their local legislature and separately to run the government's administration. In 1908 the town of Staunton, Virginia, hired a manager, a trained expert, to run their city. Hundreds of smaller cities adopted these commission and city-manager plans. Other cities acted to strengthen their mayors against the city councils and aldermen. Everywhere political parties and their corruptions were the enemy. The main thrust of urban reform was to give power to more expert, more businesslike, and better-educated people. It was, in part, a revolt of the suburbs (then still within city limits in most cases) against the center cities. It improved the tone and the performance of government, and in the process helped many of the poor. It brought efficiency and sometimes social justice. But democracy—if by that we mean popular participation in politics, including by the poor— was more the urban progressives' slogan than their achievement.

Immigrants Part of this distrust of the urban masses stemmed from widespread fears of an "undesirable" foreign element, immigrants from southern and eastern Europe, whom the commissioner of immigration officially labeled as "indigestible." The years between 1903 and the outbreak of the European war in 1914 saw an average annual migration of just under a million people. About two-thirds came from Russia, Poland, Austria-Hungary, the Balkans, and Italy. To most Americans these were disconcerting people, speaking strange tongues, practicing alien religions, possessing little of what passed for American manners or civic ideals. Men outnumbered women or children in the new migration by about two to one, and many

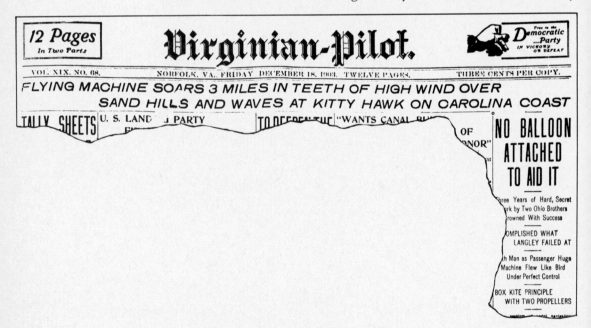

Public comfort stations,
Indianapolis—a Progressive Era
reform. *Bass*

of these were so-called birds of passage, content to earn a nestegg and then return to their native lands. They settled in the cities, another cause for suspicion among pastoral-minded Americans. Here the immigrants formed the voting fodder for political machines, the labor force to undercut domestic workingmen, and the potential public for agitators.

Progressives had no single response to the new immigrants. Municipal reformers often encountered them as political enemies, but settlement house workers and other welfare reformers frequently sympathized with their plight, identified with their aspirations, and eventually learned to appreciate some parts of their cultures. Despite racist ideas and a constant movement in favor of laws sharply restricting entry, most progressives remained optimistic and wanted only the most inconsequential restrictions on immigration. That generation belonged to the pioneers in social work, education, and city government who continued to work for the eventual "Americanization" of these new members of the nation. The restrictionists' turn would come soon enough.

The muckrakers   Americans everywhere suddenly became aware of this municipal reform movement in October 1902 when *McClure's Magazine* published Lincoln Steffens's "Tweed Days in St. Louis." The battle of idealistic reformers against municipal corruption was a highly dramatic, highly moralistic story. Steffens's series of articles on urban problems covering many cities set the theme: the common guilt for corruption, the common responsibility to eradicate it. Journalists themselves could be the heroes of the piece: Ida Tarbell disclosing the crimes of Standard Oil, Upton Sinclair exposing the meat-packing industry, Ray Stannard Baker teaching the public about labor racketeering. Theodore Roosevelt, one of the great phrase makers of American history, came up with the name (in derision) that stuck to this school of writers: muckrakers.

Muckraking dominated American journalism between about 1902 and 1906. About ten mass-circulation magazines and many newspapers featured exposés touching on almost every part of American society, and a number of widely sold books, such as Upton Sinclair's *The Jungle* (1906), spread the curiously optimistic message that, although American institutions had massive faults, Americans were fighting to correct them. This trend reflected the growth of a literate audience convinced that it could understand the world around it. The literature of exposé was not new—*Harper's* had "muckraked" the Tweed Ring in the 1870s—but the style and scope of this journalism in the progressive era was novel. Nobody had expected so large an audience for reform, and there had never been such a corps of bright, young journalists with time, enthusiasm, and financial backing to look into the dirty corners of American life. The size and enthusiasm of the audience (people read Steffens and then joined municipal reform movements) convinced many of the people uncovering societies' prob-

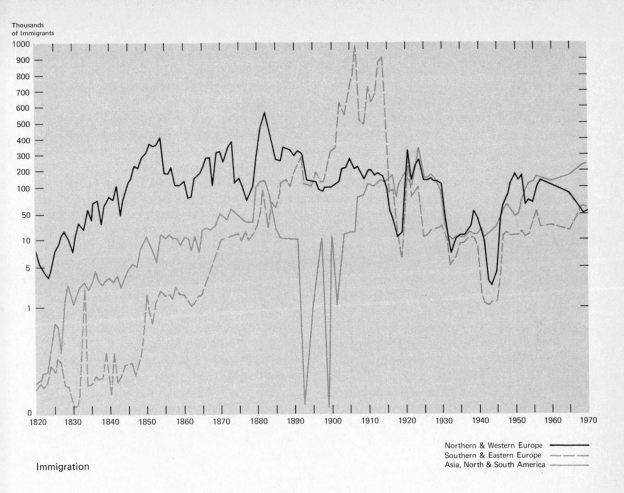

Thousands
of Immigrants

Immigration

Northern & Western Europe
Southern & Eastern Europe
Asia, North & South America

lems that this exposure was itself curing the nation's ills. In fact, people detected progress so quickly that the craze for exposure soon faded. And as the public lost some of its enthusiasm, magazines, now caving in before pressure from their advertisers, switched to less controversial topics.

STATE PROGRESSIVISM

Urban reformers characteristically pursued a trail of corruption from City Hall to the state legislature. Moreover, the limitations of most city charters narrowed the possibility for local reform. State legislatures controlled most taxes, often times local police, sometimes municipal franchises. And they could be bought: the street car magnate refused a hearing in Chicago might still win his battle by bribing legislators downstate in Springfield. Urban progressives beginning with Pingree, who became governor of Michigan in 1897, found the trek to the statehouse as natural a part of their ideals at it was of their ambitions.

439

State progressivism had clearer claim to the title of democratic reform. Efficiency-minded reformers found agrarian interests dominating many state legislatures; to get a hearing for their programs, the progressives worked to open the political system; in coalition with rural and small-town reformers, they displayed greater concern for economic legislation. Their chief instrument for political reform was institution of the direct primary, in which parties selected their candidates for major offices through elections instead of conventions. Another weapon in the progressive arsenal was the initiative and referendum, which allowed citizens to bypass an unresponsive legislature by petitioning for propositions to be included on the ballot. A more extreme method was the recall, by which citizens could get rid of an official who displeased them before his term of office ended.

In states where progressivism went furthest, such as Wisconsin under Robert La Follette, progressives not only made changes in the structure of government, but also passed positive social legislation. These measures included railroad and grain-elevator rate commissions, higher taxes on corporations, improved banking laws, factory-inspection acts, workmen's compensation, limitations in the hours that women and children could work, and improvements in school and park systems.

National needs   Even statewide progressivism was not enough to meet the many problems transcending state boundaries. For one thing, federal courts had the power to approve states' social legislation, and in this era courts all too often struck down reform efforts. In *Muller* v. *Oregon* (1908), however, the Supreme Court accepted a state law limiting women's working hours to ten a day. Louis D. Brandeis presented the Court with 102 pages of sociological data on the effect of work upon women and the state's need to protect their health and welfare, and he then limited himself to only two pages of legal precedent. This "Brandeis brief" became a model for the new school of "sociological jurisprudence," popular in law schools but far less so among older court judges. Courts still invoked the rights of property and the sanctity of private contract to restrict the states' power to police their citizens in the interest of the general welfare.

Congress, too, had a role to play. Areas that had voted for prohibition of alcoholic beverages wanted federal laws to prevent shipments entering from other states. Cities that had launched crusades against prostitution wanted an end to "white slavers" bringing in girls from across the river. Nor could states adequately protect the purity of their meats or drugs. And progressives winced each time a United States senator had to be elected. States sought means to make this a direct election rather that a decision of purchasable state legislatures. The Seventeenth Amendment, ratified in 1913, at last achieved this goal. Finally, there were inherently national issues which deeply concerned the progressives: tariff schedules, banking policy, conservation, nationwide railroad regulation, and the control of interstate corporations. Here were areas for Congress to act and for a president to lead. Fate gave the progressives a president they could follow.

THEODORE ROOSEVELT

On September 6, 1901, Leon Czolgosz, a poor, demented misfit with vague notions of anarchism, fired two shots at President McKinley, whose death a week later brought into the White House the youngest and most unusual president America had so far known. Hero of San Juan Hill, rancher and author of books about the West, Theodore Roosevelt had also prowled the nighttime streets of New York in a long cape to sweep down dramatically on corrupt policemen. A governor of New York whose progressive record had induced Republican bosses to exile him to the inanities of the vice-presidency, he was not one of those faceless "available men" who had made careers of not giving offense to people. He was a leader for the new generation of self-righteous young crusaders. An aggressive moralist, he turned the White House into a "bully pulpit." An activist, he used his office to shape opinion and influence legislation. And in some areas, such as foreign policy and conservation, he seized upon long-dormant executive powers to mold the presidency into something like the mighty office it has since become.

Sensing the uncertainty and potential hostility of party leaders, Roosevelt quickly promised to continue McKinley's policies and retained almost all of his cabinet. Throughout his tenure, he struggled to keep good relations with the powers in Congress, especially the leading Republican senators, Nelson Aldrich, John C. Spooner, Orville H. Platt, and William B. Allison. These four men in their almost nightly gatherings over cards and billiards determined the course of the Senate. Along with Mark Hanna and, after 1903, the iron-handed Speaker of the House Joseph Cannon, these conservatives kept a tight rein on the national government. Roosevelt never fought them directly, but he found new resources in the presidency that eroded their position and prepared the way for a more liberal Congress which would enable his rival Woodrow Wilson a decade later to rush into legislation much of the progressive program.

Trustbuster Roosevelt moved cautiously, especially in his first term. Yet he made even his caution seem dramatic. His action against the "trusts" especially created the image of the beloved "Teddy," the most admired American since Abraham Lincoln. Old fears of monopoly had gained fresh impetus from developments late in the nineties. In 1897, at the depression's end, eighty-six large corporations capitalized at about $1½ billion. By 1904 318 were worth $7½ billion, and they included the gargantuan United States Steel Corporation, the first billion-dollar company. Trusts were so huge

Roosevelt with Booker T. Washington at National Negro Business League. *Culver Pictures*

that the public feared that they could force up prices in order to realize their exaggerated expectations of profit. Consumers, helpless in the marketplace and baffled by inflation, soon looked to government for aid.

Roosevelt began by pressing for new laws to require national licensing of corporations and to increase the power of the Interstate Commerce Commission (ICC) over the railroads. He got laws from Congress —creating a Bureau of Corporations and limiting railroad rebate—which were clearly too weak to affect the large corporations. He then turned to executive action, making use of the Sherman Antitrust Act to prosecute the Northern Securities Company, a new, overgrown, and unpopular railroad holding company.

With the stock market reeling at the news, J. P. Morgan offered to have underlings get together to "fix it up." Roosevelt noted that the financier regarded him "as a big rival operator." The president would have none of it: the whole point was to demonstrate the superior power of government over any private concern. And Roosevelt gained his point: the courts eventually dissolved Northern Securities. Occurring at the same time as Roosevelt's equally vigorous action in the anthracite-coal strike of 1902, this landmark prosecution convinced the public that they could turn to government as an arbiter above the conflicts of private interests, however huge. Roosevelt considered this an important lesson, which he drove home in a series of speeches preaching his "Square Deal."

Roosevelt could now use the threat of antitrust prosecution to demand cooperation from big business, and he believed in such cooperation far more than he did in conflict. In 1905 he and United States Steel struck a "gentlemen's agreement" which set a pattern for government-industry relations. Steel agreed to cooperate with the Bureau of Corporations, and in return the government would allow the corporation to correct any breaches of federal law without recourse to litigation. Historians still argue over whether this was a triumph for the forces of reform seeking to check the trusts or a victory for big business in search of a painless way to regulate their industries and buffer themselves against public anger.

Workers   While perhaps less upsetting than the spectre of rapacious trusts, the new strength of labor unions represented another threat to the middle class to which Roosevelt responded. William Dean Howells had expressed a popular sentiment: "The struggle for life," he wrote, "has changed from a free fight to an encounter of disciplined forces, and the free fighters that are left get ground to pieces between organized labor and organized capital." Unions, weak since the debacle of 1886, began a steady and this time more permanent rise in membership and power during the same period trusts were forming. Inflation began to eat away at the gains that skilled workers had made in the long era of sinking prices, driving them into unions. Businessmen, fearful of halting the advance of prosperity and in a position to pass along labor gains as price increases, offered a less desperate resistance than in the past. The American Federation of Labor gained most, growing over 700 percent in the twenty years after 1897, with the sharpest growth in 1897–1904, the years of industrial concentration. AFL leader Samuel Gompers tirelessly announced the conservative goals of labor; but with prices rising, 2½ million workers organized, and various active socialist and anarchist movements outside Gompers's control, middle-class Americans worried that they were caught between two great organized interests, above and below them. "The unorganized public," lamented a leading progressive, "where will *it* come in?"

Coal strike   Roosevelt found his opportunity to define the kind of labor activity of which he approved and to establish the presidential role in labor disputes during the anthracite coal strike of 1902.

The miners, seeking higher wages and a union contract, held out for five months, maintained their discipline, and kept the strike from spilling over into the soft-coal fields (whose workers steadily contributed funds to the striking hard-coal miners). This excellent strike management by the twenty-nine-year-old United Mine Workers leader John Mitchell paid off. Roosevelt dramatically summoned the owners and Mitchell to the White House in an attempt to settle the strike. The owners came, but refused to speak to Mitchell. Infuriated, TR regretted that the dignity of his office precluded his taking the owners' spokesman, George F. Baer, "by the seat of the breeches and the nape of the neck" and defenestrating him. Roosevelt did the next best thing. He pressured Wall Street to push the unwilling owners into mediation and to get the willing workers back into the mines. While the public rejoiced over household furnaces again stoked with hard coal, the carefully selected board of arbiters gave the union a 10 percent pay raise and management a similar price hike. Although the miners had actually lost their prime demand—union recognition—the labor movement had scored a triumph in showing the nation that workers could strike without disorder or threats of revolution. And the president, of course, had demonstrated his authority.

Leader of the   Roosevelt was in a strong position going into the election year of 1904.
progressives   Progressives, perhaps making comparisons with his predecessor, accepted the limited reforms of his first term. Conservatives, certain that he was no radical and pleased at his deference toward leaders like Aldrich and Cannon, offered their cautious backing as well. The Democrats, not wanting a third straight Bryan campaign, turned to a conservative, Judge Alton B. Parker of New York. This did not prevent business from heavily financing Roosevelt's campaign. With the Republicans a clear majority nationally, Roosevelt swept to an enormous victory—as did numerous progressives in state contests.

Intoxicated by the breadth of his victory, Roosevelt became bolder. He proposed that Congress make the District of Columbia a model community, clearing slums, inspecting factories, banning child labor. He called for stricter regulation of the railroads and a minimum wage for trainmen. But Congress remained nearly as conservative as before, and few of Roosevelt's programs made any headway. The president responded by picking a single objective, railroad regulation, and sticking to it. Here he showed great political skill. Threatening the party's leadership with a divisive fight on the tariff, he forced action on a bill that allowed the ICC to fix railroad rates. He had to accept several conservative amendments allowing judicial review of the commission's findings, but the resulting Hepburn Act (1906) was the first effective law regulating the railroads. The following year Roosevelt skillfully piloted through Congress the Pure Food and Drug Act and the Meat Inspection Act, both obvious and long-delayed necessities in an industrial society. Americans had taken a tentative step toward a welfare state.

Conservationist　Conservation and foreign policy were both open fields for a determined president, and both were Roosevelt's passions. He had written feelingly of the West and of the wilderness and sincerely desired their preservation. Still, this romantic mentality never dominated his conservation activities. He stood for the efficient administration and rational use of the nation's resources. Roosevelt set aside nearly 150 million acres of public lands as national forests and removed over 80 million acres of mineral land from public sale as well as 1½ million acres of water-power sites. Those resources, when leased to private interests, could now be used for long range economic goals set and regulated by conservation-minded national administrators. Roosevelt also created five national parks, sixteen national monuments, and fifty-one wildlife refuges. His activities made conservation a national enthusiasm. Most states launched conservation commissions, and many private organizations formed to advance the cause. Nowhere else was the progressive mentality, mixing standards of rational efficiency with romantic sensibility and moral crusading, so evident as in the conservation movement. And nowhere else were Roosevelt's achievements so large, so permanent, and so unquestionably helpful.

THEODORE ROOSEVELT'S FOREIGN POLICY

In foreign policy, Roosevelt enjoyed great freedom. Few Americans believed that they had any significant stake beyond the nation's borders. Roosevelt had only to avoid offending the public's vague preconceptions about our role in the world. Otherwise, he could do pretty much as he pleased.

Roosevelt and his circle set directions in American foreign policy for decades to come. Elihu Root reorganized the army during his stint as secretary of war. Alfred Thayer Mahan effectively argued for a strong navy to maintain and extend national power. He not only convinced Roosevelt, but he influenced an entire generation of leaders who moved the nation from a weak naval power to one of the world's leading forces at sea. Henry Cabot Lodge supported an active diplomacy from his post as chairman of the Senate Foreign Relations Committee. John Hay, who remained as secretary of state until 1905, left the legacy upon which Roosevelt built. And all were his close personal friends.

The Far East Like Hay, Roosevelt worked to maintain America's commercial position in China. This required a constant fine tuning of the balance of power in Asia, no mean feat in the face of growing Japanese naval power and the uncertain strength of tsarist Russia. This delicate balance collapsed in 1904 when Japan launched a surprise naval attack and proceeded to crush the Russians by land and by sea. However, the Japanese lacked the resources for a long war and welcomed Roosevelt's mediation. With considerable tact, Roosevelt succeeded in convening a conference at Portsmouth, New Hampshire in 1905, and then persuaded the Japanese to accept a compromise peace settlement.

Roosevelt's triumph at Portsmouth—he won a Nobel Peace Prize for his efforts—created problems with Japan. The Japanese public blamed Roosevelt for how little they gained from the war. The president found further need to placate Japan when the San Francisco school board ordered all its Oriental students into a segregated school. It took a White House conference to change the school board's policy and a "gentlemen's agreement" with Japan to halt the flow of Japanese laborers into the West Coast. Then Teddy, fearing he had made too many concessions, tried a threatening gesture by sending the American fleet—second largest in the world—on a visit to Japan. This tour of the "Great White Fleet" was another Rooseveltian production: failing to intimidate anyone, it was nonetheless wildly popular, a masterpiece of grandstand diplomacy.

Latin America Closer to home, Roosevelt was more aggressive. He put an end to European interventions in Latin America. Henceforth the United States would be the hemisphere's bill collector. In 1903 when the Dominican Republic defaulted on $40 million in bonds held by European investors, Roosevelt took over the Dominican customs service to pay off the debts and incidentally to control the Dominican government. This policy soon achieved the status of a "corollary" to the Monroe Doctrine: in the face of "chronic wrongdoing" or "impotence," the president announced to Congress, we would exercise "an international police power." Under the terms of the Roosevelt corollary, American interventions in Latin America became more frequent, and American economic penetration, especially in the countries washed by the Caribbean, increased substantially in the first two decades of the twentieth century.

The high point of Roosevelt's diplomacy was the construction of the interocean canal across the isthmus of Panama. Here he was not playing to the grandstand but pursuing an obvious national interest. The growth of our naval power had revitalized the long-standing desire for a closer water link between the two American shores. In 1901 the Hay-Pauncefote Treaty cleared the way for an American canal by ending an old obligation to share control of such a canal with England. Then the battle was on to select a route: partisans of the water-level route through Nicaragua lost out to skillful lobbyists for a French-owned canal company that possessed legal rights and a few excavations through the rough fifty miles between the oceans in Panama—then still a province of Colombia. Hay proceeded to negotiate a treaty with Colombia providing for a ninety-nine-year lease for a six-mile-wide strip across the isthmus. The Colombian Senate unanimously decided that the treaty offered insufficient compensation and rejected it.

Roosevelt was furious. Dealing with those "dagoes," he bellowed, was like trying to "nail currant jelly to a wall." The canal company then took a hand, persuading the Panamanians to revolt against Colombia. They had tried before, but this time, with an American cruiser quickly sent to the area, their former rulers were helpless. The United States instantly recognized the new republic and rapidly signed a treaty for a permanent lease on a ten mile-wide zone for the same terms offered Colombia—$10 million outright and a quarter-million-dollar annual rental. Through it all, Roosevelt never lost his self-righteous aplomb. Many Latin Americans refused to forget his arrogance and disdain. Few incidents generated such long-term hostility. Eventually the United States, in 1921, gave Colombia $25 million—a monetary apology for Roosevelt's behavior. Colombia then recognized the Panamanian Republic. Meanwhile, the canal opened to traffic in 1914 and the United States dominated the Caribbean.

WILLIAM HOWARD TAFT

Roosevelt ended his administration in a posture of futile crusading against a conservative Congress. Nonetheless, he retained so much popularity that he was the first president since Andrew Jackson able to name his successor. William Howard Taft was the man, all three hundred pounds of him and more. Taft had been a good federal judge, a competent governor of the Philippines, an effective secretary of war, and, most important, a loyal Roosevelt man. A distinguished legal thinker and an excellent administrator, his chief liability was a distaste for politics: he lacked the necessary energy, joy of combat, and ability as a campaigner.

President Taft. *Brown Brothers*

His election, however, was a foregone conclusion. Taft ran as a careful progressive against William Jennings Bryan, and his administration was supposed to be a workmanlike orchestration of Rooseveltian themes. It did not work out that way.

Foreign affairs

In foreign policy, Taft tried to follow Roosevelt and yet make his own mark. Taft gave his tactics a new and unfortunate name: "dollar diplomacy." He meant this in a positive sense: an alternative to diplomacy by bullets and a boost for underdeveloped economies. But history has taken the phrase as a blunt rationale for an informal American Empire. In a few areas Taft went beyond his predecessor: he sent marines into Nicaragua in 1912, a small contingent of them remaining until 1933. He tried without success to put American bankers in charge of the finances of Haiti, Honduras, Costa Rica, and Guatemala. And he was equally unsuccessful in creating an American economic presence in Manchuria.

Taft and the progressives

Domestic policy proved even more difficult for Taft. TR's last programs had enhanced the expectations of the progressives and sharpened the caution of the Old Guard. Taft lacked the smoothness to run with both forces the way Roosevelt had. And he lacked the progressive style Roosevelt had flourished even at his most cautious. Taft, for instance, initiated far more antitrust prosecutions in his four years than Roosevelt had in seven, yet Taft remained in the public eye the friend of the corporations. So too, Taft's reform accomplishments far exceeded Roosevelt's: further railroad-rate regulation in the Mann-Elkins Act of 1910, a postal savings plan, industrial safety measures, the establishment of a Children's Bureau, and an eight-hour day for federal employees. He also had a hand in the passage of the Sixteenth Amendment, allowing a federal income tax—a necessity for later social legislation. Yet he goes down in history, as he went down with his contemporaries, a conservative.

Much of this rests on Taft's political ineptitude. He could not sell himself or his policies to the public. Somehow he always managed to alienate even the progressives, who gave the strongest support to the reforms he achieved. He never learned TR's trick of holding them back to get a passable bill without earning their enmity. And they could sense that he never liked them: the conservative leaders, especially Aldrich, simply appealed more to him as people. They weren't so evangelical, so pushy, so insistent; they were more his kind, appreciating good food and leisure and a friendly round of golf.

Several incidents divided Taft from the progressives. He failed to support George Norris's successful attempt to break "Boss" Cannon's hold on the House of Representatives. Then Taft botched the Payne-Aldrich Tariff of 1909. He had pushed for sharp reductions to benefit consumers, but when Aldrich's Senate committee tacked on 847 amendments, most of them raising rates, Taft failed to aid the progressive senators who resisted. When the crippled bill went through, he not only signed it, but told a tariff-conscious Minnesota audience that it was "on the whole...the best bill that the Republican party ever passed."

Then in one final disaster Taft fell into a position which appeared to be flatly anticonservationist and anti-Roosevelt. This was the dizzily complex Ballinger–Pinchot affair. Roosevelt and his chief forester, Gifford Pinchot, Taft believed, did not always use "the legal way" of reaching their conservationist goals. Taft had appointed as secretary of the Interior Richard A. Ballinger, a western lawyer who would follow the law strictly. Eventually conflict had to come, and when it did Taft let it grow from an intramural argument between Ballinger and the chief forester into a public scandal resulting in Taft's firing of Pinchot—the symbol of conservation and one of TR's intimate friends.

Reenter Theodore Roosevelt

Roosevelt returned in 1910 from a long hunting trip to Africa laden with big-game trophies and a trunkful of mail from unhappy progressives. Once home, he found Taft cool and the party hot with discontent. After a brief period of uncharacteristic silence, TR boomed out a new progressive platform in a speech at Osawatomie, Kansas, in August. Calling for a "New Nationalism," Roosevelt coupled the "Square Deal" program left over from the end of his presidency with a general call for an extension of federal power. The executive branch in particular, he argued, must become "the advocate of human welfare." Once again the progressives had their familiar hero.

By 1911 Roosevelt had leapt into the ring, smashing Taft in primary after primary. Nevertheless, Taft kept a thin margin of control over the Republican convention, beating back a number of credentials challenges and securing renomination on the first ballot. Roosevelt, claiming that he felt as fit as a bull moose, then accepted the nomination of the new Progressive party of 1912, which quickly became popularly known as the "Bull Moose" party. Their convention in August was more like a religious revival than a traditional political meeting. Adopting a platform that became a major text in the history of twentieth-century reform, the "New Nationalist" Progressives called for strict regulation of large corporations (rather than continuing the effort at breaking them up), progressive changes in the mechanics of government, and virtually all the economic and social legislation that had been suggested by progressives in the previous decade.

Enter Woodrow Wilson

With the Republicans divided, the Democrats saw their first real opportunity in twenty years; as much by luck as by design, they finally took it. After forty-six ballots they nominated Woodrow Wilson, by any test their ideal candidate. Born in Virginia and raised in the South, Wilson had landed on the national scene like some meteor from another world. Two years before he was known principally among educators for his role as the dynamic president of Princeton University and among political scientists and a small segment of the literate public as an author of several books on political theory and history. Then he had been elected governor of New Jersey in 1910. An instant success, he pushed through a full progressive program and impressed a large public with his high-minded oratory. His call in 1912 for a "New Freedom" for individuals to compete with large organizations spoke directly to the hopes and fears that industrial America had stirred.

The election of 1912

Nineteen twelve was the high point of progressive sentiment. Even Taft, the most conservative of the three candidates, stood for many reforms. But Roosevelt and Taft had made each other's cause hopeless. The Republican majority divided, and Wilson won easily with only a little more than 6 million out of nearly 15 million votes cast. Roosevelt's new party actually outpolled the Republicans, with the Socialist party candidate, Eugene V. Debs, also receiving almost a million votes. If many Americans wanted no more changes, they were profoundly silent about it. The mandate seemed all for progress. Few noticed that this had been the smallest voter turnout (in proportion to population) since the rise of the modern two-party system in Jackson's time.

THE WILSON ADMINISTRATION

Woodrow Wilson presided over the flowering of national progressivism and oversaw its demise. But in the first years everything, or at least everything domestic, rolled on in splendor. The Democrats, controlling both houses of Congress, were prepared to follow their president. Wilson instantly seized the initiative. His inaugural address set the tone of high idealism that was to characterize his presidency and established areas for legislation: tariff reform, a new banking and currency system, industrial regulation, and conservation of natural and human resources.

A new financial system

Congress, prodded by an aggressive president, made good on most of these promises. Wilson called them into special session to reform the tariff and broke precedent by appearing in person to present his program —a daring act Theodore Roosevelt must have envied. The speedily

Orpen's portrait of Thomas Woodrow Wilson. *Library of Congress*

passed Underwood Tariff not only cut rates, it also enacted a federal income tax. The president then held Congress in session throughout the summer—a cruel undertaking before the days of air-conditioned chambers —to enact currency and banking reform. The movement for a new financial system had recently gained impetus from a congressional committee's sensational reports of the power and extent of the "money trust." The investigation, conducted by Representative Arsène Pujo, showed that the interconnected interests of J. P. Morgan and John D. Rockefeller controlled over $22 billion of the nation's wealth. Riding this current, Wilson pushed through the Federal Reserve Act, unquestionably the domestic triumph of his administration.

The Federal Reserve Act created a national banking and currency system to replace the largely private system that had endured since Jackson's time. The Federal Reserve system consisted of twelve Federal Reserve banks—essentially banks for bankers that could issue currency in exchange for secured notes which banks received from their borrowers. A Federal Reserve Board, appointed by the president, exercised control over the commission—called the rediscount rate—that banks paid for the privilege of changing their notes into Federal Reserve bills. The result was a somewhat more decentralized currency system (no longer were all assets tied to Wall Street), a more flexible currency—no longer directly fluctuating with the price of gold—and a banking system under some measure of public control through the Federal Reserve Board.

It was hardly a radical measure. Bankers named a large minority of directors of district banks, and Wilson put conservative bankers on the Reserve Board. The act substantially removed the currency and banking issue from the national arena and offered at least the start of a reliable banking system. Whether the system took public control of banking or simply lent the power of government to the bankers themselves remained to be seen.

Progressivism at its height

Wilson continued to press important legislation. The Smith-Lever Act of 1914 financed the valuable work being done by the agricultural extension services to improve farming methods. It also, inadvertently, paved the way for an organization of American farmers much like comparable groups in American industry and labor: the American Farm Bureau Federation, an organization of, by, and for the most prosperous farmers. The Federal Trade Commission Act replaced Roosevelt's Bureau of Corporations with an independent regulatory agency with far more power than any agency had had before. Wilson staffed it with men reluctant to interfere with the needs of business as businessmen saw them. Then the Clayton Antitrust Act strengthened and made more definite the provisions of the old Sherman Act as well as vaguely promising labor some protection from antitrust actions and injunctions. Even so, as con-

Keystone capers gently satirized authority. *Culver Pictures*

gressional progressives had predicted, many of the law's restraints on big business eroded under court decisions. And what Samuel Gompers had hailed as labor's "Magna Carta" quickly proved but another weapon in the arsenal of the corporations battling the unions. As Mr. Dooley, fictional creation of the era's favorite political satirist said, "What looks like a brick wall to a layman is a triumphal arch for a corporation lawyer."

Essentially the American system had become one of voluntary cooperation between business and government punctuated by occasional bouts of open conflict. Perhaps the goal, which Wilson and Roosevelt each in his own way stated, of making business behave should be taken quite literally: businessmen were learning caution and a small measure of social responsibility. This rather small price was all the progressives asked of them, despite their rhetoric of being at Armageddon battling for the Lord.

A balance sheet National progressivism had largely run its course before the nation turned its attention to foreign affairs in 1914, when war broke out in Europe. Here and there later laws extended some of its directions: in 1915 the humanitarian La Follette Seaman's Act improved conditions in the merchant marine; the Federal Farm Loan Act (1916) and the Warehouse Act (1916) brought some relief to the eternal problem of farm credit; the Keating-Owen Act outlawed child labor—until the Supreme Court voided it in 1918; the Adamson Act raised railroad workers' salaries. And there were others. Nonetheless, the Wilson administration, by bringing the progressive movement to fruition, also pointed sharply to its limitations. It had been a movement for and by the middle classes. Quite aware of the existence of poverty, in general progressives were nevertheless rarely more than cautiously paternalistic toward the poor. In some areas, as in agriculture, by improving the conditions of those on top, they deflected concern for those in more serious need. And their definition of the public was sharply limited. Many immigrants did not fit the progressive model of a good citizen. Worse yet, except for a few noble exceptions, the progressives were no more responsive than their less moralistic compeers to the needs of Afro-Americans. In fact, their era coincides with the very lowest point in the Negro's search for a place in modern American life.

BLACK AMERICANS DURING THE PROGRESSIVE ERA

Progressivism was for whites only. Southern progressives were in the forefront of the movement to disfranchise blacks as a means of purifying the ballot in their states. Nationally, the Republican party offered little to their loyal black constituents. Theodore Roosevelt pleased blacks by allowing Booker T. Washington to dine at the White House, but when this raised a storm of protests he never repeated the invitation. Roosevelt distributed some patronage to loyal blacks—but only if they had Washington's approval, meaning that they were not loudly calling for either social or political rights. And Roosevelt scandalized blacks by dishonorably discharging three companies from a highly decorated Afro-American battalion on the basis of unproven charges against them—a miscarriage of justice that remained uncorrected for sixty-six years before the army changed the discharges to honorable in 1972. Taft's policies offered blacks no more, and black politicians supported him largely because they had no place else to turn: Roosevelt's Progressive party of 1912 was lily white, and the Democrats were even worse on racial issues.

The return of the white South to the seat of national government during the Wilson years spelled disaster for blacks. Wilson himself was a bigot, pleased to support his cabinet's rigid segregation of the federal civil service. During his tenure in the White House, more militant black leaders came to the fore, and their clashes with Wilson were particularly violent. In one celebrated incident involving William Monroe Trotter, the aggressive editor of the black newspaper the Boston *Guardian*, Wilson ordered Trotter from his presence for using "insulting" language in protesting segregation in the civil service.

Such limited political prospects for blacks help explain Booker T. Washington's success. His disillusionment with the possibilities of political achievement for blacks extended to most of his community. Poor blacks had little faith in their political leaders. In so far as anyone knows what they felt, their hearts seemed to be with the prophets of black nationalism or a return to Africa, men like the rough-hewn Bishop Henry M. Turner, who called for a black exodus from the United States. And even middle-class blacks, especially in the South, saw their future principally in education and economic advancement, judging that political assertion would only increase the violence and hostility directed against them. The best policy seemed to be Washington's: to keep the white oppressors off their backs while developing community strength and economic power.

A new activism   One of Washington's opponents, Adam Clayton Powell, Sr., asked in 1906: "What are the results of Washington's leadership?" He answered:

> *Lynchings are increasing and riots are more numerous. The race is humiliated by Jim Crow laws, and woefully handicapped in its intellectual and moral development by inferior schools. In a word, under Dr. Washington's policy the two races in the South are a thousand times further apart than they were fifteen years ago and the breach is widening every day.*

While it was unfair to blame Washington's policy for this state of affairs, Powell's description of the situation was undeniably accurate. A prominent New York minister and community leader, Powell was typical of the new men coming to oppose Washington for both his submissive style and his policy. Powell's son, Adam Clayton Powell, Jr., would have an extraordinary and controversial career dedicated almost wholly to eradicating from both black and white minds the Booker T. Washington image of the black leader.

W. E. B. Du Bois and the "color line"

The greatest of Washington's opponents in every respect was William Edward Burghardt Du Bois. As a publicist, scholar, author, and one of the founders of the modern civil rights movement, Du Bois left a large imprint on American life and thought. Massachusetts-born, educated at Fisk and Harvard, arrogant and brilliant, he rapidly emerged as the great interpreter of Afro-American life. In 1900 he issued the warning that continues to echo:

> The problem of the Twentieth Century is the problem of the color line, the question as to how far differences of race, which show themselves chiefly in the color of the skin and the texture of the hair, are going to be made, hereafter, the basis of denying to over half the world the right of sharing to their utmost ability the opportunities and the privileges of modern civilization.

Du Bois argued that black Americans had to build their own enterprises to achieve racial pride (he was also one of the first theorists of Pan-Africanism). Yet blacks could not achieve this manhood without an assertion of their rights, without striving for and achieving full equality in American life. Du Bois saw the need for both the self-help tradition of Washington and the integrationist philosophy of Frederick Douglass. Everything had to be done at once: to wait for political rights as Washington counseled was to risk losing self-respect; to reach for them without economic and moral force behind them—as in Reconstruction— would be to court disaster. And Du Bois, who had thoroughly studied his people's past and their present circumstances, knew that life behind the veil of segregation had denied them most of the resources they required for the gargantuan task.

Founding the NAACP

Du Bois's answer was sharply elitist: men like Du Bois himself—what he called the "talented tenth" of the black population—would have to save the race. There was a harsh realism to Du Bois's views. He helped to build a generation of black leaders. This meant attacking Washington for his industrial-education theories: the community's limited resources had to go into educating the talented tenth, not raising "the man farthest down." It meant insisting on political rights and social privileges. Under Du Bois's inspiration a group of men disenchanted with Washington's leadership gathered at Niagara Falls in 1905. The Niagara Movement formulated demands which set the tone for a half-century and more of protest: an end to racial discrimination in employment, in the courts, in business, and in labor unions; universal suffrage; the demolition of the Jim Crow system; and higher education for the able. The movement attracted no mass following, but it did stir some white liberals such as John Dewey and Jane Addams to join with Du Bois in founding the National Association for the Advancement of Colored People, an inter-racial organization dedicated to ending legal and political discrimination. Du Bois became editor of its journal, *The Crisis,* and before leaving to seek more radical alternatives he had made of it the first permanent and effective lobby for black rights.

Black renaissance   Du Bois's efforts were part of a renaissance in Afro-American life. As if in challenge to the rising white racism, black leaders and artists showed a new militancy and a fresh pride in their common experience. Around the turn of the century a number of important works by black authors and artists suddenly began to appear: the sculpture of Meta Warwick

W. E. B. Du Bois, an intellectual of first rank

Marcus Garvey led a "Back to Africa" movement after the war. *UPI*

Fuller, the poetry of Paul Lawrence Dunbar, Charles W. Chesnutt's novels, Du Bois's writings. One of the greatest works of black literature in this period, James Weldon Johnson's *Autobiography of an Ex-Colored Man,* was published anonymously in 1912. It showed an acceptance of black folkways and especially black music—ragtime and jazz—that earlier black writers had avoided in deference to white critics. Other signs of growing racial pride were the rising popularity of black dolls around 1910, calendars with black themes, and—in a rather different area—the founding in 1915 of the *Journal of Negro History,* which joined Du Bois's Atlanta University publications as a vehicle for the investigation of the black experience in America.

A new age Booker T. Washington died in 1915. His power had been steadily waning in the black world for several years, and his passing marked the end of an era. In fact, the symbolism was peculiarly apt. Washington's world was passing in the most fundamental sense. The Great War had broken out in Europe, and it affected blacks even more than other American citizens. With war production opening new opportunities in the factories and cities, the steady trickle of black families northward suddenly turned into a flood. From 1915 onward increasing numbers of blacks moved into northern cities, creating raw new urban ghettos and spawning a new culture and politics. A "new Negro movement" among black intellectuals sparked a Harlem literary renaissance which became a rage in New York literary circles during the 1920s. A new prophet, Marcus Garvey, led a massive but short-lived nationalist movement, the Universal Negro Improvement Association. At its height, during 1920 and 1921, some 4 to 6 million Afro-Americans supported his attempt to form a beachhead for black Americans in Africa. Garvey extolled everything black and rejected the white world and any attempt to become assimilated by it. His uniforms and parades and his swagger filled emotional needs among lower-class blacks that the interracial civil rights groups could not. When his plans for an African kingdom went awry and the federal government sent him to prison for some of his dealings in connection with this project, the movement collapsed. He remains, however, a hero of black nationalists.

WILSON AND THE WORLD

Missionary America Wilson, although he expected to make his mark in domestic affairs, never doubted that he had lessons to teach the rest of the world as well. He was determined to raise the moral tone of American diplomacy by turning from cynical professional diplomats to idealistic amateurs, avoiding the imperialism and dollar diplomacy that had marred America's recent role in the world. In meeting party obligations by naming William Jennings Bryan secretary of state, he made a good start in this direction:

wholly without experience in diplomacy, Bryan retained the high moral tone of his great crusading days, and he planned to fill critical places in the State Department with "deserving Democrats."

Wilson's foreign policy generally continued that of Roosevelt and Taft under a different name and rhetoric. Intent on achieving American-style democracy in the rest of the world, he intervened as freely as his predecessor in the Caribbean: the United States stayed in Nicaragua, reentered Santo Domingo, and virtually took over Haiti. Wilson continued to defend the Open Door in China, and policy there still fluctuated with the perceived threat that Japan posed to our interests. Wilson began his administration intent on maintaining a balance of power in Asia. He concluded the Lansing-Ishii Agreement in 1917 by which we vaguely condoned Japanese penetration into China, and Japan just as vaguely promised to abide by the Open Door.

Wilson and revolution Wilson's primary departure in foreign affairs came in Mexico. The revolution there, which began in 1910, was no minor coup or change in dictators. A whole generation struggled for and against social and economic change and constitutional democracy. Here was a serious test of Wilson's idealism.

American investors had long prospered in Mexico under the dictatorship of Porfirio Díaz, who encouraged foreign investment and kept the lid on popular discontent. The democratic reformers who took power in 1910 were less accommodating, and when their leader, Francisco Madero, was murdered in 1913 by Victoriano Huerta, foreign investors and European governments scarcely shed a tear. But Wilson refused to follow the path of the other powers and the unbroken American tradition of recognizing whichever government was in power. He would not recognize Huerta's "government of butchers."

Wilson hoped this new policy of nonrecognition would bring down the Huerta government, which in any case controlled only part of Mexico. When Huerta survived, Wilson found himself without a policy. Those he had hoped to help rebuffed offers to mediate and even to intervene. Wilson was troubled by the contradiction of trying to settle a nationalist uprising from outside: opposing factions became friends facing this clumsy embrace from the north. Meanwhile, the American fleet ominously patrolled the Mexican coast in watchful wait for their orders or an incident.

In April 1914 a minor Mexican official arrested some American sailors who had gone ashore in Tampico. His superior promptly released them and offered apologies. The United States admiral demanded a twenty-one gun salute to the American flag, and Huerta refused. Wilson thought he had to back his admiral and sent more naval force to the area. Hearing of a German ship on its way with munitions for the Mexican government, Wilson ordered his fleet to seize its port of destination, Vera Cruz. Gunboat diplomacy, so often a farce, suddenly turned to tragedy. To Wilson's horror, the Mexicans dared to resist. Casualties for both sides ran into the hundreds: Wilson had blundered to the brink of a senseless war with our southern neighbor. Only an offer to mediate by Argentina, Brazil, and Chile allowed Wilson a last-minute escape hatch. As negotiations dragged on, tempers cooled. Then in July, democratic forces under Venustiano Carranza finally succeeded in driving Huerta out of Mexico City.

This was America's first experience of responding to a modern national revolution. Wilson's effort was long on ambition but short on achievement. In fact, even Carranza's victory did not end Wilson's Mexican embroglio. He foolishly mistook the swashbuckling bandit Pancho Villa for a Wilsonian progressive, realized his error, and then had General John J. Pershing chase Villa's army three hundred miles into Mexico. His mistake here was of a piece with the rest of his Mexican policy: he grasped at whatever in the uncertain course of revolution looked familiar, progressive, and American, then discovered that it was none of these things. That was not how the rest of the world behaved, a lesson Wilson learned later and to his sorrow.

WAR IN EUROPE

In late summer 1914 a Serbian nationalist assassinated Austrian Archduke Franz Ferdinand. This seemingly minor incident of isolated violence provoked a chain reaction through the complex system of European alliances and led Britain, France, and Russia into war against Germany and Austria-Hungary. The resulting conflict, the climax of decades of increasingly serious confrontations around the globe, would weaken Europe and touch off at least half a century of worldwide turbulence and instability.

Like Germany, the United States was a relative newcomer in the club of world powers. But unlike its Central European counterpart, America was not surrounded by established powers and felt few constraints upon its expansionist muscles. Isolated by two oceans, Americans initially saw little reason for the European war to affect them directly. When brutal military stalemate shattered the widespread expectation of rapid victory and a speedy peace, Americans began more thoughtfully to assess their own position and the fate of the corrupt and greedy Old World states. Deadlocked pairs of bleached horns which littered the western plains taught Americans that the only victor from a struggle between equals was the outsider, the noncombatant. And during the early years of the war Americans reveled in their neutrality, cherished their isolation, and watched themselves grow stronger as Europe exhausted itself. The refrain of a popular song expressed a common attitude:

I didn't raise my boy to be a soldier,
I brought him up to be my pride and joy,
To live to place a musket on his shoulder,
To shoot some other mother's darling boy....
There'd be no war today
If mothers all would say
I didn't raise my boy to be a soldier.

The barbarism and lawlessness of the war shocked Americans. The horrors of trench warfare and the deadly new gases revealed rationality and civilization as only thin veneers, the gilt on modern man rather than his substance. And, almost unconsciously, Americans began assigning responsibility for the awful events. Feeling more comfortable if they could distinguish between outlaw and victim, evil and righteousness, they gradually dropped their impartiality. Although America's own superiority to both sides remained unquestioned, between the combatants Germany emerged the greater villain. The United States had fewer economic and cultural ties with Germany than with England, and Germans seemed more clearly to have violated international law. They followed the invasion of neutral Belgium with the introduction to warfare of the submarine, a weapon which ignored traditional rules requiring ships to warn and search enemy vessels before sinking them. With some exceptions—such as socialists and German Americans—most people in the United States sympathized with Great Britain. But beyond this vague pro-British leaning and a general belief in America's higher morality, there was little consensus on how Americans should respond to the war.

Pacifists and interventionists

The large prewar pacifist movement viewed the conflict as a ghastly mistake to be avoided even at the cost of abandoning certain traditional neutral rights. Secretary of State Bryan, for example, privately favored Great Britain but valiantly strove for absolute impartiality. He sponsored the Wilson administration's early ban on loans to belligerents and urged the president to forbid American citizens from traveling on the ships of warring nations. He warned that extending credit—which as a practical matter would go mostly to Britain and France—and allowing Americans on British ships would inevitably lead to conflict with Germany. But Wilson moved away from Bryan's position of careful non-involvement and insisted on observing only theoretical neutrality. When the president lifted the ban on loans and demanded that Germany safeguard the lives of Americans on British ships, Bryan resigned from the cabinet. He and many pacifists charged the president with abandoning neutrality in practice on the pretext of upholding it in principle.

A more vocal and colorful coalition argued that Wilson's policies were not strong enough and advocated increased military "preparedness." Labeling Germany as the troublemaker and Britain as a guardian of civilization, interventionists felt that America's national honor would eventually require entry into the war. The most bombastic and influential spokesman for preparedness was America's beloved ex-President Theodore Roosevelt. Trumpeting his conviction that Americans were becoming "soft" and deriding pacifism as unmanly, Roosevelt believed that a firm stand and a righteous war would strengthen America's moral fiber and earn the nation new respect around the globe. The advocates of preparedness lobbied for military appropriations and for a harder line against German submarine warfare.

Wilson's neutrality   Steering a middle course, Wilson sought to uphold traditional neutral rights yet avoid war. The two goals proved irreconcilable. Freedom of the seas was a neutral right, but with the British navy enforcing a tight blockade of Germany, America's "neutral" trade benefited only Britain and its allies. When shortage of capital threatened to limit British and French purchases in the United States, Wilson permitted Americans to extend credit to these belligerents and loftily justified growing Anglo-American economic ties as perfectly consistent with neutrality. America's rigid insistence on neutral rights assisted Britain and France while it worked against Germany by threatening the effectiveness of its major weapon, the submarine. Wilson demanded that Germany abandon surprise attacks and follow the traditional procedure of first warning and then removing passengers from a besieged ship. He announced that Germany would be held to "strict accountability" for any loss of American life on the high seas.

But the German government depended upon its submarines to cut off supplies to Great Britain. It could only warn Americans that they traveled on English vessels at their own risk. When in May 1915 a torpedo sank the *Lusitania,* a British passenger liner which also carried munitions, hundreds of innocent people died, among them many Americans. The deed outraged the country and strengthened the forces favoring preparedness, but the president maintained that there was an admirable quality of being "too proud to fight" and continued trying to negotiate neutral guarantees. After the sinking of the French passenger ship *Sussex* in March 1916, Wilson finally delivered an ultimatum: the United States would sever relations unless Germany ceased its methods of submarine warfare. Reluctant to bring America into the war, Germany acceded to the demand, promising to uphold the rules of visit and search. Wilson's supporters in the election of 1916 could claim that he had "kept us out of war."

The *Sussex* pledge was not a workable formula for peace. Wilson's ultimatum made the issue of war or peace dependent upon decisions in Berlin, and German military officials ultimately considered the submarine campaign more important than the risk of American involvement. In January 1917 Germany announced the resumption of unrestricted sub-

Eugene Debs, a Christian
Socialist, said to the jury that sent
him to prison: "Gentlemen, I
abhor war. I would oppose it if I
stood alone." *Brown Brothers*

marine warfare. Wilson had warned in an earlier address that a moment might come when the United States could not preserve both honor and peace and asked Americans not to "exact of me an impossible and contradictory thing." Now the country knew that war lay only one torpedo away.

Wilson's hopes   The issue of neutral rights did not alone bring America into the war. Wilson nurtured a growing desire to have a hand in shaping the postwar peace. Like most Americans, the president believed deeply in the superiority of the American way and in the corruption of the Old World. The war revealed the disastrous consequences of the old diplomacy of secret treaties, diplomatic intrigue, and spheres of influence. Wilson shared the progressives' faith that the world was marching upward on an evolutionary path toward democracy, liberalism, and open diplomacy. A devout Presbyterian, he believed that the years of horror and devastation should be put to a higher end and become a transitional phase to this new and better order. As war weakened the European powers and America emerged stronger, Wilson began to believe he could act as a peacemaker— not just as an ordinary mediator but as an impartial architect with power to construct the new world on the ruins of the old. The president at first attempted to use America's neutral position to bring the warring nations to the conference table. He sent his close personal friend and special emissary, Colonel Edward House, to meet with European leaders, but neither side was interested in a compromise settlement.

Wilson realized that he could play a major role in a postwar peace conference only if America jointed the war as a belligerent, and his own personal sympathy for England together with the submarine issue made this alternative more and more likely. In March 1917, shortly after Germany's declaration of unrestricted submarine warfare, Great Britain turned over to the State Department a telegram from German foreign minister Alfred Zimmermann inviting Mexico to declare war against the United States in the event of hostilities. This revelation of German designs to disrupt the vulnerable southern border outraged Americans; anti-German sentiment flooded the country, and in April 1917 Wilson went before a special session of Congress to ask for a declaration of war.

Wilson had already articulated the purposes for which he believed America should fight: not for victory, but for a "peace without victory." Through war, Americans would bring to the world "American principles, American policies," which "are also the principles and policies of forward-looking men and women everywhere. . . . They are the principles of mankind and must prevail." The sense of mission and the desire to spread the American way worldwide stretches from John Winthrop to Richard Nixon, but these goals had no more eloquent or dedicated champion than Woodrow Wilson.

AMERICA AT WAR

In 1917 and 1918 Americans no longer hummed "I didn't raise my boy to be a soldier." They sang "It's a long way to Berlin, but we'll get there" or the famous patriotic bombasts of George M. Cohan, such as "Johnny get your gun, . . . take it on the run, . . . hear them calling you and me, every son of liberty. Hurry right away, no delay, go today. . . over there!"

Americans made a small but significant contribution to military victory. The American Expeditionary Force in France, commanded by General John J. Pershing, relieved some of the pressure on British and French forces and helped launch a series of counteroffensives which eventually led to an armistice. On the sea, where German submarines threatened British supply lines, America's small navy and large shipbuilding capacity helped maintain Allied control of the Atlantic. America's economic potential and financial power were its most important wartime assets, and their employment in the Allied cause had lasting consequences. Private financiers granted millions of dollars of credit to England and France before America joined the war, and after American entry Congress authorized the federal government to extend financing directly. In 1914 British investors had a huge investment stake in America: by 1919 the United States had liquidated this indebtedness and reversed the tables, becoming a great creditor to Britain. By the end of the war, various nations of the world owed America over $10 billion. This loaned money was a stimulant, not a drain on the American economy, for most of it went into the purchase of products made in the United States. Industry boomed and huge commercial farms expanded agricultural production. World War I made America the richest and most productive country in the world, a transformation which led directly to the consumer society of the twenties, to farm overproduction, and to the complex war-debt problem which plagued future diplomacy.

Wilson's peace plans   Wilson participated in the war effort wholeheartedly, but he believed America's goals differed significantly from those of its allies and took care not to identify their cause with his own. Insisting that the United States was an "associate," not an "ally," the president operated American troops as a separate entity and refused to merge them into a unified command. When the Bolsheviks overthrew the tsarist government in Russia and published the secret agreements among Allied governments, Wilson had even more reason to dissociate America from Allied war aims. He promulgated his own peace program, the famous Fourteen Points. This articulation of traditional American principles called for open diplomacy, freedom of the seas, armament reductions, free trade, an adjustment of colonial claims, self-determination, and a League of Nations to guarantee independence and territorial integrity. It was Wilson's vision of a purified, harmonious, and liberal world.

But Wilson did not expect a just and peaceful world to appear automatically out of his good intentions. Like others of his generation, he believed that fact gathering, detailed study, and scientific problem solving provided the means to reorder the world. Early in the war he created The Inquiry, a commission charged with drawing together information and plans to bring to the peace conference. It attracted some of the foremost experts and intellectuals of the day, all rallying to help the former president of Princeton construct a new world. Today, when governmental reports and investigatory commissions are commonplace, The Inquiry hardly seems a unique undertaking. In the early twentieth century, it was an exciting new experiment in governmental activity. Financing studies of incredible detail, The Inquiry compiled information on such subjects as boundary disputes, ethnic distribution and relations, land tenure patterns, and rainfall and topography. Although created to provide

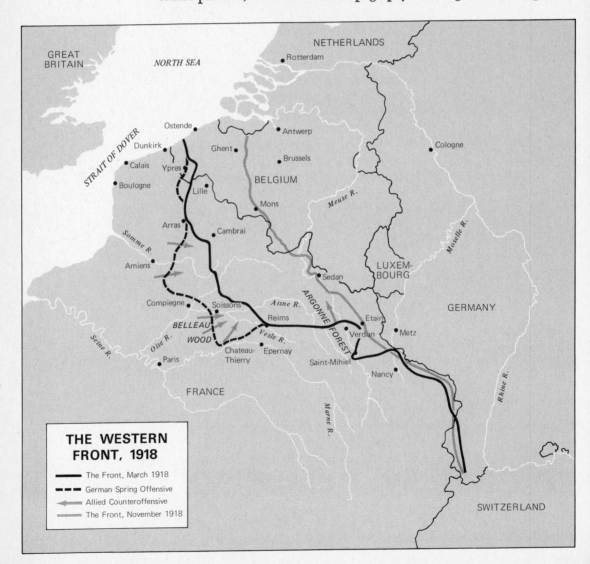

THE WESTERN FRONT, 1918

—— The Front, March 1918
- - - German Spring Offensive
←— Allied Counteroffensive
—— The Front, November 1918

advice for the peace conference, it went far beyond European affairs (many of its reports, for example, dealt with Latin America), and no subject or part of the world was beyond its scrutiny. The Inquiry symbolized the progressive era: its bureaucratic attention to detail; its energy and optimism; its conviction that the world's problems could be catalogued, understood, and solved; its belief that the war would usher in a new era of American leadership in a more moral and rational world.

The home front

The Inquiry was not the only new governmental bureaucracy. The War Industries Board nationalized raw materials and production; the War Trade Board controlled imports and exports; the Food Administration monitored farm production and urged Americans to observe "wheatless" and "meatless" days. The government regulated prices, supervised fuel supplies, and ran the railroads. The war brought America's first major experiment with a government-directed economy, and many of the experts who manned the wartime emergency boards would later use the experience to fight the economic depression under the next Democratic president, Franklin Roosevelt. One of the small group of radical intellectuals who opposed the war, Randolph Bourne, characterized the men who staffed the wartime bureaucracies:

> *The war has revealed a younger intelligentsia, trained up in the pragmatic dispensation, immensely ready for the executive ordering of events, pitifully unprepared for the intellectual interpretation of the idealistic focusing of ends. . . . They are a wholly new force in American life, the product of the swing in the colleges from a training that emphasized classical studies to one that emphasized political and economic values. . . . There seems to have been a peculiar congeniality between the war and these men. It is as if the war and they had been waiting for each other.*

100 percent Americanism

The most controversial of the new agencies was the Committee on Public Information, headed by journalist George Creel. In preceding decades, journalism, like everything else in American life, had undergone extensive centralization. National news services, the Associated Press and the United Press, provided the national and international stories for local papers throughout the country, making news dissemination more efficient, more accurate, and less costly, but also rendering it easier to control from above. Working through the AP and UP, which agreed to voluntary censorship, Creel found wartime news management a less difficult task than it had been during the Civil War or than it might have been in the previous decade of fiercely independent, sensationalist newspapers. And just as The Inquiry attracted many scholars and intellectuals, George Creel also hired hundreds of artists and writers willing to turn their talents to wartime propaganda. The Creel committee's "informational" pamphlets flooded the country and advertised the Allied cause throughout the world. In fact, many critics charged that it oversold the war, creating a spirit of intolerant "100 percent Americanism."

German-American citizens were the most obvious target for the patriotic frenzy. Comprising the country's largest single group of foreign born, German immigrants numbered more than 2.3 million. Many schools banned German language from the curriculum; sauerkraut became "liberty cabbage"; and people of German origin felt the suspicion, scorn, and hatred of their neighbors. The president himself capitulated to the "antihyphenate" hysteria, striking out against those aliens who "poured the poison of disloyalty" into America and proclaiming that "such creatures of passion, disloyalty, and anarchy must be crushed." Thousands of German aliens were arrested and placed in internment camps.

The pressure for total conformity also bore down upon pacifists and radicals, whose opposition to the war was quickly branded as unpatriotic. Local vigilante groups sprang up to safeguard American life against "aliens" and "radicals." The American Protective Association, a private group which persecuted dissenters of any sort, enjoyed semiofficial governmental sanction. And the government itself led the crusade. The attorney general organized raids on IWW halls and against the Industrial Workers of the World and arrested many members of this radical labor union; the postmaster general banned socialist publications from the mails; and the government prosecuted and imprisoned Eugene Debs, the aged socialist leader, for a relatively innocuous statement questioning the goals of the war.

This widespread violation of traditional civil liberties raised concern among some libertarians. They organized the American Civil Liberties Union, a private pressure group which has continued to champion the rights of the individual, including that of dissent, to the present day. There were others, too, who had reservations about the ethical consequences of the war. Franklin K. Lane, Wilson's secretary of the interior, refused to give the New York *World* an interview on the "moral benefits of the war." He wrote:

> This would be sheer camouflage. Of course, we will get some good out of it, and we will learn some efficiency—if that is a moral benefit —and a purer sense of nationalism. But the war will degrade us. That is the plain fact, make sheer brutes out of us, because we will have to descend to the methods that the Germans employ.

But such expressions were rare and seldom made publicly. To most Americans, the war provided an opportunity to Americanize America completely and bring the same values to the rest of the world. It was a chance for achieving purification, patriotism, and peace, even if these goals had to be reached through intolerance, oppression, and war. The repression of the postwar Red Scare and the disillusionment of the twenties were legacies of the crusade "to save the world for democracy."

AMERICA GOES MODERN

"The fiddles are tuning . . . all over America," said a visitor in 1912. Indeed they were, and making strange sounds. Charles Ives, the first important American composer, experimented with tonalities similar to those Stravinsky and Schönberg were using in Europe. Scott Joplin created ragtime, which quickly passed into popular music. W. C. Handy elaborated black American blues into a complex idiom. White Americans discovered Dixieland jazz.

A number of American painters tried to transfer progressive ideals onto canvas. Called the "ashcan school" because they insisted on depicting the grimier sides of modern life, their great contribution to a new style was the art show they organized in 1913 at the Sixty-ninth Regiment Armory in New York City. Here Americans—some quarter-million of them—met modern art. The show was large and conservative overall, but it contained a sampling of the works of Cézanne, van Gogh, Matisse, Rouault, and Picasso. These artists, whose classic works now hang in even the most staid museums, then seemed shocking. They were nonrepresentative, or sensual, or distorted—strange mirrors reflecting an even stranger world that most Americans hesitated to see as their own. Critics had a field day: Theodore Roosevelt preferred the Navaho rug hanging in his bathroom (a derogatory judgment in 1913) to the cubist art he saw in the armory. Yet he found the show a relief from the dullness of most works of art, a sign that the American public might soon see things the same way.

"The Village" Poets, artists, novelists, and critics gathered in little knots, experimenting with new forms of art and new ways of life. A vigorous bohemian culture flourished in New York's Greenwich Village. For six or seven years before the war "the Village" was what it has since been reputed to be: the home of social experimentation, serious writing, and men in flannel shirts living in what was then called "sin" with cigarette-smoking women with short hair. People discussed the new ideas of Sigmund Freud in apartments painted orange and black, they attended plays, parties, and impromptu events.

It was not an idle game: Floyd Dell, Max Eastman, and John Reed published *The Masses*, the best radical journal in American history. The Provincetown Theater produced Eugene O'Neill's remarkable dramas with their naturalistic dialogue and heavy symbolism. Isadora Duncan danced, and Edna St. Vincent Millay acted and wrote poetry. Many progressives hung around, enjoying the scene. The Village offered a good and richly productive life. And a very short one. By 1917 everything about the Village was in decline except the rents, the prices in the restaurants, and the tourists.

This bohemia was America's first try at being "modern." These practitioners of "liberation" sought changes more radical than the progressives. They questioned the possibility of an adequate moral code to guide the world. They expressed skepticism about man's progress. They wondered if they were in fact superior to the non–Anglo-Saxons living around them. Most Americans did not entertain such doubts. To the progressives in particular, these attractive new voices could only be nagging irritants, suggesting that perhaps all might not be well even after they had fought their good fight. Yet these vivid splotches of experimentation fitted closely into the rest of American life. Almost every magazine contained articles worrying about the rising divorce rate, the sinking birth rate, and the restless "new woman." Everyone seemed to know that profound changes were taking place in these sensitive areas of sex, family, and culture. Decades later, in 1947, the Kinsey Reports documented that the sharpest changes in sexual behavior—the sexual revolution that every generation considers its own contribution to American culture—occurred in the generation coming of age in these years. While others worried, the Village experimented. America quickly discovered its bohemia: fashionable urban Americans worked hard in the 1920s to copy its style.

THINGS TO THINK ABOUT: 1900–1918

Who were the progressives? George F. Mowry, *The California Progressives* (1951) and *The Era of Theodore Roosevelt* (1958) describe the typical "progressive profile." Richard Hofstadter, *The Age of Reform* (1955) suggests some sources of progressivism. Robert H. Wiebe, *Businessmen and Reform* (1962) describes a different group of progressives. Russell B. Nye, *Midwestern Progressive Politics* (1951) deals with an important tradition. William L. O'Neill, *Everybody Was Brave* (1969) is the most detailed account of women in the movement. On the Muckrakers, see David M. Chalmers, *The Social and Political Ideas of the Muckrakers* (1964). Best of all, read the progressives' own writings. Lincoln Steffens, *The Autobiography of Lincoln Steffens* (1931) and Jane Addams, *Twenty Years at Hull House* (1910) are both splendid.

How did the progressives deal with the problems of the cities? Were they democratic or elitist? Samuel P. Hays, "The Politics of Reform in Municipal Government in the Progressive Era," *Pacific Northwest Quarterly* 55 (1964): 157–69 and J. Joseph Huthmacher, "Urban Liberalism and the Age of Reform," *Mississippi Valley Historical Review* 49 (1962): 231–41 take diverging viewpoints. Both articles have been widely anthologized. On particular cities see Melvin G. Holli, *Reform in Detroit* (1969) and William D. Miller, *Memphis During the Progressive Era* (1957).

Did the progressives succeed in revitalizing state government? There are studies of many states. Among the best are Richard M. Abrams, *Conservatism in a Progressive Era: Massachusetts* (1964), Mowry on California, cited above; Sheldon Hackney, *From Populism to Progressivism in*

Alabama (1969). Robert LaFollette, *LaFollette's Autobiography* (1913) catches the flavor of Wisconsin's advanced progressivism.

Was national government conservative or progressive in the era? Roosevelt, always fascinating, has attracted many biographers. Henry Pringle, *Theodore Roosevelt* (1931), John M. Blum, *The Republican Roosevelt* (1954), and William H. Harbaugh *Power and Responsibility* (1961) are all excellent. William Manner, *TR and Will* (1969) studies his relationship with William Howard Taft. Henry Pringle, *The Life and Times of William Howard Taft* (1935) is a fine large-as-life portrait. Richard Lowitt, *George W. Norris: The Making of a Progressive* (1963) presents a leading national progressive. Gabriel Kolko, *The Triumph of Conservativism . . . , 1900–1916* (1963) offers harsh judgments on national progressivism.

Woodrow Wilson in war and peace: was the New Freedom a policy both for the nation and the world? Arthur S. Link, *Woodrow Wilson and the Progressive Era* (1954) is a fine introduction; Arthur S. Link, *Woodrow Wilson* (5 vols. to date, 1947–   ) is magisterial; Alexander L. and Juliette L. George, *Woodrow Wilson and Colonel House: A Personality Study* (1956) is psycholanalytical and fascinating; John M. Blum, *Woodrow Wilson and the Politics of Morality* (1956) is elegant and thoughtful. On Mexico see Robert E. Quirk, *An Affair of Honor* (1962). The best introduction to Wilson's diplomacy is Arthur S. Link's *Wilson the Diplomatist* (1957). The best source for material about the home front is Frederick L. Paxson, *American Democracy and the World War* (3 vols., 1936–48).

1918-1932

eleven | THE BOUYANT TWENTIES

AL CAPONE

Among the great celebrities of the 1920s was the gangster Al Capone. He received fan mail from all over the world, including requests to "rub out" irritating neighbors. The lucky visitor to Chicago might catch a glimpse of the "big fellow" lolling in his seven-ton, silk-upholstered limousine complete with bodyguard in the front seat nursing a machine gun on his lap. The extravagant Capone customarily wore a fifty-thousand-dollar diamond ring and carried fifty thousand in cash in his wallet. Meticulous and fond of personal luxury, Al slept between monogrammed silk sheets; his solid silver toilet seat also bore his initials.

Born in 1899 in Brooklyn, Capone learned about life from the city streets. No boy would linger an instant longer than necessary in the fetid tenements, and the schools and churches gave scant attention to poor Italian immigrant children. The street gangs offered escape, adventure, and violence. In his teens Capone joined the notorious Five Pointers of Manhattan's lower East Side. The police arrested him three times in New York, once for disorderly conduct, twice on suspicion of homicide. Capone became a protégé there of the gangster Johnny Torrio, who summoned him to Chicago after the World War.

Under the benevolent eye of Chicago's antiprohibition Mayor "Big Bill" Thompson ("I'm wetter than the middle of the Atlantic Ocean"), Capone engineered perhaps fifty of the city's five hundred gangland slayings in the course of the twenties. Best known for bootlegging liquor, he also dabbled in the protection and prostitution rackets. The brutal slaying of seven North Side gang members on Saint Valentine's Day, 1929, Capone dismissed with characteristic brio as "bad public relations." "A real goddam crazy place," remarked his Five Pointers pal Lucky Luciano after a visit to Chicago: "Nobody's safe in the streets."

Capone always lived with danger. He acquired a country estate in Wisconsin and added machine gun emplacements to a lookout tower near the main house. Later he built a shore-front home near Miami, Florida, and offered to join the local Rotary Club—but time was running out. In 1929 President Herbert Hoover, between *thwunks* of early-morning exercise with a medicine ball, ordered Secretary of the Treasury Andrew Mellon to "get" Capone. The ensuing battle sounded more exciting than it was. A melodramatic government agent named Eliot Ness grabbed the headlines, and Capone, to the dismay of his associates, planned wholesale murder of the Chicago branch of the Internal Revenue Department. Meanwhile, quiet work by Internal Revenue agents bore results. Capone drew an eleven-year prison sentence for tax evasion and eventually went to Alcatraz. Afterwards he survived with his family in rural Pennsylvania until 1947, when syphilis conquered his brain. The writer Rafael Sabatini conceded Capone to have been "a center of that atmosphere of treachery, intrigue, shots in the dark, and raw power in which historical romance best grows," but disqualified him as a hero because "he really seems to have no ideals."

Capone once described his career as "heroic." Theodore Roosevelt's heroic Americans were hunters, cowboys, frontiersmen, soldiers, naval heroes; but in the crowded slums gangsters were heroes. Capone rivaled New York's Governor Al Smith as the first successful public figure of recent immigrant stock. Purveying liquor and women was a career open to talent: Capone was only twenty-nine at the height of his power.

Crime offered the immigrant American denied other opportunities a risky but rewarding path of advancement. Organized crime also fed on the cleavage between the big city and the small town. In making unlawful certain elements of urban night life such as drinking, gambling, and prostitution, rural legislatures opened the way for a new kind of American entrepreneur. Then, as always, Americans loved a man who got ahead. Not only did newspaper headlines and crime stories bespeak America's fascination with these new celebrities: one of the finest novels of the age, F. Scott Fitzgerald's *The Great Gatsby*, reached into this lurid world of bootlegging and racketeering to find a hero about whom some spoke in whispers "who had found little that it was necessary to whisper about in this world."

Jack Levine, *Gangster Funeral.* Collection of Whitney Museum of American Art, New York

1918-1932

1918	Republicans gain control of Congress, November 5
	Armistice Day, November 11
1919–early 1920	Red Scare
1920	Palmer Raids, January 2
	Warren Harding (Republican) elected president; defeats James Cox
	Sinclair Lewis, *Main Street*
1921–22	Washington Naval Conference (November 12–February 6)
1923	President Harding dies, August 2; Calvin Coolidge becomes president
1924	Immigration Restriction Acts
	Calvin Coolidge (Republican) elected president; defeats John W. Davis
1925	F. Scott Fitzgerald, *The Great Gatsby*
1927	Charles Lindbergh flies solo across the Atlantic
1928	Herbert Hoover (Republican) elected president; defeats Alfred E. Smith
1929	Black Thursday, October 24 (stock market crash)
	Ernest Hemingway, *A Farewell to Arms*
1930	London Naval Conference, January 21–April 22
1931	Hoover Debt Moratorium, June 20
1932	Stimson Doctrine, January 7
	Franklin Delano Roosevelt (Democrat) elected president; defeats Herbert Hoover

THE RED SCARE

America's brief participation in World War I had lasting effects. In the disturbing times just afterward—the era known as the "Red Scare"— shocking events moved hard upon one another, and groups of people reacted almost primitively in fear or hatred or simple ignorance. The war passion, so well orchestrated by the Committee on Public Information, endured longer than the brief fighting, releasing emotions which sought out new enemies on which to spend themselves.

In a very rapid demobilization the government released half a million soldiers at once and over the course of the year 4 million more. The economy fluttered about and prices rose. In the labor market uncertainty came to seem almost normal: some 9 million men moved from wartime jobs to work in a peacetime economy, and strikes hit industries that were no longer under federal constraints. Across the Atlantic a new spectre rose to replace the defeated Hun—Russian communism (then called bolshevism). A few thousand American soldiers actually engaged Russian troops in Siberia early in 1919.

Viewed as a band of nihilistic fanatics, American Bolsheviks were accused of influencing the first great domestic drama of 1919, the general strike in Seattle, Washington. The very idea of a "general" strike, when all workers would rally in defense of a few, had almost no precedent in the United States. A "Committee of Fifteen" set up to supervise the operation, even when it conscientiously attended to problems of public safety and health, sounded vaguely foreign and sinister. The strike crippled Seattle: its "pulse . . . had ceased to beat," wrote one journalist after seeing the deserted downtown streets. Yet the shipyard owners, the target of the strike, suffered no special deprivation. Mayor Ole Hanson portrayed the strike leaders as Bolsheviks, and gradually public opinion came to support his employment of private police to insure public order. Lacking a well-defined goal and the means to accomplish it, the strike dissolved after just two weeks.

During that episode Mayor Hanson's actions had earned for him the reputation of a vigorous anti-Communist. In late April, while he was away on a Victory Bond tour, his office received a package wrapped in brown paper. Some liquid leaking from the box burned a table. The liquid proved to be acid, the package a bomb. In Georgia Senator Thomas Hardwick's maid picked up a similar parcel which exploded in her hands and face. These events, trumpeted in newspaper headlines, caught the eye of a clerk from the New York City central post office as he rode the West Side subway home. After reading the description of the packages, he dashed from the train at the next station and caught the downtown express. Back at the post office he found more than a dozen similar packages he had set aside for insufficient postage three days earlier. All contained homemade bombs. Additional explosives were discovered in transit. The press compiled a "bomb honor list" of famous citizens, including Supreme Court justices and John D. Rockefeller, Jr. In June bombs went off in eight major cities, and an Italian anarchist blew himself to bits with his own device when he stumbled on the stone steps of Attorney General A. Mitchell Palmer's house in Washington, D.C.

These bomb-throwing cranks gave the American Left a reputation for vitality far out of proportion to its actual strength. The number of Communist party members in America during 1919 was relatively small—something like fifty thousand. And the larger Socialist party's idea of revolution was one of gradual, democratic ascendance through the electoral system. Its eloquent leader, Eugene V. Debs, languished in the Atlanta federal penitentiary for actively opposing the war. Yet this shrinking Left became the principal object of popular fears.

Further events contributed to social tensions during 1919. On a hot August day, a black teenager in Chicago accidentally floated over an invisible line and into a bathing area reserved for whites. Greeted by a barrage of stones, in confusion he abandoned a floating railroad tie, swam away a few strokes, sank, and drowned. The episode, seen by hundreds of bathers, sparked full-scale rioting in Chicago that ended with thirty-eight dead—twenty-three blacks and fifteen whites. Another race riot had erupted in July in Washington, D.C.; later disturbances came in Knoxville and Omaha. All were related to the vast migrations of blacks to cities and to the North for jobs during World War I, to new militancy as a result of military service, and to the resistance of all-white neighborhoods to black encroachments.

In early September the Boston police, infuriated by an autocratic chief, walked off their jobs, leaving the city defenseless. As in Seattle, the Bolsheviks were blamed. President Wilson called it a "crime against civilization." The chief simply hired a largely new force to maintain public order. A few weeks later labor strikes paralyzed the steel and coal industries. Many steel workers still put in a twelve-hour day and a six-day week, while in the coal mines conditions were unsafe and unhealthy. These strikes, like thirty-six hundred others that broke out in 1919, aimed primarily at preserving collective bargaining or the simple economic gains of the war. The corporations, aggressively resisting unionism, promoted the "American plan" or nonunion open shop. Like most of the other walkouts, those in steel and coal ultimately failed; the steel companies refused even to discuss terms with the striking workers and resisted unionization in their industry until the 1930s. Throughout the twenties labor unions never regained the influence and membership they had achieved under a friendly wartime administration. An Industrial Conference held in Washington in November 1919 dramatized the stubbornness of the big corporations; they refused assent to the principle of unrestricted collective bargaining. Many insisted that laborers choose their spokesmen from within the factory, seeking to avoid all but company-oriented unions.

The Palmer raids Many of the charges linking labor strikes with bolshevism Attorney General A. Mitchell Palmer knew to be wild exaggerations. But Palmer soon joined the popular clamor. In September the Justice Department deported to Finland and Russia some two thousand undesirable aliens, mostly Russian Jews, on the S.S. *Buford*. One newspaper reported the hysterical entreaties of wives and children left behind at the departure as "Reds Try to Free Commie Pals." The evangelist Billy Sunday wanted more Bolsheviks sent to sea in "ships of stone with masts of lead." Another 249 aliens embarked to Finland in November.

On the night of January 2, 1920, acting almost simultaneously in thirty-two major cities, agents from the Justice Department and local police rounded up thousands of alleged Communists. Often held in violation of constitutional rights, sometimes denied food, water, heat, or sanitary facilities, a few of the prisoners succumbed to serious disease

Yesterday

or death. A Detroit paper photographed a man kept in filthy surroundings for some days, without water to wash or shave, and labeled the picture "Unkempt Bolshevist."

The Palmer raids were the high point of the Red Scare. A few days later the New York State Assembly refused to seat five duly elected Socialist members, but former Supreme Court Chief Justice Charles Evans Hughes and other prominent Americans protested vigorously. In Washington acting Secretary of Labor Louis F. Post refused to deport many of the aliens Palmer had rounded up. As depression approached, people turned from dramatic public events to the pressing need of making a living. Suppression, too, had its effects in bringing agitation to an end. Those wanting social change were dispirited; reformers retreated into private worlds of business, writing, and the arts.

THE LEAGUE OF NATIONS

The postwar period was a time of innocence assaulted by experience. Having finished a war it thought it could handle on the simplest and purest moral terms, the nation discovered that these terms meant little to Europe, a continent it thought oddly ungrateful to the United States and unresponsive to an eminently reasonable and virtuous American guidance.

President Wilson himself had cast the national interest into a perfectly honest, if self-deceptive, rhetoric of liberal internationalism. He envisioned a world peace-keeping organization hospitable to capitalism and free trade, with the United States occupying the key leadership position. This League of Nations would control both old-fashioned imperialism and new threats of social revolution.

Even though cheering throngs greeted him in London, Paris, and Rome, Wilson soon discovered that promising a lasting peace was easier than creating one. In Paris he met with representatives of Great Britain, France, and Italy to draft the Treaty of Versailles and construct "a just and lasting peace." Wilson was most effective in scaling down Allied territorial demands and in setting boundaries that conformed in the main to lines of nationality. He himself desired punishment for Germany, but opposed the exorbitant reparations the Allies successfully demanded. On this and other matters, he believed that an American presence in a League of Nations, which he fused with the Versailles treaty, would remove persisting inequities.

America stays out Yet Wilson did little to prepare the Senate or the American people for acceptance of the League; initial support disintegrated in a year of controversy. On his mission to Paris he failed to take along Senate Republicans—now the majority party following the 1918 congressional elections

—and showed open contempt for the new chairman of the Senate Foreign Relations Committee, Henry Cabot Lodge of Massachusetts. Anti-League senators he called "bungalow-minds," their heads "knots tied to keep their bodies from unraveling." Besides Wilson's slights, the Republicans also had selfish reasons to suspect the League. If the Wilson cause triumphed here as it had in war, they would have less hope for success in the next elections. Senator Lodge, who had endorsed limited American participation in some kind of international group as early as 1915, proposed a series of reservations that would have exempted the Monroe Doctrine and other traditional American policies from League jurisdiction. The central point of controversy between Lodge and Wilson was Article X of the League Convenant, which seemed to compel America into a collective-security arrangement. The president's partisan attitude, his insistence on making it a "Wilson" League, and his refusal to accept any reservation coming from Lodge forced the Republicans into various forms of opposition, and ultimately doomed the chances for Senate ratification of the Versailles treaty.

Republicans were not the only group estranged from the League. Young men and women active in the Progressive Era had wanted the League to spread the moralism of Wilson's Fourteen Points throughout the world. But the compromises forced on Wilson at Paris discouraged these idealists and led them away from political involvement. Some concluded that the Fourteen Points were merely propaganda to counter Russian Bolshevik allegations about secret Allied agreements concerning the postwar division of spoils. Even in setting eastern European boundaries along ethnic and national lines, Wilson was suspected of creating buffers against Russia.

Wilson lost the support of several traditionally Democratic immigrant groups who violently rejected the Versailles treaty. Irish Americans joined their homeland in fearing the large number of votes the English controlled in the League Assembly, which they supposed would slow the movement for Irish independence. Italian Americans resented giving Fiume to the new state of Yugoslavia. Versailles ignored the Jewish campaign for a new national homeland. German Americans saw the reparations as punitive. All these ethnic groups would vote Republican in 1920.

Although weakened by influenza, Wilson attempted to revive flagging support for the League by a direct appeal to the people. He went west on a speaking tour. Admitting that the treaty was flawed but claiming that the League would correct inequities, Wilson, after some thirty speeches, felt the tide running in his direction. But on September 25, 1919, he suffered a breakdown in Colorado and, a few days after returning by darkened train to the White House, a paralyzing stroke. Had he died then, the Treaty of Versailles with the League built into it would have sailed through the Senate. As it was, people gossiped about the president; it was whispered that the barred windows of the White House held a demented man within. (They had been put there to prevent Teddy Roosevelt's boys from breaking windows with wayward baseballs.) Although Wilson had earlier drafted acceptable amendments to the League Covenant, now he stood fixed against compromise. When in November the Senate voted on the treaty with the Lodge reservations, administration Democrats joined the League's opponents to defeat it. Again, in March 1920, southern Democrats combined with outright adversaries rather than accept the taint of Lodge's hand.

Was our failure to join the League a tragedy? No one can say with certainty. League membership might have quickened our will to act against fascist aggression in the 1930s. On the other hand, America played a vigorous international role in the 1920s and could act swiftly and more freely outside the League in the thirties. It cannot automatically be assumed that staying independent was either a disaster or a boon to world peace. The uncertainty of the debate over collective security in 1919 remains an uncertainty now.

ECONOMIC INTERNATIONALISM

The Senate's refusal to ratify the League of Nations represented not so much a victory for isolationism as the work of a successful coalition ranging from the anti-imperialist Senator William E. Borah to the expansionist Henry Cabot Lodge. Even those Republicans who opposed the League often shared the central vision of Wilsonian internationalism: a free-trading world with equality of competition and respect for property rights. Wilson's Republican successors agreed on the importance of keeping the world safe for America's peaceful economic expansion, and they pursued a vigorous involvement in world economic affairs.

World War I ushered in a decade of rapid economic growth. During the war young, highly trained professionals found a niche for their talents within the bureaucracy of government. There they worked in league with businessmen to heighten production and, after the war, to promote prosperity and economic expansion abroad. Postwar fears of widespread economic disruption and unemployment made business expansion an imperative means of warding off social revolution. Herbert Hoover, infatuated by the guiding power of government which the war revealed, constructed during the twenties an active Department of Commerce, whose job was "to inspire and assist in cooperative action" the expansion of the American economy.

During the 1920s Americans generally believed, somewhat mistakenly, that their own consumptive capacity could not absorb the high production that their factories now maintained. Businessmen joined with government in directing concerted drives to expand exports and to encourage investment of capital in foreign lands. Investment served two purposes: foreigners would inevitably use a portion of the borrowed capital to purchase American exports; and investments, by helping the debtor country build up its economy, served as a bulwark against social revolution and the spread of bolshevism. Economic expansion, not political instruments such as the League of Nations, came to be seen as the best road to world stability.

Economic expansion abroad

Before World War I the United States had almost no capital invested abroad and presented only a distant competitive threat to the major exporting countries of the world. After the war, European nations which had contracted vast debts in the United States undertook agonizing programs of economic reconstruction. The United States, physically untouched by combat and greatly enriched by wartime profits, became an important industrial exporter and a powerful creditor for the first time in its history.

Industrial products, rather than agricultural goods, now constituted the bulk of American sales abroad. Just as the age of the automobile characterized life at home, so the expansion of America's foreign trade was based to a large degree upon the export of automobiles, automotive accessories, and petroleum for the relatively new internal-combustion engine. By 1928 these products made up over 20 percent of American exports, although before the war they had constituted a bare 7 percent.

In the realm of finance, New York began to replace London as the hub of the world's credit market. For the first time in their history, Americans loaned billions of dollars abroad, particularly in Germany, to assist foreign governments and industry. In Latin America, a new form of investment was perfected—the branch business. Rather than loaning capital to Latin Americans to build their own factories, mines, or agricultural enterprises, Americans simply established branches of industries whose home offices lay within the United States. This mode of business organization—the multinational corporation—permitted American businessmen to take advantage of cheap foreign labor supplies and to avoid tariff barriers in the host country. The long-term consequence of the establishment of branch businesses in Latin America, a trend which would extend worldwide after World War II, was the development of a particularly virulent strain of "Yankeephobia." Companies such as Standard Oil, RCA, United States Steel, Anaconda Copper, Swift and Company, and United Fruit became synonymous with "Yankee imperialism" to many Latin Americans during the twenties.

America's new technology brought in its wake a new cultural influence abroad. Motion pictures were surely among the most popular

American export products, and the entire globe joined Americans in idolizing the great screen stars of the twenties. The way in which movies spread, popularized, and distorted the image of America in foreign lands has had a lasting, if difficult-to-define, impact upon the United States' relations with other peoples.

Disarmament   In 1921 Secretary of State Charles Evans Hughes invited Britain, France, Italy, the Netherlands, Belgium, Portugal, China, and Japan to a conference on naval disarmament and Far Eastern questions. It was the first major international conference ever held in Washington (another sign of America's new prominence). Before a startled audience at the opening session, the imposing and dignified secretary of state wasted few words on the formalities of welcome and, quickly abandoning platitudes, offered specific proposals for the suspension of naval construction and the scrapping of existing ships. Hughes in thirty-five minutes sank "more ships than all the admirals of the world have sunk in a cycle of centuries." The time did seem propitious for naval disarmament. In each country there were pressures for economy in government and fears of an arms race similar to the one which preceded World War I. Still, the naval agreement reached in Washington was remarkable in its scope. The nations agreed to scrap over 2 million tons of vessels and to limit their tonnage to precise ratios: 5 for the United States, 5 for Great Britain, 3 for Japan, and 1.67 each for France and Italy.

The initial foreign policy interest of Warren G. Harding's new Republican administration was in naval matters, but the Washington Conference also tried to deal with the uncertain balance of power in the Far East. In a four-power treaty the United States, Britain, France, and Japan agreed collectively to guarantee the status quo in Asia. A nine-power treaty provided a pledge to maintain the Open Door in China and outlawed spheres of influence. These agreements, never supported by Japanese militarists, would be violated by them within less than a decade.

The Washington treaties (there were nine in all) represented a major contribution to disarmament, and they spurred a peace movement which reached fruition in the Kellogg-Briand Pact of 1928. France originally proposed a bi-national renunciation of war to the United States, and Secretary of State Frank B. Kellogg expanded upon the idea. He suggested that all nations of the world sign a declaration outlawing war as an instrument of national policy. With its lack of enforcement procedures, the unrealistic pact reflected the well-intentioned hopes of the period. Together with the League of Nations and the Washington treaties, it created an international structure which most Americans hoped would keep the peace. But these arrangements proved inadequate in the 1930s to deal with international disruptions growing out of worldwide economic depression and resurgent nationalism.

REPUBLICAN POLICY

After the war President Wilson seemed to fade from public view. Between December 1918 and July 1919 he stayed abroad at the Paris Peace Conference, returning home once for a brief ten-day trip in March. After his cerebral hemorrhage in the fall, he remained secluded in the White House. He could no longer provide the domestic leadership the nation and his party sorely needed.

Wilson retained, however, a jealous interest in the selection of his successor, asking that the coming election be a "great and solemn referendum" on the League. Then he cavalierly dismissed the other likely Democratic candidates as they acquired prominence and finally decided he would have to run again. But friends in the party would not consider a third term, and although he lived on until 1924—outlasting his replacement Warren Harding—his influence was at an end.

The strongest Democratic presidential candidate was Wilson's own son-in-law William Gibbs McAdoo, secretary of the treasury until he resigned late in 1918. Ambitious to a fault, McAdoo stood high in public opinion polls; but Wilson would not support him and the canny McAdoo divined that 1920 would be an inauspicious year for the Democratic party. Another Wilsonian, Attorney General Palmer, hoped to use the Red Scare as a means to the presidency. But as the hysteria subsided, so did Palmer's presidential prospects. The candidate actually chosen at the Democratic convention was Governor James Cox of Ohio. Although the favorite of anti-Wilsonian machines bosses in New York, Chicago, and Indiana, the moderately progressive Cox adopted an administration position in his lackluster campaign. The vice-presidential candidate Franklin D. Roosevelt, a relatively obscure New Yorker but for his surname, proved a more attractive campaigner than Cox.

The Republican nomination was much sought after. By 1920 the Democrats were receiving blame for everything from the war settlement to the high cost of living, from worsening unemployment to declining farm prices. General Leonard Wood was a popular candidate who had been favored by the late Teddy Roosevelt, and Governor Frank Lowden of Illinois had important agrarian support. But the two men, especially Wood, indulged in an orgy of campaign spending that received bad publicity and deadlocked the convention voting. The handsome Ohio Senator Warren G. Harding stood waiting in the wings. With the help of prominent senators and party bosses, Harding won the nomination. Governor Calvin Coolidge of Massachusetts was a natural choice for vice-president; he had become famous during the Boston police strike for his injunction, "There is no right to strike against the public safety by anybody, anywhere, anytime."

Cox was no match for Harding in 1920. The expansive newspaper publisher from Marion—dubbed the "Ohio Marionette" by opponents—

President Harding—a much loved man—and Mrs. Harding in Ohio. *Photoworld*

obfuscated the issues, talking around them. He even tried to take both sides on the question of United States membership in the League of Nations, but gradually adopted a clearly negative position. While Cox and Roosevelt hustled around the country pumping for the League, Harding stayed near the front porch of his Marion home. The strategy worked for Harding, as it had for William McKinley, and the votes came pouring in on election day; Harding won by nearly a two-to-one margin.

Harding   Presidents Harding and Coolidge were ill equipped to understand the economic and industrial complexities of the 1920s. The task was too much for the affable Harding, but he worked hard and showed himself capable of some remarkably good judgments. A few members of Harding's cabinet were top-flight: Charles Evans Hughes, formerly governor of New York and Supreme Court justice, became secretary of state; Herbert Hoover took the post of Commerce, Henry C. Wallace that of Agriculture. Andrew Mellon, head of the Treasury Department, was an able spokesman for business.

488

But the presidency never went well for Harding. During his first two years in office the economy was in severe depression following its deflation by the Federal Reserve Board. Because of the hard times, voters almost gave the Democrats control of Congress in the off-year elections of 1922. Worse still for Harding, it gradually became apparent that a number of his appointees were crooks. Trouble came first in the Veterans' Bureau under Charles R. Forbes, who later spent a term in prison for embezzling a quarter-million dollars of public funds. The corruption under Harding reached up to the cabinet. Secretary of the Interior Albert Fall had managed to make improvements on his New Mexico ranch at a cost of a hundred and seventy thousand dollars even though his annual salary was only twelve thousand dollars. Fall had persuaded the naive Navy Secretary Edwin Denby to transfer out of the public domain oil reserves at Elk Hills, California, and Teapot Dome, Wyoming. For this service the grateful oil magnates who leased the properties, Edward L. Dohney and Harry F. Sinclair, had "loaned" Fall considerable sums. The trail of corruption even skirted the offices of the president's confidante Attorney General Harry Daugherty, when Jesse Smith, a notorious "fixer" with an office in the Justice Department, committed suicide in Daugherty's apartment and left a joint bank account of fifty thousand dollars. The Harding scandals may have been exaggerated in extent, but certainly they were dramatic.

President Harding learned something of the scandals before he started out on a trip to Alaska in the summer of 1923. During the long train ride west he played bridge incessantly and seemed deeply troubled in mind and body. After a speech in Seattle, he became sick while enroute to San Francisco. There, confined to his hotel bed, he died on August 2 when a blod clot reached his brain.

Coolidge The new president, Calvin Coolidge, was a flinty little man of straitlaced habits and overpowering rectitude; he would not be betrayed by his intimate friends, for he had none. Famous as a public man of few words and frigid disposition—when told that Coolidge died, someone asked, "How can they tell?"—his exterior was somewhat misleading. In reality, he was almost affable and possessed a calculating political sense bred by years of experience in Massachusetts politics. Coolidge gradually eased Daugherty out of the cabinet and appointed a bipartisan committee to investigate the "Harding scandals."

The deceased president served as scapegoat for the scandals, and the Democrats, with the 1924 election approaching, ran into problems of their own. It was found that William Gibbs McAdoo, the candidate of western and southern Democrats, had received considerable sums in legal fees from Doheny and was promised far more. McAdoo's opponent at the Democratic convention in New York City in June 1924 was the state's reform governor, Alfred E. Smith, a spokesman for the new urban constituency of ethnic Democrats. The candidates, representing rural and urban America, battled to a hundred-ballot stalemate, appalling the country and wrecking their party's hopes. The compromise nominee, lawyer John W. Davis, lost badly to Coolidge. A third-party candidate, Senator Robert La Follette of Wisconsin, earned 5 million votes for his reformist and foreign-policy views.

By and large, the Harding and Coolidge programs were of a piece. Both men opposed reforms that might dampen the business climate. The progressive impulse had been vibrantly alive as late as 1916 with the passage of the Adamson Act that prescribed an eight-hour day for railroad workers. But late in 1919 the journalist Walter Lippmann asked: "Can anyone name a single reform initiated or carried through since the Armistice?" Basically, progressivism had depended on presidential leadership, and although a reform impulse survived in Congress as well as in some local and state governments, it served mainly to restrain business-oriented national administrations rather than to initiate programs of its own.

Congressional opposition, for example, thwarted the plans of Treasury Secretary Andrew Mellon for years. A Pittsburgh industrialist and one of the world's richest men, Mellon sought to lower federal taxes

Andrew Mellon was known to contemporaries as the greatest Treasury Secretary since Alexander Hamilton. *Culver Pictures*

on the wealthy. This would free capital, he reasoned, for industrial investment here and abroad. But only after seven years in the cabinet did he accomplish the chief goals he had set forth in 1921. Opposition from progressive midwestern Republicans stymied Mellon until the Democrats, sensing the popularity of his efforts, joined up in 1927 and 1928.

Congress also resisted the White House in other areas. It had cooperated in the early twenties on some important legislation to help the farmers: the Capper-Volstead Law of 1922 exempted farmers' cooperatives from prosecution under the antitrust laws; the Fordney-McCumber Tariff passed in the same year protected agricultural produce; and the Agricultural Marketing Act of 1923 offered intermediate term credits. Actually, many if not most farmers fared reasonably well during the twenties. But the major farm issue of the decade sharply divided the two branches of government. Proponents of the McNary-Haugen Bill wanted the Agriculture Department to assure a minimum price for produce. To control foreign marketing, a government-owned corporation would purchase all surplus agricultural crops at a good price and then sell them abroad. As a result of artificially created scarcity, domestic prices would rise; farmers would pay the government an equalization fee to offset its expenses. Twice the bill passed Congress, twice President Coolidge vetoed it.

A similar stalemate developed over construction of an electric-power and nitrate plant at Muscle Shoals on the Tennessee River in northern Alabama. During World War I the federal government had produced nitrates there, and the question was how to dispose of uncompleted government facilities on the river. Henry Ford offered to lease the plants and construct "a great new Detroit" in the Tennessee Valley—a mixed blessing, some said. He withdrew his offer, however, in the face of congressional opponents who saw his demand for a ninety-nine-year lease as a "giveaway" of public lands and water power. Then Senator George Norris of Nebraska helped expose a gambit by General Electric, under the guise of private power companies, to take over the region. Finally, Congress passed Norris's own bill for government operation, which Coolidge angrily vetoed in 1928.

Harding and Coolidge found more success in their attempts to aid business through appointments to the federal regulatory agencies. By the end of the decade, the Federal Reserve Board, the Federal Trade Commission, and the Interstate Commerce Commission had majorities who generally subverted the regulatory functions for which the agencies had presumably been created. They conceived of their powers as created to aid business and promote prosperity. The Supreme Court, changed considerably after four new appointments by Harding alone, usually adopted a "hands-off" attitude toward business. One reason unions fared so miserably in the twenties was unsympathetic treatment by the courts. In *Bailey* v. *Drexel Furniture* (1922) the Supreme Court even rejected a law regulating child labor. *Adkins* v. *Children's Hospital* (1923) declared invalid a District of Columbia minimum-wage law for women on grounds that it interfered with liberty of contract.

THE ECONOMY

The economy of the 1920s had its soft spots—notably the textile industry in New England, coal mining in Pennsylvania and West Virginia, and wheat farming in the western Middle West—but in general it was vibrant and strong. Great productivity brought the price of automobiles, radios, household appliances, and even houses within reach of most American families. The number of automobiles in the course of the decade tripled, from 9 to 27 million, and led to a boom in highway building and real estate. Electricity and interior plumbing became customary items rather than luxuries in all except rural homes. Productivity and economic growth were hallmarks of the decade.

The coming of plenty owed a great deal to the war itself. The invention of new machines and concepts of engineering management go back to the last century, but their use became essential in 1917–18. Mass production proved itself in building ships and airplane motors. The plants themselves, as well as standardized production along the assembly line, lasted into peacetime. Electricity also speeded the revolution in production: in 1914 some 30 percent of manufacturing was electrified, in 1929 70 percent of all factories benefited from the ease and versatility of the new power source. Everything became mechanized: loading devices, highway pavers, an important new warp-tying machine in textiles. Higher wages were a cause as well as a result of technical advance, making the introduction of still more labor-saving machinery desirable. And the government helped. High tariffs aided the young chemical industry; subsidies sustained the airlines. The Department of Commerce worked to extend American markets abroad and at home it provided businessmen with all varieties of useful statistical data. Trade associations, encouraged by the Republican administrations, helped to control the domestic market and maintain prices through the use of shared cost-accounting procedures; efforts to simplify sizes and designs helped eliminate waste in industry.

The consumer The film and radio played a principal part in the formation of the postwar mass-consumer society. They wore down old ideals of thrift and self-denial and suggested hedonistic roles to replace them. The life style of the movies was open to all through consumer credit—"a dollar down and a dollar forever." While in 1920 only 5 percent of the twenty largest corporations directly served the consumer public, by 1929 the figure had risen to 45 percent, headed by the automobile industry. All this meant that the average American was the best-fed and best-clothed man in history.

Fields remarked that his father, one of the "Great Immorals," held the Chair of Applied Electricity at state prison. *Culver Pictures*

Ordinarily, he owned both an automobile and a radio, both of which, along with the movies, increased his mobility and destroyed the isolation of village and farm. Sports heroes and movie stars became national heroes. Some women entered business and the professions. Modern America was being born.

The economy of the twenties also posed the question of the relationship of industrialism to the environment. Economic growth was an ambiguous thing. With it came a level of consumption that tore the tops off the nation's forests and despoiled many natural resources. *I'll Take My Stand* (1930) was a protest by southern writers against mass-consumption values and material progress. They preferred the land, perhaps a farm or a village community, to the intangible world of credit. The brutal tempo of the assembly line destroyed the amenities of daily life, and the illusion of power over nature forced an abandonment of the religious sense—a feeling for a fairly mysterious nature and its awesome strength. For the most part, however, Americans did not foresee what would happen to the air and water and forests of the land, nor did they feel the subtle changes wrought by servitude to the machine.

Welfare capitalism One area of socially conscious practices came about among the large corporations. The first sustained corporate attempt to treat human problems resulting from industrialization, the movement known as welfare capitalism had origins in the nineteenth-century paternalistic strain of men like Andrew Carnegie and George Pullman (who built a model

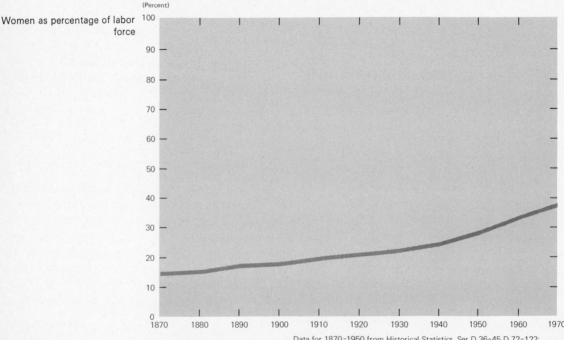

Women as percentage of labor force

Data for 1870–1950 from Historical Statistics, Ser. D 36–45, D 72–122;
Data for 1960 and 1970 from Statistical Abstract of the United States 1971,
No. 347. Alaska and Hawaii are included in 1960 and 1970 Figures.

town—Pullman, Illinois—for his railroad works' employees). It also drew strength from the progressive era (by which time most of the business leaders of the twenties had come to maturity) and from the war with its spirit of sacrifice for the general good. Especially after the deadly combat with labor in 1919 and the depression of 1920–22, some businessmen saw the importance of avoiding strikes in order to maintain high levels of purchasing power and demand for consumer goods. The prestige of businessmen has never been higher than it was in the twenties. Once considered inferior in status to the medical and legal professions, they now took on an aura of professionalism: even Harvard University had founded a School of Business. A managerial revolution stemming from widespread distribution of stock placed the direction of giant industries in the hands of executives (not owners) with larger interests than immediate profit.

Welfare capitalism took varied forms in the 1920s. Accident, illness, and death benefits became quite common, as was provision for plant safety and on-the-job medical services. Several hundred companies offered pension plans and a few even tried profit sharing. Some companies gave relief payments to laid off employees; Procter and Gamble experimented with a guaranteed annual wage.

For all the promise of welfare capitalism, it was regarded suspiciously by unions. What would happen in hard times? Under the weight of the Great Depression the various plans in fact collapsed. Moreover, the movement promoted company unions with leaders chosen from among the workers; the $1\frac{1}{2}$ million members (in 1929) of these unions had little bargaining power, for they could not strike. Nor had the laboring man made enormous strides in the twenties. Although real wages were up about 15 percent, the wealthy were taking a proportionately much greater share of the increased profits. The average work week declined from six to five-and-a-half days, while the rapid growth in technological efficiency led to a substantial rate of unemployment. Had prosperity continued, labor might perhaps have received a more equitable share of profits; the Depression prevented a completely fair test of corporate welfarism.

Labor in retreat   Organized labor had great difficulties in the face of mass-produced consumer goods, rising wages, and welfare capitalism. Membership fell from over 5 million in 1920 to 3,444,000 in 1929. Defeat in the strikes of 1919 had depleted union treasuries and discouraged militant action throughout the decade. The American Federation of Labor looked after skilled workers in elite unions rather than organizing the new mass-production industries. Even the successful drive to abolish the twelve-hour day in the steel industry owed far more to Secretary of Commerce Hoover than to union agitation. Toward the end of the decade, however, the AFL supported efforts to organize southern textile workers. Conditions in the South were deplorable: in Elizabethton, Tennessee, young girls worked fifty-six hours a week for sixteen to eighteen cents an hour. In Marion, North Carolina, textile owners evicted strikers from their homes and prevailed on state troops and county sheriffs' deputies to guard the mills. Statistics tell a story at Marion: one outbreak of violence saw six strikers killed and twenty-five wounded; in an ensuing trial, the law-enforcement officers involved won acquittal while the local union leader was sentenced to prison. Unionism eluded much of the southern textile industry for many years.

SOCIAL THEMES

Social history is at the core of the 1920s. Even some of the dominant political issues—immigration restriction, the Ku Klux Klan, prohibition, the presidential hopes of New York's Roman Catholic Governor Al Smith, the Sacco-Vanzetti case—were at heart questions not of the political or economic process but of what kind of country America should be. Different segments of the electorate took varied positions on these issues. But the main camps were of city against country, foreign against native-born, "wet" against "dry," Catholic against Protestant.

Rural areas, especially the South and its heartland in the fundamentalist "Bible Belt," had long resented the economic advantages of the cities. Now, in the 1920s, as the radio and automobile spread the urban culture and prosperity and sophistication bred urban condescension, the ruralists felt themselves a beleaguered minority in a hostile nation that had once held their values. They fought back on a variety of social issues.

Prohibition

The Prohibition Amendment, added to the Constitution in 1919, had passed quickly in state legislatures because drinking "German" beer or diverting money from the war effort for liquor seemed unpatriotic. But prohibition was above all an inheritance from the progressive era and a movement that inspired great hope. Social workers promised that asylums and jails would be emptied. In a time when people and notably intellectuals believed naively in "science," the eugenicists announced that banning alcohol would improve the race. Doctors no longer raised the spectre—seriously advanced in the nineteenth century—of spontaneous combustion, but they did confuse morals and medicine in their professional opinions. In addition, taxes would fall, husbands would leave the dirty saloons and return to their families. Prohibitionists promised a "sort of millenial Kansas afloat on a nirvana of pure water."

Instead America got poisoned whiskey and a growing problem of organized crime. But the fanatical prohibitionists had perhaps gotten what they wanted: first, a way of exercising control over the immigrant by closing his saloons, and second, the kind of gratification a deeply felt

Yankee Prisoners at Salisbury, N. C.
Prints Division, The New York Public Library

Lee McKay. *Steeplechase Park, Coney Island.*
Museum of the City of New York

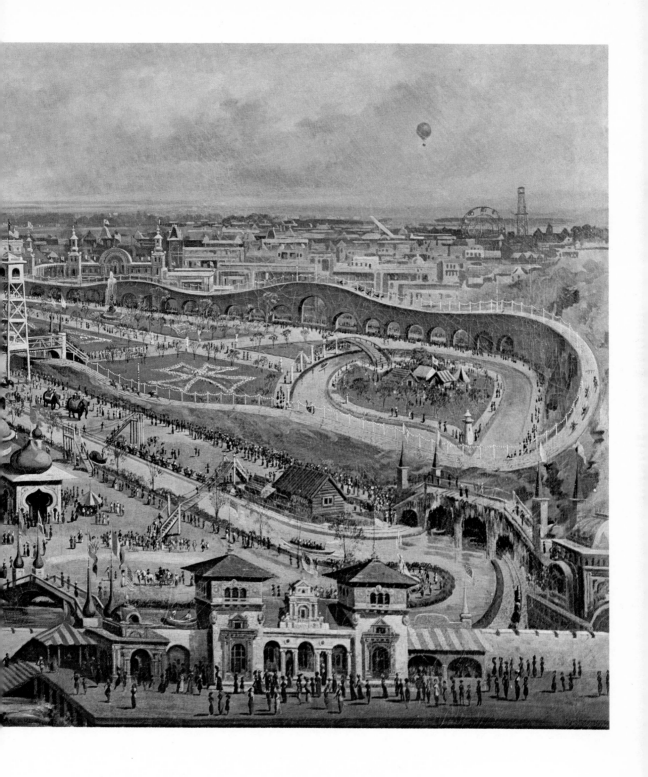

Curry's Fresco, "Comedy." *King's Highway Elementary School,
Westport, Conn.*

John Steuart Curry, *Baptism in Kansas.* Collection of Whitney Museum of American Art,
New York

cause can give—a sense of personal purification and moral glory. Many of the more honest "drys" eventually admitted that the "noble experiment" had failed, and when the Depression brought a compelling need for liquor tax revenues, prohibition was repealed in 1933.

The Ku Klux Klan   The white-sheeted fraternal order of the Ku Klux Klan flourished and then disintegrated during the course of the decade. Founded in 1915 in Georgia as an imitation of the Reconstruction Klan, the new organization gathered its 2 million members chiefly during the early twenties. It was anti-Negro in the South but mainly anti-Catholic both there and in the rest of the country. The Klan's popularity came from the lure of secrecy and from association with religious and patriotic institutions. One of the Klan's most popular songs, sung to the tune of "The Battle Hymn of the Republic," combined symbols of both:

> *We rally round Old Glory in our robes*
> *of spotless white,*
> *While the Fiery Cross is burning in the silent,*
> *silv'ry night,*
> *Come join our glorious army in the cause of God*
> *and Right,*
> *The Klan is marching on.*

The Klan lost face when financial and sexual scandals struck some of its leaders in the mid-twenties. Decline also resulted from success. One of the Klan's triumphs came in helping to insure that Governor Al Smith of New York would not win the Democratic presidential nomination in 1924. The Klan did its part to spread anti-Catholic rumors that the pope, crowded in the Vatican, aspired to new headquarters in the Mississippi Valley and that his minions were tunneling their way under the Atlantic Ocean to give orders to Smith in New York. Wily Jesuits had killed President Harding with "hypnotic-telepathic thought waves," and even the dollar bill bore a rosary cleverly inscribed in the background.

The Klan—which could with some justification claim to have "elected" a number of congressmen and senators in the South and West —also contributed some small part, along with organized labor and most social workers, to ending the decades of immigration that had contributed so much to variety and mobility in American life. In 1921 Congress passed a law setting immigration quotas based on the proportion of each ethnic group to the general population in 1920. When the formula proved too generous to southern and eastern Europeans, quotas were reduced and the date of computation was set back, by the Johnson Act of 1924, to the census of 1890, when fewer aliens had infected the "pure" American culture. In the following quarter-century fewer European immigrants came to the United States than in the single year of 1907.

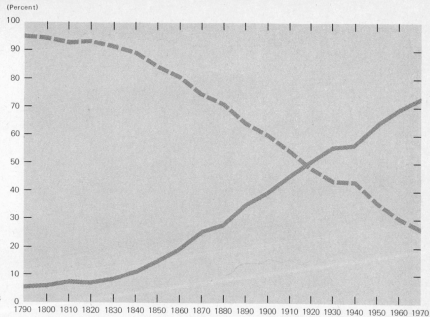

(Percent)

Urban and rural populations

Urban
Rural

Alaska and Hawaii are included in the 1960 and 1970 figures.
Data from Statistical Abstract of the United States, 1971

Rural-urban tensions The antiforeign and antiradical sentiments of the postwar years found near-perfect expression in the Sacco-Vanzetti case. Nicola Sacco and Bartolomeo Vanzetti had been found guilty in 1921 of murdering a factory paymaster and a guard during a robbery in South Braintree, Massachusetts. Recent evidence suggests that Sacco alone was guilty of the crime, but it is plain from the court transcript that Judge Webster Thayer permitted the prosecuting attorney to exploit the defendants' draft evasion and anarchist beliefs in order to secure a conviction. Numerous appeals and finally a special investigatory commission headed by the president of Harvard University merely postponed their execution until 1927. In the meantime, Vanzetti's touching letters from prison, along with publicity given the case by radicals, made it a *cause célèbre* throughout Europe as well as among American intellectuals.

The Scopes trial in Dayton, Tennessee, became a symbol for the decline of the old ways. In 1925 John T. Scopes, a high school biology teacher, challenged the Tennessee law that forbade the teaching of Darwinian evolution in public schools as contrary to biblical literalism. When Scopes was indicted, the ruralists' great champion William Jennings Bryan volunteered to help the prosecution. Now increasingly given to the defense of prohibition and to religious fundamentalism, Bryan was confronted in Dayton by the famous criminal lawyer and agnostic

City Voices. *Minnesota Historical Society*

Clarence Darrow. During one sultry day Judge Raulston of Gizzard's Cove moved the proceedings out onto the courthouse lawn, and there Darrow exposed Bryan's simplistic religious beliefs. Actually, Darrow displayed an equally childlike faith in science, and Bryan's rural provincialism had its counterpart in the lawyer's urban narrowness. Bryan died ten days after the trial, and with his passing much of the heart went out of the rural crusades.

In the long view, the new urban culture was winning out. The census of 1920 was premature in declaring that more people lived in the cities than in the country; it took as its definition of "urban" a population of twenty-five hundred or more, which included many a hinterland village. By 1930, however, metropolitan areas had increased greatly in size at the expense of rural America. Young people left the farms to seek excitement and their fortunes in the city, and economic needs drove whole families to a city factory life. The cities' victory over the countryside went deeper even than population figures suggest. The countryside's moral victories such as antievolution laws and prohibition were short-lived. Urban culture had all the big weapons: advertising, the new mass media of radio and the movies, and the products—such as the automobile —that tied the countryside to urban styles, markets, and values. *Variety,* a show business newspaper, conducted a survey of popular taste in motion pictures and discovered that even country people did not want movies on country subjects: "Stix Nix Hix Pix" read the famous headline.

Above all, the needs of a mass-production economy forced the old ways aside. The rural values of thrift and restraint fell before the need for consumer credit as a device to extend consumption. The film, broadcasting, and advertising industries increased the expectations of the masses and turned them toward the leisure and pleasure patterns of modern urban America. With the values of rural America increasingly flouted and its economic health in jeopardy, bigotry and intolerance predictably resulted. Ironically, the Catholic, Jew, and Negro had less to do with destroying the old values than the mass-production and mass-consumption needs of the new corporations.

Women and the family

By the 1920s many of the institutional functions of the family had declined. Recreation moved outside the home to the movie house and the automobile. The family itself was becoming smaller—particularly in urban areas, where an increase in apartment living also substantially reduced the time traditionally used in maintaining a home. Concurrent

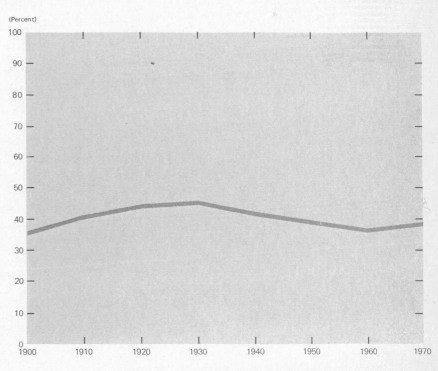

Women as percentage of professional, technical labor force

with changes in family size came a more subtle but equally important change on the domestic scene. The family was beginning to turn inward toward a greater preoccupation with the proper upbringing of children, the growth of their personalities, and their education. Such a concern brought with it a new emphasis on the role of the woman, her place as mother, household manager, and consumer tending to supersede that of household worker.

At the same time, while young unmarried women tended to predominate in the female work force, the percentage of working married women increased steadily, as did the number endeavoring to remain at their jobs after marriage. Between 1900 and 1930 the total number of employed women doubled, but the number of employed married women increased fourfold. In the same years their work shifted away from domestic services and manufacturing and more toward clerical, professional, and trade-oriented work. Some clerical occupations have ever since been considered "women's work."

The early twenties appear to have been a peak period for professional gains among women, most of which had been accomplished before World War I. While there has been an absolute gain in the number of professional women since that time, women's position relative to men has steadily declined since the twenties. One Ph.D. in seven went to a woman in 1920; this dropped to one in ten by 1956. The percentage of women on college faculties fell from 30 percent in the mid-twenties to 24 percent in the mid-sixties.

With increased employment came an increasing variety in female dress and a greater sexual freedom. Yet in today's view the short-skirted "flapper" was not really free but a frivolous object in a masculine world. Nor did the vogue of Freudian psychology contribute to the liberation of women. Freud and other psychoanalysts, each in his own way, stressed the uniqueness of feminine sexuality and inadvertently made women relatively ineffectual as professional and social beings.

Granting women the vote was really not such a great stride forward. For after the Nineteenth Amendment took effect in 1920 the threat of a women's political coalition dissolved: women simply voted as their husbands did, and even the League of Women Voters took a position of political neutrality. Once again it was shown that there is no conspiracy against women in which they themselves are not co-conspirators.

The women's rights movement, so prominent in the activity of suffragettes fighting for their vote during the progressive era, became divided in the twenties. After gaining the vote their first goal was to fight against discriminatory practices and legislation; a state and national campaign began for the passage of equal employment laws. But to those women who had desperately fought for social welfare legislation to protect their hours and conditions of labor, the new campaign threatened to jeopardize hard-won victories. In short, by the twenties the accomplishments of women were paradoxical: they went to work but did "women's work"; they consolidated some of their sexual freedom, but a new view of women emphasizing their feminine roles seriously minimized chances for fruitful social careers.

Literary achievement   The 1920s was no aesthetic wasteland. America's most culturally productive period since the 1850s, the decade produced a great quantity of fine writers and artists. The novels of Sinclair Lewis, F. Scott Fitzgerald, and Ernest Hemingway are of particular importance for an understanding of the period. Lewis's characters are sometimes burlesques, but he is often brilliant in observing the small things that contain the culture of a people. Lewis possessed a phonographic, as well as a photographic, memory. In *Main Street* (1920), which satirized the dullness of a small mid-

A first step: women win the vote. *Brown Brothers*

western town, and in *Babbitt* (1922), which parodied the materialistic businessman, he studied the surfaces of life and mined the native American vein of self-criticism. Both bestsellers, their success illustrates our profound attachment for didactic literature and especially for criticism of ourselves. Lewis's popularity suggests that many Americans stirred restlessly in the twenties.

F. Scott Fitzgerald treated the wealthy, whose glamour and vitality tantalized and disturbed him. *The Great Gatsby* (1925) studies a powerful and vulnerable figure—Jay Gatsby, authentic American, self-made man 1920s style—a bootlegger who aspired to success and love

The first cover of Sinclair Lewis's *Main Street,* a feminist novel about life in a small Western town

through sheer will and determination. In Gatsby the American genius attempted to force reality itself to bend and be shaped anew. This arrogance was a deep-seated trait in the American psyche and a powerful force in a nation that so far had conquered all before it.

Ernest Hemingway, the master of short, crisp dialogue, revealed in *The Sun Also Rises* (1926) and *A Farewell to Arms* (1929) the capacity for both heroism and disillusionment that war could produce. Hemingway wrote about a generation of American young men and women born around the turn of the century and brought to maturity during the war. The phrase "lost generation" was usually applied to the American writers who lived in Paris after the war. They had lost not only their own sense of country but also the restricting past; found was the revelation through art of new concepts that the older generation could not accept.

Intellectuals generally were critical of American life in the twenties. H. L. Mencken attracted many with snide remarks about the "puritanism" of the American "booboisie." Asked why he stayed in America if he despised it so much, he replied: "Why do people go to the zoo?" Some writers cited the newly popular cult of Freudian psychoanalysis in attacking what they saw as America's repressive small-town morality. They turned to European culture protesting America's hostility to new ideas and to the worship of art protesting its smug materialism. A few, such as Joseph Wood Krutch in *The Modern Temper*, went beyond criticisms of American culture to a bleak view of all industrial society, civilized out of all belief and in need of some rejuvenating force.

A number of intellectuals saw this hoped-for rebirth in the very social changes that frightened other Americans. The city with its strange new peoples could offer the diversity that American writers found lacking in the villages. Some, like Randolph Bourne, envisioned America as a salad bowl of races and groups rather than a melting pot, a variegated world in which each exotic group preserved its own life and culture for the enrichment of all. This cultural pluralism would become increasingly important in the twentieth century.

Behavior   The twenties digested startling changes in American manners and morals, as standard notions of propriety disintegrated. The world war played a major role in this process through the disruption of social patterns which had been based on Victorian ideals, but it did not create the ideas and movements of the twenties. The new thought and behavior blossomed from prewar seedlings and often employed or reflected the advancing technology of the period.

In the cultural development of the twenties, few events were of more significance than the arrival of the "new psychology." This movement received impetus as early as 1909 from the American tour of its greatest prophet, Sigmund Freud, but came to fruition in the professional and popular mind only during the postwar decade. In its variously distorted forms, Freudianism quickly became an apparent influence in most literature and entertainment, affecting thousands who had never heard of Freud.

The influence of sex and repression in human behavior dominated the national understanding of the new psychology. Sexual restraint preached by late nineteenth-century social guardians seemed now positively counterproductive; social problems stemmed from an unhealthy containment of sexual urges. To be unrestrained, to release inner desires and tensions, became a worthy goal. Such conclusions in general psychological theory provided a ready rationalization for ignoring custom and violating taboos.

The general currency of Freud's ideas and his intellectual respectability were important in making sex a fit subject for mixed-group discussion among the sophisticated. Men and women at the modish cocktail parties of the twenties talked about sex under the guise of science, spicing their remarks with choice selections from tempting psychoanalytic vocabulary. The desire to be shocking encouraged daring rather than caution; with this accelerator, the subject of sex moved in a few years from nonentity to notoriety. The new psychology was not alone in its support of the revolution in manners and morals. Other more tangible influences, affecting the young in particular, shaped innovative social patterns.

Automobile ownership spread rapidly in the twenties and provided a mobility previously unknown. Yet the family car could be used for more than commuting to work or driving about on a Sunday. As closed cars increasingly dominated the market, the automobile became in effect a room on wheels, a room which could be moved and stopped where prying eyes and interruptions were unlikely. Soon automobiles were being held directly responsible for a portion of the birth statistics. Sexual experimentation was not, of course, limited to parked cars. Petting parties were in vogue before the war and magazines discussed the "petting question" throughout the twenties. Yet the automobile provided a uniquely available vehicle for the passionate and the curious.

The subtle social infiltrations of sex were by no means confined to covert couplings. Wary guardians of morality were shocked to find sex barely disguised in brazen forms of popular culture, such as jazz—immediately suspect for its Negro origins. Beyond that, defenders of hymnal and hearth quickly saw insidious sensuality within the music itself. Jazz often featured the "passionate crooning and wailing" of the saxophone—a far cry from the parlor piano—and no one could doubt the corruption and disarray evidenced in the threatening evil of syncopation. Dancing in the twenties passed from fad to fad in a fury of exuberant creativity, including early dances like the Horse Trot, the Grizzly Bear, and the often berated Bunny Hug, while the famous Charleston came

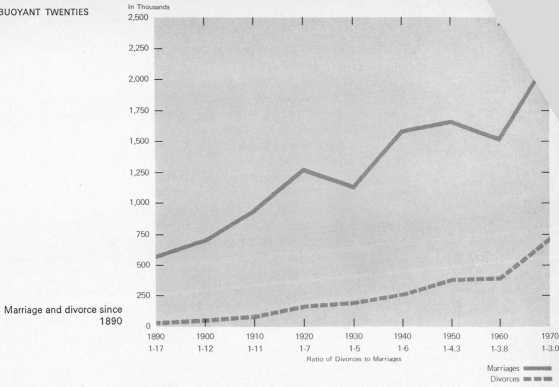

In Thousands

Marriage and divorce since 1890

	1890	1900	1910	1920	1930	1940	1950	1960	1970
	1-17	1-12	1-11	1-7	1-5	1-6	1-4.3	1-3.8	1-3.0

Ratio of Divorces to Marriages

Marriages
Divorces

later in the decade. One religious newspaper tied together music, sex, and the new dances in one broad condemnation: "The music is sensuous, the embracing of partners—the female only half dressed—is absolutely indecent; and the motions—they are such as may not be described, with any respect for propriety, in a family newspaper."

The growing mass culture industries of the twenties may have heard the critics, but they listened to the demands of their audience. During the day radio stations aired a variety of programs including inspirational and educational material; but in the evenings, during "prime time," most stations concentrated on popular music, especially jazz. Similarly, the motion picture industry churned out a mixed product, but the movies which drew the largest audiences relied heavily on sex as a theme, some of the earliest pictures being the most explicit. Yet even after luring Postmaster General Will Hays from the Harding Cabinet to maintain moral standards the industry, in many pictures, conforming on the surface to the old morality and the happy ending, nevertheless depended for their appeal on plots permeated with sexual innuendo.

On the newsstands the evidence of a new kind of popular literature glared: the confession and sex magazines. *True Story*, founded in 1919, achieved the most spectacular success in this genre, by 1926 reaching a circulation of nearly 2 million on the strength of such stories as "What I Told My Daughter the Night Before Her Marriage" and "The Primitive Lover." Frequently, as in the movies, these provided a moral ending or gratuitous preaching of trite homilies, but the subject was clearly the same. Interestingly, remarkable similarities appeared between the "confessions" in pulp magazines and the case studies of popular psychoanalysts, revealing perhaps one more unintended influence of Freudian theory.

Many of the cultural clashes of the twenties stood clearly revealed on the battlefield of women's fashion. Social conservatives idealized the nineteenth-century woman, her skirts reaching the ground, a face plain and scrubbed, with her long hair in a bun. Any change in such an appearance represented obvious sexual impurity. Nonetheless, fashion trends in the twenties embraced the same freedom from old forms implied by the changes in music, dancing, and entertainment; and in doing so, they came into direct conflict with the older image of woman. Skirts rose from ankle to knee in the first half of the decade; bobbed hair became stylish, first among the young but soon for women of all ages; cosmetics came to be not only permissible but also essential—the beauty industry expanded astonishingly during the twenties. In her early exaggeration of these trends, the "Flapper" symbolized the tide of sexuality and experimentation that so disturbed those who were not busy participating.

Not everything in the twenties revolved around explicit sexuality or the rejection of older values. Feeding on increasing leisure and prosperity, various sports claimed far greater public attention than ever before. Some encouraged participation; golf, for instance, aided by the developing role of the country club as a social center, became especially popular. But the era showed a tendency to watching professional athletes. Golf itself boasted Bobby Jones and Walter Hagen; tennis proclaimed Bill Tilden; in football Red Grange should perhaps top any list; the boorish Babe Ruth gave a lift to baseball; boxing fans thrilled to two Dempsey-Tunney fights. Huge crowds attended college football games and millions heard the first professional sportscasters on their radios. Spectatorship emerged as an art.

The cultural turmoil of the twenties was inescapable. By the end of the decade, even a religiously and socially conservative family in some obscure hamlet might well have owned or at least listened to a radio. Such slight exposure still changed their world. No earlier decade had so stirred American society.

HOOVER AND THE DEPRESSION

For inscrutable reasons President Coolidge declared in 1927: "I do not choose to run again." His successor would be Secretary of Commerce Herbert Hoover, who had won enormous fame as an engineer and humanitarian. Against Hoover the Democrats ran Alfred E. Smith, the able governor of New York. Hoover would probably have won the 1928 presidential election because of "Republican" prosperity no matter who was the Democratic nominee, but his opponent had special liabilities. A Roman Catholic and antiprohibitionist, Smith drew solid support from the "ethnics" in the big cities, but bigotry lost him normally Democratic votes in the South and elsewhere. Moreover, Smith had a strain of urban provincialism that prevented him from reaching out to decent Americans of the West and South in gestures of compromise and friendship. A reporter asked him about the needs of the states west of the Mississippi. "What are the states west of the Mississippi?" Smith, half-jokingly, replied. Smith polled an impressive vote in the big cities, but Hoover became president.

Herbert Hoover, who perfectly catches the twenties' image of restless productivity, is an ideal American success story—it is a supreme irony that the Depression overtook his presidency. Born in the Quaker hamlet of West Branch, Iowa, in 1874, Hoover lost his mother and father while yet a child. He grew up with the country in Iowa, Oregon, and California. At Stanford University he studied geology and soon after graduating embarked on ship to work as a mining engineer on the goldfields of Western Australia. From 1897 to 1914 Hoover circled the globe no less than eight times, maintained offices in London, New York, San Francisco, Shanghai, Mandalay, and Saint Petersburg, and accumulated a modest fortune.

The new president dreamed of abolishing poverty in America. Like Frederic Winslow Taylor and other great technicians of his day, Hoover was a practitioner of industrial rationalization—the complete ordering and standardizing of production. He set out to rationalize the operations not of a single plant but of an entire technological economy. In his little book *American Individualism* (1922) he sometimes sounds like a reformer out of the progressive era: he wanted "pioneers" to invade "continents of human welfare of which we have penetrated only the coastal plain."

Hoover and his predecessor Coolidge presented a striking contrast. Coolidge would not have a telephone in his office, Hoover had several. Coolidge never smoked, Hoover smoked incessantly. Coolidge slept almost twelve hours a night, took a long nap in the afternoon, and still complained of being tired. Hoover got up at six-thirty, played with a medicine ball for exercise, and often worked eighteen hours. He believed in an activist government, helping business and controlling its worst excesses.

While Hoover opposed having the government dictate solutions to social problems, he did not object to extensive government activities; his use of the Commerce Department was an advance in governmental involvement. His concept of organization blended a taste for voluntarism and individual decision with a commitment to collective effort. He believed that rational and decent people would freely cooperate if shown the necessity of doing so; the large units essential to an industrial society would receive their energies from the bottom up and their efficiency from the top down. The ends in view were always the potentially contradictory ones of productivity and freedom. Hoover worked toward a justification for American business and took credit for the great material advances made in the twenties.

The great crash For some time Hoover had been warning against the possibility of a day of reckoning in the economy. There had been numerous signs of impending collapse. Speculative excesses in real estate and the stock market created a dangerous probability of rapid deflation. In 1928 consumer spending fell off, housing construction declined, and inventories increased. These trends led to a cutback in production—the clearest warning of all.

The Federal Reserve Board did little to discipline the stock market speculation of the late twenties. Open market operations (the selling of government securities to decrease the amount of money in circulation) began in earnest in 1928; but the inventory of these debts was too slight to deflate the boom. Raising the rediscount rate (the interest charged member banks for loans) came too late to have much effect. By 1929 loans from nonbanking sources eclipsed those from banks. Money from all over the world came to Wall Street, where brokers were willing to pay a whopping 12 percent interest for short-term financing. Raising the government interest rates penalized small businessmen and farmers and scarcely deterred speculators accustomed to borrowing at any rates. The crash came suddenly on Thursday, October 24, 1929.

The stock market revived a bit during the winter of 1930, but once spring came it dropped precipitously again and continued to drop, month by month, until it reached bottom in 1932. The *New York Times* index average of stocks sank from around 300 at its height in 1929 to 38 by July 1932. Some individual stocks did far worse; Montgomery Ward plummeted from 138 to 4. Many corporations went bankrupt. A few tycoons committed suicide—the head of Rochester Gas and Electric took gas. Samuel Insull, whose jerrybuilt structure of holding companies had collapsed like a deck of cards, fled to Europe.

The stock market crash alone was not responsible for the Great Depression. John Kenneth Galbraith in his study of the crash lists five fundamental weaknesses in the economy. (1) *The unequal distribution of income:* In 1929 5 percent of the population with highest incomes received about one-third of all personal earnings. Because their spending could be reduced more abruptly than that of ordinary people, the rich, once the market crashed, contributed quickly and decisively to deflation.

(2) *The bad corporate structure:* Holding companies and investment trusts could not have been better designed to fall into a deflationary spiral once a weakening of dividends curtailed operating investments. (3) *The weak banking structure:* Too many independent banks meant that when one failed and its assets were frozen, others felt the repercussions; once several failed, a domino effect ensued. (4) *The foreign balance* (see page 485). (5) *The miserable state of economic knowledge:* Both political parties endorsed the gold standard and the balanced budget. The kind of public spending that we now suppose helps to alleviate bad times was forbidden by economic authorities whose influence on politicians was nearly absolute. Worst of all, the money supply itself virtually dried up.

Willing and anxious to use the government within certain limits to cushion the Depression, the activist Hoover abandoned laissez faire (which never really existed in pure form in America) and tried to avert the impending disaster. He persuaded a conference of governors and mayors to speed up their own works projects. A group of leading businessmen agreed not to reduce wages. Hoover made reassuring public

Hoover got all the blame. A "Hooverville" in Seattle. *Wide World*

statements and asked Congress for legislation to regulate the banking system. He gave promise of doing whatever was necessary to end the hard times.

The Hoover program   Before the Great Crash the president had signed into law the Agricultural Marketing Act of 1929, which embodied his favorite notion of cooperative marketing. If farmers could control their production and marketing, they could obtain higher prices. To assist them, the new law set aside a half-million dollars to fund large marketing cooperatives. Unfortunately, the scheme never received a fair chance. The Depression affected farmers so ruinously that the government money simply went down the drain. The Act was not equipped to deal with continuing surplus, and this was another major problem. Another idea, popular among congressional progressives, was a domestic allotment program that would restrict the amount of a crop sold on the domestic market. Some features of this plan, along with some from McNary-Haugen, came into practice during the New Deal. The Smoot-Hawley Tariff of 1930 also aimed to help farmers by raising import duties.

Hoover believed that if businessmen would have faith and cooperate for the social good, then public confidence would be restored. To encourage business he at first lowered taxes and reduced government spending, but these formulas proved inadequate. Early in 1932 and after

MacArthur, disobeying Hoover's orders, routed the veterans from their camp on Anacosta Flats

some hesitation, Hoover signed into law the Reconstruction Finance Corporation, which he later termed his most important antidepression measure.

The RFC could loan money to financial institutions in industry, commerce, and agriculture. Since nearly twenty-three hundred banks had gone under during 1931, the RFC loaned over $1 billion to banks and trust companies and brought renewed stability to the financial system. When unemployment continued to rise, the RFC was empowered to make loans to states for relief and public works projects. Yet Hoover himself appointed to its board cautious men who did not spend the vast sums available to them. As a result, these activities of the RFC created few jobs and seemed a failure. Yet many of its institutional divisions were direct precursors of various New Deal agencies.

Lack of jobs had caused three thousand workers to march from downtown Detroit in March 1932 to the Ford plant in Dearborn. When they reached the township line and refused to turn back, the police opened fire with revolvers and then a machine gun. Four Communist marchers died, and scores lay injured. In the spring veterans began to march on Washington to demand early payment of their soldiers' bonus, due in 1945. When the Senate defeated the bill in June, as many as fifteen thousand men stayed on, camping just outside Washington on Anacostia Flats. After an incident General Douglas MacArthur, disobeying Hoover's explicit order, moved on the veterans' shacks, which were set afire. The veterans dispersed, a baby died from other causes shortly afterward, and Hoover took all the blame.

Depression diplomacy   Americans hummed throughout the twenties an optimistic refrain of rising production figures, growing consumption, and economic expansion abroad. But just as government leaders failed to see the warning signs of impending economic collapse at home, the frailty of international prosperity likewise escaped them.

The Great Depression, in its international dimension, had roots reaching back to the war-debt and reparations settlements of the Treaty of Versailles. The United States had loaned various Allied governments over $10 billion, and even though most of this money had been used to purchase products in this country the Republican administrations insisted that the debt be repaid. Allied governments and a few sympathetic Americans argued that repayment was both impossible and unfair. The Allies were burdened with vast, expensive programs to reconstruct their devastated countries and economies. If Europeans were required to send tax money to the United States, which had already reaped tremendous profits from the war, the recovery of world commerce would be slowed and everyone would suffer. Moreover, the borrowed money had been expended in a common effort, and Europeans pointed out that they had made a much costlier sacrifice in terms of human lives than had the

United States. Finally, the United States' high tariff barriers hampered the Allies' ability to sell their exports in the United States. With their taxpayers already overburdened and the large American market virtually closed, the Allies could raise the revenue needed to pay the United States only through high reparations—the payments exacted from Germany for wartime damages.

Americans opposed high reparations that would cripple the German economy for years to come, but presidents from Wilson to Hoover all refused to relate the obviously interdependent questions of war debts and reparations. Rather than substantially scaling down war debts, which would have permitted a realistic reduction of Germany's reparations, the United States informally assisted Germany in meeting its payments by encouraging private American investment in German bonds. Until the late 1920s this arrangement worked: the United States loaned money to Germany; Germany used the loans to pay the European Allies; the Allies could meet their war debts to the United States. The great weakness of the arrangement was that Germany's economic wellbeing and all of Europe's ability to meet financial obligations depended, to a great degree, upon a continued outward flow of American investment capital.

International depression The collapse of the New York Stock Exchange in 1929 signaled an abrupt end to the expansive American economy and the beginning of grave problems for international finance. As credit dried up, American businessmen began to recall capital invested abroad, particularly in Germany. Plagued by financial difficulties ever since the war, the German government now faced total bankruptcy. Without new funds from the United States, Germany suspended its reparations payments and threatened to default on the huge volume of bonds which American investors and bankers had bought throughout the twenties. And the European Allies could not hope to meet war-debt obligations without reparations. The structure of world prosperity was crashing down. President Hoover bowed to reality and announced in June of 1931 a one-year moratorium on all intergovernmental debts. But just as Hoover's measures to cope with the domestic economic crisis seemed too late and too limited, so this eleventh-hour gesture, delayed even longer by French opposition, did little to halt the worldwide financial contraction from plunging into deep depression. Suspension of debt payments, in fact, augmented the alarm among international financiers, who rushed to convert their assets into gold. Unable to maintain liquidity, England was forced to abandon the gold standard.

International depression initiated a decade of global instability and threats to peace, ultimately culminating in World War II. Although the League of Nations, the Washington treaties, and the Kellogg-Briand

Pact contributed little to the maintenance of peace in the thirties, these instruments were not wholly to blame for the crises which led to World War II. The most basic cause of international problems was economic disruption. Hard times led to a worldwide upsurge of nationalism, and in Italy, Japan, and Germany this trend took the form of territorial expansionism. Elsewhere, including the United States, economic problems created a desire to avoid foreign involvement in order to concentrate on difficulties at home.

The Far East The first major diplomatic crisis following the onset of the Depression occurred in the Far East. Japan's economy, which had been in difficulty even before 1929, deteriorated further from the effects of worldwide depression. The consequent social and economic unrest strengthened militant nationalists, who charged that civilian government had compromised Japanese security in the naval disarmament agreements of the Washington treaties. In the Mukden Incident of September 18, 1931, a few staff officers of the Japanese Kwantung army in Manchuria blew up a Japanese-owned railway and falsely proclaimed that the Chinese had committed the deed. In "retaliation," the commander of the Kwantung army quickly defeated the local warlord and conquered Manchuria without the knowledge or approval of the civilian government in Tokyo. At first, the Hoover administration seemed not to notice this violation of the Washington treaties and the Kellogg-Briand Pact. Secretary of State Henry Stimson hoped that the civilian administration in Tokyo, which was friendly to the United States, would be able to resume control over the Kwantung army and order its withdrawal. When this government was replaced with one that gave belated approval to the military's conquests, the situation took on a more somber tone.

The international responses to the Mukden Incident and Japanese aggression revealed the extent to which world economic crisis debilitated the collective-security arrangements constructed during the twenties. Although the League of Nations dispatched the Lytton Commission to investigate events in Manchuria and subsequently condemned the Japanese action, no government was willing to employ force against the Japanese. The League of Nations charter, the Washington treaties, and the Kellogg-Briand Pact had all been violated, but collective security apparently worked only if it reflected the national interests of the states involved. By 1931 European and American leaders believed that their countries' paramount interests lay in avoiding foreign difficulties and concentrating on domestic ills.

Washington's ultimate response to Japan's occupation of Manchuria took the form of nonrecognition, a concept later affirmed by the League of Nations. This Hoover-Stimson Doctrine professed refusal to recognize the legality of any move violating treaty agreements concerning the sovereignty of China and the maintenance of the Open Door. Non-recognition permitted the United States to make clear its moral opposition to Japanese actions while, at the same time, making no commitment to back up its opposition with force.

Because Japan and Germany continued their expansionism throughout the thirties, it has been easy to condemn the United States and other major powers for not taking a stronger stand against Japanese activities in 1931. Yet if nonrecognition seems an unrealistic method of halting aggression, how much more unrealistic was a policy of military force against the Japanese? How would an American president, least of all one as unpopular as Herbert Hoover, have convinced Congress and the American people that, despite the daily closing of banks and the rising rate of unemployment, the national interest required a costly war in China? Even the frequently suggested alternative of establishing economic sanctions against Japan takes on an air of unreality when considered in the context of the Depression. With the United States and European countries all trying to boost exports, the governments could not seriously entertain the idea of voluntarily suspending sales in a lucrative market. In fact, many American businessmen believed, in view of continued instability in China, that a strong Japanese dominance on the mainland might be beneficial to United States trade and investment. Theodore Roosevelt had pursued such a pro-Japanese policy some twenty years earlier when he had acquiesced to Japan's occupation of Korea. The United States had always had far more important economic ties with Japan than with China.

While the Japanese action offended the morality of Hoover, Stimson, and many other Americans, it did not represent a serious challenge to American economic or strategic interests. On the whole, the Hoover-Stimson policy seemed well tailored to America's needs: it expressed disapproval without committing the United States to any course which would have proved militarily and economically unwise.

By the time Hoover left office, the role of the United States in the world had changed greatly. No longer the expansive, self-assured power of the twenties, the country was drawing inward, politically and economically. The issue of war debts and reparations remained unsettled; the status of the Japanese in Manchuria and the future of China remained cloudy; and the growth in many countries of nationalist parties of the extreme Right and Left threatened to transform the relatively calm political world of the 1920s.

Hoover and Roosevelt   Bad luck and poor political judgment plagued Hoover. His socially conscious efforts in some areas went unnoticed under the burden of the Depression. He so lacked political sensitivity that he allowed photographers to snap him feeding meat to his dog on the White House lawn while people neared starvation throughout the country. Before a large audience

Hoover was uninspiring. He read his speeches in a low, monotonous, almost inaudible tone; standing stiffly with one hand in the pocket of his blue serge suit, he made no gestures, and spoke rapidly without expression. The nation needed someone with the more informal gifts of political statesmanship. Franklin Roosevelt, who could say "My old friend" in a dozen languages, provided the presence and the skill. Nourished by much the same economic and social philosophies, the different personalities of these two men largely determined their differing responses to the economic crisis.

THE TWENTIES: A LESSON
IN HISTORICAL STEREOTYPING

The 1920s—the first decade when celebrities became a major attraction—remain vivid in the historical imagination. The generation often saw itself as heroic, risqué, extravagant: it lived in the newspapers. In the southern

Lucky Lindy represented the new technology and the old individualism. *Brown Brothers*

Indiana town of Kokomo in 1923, one famous celebrity, the Ku Klux Klan's Grand Dragon of the Realm, descended by plane to join a gathering of some two hundred thousand devoted followers. Although he wore white robes to symbolize moral purity, this Grand Dragon was to serve a score of years in prison for assaulting his secretary and driving her to suicide by poison. Four years later, in New York City, swirling crowds enveloped the shy Charles Lindbergh, who had just completed the first solo flight from New York to Paris. Lindbergh's flight was a triumph of the machine age; yet it occasioned a feeling of regeneration, a momentary rebirth of the American pioneer spirit. Abroad, on the French coast of the Mediterranean at Cap d'Antibes, the American novelist F. Scott Fitzgerald and his wife Zelda danced late at night on a moonlit patio strewn with broken champagne glasses. Such moments beg to be relived and felt anew in more complex and less romantic times. The twenties have become one of our enduring legends. Yet to leave it as legend is to fail to understand that era as well as the decades following it.

Because the 1920s are seen through the decade's own flashing images, its real self is hard to recapture. Each age has had its own vision of the twenties. Contemporaries viewed the period as one of cultural conflict: countryside versus city, Anglo-Saxon versus immigrant, tradition versus modernity. During the Great Depression, many writers who believed in the public drama of the twenties saw it as a hedonistic "jazz age," a national sin of frivolity for which the hunger and unemployment of the thirties were retribution. The decade was a youthful fling, an aberration in the serious march of American history. By the 1950s this garish portrait had been softened by nostalgia: the escapades had been fun. Besides, not all Americans had spent their time in seven-day bicycle races or ninety-day flagpole sits. Some had found the years after World War I rewarding because —like the years after World War II—they had been just that: a spreading economic plenty, marked by a million homes electrified, a million cars to drive over mile upon mile of new highway. Everywhere there were more and better houses, appliances, movies. Essentially, what was good about the twenties was what was also good about the fifties, and if a few intellectuals wanted to complain, let them.

Viewing the twenties from the seventies, we can see clearly yet another aspect—the beginning of the age in which we live, the age of mass comsumption, spreading cities, national media and markets, standardized products available to the millions, and a sometimes equally standardized culture just as available. Very much in the American mainstream, the twenties posed all the modern hopes and problems—of the city, of intergroup relations, of the relationship of industrialism to the environment —with which we have striven to live since.

THINGS TO THINK ABOUT:
1918–1932

Was the United States better off for not entering the League of Nations?
For a variety of viewpoints see Arthur Link, *Wilson the Diplomatist* (rev.
ed., 1963), N. Gordon Levin, *Woodrow Wilson and World Politics* (1968),
and Arno J. Mayer, *Politics and the Diplomacy of Peacemaking* (1968).

How can one account for the severity of the "Red Scare" of
1919? Stanley Coben's *A. Mitchell Palmer* (1963) and his article "The
American Red Scare of 1919–1920," *Political Science Quarterly* (1964)
are keys to understanding this phenomenon.

How did the thinking of Harding and Coolidge differ from that of
Herbert Hoover? The best book on Harding is Robert K. Murray, *The*
Harding Era (1969); the best on Coolidge is Donald McCoy, *Calvin*
Coolidge (1967). Perhaps Hoover's own *Memoirs* (1952) give the best
introduction to his thinking, but see the sophisticated interpretation in
William Appleman Williams, *The Contours of American History* (1962),
and Joan Hoff Wilson's *Herbert Hoover* (1974).

How did prohibition help to promote social change during the
1920s? An entertaining and often insightful account is Andrew Sinclair,
Era of Excess (1962).

What role did the automobile play in the decade's economic and
social history? See Allan Nevins and Frank E. Hill, *Ford: Expansion and*
Challenge, 1915–1933 (1957).

What was the role of the stock market crash in the Great Depres-
sion? John Kenneth Galbraith has written a fascinating account, *The Great*
Crash (1955), but also consult George Soule, *Prosperity Decade* (1947).

What forms did economic diplomacy take in the twenties and
what was its role in bringing on the Depression? See Joan Hoff Wilson,
American Business and Foreign Policy, 1920–1933 (1971).

1932-1940

TWELVE | a new DEAL, NOT a new DECK

WOODY GUTHRIE

Today Woody Guthrie looms as one of America's larger-than-life heroes, a folk balladeer who inspired two generations of singer-activists. Woodrow Wilson Guthrie was an authentic voice of the troubles, and the hopes, of the Great Depression. Growing up in rural Oklahoma, he developed his unique guitar style listening to his relatives and to radio broadcasts of the famous Carter family. In the early thirties he watched the Great Plains turn into a giant Dust Bowl and experienced first-hand the descent into poverty. Like the Joads of John Steinbeck's *Grapes of Wrath*, Woody hit the road to California. His encounters with other people undergoing "hard travelin'" (as he put it) sharpened his social consciousness and shaped the lyrics of a flood of songs, over a thousand by some people's count. With his folksinging sidekick Cisco Houston and actor Will Geer, Woody rambled around migrant labor camps, singing and raising money for the impoverished workers. If the "Okies'" potato stew "had been just a little bit thinner," he wryly observed, "some of our senators could have seen through it." Particularly struck by the exploitation of Mexican migrants, he asked in his song "Deportee," "Is this the best way we can raise our good orchards? Is this the best way we can grow our good crops?"

As his radicalism deepened, Guthrie began writing for the left-wing *People's Daily World*, but music remained his true medium. During the thirties he wrote a set of songs for the Oregon Department of Interior, including "Grand Coulee Dam" and "Roll on Columbia," extolling the virtues of public power projects. Later in the decade New York City intellectuals "discovered" Woody as a true proletarian minstrel, and he joined the left-wing urban folk revival. But unlike some other artists, such as Burl Ives and Josh White, Woody generally shunned commercial performances. He preferred the freedom of the open road and working-class audiences. With Pete Seeger and several other politically radical musicians, he formed the Almanac Singers who toured the country singing to farm and factory laborers and participating in unionization campaigns.

Increasingly Woody became concerned with the spread of fascism, and songs such as "The Sinking of the Reuben James" expressed his fervent desire for American intervention in the European war. In 1943 he joined the Merchant Marine, participating in several invasions and having two ships torpedoed from under him. Still, he considered song his most potent weapon, and his battered guitar carried the slogan, "This Machine Kills Fascists."

A wiry little man with bushy dark hair, Woody Guthrie, like Franklin Roosevelt, never lost faith in the country during the depression. "I hate a song that makes you think that you're not any good," he once said. "I'm out to fight those kinds of songs." But unlike Roosevelt, Woody embraced socialism as the solution to the nation's plight. His radicalism sprang from the American heartland and, in many ways, looked backward. Woody believed that the dry, blistered prairie could be revived and that the weather-beaten people could recapture the pioneer spirit and regain the seats of power. Ballads such as "The Oregon Trail" and "Oklahoma Hills" reflected his pride in America's rural heritage. His hope lay in a people's socialist revolution. Commonly viewed as a lyrical description of America's natural beauties, his most famous song, "This Land is Your Land," also prophesied an end to acquisitive capitalism:

> As I was walkin' a dusty roadway,
> The sign before me said private property,
> But on the other side it said nothing.
> This land belongs to you and me.

1932-1940

1933	"Hundred Days" session of Congress; beginning of the New Deal
	Agricultural Adjustment Act
	Tennessee Valley Authority
	National Industrial Recovery Act
	21st Amendment ratified, repealing prohibition
	National Labor Relations Act
1935	Social Security Act
	Supreme Court declares some New Deal laws unconstitutional
1935–36	Roosevelt elected to second term
1936	Fight over Roosevelt's "court-packing" plan
1937	Administrative Reorganization Act
1939	War breaks out in Europe
	Roosevelt elected to third term
1940	United States preparedness and defense measures

FDR

In the 1928 presidential campaign Herbert Hoover had taken credit for the decade of Republican prosperity; when the economy collapsed, he got the blame. By early 1932 Hoover's chances for reelection appeared dismal. The dispersal of the Bonus Marchers—which seemed to reflect an indifference to human misery—made his chances hopeless.

Among the Democrats Franklin Delano Roosevelt was the front-runner, but the popular New York governor could not trace an unobstructed path to the nomination. Al Smith, by 1932 Roosevelt's confirmed enemy, retained significant support, especially in the Northeast. John Nance Garner of Texas, Speaker of the House, commanded strength in the South and also enjoyed the backing of the powerful newspaper publisher William Randolph Hearst. Roosevelt entered the Chicago nominating convention burdened by a three-to-one defeat to Smith in the Massachusetts primary and a loss to Garner in California. Through the first three ballots, Roosevelt failed to achieve the necessary two-thirds, but then William Gibbs McAdoo switched the California delegation from Garner to FDR, who went over the top on the fourth ballot and chose the Texan as his running mate.

The campaign sharpened the great contrast between the buoyant Roosevelt and the dour Hoover. The president campaigned with energy and determination but failed to project any sense of optimism or confidence. Roosevelt suggested the opposite mood. Immediately after the fourth ballot, the new Democratic nominee bravely boarded a plane that

In fine spirits. *Wide World*

FDR and Herbert Hoover, 1933. *UPI*

bucked stormy weather over the Great Lakes and, breaking with tradition, arrived in Chicago to accept the nomination in person. "Let it be now the task of our party to break foolish traditions," he proclaimed to the cheering delegates. Running against the unpopular incumbent, Roosevelt could be dynamic and vague at the same time—a technique making some fear that he lacked the requisite intellectual depth to be president. Yet in the time of crisis this superficiality appealed to the voters, while Hoover's ideological hardness made them uneasy. Roosevelt overwhelmed Hoover on election day, the Republican president winning only six of the forty states he had carried four years before.

FDR and the depression

During the four months between the voters' repudiation of Hoover and the swearing-in of the new president, the depression exacted its cruelest toll upon a leaderless nation. By 1933 more than 25 percent of the civilian labor force lacked jobs, but economic statistics cannot adequately convey the gloom and despair. To people who thought economic progress inevitable, the hard times threw into question traditional American values. The collapse of thousands of banks—by Roosevelt's inauguration forty states had closed all banks—revealed how quickly savings acquired through hard work and sacrifice could vanish. But the nation's mood was one of resignation, the economic calamity seemed to defy human powers. A popular country-music song reflected the general spirit of hopelessness: "For fear the hearts of men are failing. . . . The Great Depression now is spreading, God's will declared it would be so." Meanwhile, Roosevelt and Hoover circled each other like wary gladiators, coming together only in two brief and unproductive meetings. The president elect refused to accept Hoover's proposals and remained vague about his own solutions.

The pampered son of an aristocratic New York family, FDR grew up in a handsome white house at Hyde Park on the Hudson River. Supremely confident of the country's future, young Franklin learned to be a fierce competitor, not in the harsh business world but on the playing fields of Groton Academy and later at Harvard. FDR's school days, especially at the Reverend Endicott Peabody's Groton, ingrained the notion that members of his social class should offer their talents in service to those less fortunate. Roosevelt, however, was no student. Fraternities and athletics seemed more important to the editor of the Harvard *Crimson,* and he left college unencumbered by fundamental doubts. His uncomplicated creed consisted of love of school, God, and country. Such an upbringing and privileged position had never forced him to question traditional American pieties. His later life did little to shake his self-assurance. The young country squire won his first contest for public office in his Dutchess County home territory; married a distant cousin, a niece of President Theodore Roosevelt; survived revelation of an affair with his secretary; and took over TR's old job as assistant secretary of

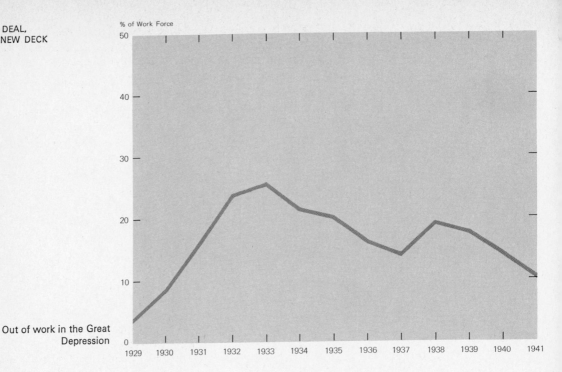

% of Work Force

Out of work in the Great
Depression

the navy. In 1920 the Democratic party nominated him for vice-president. He met his only serious setback, a severe attack of polio which left his legs paralyzed for life, with characteristic courage and even turned the handicap into a political asset. Cheated by wealth out of birth in a log cabin or even above the family drugstore, FDR's crippled legs gave the Hudson River aristocrat the underdog's image. For a nation requiring reaffirmation of basic values as much as sophisticated analyses of economic problems, FDR was the perfect evangelist for the glories of democratic capitalism.

Roosevelt takes control   Immediately after taking the oath of office, Roosevelt sounded the dominant themes of the first years of his presidency. He rallied the nation to a war against depression, comparing the battle to the one it had successfully fought against the Kaiser's Germany little more than a decade earlier. Americans had to act "as a trained and loyal army," and he himself would ask Congress for "broad Executive power to wage war against the emergency, as great as the power that would be given to me if we were in fact invaded by a foreign foe."

FDR freely invoked his persuasive talents to cheer a discouraged people and to rally them with the combative spirit he had always displayed. The first president to make effective use of radio, Roosevelt, an affable and winning conversationalist, delivered "fireside chats" from the White House to advise listeners of new programs and to assure them that government was taking bold action. No longer an abstraction hidden away in Washington, the president sent soothing messages and inspirational little pep talks into homes throughout the nation.

All the president's vibrant tones, however, would have soon sounded flat had he not been able to offer some concrete successes. Roosevelt's campaign and early presidential speeches predicted swift and decisive action against depression. After the November election a variety of advisors—the "Brains Trust"—went to work on myriad programs. FDR and his advisors labeled their actions the "New Deal," a catchphrase emphasizing FDR's departure from the ways of the past.

The New Deal was primarily a product of the personality, style, and values of the president. Unaffected by grand theories or philosophical subtleties, FDR saw his job as achieving rapid economic recovery. Rather than probing alternative means of organizing and ordering a complex technological society, Roosevelt vigorously employed the power

Unemployed men. *Brown Brothers*

of the executive in a not-always successful or coherent search for prosperity. The result of his efforts was an ever-chaotic, frequently unpredictable, and sometimes contradictory set of programs. The New Deal ultimately assured economic security for the upper two-thirds of society and erected institutional barriers against further economic collapse. It brought the welfare state to America while preserving the traditional values of a capitalist economy and a democratic political system. At a time when economic disaster forced some nations of the world to abandon one or both of these latter institutions, FDR's achievement was not small.

THE HUNDRED DAYS

Moving on a broad front during the first one hundred days of FDR's administration, the New Dealers attempted to revive the confidence of both businessmen and consumers and to stimulate growth in all phases of the economy. They hoped to restore the cycle of mass production and mass consumption, the basis of prosperity during the twenties.

The chaotic banking system demanded immediate attention. State decrees had already closed banks in most areas, and Roosevelt quickly dramatized his leadership by declaring a national bank "holiday," a move affecting only eight additional states. The holiday, together with a banking bill rushed through Congress in emergency session, set the style for the early New Deal. FDR's inaugural address had contained tough talk about driving money changers from the temples, but the suspicion that he meant nationalization of banks, a step some advisors urged, proved illusory. Large banking interests drafted much of the Emergency Banking Relief Act, which extended governmental aid to existing financial institutions. A familiar Roosevelt pattern emerged—extravagant rhetoric followed by much less radical action. Congressmen shouted approval of the measure even before a copy of the final bill appeared, and the act itself gave the executive branch complete authority over the movement of gold. The bank holiday, the essentially conservative legislation, and FDR's soothing assurances restored faith in the banking structure.

During the rest of the "Hundred Days," FDR offered a bewildering array of programs. The Civilian Conservation Corps (CCC), a personal favorite of the president, paid young men to work on forest and other reclamation projects. The Public Works Administration (PWA), administered by Secretary of Interior Harold Ickes, financed a variety of programs to create fresh job opportunities across the country. And more grants went to the states for relief programs.

FDR also launched a broad experiment in regional planning in the six-hundred-mile-long Tennessee Valley. During the 1920s Senator George Norris of Nebraska had attempted to introduce direct govern-

George Bellows, *Dempsey and Firpo*, 1924.
Collection of Whitney Museum of American Art

Buster Brown. *Sy Seidman*

Sailboats with the John Hancock Center in Chicago in the background.
Wide World Photos

mental development of the area, but not until the early New Deal did such a project come to fruition. The Tennessee Valley Authority (TVA) built fifteen dams, providing government-owned electric power plants and flood control. Although it also produced phosphate fertilizers, sponsored innovative farming techniques, and encouraged new business enterprises, low-cost power remained TVA's best-known function. Serving as a yardstick by which the government could measure private-utility rates, TVA drove down the price of electricity throughout the area.

The New Deal also tried to eliminate or at least minimize some of the risks which capitalism imposed on the average citizen. The Federal Deposit Insurance Corporation (FDIC) made the federal government ultimate insurer of deposits (up to five thousand dollars) in savings institutions. The Securities Exchange Act required companies to disclose information about all stocks and bonds sold on the market and created the Securities and Exchange Commission (SEC) to protect investors from fraudulent practices. The Home Owners Loan Act authorized a federal agency to rescue property owners from foreclosure, and farmers received similar assistance from the Farm Credit Administration. In less than two years the government refinanced about one-fifth of home and farm mortgages. Measures such as these offered immediate relief and some promise of future security; but the New Deal's main hopes for lasting recovery rested upon its agricultural program and its most sweeping measure, the National Industrial Recovery Act.

The Line Storm, John Steuart Curry. *New York Public Library*

Mrs. Perkins. *Wide World*

The AAA and NRA New Dealers tried to solve the perennial agricultural dilemma of surpluses and low prices. After resorting to the unpopular expedients of destroying crops and slaughtering baby pigs in order to boost farm prices, they turned to the less controversial method of achieving the same end through acreage reduction. Under the first Agricultural Adjustment Act the government, through the Agricultural Adjustment Administration (AAA), paid producers of several basic commodities to limit the number of acres under cultivation. A "processing tax"—including a levy on the ginning of cotton, for example—provided the revenue for the program.

The National Industrial Recovery Act (NIRA), the New Dealers' trump card in their showdown with the Great Depression, was the most comprehensive program enacted during the Hundred Days. Section 7a of this act guaranteed labor union members the right to collective bargaining and took a tentative step toward making the federal government a referee in labor-management disputes. The act authorized industrywide boards to draft "codes of fair competition" establishing fair wages, working conditions, and prices. The National Recovery Administration (NRA) undertook the unenviable task of securing compliance with the codes and encouraging consumers to support only participating businesses. The NRA adopted the American eagle (colored blue) as its symbol, and employed a bullish army officer, General Hugh Johnson, as its administrator. General Johnson organized a massive NRA parade down New York's Fifth Avenue and continually urged consumers to "buy under the Blue Eagle." "It is the women in the home—and not soldiers in uniform— who will this time save the country," he proclaimed. "Housewives will go over the top to as great a victory as the Argonne." Behind the patriotic rhetoric, the measure represented a hardheaded attempt to achieve recovery through a working partnership between large corporate interests and the federal government. Suspending antitrust laws and shelving hallowed pieties about free competition, Roosevelt and his Brains Trust moved toward a planned economy—the type of system so successful during World War I.

Results of
the Hundred Days

The Hundred Days declared total war against the Depression, but Roosevelt and his lieutenants gained only nominal victories. The economy did pick up during early 1934; yet by the spring of 1935 all the indicators revealed only minimal improvements. Unemployment remained high (nearly one-fifth of the labor force), and national income totaled less than in 1931. Many reasons accounted for the disappointing results. Too many programs worked at cross purposes or were simply ineffective. The effort to stimulate buying power through public works projects conflicted with FDR's early commitment to a balanced budget. Acreage reduction failed to decrease crops because farmers withdrew their least productive fields from cultivation and applied more intensive methods to the remaining land. Farm income rose, but the rest of society, including the unemployed and the hard-hit urban laborers, bore the cost in higher food prices.

The failure of government-business cooperation under the NRA was the Roosevelt administration's gravest disappointment. Large corporations dominated formulation of the "codes of fair competition," and the interests of labor, small businessmen, and consumers received little attention. Some of the codes seemed little more than carbon copies of large industries' informal trade agreements drafted during the 1920s. Section 7a of the NIRA proved of limited use to organized labor; businessmen could evade the wage and hour provisions and continued to establish company-dominated unions in violation of the act. Hugh Johnson's blustering façade failed to disguise his incompetence as an administrator. An official investigation, headed by the reformist lawyer Clarence Darrow in 1934, revealed a number of irregularities in the NRA, and Roosevelt secured Johnson's resignation in September. By the time the Supreme Court declared the NIRA unconstitutional in *Schecter* v. *U.S.* (1935), the decision seemed merciful.

Immediate recovery required mutual confidence between Roosevelt and big business, but large capitalists never fully trusted FDR and remained suspicious of governmental meddling in their affairs. The president sometimes gave businessmen reason to doubt his sincerity about cooperation by adopting a self-righteous tone and assailing them for greed and selfishness. The NRA, like other early New Deal programs, neither brought together all groups in the country nor stimulated the economic energy needed to lift the nation out of depression.

THE DIPLOMACY OF ECONOMIC RECOVERY

Roosevelt believed that foreign policy could contribute to domestic recovery, but like the array of programs initiated during the Hundred Days, the jerry-built diplomacy of the early New Deal lacked coherence. Seeking advice from both hard-boiled economic nationalists like Rexford Tugwell and liberal internationalists like Secretary of State Cordell Hull, Roosevelt adopted conflicting means to promote the general goal of prosperity at home.

The London Economic Conference

Before leaving office Hoover had promised United States participation in a world economic conference, and Roosevelt initially seemed willing to cooperate. Proclaiming the importance of stabilizing currencies and trade, FDR appointed Secretary of State Hull head of the United States delegation to the 1933 London meeting. In order to revive world commerce, Hull planned to commit the new administration to lower tariffs. But he was astonished to discover, upon reaching London, that the president had decided not to submit a new tariff bill to Congress. The embarrassed secretary thus "arrived with empty hands," as he phrased it. Although undercutting tariff reform, Roosevelt still appeared to favor stabilization of world currencies in relation to gold. But as the conference progressed, more nationalistic advisors finally convinced Roosevelt that any agreement in London might hamper New Dealers' efforts to manipulate the value of the dollar upward and to stimulate recovery at home. When Raymond Moley, who had superseded the disgruntled Hull in London, agreed to an innocuous joint statement approving currency stabilization, FDR abruptly and testily repudiated the action.

Roosevelt's tactless conduct toward the other participants in the London Economic Conference provoked controversy. His defenders claimed that the nations could never have reached meaningful agreement and that Roosevelt's actions simply provided a convenient scapegoat for failure. They also pointed to the importance of currency flexibility in combating domestic depression and the need for raising, rather than stabilizing, the general level of prices. But critics of Roosevelt viewed the conference as a "lost opportunity." America's resurgent unilateralism, they believed, prevented solving worldwide problems through international action, and the new president's abrupt reversal strengthened the position of

European nationalists who argued that cooperation was futile. On balance, Roosevelt did sacrifice the appearance, if not the reality, of international cooperation for measures he thougt would assist economic recovery at home. In the retrospective light of World War II, his course may seem misguided; considering his own preoccupation with domestic depression, the action appears understandable.

Efforts to encourage exports

Although America's conduct at the London Economic Conference struck a blow at free trade and internationalism, Cordell Hull continued to work for the lowering of tariffs. In a manner of speech which turned *r*'s into *w*'s, the handsome Tennessean repeatedly stressed that a "reciprocal trade agreement program to reduce tariffs" was the only path to lasting world peace. By 1934 he convinced the president that his plan would stimulate domestic recovery by keeping the world open to American exports. In the spring, over the protests of businessmen in protected industries, Roosevelt swung the Democratic Congress behind the Trade Agreements Act of 1934, which allowed him to manipulate tariff duties in exchange for concessions to American exports abroad. Like other New Deal measures, this bill gave the executive branch unprecedented control in an area previously reserved to Congress. Hull busily negotiated tariff agreements with many countries, but the reciprocal trade act proved no spectacular panacea for recovery or harbinger of peace and internationalism.

The desire to stimulate exports likewise influenced Roosevelt's decision to extend recognition to the Soviet Union. The lure of a potentially vast Soviet Russian market, from which nonrecognition had virtually excluded the United States, combined with more favorable attitudes toward the Soviet Union to permit a change in policy. The Depression had called into question America's traditional bias against governmental planning; and businessmen, intellectuals, and policymakers increasingly became intrigued with the efficiency of centralized direction. The purge of Leon Trotsky, who had advocated international revolution, and the triumph of Joseph Stalin, who concentrated primarily on building socialism at home, eroded the USSR's image as an international troublemaker. In fact, American policymakers hoped that accommodation with the Soviet Union might serve world peace by countering Japanese expansion in the Far East. In addition, the widespread default on World War I debts made Russia's refusal to pay, which had been a crucial stumbling block to recognition in the twenties, seem less onerous. In 1933, more than fifteen years after the start of the Russian Revolution, the United States finally extended recognition to the USSR.

Labor unions and businessmen joined anti-imperialist congressmen and editors in urging yet another new direction in our foreign relations. Charging that cheap labor, sugar, cotton, and other products from the Philippines hurt the United States economy, they demanded that immigration and tariff barriers be applied to the islands. The cry to free the Philippines, which American marines had brutally secured a generation earlier, now echoed throughout the United States. In the Tydings-McDuffie Act of 1934, Congress made the islands a semisovereign commonwealth and promised full independence in ten years.

The Good Neighbor Policy . Roosevelt's policy toward Latin America, touted as a new departure termed the "Good Neighbor" policy, actually originated in the Hoover administration. Government officials under Hoover and many businessmen had concluded that military intervention in Latin America brought more ill will than advantages. A leading investment banker, Thomas P. Lamont, remarked that "the theory of collecting debts by gunboats is unrighteous, unworkable, and obsolete." An ounce of good will was worth a pound of gunpowder, and the Depression highlighted the expense of armed occupation. The State Department also felt some embarrassment at strongly denouncing Japanese troops in Manchuria while United States Marines marched around sovereign states of the Caribbean. Shortly before Hoover left office, a memorandum by Undersecretary of State J. Reuben Clark officially repudiated the hated (Theodore) Roosevelt corollary, which had justified military interventions.

The principles of the Clark memorandum met a challenge in the new Democratic administration when political turmoil in Cuba threatened United States strategic and economic interests. In 1933 Hull dispatched Sumner Welles, an austere New England aristocrat who reportedly once laughed at a joke and then, catching himself, murmured: "Pardon me. You amused me." Confident of his judgment and ability, Welles sailed into Havana intending to mediate among the various factions and to set up a new government. But his plan did not go smoothly. When Ramón Grau San Martín gained the presidency and threatened measures which sounded radical to United States sugar interests, Welles urgently requested American military intervention. Roosevelt, however, refused to permit any landing of troops and, as an alternative to occupation, employed the more subtle weapons of nonrecognition and denial of economic assistance. Before Welles returned to Washington, he fanned the ambitions of Colonel Fulgencio Batista, who subsequently overthrew Grau and instituted a conservative regime which lasted until Fidel Castro's revolution in 1959. The United States quickly recognized Batista and solidified his repressive military regime by lowering the sugar duty and abrogating the unpopular Platt amendment.

The Cuban incident illustrated the nature of the Good Neighbor policy. Roosevelt sincerely wished to avoid further military incursions, and the days of American occupation of Caribbean countries were numbered. At the Montevideo conference of 1933 and again at Buenos Aires in 1936, Hull signed pledges formalizing the United States' commitment to nonintervention. Roosevelt dutifully liquidated all American protectorates in the Caribbean. But his actions toward Cuba also indicated that the United States had other, more subtle, means of getting its way. The president's new authority to lower the tariff barriers, combined with creation of the Export-Import Bank—which could extend loans to countries wishing to purchase American products—provided considerable leverage over impoverished Latin American governments. In addition, departing American troops were simply replaced by local militias trained and equipped by the United States. In every ex-protectorate, an oppressive military dictatorship sprang up to maintain the order previously guaranteed by United States Marines. Critics throughout the hemisphere began to suspect that a more accurate catchphrase for Roosevelt's policy was "Good Neighbor of Dictators."

Despite its limitations, the Good Neighbor policy did make some friends in Latin America. When relations with Mexico's Lazaro Cardenas deteriorated, Roosevelt sent a veteran of the Wilson administration, Josephus Daniels, as ambassador to Mexico. Daniel's conciliatory attitude often bordered upon insubordination toward his less flexible superiors in the State Department, but he successfully worked for accommodation over the long-smoldering issue of expropriation of American oil interests. Like other New Deal policies, the Good Neighbor policy was a mixture of expediency and idealism. It represented less a shift in objectives than a tactical change in the traditional policy of increasing the political and economic influence of the United States.

RADICAL ALTERNATIVES

In retrospect, Franklin Roosevelt towers over the politics of the thirties. But in those days other voices, with more sweeping programs and more radical solutions, challenged FDR. From the avowedly fascist Silver Shirts of William Dudley Pelly to the Communist followers of Earl Browder and William Foster, numerous agitators vied for public attention.

One of the earliest and most interesting challenges came out of the past in the person of Upton Sinclair, the muckraking author of *The Jungle* (1906). In 1934 Sinclair deserted the Socialist party and, with the support of unemployed laborers and farmers in southern California, captured the Democratic nomination for governor. Sinclair's utopian program called for converting California's idle factories and untilled farmlands into nonprofit cooperatives. He hoped that state-sponsored enterprises, operating alongside the capitalist system, would not only solve the immediate problem of relief but also demonstrate the superiority of socialism. Calling his program End Poverty in California (EPIC), Sinclair predicted that within a few years the only poor person in the state would be a hermit who voluntarily exiled himself from the cooperative commonwealth. The Roosevelt administration initially gave tacit support to its party's nominee but began to back away when established interests in California, including many party leaders, came out strongly against Sinclair. His gubernatorial chances evaporated in the face of a full-scale media campaign which viciously attacked EPIC as communistic, atheistic, and un-American. Small-time Hollywood actors who could put on an accent or play a "radical foreigner" suddenly found employment posing as Sinclair's "supporters" in campaign "documentaries." By election day the movement had collapsed. The Republican nominee swept to victory and put an end to Sinclair's dream.

Twentieth-century populists from the Great Plains demanded increased attention to farm problems. Representative William Lemke sponsored a bill calling for the national government to supply farmers with all the cash needed to repay their mortgages and to buy back and refinance every farm foreclosed after 1928. When the House, with strong White House urging, rejected Lemke's plan, he became an implacable foe of Roosevelt, eventually leading a third-party movement in 1936. Milo Reno, another veteran of farm radicalism, urged currency inflation, a traditional populist panacea. By the mid-1930s, Reno's Farm Holiday movement demanded that the government guarantee farmers their cost of production and provide greater mortgage relief. In spectacular displays, his followers blocked highways, dumped milk cans along roadways, and forcibly stopped eviction sales. Reno also called for a "farm holiday," a kind of rural general strike, and in 1935 seemed to be contemplating an alliance with Huey Long, the hero of small southern farmers.

Huey Long

Huey Pierce Long was the most enigmatic and certainly the most threatening of FDR's challengers. Raised in the impoverished hill country of northern Louisiana, a breeding ground for populist and socialist ideas, Long parlayed keen intelligence and utter ruthlessness into a mercurial political career. Elected governor at the age of thirty-five, he taxed oil companies' profits and used these revenues (or at least that portion not ending up in his own coffers) to upgrade the life of Louisianans. Even as he provided better schools, free textbooks, and more roads, Long consolidated his political control and ran the state with an iron hand.

In 1930 Long brought his considerable oratorical skills and flashy clothes to Washington and from the floor of the United States Senate began to build a national reputation. An early supporter of Roosevelt, Long quickly broke with the president and, with a slogan borrowed from William Jennings Bryan—"Everyman a King"—championed his "Share-Our-Wealth" program. Long advocated not only a radical redistribution of wealth but a reconstruction of American society. He proposed liquidating large fortunes, allowing no one to hold "more than a few millions of dollars," and redistributing them so that every family would have "a home and the comforts needed for a home, including such things as a radio and an automobile." In addition to this "homestead" idea, Long's most famous proposal, the plan included several other features. The federal government would guarantee everyone as much education, including college and professional training, as his capabilities allowed. Work hours would be regulated in accordance with consumption needs, providing every worker a minimum annual income of between two thousand dollars and twenty-five hundred dollars. The state would handle farm production much as Joseph managed the agricultural system of ancient Egypt, stockpiling grain during the years of plenty to provide for years of famine. When farm warehouses contained enough for current demands and the needs of the near future, farmers could work on public improvement projects or even return to school for a time.

Part buffoon, part demagogue, and at least one part democratic leader, Long attracted a great deal of support. While his associate Gerald L. K. Smith, a spellbinding evangelist (a famous journalist called Smith "the gutsiest and goriest, loudest and lustiest, and deadliest and damndest orator ever heard on this or any other earth"), preached the gospel across the South, Huey the "Kingfish" attracted a national following. More than twenty thousand Share-Our-Wealth clubs sprang up and the organization claimed over 7 million members. Some believed that Long was preparing for a full-scale presidential bid in 1936, but he probably aimed at the 1940 balloting. Roosevelt's political advisors considered Long a dangerous adversary. Then one day after leaving Governor O. K. Allen's office in the skyscraper capital at Baton Rouge (a journalist's observation of Allen: "A leaf blew in his window, he signed it"), as Long strode down the marble corridors an assassin's shot rang out, and Long fell dead. Gerald L. K. Smith tried to keep the movement alive, but bereft of Long's unifying presence, "Share Our Wealth" quickly fizzled.

Huey Long at play

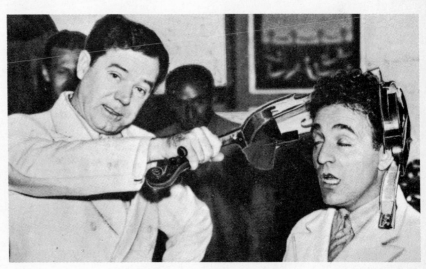

Long's chief rival was the Roman Catholic priest Father Charles Coughlin. Employing a melodic Irish brogue, Father Coughlin broadcast weekly his increasingly political radio messages. Challenging FDR at his own game, the radio preacher became one of the most popular figures on the airwaves. When CBS, alarmed at his growing militancy, dropped his show, Father Coughlin broadcast independently the "Golden Hour of the Little Flower" from the Shrine of the Little Flower in Royal Oak, Michigan. In 1934 his volume of mail exceeded that of the president and Amos 'n' Andy. Forming a movement called the National Union for Social Justice, Father Coughlin advanced a vague, often contradictory list of programs which emphasized inflating the currency with silver and nationalizing the banking system. His popularity, especially among low-income Catholics in middle western cities, led to more and more extravagant rhetoric. Some sermons touched anti-Semitic as well as anti–New Deal themes. Finally, Coughlin openly entered politics as one of the formers of the ill-fated Union party of 1936.

Another founder of the Union party, Dr. Francis E. Townsend, was the most unlikely looking radical of all. This white-haired country doctor, then living in California, spearheaded a sweeping recovery-retirement scheme. The Townsend plan provided that the government give everyone over the age of sixty a monthly pension, the only conditions being that the recipient quit work and spend the entire sum within the month. The program promised to provide relief and security for the elderly, to create jobs for younger workers, and to stimulate general economic recovery through its forced-spending provisions. Many people over sixty embraced the plan with almost religious fervor, and Townsend clubs sprang up throughout the nation singing "Onward Townsend Soldiers." The good doctor's followers formed an important political constituency that not even passage of the Social Security Act could eliminate. Few people questioned the dire need of the nation's elderly, but the program's detractors correctly pointed out that the monthly payments would have eaten up over half the federal government's income and supported only about 10 percent of the population. Even Dr. Townsend's best economic minds stumbled over the problem of financing his plan.

None of these figures achieved his hopes for personal power, and their movements had little lasting impact. Some peddled inflated oratory rather than serious programs; others sounded ugly strains of racism. Dr. Townsend's right-hand man viewed the old people's campaign as an opportunity to turn a quick buck, and Milo Reno referred to the New Deal as the Jew Deal. But all of the agitation should not be dismissed as the work of demagogues or cranks. Despite his great appeal, Franklin Roosevelt had failed to win his war against the Depression, and the despair of 1933 became anger and frustration by 1935. The proposals of Long, Coughlin, and others indicated deep-seated discontent and growing pressure for more radical measures. The popularity of unusual programs which seemed to promise social justice for the common man clearly reflected a widespread antibusiness sentiment.

Carefully gauging the political winds, Roosevelt after 1935 abandoned phrases about cooperation with the business community. The president's harsh campaign attacks on "economic royalists" signaled no movement toward a government takeover of the economy or toward any significant redistribution of the nation's wealth, but they did blunt the radical challenge. Rather than destroying or revolutionizing the old order, Roosevelt offered a series of measures designed, through greater government intervention, to remedy the grossest inequities of the capitalist order. The New Deal's legacy proved not to be socialism or fascism but an Americanized version of the capitalist welfare state.

THE WELFARE STATE

By the spring of 1935 Roosevelt confronted a number of difficulties. The economic picture appeared brighter than two years earlier, but New Deal programs had not stimulated enough recovery to forestall attacks from both the Left and the Right. A mixed group of radical spokesmen demanded that FDR translate his tough talk into positive action against giant capitalists. On the other side, corporate interests were disillusioned and not a little frightened. The American Liberty League, a pressure group dominated by leading industrialists, launched a full-scale assault against almost every New Deal measure.

Rising discontent, failure of the NRA, and the elusiveness of economic recovery might have deterred and embittered a person of less confidence and optimism, but Roosevelt began searching for other ways to meet the challenge. In June 1935, as congressmen prepared to escape the humid Washington summer, the president demanded that the lawmakers act on a series of brand-new measures, including greater relief expenditures, labor legislation, a tax bill, and Social Security. His message to Congress sounded what some historians call "The Second New Deal," signifying a fundamental philosophical shift toward smashing large economic units, and what others term "the Second Hundred Days," indicating another sudden rush of legislative action. The second phrase seems more accurate. Roosevelt never established clear-cut ideological guidelines, and the bills coming out of Congress and the White House lacked any unifying concept. If a pattern emerged from the new acts it was that of a welfare state: a series of government programs designed to protect some of the groups and individuals who could not adequately fend for themselves in a capitalistic society.

The idea was not new. Bismark's Germany began such a program in the late nineteenth century, and the British Liberal party of Lloyd George implemented a similar policy between 1906 and 1914. Few Americans maintained that the national government bore no responsibility for its citizens' well-being, but reasonable men could differ over how far its jurisdiction extended. Rigid ideologues maintained that greater *federal* charity and protection would destroy individual initiative, sap moral vitality, and destroy the political independence necessary for democratic government. But recovery from the Depression (and the political fortunes of Roosevelt and his party) seemed to require a greater extension of national power, and after 1935 FDR began to graft a welfare state onto a market economy.

Welfare measures

To aid unemployed workers and to boost the economy in general, Congress granted Roosevelt's request for much larger relief expenditures. Almost $5 billion, a sum totaling over half the 1936 federal budget, went mostly to Harry Hopkins's Works Progress Administration (WPA), which financed a variety of conservation and public works programs. In addition to the much-caricatured leaf-raking and ditch-digging jobs, Hopkins's agency employed millions of workers building bridges, post offices, city halls, and local recreation centers. The vast infusion of national revenues, in the absence of large business investments or a high level of consumer spending, effectively stimulated the economy.

The Social Security Act of 1935 created a complex system of income maintenance for people facing financial disaster. In addition to

Percent of National Wealth
held by Richest 1%, 1922–1956

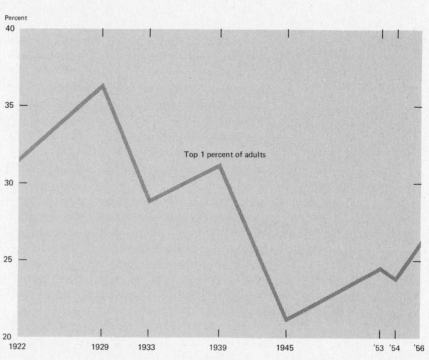

Reprinted by permission of National Bureau of Economic Research, Inc.

the well-known retirement benefits, the law extended aid to dependent children, assistance to the blind, and money for unemployment payments by state and local governments. Social Security, a major pillar of the welfare state, suffered from significant limitations. Financed largely through payroll taxes, it reduced already-slim take-home salaries and exempted many workers, including agricultural laborers and most public employees. Nevertheless, it did place an economic floor under a sizeable portion of the population and was probably the most popular of all federal programs.

Another New Deal measure of 1935, the so-called Wealth Tax, attempted to shift the federal revenue burden to persons whose income and accumulated wealth enabled them to pay most easily. Roosevelt proposed increased inheritance taxes, gift taxes, and steeply graduated levies on corporations and large individual incomes. The program raised a tempest among the wealthy, and Congress pared down some of the bill's features, rendering it ineffective in redistributing wealth or in tapping many new sources of revenue. Despite its limitations, the act did establish a precedent for government action affecting income redistribution.

Several other significant pieces of legislation came during the Second Hundred Days. The Public Utilities Holding Company Act authorized the Securities and Exchange Commission to break up monopolistic utility companies. The Banking Act of 1935 strengthened the Federal Reserve System, giving a central Board of Governors greater control over regional banks, and increased federal authority over currency matters. Establishment of the Rural Electrification Administration (REA) created a government agency offering low-interest loans to nonprofit power cooperatives in farm areas. Since private electrical lines then reached only one out of every ten farms, the REA brought rural life into the twentieth century. Electricity and running water, amenities taken for granted in urban America, finally became realities on the farm.

In these and other laws FDR and Congress hammered out the basis of the modern American welfare state. Other presidents and Congresses have added bits and pieces, but the New Deal's assertion of the national government's responsibility for the well-being of citizens remains unchallenged.

Later New Deal measures expanded the welfare programs. Housing legislation of the early thirties had simply guaranteed residential mortgages, but in 1937 Roosevelt finally supported creation of the United States Housing Authority (USHA), a federal corporation authorized to construct low-cost units. The USHA completed only a few complexes before 1941, and, like other well-intentioned New Deal ventures, it promised considerably more than it delivered. The Fair Employment Standards Act of 1938 established minimum wages and maximum hours for employees in interstate businesses. The law contained numerous exemptions and provided a minimum rate of only forty cents per hour, but it did carry forward the New Deal's commitment to its blue-collar constituency. Finally, the Agricultural Adjustment Act of 1938 brought together and updated a number of farm programs. This second AAA relied upon broader controls over production and higher price supports for basic commodities. Although often revised and augmented in the direction of greater reliance upon acreage retirement (the soil bank), the second AAA remained the heart of the government's farm program into the 1970s.

The New Deal and Labor

The New Deal came out fully behind organized labor in 1935. For several years Senator Robert F. Wagner of New York had campaigned, without White House support, for a new federal act protecting labor unions, and in the spring of 1935 FDR finally endorsed the crusade. Signed into law in July, the National Labor Relations Act (the Wagner Act) guaranteed workers in interstate businesses the right to unionize and to bargain collectively through their own representatives. A National Labor Relations Board (NLRB) was created to enforce the act's provisions and to prevent management from engaging in a number of "unfair" labor practices, such as establishing their own company-dominated unions.

Enactment of the NLRA coincided with a great expansion of labor unions. The American Federation of Labor's long-standing commitment to trade unionism grew increasingly less tenable in a complex industrial economy. Dissidents within the AFL urged formation of unions encompassing all laborers, regardless of trade, in a specific industry. By 1935 the Committee for Industrial Organization (which later became the Congress of Industrial Organizations, CIO), led by unionists such as crusty John L. Lewis of the United Mine Workers and David Dubinsky of the International Ladies Garment Workers, split off from the parent AFL. The CIO chose the auto industry as one of its first targets. Section 7a of the NRA had already stimulated some unionization there, and CIO organizers, building upon this foundation and employing the new tactic of the sit-down strike, won significant victories against General Motors and Chrysler in 1937. Shortly after GM came to terms, another industrial giant, United States Steel, capitulated without a fight. Several "Little Steel" companies refused to settle, provoking a violent Memorial Day confrontation at Republic Steel's Chicago plant. But by the outbreak of World War II, organized labor's new militancy, together with the Wagner Act, resulted in unionization of most major industries.

Election of 1936

The welfare state proved an immediate political success in the presidential election of 1936. The Republican candidate, Governor Alfred M. Landon of Kansas, offered solid progressive credentials extending back to the Bull Moose days of Teddy Roosevelt. Hesitant to attack New

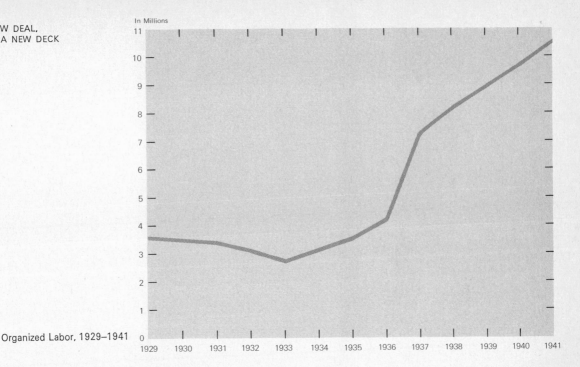

In Millions

Organized Labor, 1929–1941

Deal measures too vehemently, the colorless Landon did little more than promise to administer them more efficiently. A rag-tag third party headed by Congressman William Lemke brought together many of the remnants of FDR's radical opposition. Father Coughlin, Dr. Townsend, and Gerald L. K. Smith backed the Union party, but without the magnetism of the fallen Huey Long and undercut by New Deal welfare measures the party drew less than a million votes. Roosevelt won a smashing victory, driving the Republican party back to the two lone bastions of Maine and Vermont, the only states Landon carried against the president. Roosevelt's Democratic bandwagon also rolled successfully through congressional districts. When the new Congress convened, only nineteen members of the GOP sat in the Senate and 197 in the House of Representatives.

THE WANING OF THE NEW DEAL

The electoral landslide of 1936 gave FDR an overwhelming popular mandate and provided him with a solid working majority in both houses of Congress. The November victory marked the height of his political strength, but events soon conspired against the president. A head-on collision with the Supreme Court in early 1937 put the first major dent in the New Deal steamroller.

"Nine Old Men"—The Supreme Court of 1935. *Underwood and Underwood*

The court fight From the beginning, the traditionalists on the Supreme Court obstructed Roosevelt's efforts to meet the Depression. A solid bloc of four justices—Willis Van Devanter, James McReynolds, Pierce Butler, and George Sutherland—carried their nineteenth-century judicial and social philosophies into the debate over twentieth-century problems. These aged judges, all in their late seventies, viewed with suspicion any program—state or national—which extended governmental power into areas traditionally reserved for private business decisions. The Four Horsemen, as their critics labeled them, were balanced by another bloc of three justices who generally favored governmental measures to deal with the economic crisis. In the middle sat Chief Justice Charles Evans Hughes, a skilled judicial politician whose views sometimes seemed to fluctuate according to the way the majority of associate justices leaned, and the enigmatic Owen J. Roberts. When Roberts lined up with the traditionalists in 1935 and 1936, the acts underlying a number of key New Deal programs, including the

NRA and the AAA, were declared unconstitutional by the Supreme Court. Speaking for a unanimous bench in the NIRA case, Chief Justice Hughes appeared to lay down an exceedingly narrow view of the national government's authority over economic affairs, causing FDR to fume about the justices' "horse and buggy" interpretation of the Constitution.

The gravest constitutional crisis came over the Court's position toward the New Deal measures enacted in 1935. Justice Roberts's earlier decision invalidating the processing tax of the first AAA and Justice Sutherland's vitriolic opinion striking down an act regulating the coal industry suggested that few pieces of legislation would pass the Court's scrutiny. Needing only to attract the vote of Roberts, the Four Horsemen seemed to constitute a formidable barrier against the popular sentiment expressed in Roosevelt's 1936 landslide.

Buoyed by victory and anxious over the future of his programs, Roosevelt moved against the Court in February 1937. Initially, he avoided a frontal assault in favor of an all too transparent ploy. In a message asking Congress to reorganize the entire federal judiciary, the president argued that due to the justices' advanced years there was a serious backlog of undecided cases. He proposed that Congress allow the executive to appoint as many as six new justices to the Supreme Court if judges over the age of seventy failed to retire. Under the guise of assisting the Court, Roosevelt's plan would have allowed him to add up to six new justices to the Supreme Court and to override the anti–New Deal bloc then threatening such legislation as the Social Security Act.

The "court-packing" scheme raised an immediate furor. The president's opponents—and even some of his Democratic supporters— saw it at a naked political assault upon the Constitution. During congressional hearings on the bill, a string of distinguished witnesses spoke out against the plan and urged representatives to reject any change in the number of Court members. Chief Justice Hughes, whose carefully manicured goatee enhanced his magisterial image, proved to be as resourceful an infighter off the bench as on it. In a letter replying to a query from Senator Burton K. Wheeler, Hughes threw the Court's prestige against Roosevelt without openly entering the fray. Citing the justices' record of speedy decision making, Hughes demolished FDR's claim of a backlog of cases.

Forced to retract earlier justifications, by the spring of 1937 FDR openly admitted that his plan aimed at obtaining a majority of justices favorable to his programs and at reversing the political decisions of the five obstructionists. In effect, Roosevelt challenged the old Federalist idea that the American policy consisted of carefully balanced institutions, the Supreme Court operating to check the excesses of a popular majority. Stripped of rhetoric about crowded dockets and superannuated justices, the court-packing plan appeared as a means of enforcing a popular dictum that the Court should follow election returns, in this case the referendum of 1936. FDR was insisting that the Supreme Court accept his and the Democratic Congress's view of constitutional interpretation and not make their own independent judgment on social and economic questions.

In late March 1937 the plan suffered a serious setback when the Supreme Court upheld a Washington state minimum-wage law almost identical to one it had invalidated only a year before. Owen Roberts, the Court's swing man, sailed back into the pro—New Deal camp, reversing his earlier position. The reasons for Roberts's quick shift are unclear. Apparently he changed his mind sometime after the 1936 elections but before FDR announced his court-packing plan. Quickly labeled as the switch in time to save nine, Roberts's flip-flop in *West Coast Hotel* v. *Parrish* (1937) undercut much of the necessity for Roosevelt's radical assault upon the Court. The *Parrish* decision suggested that the new five-to-four majority might look more favorably upon government regulation of the economy.

Roosevelt continued to push his measure but only met further rebuffs. In May Justice Van Devanter's long-expected retirement gave the president an opportunity to make his first appointment. Following Van Devanter's resignation, the Senate majority in favor of court packing nearly vanished, but Roosevelt still persisted. He had firmly committed his prestige to the fight and had no assurance that Justice Roberts would stay with the New Deal. In addition, the president had long ago promised the first vacancy to Senate Majority Leader Joseph Robinson, a sixty-five-year-old southern conservative whose enthusiasm for innovative programs was less than overwhelming. Assured of his long-coveted judgeship, Robinson kept the Senate in session through the hot summer months, hoping to ram through at least a compromise measure. Suddenly, in mid-July, overworked from leading the floor fight on the bill, Robinson suffered a heart attack and died. His death killed the Court bill.

The "depression" of 1937

The Court fight had scarcely ended when FDR was faced with another challenge—renewed economic depression. In late 1936 and during the first half of the following year, conditions had gradually improved, but in August of 1937 the economy suddenly nose-dived. Business indices plummeted even faster than under Herbert Hoover, and Republicans gleefully labeled it "Roosevelt's depression." By New Year's, the stock market showed a decline of over 40 percent, industrial production slipped by almost one-third, and unemployment rolls lengthened. As prosperity vanished, America's poor once again faced hunger.

What caused the economic downturn? The brief post-1935 prosperity had lacked a solid base. Unemployment stayed high and the important construction industry remained weak. The volume of long-term investment lagged behind short-term commitments because many businessmen questioned Roosevelt's ability to manage the economy. Several government actions which contributed to the downturn indicated that the New Dealers had not yet solved the mysteries of the economic cycle. FDR's attachment to a balanced budget forced a sharp cut in relief expenditures, including termination of the PWA. This contraction of consumer spending coincided with the beginning of Social Security taxes, which further diminished purchasing power. The administration succeeded in simultaneously shaking businessmen's confidence and reducing buyers' ability to purchase goods.

Beset by conflicting advice, FDR vainly searched for a quick solution. Initially blaming the problem on business's reluctance to invest —a "strike of capital," as he called it—the president considered more vigorous antimonopoly actions. But eventually he returned to the path of greater government expenditures, a course which forced him to abandon his predilections for a balanced budget. In 1938 Roosevelt successfully asked Congress for slightly under $4 billion in relief funds, and he revived the PWA and refilled the WPA's job-creating pipeline. This strategy of "priming the pump," which paralleled the theories of the English economist John Maynard Keynes, substituted federal government expenditures for private investment and purchases. By midyear the economy began to catch hold again, and conditions steadily improved through 1939 and 1940, when international dangers produced substantial increases in military spending. Ultimately, the vast outlays during World War II represented a massive government subsidy which finally pushed the economy above pre-1930 levels.

The conservative coalition

Following close upon the Court fight, the depression of 1937 marked another setback for the New Deal. It indicated the essential failure of Roosevelt's programs to restore prosperity and strengthened the hand of the president's critics in government and business. Although voters still supported FDR, they opposed any fundamental extensions of New Deal measures, and the rise of a more substantial congressional opposition soon demonstrated the limits of Roosevelt's power.

The president considered some Democratic congressmen, especially a number of southerners, more troublesome than some Republicans. FDR sought revenge against these Democrats who accepted the New Deal's standard in election years but deserted it during congressional rollcalls. In one of his "fireside chats," he compared his Democratic opponents to the "copperheads" of the Civil War era and threatened to purge the worst traitors in the 1938 off-year elections. Picking several senators, mostly southerners, as his main targets, Roosevelt supported rival Democratic nominees in the state primaries. The move backfired. His intrusion into local politics gave incumbents a good issue; they emphasized their support for the majority of New Deal measures and also asserted their independence from presidential dictation.

Following the attempted "purge" of 1938, the president confronted a sizeable opposition force composed of anti-Roosevelt Democrats and an augmented GOP. This so-called conservative coalition never amounted to a solid bloc—its composition shifted with specific issues—but Roosevelt found it increasingly difficult to push bills through Congress. During the 1939 session, for example, Congress stopped relief appropriations, voted to investigate several New Deal agencies, and narrowly failed to add crippling amendments to the National Labor Relations Act.

In one sense, emergence of a more effective opposition marked a return to normality. Later relations between the executive and legislative branches rarely went as smoothly as during Roosevelt's early years. With the passing of economic crisis, congressmen became less willing to give the president the latitude he enjoyed during his first years in office.

The End of Reform   By 1939 the era of reform had ended. The New Deal's piecemeal approach, held together primarily by Roosevelt's commanding presence and personality, required broad-based support from normally conflicting interests. Once initial recovery began, groups whose stake in the capitalist order once again seemed secure proved reluctant to sanction new measures or to extend existing programs. Although total economic recovery remained elusive, the New Deal became, in effect, the victim of its own partial success. Farm interests, for example, who had received large subsidies from the national government, generally opposed programs designed to aid the urban poor. Southerners remained wary of any proposals which threatened racial control in their region, coming out particularly strong against an antilynching bill.

The New Deal also confronted the traditional American resistance to change. The desperate conditions of 1933–34 supplied the primary impetus for the furious pace of legislative action. The New Deal did not erase old ideas about balanced national budgets, limited federal action, and individual initiative; it proceeded despite them. By the late thirties the economic situation no longer seemed as grave, and businessmen's claims that excessive New Deal interference blocked final recovery seemed more reasonable than they had several years earlier. Even during the 1937 recession, demands for decisive governmental action remained muted. Only in times of great crisis—war, economic disaster, or domestic upheaval—do the majority of Americans demand that their representatives seek bold solutions to basic problems. By 1938 such a time had passed.

THE CULTURE OF DEPRESSION

The Depression confirmed many intellectuals' and writers' estrangement from bourgeois society. During the 1920s they had became increasingly disillusioned with American life; the Sacco-Vanzetti affair crystalized this mood. If the alleged frame-up of two poor Italians destroyed faith in America's political system, the Depression revealed the chimera of capitalism. The collapsing system indiscriminantly dragged people under and trampled them without regard to their own will. Individual action, it seemed, counted for nothing, and the plight of the faceless people brought to life in John Steinbeck's *Grapes of Wrath* seemed to demand collective action. Searching for a solution, many writers shed their "virus of liberalism" and embraced socialism or communism. In 1932 when Communist William Z. Foster ran for president, his endorsements included fifty-three writers and artists, including Sherwood Anderson, John Dos Passos, Lincoln Steffens, Edmund Wilson, Granville Hicks, Sidney Hook, Langston Hughes, and Matthew Josephson.

Among many writers, the infatuation with communism was short-lived. John Dos Passos quarreled with the party in 1934, beginning his swing to the right, and T. S. Eliot, Joseph Wood Krutch, Edmund Wilson, and Sherwood Anderson all became critics by the mid-'30s. Their dissatisfaction stemmed from a distaste for the new form of "proletarian" literature, which seemed to demand that art be the servant of social change and the instrument of massive class upheaval. They found it difficult to reconcile the roles of a serious writer and a social agitator. Choosing the former, they abandoned the politics and the ideologies of collectivisim in favor of individual expression and the pursuit of artistic excellence.

Proletarian literature   Yet proletarian literature set the distinctive tone of the decade. Granville Hicks, dean of the new style, suggested that anything which deserved the name "art" should contain elements of the class struggle and impel the reader to identify with the oppressed, but ultimately victorious, hero. Authors, Hicks proposed, should consider themselves members of the proletariat. The plots of proletarian novels and plays were often as stereotyped as the Horatio Alger fantasies of a previous generation. Heroic workers called a strike against villainous employers; brutal repression illuminated the class struggle; in a glorious moment of conversion, workers perceived the benefits of a collectivist state and triumphantly joined the worldwide proletarian upheaval. The basic plot could be spiced with special effects. In a proletarian stage adaptation of Theodore Dreiser's *American Tragedy*, for example, a loudspeaker periodically droned, "We have given a name to Fate. It is the Economic System."

The playwright Clifford Odets and novelist John Steinbeck were the best practitioners of this style. Odets wrote *Waiting for Lefty* in response to a request for a simple play workers could stage at any meeting place. But his popularity transcended the union halls, reaching to successful Broadway productions. Steinbeck generally avoided crude stereotypes and single-minded economic motivation but still basically adhered to the new art form which emphasized class struggle. The Joad family of *The Grapes of Wrath,* driven from the misery of dusty Oklahoma to a nightmare of unemployment and repression in California, remains a popular symbol of dispossessed people.

Left-wing musicians made a similar effort to blend their art form into the working-class struggle. During the early thirties a group called the Composers Collective tried to create a new proletarian music in which both words and melody would express militancy. "Music is propaganda—always propaganda—and of the most powerful sort," wrote a member of the Collective. Several years later other radical intellectuals began discovering working-class militancy in native American folk music. Activists found a whole new range of songs and folk artists such as "Aunt Molly" Jackson, an organizer for the National Miners Union, and Jim Garland, a miner in the Kentucky coal fields. These agitator-performers sang about America's "common folk" and added their own radical themes to traditional tunes. Jim Garland used the music of "Greenback Dollar" for his attack upon the capitalist system:

> We worked to build this country, mister,
> While you enjoyed a life of ease;
> You've stolen all that we built, mister;
> Now our children starve and freeze.

Edward Hopper, *Gas, 1940. Collection, Museum of Modern Art, New York, Mrs. Simon Guggenheim Fund*

By the end of the decade, the American Left fully embraced the folk music of proletarian minstrels such as Garland, "Aunt Molly," and Woody Guthrie.

Movies While some literary figures and musicians puzzled over the relationship between art and social action, motion picture makers catered to the desires of millions. Nobody reads the proletarian novelists any longer, but the movies of the 1930s remain part of our contemporary culture. Stars who dazzled two earlier generations now awe and entertain a younger group of admirers. W. C. Fields, the Marx brothers, and even John Wayne's early westerns still enjoy both critical and popular acclaim. More than the faded memories of FDR, the now-slightly-blurred images of the great figures of the silver screen provide a link with the past, a reminder of the contrasting moods of the decade of the Depression.

One popular type of movie reflected the hard-boiled exterior of the thirties. Viewers displayed a particular affinity for gangster heroes. James Cagney and Edward G. Robinson often portrayed them, and toward the end of the decade Humphrey Bogart made the role his own. Hardly the Valentino matinee idol, these actors exuded a tough-minded attitude toward life's problems and opportunities. In an age of a fading American dream, Bogart and Cagney represented the survival of the self-made man who, without moralizing or equivocating, lifted himself out of poverty. They portrayed both the cynical opportunist and the eternal humanist. Cagney could push a grapefruit into a troublesome girlfriend's face and weep over his kindly old mother; and Bogart, as a small-time crook on the lam, could furnish the money to straighten a crippled girl's foot. Although the analogy should not be pushed too far, such movies paralleled the New Deal's often opportunistic yet basically humanitarian reaction to the problems of the Depression.

If some movies reflected the hard-boiled tone of the thirties, others offered escape from the problems of the day. The intricately staged musicals of Busby Berkley, with hundreds of chorus girls dancing in perfect harmony, provided hours of beauty and symmetry for people whose lives contained too little of either. The enormously popular *Flash Gordon* serials carried viewers into futuristic struggles between forces of light and darkness for control of sophisticated technology. As the comic-strip hero, bleached-blond former swimming star Buster Crabbe typified the all-American boy, while Charles Middleton as "Ming the Merciless," personified the yellow, red, and almost every other menace who ruled twenty-first-century Mongo. The action-filled "B" Western entranced would-be cowboys all across the country. By the opening reel every Saturday matineegoer could spot his white-hatted, two-gunned hero, be he Ken Maynard, Hopalong Cassidy, or a more obscure wrangler such as "Crash" Corrigan. And no one could miss the outlaw gang — generally led

Count Dracula (Bela Lugosi).
Culver Pictures

"The Mask of Dimitrios" (Sidney Greenstreet and Peter Lorre). *Culver Pictures*

Young John Kennedy, London. *Magnum Photo Inc.*

by smartly dressed lawyers, bankers, or railroad men who threatened the decent people of the community. Whether riding past the same clump of trees, leaping off the same cliff, or firing scores of shots without reloading, the good guy invariably survived the most bloodless violence ever put on film.

THE LIMITS OF THE NEW DEAL

The New Deal offered the most to Americans whose income and accumulated wealth placed them in approximately the upper two-thirds to three-fourths of the economic structure. For those at the very top, it eventually revived business prosperity without any radical redistribution of vested wealth or serious interference with the capitalist economy. Through more vigorous governmental intervention, the national administration became the promoter of economic growth and the agency charged with preventing any repetition of the Great Depression. For middle- and lower-income groups, the New Deal offered a variety of programs which, in addition to promoting general prosperity, guaranteed minimum wages, encouraged unionization, financed home construction, underwrote farm income, and provided support for the aged and temporarily unemployed. Roosevelt thus extended concrete assistance to meet the exigencies of the thirties and established some degree of insurance against future disasters.

Creation of a welfare state represented no small accomplishment, but when the pace of domestic change slowed in the late 1930s, much remained undone. In addition to a period of recovery and reform, the decade was also a time of unfullfilled hopes and all-too-limited advances.

One of the New Deal's most obvious shortcomings was the failure to deal with the hard-core poverty infecting many areas of the country. In his 1937 inaugural FDR himself promised to meet the needs of the one-third of Americans who remained ill-clothed, ill-housed, and ill-fed. All too often, though, opposition from more powerful and better-organized political and economic interests frustrated efforts to aid the very poor. As the nation would discover during the early 1960s, three decades of federal welfare programs still left millions of needy people largely unassisted. Appalachia, the black belts in the south, and urban ghettoes serve as a bitter reminder of the limits of liberalism in the United States.

Blacks in the great depression The New Deal's relationship to black people illustrated both the positive impact and the shortcomings of reform measures. Already on the bottom of the socioeconomic ladder, black workers were hit particularly hard by the Depression. Roosevelt himself developed a strong appeal to black voters, reversing traditional voting patterns. Eleanor Roosevelt served as the president's unofficial emissary to blacks, and she displayed a genuine desire to deal with America's long-standing racial dilemma.

But the New Deal had no consistent policy to meet the special problems of black Americans. Each bureau followed its own approach, and assistance varied according to the interest and concern of the persons in charge. Harold Ickes's PWA and Harry Hopkins's WPA supplied badly needed jobs and showed sensitivity to the plight of black workers. After some hesitation, Hopkins issued a general ban against discriminatory hiring practices, and during the late thirties and early forties blacks comprised a sizeable percentage of the WPA work rosters. But some recovery programs actually worked against the interests of blacks. Payments in exchange for restriction of cotton acreage reduced the number of black laborers and sharecroppers required on southern plantations, and AAA officials failed to prevent white landlords from retaining funds intended for black tenants. As long as many unions maintained segregation, federal legislation advancing the rights of organized labor rebounded against black workers. In fact, growing unionization and minimum-wage laws often resulted in layoffs of blacks. And always mindful of southern Democratic support, many New Dealers proved reluctant to overturn Jim Crow practices on federal projects. On some WPA sites black and white laborers drank from segregated buckets with separate dippers.

The New Deal's ambivalent record divided the leadership of the black movement. Old-line NAACP leaders, especially Secretary Walter White, faced challenges from younger and more militant spokesmen. The "young Turks," who included Ralph Bunche and sociologist E. Franklin Frazier, wanted the NAACP to modify its traditional preoccupation with

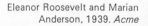

Eleanor Roosevelt and Marian Anderson, 1939. *Acme*

civil and political rights and exert greater pressure for basic economic assistance to blacks. Being able to sit front and center in a desegregated theater, dissidents reasoned, meant little to a black family lacking money for a decent meal. Some militant NAACP members encouraged black-white cooperation through the more egalitarian CIO unions and advocated a class-based drive for a greater share in the capitalist economy. Breaking completely from the organization he had helped to create, the historian and writer W. E. B. Du Bois urged blacks to avoid white-owned businesses and to establish nonprofit cooperatives within their own communities. Dominated by the black elite and closely tied to white philan-throphists, the NAACP rejected such new directions and maintained its traditional crusade against legal discrimination, placing renewed emphasis upon a national antilynching law. Without a Marcus Garvey to ignite the masses, most blacks remained unorganized and received limited benefits from the New Deal.

The limits of planning   The absence of any program or guidelines to deal with racial questions reflected a more general failure of the New Deal—the lack of coherent planning and organization to meet fundamental problems. Some members of the administration—particularly Rexford Guy Tugwell, who served in a number of capacities—urged more attention to planned development, but such efforts ran into numerous constitutional, political, and fiscal difficulties. Several outstanding examples of frustrated programs—such as the broad regional aims of the Tennessee Valley Authority and the Resettlement Administration's "greenbelt" towns for low-income families—illustrate the opportunities lost.

TVA's dams reduced the danger of floods, and its generators brought billions of kilowatts to the valley's residents. But the broader hopes of TVA's major architect, Arthur Morgan, became subordinated to the fight to extend public power. Morgan hoped that TVA would provide the basis for a general rehabilitation of the region—planned communities, folk-art programs, and new industries. Morgan's vision, however, simply cost too much money and presented too many political obstacles. Cheaper electrical rates offered a less ambitious yet politically attainable goal.

The history of the Resettlement Administration offers another example of lofty ideals and less grandiose accomplishments. Established in 1935 and headed by the controversial Tugwell, the agency provided loans and assistance to poor farmers untouched by other programs. The RA also ran a number of camps for migratory workers in California. Tugwell's most ambitious endeavor called for governmental construction of planned communities to resettle poor families near metropolitan areas but outside the teeming slums. Suburban projects, it was believed, would provide both low-cost housing and grassy spaces generally available only to the more affluent. The back-to-nature bias of the program raised hopes that the towns' residents would develop a type of participatory democracy and a vigorous communitarian spirit. With his own agrarian preferences, Roosevelt showed a great interest in the greenbelt towns, but the planners' dreams soon ran into hard political and economic realities. Local politicians, land developers, and wealthy suburbanites comprised a complicated pattern of vested interests who blocked land acquisition. The extensive federal direction associated with the communities allowed critics to label them as communistic and un-American. Tugwell's radical image lent credence to such charges, and the program never proceeded beyond one town each in Maryland, Wisconsin, and Ohio. This attempt to reserve the influx of the poor into decaying central cities and to establish a more decentralized pattern of settlement thus ended in failure.

Any assessment of the New Deal depends upon the writer's position and perspective. Persons who benefited from New Deal measures display a fierce loyalty to Roosevelt and deeply resent almost any criticism of his presidency. Republican businessmen who traditionally considered FDR and his "alphabet agencies" the height of Democratic "socialism" may now see how his essentially conservative measures aided many enterprises and shored up the entire capitalist structure. Most historians, generally Democrats, focus upon Roosevelt's antibusiness rhetoric and humanitarian goals, concluding that he was the epitome of a progressive reformer. Recent events have revealed the limitations and flaws inherent in Roosevelt's programs—particularly the failure to develop any permanent apparatus for dealing with the problem of poverty—and a younger generation of interpreters often fault the restricted vision and halfway solutions of the 1930s.

Recognizing the complexity and subjectiveness of many judgments, several general conclusions still emerge. Most obviously, FDR and his aides, although averting total collapse and providing the beginnings of economic revival and a welfare state, never achieved real recovery until the massive government spending during World War II underwrote greater production and fuller employment. The New Deal provided security for a sizeable part of the population, but it also missed a number of opportunities to do more and preserved far more of the economic system than it transformed. The 1930s truly represented a "new deal, not a new deck," for the American people.

A RESURGENT NATIONALISM

The worldwide economic crisis of the thirties destroyed the internationalist spirit of the twenties. Attempts to cope with domestic problems encouraged expansionist adventures in Germany, Italy, and Japan and withdrawal from world concerns in England, France, and the United States. The resurgent nationalism of the Depression decade washed away collective-security arrangements and crested in another world war, leaving the debris of violated treaties and broken promises in its wake.

In the United States, economic stringency led to a retreat from formal empire, a concentration upon trade expansion, and a sentiment favoring political isolationism and nonentanglement. The desire to remain aloof from foreign wars had existed throughout the twenties, but the outbreak of fighting in Manchuria and Italy's bellicose gestures toward Ethiopia deepened American determination to avoid distant conflicts. Reflecting the growing isolationist mood, Congress in early 1935 soundly defeated Roosevelt's proposal to join the World Court. During the debate, a Minnesota senator who feared that membership in the international body would impair American sovereignty shouted, "To hell with Europe and the rest of those nations." As a means of deterring invasions and preserving world peace, Roosevelt requested congressional authority to institute an arms embargo against aggressors. Instead, isolationist senators passed a bill requiring that any embargo apply equally to all belligerents. They hoped that this Neutrality Act of 1935 would preserve impartiality and preclude involvement in foreign disputes.

As Americans turned inward, the Italian dictator Benito Mussolini sought to alleviate his country's domestic ills by enlarging its African empire. In October 1935 his armies marched into Ethiopia, a proud

Lou Gehrig and Babe Ruth, 1939

kingdom which had never succumbed to colonialist rule. Isolationists praised Roosevelt for quickly invoking the Neutrality Act, but the president intended that the "impartial" arms embargo work primarily against Italy, a country with which the United States normally traded. Roosevelt next called for a "moral embargo" on all strategic commodities. In this way, United States policy paralleled the League of Nations's recommendation of economic sanctions against the aggressor. But the height of the Depression proved a poor time to expect voluntary curtailment of exports. In the end, neither the United States nor members of the League enforced an effective boycott, and each lamely blamed the other for failure to halt aggression. Italy's invasion, like Japan's incursion a few years earlier, met nothing more than worldwide moral outrage.

A reappraisal of America's role in World War I provided support for the policy of insularity. A new school of revisionist historians contended that Americans in 1917 had been tricked into a war in which they had little national interest. According to this interpretation, Wilson and his advisors were never neutral and steered the United States into belligerency because of their own sympathy for England. Moreover, by permitting American bankers and munition makers to incur heavy debts to Allied nations, the government had encouraged an economic tie that made neutrality virtually impossible. Walter Millis's influential *Road to War* (1935), a Book-of-the-Month Club selection, was perhaps the most scholarly of the revisionist works, but more sensationalist treatments bore such titles as *Blood and Profits* and *Merchants of Death*. In a decade of high unemployment and business collapse, Americans readily accepted the proposition that an unholy alliance between bankers and businessmen had plunged the nation into the world war. Between 1934 and 1936, a Senate investigating committee headed by Republican Gerald Nye of North Dakota publicized sensational exposés of businessmen who profited from arms races and war. The Nye committee's reports transformed the image of the crusade to save the world for democracy into an ignominious intrigue to fill the coffers of unscrupulous businessmen. The "munition makers' conspiracy" became an easy explanation for world turmoil, and decent Americans resolved never again to be maneuvered into foreign quarrels or to sacrifice their sons for profiteers.

The revisionist interpretation of World War I and the Nye committee's findings briefly redeemed Germany. The picture of the hated Hun softened into one of an unfortunate victim of an unjust peace. If Adolf Hitler's anti-Semitism and militarism alarmed Americans, his desire to reunite German-speaking peoples and his repudiation of the Versailles settlement seemed understandable. Late in 1933, following the virtual collapse of a World Disarmament Conference in Geneva, Hitler terminated Germany's eight-year participation in the League of Nations and began to rearm in contravention of the Versailles treaty. Quickly boosting military expenditures by 90 percent, he restored compulsory military service, built an air force, and planned an army that would out-number France's. In March 1936 Nazi troops reoccupied the strategic Rhineland, in further violation of the Versailles agreement. Fascist armies were on the move, but their threat seemed distant to most Americans and did not yet impair vital economic or strategic interests.

The Spanish Civil War   A few months after Hitler's legions goosestepped into the Rhineland, civil war broke out in Spain, providing further experience for the military machines of Hitler and Mussolini. Lending sophisticated weaponry and thousands of soldiers, the two fascist leaders supported the uprising of General Francisco Franco, who promised to institute a fascist state and restore traditionalism on the Iberian penninsula. Loyalist (republican) forces appealed to the world for assistance in crushing the rebellion, but only the Soviet Union sent aid. Britain, France, and the United States, fearful that the conflict might spread if more foreign powers took sides, adopted policies of nonintervention. The United States Congress extended the arms embargo to cover civil wars, an act which departed from traditional practice by denying weapons to legitimate governments as well as to rebels. Gradually Franco's superior fire-power wore down the Loyalists, and the ultranationalist, conservative regime which would govern Spain into the 1970s assumed power.

The Spanish Civil War provoked some Americans to revaluate the policy of nonentanglement. Catholic groups passionately backed Franco, whom they viewed as a strong anti-Communist fighting to maintain religion and order. Many left-wing American intellectuals took up the Loyalists as a *cause célèbre*. Disillusioned with the depression-riddled capitalist system and fearful of the repressive and demagogic fascist regimes, young writers and artists fervently supported the Soviet-organized international brigades which assisted the republicans in Spain. Caught up in the romanticism of the crusade, cadres of Americans such as the "Abraham Lincoln Brigade" crossed the Atlantic. Many of these men died cursing their country for its indifference to the plight of free Spain.

Aggression in the   As Germany and Italy carved out spheres of influence, Japan continued
Far East and Europe   its expansion. The island nation, confronted with population pressures and a shortage of raw materials, followed its longing glances toward the vast Chinese mainland with an invading army. In the summer of 1937, following an exchange of shots between Chinese and Japanese troops stationed near the Marco Polo Bridge, Japanese columns swooped southward through Peking, Shanghai, Nanking, and Shantung. The weak Nationalist government led by Chiang Kai-shek failed to halt the invaders and retreated to the interior city of Chungking, leaving the important seaports to the enemy. Japan announced a plan for an East Asian Co-Prosperity Sphere and demanded that China accept a position of political and economic subserviency.

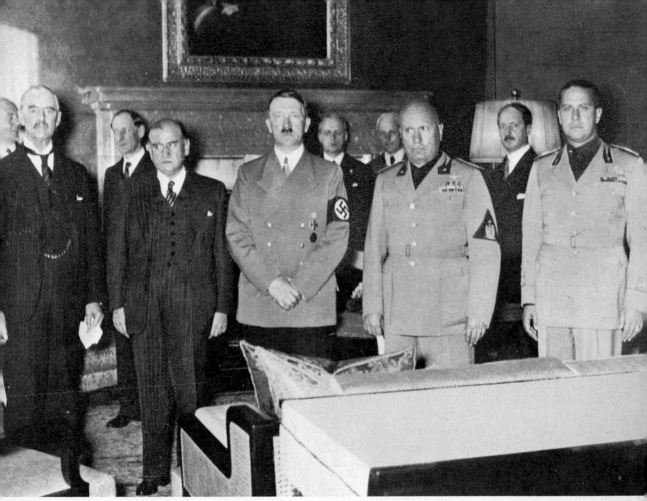

Munich. *Wide World*

The attack against China and the collapse of the Washington Treaty agreements stunned many Americans, but events in Europe distracted them from Far Eastern problems. Hitler and Mussolini formalized their friendship into an Axis; Italy withdrew from the League; and in mid-1938 Hitler proclaimed Austria as part of the Third Reich. While Franco triumphed in Spain, Hitler announced his intention to annex the Sudetenland, a portion of Czechoslovakia which contained 3½ million Germans. Hitler's new move threatened a direct confrontation with France and Britain. But these countries, beset by political instability, economic trouble, and military inadequacies, were unprepared for a showdown. Desperately wanting peace, British and French leaders hoped that Hitler's desire for *Lebensraum* ("living space") would be appeased once he gained the Sudeten territroy. Meeting Hitler at Munich in September 1938, they agreed to German occupation of the Sudetenland, and Hitler assured them he would seek no more territory.

561

The Munich settlement soon joined the collective-security structure of the twenties on the rubbish pile of false hopes. Within the next year, Germany annexed the rest of Czechoslovakia, made demands on Poland and Lithuania, formed a military alliance with Italy, and secured its eastern flank by signing a nonaggression pact with the Soviet Union. On September 1, 1939, German troops stormed into Poland. England and France drew the line at further appeasement, and the world plunged into the second major war of the century.

The American response to the kaleidoscopic events preceding the invasion of Poland had been ambiguous and ineffectual. A gap of perception widened between the White House and Congress, while Americans stood, leaderless and vaguely bewildered, wishing the eastern hemisphere would just go away. In 1937 Roosevelt had murmured some cautious phases about "quarantining" aggressors, but Congress just passed another Neutrality Act aimed at preserving noninvolvement. When the president asked for funds to develop naval bases in the Pacific, the House recoiled for fear of provoking Japan. Roosevelt desperately pressed for modification of the Neutrality Act, but many congressmen became convinced that he, like Wilson, was maneuvering the country into an alliance with Britain and France which would drag the country into a remote war. Official dispatches from Europe urging a stronger stand and predicting war flooded the State Department; yet William Borah, chairman of the Senate Foreign Relations Committee, roared that he possessed better sources of information and did not believe a crisis was imminent.

The economic depression and rising nationalism of the thirties resulted in cycles of aggression and appeasement which would haunt postwar diplomats and fascinate historians. Searching for an explanation of appeasement, analysts have flung indictments in all directions. Some assign almost total responsibility to Britain and France, portraying the United States as an innocent bystander. Others blame the United States' irresponsible isolationism, pointing out that Britain and France lacked the military and economic might to make a strong stand wthout American cooperation. Most would probably agree that the American desire for nonentanglement, if not the direct cause of appeasement, was certainly its handmaiden.

Looking back on what now seems a clear course of open-ended aggression, postwar historians and policymakers have generally viewed negotiations such as the Munich Conference as foolish policies which whetted expansionists' appetites rather than satisfying them. And just as the misapplied historical lesson of World War I guided an unfortunate course of noninvolvement during the thirties, the disastrous consequences of appeasement contributed to a postwar orthodoxy of inflexibility. After Munich, compromise became associated with appeasement and war; hard-line stands came to characterize postwar diplomacy regardless of their appropriateness. Perhaps the real significance of the thirties lies not in determining who was responsible for appeasement or why, but in the revelation that Americans in the twentieth century have persistently tried to relive and redeem past mistakes in present situations. Ghosts of previous failures—a "munitions makers' conspiracy" or a "Munich"—have substituted for policies based upon contemporary realities.

RADIO

The decade of the depression marked radio's emergence as a truly mass medium. During the twenties many people considered radio a novelty : they tinkered with primitive crystal sets, searching for distant stations through a bewildering maze of signals. Just before the Depression the national government regulated wireless transmissions—assigning wavelengths and setting power levels for individual station—and manufacturers reduced the size, complexity, and cost of radio receivers. Between 1930 and 1940 the number of homes with sets more than doubled, and business found the medium an effective means of reaching large numbers of people. Advertisers, euphemistically known as "sponsors," began presenting a wide variety of programs, many of them beamed nationwide over the two major networks, NBC and CBS. Mass audiences meant higher-priced entertainers. Bob Hope, Bing Crosby, and Jack Benny replaced such lesser-known radio acts as the "Cliquot Club Eskimos."

Radio offered a wide range of attractions, but market demands dominated programming tastes. Most sponsors measured artistic value by ability to attract listeners and sell products. Certain subjects, particularly sex, were taboo. A mildly suggestive sketch involving Mae West and a wooden dummy, Charley McCarthy, outraged enough people so that Miss West's voice was subsequently banned from the airwaves. Some series attracted millions of loyal fans. Two white vaudevillians created a show based upon black characters : "Amos 'n' Andy" remained on the air for more than thirty years, burlesquing black lives for largely white audiences. "Soap operas," involving the exciting careers and carefully sanitized loves of larger-than-life heroines, spiced housewives' daily routines. A Detroit entrepreneur, George Trendle, invented "The Lone Ranger," a nondrinking, noncursing, nonkilling hero who quickly rivaled Saturday matinee cowboys for juvenile acclaim. Following this success, Trendle introduced "The Green Hornet" and "Sergeant Preston of the Yukon" (and his lead dog "Yukon King"), two other nightly favorites that ran for almost twenty years.

Radio did offer a limited amount of more serious entertainment. CBS carried the New York Philharmonic, and NBC the Metropolitan Opera on Saturday afternoon. Later in the decade NBC formed its own symphony orchestra, a distinguished group of musicians under the direction of Arturo Toscanini. Several theater-radio programs offered top-name talent—such as Charles Laughton, Clark Gable, and Cary Grant—in first-rate productions. Other projects concentrated upon developing material uniquely suited to radio; Orson Welles's "Mercury Theater of the Air" provided a number of aural innovations, some of which he adapted for the screen in his classic motion picture *Citizen Kane*.

Perhaps radio's greatest impact came through its ability to bring far-off events into people's homes. On-the-spot newscasts dramatized spectacular events of the thirties—the Munich Conference, the explosion of the dirigible *Hindenburg* over a New Jersey airport, and Joe Louis's rise to the heavyweight championship. Some skillful broadcasters even improved upon reality. When Bill Stern, breathlessly describing a thrilling, zigzag run by "Crazylegs" Brown, discovered that "Breakaway" Smith was actually carrying the ball, the fast-talking sportscaster simply invented a last-second lateral, and the proper ballcarrier skipped across the goal line. Imaginative baseball announcers such as the semiliterate fireballer Dizzy Dean routinely turned easy outs into spectacular catches and lazy fly balls into booming drives. When Orson Welles presented his radio adaptation of *War of the Worlds*, an H. G. Wells story of a Martian invasion, he created pockets of hysteria across the nation. Frantic callers jammed CBS's phone lines, and Welles had to go back on the air specifically to assure people that his production was pure fiction.

THINGS TO THINK ABOUT:
1932–1940

How did the Depression affect the nation? In addition to the more scholarly works listed below, two journalistic accounts provide readable surveys: Frederick Lewis Allen, *Since Yesterday: The Nineteen-Thirties In America* (1939), and Edward R. Ellis, *A Nation in Turmoil: The Great American Depression, 1929–1939* (1970). Studs Turkel's *Hard Times: An Oral History of the Depression* (1970) contains reminiscences as well as other perspectives on the difficulties of the 1930s. Compare Hoover's presidential leadership with FDR's leadership and style. Hoover still lacks a scholarly biography, but his own works, *The Memoirs of Herbert Hoover: The Cabinet and the Presidency 1920–1933* (1952) and *The Great Depression, 1929–1941* (1952), provide insights into this often-misunderstood man. Albert U. Romasco, *The Poverty of Abundance* (1965) is a good study of Hoover's response to the Depression. Two leading historians, Arthur Schlesinger, Jr., and Frank Freidel, are writing multivolume studies of Roosevelt, and each has published several volumes. Perceptive accounts of Roosevelt are James M. Burns, *Roosevelt: The Lion and the Fox* (1956) and Rexford G. Tugwell, *The Democratic Roosevelt* (1957).

How did the New Dealers try to solve the nation's social and economic problems? How successful were their efforts? William E. Leuchtenburg, *Franklin D. Roosevelt and the New Deal, 1932–1940* (1933) offers a generally positive assessment and remains the best one-volume treatment of the New Deal. Edgar E. Robinson, *The Roosevelt Leadership,*

1933–1945 (1955) criticizes the New Deal for going too far; and Paul K. Conkin's influential survey, *The New Deal* (1967), criticizes reformers for not doing enough. Ellis Hawley, *The New Deal and the Problem of Monopoly: A Study in Economic Ambivalence* (1965) provides numerous insights into the New Deal. James T. Patterson, *Congressional Conservatism and the New Deal* (1967) discusses Roosevelt's growing opposition in Congress. Raymond Wolters, *Negroes and the Great Depression: The Problem of Economic Recovery* (1970), and David Conrad, *The Forgotten Farmer: The Story of the Sharecroppers and the New Deal* (1965) are basic works. Donald McCoy, *Angry Voices: Left-of-Center Politics in the New Deal Era* (1958); David H. Bennett, *Demagogues in the Depression* (1969); and T. Harry Williams, *Huey Long* (1969) treat FDR's rivals on the Left.

What happened to American culture and society during the 1930s? Daniel Aaron and Robert Bendiner, eds., *The Strenuous Decade: A Social and Intellectual Record of the 1930's* (1970) is a valuable collection of primary materials. Charles C. Alexander, *Nationalism in American Thought, 1930–1945* (1968) offers a concise interpretation of many social and cultural developments. Daniel Aaron's *Writers on the Left* (1961) discusses literature, and Andrew Bergman's *We're in the Money: Depression America and Its Films* (1971) treats motion pictures. One can gain an appreciation of Woody Guthrie through his book, *Bound to Glory* (1964), as well as through his many songs. *Dust Bowl Ballads* (1964), a one-record album, and the three-record Library of Congress Recordings (1964) are valuable social documents from the 1930s.

How did FDR's foreign policy from 1937 to 1939 reflect domestic as well as global pressures? John E. Wiltz's *From Isolation to War, 1931–1941* (1968) and Robert A. Divine's *The Illusion of Neutrality* (1962) are convenient summaries. Arnold Offner, *American Appeasement: United States Foreign Policy and Germany, 1933–1938* (1969); Dorothy Borg, *The United States and the Far Eastern Crisis of 1933–1938* (1964); and Lloyd Gardner, *Economic Aspects of New Deal Diplomacy* (1964) are more specialized studies. Manfred Jonas, *Isolationism in America, 1935–1941* (1966) is a recent interpretation of isolationist sentiment.

1940-1953

Thirteen | COLOSSUS OF THE WEST

DOUGLAS MACARTHUR

"To join the Long Gray Line had been the lodestar of all my hopes since the sound of the bugles ushered me into the world," Douglas MacArthur once reminisced. Born at a western frontier garrison in 1880, MacArthur literally grew up along with the modern army, spending all but the last thirteen of his eighty-four years actively associated with the military. His father rose through the ranks to major general, winning the Medal of Honor during the Civil War, fighting Indians on the Great Plains, and serving in the Philippines during the Spanish American War. "Always before me was the vision of West Point, that greatest military institution in the world," MacArthur later wrote. Also encouraged by his mother "Pinky," an aggressive army wife, young Douglas entered West Point in 1899. While his mother lived nearby during his four years at the Academy, MacArthur compiled an outstanding scholastic and athletic record. Upon graduation, he astutely chose the Engineer Corps, a branch offering the best chance for rapid advancement.

As President Hoover's army chief of staff, MacArthur achieved national attention when he directed the dispersal of the Bonus Marchers in 1932. He considered the demonstration a Communist plot and feared that "an incipient revolution [was] in the air." Attired in his heavily decorated uniform, the general watched the action personally. "It was a good job, quickly done, with no one injured," he told a reporter during a lull in the operation. But before the day ended, scores of persons lay injured. Still, MacArthur declared, his vigorous campaign was a great success and was welcomed by the "distressed populace" Many other observers, however, did not share his enthusiasm. Democratic presidential aspirant Franklin Roosevelt linked MacArthur with Huey Long, privately warning that they were the two most dangerous men in the country. People wanted strong direction, FDR claimed, and MacArthur provided "the famous symbolic figure—the man on horseback." But Roosevelt's own kind of leadership obviated the need and the desire—if any such mood really did exist in the thirties—for MacArthur's style of command. FDR retained MacArthur as chief of staff until 1935, when the general became military advisor to America's new commonwealth, the Philippines.

From 1935 until 1951 MacArthur's career was linked to the Far East and to war; he finally assumed the Napoleonic role denied him at home. In 1937 he even resigned from his beloved army, preferring the Philippines to another stateside assignment, and became field marshall for the Philippine government. The only American ever to hold such a rank, MacArthur designed his own gold leaf–encrusted garrison cap, later adding the sunglasses and corncob pipe which became his trademarks during World War II. Shortly before Pearl Harbor he returned to active duty and directed the unsuccessful defense of the Philippines. In 1942, officials ordered him to evacuate his underground headquarters on Corregidor, and with his dramatic farewell, "I shall return," he regretfully left for Australia. He continually urged an American war effort centered on recapture of the islands, and in 1944 he finally waded ashore at Leyte, announcing: "By the grace of Almighty God, our forces stand again on the Philippines." And a year later MacArthur presided over the Japanese surrender ceremonies aboard the battleship *Missouri*. "Show him where to sign," he snapped to his chief of staff when the Japanese representative stopped to read the surrender document.

Sent to Tokyo as supreme commander of the occupation of Japan, he took complete charge of the radical reconstruction of Japan's society, government, and economy. He later said that he wished history to remember him as "one whose sacred duty it became once the guns were silenced, to carry to the land of our vanquished foe the solace and hope and faith of Christian morals."

The general was in Tokyo when the Korean conflict broke out in 1950. His brilliant marine invasion behind North Korean lines at Inchon showed that he had lost none of his military daring, but his arrogant attitude toward President Truman as well as his cavalier disregard for Chinese intervention indicated a growing sense of omnipotence. Openly criticizing the Truman administration's policy of "limited warfare," he pushed for an all-out effort, telling sympathetic Republican supporters that there was "no substitute for victory." Meanwhile, other military experts questioned MacArthur's own tactical and strategic decisions, and even foreign observers commented upon his open disregard of the military's traditional deference to civilian control. When President Truman flew all the way to Wake Island (five thousand miles) to meet with the general, who had traveled nineteen hundred miles, British Prime Minister Clement Atlee remarked, "I thought it a curious relationship between a government and a general." MacArthur continued to challenge the president, his commander-in-chief, until Truman finally recalled him in 1951.

Amid great popular acclaim and sympathy, MacArthur returned to the United States, but unlike Generals De Gaulle and Eisenhower he never could grasp the elusive ring of political power. A candidate for the 1952 Republican nomination, he gave the keynote address to the delegates who selected Eisenhower. Touring the nation with his wife and young son, MacArthur tried to summon support for the old virtues—what he called "the simple, eternal truths of the 'American way'"—but the aristocratic MacArthur lacked Ike's common touch. Reflecting upon his career, MacArthur once concluded, "I believe it was destiny."

Iwo Jima Cemetery. *Culver Pictures*

1940-1953

1941	Battle of the Atlantic
	Lend-Lease Act
	Japanese attack Pearl Harbor, December 7
1942	Domestic war mobilization
	Allied campaign in North Africa
1944	Invasion of Europe; landing at Normandy, June 6
	Roosevelt elected to fourth term
1945	Atomic bomb dropped on Hiroshima, August 6
	Vice-President Truman becomes president on Roosevelt's death
	United Nations formed
1946–47	Deterioration in U.S.-Soviet relations; beginnings of Cold War
1947	Marshall Plan put into operation
	Truman Doctrine announced
1948	Truman elected in his own right
1949	North Atlantic Treaty Organization formed
1947–51	Loyalty campaign and trials of several Communists or spies
1950	Outbreak of Korean conflict
	Rise of Senator Joseph McCarthy as popular anti-Communist
1951	22nd Amendment
1952	Eisenhower elected president

AMERICA'S ROAD TO WAR

From September 1939, when Britain and France came to Poland's defense, until April 1940, when the German *Blitzkrieg* ("lightning war") swept westward, an eerie quiet settled over Europe. The nations watched each other warily, preparing their defenses and perfecting their war machines, but there was no sign of battle. "There is something phony about this war," Senator Borah remarked. In the United States, the Roosevelt administration and much of the public began hastily to discard the isolationism that had enshrouded their foreign policy for at least a decade.

Roosevelt quickly asked Congress to replace the Neutrality Act's arms embargo with a "cash and carry" provision requiring belligerents to pay cash for American products and to transport them in non-American ships. The Neutrality Act actually imperiled neutrality, the president argued, because American merchantmen could still enter hostile waters with nonmilitary goods and be subjected to some "incident" leading to war. Despite such assertions, most congressmen realized that, since Britain and France controlled the Atlantic, they were the only countries that could possibly benefit from "cash and carry." Yet this alteration of the

Neutrality Act, which had been stalled in Congress before the invasion of Poland, now passed by a wide margin. The new bill took America a giant step away from nonalignment.

On April 9, 1940, the derisively termed *Sitzkrieg* ("sitting war") exploded into action. Within two months, German troops overran Denmark, Norway, Holland, Belgium, and Luxembourg, and thundered into Paris. Italy joined the attack, hurling armies into France from the south. Three weeks before Bastille Day, in the same railway car in which the Germans had capitulated over twenty years earlier, French leaders signed an armistice. The rapid fall of France, creating a myth of Nazi invincibility and raising the possibility of England's early defeat, shattered American illusions about noninvolvement. Congress quickly passed rearmament appropriations and a Selective Service Act. The executive branch, given a bipartisan flavor by the appointment of Republicans Henry Stimson as secretary of war and Frank Knox as secretary of the navy, abandoned all pretense of neutrality by supplying war materiel directly to Great Britain. After the German *Luftwaffe* began to bomb English cities in the Battle of Britain, the new Prime Minister Winston Churchill appealed for even more aid. With scarcely a glance at the Constitution, FDR transferred fifty World War I destroyers to England in return for British naval bases in the western hemisphere.

Domestic debate over foreign policy

The election of 1940 showed broad support for the president's policy. Bypassing several stalwart isolationists, the Republicans nominated Wendell Willkie, an internationalist who strongly favored the Allied cause. Willkie campaigned primarily against a third term for Roosevelt and the weak economy. "Twice is enough for any man," read one Republican campaign button. As election day approached, however, Willkie grew more desperate: he charged that a vote for Roosevelt was a vote for war, and the president countered with the extravagant promise that "your boys are not going to be sent into any foreign wars." But the election was neither fought nor won primarily on issues of foreign policy. The nation seemed content assisting England with measures short of war.

Yet opposition to any foreign involvement persisted. Some senators warned against a replay of the presidential maneuvering which they believed had led the nation into World War I. During debate over repeal of the arms embargo, men as diverse as the aviator-hero Charles A. Lindbergh, the socialist Norman Thomas, and former President Hoover conducted radio appeals against revision of the Neutrality Act. After the controversial destroyers-for-bases deal, General Robert E. Wood of Sears Roebuck organized the America First Committee. This isolationist group contended that Hitler did not menace United States security and that all-out aid to Britain would make intervention a certainty.

Pro-Allied spokesmen countered America First and isolationist sentiment with jeers and organizations of their own. During the 1940 campaign, FDR spiced his speeches with rhythmical barbs against "Martin, Barton, and Fish," three prominent Republican isolationists. The folk singer Woody Guthrie set his political criticism to a catchy tune:

> Hitler wrote to Lindy [i.e., Lindbergh]
> Said do your very worst
> Lindy started an outfit
> He called America First....
>
> Lindy said to Hoover
> We'll do the same as France
> Make a deal with Hitler
> And then we'll get our chance....
>
> I'm gonna tell you workers
> Before you cash your checks
> They say "America First"
> But they mean "America Next!"

On a more practical level, Kansas newspaper editor William Allen White organized the Committee to Defend America by Aiding the Allies. Expanding to three hundred local chapters within a few weeks, its contributors included the wealthy banker J. P. Morgan and the militant labor leader David Dubinsky. Members of White's group had originated the destroyers-for-bases idea, and some urged the president to take even more decisive action against fascism.

America as an arsenal of democracy

Germany's aerial assault did not crack England's will but did severely strain its economy. In December 1940 Churchill warned Roosevelt that Britain's ability to purchase goods in the United States would soon be exhausted. In response, Roosevelt set forth a new plan to "lend-lease" munitions to the Allies. Drawing a homey analogy, Roosevelt reminded Americans that if a neighbor's house catches fire, "I don't say...'Neighbor, my garden hose cost me fifteen dollars; you have to pay me fifteen dollars for it.' No, I don't want fifteen dollars—I want my garden hose after the fire is over." In a fireside chat a few days after Christmas, he further justified his program, explaining that the only way to avoid "the agony and suffering of war which others have to endure," was to become "the great arsenal of democracy." The lend-lease bill, cleverly numbered H.R. 1776, passed Congress overwhelmingly, though isolationists grumbled that lending war supplies was similar to lending chewing gum.

As isolationists charged, it was unrealistic to suppose that the United States could support the British cause without eventually becoming a belligerent, and FDR was less than candid about the obvious dangers of all-out American aid. While he assured Americans that assistance to Britain would keep the country out of war, military officials recognized the risks and made preparations. In the early months of 1941 British and American military strategists secretly coordinated plans to concentrate upon Europe first in the event the United States entered a two-front war against both Germany and Japan.

Hitler's relentless pressure on Great Britain suddenly subsided after he made his fateful decision to invade the Soviet Union. Most isolationists believed the Bolshevik regime represented a greater threat than the Nazis and hoped the two countries would destroy each other in a protracted struggle. But Soviet Russia's entry into the war did not reduce Roosevelt's determination to aid the Allies; rather, it strengthened his hope that Hitler could be defeated without America entering the struggle. To the horror of most conservatives, FDR stretched the concept of an "arsenal of democracy" and extended Lend-Lease to Joseph Stalin.

The crowning point of Anglo-American cooperation came in the Atlantic Conference of August 1941, when Roosevelt and Churchill met on a destroyer off the coast of Labrador. Roosevelt and Churchill issued an eight-point declaration of principles, the Atlantic Charter. Like Wilson's Fourteen Points, the charter disavowed territorial expansion, upheld self-determination and free trade, and proclaimed the need for "a wider and permanent system of general security." American leaders exacted a price for this alliance. During the Depression, England had moved toward a system of imperial preference, preserving markets and raw materials within the empire from outside competitors. The United States, anxious about its own international economic position, vigorously opposed carving the world into restricted spheres. With England's survival now dependent upon United States cooperation, the Roosevelt administration succeeded in gaining assurances that Britain would keep trade and access to raw materials open equally to all nations.

In an effort to ensure the arrival of Lend-Lease supplies, Roosevelt next ordered the navy to convoy American goods as far as Iceland. When German submarines sank several American vessels in the Atlantic, the president condemned these "outrages," sometimes distorting events by telling Americans that German attacks were unprovoked (in at least one incident, the reverse was true). As isolationists predicted, Lend-Lease and close cooperation with Great Britain finally led to an undeclared naval war with Germany.

America goes to war   American military participation in World War II came about not through a spectacular collision with Germany but via the "back door" in Asia. Historically committed to the "Open Door" and to the territorial integrity of China, the United States had opposed Japanese expansion throughout the thirties. But it refused to back up its objectives with force. Even Japan's sinking of an American gunboat *Panay* in December 1937 provoked little public clamor for retaliation. When pressure finally mounted for some action to halt Japan's advances in China, Roosevelt threatened economic boycott. In mid-1939 he terminated the Treaty of Commerce and Navigation with Japan, leaving the United States free to curtail or prohibit exports.

When German victories left the French, Dutch, and British colonies in Southeast Asia vulnerable to Japanese pressure, Roosevelt turned his threats into actions. Claiming that America's own security required the stockpiling of strategic materials, the president banned the American sale of aviation fuel and high-grade scrap iron to Japan. After Japan firmed up its alliance with the Axis powers, Roosevelt expanded the embargo to include other strategic products, promised loans and military assistance to China, and bolstered America's Pacific defenses. But Japan pushed further into Indo-China in search of iron ore and coal. As Japanese transports steamed toward Saigon in July 1941, the president "froze" Japanese funds in the United States, placing trade between the two countries under complete presidential control. Products from the United States, particularly petroleum, remained vital to the Japanese economy, and this new step in what Secretary of State Hull called the "general tightening up" was a direct challenge to Japan's Far Eastern policies.

The Japanese government insisted that the United States recognize Japan's special position in China and help Japan gain access to raw material in Southeast Asia. Prime Minister Fumimaro Konoye, a moderate, believed that the United States would negotiate rather than risk a two-front war. But Japan's impatient militants wanted to fight. Konoye appealed for a summit conference to break the deadlocked negotiations. Although Konoye and Roosevelt both knew that prolonging the diplomatic impasse would give the militants their war, neither leader could sacrifice what he considered vital national interests in Asia. Roosevelt refused the Japanese invitation; Konoye resigned; and militant War Minister Hideki Tojo took power.

American officials expected an attack in Indo-China or possibly in the Philippines. Confused by the welter of intelligence data and radio signals, they missed Japan's real objective. On December 7 Japanese pilots, soaring across the clear Hawaiian skies, found America's Pacific fleet neatly arranged and unprotected in Pearl Harbor. The bombs fell, and stunned Americans turned on their radios to discover that their country was at war.

THE WAR IN EUROPE

After Pearl Harbor, Germany quickly fulfilled its alliance with Japan by declaring war on the United States. Great distances, the location of allies, and the terrain made warfare in the Pacific far more expensive and difficult than war against Germany, and so Anglo-American strategists decided to concentrate on the Atlantic theater. The defeat of Japan

Attack on Pearl Harbor, December 7, 1941. *Wide World*

meant little if Germany rolled to victory in Europe, but the newly created Joint Chiefs of Staff realized that if they stopped Hitler, Japan was finished as well.

Roosevelt rejected Woodrow Wilson's example of insisting that the United States remain an "associate" rather than a full "ally." Instead, FDR merged the Joint Chiefs with a similar body in Britain to create a unified strategy. A single administration, however, did not eliminate fundamental disagreements. British planners favored nibbling at the edge of German power, expecting the Soviet Union to hold off the main thrust in eastern Europe. Churchill advocated first an invasion of French North Africa and a gradual "closing in" until the Allies could stab successfully into the German heartland. A more direct confrontation, he argued, risked a demoralizing and disastrous battlefield defeat. Americans strenuously objected, believing that the British strategy would drain energy and resources into marginal campaigns having little effect on the war's ultimate outcome. Less confident that the Soviet Union could withstand the German assault alone, General George C. Marshall argued that Anglo-American armies should relieve pressure in the east by opening a second front in France.

Roosevelt initially supported his general's recommendations, even promising Soviet leader V. M. Molotov in May of 1942 that the United States would seek a cross-channel invasion of France. But an assault could not be prepared before the spring of 1943, and Roosevelt felt that such a long delay would hurt morale at home and increase demands for an Asia-first strategy. He needed some rapid victories, and a landing in France ran a large risk of failure. Opting for quick if small successes, FDR swung his support behind Operation TORCH, the code name for the invasion of French North Africa.

Once the campaign began, another basic disagreement arose. Whichever political faction the Allies backed in French Africa would probably become the government of France following an Allied victory. Britain supported Charles de Gaulle, a relatively unknown leader of the Free French movement who denounced as traitors the Vichy regime currently governing France in collaboration with the Nazis. Roosevelt intensely disliked the egotistical and authoritarian de Gaulle. Instead, he supported Vichyite army officers in North Africa who, in return, broke with their pro-German government and convinced the French army in Africa not to oppose the American advance. Making a deal with ex-collaborationists may have been militarily sound, but liberals in the United States questioned our war aims if we were willing to install fascist-leaning elements in the future government of France. The assassination of the American-backed leader and the ascendancy of de Gaulle finally resolved this embarrassment, but America's wartime opposition to the man who would lead France during much of the next generation hurt United States—French relations long after the war.

WORLD WAR II, EUROPEAN THEATER

→ Allied Offensives

FDR liked to pilot large ships. *Wide World*

While Anglo-American forces advanced through North Africa, Soviet troops finally halted Hitler's offensive at Stalingrad. By the end of 1942, these victories augered well for the Allies, but the Soviets, who had felt the brunt of German power alone, suffered staggering casualties. Again Stalin demanded a second front; and once more Britain pressed for delay, this time in favor of a campaign into Sicily and Italy. The United States reluctantly accepted the British plan, and the Soviets became increasingly suspicious of their allies' good faith.

The Italian campaign   Allied armies landed in Sicily during the summer of 1943 and invaded Italy in the fall. Meeting heavier resistance than expected, they took great losses, and the prolonged fighting further delayed the second front. But the operation did give the United States and Great Britain a strong position in determining postwar Italian politics. The new government of Marshal Pietro Badoglio, which took power from Mussolini, represented little change in Italian ruling circles and contained no leftist or Soviet-backed elements. British and American governments supported the con-

578

servative regime without even consulting Stalin about the future of this defeated enemy.

The Italian offensive created an atmosphere of distrust among the allies which lasted long after the guns ceased firing. To allay Soviet suspicions that Britain and the United States might make a separate peace with Germany, leaving Russia to fight alone, Roosevelt announced at the Casablanca Conference in early 1943 that the United States would remain in the war until the Axis surrendered unconditionally. Britain also agreed eventually to open a front in France. But these moves hardly soothed Stalin's bitterness when he compared casualty lists and wondered if his allies purposely delayed relieving pressure on the Soviet Union. While Russian troops exhausted themselves against Germany, Anglo-American armies had pecked off a sphere of influence around the Mediterranean. In particular, Stalin carefully derived a precedent from the Italian campaign: those armies which liberated an area would decide the type of government established there. It was a lesson he would employ later in Eastern Europe, where Soviet armies would have a free hand.

Overlord   Toward the end of 1943 British strategists proposed to follow up the Italian campaign with forays into Greece, Turkey, and the Balkans. But Americans preferred invading France to hasten the defeat of Germany and avoid further delay in the Pacific theater. The proponents of a second front finally prevailed, and General Dwight D. Eisenhower, commanding the Allied Expeditionary Force in Great Britain, received orders to begin the planning and build-up for Operation OVERLORD, code name for the cross-channel assault. In a daring maneuver, with success dependent largely upon the unpredictable weather in the English channel, Allied troops landed on the beaches of Normandy on June 6, 1944. Confused by diversionary stratagems, the Germans failed to organize a successful defense, and Allied forces pushed eastward throughout the summer. Within three months, American troops liberated Paris and entered Germany; and Soviet armies swept across Poland, closing the circle from the east. A last-ditch German counteroffensive, halted in the Battle of the Bulge in December, ended the Nazi offensive. In the spring of 1945, Allied armies crossed the Rhine and headed toward Berlin as Soviet troops raced toward the German capital from the other direction. The war in Europe was swiftly drawing to a close.

WAR IN THE PACIFIC

Americans still faced a lengthy and perplexing fight in the Far East. Immediately following the attack on Pearl Harbor, Japan quickly enlarged its "Co-Prosperity Sphere": Guam, Wake, Hong Kong, Singapore, Java, and the Philippines all fell within a few months. But a decisive

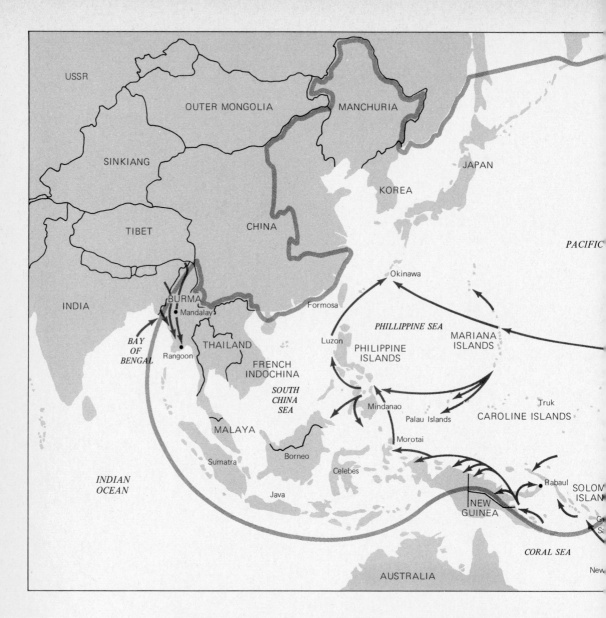

American naval victory at Midway in June 1942 forced Japan on the defensive. American forces sunk 4 aircraft carriers and shot down 275 planes. For the next three years American forces chipped away at the Japanese Empire, slowly closing in on the home islands.

The American military establishment was divided over Far Eastern strategy. General Douglas MacArthur, commander of the army in the South Pacific, urged an offensive launched from his headquarters in Australia and proceeding up through New Guinea and the Philippines to

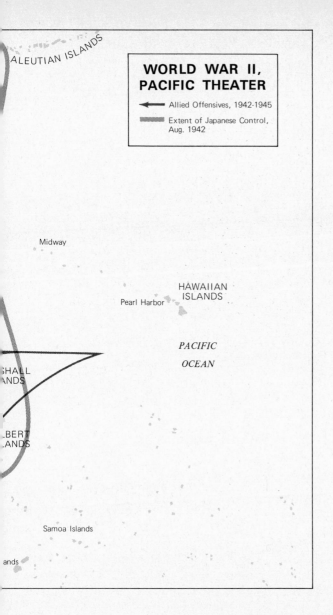

WORLD WAR II, PACIFIC THEATER

← Allied Offensives, 1942-1945

▬ Extent of Japanese Control, Aug. 1942

ALEUTIAN ISLANDS

Midway

HAWAIIAN ISLANDS

Pearl Harbor

PACIFIC OCEAN

MARSHALL ISLANDS

GILBERT ISLANDS

Samoa Islands

Japan. When Japanese troops had driven him from the Philippines in May of 1942, he promised to return as a liberator; his critics charged that his enormous vanity and personal pride colored his assessment of strategy. But MacArthur and his supporters within the army argued that the plan was both militarily sound and politically imperative. If the United States did not control the Philippines when the war ended, the radical, anti-American Huks might gain power and undercut America's future position in the Pacific. Admiral Chester Nimitz and the navy dissented from

581

MacArthur's view, advocating an advance through the smaller islands of the central Pacific as the most direct route to Japan. Beseiged by conflicting advice, the Joint Chiefs permitted simultaneous offensives along both the southern and central routes, thereby splitting Japanese defenses.

In June 1943 the two-pronged offensive began, gradually "leap-frogging" toward Japan, and in late 1944, while Nimitz's forces closed in from the center, MacArthur returned to the Philippines, attributing his success to "bomb, torpedo and strafing air attacks, timely maneuvers, and the definite partiality of Almighty God." Success in island hopping assured the United States of naval bases scattered throughout the Pacific.

The China tangle   A strong and independent China, capable of resisting Japan on the mainland as Americans moved in from the east, would have reduced American casualties and hastened victory. But chances for stability in China looked dismal. The growing Communist movement—popular with the peasants, relatively free from corruption, and militarily effective against the Japanese—alienated American policymakers with its radical economic program. Yet the American-backed Nationalist government of Chiang Kai-shek remained as incompetent, corrupt, and unpopular as it had been for decades. One American official aptly described the basis of Chiang's regime as "one-party government, a reactionary policy, or the suppression of democratic ideas with the active aid of his gestapo." While Americans urged a vigorous offensive against Japanese troops, Nationalist officials preferred to rake off profits from American aid and to oppose Mao Tse-tung's Chinese Communists. Civil war seemed as grave a threat to China as foreign invasion.

Despite the chaos in China, the United States persistently pretended that Chiang was a stable ruler and world leader. Chiang participated in Allied conferences dealing with the Far East, and Roosevelt insisted that China sit alongside the major victorious powers on the United Nations Security Council. Even Stalin promised to support Chiang rather than Mao in return for some concessions to the Soviet Union in Outer Mongolia. In early 1942, after proceeding to China to organize a military effort against the Japanese, General Joseph W. Stilwell discovered that Chiang's Kuomintang armies were hopelessly inadequate; he vainly tried to promote internal reforms and coordination with Mao's forces. Eventually, Roosevelt had to choose between backing Stilwell, who viewed Chiang as China's major problem, and Chiang, who demanded Stilwell's dismissal. Roosevelt recalled the American general and continued to pour assistance into the Nationalist cause. But all of America's moral and material support could not make Chiang effective, and Mao's forces increased their popularity by leading the Chinese military effort against the Japanese invaders. The Communist takeover of China in 1949 shocked the American public, imbued with the wartime myth of Nationalist strength. But it was a predictable result of the tangle of wartime events in China.

Looking to a postwar world

Unable to organize an effective Chinese resistance force, American leaders hoped to bring the Soviet Union into the Asian war as soon as possible. The tide of battle clearly indicated ultimate American victory, but Japan's tenacious resistance at Iwo Jima and Okinawa in early 1945 seemed to indicate that years of hard fighting and possibly a million more American casualties lay ahead. The advantages of Soviet assistance seemed to outweigh the political dangers of introducing Soviet troops into Asia. At the Yalta Conference in February 1945 Stalin promised to declare war on Japan a few months after Germany's surrender, an agreement with far-reaching consequences tracing up to and beyond the Korean war.

By early 1945 the eventual outcome of the war in both Europe and Asia appeared certain. Policymakers began to weigh the monumental problems of reestablishing an international monetary and economic system, building a more effective international organization, deciding the fate of defeated nations and colonial areas, and working out the power balance in Europe and the Far East. Dean Acheson, an important policymaker of the postwar period entitled his memoirs of these years *Present at the Creation.* If the task of rebuilding the world seemed as vast and complicated as that undertaken in those initial "seven days," Acheson, by comparing his handiwork with that of the Lord, unconsciously revealed American policymakers' shortsighted and tragic view of their own omnipotence. One consequence of this "arrogance of power" was the cold war.

THE WAR AT HOME

For Americans, World War II was more than a global military conflict. The war caused great stresses and forced significant internal changes, even though the United States was the only major belligerent whose own territory escaped the ravages of combat.

Most obviously, the conflict revived the American economy and extended the scope of government. The war, not New Deal measures, finally restored prosperity. Between 1939 and 1945 the country's total economic output almost doubled, and the massive unemployment of the 1930s became a bad dream of the past. War-related industries not only hired all able-bodied men, but eagerly sought women ("Rosie the Riveter"), teenagers, and retired persons. The fight against the Axis helped to heal old antagonisms between big business and the Roosevelt administration; "dollar-a-year" men from large corporations assumed key positions within government's wartime bureaucracies. The close relationship between big business interests and military officials often re-

Rosie the riveter. *National Archives*

sulted in an unfair apportionment of lucrative defense contracts and gave impetus to a powerful, if hard-to-define, pressure group which President Eisenhower later termed the "military-industrial complex."

The enormous increase in production raised the spectre of runaway inflation, to which the Roosevelt administration responded with a series of economic measures designed to control prices and allocate resources more efficiently. People barely familiar with the myriad New Deal agencies suddenly discovered a whole new series of "alphabet agencies" regulating the wartime economy. The Office of Price Administration (OPA) established price ceilings on goods, services, and rents. The government entirely prohibited manufacture of some products, such as automobiles, in order to conserve steel, and the OPA rationed a variety of other items, including sugar, meat, and canned goods. Price controls and rationing, following upon the lean years of the Depression, produced discontent. Families had to pool ration coupons (for items such as baby shoes) and to find substitutes for scarcities such as gasoline, although a sputtering, kerosine-powered automobile hardly made for a pleasant Sunday afternoon's drive. Under-the-counter "black market" transactions in rationed products became fairly frequent. Still, governmental regulations did prevent a dramatic inflationary spiral, and price increases remained under those of World War I.

Selling the war   As in the First World War, the government established a propaganda bureau. But remembering how the passions stirred up by George Creel's Committee on Public Information were eventually released in a postwar Red Scare, Roosevelt and his advisers avoided attempts to create a blind and chauvinistic "one-hundred percent Americanism." Neither did the

"Just gimme a coupla aspirin. I already got a Purple Heart."
Bill Mauldin

government inflame fighting men with the superpatriotic idealism of our first Great Crusade. Few soldiers set out singing patriotic ditties such as "Over There." Instead, the hard-bitten, matter-of-fact attitude of Bill Mauldin's cartoon characters, Joe and Willie, reflected the less emotional tone of the GIs of World War II. Defeating the Axis was something that had to be done, but few soldiers sloshing through Europe considered it a glorious undertaking. The war, however, did produce numerous efforts to sell the American cause at home.

Popular culture, for example, reflected the war. Comic book heroes—Superman, Dick Tracy, and even Little Orphan Annie—were among those who fought the Axis. Several famous Hollywood filmmakers produced classic war documentaries, and others turned out less artistic entertainment which glorified America's military exploits. Leading men such as John Wayne (who never actually served in the armed forces) fought up and down studio backlots liberating countless "Pacific" islands. Two popular movie serials featuring "Don Winslow of the Coast Guard" played up Japanese attempts to infiltrate the West Coast. Even cowboy stars, in addition to their normal quota of cattle rustlers and bank robbers, mixed it up with Nazi and Japanese agents. Noncombat movies also reflected the wartime atmosphere. James Cagney, who specialized in gangster heroes during the thirties, won an Academy Award for his portrayal of George M. Cohan, composer of "It's a Grand Old Flag." Backed by the greatest armada of American flags ever assembled in Hollywood, Cagney furiously danced and sang his way through "Yankee Doodle Dandy" and Cohan's other patriotic standards from the First World War. The film closed with a somber, no-nonsense meeting between a dying Cohan and President Roosevelt. *Wilson* (1944), another extravaganza, harkened back to the World War I experience and presented a none-too-subtle plea for the revival of Wilsonian internationalism following defeat of the Axis. Films such as *Mission to Moscow* portrayed the Soviet Union in a sympathetic light.

Repression of Japanese Americans

Propagandists and governmental officials generally avoided direct aspersions against Germans and Italians. Although wars are rarely a time for vigilant protection of individual rights, members of the Roosevelt administration, particularly Attorney General Francis Biddle, remembered the suppression during World War I and also the importance of immigrant votes to the Democratic coalition. Neither Italian Americans nor German Americans faced the kind of active persecution suffered by persons of German extraction during the earlier conflict. The notorious exception to the country's generally commendable record on wartime civil liberties was the capitulation to racism and popular hysteria in the treatment of Japanese Americans. No anti-German literature approached the venom of anti-Japanese tracts or the crudity of songs such as "You're a Sap, Mr. Jap."

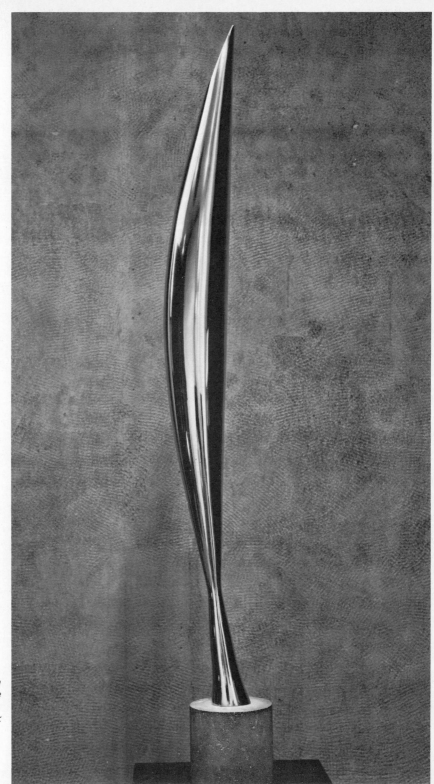

Constantin Brancusi, *Bird in Space* (1928?). *Collection, The Museum of Modern Art, New York*

Immediately following the attack upon Pearl Harbor, Japan assumed the role of archvillain. Prowar spokesmen pictured Japanese as cunning, evil, almost subhuman little men, and this image of the Oriental enemy abroad dovetailed with long-standing racial antagonism on the West Coast. In California, Japanese Americans comprised a hard-working population whose thrift, success, and physical differences made them a frequent target for attack. The war intensified racial hatred, provoking calls for a crackdown on this potentially disloyal "fifth column." In northern California a guerrilla band of almost a thousand farmers (known as the "Bald Eagles") armed themselves to put down Japanese subversion. Congressman John Rankin of Mississippi proclaimed: "Once a Jap always a Jap. . . . This is a race war, as far as the Pacific side of this conflict is concerned. . . . It is of vital importance to get rid of every Japanese whether in Hawaii or on the mainland." A West Coast newspaperman called for the immediate removal of Japanese Americans to the interior. "I don't mean a nice part. . . either. Herd 'em up, pack 'em off, and give 'em the inside room in the badlands." Amid such a climate of opinion, Americans may have accepted the moral burden of dropping atomic bombs on Hiroshima and Nagasaki with more ease than had they been targeted for Munich or Milan.

Initially civilian and military leaders resisted West Coast pressure, but ultimately they capitulated. With the cooperation of the Roosevelt administration in Washington, officials (including California's Attorney General Earl Warren) first imposed a series of restrictions upon Japanese Americans and finally instituted a full-scale removal program. Claiming that military necessity dictated their decision, the government ordered citizens and resident aliens alike to sell their possessions and relocate in segregated areas away from the West Coast. After 1942, the army forcibly moved over a hundred thousand persons to various "resettlement centers." Even the libertarian members of the Supreme Court acquiesced to this concentration camp operation, holding in *Korematsu* v. *U.S.* (1944) that the judiciary could not interfere with the executive's wartime military decisions. Only many years later did the government agree to reimburse Japanese Americans for financial losses, but nothing could erase this flagrant violation of democratic principles.

The overwhelming popularity of the war limited dissent and intensified civil rights problems. The shock of the Japanese attack and the barbarities of the Nazi regime helped defuse antiwar sentiment. A hard core of true pacifists refused to fight, but even many pacifist religious leaders, especially among the Quaker and Mennonite sects, complained that too many of their young men accepted military service.

World War II and black Americans

Antiwar sentiment did find support among a few black Americans. "What the hell do we want to fight the Japanese for anyhow?" asked one black GI. "They couldn't possibly treat us any worse than these 'crackers' right here at home." A slogan popular among draftees expressed a similar attitude: "Here lies a black man killed fighting a yellow man for the glory of a white man." Pacifist groups failed to gain large numbers of converts, but they did forge some important connections with black civil rights leaders during the war. In Chicago, pacifists and blacks established the Congress of Racial Equality (CORE), a militant but nonviolent direct action group. CORE, which became prominent during the civil rights movement of the 1960s, used the tactic of civil disobedience to desegregate public facilities in several northern cities.

CORE's activities during the war reflected a greater militancy, especially among lower-income blacks. A number of black leaders saw the war as an opportunity to force white America to live up to the democratic ideals it professed around the globe. The affinity of black voters for the Democratic party led some leaders to hope that FDR might lend support to their cause. When the president procrastinated—he basically considered blacks a group to be treated as wards of the state rather than

Lunchtime. *Library of Congress*

as people to be dealt with as equals—the black labor leader A. Philip Randolph planned a march on Washington to protest job discrimination in the burgeoning defense industry. The march's organizers enjoyed surprising success mobilizing ghetto blacks, a group generally untouched by older organizations such as the NAACP. In response to Randolph's constantly escalating estimates of the expected number of demonstrators (he ultimately predicted a hundred thousand), Roosevelt finally compromised. In return for cancellation of the march, he issued an executive order establishing a commission to deal with employment discrimination. Although the Fair Employment Practices Commission (FEPC) failed to live up to expectations, its establishment seemed to demonstrate the practical value of militant action.

The war years also brought more violent confrontations between blacks and whites. Rigid segregation in the military failed to prevent racial contact and led to serious disturbances on bases at home and abroad. Black soldiers frequently complained that while officers ignored racist attacks they considered black protest a sign of disloyalty. Friction in the armed forces paralleled massive urban disorders. Southern blacks, migrating from rural areas, offered job competition for white workers, and the conflict sometimes spilled over into the streets. In several southern cities white laborers organized vigilante organizations to prevent the hiring of blacks, and a number of northern cities experienced full-scale race riots in 1943. Smoldering racial tensions in Detroit produced numerous predictions of trouble, but city officials seemed paralyzed. "I was taken by surprise only by the day it happened," confessed Detroit's mayor. After thirty-four deaths and millions of dollars in property damage, federal troops finally restored order in the Motor City.

Despite encouragement from associates and especially from his wife Eleanor, FDR avoided any firm commitment to the civil rights cause. He offered several token appointments to blacks but never really understood the aspirations of black people. He did not wish to alienate the powerful bloc of southern Democrats in time of war and rejected suggestions that he devote a fireside chat to the riots or that Congress hold an investigation of racial tensions.

But fear of further violence led others to defuse the racial dynamite buried in urban ghettos. Apprehensive about controlling the masses, most black leaders abandoned militant tactics such as marches and demonstrations after 1943. Black magazines and newspapers toned down their rhetoric, and the NAACP urged protestors to use legal and political means. Working with white liberals, black leaders sought to build a strong interracial and nonviolent movement. Publication of Gunnar Myrdal's *An American Dilemma* in 1944 symbolized the direction of the civil rights movement for the next several decades. Sponsored by the Carnegie Foundation, this study indicted the United States for its racial discrimination but optimistically concluded that Americans could eventually live up to their egalitarian ideals. *An American Dilemma* became the guidepost for a generation of liberals who struggled valiantly, if somewhat naively, to abolish legal segregation through court tests, executive orders, and legislative actions.

Domestic politics At least two things did not change drastically during the war—the conduct of partisan politics and the popular appeal of Franklin Roosevelt. Early military reverses and more extensive federal controls provided the Republicans with potent issues during the 1942 congressional elections. And after picking up forty-six House and nine Senate seats, some GOP strategists anticipated capturing the White House in 1944. But always the canny politician, Roosevelt generally struck the image of a wartime statesman above petty politicking. At a 1943 press conference he announced that he would shelve domestic reforms and concentrate upon winning the war—"Dr. Win-the-War," he said, had succeeded "Dr. New Deal." Indicating that he would not seek but would accept his party's nomination for a fourth term, FDR abandoned his role as the Great Commander long enough to crush his much younger Republican opponent, Governor Thomas E. Dewey of New York. Just before the 1944 election, the president squelched rumors of ill health with a vigorous and highly successful campaign tour. Roosevelt and his new running mate, Harry S. Truman of Missouri, defeated Dewey by 432 to 99 electoral votes and by over 3½ million popular votes. Yet 1944 Republican gains over 1936 and 1940 were solid enough to make Dewey the man for '48. By late 1944 Roosevelt and his supporters confidently looked forward to ending the war, establishing a peaceful world order, and reviving the New Deal at home.

THE ORIGINS OF THE COLD WAR

World War II was the most destructive phase of this century of conflict; it not only toppled the old political order in Europe but also convulsed the "Third World." The European nation-states fought themselves into economic and political exhaustion, and revolutionary instability threatened much of the world. It became clear by 1945 that the Axis nations would be defeated and that the postwar world would differ radically from that of 1939.

"We are going to win the war, and we are going to win the peace that follows," Roosevelt said a few days after the attack on Pearl Harbor. But what had the long and bloody battles of World War II accomplished, and how did Americans envision the postwar world? The economic nationalism arising out of the Depression in the thirties had created obstacles to free trade, and the Roosevelt administration sought in the postwar era to reverse this trend toward restrictionism. On the battlefield, the United States challenged German, Italian, and Japanese attempts to create spheres of influence, and also made its ally Great Britain promise to move away from its imperial preference system as a price of American aid. In the Bretton Woods Conference of 1944, the Roosevelt administration revealed its blueprint for a postwar international economic system which would maximize free trade and investment flow, preventing a relapse into depression. The president opened the conference by expressing an article of faith he believed held the key to postwar prosperity and peace: "Commerce is the life blood of a free society. We must see to it that the arteries which carry that blood stream are not clogged again, as they have been in the past, by artificial barriers created through senseless economic rivalries." The subsequent Bretton Woods agreements established an international gold standard and set up the International Monetary Fund and the International Bank for Reconstruction and Development. These agencies were designed to restore commerce, promote world prosperity, and insure political stability by making capital—largely American—available for recovery and development.

American policymakers hoped that the Bretton Woods agreements, along with the plan for a United Nations devised shortly afterward at Dumbarton Oaks, would create an open world in which America's political institutions, financial resources, military power, and ideological principles could flow unrestricted. Political, humanitarian, economic, and strategic objectives, Dean Acheson observed, could not "be separated in the intellectual equivalent of a cream separator." They were intertwined in a system of liberal values which Americans sought to introduce throughout the world. Economic or political spheres of influence—except in Latin America, where the United States jealously guarded one of its own—ran counter to American interests. Never doubting that if given the chance all peoples would emulate the American way, Americans believed that an open world, their goal in peace and their aim in war, would be an Americanized world in which they could remain both prosperous and secure.

Divisions within the Grand Alliance between Great Britain, the Soviet Union, and the United States threatened America's postwar plans. Churchill sought to protect Britain's far-flung empire, particularly the rich oil fields of the Middle East and the Indian subcontinent, and his wartime strategy had reflected this goal. Stalin envisioned elimination of any future German threat and creation of a series of friendly pro-Soviet governments in Eastern Europe. These two leaders, both at home with the idea of swapping and balancing spheres of influence, reached an informal agreement in 1944 permitting Soviet predominance in Rumania and Bulgaria in return for British preeminence in Greece. But American policymakers feared that American influence would be shut out and hestiated to endorse such backroom diplomacy. As the war drew

Churchill, Roosevelt, Stalin at Yalta. *Wide World*

Why was the atomic bomb used on Japan? *Wide World*

to a close, discrepancies in postwar political and economic aims surfaced, widening schisms among the Allies.

Yalta and international tensions

At the Yalta Conference of early 1945, Churchill, Stalin, and Roosevelt reached vague agreements to divide occupied Germany and to hold free elections in Eastern Europe. But the course of battle and the destruction of old power arrangements, rather than formal wartime agreements, shaped the course of events. Stalin's forces drove into Berlin about the same time as the American army advanced through Germany from the west, and Germany was eventually divided into four zones of occupation. Anglo-American troops occupied zones of influence around the periphery of Europe, supporting friendly governments in France, Italy, and Greece. Red armies swept the Nazis out of Eastern Europe, becoming predominant in that sphere and conducting their own version of "elections." Pro-Soviet groups came to power in Rumania, Hungary, Bulgaria, Albania, Poland, and eventually Czechoslovakia. In Poland Communist-led resistance forces took total control despite Stalin's specific assurances to include an Anglo-American—backed group which had sat in London as a government-in-exile during the war. Stalin believed his military victories and his country's particular vulnerability from the west justified creation of friendly regimes in Eastern Europe. Always fearful of "capitalist encirclement," he sought to create a buffer zone of Communist states with which the Soviet Union could trade. Republican critics at home soon would denounce the Yalta Conference as a betrayal of democracy in Eastern Europe and a gift of territory to Russia, but free governments had not existed there nor had the Western allies ever occupied those lands.

To Britain and the United States, Stalin's essentially defensive conduct in Eastern Europe appeared aggressive, and his threat to an open world challenged the very principles for which Americans had fought the war. In this clash between what the United States and the USSR each defined as vital strategic and economic interests, both began to view the other as a direct threat to its own well-being. When Roosevelt unexpectedly succumbed to a massive stroke and Vice-President Harry S. Truman assumed diplomatic leadership, relations deteriorated further. Where Roosevelt had felt, perhaps naively, that Americans could get along with Stalin, the new president quickly sided with those who urged a harder line.

While a "cold war" began to develop between the United States and the Soviet Union over the nature of postwar Europe, the situation in the Far East remained fluid. Japan could not win the war, but the price of its surrender would run high. At Yalta, Stalin had agreed to enter the war against Japan, but experience in Eastern Europe made American officials increasingly less eager to draw Soviet troops into Asia. They searched for a way to save American lives without relying upon full Soviet participation. Atomic power provided the answer.

The awesome power of the new bomb, frightfully demonstrated at Hiroshima and Nagasaki, was one of the ingredients contributing to a general hardening of America's attitudes toward the Soviet Union. Wearing "this weapon rather ostentatiously on our hip," as one official put it, the United States felt it could make demands regarding Soviet conduct in Eastern Europe which Stalin could not ignore. Americans believed their economic power could also be used as diplomatic leverage. The Soviet Union badly needed assistance for postwar reconstruction, and when Stalin requested aid following the end of Lend-Lease the Truman administration again made it clear that he would have to keep Eastern Europe open to American trade and ideas. Truman's tough, anti-Soviet tone found encouragement from respected statesmen such as Churchill, top advisers such as Averell Harriman, and Americans of Eastern European decent who were an important part of the Democratic coalition. To these people, the USSR's denial of democratic freedoms, its new power position in Europe, and its support of leftist movements around the globe made it a dangerous threat to civilization. Many Americans came to believe that Stalin, like Hitler, had to be stopped, and with their overwhelming nuclear and economic power they were in no mood to compromise.

The growing cold war

As Truman's attitude grew more inflexible, Stalin's mirrored it by degrees. Russians never understood America's outrage at the Eastern European situation. They had not protested Anglo-American hegemony in Italy or Greece, and America alone occupied Japan. Surely, Stalin argued, his nation, which had suffered the greatest casualties and property damage during the war, deserved minimal guarantees for its own future security. Truman's uncompromising stance did not force Stalin to change but only strengthened his desire for security. Stalin badly needed loans, but not at the price of what he believed were his country's most basic strategic interests—keeping a tight hold over Eastern Europe. He turned instead to other solutions, announcing a new Five-Year Plan to rebuild Soviet industry. To help his reconstruction effort, Stalin expropriated what he could from the occupied European territories and closed off the area from almost all western influence.

A few groups in the United States voiced opposition to the deterioration in Soviet-American relations and condemned the Truman administration's inflexibility. Many had no sympathy for Communism but perceived that the bomb offered no realistic way to rid Eastern Europe of pro-Soviet regimes. Believing that a militant attitude would only further close trade and communication links, liberals such as Henry Wallace advocated accommodation rather than saber-rattling. In 1946

Wallace left Truman's cabinet and two years later ran for president on a third-party platform which advocated defrosting the cold war.

Wallace's views gained few converts in a world plagued with disorder and threatened by left-wing revolutionary movements. Communism grew up amid conditions of want and political disruption, and American policymakers began to postulate that it might wither away with prosperity and stability. "The only hope of stopping Soviet penetration is the development of sound economic conditions," Harriman advised Truman. When in early 1947 a Communist coup threatened the British-backed regime in Greece and Great Britain announced that it could no longer afford economic assistance, Truman undertook a massive aid program in Greece and Turkey. Overcoming resistance from congressmen who believed that replacing Britain as protector of the Greek monarchy would prove inordinately expensive and ill-advised, Truman finally received authorization for $400 million, primarily for arms. This Truman Doctrine began America's fight against revolutionary Communism through foreign aid. In the following year, Truman sought to extend economic assistance to other European nations through the Marshall Plan. This new aid program, designed to rebuild a strong Europe, including Germany, initially met strong domestic opposition, but after a Communist coup in neutralist Czechoslovakia, Congress passed it by an overwhelming margin.

Together, the Truman Doctrine and the Marshall Plan extended the fight against Communist movements throughout Europe and provided a pattern for foreign aid programs which would eventually expand throughout the world. The money brought needed assistance to many nations and provided opportunities for American trade and investment abroad, but it also committed the United States to preserving the status quo in countries swept by pressures for change. The decline of the colonial powers and Japan's bid for supremacy in the Far East had undermined old imperial structures and stirred nationalist movements. But the United States—once the champion of the right of revolution, social justice, and self-determination—increasingly fell into the uncomfortable position of supporting colonialist nations (such as the French in Indo-China) and corrupt elitist regimes (such as Chiang Kai-shek's). In its well-intentioned effort to "contain" totalitarianism, the United States often undertook the impossible task of "containing" social instability throughout the world. In the vocabulary of the cold war, the terms "free peoples" and the "free world" came to be defined purely as anti-Communist, having little to do with respect for individual liberties or democratic values. One of the ironies of the cold war was that in their determined effort to keep the world open to the spread of American ideals, Americans too often allied themselves with violators of the very freedoms they sought to uphold.

President Truman and Lauren Bacall. *UPI*

The self-perpetuating cycle of distrust between the United States and the Soviet Union gave rise to a whole new cold war rhetoric which reflected the way in which each country viewed the postwar world. Soviet charges of "imperialist war-mongering" met American cries against an "international Communist conspiracy." Fear of "capitalist encirclement" matched apprehension about "Soviet aggression" which had to be "contained." America's allies were "running dogs," and Russia's were "satellites." "Imperialist dupes" became the equivalent of "enslaved peoples" and "lackey of Wall Street" and "atheistic, Godless Communism." Which side of the "Iron Curtain" was truly "liberated" depended upon whether one looked from the East or from the West. More than a cycle of events, the cold war became a battle of rhetoric and images, filtering down from the diplomats to the man on the street. The cold war was a mentality, pervasive and convincing, which took its initial shape from events and then assumed a life of its own. The very words and expressions used in postwar years became increasingly less a description of reality and ever more a determinant of it.

HARRY S. TRUMAN

Succeeding a deceased president is always difficult, but Harry S. Truman found the ordeal of succession particularly cruel. Roosevelt, who guided the nation through the Depression and to the point of final victory over the Axis, symbolized security at home and abroad to millions of Americans. Reformers within the Democratic party considered him the heart of the New Deal tradition, and they eagerly awaited the end of the war when they could revive the battle against domestic problems. Even Roosevelt's detractors conceded his prestige and popularity both in the United States and around the world. Nothing in Harry Truman's background suggested the capacity to match either the fallen leader's personal appeal or to approach his presidential accomplishments.

Much in Truman's career invited comparison, rarely flattering, with his predecessor. A short, undistinguished-looking man who grew up in rural Missouri, Truman lacked Roosevelt's commanding presence. During the First World War FDR served as undersecretary of the navy; Truman fought in the ranks. FDR prudently cooperated with the Democratic bosses but generally rose above the seamier side of political bargaining. Truman, although untouched by personal scandals, learned his trade with the infamous Pendergast machine in Kansas City and always struggled to live down charges of bossism and cronyism. While FDR captured the spotlight during the days of the New Deal, Truman sat in the back of the Senate loyally supporting reform but never launching crusades. The 1944 Democratic convention selected Truman as vice-president primarily to replace Henry Wallace with a less controversial figure, and although Truman enjoyed his short time in that office, FDR rarely consulted him. "I don't think I saw Roosevelt but twice as Vice-President except at Cabinet meetings," Truman later confessed. When the squire from Hyde Park passed away, the man from Independence seemed all too small a successor.

An uncertain mood

One historian has remarked that a sense of uncertainty—a "mood maybe" —characterized the immediate postwar period. Remembering the difficult transition in 1919–1920, many Americans feared the reappearance of economic problems once orders for military goods stopped and soldiers glutted the job market. Both businessmen and workers eagerly anticipated the end of wage and price controls, and organized labor wanted to be released from its wartime pledge against striking. Republican leaders hoped that their party would regain some of the ground lost during almost twelve years of Roosevelt. And within Democratic ranks, many ardent New Dealers believed that Harry Truman could never offer the type of leadership which the reform cause needed to face mounting opposition.

Economic problems immediately tested the new president. Following the surrender of Japan, American consumers insisted on goods—nylon stockings, canned beer, electric toasters—which had been scarce or unavailable during the war. Demand for items such as cars and new homes quickly outstripped available supplies. At the same time, a number of labor unions struck for higher wages. The coal and auto industries shut down briefly, and only a presidential threat to draft workers into the army halted a nationwide rail walkout. Despite businessmen's calls for an end to governmental economic controls, commodity shortages and rising wages forced retention of price restraints until the middle of 1946. But the randomly enforced measures proved ineffective; prices skyrocketed and shortages increased. Wholesale meat prices in Chicago went up 22 percent in a single day—and even then customers kept buying. Large-city butchers often expected a tip for the laborious task of passing meat over the counter. Some car purchasers handed over several hundred extra dollars before a smiling auto dealer delivered one of the scarce Detroit specials. Such black market operations became a familiar part of life immediately after the war, and, as usual, people blamed the president.

The Eighteenth Congress   Wherever Truman turned, new difficulties appeared. Powerful members of the New Deal coalition, especially labor leaders, found the president a confused and vacillating executive, unable to gloss over contradictions with FDR's confident manner. Frustrated after so many years of launching futile attacks on Roosevelt, Republicans declared open season on Truman during the 1946 congressional election. "To err is Truman" and "Under Truman, Two Families in Every Garage," proclaimed Republican slogans. "Had Enough?" Republican posters asked. Millions of voters had. The GOP captured control of both houses of Congress and, outside the still solidly Democratic South, elected twenty-five governors. Republicans generally promised little; their bandwagon rolled along a trail of public frustration against an administration that seemed incapable of adjusting to the postwar world.

Truman gained strong bipartisan support for his anti-Soviet containment policy, but the president and the Eightieth Congress moved further and further apart on domestic issues. Adopting the advice of several liberal advisers, Truman escalated his militant stands as the 1948 presidential election neared. He asked Congress for a higher minimum wage, public housing construction, federal aid to education, a national health insurance plan, and farm legislation. Realizing that the Eightieth Congress would reject much of this legislation, he planned to align his administration with Roosevelt's New Deal and label GOP legislators as reactionaries.

The leader of congressional Republicans, Senator Robert A. Taft of Ohio, struggled to present an attractive alternative to Truman's ag-

Norman Rockwell's "Freedom From Want." *Reprinted with permission from The Saturday Evening Post* © *1945, Indianapolis, Indiana*

William Gropper's "House Rules Committee." *New York Public Library*

gressively liberal position. Known as "Mister Republican," Taft supported federal aid to education, some public housing, and a limited welfare program. To avoid charges that Republicans would dismantle the entire New Deal structure, he concentrated his attacks on the excessive cost of many Democratic programs and their threat to individual liberties. He suggested that Truman had gone beyond the course set by FDR, telling a nationwide radio audience that the president "has raised all the ghosts of the old New Deal with new trappings that Tugwell and Harry Hopkins never thought of." But Taft was no inflexible reactionary and labored to restrain ultraconservative Republicans in both houses of Congress.

Enactment of the important Taft-Hartley labor act, which aimed at reducing the new power of unions, illustrated both the obstacles facing Truman and Taft's crucial position in the Eightieth Congress. While the president put up an ineffective opposition to the Republican-sponsored measure, Taft skillfully maneuvered the bill through the Senate. He gained southern Democratic support and then helped soften the House's more extreme provisions in a conference committee. The Taft-Hartley Law outlawed the closed shop (which forbade the hiring of nonunion workers), prohibited political contributions out of union dues, and authorized injunctions against strikes which endangered national security. Truman immediately vetoed the bill, but Taft's fence mending paid off when Congress overrode the president's action. The law represented a victory for Taft's version of modern Republicanism, but it also handed the president a ready-made issue to attract union members in the 1948 elections.

Republicans,
progressives, and
dixiecrats

Truman and his advisers made Congress the key issue in the campaign, while the Republicans tried to avoid the question. The GOP convention bypassed Taft and selected their less controversial 1944 standard bearer, Thomas Dewey of New York. Dewey had won a landslide victory in the 1946 gubernatorial election, and coupled with the popular California Governor Earl Warren the New Yorker seemed a sure winner in 1948. Neither Dewey nor Warren could be linked directly to the Eightieth Congress. But Truman called Congress back into special session and presented a long list of "must" legislation, much of it from the Republicans' own platform promises. "They can do this job in fifteen days, if they want to do it," Truman announced, but Republican leaders passed no new legislation and adjourned Congress after several weeks. Truman accomplished his purpose: identifying Dewey with the "do-nothing, good for nothing" Republican Congress.

Division within his own party made Truman's attacks on the Eightieth Congress a desperate necessity. Some Democratic professionals considered his chances for reelection so slim that they approached

Dwight Eisenhower, unsuccessfully urging the popular general to accept the nomination. Former Vice-President and Secretary of Commerce Henry A. Wallace also led a revolt against Truman's leadership, mounting a bid for the White House under the banner of the Progressive party. The Progressive platform—which emphasized "Peace, Freedom, and Abundance"—included planks endorsing abandonment of America's containment policy, cooperation between the United States and the Soviet Union, an end to the draft, removal of racial barriers at home, and destruction of the stockpile of atomic bombs. Campaigning as the true heir to Roosevelt's foreign and domestic policies, Wallace's campaign resembled a curious mixture of urban radicalism and old-fashioned Bible Belt evangelism. Folksingers Woody Guthrie and Pete Seeger led voters in "Down by the riverside...we'll study war no more," and the Iowa-born Wallace contributed his rumpled midwestern presence. Wallace had no chance for the presidency, but his effort did threaten to undercut Truman's support among left-leaning Democrats, especially in the crucial state of New York.

An even more serious revolt occurred in the solidly Democratic South. When a coalition of liberals (led by Hubert Humphrey, then mayor of Minneapolis) and urban bosses pushed through a strong civil rights plank, some southerners walked out of the Democratic convention and launched a fourth political party. The States' Rights or "Dixiecrat" party offered Governor J. Strom Thurmond of South Carolina as its presidential candidate and pledged retention of racial segregation as the southern way of life. Much like Governor George Wallace's American party of 1968, the Dixiecrats of 1948 hoped to capture enough southern electoral votes to send the election to the House of Representatives.

The election of 1948   However limited their own chances for success, the candidacies of Wallace and Thurmond appeared to guarantee Truman's defeat. Dewey confidently held to his noncontroversial path, campaigning for fewer weeks, in fewer states, and with fewer personal appearances than the energetic Truman. He relied upon broad appeals to national and party unity. With "restoration of faith in ourselves, of competence in our Government, of unity of purpose among our people," he advised, "there is nothing, as a people, we cannot do." Such platitudes, the New Yorker hoped, would smooth over divisions within the GOP and, more important, contrast his sober positions with the "mudslinging," "cheap wisecracking," and "ranting, bombasting partisanship" of the Democratic president.

Facing predictions of disaster, Truman's attacks upon Dewey and the Eightieth Congress grew more strident. As approving Democrats yelled, "Give 'em hell, Harry," the president assaulted Republicans as "a bunch of old mossbacks,...gluttons of privilege,...all set to do a hatchet job on the New Deal." "If you let the Republicans get control of the government," he warned one audience, "you will be making

America an economic colony of Wall Street." With his down-home, Missouri stump-speaking style, Truman reminded workers of the Taft-Hartley Act and told rural voters how Republicans "stuck a pitchfork in the backs of farmers by cutting down on funds for crop storage." He assailed the press as biased and claimed their polls predicting a Dewey victory were rigged to discourage Democrats from voting. Hoping to attract black voters in northern cities, Truman endorsed the civil rights cause more strongly than in the past. In July he issued an executive order desegregating the armed forces and the departments of the national government. Shortly before the end of his campaign, he became the first presidential candidate ever to make a personal appearance in New York's Harlem.

But despite Truman's efforts, almost all pollsters and political writers predicted a Dewey victory in November. Even as early returns showed Truman leading, most experts stuck by their forecasts. A famous extra edition of the staunchly Republican Chicago *Tribune*, which hit the streets with a banner headline proclaming "Dewey Defeats Truman," became a collector's treasure when final returns showed a narrow, Truman upset. Strom Thurmond's party failed to garner enough southern electoral votes to throw the contest into the House, and Henry Wallace ran a distant fourth.

The 1948 election revealed that the proliferation of candidates and issues either failed to arouse the voters' interest or confused them into staying home. Turnout across the country was light; only slightly more than 51 percent of the electorate cast ballots. In such a "decline election" of low vote totals, Truman and the Democrats could rely upon the Roosevelt—New Deal coalition to pull them through, but the president failed to gain any real mandate for new changes. The voters had rejected the dismantling of the New Deal which the Eightieth Congress had threatened, but without calling for its further extension. The 1948 election would define the shape of postwar politics, initiating a generation of stalemate.

Measured by the accomplishments of his predecessor, Truman's reform record appeared meager; his "Fair Deal" hardly made people forget the New Deal. Congress did enact the National Housing Act of 1949 which provided money for slum clearance and authorized construction of almost a million low-income units (few were actually built). Legislators also granted Truman's request for an increase in the minimum wage (to seventy-five cents), for broader Social Security coverage, and for funds to carry on the work begun by Roosevelt's TVA and RA. But a coalition of conservative Republicans and southern Democrats blocked most of the president's requests and frustrated a number of his priority programs. Extensive lobbying by the American Medical Association helped bury his national health insurance plan under a barrage of propaganda labeling it as "socialized medicine." Southern committee chairmen and filibusters kept the president's civil rights promises effectively bottled up in Congress, and his hopes for federal aid to education foundered on the controversial issue of extending funds to parochial schools. In addition to legislative obstacles, Truman's domestic program suffered from controversy growing out of the developing cold war.

THE COLD WAR

During Truman's second term (1949–1953) deepening hostility between the United States and the Soviet Union dominated national attention. No longer was the Red menace limited to Greece and Turkey: the entire globe became the arena for conflict between the "free" and "Communist" worlds, as Americans automatically identified revolutionary movements throughout the world as part of a unified Communist conspiracy. Most leaders opposed using America's military power to roll back the Communist threat and liberate "enslaved" peoples. But the vast majority also rejected the idea of negotiation—a term which implied concession and appeasement. Memories of the rapid spread of Nazism during the late 1930s remained vivid, and American leaders feared that a Communist success in one area would quickly snowball into a worldwide Red avalanche. As the strongest nation, the United States bore the heaviest responsibility for "containing" Communist expansion. Any Munich-like compromise could send outposts of the free world tumbling like a row of dominoes. "We cannot afford any more compromises," explained Reinhold Neibuhr in a 1948 *Life* magazine article. "We will have to stand at every point in our far-flung lines."

On the other side of the so-called Iron Curtain, Stalin and his key advisers held a strikingly similar vision of a bipolar world, a world divided into two hostile camps and dominated by the two superpowers. Soviet strategists interpreted western actions as part of a hostile and long-standing anti-Bolshevik policy. As a result of this "mirror image," which dominated elites in both the United States and the Soviet Union, the postwar period of hostility and distrust expanded into an era of global conflict and crisis after 1948.

Berlin and NATO   Germany was the first battleground. American officials considered a strong, prosperous, and West-leaning Germany the key to political and economic stability in Europe. The three non-Soviet zones of occupation were merged into a single state of West Germany; the United States undertook currency reform as the first step toward reviving the German economy. When the American administrator, General Lucius D. Clay, introduced the revalued *Deutschmark* into West Berlin, a western outpost inside the Communist zone, Stalin saw the action as a threat which he could not safely ignore. The Soviet Union had suffered German invasions twice in the twentieth century, and Stalin believed that a weak, neutral Germany was essential to Russia's security. Facing what he saw as a capitalist conspiracy against his country, Stalin closed all surface access into West Berlin.

American officials reacted swiftly, interpreting Stalin's actions as a further step in his own aggressive campaign to dominate Europe. "We have lost Czechoslovakia," explained General Clay. "Norway is threatened. We retreat from Berlin. When Berlin falls, Western Germany would be next." Some of Truman's military advisers wanted to blast their way into Berlin, but the president rejected this alternative. Instead, he authorized a massive airlift; planes began flying round the clock, bringing as much as thirteen thousand tons of supplies into the city in a single day. The president reinstituted the draft; began increasing the size of the army; and sent two squadrons of B-29s, the planes which carried atomic bombs, to Great Britain. His advisers hoped that this would signal how seriously they viewed the Berlin crisis (and secondarily that it would accustom Britons to having American warplanes on their soil).

The Truman administration also moved to safeguard America's long-range economic and political interests in Europe. Creation of the North Atlantic Treaty Organization (NATO) in early 1949 formalized the new strategy. Twelve nations, including the Big Three Allies—the United States, Great Britain, and France—signed this collective-security arrangement which provided that an attack upon any member would be considered aggression against all. The treaty pledged members to develop "free institutions" and to encourage "economic collaboration between any or all" of the parties. As originally conceived, NATO lacked the ground forces to repel a nonnuclear invasion, and the United States refused to share its atomic weapons with other members. Rather than representing a spectacular strategic departure, NATO primarily offered the United States a new means for channeling aid and influence into Europe.

During 1949, a new series of events shook the United States. At home, exposure of alleged Communist spy rings—the most spectacular charge implicated a minor member of Roosevelt's administration—raised popular fears about America's internal security. In addition, Mao Tse-tung's Communist forces finally drove Chiang Kai-shek off the Chinese mainland to the island of Formosa. The United States tried to support Chiang with military assistance, but what the chief American adviser called "the world's worst leadership" and "many other morale-destroying factors" doomed the Nationalist regime. Much of their army simply melted away, and 80 percent of the American-sent material fell into Communist hands. In an official "White Paper" Secretary of State Acheson argued that Mao's victory was "the ominous result of the civil war in China" and "beyond the control of the government of the United States." But a number of Republicans charged the administration with pursuing a "no-win" policy in Asia, and some Americans, nurtured on the wartime myth of Chiang's dominance, concluded that "Reds" in the State Department had "sold us out." Finally, only months after Chiang's collapse, President Truman made another startling announcement. At a late morning news conference, he informed White House reporters that the Soviets had exploded their first atomic weapon, a revelation which signaled the end of the United States' nuclear monopoly. As Republican Senator Arthur Vandenburg remarked, "This is now a different world."

Following the events of 1949, the "year of shocks," senior advisers in the State and Defense departments searchingly reviewed United States capabilities. By the spring of the following year, these officials and members of the National Security Council produced a comprehensive blueprint for future strategy. Labeled "N.S.C. paper number 68," the document reiterated assumptions which were already conventional cold war wisdom: the bipolarity of world affairs; the aggressive nature of international communism; and the validity of the "domino theory." The paper recommended that the United States radically increase both its own and its allies' military power. Americans had to stop "trying to distinguish between national and global security," and they could not worry about costs. Arguing that the country could reasonably afford a massive military buildup (consuming as much as 20 percent of the gross national product), the framers of N.S.C. 68 concluded that the Communist threat required the United States to play the role of world policeman.

Korea   N.S.C. 68 lay before President Truman in June 1950 when Communist North Korea attacked South Korea, an informal ally of the United States. Mystery still shrouds the origins of the Korean War. The Soviet Union equipped the North Koreans and possibly encouraged their invasion of the South. Yet the Soviet delegation was boycotting the United Nations at the crucial moment of attack, an absence which allowed the United States to circumvent a Soviet veto and gain United Nations support for the American-controlled defense of South Korea. Either the North Koreans invaded without consulting Stalin, or the Soviets never expected the United States to rush to South Korea's aid. No strong evidence supports persistent charges that America's unpopular South Korean ally, Syngman Rhee, actually provoked the North Koreans in order to save his tottering regime, but Truman's massive and immediate reaction does suggest that military operations in Korea came as no surprise to American officials.

Reacting swiftly according to the assumptions contained in N.S.C. 68, Truman implemented a worldwide containment policy. The situation in Korea made it "plain beyond all doubt," he argued, "that communism has passed beyond the use of subversion to conquer independent nations and will now use armed invasion and war." Two days after the outbreak of fighting in Korea, the president announced that our Seventh Fleet would protect Chiang Kai-shek's regime on Formosa from invasion by the mainland Chinese; that the United States would send arms and a "military mission" to support the French against the guerrilla forces of Ho Chi Minh in Indo-China; that the government would give the Philippines additional assistance in their struggle against leftist Huk rebels; and that American naval and air forces would assist Syngman Rhee's government in repulsing the North Korean advance. Truman began augmenting American forces elsewhere, providing more troops for NATO in the early fall. And in a dramatic conference with British and French representatives, Secretary of State Acheson formally announced the United States' long-planned program for rearming West Germany and integrating it into the NATO system. The Korean conflict helped Truman convince congressmen to appropriate a much larger defense budget. In two years military expenditures more than tripled, making up nearly 70 percent of the 1951–52 budget.

The Korean War itself was a bloody, seesaw affair. Truman originally believed that air power could contain the North Koreans, but, as in Vietnam a decade later, strategists overestimated the military effectiveness of bombing. When the South Korean army rapidly disintegrated, the president sent in United States ground troops under the umbrella of a United Nations operation. North Korean armies still continued advancing south and sent Americans reeling back. Finally regrouping his troops, General Douglas MacArthur masterminded a brilliant marine landing behind enemy lines at Inchon and quickly reached the 38th parallel, the official boundary between the two Koreas. MacArthur then received presidential authority to move northward and "liberate" the Iron Curtain capital of Pyongyang. As United States forces neared the North Korea–China border, Chinese Premier Chou En-lai condemned the "frenzied and violent acts of imperialist aggression" and warned that China could not tolerate such a threat, but General MacArthur downplayed the possibility, or the effectiveness, of Chinese intervention. Even after encountering Chinese "volunteers," the general confided to reporters in late November 1950 that the "war very definitely is coming to an end shortly." Two days after his prediction, Chinese troops stormed across the Yalu River, driving between MacArthur's widely scattered armies and forcing the United States to retreat south of the 38th parallel once again, this time with heavy casualties. When Americans, in yet another drive northward, pressed near the 38th parallel, Truman instructed MacArthur to seek negotiations rather than to pursue full-scale invasion. But the general, hoping to carry the war back into North Korea and ultimately to China, publicly opposed Truman's idea of "limited warfare" and attempted to subvert efforts to end the war at the 38th parallel. In a dramatic clash of wills, Truman "fired" the proud general.

The Truman-MacArthur controversy reflected the administration's view that containment was a truly global strategy. Korea was simply one part of a more general struggle against Communist expansion. Policymakers supported MacArthur's first drive into North Korea, expecting a relatively easy victory, but Chinese involvement threatened an interminable Asian land war which would weaken America's ability to defend its more vital interests in Western Europe. In the later words of General Omar Bradley, a protracted engagement in Korea would have been "the wrong war, at the wrong place, at the wrong time, and with the wrong enemy."

MacArthur and the "Asia-firsters"—a loosely organized group of religious leaders, economic interests, and right-wing Republican spokesmen who urged all-out victory in Korea and liberation of Red China—made a fervent stand against the orthodoxy of containment. MacArthur triumphantly toured the country assailing the president, and his supporters called for greater efforts to roll back the Red Menace. The general warned that "the insidious forces working from within" would lead America "directly to the path of Communist slavery." But the administration rode out the storm. Senate hearings into MacArthur's dismissal revealed that most military strategists supported the president, and, after a wave of sentiment in favor of the World War II hero had subsided, most people rejected his scenario for a wider war in Asia. As Truman's presidency ended, the war continued, but at a reduced level. In Korea, negotiators for both sides were sitting around a conference table which carefully straddled the 38th parallel.

CRUSADE FOR CONSENSUS

Events of the postwar years awakened fears of a foreign-directed conspiracy, a vast Communist plot which threatened to surround the nation abroad and to undermine it from within. Although generally associated with Senator Joseph R. McCarthy of Wisconsin and his followers, this second "Red Scare" was part of a much broader quest for consensus and conformity. The most extreme anti-Communists envisioned conspirators spreading insidious doctrines into almost every area of American life. A Michigan congressman, for example, charged that modern artists, "soldier[s] of the Communist Revolution," sought to destroy people's attachment to logic and reality by saturating them with the "depraved" and "illogical" ideas of expressionism.

During the late forties and early fifties government officials and private watchdogs made searching examinations into people's ideas and actions. Both state and national governments established loyalty programs designed to unmask enemy agents and sympathizers. Inquisitors examined people's associates, organizations, and even casual acquaintances for evidence of Communist or radical ties. When no direct link could be established to Communist organizations, investigators often labeled their prey as "fellow travelers," "pinkos," or "Fifth Amendment Communists." Employing the technique of guilt by association and sometimes grossly distorting facts, anti-Communist crusaders cast a shadow of fear over the lives of a number of innocent Americans and trampled upon their basic constitutional liberties. But these twentieth-century witch hunters found few actual subversives.

Doubts about the United States' position in a rapidly changing and complex world helped to generate these exaggerated fears of a gigantic Red conspiracy. After four years of total war, Americans had suddenly found themselves unable to "return to normalcy" as after the First World War. Extension of Soviet control over Eastern Europe appeared to demonstrate the aggressive designs of Stalin's regime and raised fears about its aims elsewhere. When leaders such as President Truman equated the Communist and Nazi threats, Americans could logically conclude that the fight to save democracy had become an open-ended commitment. A Communist form of totalitarianism seemed to have replaced the fascist version.

Politics and anti-Communism

Partisan politics also fueled the hysteria. Although Harry Truman enjoyed impeccable anti-Communist credentials, fears of Republican criticism impelled him to adopt an increasingly tough position against domestic subversion. During the 1948 elections Truman emphasized his anti-Communist actions, preventing Republicans from expropriating the issue for themselves. He established a tight internal security program which failed to distinguish very clearly between persons accused of being Soviet agents and those merely suspected of holding unorthodox political ideas. Truman's attorney general warned that Communists were "everywhere—in factories, offices, butcher stores, on street corners, in private businesses." By 1950 the president himself could proclaim that the Soviet Union was a "modern tyranny led by a small group who have abandoned their faith in God. . . . We are on the right track and we will win—because God is with us in that Enterprise." Truman and his administration helped create a set of conspiratorial images and fears, elements which more extreme Republican Red baiters could carry even further when the opportunity presented itself.

After 1948 events at home and overseas encouraged new charges. Continued deterioration of Soviet-American relations, Mao's victory in China, Russia's acquisition of atomic weapons, and the Korean War put the Truman administration on the defensive. And revelations of espionage activities within the United States gave immediacy to charges of Communist penetration into sensitive government positions. Whitaker Chambers, a former associate editor of *Time,* charged Alger Hiss, a Roosevelt aide who had been at Yalta, with being a member of the Communist party and passing classified material to the Soviets in the late 1930s. In a dramatic showdown, Chambers led congressional investigators to his Maryland farm and pulled microfilmed documents from a hollowed-out pumpkin. The arrest of British scientist Klaus Fuchs on a spy charge was even more ominous; the supposed plot included several Americans and involved giving atomic secrets to the Russians. "How much more are we going to have to take?" exploded Republican Senator Homer Capehart. "Fuchs and Acheson and Hiss and hydrogen bombs threatening outside and New Dealism eating away at the vitals of the nation. In the name of Heaven, is this the best America can do?"

Enter McCarthy In this already frenzied atmosphere, a new anti-Communist spokesman made his belated debut. With a rasping voice and crude manners, Joseph McCarthy seemed a more likely candidate for the heavy in a B movie than for a United States senator. But McCarthy capitalized on his image as a political primitive and followed a stormy career as a state judge with an upset victory in 1946. The thick-set "Fighting Marine" proved a tough back-alley brawler, firing political punches in all directions. Although fading pictures and old newsreels make him appear slightly comical—with his baggy suits and ill-matched ties—the Wisconsin senator became a powerful force in the early 1950s.

Facing reelection with an undistinguished record—the Washington press galley had voted him the worst of the ninety-six Senators—McCarthy seized the Communist issue as his return ticket to the Senate. He hurriedly assembled a patchwork of old material on Communist infiltration and, by adding his own embellishments, established himself as America's most feared Red baiter. In a 1950 speech before a Republican women's club in Wheeling, West Virginia, McCarthy waved a paper purporting to be a list of Communist party members and sympathizers employed in the State Department. His exact words and figures are forever lost—McCarthy had no finished text and a radio engineer innocently erased the only recording—but the Wisconsin senator charged somewhere between 57 and 279 employees with subversive connections. Although he had no list and never proved any of his "documented cases," McCarthy continued to issue new and more sensational allegations. Claiming to name names and to present only the facts, he flung charges faster than his victims could refute them.

McCarthy set the tone for much of the political debate of the next few years. A special Senate committee, chaired by the distinguished Democratic conservative Millard Tydings, tried to deflate McCarthy but only succeeded in giving him greater publicity. Other GOP members copied his rhetoric, charging Democratic rivals with un-American sentiments and suspicious connections. Many Republicans who resisted such tactics stood by as less reticent colleagues freely used the Red brush against Democrats. In 1950 the defeat of Millard Tydings and the success of anti-Communist campaigns, such as those of senators Richard

Joseph McCarthy. *UPI*

Ike said "I'll be darned" on hearing that President Truman had fired Douglas MacArthur. *Wide World*

Nixon and Everett Dirkson, demonstrated the appeal of the Red issue and appeared to confirm the power of McCarthy and his followers.

The McCarran Internal Security Act of 1950 illustrated the near-terror with which politicians approached the anti-Communist issue. A hodgepodge of "antisubversive" legislation, the McCarran Act included sections requiring registration of Communist and Communist-front organizations and authorizing a number of detention camps to house internal enemies in times of crisis. Such provisions raised serious constitutional difficulties, but few congressmen dared provoke the McCarthyites' wrath by openly opposing the bill. Even Hubert Humphrey, normally a pillar of postwar liberalism, supported it on final passage. "I was very proud of you and your vote," he later wrote one of the seven senators who voted no. "I wish I could say the same for myself." Joined by Humphrey, a few libertarians urged President Truman to veto the measure. Truman prided himself on his desk plaque, "The Buck Stops Here," and he did reject the act, a veto which Congress quickly overrode.

As a coterie of right-wing Republicans, anti-Communist zealots, Texas oilmen, and outright racists attached themselves to McCarthy's coattails, even more sensational "revelations" unfolded. On the floor of the Senate, McCarthy strongly implied that General George Marshall, World War II hero and former secretary of state, had betrayed the American cause and sold out Chiang Kai-shek to the Communists. How else could anyone explain Communist successes, charged McCarthy, "unless we believe that men high in the Government are concentrating to deliver us to disaster? This must be the product of a great conspiracy, ...so immense as to dwarf any previous such venture in the history of man." Numerous other political and intellectual leaders felt the sting of "Senator Joe's" wild attacks, but fear of his supposed political invincibility and his unscrupulous methods silenced most potential critics. In a January 1953 editorial, the New York Post asked plaintively, "Is McCarthy untouchable?"

McCarthy only appeared unassailable. The Wisconsin senator proved to be not the leader of a dangerous mass movement, as many intellectuals of the period feared, but the beneficiary of a peculiarly favorable set of political circumstances. Old-line conservative Republicans from the Midwest formed the foundation of McCarthy's power base, and he benefited from the blessing or acquiesence of other elites in postwar society. Seeing the anti-Communist issue as a potent weapon against the Democrats, most Republican leaders either encouraged or tolerated McCarthy's extreme attacks on the opposition. The Senate's "establishment" hesitated to censure one of their own; prominent liberals kept quiet; and sensation-hunting newspapers gave McCarthy abundant coverage. And during the cold war's hottest days—the period of the Korean conflict—McCarthy's claims of Communist subversion carried additional emotional appeal.

But following the 1952 election of the new Republican president, former General Dwight D. Eisenhower, and the cessation of hostilities in Korea, McCarthy gradually lost both his elite support and popular credibility. To a Republican party out of power McCarthy was an asset; to a party in power, especially one which had ended the Korean conflict, the raucous senator proved an acute embarrassment. The Eisenhower administration initially tolerated McCarthy—Ike remarked that he would "not get down in the gutter with *that* guy"—but eventually the senator went too far. Following his charges that the United States army contained Communist infiltrators, the various elites which had once sheltered him turned against the maverick senator. Eisenhower repudiated him; many (though by no means all) conservative Republicans deserted him; the army struck back at him; and a majority of senators officially ostracized him. During thirty-five days of nationally televised hearings, a special Senate committee investigated McCarthy's charges against the army. McCarthy, overconfident and pugnacious, came across on the TV screen as the town bully. The hearings, which became daily television spectaculars, helped break McCarthy's aura of political invincibility; six months later the Senate formally censured him for conduct unbecoming a member of that august body. His fragile power broken, McCarthy ended his days a pathetic figure, dying in 1957.

McCarthy's appeal proved shallow, but a spirit of consensus pervaded the nation. During the height of the cold war, radicalism in politics, social thought, or the arts became unfashionable. Legal prosecutions for unorthodox sentiments were less important than more subtle means of coercion. Left-wing sympathizers in the Hollywood film community discovered that producers' doors were suddenly closed to them; folksingers such as Pete Seeger and the Weavers found themselves barred from the airwaves; and the intellectual establishment, lined up behind militant anticommunism and containment, trumpeted the glories of the liberal, capitalist order. Writers such as I. F. Stone, who would become a "respectable" radical during the 1960s, stood out in the consensus-ridden cold war period. Although charges that intellectuals became merely uncritical cheerleaders for America are unfair, a generation of liberals agreed with Arthur M. Schlesinger, Jr., that their proper position was in the "Vital Center."

THE ATOMIC BOMB

The development of atomic power was not the achievement of Americans alone; scientists from around the world conducted the research and made the discovereries which led to the release of atomic energy. But the fact that these efforts first reached fruition in the United States reflected America's tremendous growth as a world power and demonstrated an outstanding ability to mobilize and organize scientific resources on a massive scale.

Throughout the twentieth century, scientists worked to unravel the mysteries of the atom, once considered the smallest particle of matter in the universe. Early in the century, researchers discovered the atom's nucleus, protons, and neutrons. Elaborating upon his formula, $E = mc^2$ (energy equals mass multiplied by the square of the speed of light), Albert Einstein showed that splitting an atom would produce a tremendous force resulting from the transformation of matter into energy. By the 1930s an MIT scientist had constructed an "atom smasher" and a University of California researcher had developed a cyclotron. These machines provided the great amounts of voltage required for atomic exploration. And by the end of the 1930s the United States scientific community gained from the arrival of three important refugees from Europe: Einstein, Niels Bohr, and Enrico Fermi. The migration of these great scientists to the United States provided immediate aid in atomic research. It also symbolized a larger phenomenon—the emergence of the United States as the leading supporter of scientific and technological research.

The growing crisis in world affairs and the fears that Germany was ahead of the United States in atomic research intensified efforts to apply nuclear discoveries to military purposes. In 1940 President Roosevelt established a special committee to coordinate military research, and a year later he created the more extensive Office of Scientific Research and Development (OSRD). In addition, the president, unknown to Congress, spent over $2 billion for research on and development of an atomic bomb. Under the direction of J. Robert Oppenheimer, the collaborators on the "Manhattan Project" finally broke through the complexity of scientific problems, and in June 1945 the United States exploded a primitive atomic device in New Mexico.

Development of this new and frightful weapon presented America's political and scientific leaders with a grave choice. Some urged President Harry Truman not to employ the bomb against Japan. "If the United States were to be the first to release this new means of indiscriminate destruction upon mankind, we would sacrifice public support throughout the world, precipitate the race for armaments, and prejudice the possibility of reaching international agreement on the future control of such weapons." But in a decision which still nags the conscience of many Americans, Truman and his principal advisers decided to drop the bomb, first on Hiroshima and three days later on Nagasaki, two major Japanese population centers. The president rejected the alternatives of warning Japan about the new weapon, demonstrating its power on a barren island, or dropping it on less populated areas. He opted for maximum surprise and devastation "in order to shorten the agony of war," as he put it. The bombs did bring surrender, but America's victory had a bitter taste and left lingering doubts about our self-proclaimed benevolence.

THINGS TO THINK ABOUT:
1940–1953

Why did the United States move from neutrality to belligerence between 1939 and 1941? In addition to the works cited in the previous chapter, the basic surveys are W. L. Langer and S. E. Gleason, *The Challenge to Isolation, 1937–1940* (1952) and *The Undeclared War, 1940–1941* (1953); Basil Rauch, *Roosevelt: Munich to Pearl Harbor* (1959); and Herbert Feis, *The Road to Pearl Harbor* (1950). Paul W. Schroeder, *The Axis Alliance and Japanese-American Relations, 1941* (1958) and Warren F. Kimball, *The Most Unsordid Act: Lend Lease, 1939–1941* (1969) are specialized studies. Bruce M. Russett's *No Clear and Present Danger: A Skeptical View of the U.S. Entry into World War II* (1972) is a short interpretative essay in the "revisionist" tradition.

Assess the impact of total war upon the home front. What tensions did war produce? What changes did it bring? Chester Eisinger, ed., *The 1940's: Profile of a Nation in Crisis* (1969) is a valuable collection of source materials. Richard Polenberg, *War and Society, The United States, 1941–1945* (1971) is a general survey. Jacobus ten Broek, et al., *Prejudice, War, and the Constitution* (2nd ed., 1968) remains the best treatment of the internment of Japanese Americans. Lawrence S. Wittner, *Rebels Against War: The American Peace Movement, 1941–1960* (1969) and Richard M. Dalfiume, *Desegregation of the U.S. Armed Forces: Fighting on Two Fronts, 1939–1953* (1969) relate their topics to broader social and political trends.

What was the relationship between wartime strategy and the Allies' postwar aims? Gaddis Smith, *American Diplomacy During the Second World War, 1941–1945* (1965) and Raymond G. O'Connor, *Diplomacy for Victory: FDR and Unconditional Surrender* (1971) are short summaries of wartime diplomacy. James M. Burns, *Roosevelt: The Soldier of Freedom* (1970) and Gabriel Kolko, *The Politics of War: The World and United States Foreign Policy, 1943–45* (1968) offer differing perspectives on the conduct of the war and postwar aims.

How did both foreign and domestic considerations lead to the "cold war" between the Soviet Union and the United States? William L. Nuemann, *After Victory: Churchill, Roosevelt, Stalin, and the Making of the Peace* (1969) is a recent summary. Lloyd C. Gardner, Arthur M. Schlesinger, Jr., and Hans J. Morganthau, *The Origins of the Cold War* (1970) provides differing interpretations on this controversial topic. Three recent works are Walter LaFeber, *America, Russia, and the Cold War, 1945–1971* (1972); Stephen Ambrose, *Rise to Globalism* (1970); and Athan G. Theoharis, *The Yalta Myths: An Issue in U.S. Politics, 1945–1955* (1970).

Characterize the major developments in domestic politics between 1945 and 1953. Why did the Democrats face increasing challenges? Truman's own *Memoirs* (2 vols., 1955, 1956) are enlightening, and Cabell

Phillips's journalistic account, *The Truman Presidency* (1966) is another valuable work on postwar politics. Eric F. Goldman's *The Crucial Decade—and After: America, 1945–1960* (1960) offers some insights, and Richard Neustadt's *Presidential Power: The Politics of Leadership* (2nd ed., 1969) contains an analysis of Truman. The essays in Barton J. Bernstein, ed., *Politics and Policies of the Truman Administration* (1970) are more critical. Ronald J. Caridi's *The Korean War and American Politics: The Republican Party as a Case Study* (1968) crtiically analyzes Truman's opposition.

Why must any explanation of McCarthyism consider a variety of political, social, cultural, and foreign policy developments? Richard Rovere, *Senator Joseph McCarthy* (1959) is a useful account. Michael P. Rogin, *The Intellectuals and McCarthy* (1967) summarizes previous scholarly interpretations of McCarthyism and offers a critique of these views. Three recent studies are Alan D. Harper, *The Politics of Loyalty: The White House and the Communist Issue, 1946–1952* (1969); Robert Griffith, *The Politics of Fear: Joseph R. McCarthy and the Senate* (1970); and Richard M. Freeland, *The Truman Doctrine and the Origins of McCarthyism: Foreign Policy, Domestic Politics, and Internal Security, 1946–1948* (1972).

1953-1973

FOURTEEN | recent America

MARTIN LUTHER KING, JR.

Few men have ever been so privileged as to hold an entire nation in their moral debt. A national commitment to end legal segregation made in the 1940s and '50s found no mechanism that could move at more than a glacial pace until the Reverend Martin Luther King's nonviolent protest movement galvanized black and white Americans into effective action.

Born in Atlanta in 1929 to a family of middle-class black Americans, King chose his father's career, the Baptist ministry, rather than his mother's schoolteaching. King graduated from Morehouse College at the age of nineteen, earned a Bachelor of Divinity at the interracial Crozer Seminary in Pennsylvania, and in 1955 completed a Ph.D. in systematic theology at Boston University. While in Boston he met his future wife Coretta, an Antioch College graduate attending the New England Conservatory of Music. Returning to Montgomery, Alabama, King became pastor of the Dexter Avenue Baptist Church and led the successful city bus boycott of 1955–56. King's life was threatened and his home bombed as a result of his activities, but in 1957 he organized what later became the Southern Christian Leadership Conference. Working after 1960 from Atlanta's Ebenezer Baptist Church, King became internationally

621

famous for his nonviolent philosophy in seeking social change. He stood out as the main figure in confrontations at Birmingham and Selma, Alabama. As the principal speaker at the historic 1963 March on Washington, King delivered his famous "I have a dream" oration.

> I have a dream that one day on the red hills of Georgia the sons of former slaves and the sons of former slaveowners will be able to sit together at the table of brotherhood. . . . I have a dream that one day even the State of Mississippi, a desert state sweltering with the heat of injustice and oppression, will be transformed into an oasis of freedom and justice. . . . . I have a dream that one day the State of Alabama . . . will be transformed into a situation where little black boys and black girls will be able to join hands with little white boys and girls and walk together as sisters and brothers.

In Stockholm the next year King received the Nobel Peace Prize —becoming the youngest peace laureate in history. But there were limits to King's movement and he found himself in deep trouble after 1965. In 1967 he spoke out against the Vietnam War. The next year he was assassinated, at the young age of thirty-nine, while in Memphis to encourage striking refuse workers.

Where King could go no further, neither could the nation; the very successes of the civil rights movement revealed all that still remained to be done. It would be foolish either to discount the accomplishments of that movement or to be complacent with what it achieved. King himself understood this as well as any of his critics. The civil rights movement had achieved largely legal, not economic, gains and directly benefited middle-class blacks rather than the more desperate ghetto dwellers. Yet before King the streets of Watts and Harlem had had no effective voice and afterward a babel of voices sought to lead, direct, use, or uplift. These voices usually did not speak the idiom of Martin Luther King, but they might never have been heard in a community lacking the expectations and hope that black and white Americans had developed by the mid-sixties. King had a rare ability to articulate and dramatize ideas. He lived by the principles he had recommended to an audience at his church on the first night of the Montgomery bus boycott:

> If you will protest courageously, and yet with dignity and Christian love, when the history books are written in future generations, the historians will have to pause and say, "There lived a great people—a black people—who injected new meaning and dignity into the veins of civilization."

1953-1973

1953	Stalin dies, March 5
	Korean ceasefire, July 27
1954	SEATO Pact, September 8
	Senate censure of Joseph F. McCarthy
1955	Geneva Summit Meeting, July 18–23
	Montgomery Bus Boycott, December 1–January 1956
1956	Eisenhower sends paratroopers to Little Rock, September 24
	Eisenhower reelected president; defeats Adlai E. Stevenson
1957	Eisenhower Doctrine, January 5
1960	John F. Kennedy (Democrat) elected president; defeats Richard M. Nixon
1963	Kennedy is assassinated, November 22; Lyndon B. Johnson becomes president
1964	Gulf of Tonkin Resolution passes Senate with two votes against it
	Lyndon Johnson reelected president; defeats Barry Goldwater
1968	Tet Offensive in Vietnam, January–February
	Martin Luther King is assassinated, April 4
	Richard M. Nixon (Republican) elected president; defeats Hubert Humphrey
1969	Moon landing, July 20
1972	Richard M. Nixon is reelected; defeats George McGovern
1973	Vietnam ceasefire signed, January 15

EISENHOWER'S FOREIGN POLICY

President Dwight D. Eisenhower presided over something rare in recent American history: a brief era of peace. Behind his administration stretched the agonizing pasts of the cold war, the Second World War, and the Great Depression—itself a war against want. Ahead lay the heated debates of the 1960s and the debacle of Vietnam. The foreign policy tone of the fifties—characterized after Korea by the near-absence of foreign conflict, real or impending—is nicely captured by the American general who wished, above all, to be remembered as a man of peace.

A Kansan who enjoyed undergraduate days at West Point, Eisenhower had gone on to academic honors at Command and General Staff School. During World War II he demonstrated his military acumen commanding first the invasion of North Africa and later the second front assault on Normandy; Montgomery of England and de Gaulle of France praised his skills at strategic maneuver. Concealing a determined will behind a self-effacing manner, General Eisenhower continually inspired confidence among his troops and with homefront Americans. Yet after the peace he showed no desire to impose his own military background on the demobilized nation. In Europe the general had learned the horrors of war. His *Crusade in Europe* recounts the entry into the Falaise Gap Zone in Normandy in 1944: "It was literally possible," he wrote, "to walk for hundreds of yards at a time, stepping on nothing but dead and decayed flesh."

After the war Eisenhower served briefly as president of Columbia University where he set up an academic "chair of peace" and inaugurated the American Assembly, a cold war "think tank" that would study international problems. In 1950 Truman appointed him commander of the new North Atlantic Treaty Organization. Then, a group of eastern Republicans led by Thomas E. Dewey and Senator Henry Cabot Lodge, Jr., persuaded him to run for president in 1952. Eisenhower later said that he ran to prevent the nomination of Ohio Senator Robert A. Taft who believed in less, rather than more, foreign involvement as the surest way to peace. Taft opposed the export of American institutions and believed the country should sustain itself on domestic markets protected by high tariffs—isolationist attitudes which Eisenhower thought selfish and immoral.

"Ike's" military glamour and easygoing personality made him an ideal presidential candidate in 1952. He handily defeated Adlai E. Stevenson, the Democratic governor of Illinois, who had cracked down on gambling and modernized his state's government. The play of Stevenson's intellect failed to reach the voters; Eisenhower's simple approach—his promise, for instance, to "go to Korea"—did. And the Democratic candidate had to contend with corruption in the Truman administration and with Republican charges that the Democrats were "soft" on communism.

Presidential diplomacy President Eisenhower pursued a rather steady course of detente in foreign affairs. Perhaps the most important element in the so-called thaw was Eisenhower's dramatic reversal concerning the Korean imbroglio. The thorny prisoner-of-war issue had brought armistice negotiations to a stalemate. America maintained that some one hundred thirty-two thousand captured soldiers did not want to return to North Korea and China; the Communists were understandably reluctant to leave South Korean president Syngman Rhee a highly trained army. Eisenhower and his Secretary of State, John Foster Dulles, decided on a daring tactic: the secretary informed neutralist Prime Minister Jawaharal Nehru of India that the United States might resort to atomic warfare in Korea and Manchuria if an agreement were not reached "very shortly." The Communists gave in on the POW issue but launched a major ground offensive only two weeks later. This heavy attack demonstrated the Communists' impressive military strength, but after a short time both sides avoided any further escalation. On July 27, 1953, American General Harrison and North Korean General Nan II initiated an armistice agreement which, for

Eisenhower's favorite pastime.
U.S. Army photo

all practical purposes, restored the prewar status quo. Though the Korean War ended amid atomic threats and military clashes, the fact of peace overshadowed the sputtering cold war tactics.

Events in the Soviet Union aided Eisenhower in his apparent desire to resolve the victors' clash over the spoils of World War II. The Soviets detonated a hydrogen bomb in 1953, which meant nuclear stand-off. On March 5, 1953, Stalin died; his nominal successor, Georgi Malenkov, acted to ease tensions. And by the later fifties, with the First Secretary of the Communist party, Nikita Khruschev, in control, the new doctrine of peaceful coexistence had replaced the older faith in Marxist militance. Discord did not suddenly melt away, but fresh conditions and leaders signaled an end to the most hostile phase of the cold war.

In Washington the Senate censure in 1954 of Joe McCarthy—for his unorthodox "hearings" accusing public figures of Communist affiliations—eased the public malaise and congressional carping that had plagued the Truman administration. At times Secretary Dulles seemed a throwback to an era of a fervent, crusading foreign policy. Eisenhower had to restrain his secretary from intervening in Vietnam and in the Formosa Straits. Dulles would go "to the brink" to contain communism, but he avoided the abyss—perhaps with more careful calculation than his critics allowed him. Despite Republican rhetoric about freeing the "captive nations" behind the Iron Curtain, Dulles worked to stabilize the political situation in Europe. When West Germany entered NATO, the Soviets responded with the Warsaw pact—a parallel agreement to formalize the Communist alliance in Eastern Europe. The treaty to reunite Austria also came under the secretary's tenure. The greater reliance of Eisenhower and Dulles on nuclear weaponry suggested that only a major world crisis would set off another war. This conservative intention, to achieve a holding action by gripping and controlling potentially dangerous forces, resulted in a peculiar anomaly: alongside the inflamed rhetoric of Secretary Dulles, Eisenhower exhibited in place of ideology a prudent attitude toward power. The United States sought to exercise intricate strategies in foreign relations, to deploy exact military force to balance that of the Soviet Union, and above all to live rationally with the fact of devastating power—in short, to regard the threat of apocalypse as a close, abstract intellectual problem.

Clear indication of a break with the earlier Truman-Acheson policy came when Eisenhower met Soviet leaders face-to-face. At Geneva in 1955 began an increased communication between East and West—the exchange of "people, ideas, and goods"—that has steadily grown since that time. There Eisenhower offered his "open skies" disarmament proposal: mutual aerial surveillance and an exchange of military data. The Soviets demurred (the American Senate, given the opportunity, might have done likewise). Nevertheless, Geneva produced a welcome change of mood. Tensions remained, but peace—meaning simply the absence of war—seemed possible.

Presidential diplomacy: the later years

In the last part of the decade Eisenhower responded cooly to a series of potentially explosive events. After the Poles won greater autonomy from Moscow, the Hungarians demanded political independence as well as economic reform, and in October 1956 a revolution broke out, which the Soviets put down with heavy military force. They simply could not allow the breakup of the Warsaw Pact bloc. President Eisenhower never considered intervention. The West, in fact, was soon divided over an Israeli-Anglo-French attack on Egypt in early November. This conflict had all the characteristics of a preventive war though with the stated aim of reopening the Suez Canal which Egyptian President Abdul Nasser had nationalized a few months earlier. Eisenhower condemned the colonialist attack and forced Prime Minister Anthony Eden to withdraw British troops. Then on October 4, 1957, the Soviet Union launched its first *Sputnik* earth satellite. A second heavier instrument soon followed, and America suffered a major propaganda defeat. Instead of reacting belligerently, Eisenhower chose to "wage peace" as he phrased it in the subtitle to volume II of his *Memoirs*. Dulles, now seriously ill with cancer, resigned in 1958, and the president increasingly employed his own favorite brand of diplomacy—personal meetings with foreign heads of state. Khrushchev's visit to America in 1959 had a relaxing effect, and another summit meeting was planned for the spring of 1960.

Yet Eisenhower disliked pacifism, believed in collective security, and never doubted that communism was a hostile force which threatened the nation's security. He shored up the European alliance and gave Germany a nonnuclear role in NATO. In the Middle East he even offered American soldiers, on request, to resist communism. During 1958 several thousand marines actually landed in Lebanon; their work was done swiftly and with little bloodshed. In Guatemala the United States arranged the overthrow of a left-wing government, and the CIA laid contingency plans for a refugee invasion of Cuba which later failed miserably. Approved aerial reconnaissance of the Soviet Union backfired when one of the spy planes was shot down just in time to wreck the proposed 1960 summit meeting. Nonetheless, until John Kennedy during the 1960 campaign raised the question of a "missile gap" and then as president embarked on various military adventures, the world for a time seemed at greater peace.

THE 1950s AT HOME

Raised in the Midwest at the beginning of this century, Dwight Eisenhower never gave up most of the economic and social verities of that

Theodore Roszak, *Sea Sentinel.*
Collection of Whitney Museum
of American Art, New York

region and time. Although the theater of World War II schooled him away from isolationism, his views on domestic issues underwent no such change and resembled those of another midwesterner—the conservative Senator Robert Taft of Ohio, his unsuccessful opponent for the 1952 Republican presidential nomination. As Eisenhower once remarked: "I laughed at [Taft] one day, and I said, 'How did you ever happen to be known as a conservative and me as a liberal?' "

The Eisenhower years at home have been characterized as a time of political and social stasis. If America did enjoy a rest during the fifties its duration was short-lived. The so-called placid decade began only after the end of the Korean War in 1953 and the Army-McCarthy hearings of 1954; and it seemed to close in 1957 with the Soviet achievements in space and discouraging economic recession at home.

The economy of the 1950s

Business interests had favored Eisenhower's election, but the economic climate during his administration left something to be desired. Republicans still employed the rhetoric of classical economists, but now they also trusted in the Federal Reserve Board to regulate the economy with fiscal and monetary tools. Because the Board's efforts were halfhearted and tardy, three recessions plagued the Eisenhower years in 1953, 1957, and 1959. Even after their onset the administration reacted slowly; as a result high rates of unemployment persisted throughout the decade, rising to more than 7 percent in 1958. Yet the president worried more about inflation than about the slow rate of economic growth and the resulting job scarcity. (The Soviet gross national product was increasing half again as fast as that of the United States.) Important social needs in health and other welfare areas required an active and growing economy—the kind that a business-dominated Republican party might have been expected to provide. Corporations, however, preferred a more limited and assured volume of sales, technically called the "administered price." Unionized craft workers found contentment in their own rising wages passed on to consumers in the form of higher prices. The poor suffered most by the absence of new investments and jobs. Blacks, Mexican-Americans, Indians, and some old people, shut away in ghettos, migrant camps, or reservations, were "invisible." They lacked any political representation, even in the Democratic party with its labor union base.

A major irony of the fifties was that the business-dominated Republicans appeared fearful of stimulating rapid economic growth, while the Democrats, especially in the political campaigns of 1958 and 1960, made it a central goal. Dwight Eisenhower was the first Republican president since Herbert Hoover; his party seemed to be recovering very slowly from the trauma of holding office during the Great Depression.

After twenty years of Democratic rule and virulent Republican criticisms, the nation might have expected some far-reaching changes in governmental operations. Few occurred. During his eight years as president, Eisenhower and his predominantly Democratic Congresses actually extended many New Deal laws such as Social Security. By the end of the decade only a tiny minority of Americans seriously considered repealing the legislative work of the thirties.

All through the fifties, in fact, important groundwork was laid for the Great Society legislation of the sixties. Laws were drafted; Congress held interminable hearings. Aid to public education, sponsored by Senator Taft, would have been passed but for controversy over issues of race and of church and state. The American Medical Association prevented passage of any national health care programs, but retreated by endorsing broadly based private health plans subsidized by government. Toward the end of his second term the president vetoed housing and water pollution control bills. But Eisenhower and his "free market" Secretary of Agriculture Ezra Taft Benson could not reverse the entrenched farm subsidy programs; total government payments to farmers increased during the Republican administration.

Signs of unrest   American in the fifties lacked a political Left; the conservative administration was able to go its own way without having to accommodate itself to serious dissent. Many of Eisenhower's advisers, including Vice-President Nixon, urged more progressive domestic policies, but the president would rarely support such programs when threatened with congressional opposition. Although Eisenhower in 1956 won reelection against Stevenson by over 9 million votes, the 1958 congressional elections heralded a resurgence of Democratic strength. For most of the fifties the Democrats had kept control of the House of Representatives by a slim margin. But in 1958 they captured 65 percent of the seats. Many older Republican standpatters involuntarily retired from the Senate, their places taken by younger men less content with the status quo. The 1958 vote signaled dissatisfaction with the sluggish economy as well as the Russian coup in space. Eisenhower's great personal popularity never extended to his party.

The sociological dimension of the decade also reveals a turbulence beneath the thin crusts of conformity. To accommodate their burgeoning families and to benefit from generous tax breaks on mortgages, the middle class accelerated its flight to the suburbs in the 1950s, while many blacks, impoverished whites, and Puerto Ricans were moving cityward where they would become an important force in the next decade. These two movements, inward and outward from the cities, sharpened the contrasts by race and class between the core cities and suburban communities—and helped to precipitate the urban crises of the 1960s.

The standardized suburban housing and shopping centers of the fifties spawned a vast assortment of new subcultures. Without small-town leaders to enforce traditional values, the new suburban dweller—often moved by his corporation or the military from one end of the country to another—was thrown more upon his own professional skills for a sense of personal identity and status. "Packaging" in housing, leisure, and food compensated perhaps for some of the strain and flux. But the "roots" to which these mobile people had made reference in the past were rapidly vanishing.

The rising birth rate was perhaps another symptom of a striving for roots. For at least 150 years, the American birth rate had been declining, and since about the 1890s middle-class families of the towns and cities had been leading the way, limiting the number of their children and investing heavily in each boy to fit him for the complicated tasks of business, management, or the professions. During the same period the urban lower class as well as country dwellers of all stations produced large families from which the city factories drew much of their labor. No one has satisfactorily explained why in the middle of the century the trend among the middle classes was temporarily reversed. It may be that the United States was simply approaching a postindustrial economy in which economic decisions are determined more by the wishes of consumers than by the sterner logic of industrial needs. Whatever the reasons, the birth rate soared to levels approaching those of the under-developed world; at such a pace the population would double every thirty-five years. Then, during the 1960s, births abruptly fell.

As the surface consensus of the fifties broke apart, group after group began to assert its separate identity. In addition to the growing civil rights movement spurred by the Supreme Court school desegrega-tion decision of 1954 (see pp. 634–635), there was a distinct group of adolescents with values for the first time largely separate from those of the adult middle class. A small community of rebels, the "beats," pitted their devotion to poetry, drugs, jazz, and handicrafts against the tempta-tions of Mammon. Another enclave, the "radical" Right, emerged chiefly from among southern Democrats and from Republican conservatives convinced that Eisenhower betrayed them by failing to repeal New Deal legislation and to confront communism more militantly. Working in tiny patriotic groups, these Americans promoted anticommunism in thou-sands of communities across the nation. Their interest in local, small-scale approaches as opposed to bureaucratic solutions for social problems, ironically became a characteristic of the New Left in the 1960s.

The social problems of the sixties by and large existed in the fifties as well. Not until toward the end of the Eisenhower years, how-ever, did publicists begin the task of educating the public and promoting legislative action. In *The Affluent Society* John Kenneth Galbraith at-tacked a wealthy nation that disregarded public needs. One of the most influential works in the muckraking genre did not even appear in book form until 1962, Michael Harrington's *The Other America*. One of Harrington's special concerns was the exploited "chicanos," the Mexican Americans, of the western states.

Mexican Americans Mexican Americans occupy a unique situation. This "charter-member minority" resided in the Southwest for centuries before Mexico ceded the area to the United States as a consequence of its defeat in the war of 1846–48. Differences in skin color, language, and religion exacerbated war-induced antipathies between native Mexicans and immigrating Anglos. Successive waves of settlers in search of easy riches in mining, cattle ranching, and cotton farming soon overwhelmed the relatively small Spanish-speaking population. Land-hungry Americans had toppled Mexican predominance in Texas as early as the 1820s. Next, the gold rush of the 1850s sprinkled Anglos all over northern California. Thirty years later, the new Southern Pacific Railroad brought yet another hoard of Americans into the Los Angeles area. Immigrants to America's last frontier long avoided Arizona and New Mexico because of their isolation, recurrent Indian wars, and unsuitability for commercial farming. Even today, large parts of New Mexico remain predominately Mexican American.

The white settlers radically altered the economic life of the entire region. Supported by indulgent courts, eastern money, and a ruthless ethic, the Anglos soon displaced the small-scale, isolated pastoral and mining life of most Mexicans with highly-capitalized business enterprises of enormous scope. The spread of large-scale ranching eliminated agriculture based on ownership of animals, not land. The economic efficiencies of size and technology destroyed independent, Mexican-owned mining operations. After big business won influence with state governments and white prejudice walled off social equality, the indigenous population, except in New Mexico, had no choice but to accept exploitation.

Immigrants from Mexico first entered the United States in large numbers at the beginning of the twentieth century. Many came to escape rural overpopulation, political instability, and severe poverty in their native land. Mexican immigration corresponded with the development of labor intensive oil industries in Texas and the agribusinesses of California's valleys. Between 1910 and 1917, with the advent of World War I, the "pull" of American labor shortages reinforced the "push" of the Mexican Revolution. Much of the economy of the Southwest came to depend upon this cheap, docile labor force—cheap because they had no jobs at home, docile because many had entered the country illegally. During the 1920s, nearly a million Mexicans worked, at least part of the year, in the United States, and over five hundred thousand became permanent residents.

The Depression years temporarily upset the labor economics of Mexican supply and American demand. A large segment of the seasonal, migratory work force came to be composed of displaced farmers from

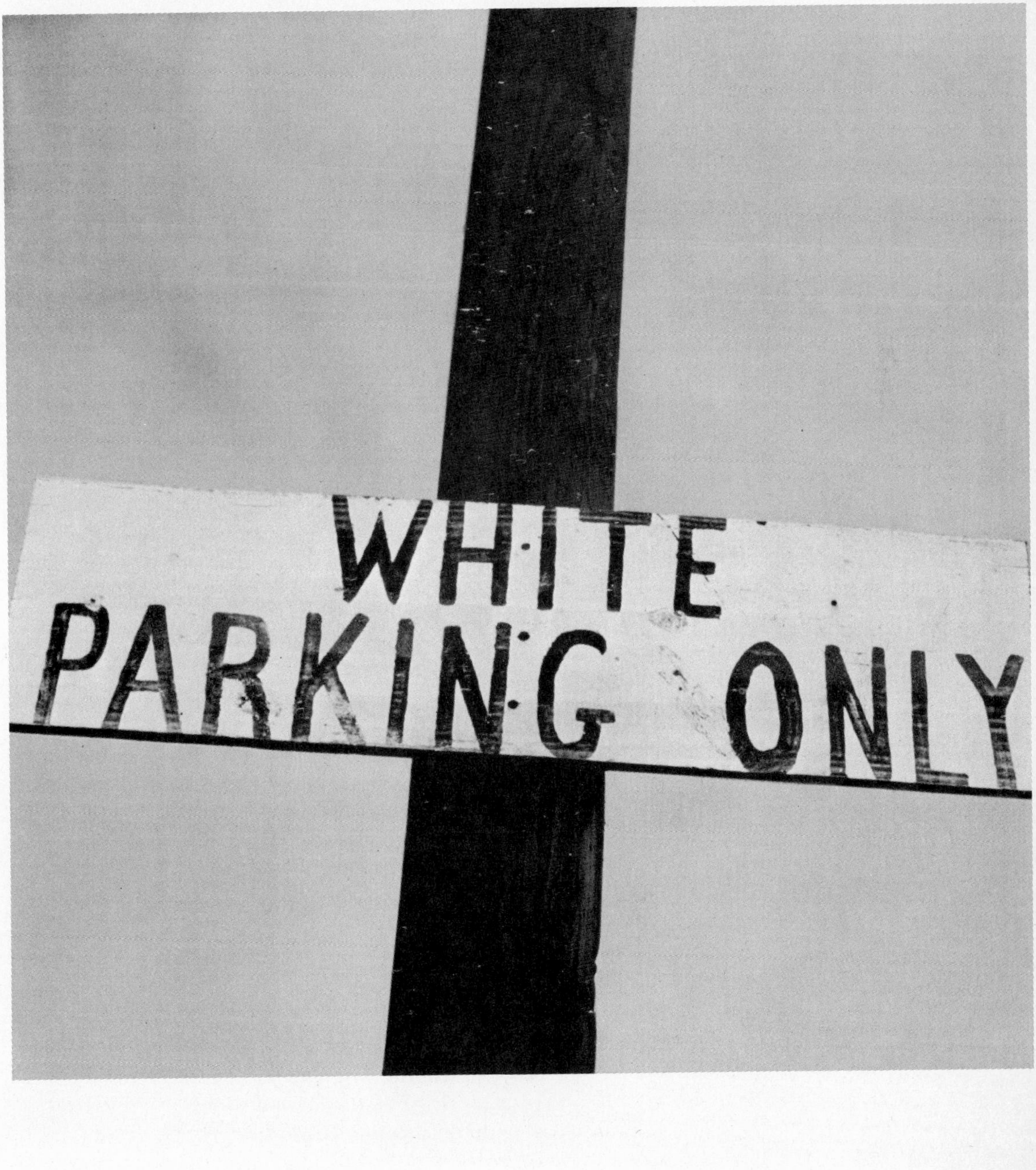
WHITE
PARKING ONLY

Oklahoma, Arkansas, and Missouri, the "Okies" or Dust Bowl refugees who went to California for the same reasons as their Mexican predecessors. John Steinbeck immortalized their journey and their hardships in *The Grapes of Wrath* (1939). When burgeoning World War II defense industries sopped up white labor, once more there was room at the bottom and once more Mexicans moved to fill it.

Beginning in 1943, the United States government supervised the seasonal flow of labor into the Southwest. The "bracero" program allowed Mexican nationals to help with peak harvests or to fill temporary, unskilled industrial jobs and then return home. Under pressure from agribusiness, Congress passed Public Law 78 in 1951, which stabilized the migratory work force at four hundred fifty thousand. This reservoir of cheap labor kept wages low for all farmworkers. Substandard working and living conditions inevitably created a domestic shortage of labor which justified importing Mexicans and accepting the labor of illegal entrants or "wetbacks." Despite efforts at reform during the early years of Johnson's presidency, California ranchers evaded laws requiring decent housing and minimum wages.

Mexican Americans, under leaders like Cesar Chavez, worked to improve their lot using the traditional weapons of American labor. Tensions between Mexican immigrants and Mexican American citizens, together with the hostility of most organized labor and the Roman Catholic Church, hampered the effectiveness of this effort. Nevertheless, as "Boycott grapes" gave way to "Boycott lettuce," one campaign after another won limited but distinct successes for the Chicanos.

THE WARREN COURT

The Supreme Court headed by Chief Justice Earl Warren, who served from 1953–69, was notable for a series of dramatic decisions. During that time, increasing conflict over civil rights and in race relations prompted critics to maintain that the Court was usurping legislative powers and involving itself in social transformation. Yet the involvement in social issues was neither new nor unusual. The Court can only rule on the issues which come before it, and those decisions historically memorable have always ruled on important social problems. Surely the Court's enunciation of the doctrine of "separate but equal" in *Plessy* v. *Fergusson* (1896) remains as political an act as the decision which overturned it, *Brown* v. *Board of Education* (1954).

Although the Court did not invent racial tensions or succeed in mitigating them, the Brown case, the first major decision of the Warren Court, served as a reference point throughout the civil rights crisis of the 1960s. The NAACP team of lawyers, headed by Thurgood Marshall, later to become the first black justice on the Court, had been attacking "separate but equal" for fifteen years and the Court had responded by tightening the promised equality provisions. Then the Warren Court unanimously held in *Brown* v. *Board of Education* that "separate educational facilities are inherently unequal," and that implementation proceed "with all deliberate speed"—a vague phrase permitting a further decade of inaction.

Some of the Warren Court's most controversial decisions came in the areas of criminal procedure and the rights of the accused. In a long series of cases the liberal majority ruled that the principle of equality before the law, the heart of the Brown decision, covered almost every action of government and held that the constitutional guarantee of due process ensured citizens fair treatment from governmental agencies. In *Gideon* v. *Wainwright* (1963), the Court guaranteed in all felony cases the right to counsel in the courtroom. Clarence Earl Gideon, a white southerner with a long criminal record, had been accused of breaking and entering a Florida poolroom and convicted at a trial in which he had been forced to defend himself owing to poverty. Three years later the guarantee of courtroom counsel was extended to the police station in *Miranda* v. *Arizona;* here the Court ruled that police interrogators must inform a suspect of his right to hire a lawyer (or have the state provide one), tell him of his right to remain silent, and warn him that any statement can be used against him.

The Court set off a religious furor when it again ruled on education in a series of cases in 1962–63 outlawing compulsory prayer and Bible reading in the public schools of several states. The Court upheld the rights of the individual student against the imposition of a particular morality and also the separation of Church and State.

A group of obscenity convictions was set aside by the Court with the notable exception of *Ginzburg* v. *United States;* the sentence of Ralph Ginzburg, the publisher of some rather pretentious, high-art erotica, was sustained. A directly political decision of the Warren Court also had individualist implications: the enunciation of the doctrine of "one man, one vote," which required that both houses of state legislatures reflect the actual distributions of population. The first such case, in 1962, was *Baker* v. *Carr.*

By the end of the 1960s, the "Warren majority" had begun to leave the Court; Warren's own retirement and Hugo Black's death removed two of the four central figures. Warren, who had come to the bench after two terms as Governor of California and an unsuccessful bid for the Vice-Presidency in 1948, appeared to be a moderate Republican when appointed by President Eisenhower in 1953; at the time no one expected him to become a social engineer. Another Eisenhower appointee, William Brennan, proved to be a staunch defender of individual freedoms. Black, a Democratic Senator from Alabama appointed to the Court by FDR, had been an honorary Klansman at the time; surprisingly, he staunchly and consistently defended civil liberties. William O. Douglas, the fourth judge who helped make the far-reaching social decisions, had worked as a Wall Street lawyer and headed the Securities and Exchange Commission; some feared when he was appointed in 1939 that he would be subservient to corporate wealth. Yet these men gave the Court its "liberal" cast, and they gained important votes from some of the justices appointed by Kennedy and Johnson during the 1960s.

JOHN F. KENNEDY

An assessment of John Kennedy's three-year presidential term remains difficult. His administration was marked by few concrete legislative accomplishments and not until his last year did he exercise any strong executive leadership on such critical domestic issues as the rights of black Americans. Instead, Kennedy preoccupied himself with international tensions and seemed almost to welcome foreign challenges; he clearly raised the stakes in Vietnam. On the other hand, the youngest man (at forty-three) ever to be president, he touched chords in American society which Eisenhower, for all his warm qualities, could not have hoped to sound. Kennedy's personal style reflected America's own transformation from the private pursuits of the fifties to the greater social awareness of the sixties. The unfulfilled promise of Kennedy's thousand days in office is nearly impossible to measure.

Former Ambassador to Great Britain Joseph Kennedy, Jr., taught his Irish Catholic children a gospel of competition and a distrust of the Soviet Union which he shared with his friend Senator Joe McCarthy. The boy John Kennedy displayed a bookish turn—his father published his senior thesis at Harvard as *Why England Slept*—and while serving in World War II won a purple heart in an authentic, lonely act of heroism. As Massachusetts congressman and senator in the late forties and fifties, John Kennedy charted a stern anti-Communist course in response to early cold war conditions. Yet he stood aloof from Senate cliques and liberal or conservative cabals; he had about him a sense of unpredictability. At times Kennedy's actions appeared the purest expedience—he hospitalized himself during the vote to censure Joe McCarthy and did not pair against him—but he was capable of forthright independent thinking. It was this contradictory man who, with the help of his father's money and his own charm, good looks, and intelligence, emerged the winner of the Democratic presidential nomination in 1960.

The election was bound to be close. No Roman Catholic had ever been president, but Kennedy carefully balanced his ticket with the Senate majority leader, Lyndon Johnson of Texas. The Republican nominee, Vice-President Richard Nixon, experienced bad luck and committed serious errors. Perhaps the worst of these was agreeing to face the younger and more photogenic Kennedy in a series of television debates.

Lyndon and Lady Bird get mad. *Stern*

In a medium that subordinates the message, Kennedy outshone the tired-looking Nixon. Kennedy also employed the religious issue in an effective, if somewhat devious, way. He promised not to let his religion influence his decisions in the White House, and he specifically said he would oppose federal aid to parochial schools. Yet during the primaries he also implied that a vote for him would demonstrate a lack of religious bigotry. Kennedy probably lost more votes than he gained on account of his religion, but the factor helped him carry important states with large Catholic populations like Illinois. Kennedy won the election by a hair's breadth.

With no clear popular mandate, Kennedy moved cautiously. He retained such stalwarts as J. Edgar Hoover of the FBI and Allen Dulles of the CIA. Such decisions indicated not only a desire for governmental continuity, but also a patience with conservatism that unsettled his liberal supporters. The narrowness of his victory in enlarging the size of the obstructive House Rules committee reinforced his prudence. On civil rights Kennedy worked with special care, for Nixon had won almost half the votes of the South. The president lacked—or so he thought—an ideological majority in Congress.

Cuba Unwilling to jeopardize his precarious popularity and hemmed in by various forces, Kennedy gave greatest attention to foreign policy. Here he inherited a number of serious problems from Eisenhower; the most pressing was Cuba, now in the hands of Fidel Castro. Unknown to Kennedy the presidential candidate, some thousand Cuban refugees had been trained high on a coffee *finca* in the Guatemalan mountains for an invasions of their homeland. It was a contingency plan, but one that generated its own momentum. Sensitive to the charge of weakness, Kennedy wanted to act firmly. So, with the encouragement of the CIA and the Joint Chiefs of Staff, and in the face of a noncommittal stance from Secretary of State Dean Rusk, he determined in April 1961 to go ahead. The result was a fiasco. The refugees landed at the well-defended Bay of Pigs with no escape route to the mountains in case of trouble. Their most important supplies went into a single boat which was sunk. Air cover was inadequate. But Kennedy must at least be credited with resisting the entreaties of his military advisers to employ American troops and massive bombing.

Why did Kennedy believe such an effort would destroy Castro? Bad advice and inexperience no doubt played a part. So did the hope of recapturing lost properties for American corporations. Hearing often from his family and church and on the floor of Congress about "liberating" Eastern European nations, he may even have been simply naive. If people living under communism yearned for freedom and if communism was evil, the oppressed masses of Cuba would surely revolt at the first opportunity. But such an analysis neglected, among other things, the wretched conditions of the peasantry under dictator Fulgencia Batista, whom Castro had replaced.

After the Bay of Pigs failure, Kennedy became all the more convinced that his administration faced an important testing period demanding great self-sacrifice. He urged and got from Congress more funds for military purposes. He then attended a summit meeting in the fall of 1961 with Soviet Premier Khrushchev in Vienna but the two men, both in bellicose mood, got on badly. On his return Kennedy stepped up the draft and called for the building of bomb shelters. Accepting advice from former Secretary of State Dean Acheson, he probably overreacted when East Germany constructed the defensive Berlin Wall. In the spring of 1962 Kennedy followed the Soviet lead in resuming nuclear tests. A compromise of sorts was reached with the USSR over Laos, yet the American troop commitment in neighboring Vietnam grew from some nine hundred men in 1961 to over sixteen thousand two years later.

But the most dangerous and dramatic event of Kennedy's administration occurred closer to home in the fall of 1962. Reacting in part to a United States boycott of Cuban sugar, Fidel Castro decided to let the USSR place intermediate-range missiles in Cuba. When Kennedy finally discovered them, he interpreted the act as a blatant challenge to the existing world balance of power. Some advisers recommended an attack on Cuba, but his brother, Attorney General Robert Kennedy, argued that it was not in the American vein to bomb a small island as the Japanese had bombed Pearl Harbor. After rejecting a Soviet compromise calling for a reciprocal withdrawal of American missiles in Turkey, President Kennedy set up a naval quarantine against additional missile shipments. As the world watched breathlessly, a Soviet ship carrying technical equipment turned back. In exchange for the Soviet missile withdrawal, Kennedy pledged no further aggression against Castro. Before the nation Kennedy appeared courageous, and the episode helped the Democrats in the off-year elections. But he had carried the world to the brink of nuclear disaster.

Following the trauma of the missile crisis Soviet-American relations underwent a thaw. A "hot line" assured emergency telephone communication between Washington and Moscow. The Test Ban Treaty of 1963 outlawed nuclear testing. Khrushchev rejected Chinese militance, reaffirming his belief in peaceful coexistence. America sold $250 million of surplus wheat to the Soviets who had suffered crop failures. Kennedy, in a speech at American University, welcomed a new era of cooperation. Unfortunately, the widening war in Vietnam quickly put an end to this brief interlude of good feelings.

Domestic problems The foreign crises of his administration diverted Kennedy from pressing domestic problems; even so, he seemed unwilling to proceed in these areas because of his thin electoral victory. In 1961, however, Congress passed administration bills for a Peace Corps, lower- and middle-income housing, a higher minimum wage, water pollution control, and area redevelopment which provided funds for retraining the unemployed. By 1963 the president seemed nervous about his poor record in domestic policy and at last awakened to the issue of civil rights (see pp. 642–645). He also emphasized the need for tax reform and tax reduction to stimulate spending.

Kennedy had treated large corporations well, and so in April 1962 when the head of United States Steel broke his promise not to raise prices, Kennedy became furious. Several government departments canceled their steel orders, and the Justice Department hinted darkly of antitrust action. After Kennedy himself appeared on television to denounce the big steel interests, the increase was grudgingly rescinded. Many in the business community never forgave the president, although he signed a generous depreciation allowance for that year and reduced corporate income taxes by 20 percent in 1963. Kennedy's important tax-cut proposals for businesses and individuals went into effect in 1964 and, by stimulating the economy, helped to finance the social welfare programs of President Lyndon Johnson's Great Society.

Assassination In Dallas, on November 22, 1963, Lee Harvey Oswald assassinated Kennedy. Immediately there was a tidal wave of grief and affection for the martyred president. Streets and schools and airports were named for him, and millions transferred their affections to his younger brothers Robert and Edward. Congress finally passed most of JFK's programs. Among some scholars a reaction eventually set in against Kennedy, mostly for his aggressive foreign policy. It seems an indisputable point. But if it is generally hard to employ such terms as liberal and conservative, it is useless to think of Kennedy in this perspective. What can one say about the eager young Kennedy who excitedly denounced the labor boss James Hoffa on grounds that he had "no discrimination or taste or style"? He remains an enigmatic figure.

THE CIVIL RIGHTS MOVEMENT

The movement for the equal rights of black people is embedded within the history of twentieth-century American liberalism. For years white liberals supported and staffed important civil rights organizations such as the NAACP and the Urban League. The liberal goal of integration presupposed the superiority of white institutions. In the mid-sixties the coming of black nationalism would challenge liberal values. But in the meantime—from about 1954 to 1965—the civil rights movement seemed to fly forward in a momentous effort to undo our entire history.

Even before the Supreme Court school desegregation decision

of 1954, many events prepared the way for the movement: rising incomes and employment opportunities for blacks during World War II; President Truman's order desegregating the armed forces; the Democratic party's insistence on including in its 1948 platform a "fair employment" recommendation; the general drift toward economic security for middle-class blacks in a more urban, industrialized South; and a perceptible growth in social and legal safeguards for individual blacks, achieved through their power in the northern Democratic party. Yet the Court's decision in *Brown* v. *Board of Education of Topeka* (1954) provided an essential catalyst, for it concerned the schooling of the young and threatened the traditional American belief in black inferiority. The case even raised the controversy of racial miscegenation—blacks marrying whites—after being thrown together in schools at an impressionable age. *Brown*, in effect, was the culmination of a series of cases reversing the "separate-but equal" doctrine set in *Plessy* v. *Ferguson* (1896), which upheld segregation in public accommodations—and therefore all other forms of racial dis- crimination.

When the decision came, most of the South reacted predictably. Racist "White Citizens' Councils" sprang up. Politicians vowed defiance of the Supreme Court decision even though it allowed gradual accommodation with the law. But the courage of small black children—who defied local customs and attended previously all-white schools—inspired the entire black community.

The great events The first great victory of the civil rights movement occurred not in the schools but on the buses of Montgomery, Alabama, in 1955. For more than sixty years Montgomery's black people had ridden in the back of the city's buses. Then, one evening, Mrs. Rosa Parks, a handsome black seamstress in rimless glasses, took a seat near the front of the bus. When she refused the driver's order to relinquish it to a white man and move to the crowded rear, she was arrested, jailed briefly, and ordered to trial. In response, the pastor of the Dexter Avenue Baptist Church, Martin Luther King, Jr., organized a bus boycott, which proved 90 percent effective. Day after day, blacks walked to and from work or joined in car pools. This Christian tactic of passive resistance troubled the white community—and the bus company almost went bankrupt. Nearly a year later the Supreme Court ruled bus segregation unconstitutional and the city was forced to concede defeat.

The next important episode, in 1957, put the federal government squarely behind the fledgling movement. In Little Rock, Arkansas, Governor Orval Faubus posted National Guardsmen outside Central High School to prevent the attendance of black students. President Eisenhower, who lacked a moral feeling for the issue, at first backed off. Then, goaded by the governor's challenge to the supremacy of the federal government, the president determined to uphold the law. When a howling mob replaced the Guardsmen, he sent a thousand paratroopers to Little Rock to enforce the court order. Senator Russell of Georgia fulminated at "Hitler's storm troopers," but Congress in that year managed to pass a timid Civil Rights Act—the first in almost a century.

The movement then adopted a new method: nonviolent direct action. In Greensboro, North Carolina, early in 1960, two black college students sat down at a Woolworth's lunch counter and ordered coffee. Local lunch counters served one color only, but the blacks stayed seated at this white counter all afternoon. They were joined the next day by sixteen fellow students and the following day by fifty, including a few whites from the Women's College of North Carolina. By the end of the week the technique had spread to other stores and then to other cities. The effect was electric. Many stores gave way, and—buoyed by the movement's genuine moral strength—many students searched for fresh antagonists.

So far the work seemed easy; the goals could be accomplished instantaneously. In a moment a cup of coffee could be served or a bus desegregated. Rarely in modern times has the commonplace had such dignity conferred upon it. By their simplicity such acts paralleled the drama and immediacy of Christian conversion: with such small gestures, a society might give signs of its regeneration. Blacks and whites could join hands and create an instant community singing "Deep in our hearts, we do believe, we shall overcome some day." But harder days lay ahead.

Attention shifted to the Deep South, especially to Mississippi and Alabama. In 1961 "freedom riders," black and white, daringly traveled together on interstate buses and integrated transportation facilities throughout the South. After numerous acts of violence, Attorney General Robert F. Kennedy sent federal marshals into Alabama to protect the riders and requested the Interstate Commerce Commission to ban segregation in bus depots and airports. Then, in 1962, federal troops went to "Ole Miss"—the University of Mississippi—to stop serious rioting and to secure the enrollment of James Meredith, the school's first black student. The following year a confrontation over local issues in Birmingham, Alabama, sparked the use of police dogs, fire hoses, and mass arrests, and later the same year the bombing of a black church killed four small girls. In 1964 in Mississippi three civil rights workers were brutally murdered. FBI men implicated the sheriff, his deputy, and sixteen others, but the local all-white jury would not convict them. Lower-class blacks, now involved in the movement for the first time, began to fight back. The period of urban rioting had begun.

Birmingham at last aroused President Kennedy to belated action. He spoke movingly to the nation in a televised speech and urged the enactment of a civil rights law that would end segregation in most places of public accommodation. The Democratic party had finally embraced the civil rights movement. The March on Washington of August 23,

John F. Kennedy. *Elliott Erwitt,*
Magnum

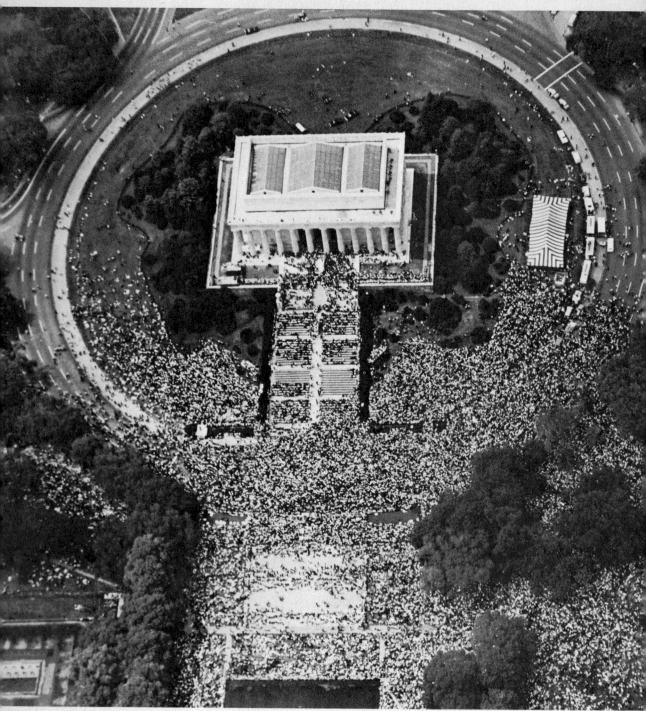

March on Washington, 1963. *UPI*

1963, brought a gentle army of over two hundred thousand in support of federal legislation. But it took Kennedy's death to bring quick action; the first meaningful Civil Rights Act was passed in 1964. Further laws in 1965 and 1966 guaranteed voting rights and prohibited discrimination in housing. But in these same years rebellions broke out in urban ghettos. By 1966 the civil rights movement, once it had moved outside the South, was dead. Lower-class whites and blacks perceived even less community of interest than did their middle-class compeers. Instead, they confronted each other over economic matters, for the rising material expectations of both groups remained unfulfilled.

Black Power The new slogan "Black Power" seemed to promise more violence; it built upon the earlier civil rights movement while at the same time rejecting it. Between 1965 and 1968 large-scale riots took place in Detroit, Los Angeles, Newark, and Washington, D.C. The old moderate organizations like the NAACP gave way to Stokely Carmichael's militant following. "Black is beautiful" implied that assimilation into white society would no longer do. The Black Muslims, a small but growing nationalist sect that first gained nationwide attention in the 1960s, became exceedingly prominent even without its martyred leader, Malcolm X. In a new search for identity blacks dug into the African past, and the ghettos became quiet as they turned in upon themselves.

But the problems of blacks continued to increase with the widening gap between expectations and reality. One young man, George Jackson, symbolized much of the despair. Born in poverty to a black family in 1941, he got in trouble with the police before he was sixteen. Permanently incarcerated since 1960, self-educated largely in solitary confinement, charged with the murder of a prison guard in 1970—and author of a notable book that same year—he died violently in September 1971 in San Quentin Prison, an enigmatic and contradictory symbol to all Americans. To some he was an image of violence and lawlessness. He led others to violence in his wake: his own younger brother Jonathan died in a wild attempt to gain George's freedom by taking a judge hostage, his lawyer accused of smuggling a gun to him in prison. But to many champions of black power George Jackson symbolized man's indomitable will, particularly the black man's struggle to retain identity and force in the face of brutalizing circumstances. Many admire the brilliance of his untutored writing. To men and women on the Left the appeal lies in his revolutionary political philosophy; to ghetto dwellers he is the prisoner who never could be cowed into any submission: "He wasn't a good nigger, that's for sure," says his mother, "and that's the reason I'm proud of him." For all that he wrote and for all that has been written about him, we know almost nothing and understand even less about this permanent prisoner who, as he wrote, could "still smile sometimes."

LYNDON JOHNSON

In Lyndon Johnson heroic vision vied with petty willfulness. Born in rural Texas, he worked his way through college and then briefly taught poor people in a country school. Extremely ambitious, he was elected to Congress, first the House and then the Senate. There he worked for his native state's oil, natural gas, and aircraft industries; he was one Democrat who always remained in the good graces of businessmen. As Senate Democratic leader in the 1950s, he bent with the times, at first cooperating with Eisenhower and then deserting him as Democrats became more assertive late in the decade. Johnson found the vice-presidency under Kennedy a dull job, although it was a national position that transcended his regional identity and brought him closer to the White House.

The office of president might have been especially designed for Lyndon Johnson, so readily did he settle into its manifold powers. Remembering the brevity of the 1933–35 New Deal coalition, he lost no time in pushing for the tax cut that would stimulate the economy and provide tax receipts for his myriad Great Society programs. Just six years before with the country in the midst of recession, Congress had overwhelmingly rejected a pump-priming cut; in 1964 it easily passed one. A year after corporate and personal taxes went down sharply, treasury revenues from taxation actually increased.

During Johnson's presidency Congress passed more laws aiding minorities and the poor than during any comparable period in history. In part the national mood after Kennedy's assassination demanded the enactment of these proposals. But even before his death a liberal coalition had begun to form that would provide the approving votes in Congress; it included organized labor, moderate southerners, blacks and other minorities, the poor, middle-class liberals, and even many businessmen. These groups allied with a master politician in the White House.

Johnson's favorite Great Society project was the Economic Opportunity Act of 1964—the basis for his "War on Poverty." A perfect issue for the fall campaign, the poverty program brought together and extended a number of laws passed under Kennedy: area redevelopment, retraining of the unemployed, public works, youth employment. Added to these were the Job Corps emphasizing vocational education; VISTA—Volunteers in Service to America, a domestic Peace Corps; and the community action agencies, which in some places sparked alternatives to decaying political machines. The twin goals of providing opportunity and eradicating poverty had wide appeal. In the election year a near-billion-dollar appropriation launched the new programs in grand style.

The 1964 election   Johnson had set the stage for his election: government largesse to the poor, a civil rights bill, and a tax cut for the middle class and for corporations. What Republican candidate could hope to challenge the man

Lunch counter sit-down protest, 1960, Portsmouth, Va. *James A. Walker, Jr.*

Fire-gutted buildings in
Washington, D.C. *Wide World*

who, in addition to all this, would campaign on a platform of atonement for the death of John Kennedy? The Republicans came up with a long shot: Senator Barry Goldwater of Arizona. A leader of the radical Right, Goldwater favored a return to modest government spending except for purposes of national defense. He hoped to attract working-class Democrats unhappy over "give-aways" to the poor and to the blacks. And perhaps even a hitherto invisible group of nonvoters would answer his call on election day.

Goldwater ran a unique campaign. At the convention, in tones of highminded exclusion, he rejected those "who do not care for our cause." In impoverished West Virginia he condemned the poverty program; in Tennessee he stood by his earlier promise to sell parts of the Tennessee Valley Authority (TVA); in Florida he criticized Social Security. The Democrats eagerly publicized his offhand remark in the primaries about defoliating Vietnam jungles with tactical nuclear weapons. Using such statements, they easily portrayed Goldwater as a reckless man lacking true conservative principles. The president deflected attacks on his foreign policy by bombing North Vietnam for allegedly firing on an American destroyer in the Gulf of Tonkin. Johnson won by almost a two-to-one popular margin, an edge nearly as great as FDR's over Alf Landon in 1936.

The Johnson coalition What liberal legislation had not been passed before the election Congress rushed through in the next session. The major new programs of 1965 were aid to public schools and Medicare (health insurance for the aged under Social Security). Other laws provided funds for model cities, regional health centers, and rent supplements for lower-income families. Big business especially welcomed programs such as job training, which provided skilled workers in areas of scarcity. During the Johnson years, corporations even loaned personnel to job-training centers—in fact a government subsidy to business. Public awareness of ecology lagged, however, and the Great Society appropriated little money to fight water, air, and noise pollution. This, perhaps, marked the limit beyond which businessmen would not go for fear of violating their own self-interest.

The Johnson coalition split apart during 1966. The Vietnam War demanded more and more of the national budget, cutting deeply into domestic appropriations. The president promised "guns *and* butter" but could not deliver both. Additional civil rights acts in 1965 and 1966 troubled the industrial workers in the Democratic party for the movement had spread to the North, threatening white enclaves and *de facto* school segregation. The civil rights cause also became a scapegoat for major ghetto insurrections—in New York (1964), Los Angeles (1965), and Newark and Detroit (1967)—as well as the violent rhetoric of black power. No longer were blacks and union-oriented whites capable of easy coexistence within the Democratic party; and no political coalition can long survive unless its members live in reasonable harmony. The "white backlash" influenced several contests during the 1966 congressional elections; it was a climate for which the Goldwater candidacy had been premature.

VIETNAM

While the American interest in Southeast Asia goes back only a few decades, other western countries with rival empires and ideologies began competing there more than a century ago. After the 1860s French colonialism in particular shaped the area's economic and social growth, producing a feudal political structure, a near-absence of industry, and agriculture polarized between subsistence farming and large scale production of export crops. Nor surprisingly, this exploitation prompted nationalist resistance almost from the start. After World War I, in re-

Barry Goldwater wore glasses without lenses. *UPI*

sponse to French refusal to endorse moderate reforms, Vietnamese nationalists adopted more militant tactics. Under the leadership of the youthful Ho Chi Minh, nationalism and communism blended inseparably. Emerging as the strongest native leader at the end of World War II, he declared Vietnam's independence.

Still unwilling to reliquish their influence, France and Britain struggled to impose neocolonialism in Asia. Anglo-French occupation troops set up a puppet government in Vietnam, and the French began a war of reconquest. With American military aid coming in 1950 after the fall of China to the Communists and the outbreak of hostilities in Korea, France lasted against Ho until the collapse of the major inland fortress of Dien Bien Phu in 1954. President Eisenhower resisted pressures from his advisers to intervene, while other conferees meeting at Geneva temporarily divided Vietnam to expedite military disengagement. Yet the Republican administration sabotaged the Geneva agreement to determine the country's future through free elections. By granting enormous sums of economic aid to Premier Ngo Dinh Diem, who in turn prevented meaningful elections, America committed itself to the establishment of a non-Communist South Vietnam. Progress made in the South from 1954 to 1957, however, was more than offset by indigenous Communist gains at the end of the decade. Eisenhower admitted to the incoming President Kennedy that foreign affairs were a "mess," particularly in Southeast Asia.

One of Kennedy's major campaign thrusts against Eisenhower had been the Republicans' reliance on nuclear weapons. Time and again, the new president stressed the need for flexible approaches to guerrillas fighting "wars of national liberation." Vietnam was the ideal test of this flexibility. Kennedy began to provide artillery and fighter-bombers to bolster Premier Diem's personalist regime. More important, some sixteen thousand American "advisers" went to Vietnam in an attempt to do what Diem and his followers could not. Initially, these steps augured well; the communist Vietcong lost territory in 1962. The Kennedy troop increment, following the pledges of the Eisenhower administration, was the second critical decision committing the United States to victory in Vietnam. Kennedy agonized over these decisions. He knew that once additional troops went in, the logic of redeeming the investment with even more men would be compelling. Ultimately Americans judged Diem a liability and America withdrew support for him just before his own assassination in 1963.

A broader war   When Lyndon Johnson assumed the presidency, a reversal of American policy in Vietnam might have meant political suicide. Johnson inherited not only the war itself and a shaky government in Saigon dependent on vast American aid, but also Kennedy's principal foreign policy advisers

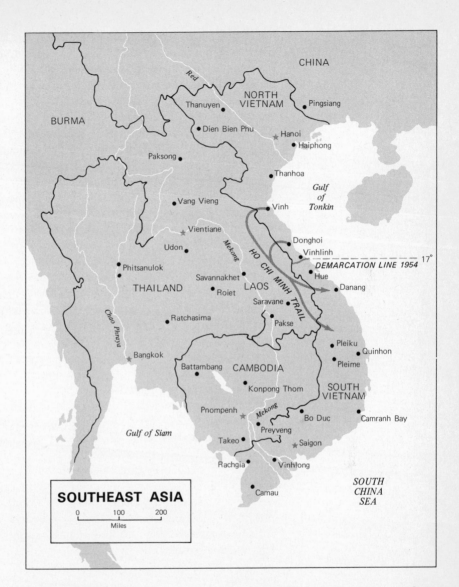

SOUTHEAST ASIA

0   100   200
Miles

and a domestic political climate requiring that a Democratic president avoid "appeasement" in world affairs. A pretext to bomb North Vietnam came in August 1964 when its ships allegedly attacked at least one American destroyer some twenty miles out to sea. This prompted the Senate to pass with only two dissenting votes—those of senators Wayne Morse of Oregon and Ernest Gruening of Alaska—the "Gulf of Tonkin resolution" which granted the president extraordinary powers to pursue the war. During the last months of 1964, air attacks sought to improve morale in the South, but bombing never brought the settlement its leading proponents anticipated.

After the 1964 election, Johnson moved toward full-scale war. He took action, his memoirs report, "to protect our interests and keep our promises." More than the elusive hope for victory drove Johnson on. A steady, calculated American effort—so the constant refrain went—would convince the North it could not win. (The use of force in 1965 had prevented an alleged communist takeover in the Dominican Republic.) This argument expanded into a philosophy about the entire Far East. The heightened American presence (which would exceed five hundred thousand troops by 1967) would "contain" China, and it would have a demonstration effect, convincing Communists elsewhere of America's intent to deter attack. Finally, so the reasoning went, no other course was possible since a withdrawal would produce the "domino effect" Eisenhower had warned of in eastern Asia: if Vietnam became Communist, other nations would inevitably follow. At home, the Pentagon had developed scores of innovative military techniques that could now be tested. And further pressure came from the Pentagon's new constituency—corporations and labor unions from defense-industry areas who lobbied in Congress for larger and larger military budgets.

Attempts at negotiation failed as long as either side thought it held the upper hand. In 1964 U Thant, Secretary General of the United Nations, persuaded most of the major powers to reconvene the Geneva Conference. Johnson demurred. His demand for a non-Communist government in Saigon precluded any hope for an early settlement. At the end of 1965 the president announced a thirty-seven-day bombing halt, a cynical maneuver to silence war critics. Nothing came of his accompanying diplomatic flourishes; nothing was expected. Renewed air attacks concentrated on cutting the flow of supplies to the Vietcong. Another effort to rally American opinion in behalf of the war came in a February 1966 meeting between Johnson and the South Vietnamese regime at Honolulu. There President Thieu and Vice-President Ky promised economic reforms and democratic elections. But the Constituent Assembly that resulted remained captive to the same generals who ran the country.

The antiwar movement

A growing antiwar movement in the United States questioned the purpose of the frustrating conflict (as did nearly all of our western allies). Senator J. William Fulbright attacked the "arrogance of power," writing that "power tends to confuse itself with virtue." America's history of victory, strength, and prosperity made it self-righteous and ready to distort reality. Vietnam taught us, the senator argued, that our political institutions and methods of political bargaining could not flourish in an alien culture. Above all, young people and educators condemned the immorality of the war: the use of napalm which fastened to the skin and burned into the body; cluster bombs; the defoliation of the countryside.

Mangrove Forests in Vietnam
before and after defoliation. *UPI*

In October 1967 some two hundred thousand Americans demonstated in Washington against the war—and against President Johnson.

Growing doubts became convictions after the Tet offensive of January–February 1968. Striking simultaneously at all the major cities of the South, the Vietcong inflicted severe casualties and seriously threatened Saigon itself. The American embassy underwent heavy attack. Hue, the ancient capital near the northern dividing line, became enemy territory for several weeks. The efficiency and secrecy of these maneuvers made plain the ineptness of the South Vietnamese troops. Although a bloody counteroffensive resecured the cities, the Vietcong had scored a notable propaganda victory by demonstrating their strength and determination. Tet also destroyed many American illusions concerning the effectiveness of a limited campaign of firepower from the air and "search and destroy" missions on the ground.

With military victory still not in sight and with the domestic economy in the grip of runaway inflation—the war was costing $30 billion annually—the Johnson administration resolved to try diplomacy. Rejecting the American commander General Westmoreland's request for still more troops, Johnson, after his relatively weak showing in the New Hampshire primary in late March 1968, announced that he would not seek reelection and instead would concentrate on seeking peace. Yet he almost immediately seemed to regret offering to meet with the Communists; they were unresponsive at meetings in Paris and maybe a little more pressure would, after all, bring success. The change in policy initiated by Johnson—sharply limited bombing, troop reduction, and "Vietnamization" of the war—determined the course of events during four subsequent years. Talks which began in Paris on May 10, 1968, stalled for five months as both sides made impossible demands. Just before the American elections an agreement came, but South Vietnam quickly renounced it. This disunity brought more complications, including a quarrel over the shape of the bargaining table; Johnson's need for even partial victory impeded his quest for peace.

From the outset the new Republican president, Richard Nixon, pursued the Johnsonian goal of limited victory. And the war dragged on. In June 1969, after a meeting with President Thieu in Guam, Nixon announced his "doctrine" that Asians would have to fight their own wars without the support of American ground troops. But in April 1970 American and South Vietnamese troops briefly invaded Cambodia to destroy enemy supplies and sanctuaries; in February 1971 a similar offensive was launched in Laos. The Senate demonstrated its changed mood by repealing the Tonkin Gulf resolution, eighty-one to ten, and by threatening to impose a cutoff date on the presence in Vietnam of American troops. Then in June 1971 the *New York Times* began serial publication of a secret report commissioned by Secretary of Defense Robert McNamara in 1968; these exhaustive *Pentagon Papers,* which traced the history of American involvement in the war, exposed the dubious assumptions and blunders of a generation of American leaders. The Nixon administration unsuccessfully attempted to halt their publication and prosecuted Daniel Ellsberg for releasing them. Another revelation concerning Vietnam exposed the unmitigated horror of the massacres at My Lai and Song My. In what appears to have been "a slaughter caused by mass psychosis," American soldiers killed scores of defenseless civilians in these towns. The killings, which were covered up by superior officers, occurred in the early spring of 1968—just a short time after the frightening experience of Tet.

In 1972, while Nixon hoped for a quiet winding down of the war, North Vietnamese troops in the South attacked major northern cities. The war started up all over again, although fewer than 50,000 American troops were in Vietnam on June 30, 1972—a 90 percent reduction from 1968. Nixon mined North Vietnamese ports including Haiphong and bombed the North brutally. At the same time he promised to withdraw all American troops four months after the release of American prisoners of war. Peace talks became serious around election time, 1972, when Nixon and Kissinger sincerely believed a settlement was at hand. When they were disappointed, the President in December ordered the bombing of Hanoi; his planes hit a hospital and populated areas of the city. Heavy criticism, from both at home and abroad, may have caused him to suspend the bombing; but the incident revealed his unpredictability. Whether the bombings had the desired effect is unclear. Perhaps in spite of them a truce finally came to Vietnam on January 27, 1973.

The 1968 election   Johnson's popularity plummeted on foreign policy. As the Vietnam War raged interminably—bringing a cost in lives and money far out of proportion to any advantage that might accrue—a distrust for established institutions spread, particularly among young people. Momentarily, hopes rose for purgation of the Democratic party as Senator Eugene McCarthy of Minnesota and Senator Robert Kennedy of New York spoke out against the war. The dramatic Vietcong offensive early in 1968 during Tet (the Vietnamese lunar New Year) gave their message the tang of truth. McCarthy, with his white hair and handsome profile, looked a gallant man. His impressive showing against Johnson in the early New Hampshire primary probably contributed to the president's decision to withdraw from the coming election and to reduce the bombing of North Vietnam. But McCarthy lacked political savvy and could not compete with Kennedy, who attracted blacks and Mexican–Americans—essential constituencies, he believed, for any Democratic presidential candidate. On the night of his victory in the all-important California primary, Robert Kennedy was killed by a Jordanian immigrant, Sirhan Sirhan, who thought him anti-Arab. With Martin Luther King's slaying by a white racist just weeks before it all seemed a nightmarish reflection of the war itself.

Mrs. Coretta King in
mourning. *Wide World*

The Republican candidate for president in 1968, Richard Nixon, had a long career of government service. He became nationally famous during the forties when his relentless prodding during congressional hearings revealed that an important figure in the Roosevelt administration, Alger Hiss, had probably been a Communist. Nixon coasted into the Senate following a 1950 California campaign in which he permitted his manager to characterize his female opponent as the "pink lady." (Some of her people called Nixon an anti-Semite.) With a voting record that alarmed neither Republican conservatives nor liberals, Nixon became Eisenhower's vice-president and then nearly defeated Kennedy in 1960. His second chance came in 1968.

The Democratic nominee turned out to be Vice-President Hubert Humphrey—not a man to chart an abrupt new course for his party. He had too consistently and vehemently supported President Johnson on Vietnam. The young turned out in force at the Chicago Democratic Convention to precipitate what an eminent study group later termed a "police riot." In the last weeks of his campaign Humphrey finally called for a halt to all bombing of North Vietnam and for immediate peace negotiations, but Nixon, too, had a "plan" for ending the war. Nixon also hit hard at the decisions of the Supreme Court under Chief Justice Earl Warren. In a "law and order" campaign the Court's decisions protecting the rights of suspected criminals were blamed for steeply rising crime rates. With Alabama Governor George Wallace's American Party drawing conservatives away from Nixon, Humphrey almost won a victory in November. Wallace, employing anti-black and economic themes, received almost 10 million votes. But in an election a near-miss is as good as a mile, and Richard Nixon, elected with 43 percent of the vote, would make the critical decisions that lay ahead.

THE SOCIAL SPECTRUM

Many Americans in the 1950s shared a mood of cultural exhaustion with the rest of the world. It was partly a matter of catching up on material things lost in depression and war, and partly a revulsion against the excesses of ideology. Both communism and fascism seemed absurd romantic visions, vast oversimplifications to apply to a complex and varied society. The sociologist Daniel Bell proclaimed an "end to ideology." The managers and piecemeal reformers alone fit the new era.

Against the technicians' view of things—so naturally suited to the gradual and "sensible" steps in the escalation of the Vietnam War— sprang up a romantic temperament among the young of the middle and later 1960s. This inchoate counterculture grew in part from the adolescent styles of the 1950s, and especially the defining of young people as separate from the rest of society rather than simply as apprentices to adult roles. The youth culture also grew because of its opposition to the conventional temper of bureaucracy. The young people in the civil rights movement had acquired a moral passion and communal vision incompatible with the routine impersonality of social institutions. The university revolts came in part from the practicing of a virtue that universities have traditionally preached but perhaps too often strayed from: relentless and open inquiry even at the expense of breaking with established intellectual forms.

In the early sixties the youth movement was largely a phase of American reformism. A moderate peace movement, beginning in the 1961 Berlin crisis and ending in the 1963 signing of the nuclear test-ban treaty, worked through organizations of the old Left. Even the militant SNCC (Student Non-Violent Coordinating Committee) originated in and cooperated with the civil rights movement. Students for a Democratic Society, the radical SDS of the later sixties, also began on a standard liberal course with roots in older reformist groups. But SDS was reborn in 1962 at Port Huron, Michigan, where two University of Michigan graduate students drafted the "Port Huron Statement." Its call for the rehabilitation of existing institutions was familiar, but its tone—communal, antibureaucratic, student-oriented—anticipated the new styles and militance of the years ahead.

The universities One of the places where radicals could exercise their own right of free speech was the university. Such schools as Wisconsin and Berkeley cherished a reform tradition and even in the fifties bred a bohemian radical fringe. But at Berkeley in the fall of 1964, after a raucous demonstration against a House Un-American Activities Committee hearing and a restriction on campus political recruiting, a full-scale student revolt threw the university into turmoil for months. Similar outbreaks occurred elsewhere, in protest against the Vietnam war, notably at Columbia in 1968 and at Harvard in 1969.

Put simply, the universities still depended on regulations imposed from above, while the student activists wanted participatory democracy. The administrators favored bureaucratic procedure through which to express grievances; faced with institutional inertia, students turned to demonstrations. Many faculty sympathized with the cry for more elective courses and varied curricula, which could rest on the traditional commitment to imaginative inquiry. But the demand to address social problems beyond the university distressed professors who wished to escape the burdens of outside involvement or who saw a conflict between them and liberal studies. Student power in fact raised the question of how

George Wallace. Richard Howard, *Bethel*

much authority the faculty itself exercised. Universities such as Michigan State had cooperated on military intelligence projects of dubious academic value, and had even tolerated classified research, violating the spirit of free inquiry.

Drugs A number of influences worked against the activists' political goals. Many students were simply apathetic; for others, the world of drugs satisfied the urge to break with convention and created an air of comradely danger that drew a clear line against most adults. Smoking marijuana particularly created a feeling of community and, for many, seemed to blur the outlines of individual identity. Stronger "head" drugs—mescaline, LSD, STP, speed—enjoyed a more ephemeral popularity, presumably because of their occasional tendency to induce transient psychoses. The use of heroin spread, especially among the poor: its thoroughly addictive character fed a rising crime rate and disrupted social cohesion in large cities.

The centers of drug use—the famous hippie colony of Haight-Ashbury in San Francisco and the East Village in New York—rapidly fell prey to exploitive commerce or pervasive crime. Events such as the Woodstock, New York, rock festival in 1969, though tainted by middle-class adventure, caught some of the good commerce among the young. But only a year later, at Altamont, California, a Hell's Angels motorcycle gang injured many people and committed a pointless murder during a Rolling Stones rock festival. Altamont was, in the phrasing of the young rock poet Don McLean, "the day the music died." The unwanted ingredient that apparently destroyed the counterculture was violence—so foreign to the life style the young attempted to practice and yet, in the words of black militant H. Rap Brown, "as American as cherry pie."

Many of the American arts, nevertheless, reflected the pervasive influence of the youth culture. Folk music, which enjoyed a revival during the late fifties in Greenwich Village, was especially adaptable to political statement and so used by such performers as the young Bob Dylan, a conscious imitator of Woody Guthrie. Some of the early protest songs, sounding pastoral notes of innocence and pacifism, carried their listeners back over the fifties and Second World War to the Great Depression and the early labor movement. Rock 'n' roll music of the fifties, embodied in Elvis Presley, combined with folk to create folk rock. Hard rock was a curious fusion of opposites: folkish melodies and the modern technology of electrical amplification. One group, the Who, experimented with rock opera; the musical *Hair* spawned a score of imitators; and Catholic churches conducted folk-rock masses.

The arts Movies also catered to the young, for most moviegoers are under twenty-five. While slick films appeared more frequently than ever for the sole purpose of making money, the outstanding productions recalled the industry's great interwar achievements. Stanley Kubrick's *Doctor Strangelove* and *2001* with their mad fantasies and psychedelic visions, or Arthur Penn's *Bonnie and Clyde,* interspersing blandness and violence with the comic, especially captured some of the nation's darkest thoughts. *Alice's Restaurant* and *Zabriskie Point* were serious attempts at portraying the shortcomings as well as the virtues of the counterculture. *Easy Rider* capitalized on a vicious stereotype of the South, while Norman Mailer and Andy Warhol brought new techniques of timing and subject matter to the experimental film world.

Drama as well as cinema fell victim to the pervasive interest in nudity. Some of the most interesting plays not only emphasized sexual freedom, such as *Dionysus in '69,* but also contributed lively innovations in staging and sometimes drew audiences into the play. But although off-Broadway theaters staged interesting works by such native talents as Edward Albee and Leroi Jones, foreign authors predominated.

In painting, a fresh new influence came into view in the fifties: Jackson Pollock practiced an impulsive yet purposeful style dubbed "action painting." He splashed paints onto a huge canvas, employing the motions of his whole body and aiming the colors with raw energy rather than carrying them on the tip of his brush. Pollock's radicalism concretely expressed the varied strains of the sixties. "Happenings" enjoyed a vogue, including a 1963 piece that gradually destroyed itself by burning, sawing, and beating itself to death. In his "pop" art Andy Warhol—who most successfully commandeered the media in the name of art—took inspiration from Roy Lichtenstein's cartoon parody: maddening rows of Brillo cartons, an eight-hour film of a man sleeping. Such names as Mark Rothko, Jasper Johns, and Frank Stella show the varied directions of modern American painting.

Women's liberation

During World War II women had taken "men's jobs" and made some short-term economic gains, but generally by the fifties the force and conviction of the turn-of-the-century feminist movement had been forgotten. Time, transportation, and babysitting problems discouraged all but the most determined women from combining a socially mandatory marriage with professional training. In 1955, for instance, a smaller percentage of graduate students were women than thirty years before; and women in college took typically "feminine" courses in elementary education, home economics, or secretarial skills.

Although many men in the youth culture or radical movements of the mid-sixties were able to reject regular jobs, most women continued to perform the traditional chores. In the film *Alice's Restaurant* women appeared either as cooks or as rejected sexual objects. Similarly, the world of rock music had been overwhelmingly a man's domain with women no better off than in middle-class culture. Janis Joplin worked for a group

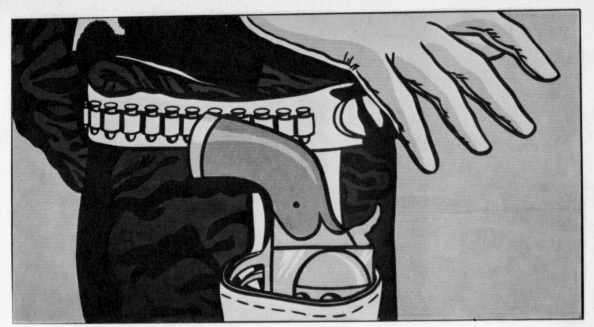

Roy Lichtenstein, *Fastest Gun. Courtesy of Betty Asher*

called Big Brother and the Holding Company, and females were notably present only in country-western or folk music and as black or "soul" singers.

Many women in the later 1960s rather suddenly concluded that their male counterparts had exploited them as cooks, secretaries, and bed partners. The new women activists of the late sixties sought no less than a transformation of their place and image in American society. One of the first major American books on the subject, Betty Friedan's *The Feminine Mystique* (1963), was an attack on the restrictions of domesticity. For too long the problems of suburban living, the child-centered philosophies of psychologists, and the pronouncements of Freudian analysts as a hard sell in the women's magazines had conspired to frustrate the independence and creativity of women caught up in an inflexible family structure. The year following publication of her book Friedan organized NOW, the National Organization for Women, which lobbied for equal pay for performing identical jobs, child care centers, and the reform of abortion laws. WITCH (originally the Women's International Terrorist Conspiracy from Hell), perhaps the most notorious of the women's liberation groups, swept into existence on Halloween 1968 in New York City. This group, with "covens" in major cities, demonstrated at the Bridal Fair held in Chicago in February 1969, asserting that the bridal industry and its magazines (edited principally by men) helped to perpetuate the myth that a woman's fulfillment is found only through a

661

husband and children. At Atlantic City a year earlier, women had picketed the Miss America pageant. Miss America, they believed, represented "the degrading mindless-boob-girlie symbol" and was a walking commercial for the pageant's sponsors.

The psychological barriers between women and men are reinforced continually in the media. Advertising affects men as well as women, but women purchase 75 percent of consumer goods. Women's magazines are best sellers; they aim, say the feminists, only to make women buy material goods. Television soap operas, too, attempt to support women's role as superconsumers; the males are professionals and the women homemakers. Even children's programs offer mostly stereotyped, passive females. Feminists argue that the so-called sexual revolution, glamorized by Hugh Hefner's *Playboy,* has not freed women but simply made them more available. They resent advertisements presenting women as "sexual objects," and especially ads that place women in sexual competition; nudity in movies, they hold, also reduces women to subjects of display.

Women began in the mid-sixties to meet in small groups for "consciousness raising," a frank and personal sharing of experiences. The reliance on personal contact makes those reached more militant and committed to the cause, for it exposes the indignities they encounter. An important part of the experience comes in breaking down the kinds of distrust bred by a system wherein the attachment to an individual man is expected to be the ultimate in a woman's experience.

Some of the literature by women on their freedom is philosophically akin to the radical Left in its assumption that only revolution against the capitalist system to produce socialism will bring about equality for women. Many radical feminists believe that a drastic change in our economic values must precede a turnabout in the traditional mascu-

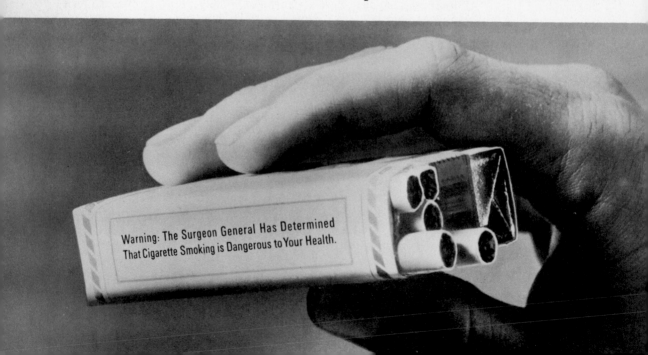

Warning: The Surgeon General Has Determined That Cigarette Smoking is Dangerous to Your Health.

line view of women. They argue that equal pay for identical jobs performed by men and women is, by itself, tantamount to the "token" integration blacks have experienced in their efforts to win equal status within the social system.

NIXON'S FIRST TERM

At his 1968 inaugural Richard Nixon offered hope mainly for an improvement in foreign relations. "We are entering," he correctly noted, "an era of negotiation." A month after taking office he flew to Europe, where he encouraged West German leaders in their search for an easing of tensions with the East and also attempted to improve relations with Charles de Gaulle of France.

But Nixon's greatest ambition was an agreement with the Soviets on strategic arms limitation. Believing in negotiation from a position of strength, he first urged Congress to pass a $2.5 billion antiballistic missile (ABM) plan, which edged through the Senate in 1970 by a single vote. ABM sites already protected Moscow, which had also deployed sophisticated missiles with twenty-five-megaton MIRV multiple-reentry warheads. As Nixon predicted, strategic arms-limitation talks (SALT) in Helsinki led to a treaty, signed during the president's visit to Russia in May 1972. Subsequently approved by the Senate, the settlement with Premier Kosygin also contained provisions for limiting certain offensive weapons.

Except for a resurgence of trouble in Vietnam during 1972 (see page 655), President Nixon seemed to be making headway against international tensions throughout the world. Major powers, following West German Chancellor Willy Brandt's lead, signed an important treaty in 1971 neutralizing Berlin and recognizing a Polish boundary claim. In Africa Nixon stayed clear of the Nigerian Civil War but afterward tried to provide food for Biafra and other areas. Developments went badly for the United States in Latin America; in the face of adverse events in Chile, Peru, and Ecuador, Nixon seemed ready to accept the desire there for economic and political independence, but "unofficial" trade pressures were exerted.

In the Middle East trouble continued unabated throughout Nixon's term. The Arab states demanded Israeli withdrawal from territory occupied during the Six-Day War of 1967. Israelis first wanted assurances of future security; some even wanted permanent possession of Jerusalem and the west bank of the Jordan River. Sporadic violations of the cease-fire occurred almost daily. In 1969 Nasser of Egypt proposed a plan embodying nonbelligerence and territorial integrity for all nations; on the same day Nixon accepted a French offer for Big Four talks at the United Nations. But Israel rejected Nasser's proposals and resisted American pressures to negotiate. In 1970 Secretary of State William Rogers finally arranged for a renewal of indirect talks. But

Palestinian Arab guerrillas ignored the cease-fire and fighting broke out in Jordan. The Palestinians hijacked a total of four commercial jetliners, holding them hostage and then blowing up the empty vehicles. Secretary Rogers tried to maintain middle ground against strong pro-Israeli groups in the United States; he backed Israel's desire not to relinquish territory before a settlement but also advocated a partial Israeli pullout in the Sinai peninsula and the reopening of the Suez Canal. No significant progress toward peace came about in the area.

A briefer conflict flared in Asia during 1971 as a result of a political and religious struggle between East and West Pakistan. Culminating in the defeat of West Pakistan, the short war led to the creation of the new nation of Bangla Desh in the area formerly known as East Pakistan. Ironically, the United States and the People's Republic of China found themselves both supporting the defeated West Pakistanis. In his State of the World message of February 1971, Nixon had already made the most explicit of a series of friendly overtures to China. In April an American table tennis team and three newsmen visited Peking. Prime Minister Chou En-lai stated that more newsmen would be welcome, and Nixon on the same day announced the end of certain trade restrictions against China. Then Henry Kissinger, Nixon's influential head of the National Security Council, secretly visited Peking in July 1971. Finally, in October, Communist China entered the United Nations and Taiwan (Nationalist China) was expelled.

From these salutory developments emerged President Nixon's stunning goodwill trip to China. He landed in Peking on February 20, 1972. At the end of five days of conferences Nixon and Chou En-lai issued a joint communiqué pledging peaceful coexistence and recognizing Taiwan as an "internal" Chinese issue. It was an amazing and, for most Americans, a welcome feat by the man who had become nationally prominent riding the crest of a pervasive anticommunism in the late forties and early fifties. The trip to China and the subsequent trip to the Soviet Union raised hopes for world peace.

Legislative problems   Nixon's domestic problems required something more than even his considerable political skill could provide. His worst difficulty was a dangerous inflationary spiral. The president's economic advisors, Paul McCracken and Arthur F. Burns, attempted to scale down the budget without precipitating severe recession. Johnson's Great Society programs suffered sharp cuts and defense spending declined, although enormous federal budget deficits persisted. "Tight money" (high interest rates)—accomplished by a raising of the Federal Reserve banks' rediscount rate—completed the first steps of Nixon's economic program. Congress by only a narrow margin refused support for Nixon's controversial and costly aircraft, the supersonic transport (SST), which threatened harm to the

Richard Nixon speaking
extemporaneously, September
1968. *UPI*

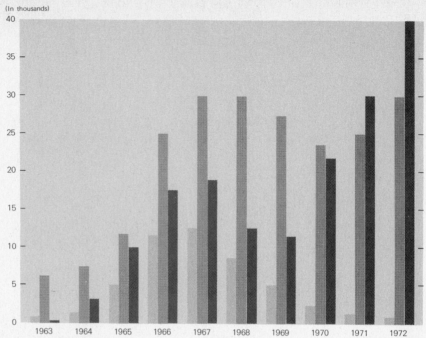

(In thousands)

War in Vietnam 1963–1972

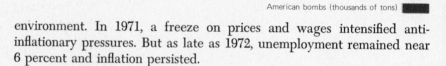

American casualties in Vietnam
Vietnamese casualties, including civilians
American bombs (thousands of tons)

environment. In 1971, a freeze on prices and wages intensified anti-inflationary pressures. But as late as 1972, unemployment remained near 6 percent and inflation persisted.

Nixon also moved to balance the American trade deficit with foreign countries. When West Germany "floated" the mark to curtail the inflow of dollars, the United States in August 1971 took steps to devalue the dollar internationally, contingent upon reciprocal moves by strong-currency nations like Germany and Japan. A brief 10 percent surcharge on imports also helped to improve the balance of foreign trade and to force other countries to cooperate with Nixon's plans for the international economy.

The Republican administration received much attention for sponsoring a legislative program of welfare reform. Under the proposal the Social Security Administration would provide each family of four with a minimum annual income of $1600, with the head of the household permitted to earn another $720 without reduction of the initial amount. Liberal Democrats found the program ungenerous but tended to see it as a step in the right direction. Nixon, however, never exerted his full influence for its passage, and partisan Democrats and conservative Republicans were obstructive.

Meanwhile, Nixon's antiwar critics found reductions of troop strength in Vietnam too gradual as well as disingenuous because of a greater reliance on air power. The expeditions into Cambodia sparked nationwide campus protests, and nervous National Guardsmen killed four demonstrating students at Kent State University, Ohio, in April 1970. Nixon apparently believed himself the victim of unfair coverage on these events by the "liberal" eastern press, a message Vice-President Agnew widely disseminated in an inimitable flowery rhetoric. In the 1970 campaign Agnew singled out war protesters for criticism, praised "law and order," and chided senators who had helped defeat the nominations of the southern judges Clement Haynesworth and G. Harrold Carswell to the Supreme Court. Voters did not respond, however, and Democrats retained control of both houses of Congress as they had since the 1950s.

Nixon's actions on such domestic problems as school desegregation and water and air pollution received both criticism and applause. This public reaction suggested that he took a moderate course on controversial domestic issues. The president's own rhetoric, however, revealed

Jane Fonda. *Shelly Rusten*

the innate conservatism of his administration. He could not help revealing his feelings against the Black Panthers on trial for conspiracy in New York; he denounced Charles Manson before a jury had found him guilty of murder; he stood behind Governor Nelson Rockefeller's use of force in the brutal quelling of an Attica, New York, prison riot; he also criticized that state's liberal abortion law.

Despite little progress in human relations, Americans reached the moon during Nixon's administration. The historic landing of astronauts Neil Armstrong and Edwin Aldrin took place on July 20, 1969. The moon landing, Nixon's trips to China and Russia, and slowly returning prosperity late in 1972 all boded well for the president as the 1972 election approached. Moreover, Nixon had all the advantages of an incumbent. He raised an enormous campaign fund before a new law required disclosure of donors' names. He used his cabinet officers and Vice President Agnew to wage the campaign while he remained above the fray in the White House. He managed not to get identified with an espionage scandal against the Democrats at the "Watergate," a large apart-

Senator George McGovern

ment complex in Washington, even though all the trails led to the White House staff; later it was shown that Attorney General Mitchell knew of the dealings—and that Nixon or his staff, or both, had been directing widespread espionage and other activities reminiscent of similar acts in totalitarian states. And in domestic politics he found a decisive issue—not racism perhaps but certainly race. Pollsters agreed that Nixon's unsympathetic stance toward Negroes was the key issue pulling normally Democratic ethnic voters toward him.

To the Democratic nominee George McGovern disaster came in his choice of Senator Thomas Eagleton of Missouri as Vice President. Eagleton, despite his claim not to have any "skeletons in the closet," had been keeping secret three periods of psychiatric treatment, two involving shock therapy, for severe mental depression. Statistically speaking, mental illness recurs and the rest periods required to avoid it are not available in the Presidency. Given also its control over nuclear weapons, the presidency is almost the only office to which a formerly mentally ill person should not aspire. It was a problem that could not be solved by compassion, a fact which many of McGovern's supporters could not understand. When the disclosure came McGovern at first stood fast by his candidate; but when Eagleton would not gracefully withdraw he was forced off the ticket. Like the shooting of George Wallace, who would have drained conservative support from Nixon, this affair was a stroke of incredibly bad luck. McGovern never recovered from it. Because he backed down on supporting Eagleton, McGovern, while constantly facing the media in spontaneous situations, received ruthless criticism for any inconsistency; President Nixon, safe in the White House, could entirely avoid open meetings with the press.

McGovern's moment of recognition about the campaign may have come on October 11 en route from Boston to Minneapolis. As the 727 jet sailed over oceans of clouds, he listened to a seven-minute tape given him that morning in Boston. It contained a Vietnam veteran's emotional recollections of the continuing war:

> I don't think the American people really, really understand war and what's going on. We went into villages after they dropped napalm and the human beings were fused together like pieces of metal that had been soldered. . . . We have jets that drop rockets and in the shells they have penny nails and those nails—one nail per square inch for about the size of a football field—you can't believe what they do to a human being. . . . And what bothers me is, when you're there you accept it. You rationalize it. You condone it. You say it's right because they are the enemy.

It was the moment at which McGovern may have seen that his candidacy against the war and the president would be in vain. The American people were glad our troops were coming home, and wanted to know nothing of the intensified air war that rained terror over Vietnam. Nixon won reelection by a 61 to 39 percent majority, yet Democrats actually increased their strength in the Senate and remained well ahead in the House.

SPACE

As American astronauts Neil Armstrong and Edwin "Buzz" Aldrin walked on the moon on July 20, 1969, an estimated quarter of humanity watched via communications satellites which beamed their images to earth. To some, the achievement represented an opportunity for international progress— "One small step for a man, one giant leap for mankind," as the astronauts put it. But to others, the landing of Apollo 11 was simply the culmination of an overly expensive effort, undertaken at the cost of domestic and other scientific goals—a technological triumph which signified little.

The Apollo project, born of damaged American pride, reflected the effort to overcome an early Russian lead in the space race. Russia launched the first artificial satellite, Sputnik I, in October 1957, an event which set off deep concern in America about the country's scientific and technological capacities. In fact, it was a time of significant international cooperation among scientists—the International Geophysical Year had begun that summer—but the political atmosphere was highly charged with troop movements in the Middle East and memories still strong of the Hungarian revolt the previous year. The Soviet challenge generated not only the space race but also an overall upsurge in domestic spending for scientific education. Although the United States readily responded with its Explorer I satellite in January 1958, comfirming the existence of the Van Allen radiation belt, and with Vanguard I, in March, testing solar cells, the Russians remained ahead. Their Sputnik II (November 1957) had orbited a dog in space, making clear the possibility of manned flight. Yet Eisenhower's science advisors set no target date for a manned moon landing, maintaining that the prohibitive cost—$20 to $40 billion—would hardly be worth the limited scientific results. Nonetheless, Project Mercury, organized in October 1958, revealed plans to orbit and recover a manned craft and study the astronauts' reactions in space flight.

Then on April 12, 1961, Russian cosmonaut Yuri Gagarin orbited in space for nearly two hours, traveling once around the earth. Less than a month later, the United States responded with Alan Shepard's 15-minute suborbital flight. President Kennedy soon announced to Congress the American goal—to land a man on the moon and retrieve him safely by 1970. Yet as the decade wore on, American space efforts continued to be responses to Russian achievements. Russian cosmonaut Alexei Leonov became the first man to "walk" in space on March 18, 1965. Five days later, the National Aeronautics and Space Administration set up Project Gemini, a series of extended flights, involving rendezvous, docking maneuvers, and controlled descents and landings; within three months, an American also "walked" in space.

Despite fatalities in both the Russian and American space programs in 1967, as well as the slackening of manned efforts by the Russians, the United States proceeded towards its goal, and in October 1968 began Project Apollo. As Apollo proceeded, the initial preoccupation with beating the Soviets to the moon diminished somewhat; a lead over the Russians in prolonged flight had been established by Gemini, and Vietnam steadily replaced all other international concerns. Domestic discontent opened criticism about space program funding; the impressive technological mastery of outer space paled when ghetto rebellions highlighted pressing problems closer to home. Even scientists complained that the Apollo program took an excessive share of the government scientific budget, especially as funding leveled off in all but defense-related research at the height of the war.

As Eisenhower's advisers predicted, the effort to put a man on the moon cost over $25 billion. Meanwhile, the federal government continued to support a number of less glamorous but more potentially profitable space programs, such as the unmanned interplanetary explorations—Rangers and Surveyors to provide information about the moon, Mariners and Vikings to collect data on Mars and Venus. While Apollo got the publicity, Americans got accustomed to immediate transmission of television images around the world via satellite along with their evening weather reports. As these technological "spin-offs" became commonplace, as public opinion against government policy in Vietnam mounted, and as the ecology movement turned attention to the scarce resources of the earth, public interest in the manned space effort faded. Nearly everyone with access to television watched at least part of the first moon landing; the subsequent Apollo missions, whatever their scientific merit, fell flat as spectacle.

THINGS TO THINK ABOUT: 1953–1973

To what extent did Kennedy influence his country? Compare Eisenhower's foreign policy to Kennedy's. See Eisenhower's memoirs *The White House Years* (2 vols., 1963 and 1965) and Emmet John Hughes, *The Ordeal of Power* (1963). On Eisenhower's successor read Arthur Schlesinger, Jr., *A Thousand Days: John F. Kennedy in the White House* (1965) and the essays in Aida DiPace Donald, ed., *John F. Kennedy and the New Frontier* (1966). For social history of the 1950s see the model suggested in David Riesman, *The Lonely Crowd* (1950) and the controversial essays in Daniel Bell, ed., *The New American Right* (rev. ed., 1963).

Why did the civil rights movement give way to black power? Compare James Baldwin, *The Fire Next Time* (1963) to Theodore Draper, *The Rediscovery of Black Nationalism* (1970) and Harold Cruse, *Rebellion or Revolution?* (1968).

Compare Lyndon Johnson's record in foreign versus domestic policy. Why did we get involved in Vietnam? On domestic history see James L. Sundquist, *Politics and Policy: The Eisenhower, Kennedy, and Johnson Years* (1968), Alfred Steinberg, *Sam Johnson's Boy* (1968), and *Vantage Point* (1971) the memoirs of Lyndon Johnson. Henry Brandon discusses the background of the Vietnam War under three presidents in *Anatomy of Error: The Inside Story of the Asian War on the Potomac, 1954–1969* (1969); a historical account covering the last century is George M. Kahin and John W. Lewis, *The United States in Vietnam* (1967). Townsend Hoopes helped shape the decision to deescalate the war and tells the story in *The Limits of Intervention* (1969). Compare the hawkish Maxwell Taylor, *Responsibility and Response* (1967) to the academic critic Noam Chomsky, *American Power and the New Mandarins* (1969).

Was Barry Goldwater a radical? See the candidate's own *Conscience of a Conservative* (1960) and the more cautious *Where I Stand* (1964), and the critical essays on Goldwater in Richard Hofstadter, *The Paranoid Style in American Politics* (1965). Excellent books centering on the mid-1960s are Alexander Bickel, *The Supreme Court and the Idea of Progress* (1970) and Theodore J. Lowi, *The End of Liberalism* (1967).

Why did women's liberation become an important social movement in the late 1960s? See Betty Friedan's *The Feminine Mystique* (1963), a precursor of the movement, and the insistent essays in Robin Morgan, ed., *Sisterhood is Powerful* (1970). On the youth culture of the 1960s see the important work of Theodore Roszak, *The Making of a Counter Culture* (1969), and that of Philip Slater, *The Pursuit of Loneliness* (1970).

How much leeway in executing national policy has a conservative like Richard Nixon? See Lewis Chester, *An American Melodrama* (1966), Garry Wills, *Nixon Agonistes* (1970), and Theodore White, *The Making of the President 1972* (1973).

Abolition *The demand for immediate end to black slavery without compensation to slaveowners.*

Armistice *A truce, usually between two military opponents. Its declaration often indicates a negotiated settlement is likely.*

Artisan *A small-scale, self-employed handicraftsman, such as a blacksmith, wheelwright, or carpenter.*

Balance of Payments *The difference between the total value of goods, services, and capital exported from a nation and the total value of its imports. If exports are more than imports, the balance is positive; if exports are fewer than imports, the balance is negative.*

Banknotes *Paper currency issued by privately owned banks and backed only by their individual assets, rather than by legal guarantee or government reserves.*

Barnburners *The radical Jacksonian faction of the Democratic party in New York State, led by Martin Van Buren. The group refused to acquiesce in the more conservative, elitist views of the party and, as a result, preferred to "burn the barn down" rather than live in it.*

Bear Market *A period of consistently falling prices on stock or commodity markets.*

Black Nationalism *The philosophy and practice that blacks should not seek integration or equality with the white community but rather assert their own economic and cultural independence.*

Bloody Shirt *A post-Civil War campaign tactic used by the Republicans which obscured real issues in preference for condemning the Democrats as the party of treason and urging citizens to vote as they had fought, for the Union and for the GOP.*

Border States *Those states geographically between the South and North—Delaware, Maryland, Kentucky, and Missouri—with legalized slavery but without a plantation society based upon large-scale agriculture.*

Brains Trust *In New Deal history, a group of informal presidential advisors drawn from universities.*

Bullion *Pure gold held as reserves to back paper currency.*

Bull Market *Consistently rising prices on stock or commodity markets, often accompanied by extensive speculation with borrowed money.*

Capitalism *An economic system based upon production for private profit and dependent upon the central role of the person who controls capital for further expansion.*

Cash Crops *Agricultural crops, such as corn, wheat, and cotton, grown to be sold on a commercial market rather than consumed by the farmer.*

Charter *In American history, a legal document which grants property and sets up a government for a new colony.*

Civil Liberties (Civil Rights) *Those privileges of American citizens which limit government powers over the individual and guarantee his right to participate in the political process, to benefit from social services, and to legal equality. Black Rights The effort to secure those civil liberties denied to black citizens because of racial prejudice.*

Closed Shop *An arrangement whereby potential employees are required to join a union as a condition of employment. (See Open Shop)*

Coastal Trade *Seaborne commerce wholly within the coastal waters of the United States and not with foreign ports.*

Collective Security *A diplomatic device in which all major powers agree to oppose, collectively, any aggressive action by one nation which might disrupt world peace.*

Currency Supply *The total amount of paper money and specie in circulation at a given time. (Some economists would also include bank deposits and/or credit.) An increase in the supply of currency usually boosts prices and lowers interest rates; a decrease reverses both tendencies.*

Dark Horse *A presidential candidate who unexpectedly wins his party's nomination despite unfavorable odds.*

Deflation *A rapid decrease in commodity prices and investment values, usually because of a decline in consumer demand or because of a reduction in the supply of currency and available credit.*

Depression *An economic crisis characterized by severe unemployment, rapid deflation, agricultural overproduction, and industrial stagnation.*

Devaluation *A legal reduction in the gold value of a currency. When adopted, the device stimulates exports and discourages imports, thus easing an adverse balance of payments.*

Electoral College *Those people, selected by the citizens of every state, who formally cast each state's allotted votes in a presidential election. Their ballots are tabulated by the House of Representatives.*

Enlightenment *An eighteenth-century philosophical movement which emphasized man's rationality and his ability to impose order upon the material universe.*

Faction *A group of men loyal to a particular man or who come together briefly for a specific purpose, in contrast to a political party which unites a much larger group of people around a broad ideology for a longer period of time.*

Farm Bloc *A nonpartisan group in Congress which votes as a unit to secure laws favorable to their farmer constituents. These legislators from the Middle West often combine with southerners for mutual benefit.*

Fishing Rights *Privileges granted to fish in a nation's territorial waters and to dry the catch on its uninhabited islands.*

Freeholders *In American colonial history, people who owned land or property worth a certain amount and thus qualified for citizenship, especially the right to vote and hold office.*

Free Soil *A political doctrine that Congress should prohibit slavery in the territories of the United States, so that only "free men" would farm the land.*

Free Trade *The doctrine that governments should not impose any tariffs. In classical economic theory, this would increase world production, as each nation would specialize in what it manufactured most efficiently, thus guaranteeing the lowest possible prices.*

Fire-eaters *Southern extremists who advocated secession even if it resulted in civil war.*

Frontier *In American history, the westernmost fringe of permanent settlement.*

Fundamentalism *A movement within twentieth-century Protestantism which emphasized the literal truth of the Bible.*

Gentry *The colonial upper class which dominated politics through their social prestige and whose wealth permitted time for intellectual pursuits and government.*

Gold Standard *An international monetary system under which a government maintains the value of its currency in terms of a certain weight of pure gold by buying and selling bullion. This limits the amount of paper money in circulation and establishes the relative worth of all currencies.*

Gospel of Wealth *A moralistic justification for the concentration of riches in the hands of a few. A wealthy person must be superior; government should not interfere with his operations, since to do so would subvert "natural laws." (See Social Darwin-*

ism) Yet wisdom compelled the rich man to improve his community, primarily by helping people to help themselves.

Great Plains   *That area from the Dakotas to Texas, last to be settled, which is relatively arid and dependent upon wheat production.*

Greenbacks   *Paper money issued by the federal government to finance the Civil War. Since this currency could not be redeemed for gold, it depreciated rapidly.*

Hard Money   *Gold or silver money which derives its value from the intrinsic worth of the metal it contains.*

Holding Company   *A method of business consolidation, organized by bankers, to secure economic stability within a given industry by rigid controls over prices.*

Home Rule   *Popular municipal reform, particularly during the Progressive era, which seeks local or city self-government without interference from the state.*

Impeachment   *The Constitutional process to remove a president from office. The House of Representatives must first charge the chief executive with "high crimes and misdemeanors" and the Senate must then convict him. In each case, the vote requires a two-thirds majority.*

Imperialism   *The policy and practice of extending the dominion of one nation, usually by direct territorial acquisition or indirect economic control over other areas.*

Imperial Preference   *Economic arrangements between a mother country and its colonies which guarantee mutually favorable tariff treatment and discriminate against countries outside the empire.*

Impressment   *The illegal seizure of American sailors by British naval officers for service in the Royal Fleet.*

Industrialization   *The utilitization of machine power to increase man's productivity. In its broader sense, the economic and social consequences of the nineteenth-century technological revolution which created rapid transportation, new materials, and huge business combinations.*

Inflation   *A rapid increase in commodity prices, usually because of an increase in consumer demand without a parallel increase in industrial production or because of an increase in the amount of currency in circulation and available credit.*

Initiative   *A political device, prominent in western states, which permits voters to originate, and then adopt, laws at special elections.*

Injunction   *A court order, issued by a federal or local judge, which prohibits certain action until an investigation determines the legality of its probable consequences.*

Internal Improvements   *Federally financed enterprises to build roads, canals, harbors, and other large-scale projects which would promote the industrial development of the United States.*

Internationalism   *The belief that national interests are best served by political and economic cooperation with other countries in pursuit of the common good.*

Isolationism   *A traditional American foreign policy which seeks to capitalize upon the nation's geographical remoteness, and consequent military advantages, by avoiding active participation in world affairs.*

Jim Crow System   *Those practices and laws which enforced racial separation and, in effect, created a caste system. (See segregation)*

Judiciary   *The judges which compose the court system of any country.*

Laissez-Faire   *An economic doctrine which asserts that government must not intervene in the free functioning of the market or with individual enterprise.*

Lame Duck   *The name given to an incumbent Congress and president after the election of a new government and before its inauguration some time later.*

Legal Tender   *Any form of money which a government declares acceptable in payment of public taxes and private debts.*

Loyalists   *Colonists, often called tories, who remained loyal to Britain during the American Revolution and who often later emigrated to Canada.*

Manifest Destiny   *The belief that America's rightful, natural fate was to expand and dominate the western hemisphere, thus spreading the "empire for freedom."*

Monopoly   *Exclusive control over the supply of a commodity which enables a businessman to determine its price.*

Monroe Doctrine   *A diplomatic device, first spelled out by President James Madison, which promises America's noninvolvement in European affairs provided the colonial powers make no attempt to extend their empires in the New World.*

Moratorium   *In financial circles, a temporary halt in the installments due as repayment on a loan.*

Muckrakers   *Early twentieth-century journalists*

who probed the dark corners of American life, especially the decline of representative government, economic exploitation, and social inequality, in newspapers and mass circulation magazines such as McClure's and Collier's.

Nationalism A conscious effort to exalt one political or cultural state as superior to all others.

Natural Rights The eighteenth-century belief that man has certain privileges, particularly against arbitrary government, which no political authority can deny.

Naval Stores Raw materials, particularly pitchblend for caulking and trees for masts and hulls, necessary to maintain trading ships and naval vessels.

Navigation Acts A series of Parliamentary laws during the seventeenth century which sought to monopolize colonial trade for England's benefit.

Neutrality A diplomatic strategy whereby a nation avoids specific commitment to any country involved in a dispute with another and pledges to treat both nations equally, without favoring either one, according to international law.

Neutral Rights Those privileges and responsibilities which international law grants to countries not involved in a dispute; usually identified in American history with freedom of the seas and equal trading opportunities.

New Freedom A theory of political economy advocated by Woodrow Wilson which would break up business concentrations in an effort to restore competition and small, individual enterprise and so alleviate the social consequences of industrialization.

New Nationalism A theory of political economy advocated by Theodore Roosevelt which, while accepting big corporations, would have regulated such combinations in the public interest. The federal government would protect individuals from any adverse consequences of such an economic system.

Nonentanglement An American diplomatic tenet which proscribed United States participation in foreign affairs in an effort to avoid overseas troubles.

Nullification The theory that a state, acting under its "ultimate sovereignity," may set aside federal laws.

Populism The Populists A western and southern political and social movement of the late nineteenth century which sought to restore government responsive to its citizens and restructure capitalism in the interests of the common people.

Old Guard That faction within the Republican party which did not want to reform machine politics or ameliorate the consequences of industrialization.

Open Door Policy A major tenet in American diplomacy which opposes exclusive or imperial privileges in order to insure equal access to overseas markets by all nations. This approach favors America's economic interests as an advanced industrial power.

Open Shop A business establishment which does not require membership in a labor union as a condition of employment. (See Closed Shop)

Panic A brief financial emergency usually confined to the banking community. A "panic" often occurs during periods of tight money when institutions cannot easily borrow short-term funds to meet unexpected deposit withdrawals.

Patronage The power to make appointments to government jobs on a basis other than merit alone.

Predestination The Calvinist doctrine that God's omnipresence in past and future permits his knowledge of a person's ultimate fate. Thus God, but not man, knows whether he will end in heaven or hell.

Prohibition Outlawry of the sale, manufacture, or transportation of alcoholic beverage in the United States between 1920 and 1933. This Progressive-oriented reform reflected their belief in the usefulness of law to accomplish fundamental social change.

Progressivism A loosely coordinated political reform movement in early twentieth-century America which sought to break up monopoly capitalism, thus restoring the individual's control over his economic future, and to remold corrupt, machine-ridden government, making it responsive to the social needs of the people.

Public Works Construction projects, such as schools, roads, or dams, financed by government to facilitate economic activity or to promote public recreation.

Racism A belief that one race is superior to all others, which are themselves innately inferior.

Radical Reconstruction That period, roughly from 1866 to 1870, when radical Republicans attempted to recast Southern politics and Southern society toward a two-party system and racial equality.

Recall A Populist reform which permits the people to oust government officials at a special election held after a small number of voters petition for his removal.

Recession *A relatively short period—technically at least two quarters of economic decline—of mild unemployment, reduced investment, and production cutbacks.*

Reciprocity *Mutual reductions of tariffs between two countries on goods of specific interest to each. For example, the United States might lower its duties against Cuban sugar if Cuba reduced its tariffs on American automobiles.*

Redeemers *Those conservative whites who took over state government in the South after Reconstruction and quickly dismantled the effort to establish racial equality and economic democracy.*

Referendum *A political tool, first adopted in western states, which allows the people to vote on proposed legislation before it becomes law.*

Remonstrance *Formal objections about the Crown's administration addressed to the British Parliament by an American colony.*

Reparations *Goods and money demanded of Germany by the European victors in World War I. Economic crises during the early 1920s and again in the 1930s interrupted payments and finally destroyed the effort to collect as much as $22 billion.*

Republic *Representative government which does not share its authority or power with a king or an aristocracy.*

Restoration *The return of monarchical government to England in 1660 when Charles II came to the throne, superseding Oliver Cromwell's Puritan republic.*

Royalists *Those who favor monarchical government or the supremacy of king over Parliament.*

Saints *In Calvinist doctrine, those people (the "elect") whom God knows will be saved and go to heaven. (See Predestination)*

Secession *In American history, the theory that a state has a right to leave the Union and resume its sovereign status.*

Sedition *Any verbal or other nonviolent incitement to resist government authority.*

Segregation *A system of race relations characterized by its attempt to minimize interracial contact and insure the social predominance of whites over blacks.*

Self-Determination *In diplomatic usage, the right of an ethnic group to establish its own cultural and political institutions without interference from or domination by other nations.*

Silver Block *Six western states—Idaho, Montana, Nevada, Utah, Colorado, and Arizona—whose rep-resentatives in Congress usually voted as a unit in order to secure legislation beneficial to the mining interests which dominated state politics. In particular, they sought to make silver legal tender or to increase its price on commodity markets.*

Slave Codes *A series of state laws which locked the slave into a rigid caste system and prevented his self-improvement.*

Specie *Gold or silver coins which derive their value exclusively from the value of their metal content rather than from law as in paper currency. (See Hard Money)*

Social Darwinism *The belief that, like Charles Darwin's theories about animal evolution, struggle and the survival of the fittest characterize human society and economic relationships. Since the strong survived because they were superior, government intervention was necessarily futile and undesirable.*

Social Gospel *A humanitarian movement in American Protestantism which sought a ameliorate the abuses of industrialism.*

Socialism *In its classic, nineteenth-century meaning, socialism meant government ownership of the "means of distribution," such as railroads and banks. Since World War I, the term more often suggests government moderation of the social consequences of capitalist industrialization, particularly business regulation, and the provision of minimual, basic welfare services.*

Subtreasury Plan *The effort to establish a federally financed commodity loan system so that farmers could borrow against their crops.*

Tariffs *A tax levied on foreign goods imported into the United States.* Protective tariff *Artificially high tariffs designed to boost the prices of foreign goods, thus "protecting" domestic industries from overseas competition.* Revenue tariff *Low tariffs which encourage commerce, and thus maximize government revenues from import taxes.*

Tenancy *An agricultural practice, particularly widespread in the South, under which an absentee owner rents his land to a tenant in return for a percentage of the crop.*

Third World *Those predominately nonwhite, underdeveloped, recently independent countries who do not adopt a foreign policy or economic system favorable either to the capitalist United States or the communist Soviet Union.*

Trust *An extralegal arrangement to consolidate a particular industry organized directly by manufacturers. A trust usually pools properties, thereby achieving a monopoly.*

677

War Debts *Roughly $10 billion which the United States loaned to its European allies during and immediately after World War I. Both Republican and Democratic administrations demanded repayment with interest.*

Welfare State *The result when government guarantees certain minimal levels of social and economic well-being to its citizens. All advanced, industrial states have adopted this goal, to varying degrees, as unrestrained capitalism simultaneously creates the need for, and the money to provide, such services as education, health care, and unemployment compensation.*

Yellow Journalism *Sensational, often highly exaggerated news stories consciously published to increase circulation. William Randolph Hearst's New York Journal developed the practice during the 1890s.*

Yeoman Farmer *An independent, self-sufficient farmer. Thomas Jefferson and other founding fathers hoped that the United States would become an agrarian society based upon small landowners.*

THE DECLARATION OF INDEPENDENCE

When in the course of human events it becomes necessary for one people to dissolve the political bands which have connected them with another and to assume, among the powers of the earth, the separate and equal station to which the laws of nature and of nature's God entitle them, a decent respect to the opinions of mankind requires that they should declare the causes which impel them to the separation.

We hold these truths to be self-evident, that all men are created equal; that they are endowed by their Creator with certain unalienable rights; that among these are life, liberty, and the pursuit of happiness. That, to secure these rights, governments are instituted among men, deriving their just powers from the consent of the governed; that, whenever any form of government becomes destructive of these ends, it is the right of the people to alter or to abolish it, and to institute a new government, laying its foundation on such principles, and organizing its powers in such form, as to them shall seem most likely to effect their safety and happiness. Prudence, indeed, will dictate that governments long established should not be changed for light and transient causes; and, accordingly, all experience hath shown that mankind are more disposed to suffer, while evils are sufferable, than to right themselves by abolishing the forms to which they are accustomed. But when a long train of abuses and usurpations, pursuing invariably the same object evinces a design to reduce them under absolute despotism, it is their right, it is their duty, to throw off such government and to provide new guards for their future security. Such has been the patient sufferance of these colonies, and such is now the necessity which constrains them to alter their former systems of government. The history of the present King of Great Britain is a history of repeated injuries and usurpations, all having, in direct object, the establishment of an absolute tyranny over these States. To prove this, let facts be submitted to a candid world:

He has refused his assent to laws the most wholesome and necessary for the public good.

He has forbidden his governors to pass laws of immediate and pressing importance, unless suspended in their operation till his assent should be obtained; and, when so suspended, he has utterly neglected to attend to them.

He has refused to pass other laws for the accommodation of large districts of people, unless those people would relinquish the right of representation in the legislature: a right inestimable to them and formidable to tyrants only.

He has called together legislative bodies at places unusual, uncomfortable, and distant from the depository of their public records, for the sole purpose of fatiguing them into compliance with his measures.

He has dissolved representative houses, repeatedly for opposing, with manly firmness, his invasions on the rights of the people.

He has refused, for a long time after such dissolutions, to cause others to be elected; whereby the legislative powers, incapable of annihilation, have returned to the people at large for their exercise; the state remaining, in the meantime, exposed to all the danger of invasion from without and convulsions within.

He has endeavored to prevent the population of these States; for that purpose, obstructing the laws for naturalization of foreigners, refusing to pass others to encourage their migration hither, and raising the conditions of new appropriations of lands.

He has obstructed the administration of justice by refusing his assent to laws for establishing judiciary powers.

He has made judges dependent on his will alone for the tenure of their offices and the amount and payment of their salaries.

He has erected a multitude of new offices and sent hither swarms of officers to harass our people and eat out their substance.

He has kept among us, in time of peace, standing armies, without the consent of our legislatures.

He has affected to render the military independent of, and superior to, the civil power.

He has combined with others to subject us to a jurisdiction foreign to our Constitution and unacknowledged by our laws, giving his assent to their acts of pretended legislation—

For quartering large bodies of armed troops among us;

For protecting them by a mock trial from punishment for any murders which they should commit on the inhabitants of these States;

For cutting off our trade with all parts of the world;

For imposing taxes on us without our consent;

For depriving us, in many cases, of the benefit of trial by jury;

For transporting us beyond seas to be tried for pretended offences;

For abolishing the free system of English laws in a neighboring province, establishing therein an arbitrary government, and enlarging its boundaries, so as to render it at once an example and fit instrument for introducing the same absolute rule into these colonies;

For taking away our charters, abolishing our most valuable laws, and altering, fundamentally, the powers of our governments;

For suspending our own legislatures and declaring themselves invested with power to legislate for us in all cases whatsoever.

He has abdicated government here by declaring us out of his protection and waging war against us.

He has plundered our seas, ravaged our coasts, burnt our towns, and destroyed the lives of our people.

He is, at this time, transporting large armies of foreign mercenaries to complete the works of death, desolation, and tyranny already begun with circumstances of cruelty and perfidy scarcely paralleled in the most barbarous ages, and totally unworthy the head of a civilized nation.

He has constrained our fellow citizens, taken captive on the high seas, to bear arms against their country, to become the executioners of their friends and brethren, or to fall themselves by their hands.

He has excited domestic insurrections amongst us and has endeavored to bring on the inhabitants of our frontiers, the merciless Indian savages, whose known rule of warfare is an undistinguished destruction of all ages, sexes, and conditions.

In every stage of these oppressions, we have petitioned for redress in the most humble terms; our repeated petitions have been answered only by repeated injury. A prince whose character is thus marked by every act which may define a tyrant is unfit to be the ruler of a free people.

Nor have we been wanting in attention to our British brethren. We have warned them, from time to time, of attempts made by their legislature to extend an unwarrantable jurisdiction over us. We have reminded them of the circumstances of our emigration and settlement here. We have appealed to their native justice and magnanimity, and we have conjured them, by the ties of our common kindred, to disavow these usurpations, which would inevitably interrupt our connections and correspondence. They, too, have been deaf to the voice of justice and consanguinity. We must, therefore, acquiesce in the necessity which denounces our separation, and hold them, as we hold the rest of mankind, enemies in war, in peace, friends.

We, therefore, the representatives of the United States of America, in general Congress assembled, appealing to the Supreme Judge of the world for the rectitude of our intentions, do, in the name and by the authority of the good people of these colonies, solemnly publish and declare, that these united colonies are, and of right ought to be, free and independent states: that they are absolved from all allegiance to the British Crown, and that all political connection between them and the state of Great Britain is, and ought to be, totally dissolved; and that, as free and independent states, they have full power to levy war, conclude peace, contract alliances, establish commerce, and to do all other acts and things which independent states may of right do. And, for the support of this declaration, with a firm reliance on the protection of Divine Providence, we mutually pledge to each other our lives, our fortunes, and our sacred honor.

THE CONSTITUTION OF THE UNITED STATES OF AMERICA

We the people of the United States, in order to form a more perfect union, establish justice, insure domestic tranquillity, provide for the common defense, promote the general welfare, and secure the blessings of liberty to ourselves and our posterity, do ordain and establish this Constitution for the United States of America.

ARTICLE I

SECTION 1. All legislative powers herein granted shall be vested in a Congress of the United States, which shall consist of a Senate and House of Representatives.

SECTION 2. *1.* The House of Representatives shall be composed of members chosen every second year by the people of the several States, and the electors in each State shall have the qualifications requisite for electors of the most numerous branch of the State legislature.

2. No person shall be a representative who shall not have attained to the age of twenty-five years, and been seven years a citizen of the United States, and who shall not, when elected, be an inhabitant of that State in which he shall be chosen.

3. Representatives and direct taxes[1] shall be apportioned among the several States which may be included within this Union, according to their respective numbers, which shall be determined by adding to the whole number of free persons, including those bound to service for a term of years, and excluding Indians not taxed, three fifths of all other persons.[2] The actual enumeration shall be made within three years after the first meeting of the Congress of the United States, and within every subsequent term of ten years, in such manner as they shall by law direct. The number of representatives shall not exceed one for every thirty thousand, but each State shall have at least one representative; and until such enumeration shall be made, the State of New Hampshire shall be entitled to choose three, Massachusetts eight, Rhode Island and Providence Plantations one, Connecticut five, New York six, New Jersey four, Pennsylvania eight, Delaware one, Maryland six; Virginia ten, North Carolina five, South Carolina five, and Georgia three.

4. When vacancies happen in the representation from any State, the executive authority thereof shall issue writs of election to fill such vacancies.

5. The House of Representatives shall choose their speaker and other officers; and shall have the sole power of impeachment.

SECTION 3. *1.* The Senate of the United States shall be composed of two senators from each State, chosen by the legislature thereof,[3] for six years; and each senator shall have one vote.

2. Immediately after they shall be assembled in consequence of the first election, they shall be divided as equally as may be into three classes. The seats of the senators of the first class shall be vacated at the expiration of the second year, of the second class at the expiration of the fourth year, and of the third class at the expiration of the sixth year, so that one third may be chosen every second year; and if vacancies happen by resignation, or otherwise, during the recess of the legislature of any State, the executive thereof may make temporary appointments, until the next meeting of the legislature, which shall then fill such vacancies.[4]

3. No person shall be a senator who shall not have attained to the age of thirty years, and been nine years a citizen of the United States, and who shall not, when elected, be an inhabitant of that State for which he shall be chosen.

4. The Vice President of the United States shall be President of the Senate, but shall have no vote, unless they be equally divided.

5. The Senate shall choose their other officers, and also a president pro tempore, in the absence of the Vice President, or when he shall exercise the office of the President of the United States.

6. The Senate shall have the sole power to try all impeachments. When sitting for that purpose, they shall be on oath or affirmation. When the President of the United States is tried, the chief justice shall preside: and no person shall be convicted without the concurrence of two thirds of the members present.

7. Judgment in cases of impeachment shall not extend further than to removal from office, and disqualifications to hold and enjoy any office of honor, trust or profit under the United States: but the party convicted shall nevertheless be liable and subject to indictment, trial, judgment and punishment, according to law.

SECTION 4. *1.* The times, places, and manner of holding elections for senators and representatives, shall be prescribed in each State by the legislature thereof; but the Congress may at any time by law make or alter such regulations, except as to the places of choosing senators.

2. The Congress shall assemble at least once in every year, and such meeting shall be on the first Monday in December, unless they shall by law appoint a different day.

SECTION 5. *1.* Each House shall be the judge of the elections, returns and qualifications of its own members, and a majority of each shall constitute a quorum to do business; but a small number may adjourn from day to day, and may be authorized to compel the attendance of absent members, in such manner, and under such penalties as each House may provide.

2. Each House may determine the rules of its proceedings, punish its members for disorderly behavior,

1 See the Sixteenth Amendment.
2 See the Fourteenth Amendment.
3 See the Seventeenth Amendment.

4 See the Seventeenth Amendment.

and, with the concurrence of two thirds, expel a member.

3. Each House shall keep a journal of its proceedings, and from time to time publish the same, excepting such parts as may in their judgment require secrecy; and the yeas and nays of the members of either House on any question shall, at the desire of one fifth of those present, be entered on the journal.

4. Neither House, during the session of Congress, shall, without the consent of the other, adjourn for more than three days, nor to any other place than that in which the two Houses shall be sitting.

SECTION 6. 1. The senators and representatives shall receive a compensation for their services, to be ascertained by law, and paid out of the Treasury of the United States. They shall in all cases, except treason, felony, and breach of the peace, be privileged from arrest during their attendance at the session of their respective Houses, and in going to and returning from the same; and for any speech or debate in either House, they shall not be questioned in any other place.

2. No senator or representative shall, during the time for which he was elected, be appointed to any civil office under the authority of the United States, which shall have been created, or the emoluments whereof shall have been increased, during such time; and no person holding any office under the United States shall be a member of either House during his continuance in office.

SECTION 7. 1. All bills for raising revenue shall originate in the House of Representatives; but the Senate may propose or concur with amendments as on other bills.

2. Every bill which shall have passed the House of Representatives and the Senate, shall, before it becomes a law, be presented to the President of the United States; If he approves he shall sign it, but if not he shall return it, with his objections, to that House in which it shall have originated, who shall enter the objections at large on their journal, and proceed to reconsider it. If after such reconsideration two thirds of that House shall agree to pass the bill, it shall be sent, together with the objections, to the other House, by which it shall likewise be reconsidered, and if approved by two thirds of that House, it shall become a law. But in all such cases the votes of both Houses shall be determined by yeas and nays, and the names of the persons voting for and against the bill shall be entered on the journal of each House respectively. If any bill shall not be returned by the President within ten days (Sundays excepted) after it shall have been presented to him, the same shall be a law, in like manner as if he had signed it, unless the Congress by their adjournment prevent its return, in which case it shall not be a law.

3. Every order, resolution, or vote to which the concurrence of the Senate and the House of Representatives may be necessary (except on a question of adjournment) shall be presented to the President of the United States; and before the same shall take effect, shall be approved by him, or being disapproved by him, shall be repassed by two thirds of the Senate and House of Representatives, according to the rules and limitations prescribed in the case of a bill.

SECTION 8. The Congress shall have the power

1. To lay and collect taxes, duties, imposts, and excises, to pay the debts and provide for the common defense and general welfare of the United States; but all duties, imposts, and excises shall be uniform throughout the United States;

2. To borrow money on the credit of the United States;

3. To regulate commerce with foreign nations, and among the several States, and with the Indian tribes;

4. To establish an uniform rule of naturalization, and uniform laws on the subject of bankruptcies throughout the United States;

5. To coin money, regulate the value thereof, and of foreign coin, and fix the standard of weights and measures;

6. To provide for the punishment of counterfeiting the securities and current coin of the United States;

7. To establish post offices and post roads;

8. To promote the progress of science and useful arts, by securing for limited times to authors and inventors the exclusive right to their respective writings and discoveries;

9. To constitute tribunals inferior to the Supreme Court;

10. To define and punish piracies and felonies committed on the high seas, and offenses against the law of nations;

11. To declare war, grant letters of marque and reprisal, and make rules concerning captures on land and water;

12. To raise and support armies, but no appropriation of money to that use shall be for a longer term than two years;

13. To provide and maintain a navy;

14. To make rules for the government and regulation of the land and naval forces;

15. To provide for calling forth the militia to execute the laws of the Union, suppress insurrections and repel invasions;

16. To provide for organizing, arming, and disciplining the militia, and for governing such part of them as may be employed in the service of the United States, reserving to the States respectively, the appointment of the officers, and the authority of training the militia according to the discipline prescribed by Congress;

17. To exercise exclusive legislation in all cases whatsoever, over such district (not exceeding ten miles square) as may, by cession of particular States, and the acceptance of Congress, become the seat of the government of the United States, and to exercise like authority over all places purchased by the consent of the legislature of the State in which the same shall be, for the erection of forts, magazines, arsenals, dockyards, and other needful buildings; and

18. To make all laws which shall be necessary and

proper for carrying into execution the foregoing powers, and all other powers vested by this Constitution in the government of the United States, or any department or officer thereof.

SECTION 9. *1.* The migration or importation of such persons as any of the States now existing shall think proper to admit, shall not be prohibited by the Congress prior to the year one thousand eight hundred and eight, but a tax or duty may be imposed on such importation, not exceeding ten dollars for each person.

2. The privilege of the writ of habeas corpus shall not be suspended, unless when in cases of rebellion or invasion the public safety may require it.

3. No bill of attainder or ex post facto law shall be passed.

4. No capitation, or other direct, tax shall be laid, unless in proportion to the census or enumeration hereinbefore directed to be taken.[5]

5. No tax or duty shall be laid on articles exported from any State.

6. No preference shall be given by any regulation of commerce or revenue to the ports of one State over those of another: nor shall vessels bound to, or from, one State be obliged to enter, clear, or pay duties in another.

7. No money shall be drawn from the treasury, but in consequence of appropriations made by law; and a regular statement and account of the receipts and expenditures of all public money shall be published from time to time.

8. No title of nobility shall be granted by the United States: and no person holding any office of profit or trust under them, shall, without the consent of the Congress, accept of any present, emolument, office, or title, of any kind whatever, from any king, prince, or foreign State.

SECTION 10. *1.* No State shall enter into any treaty, alliance, or confederation; grant letters of marque and reprisal; coin money; emit bills of credit; make any thing but gold and silver coin a tender in payment of debts; pass any bill of attainder, ex post facto law, or law impairing the obligation of contracts, or grant any title of nobility.

2. No State shall, without the consent of the Congress, lay any imposts or duties on imports or exports, except what may be absolutely necessary for executing its inspection laws: and the net produce of all duties and imposts laid by any State on imports or exports, shall be for the use of the treasury of the United States; and all such laws shall be subject to the revision and control of the Congress.

3. No State shall, without the consent of the Congress, lay any duty of tonnage, keep troops, or ships of war in time of peace, enter into any agreement or compact with another State, or with a foreign power, or engage in war, unless actually invaded, or in such imminent danger as will not admit of delay.

ARTICLE II

SECTION 1. *1.* The executive power shall be vested in a President of the United States of America. He shall hold his office during the term of four years, and, together with the Vice President, chosen for the same term, be elected, as follows:

2. Each State shall appoint, in such manner as the legislature thereof may direct, a number of electors, equal to the whole number of senators and representatives to which the State may be entitled in the Congress: but no senator or representative, or person holding an office of trust or profit under the United States, shall be appointed an elector.

The electors shall meet in their respective States, and vote by ballot for two persons, of whom one at least shall not be an inhabitant of the same State with themselves. And they shall make a list of all the persons voted for, and of the number of votes for each; which list they shall sign and certify, and transmit sealed to the seat of the government of the United States, directed to the president of the Senate. The president of the Senate shall, in the presence of the Senate and House of Representatives, open all the certificates, and the votes shall then be counted. The person having the greatest number of votes shall be the President, if such number be a majority of the whole number of electors appointed; and if there be more than one who have such majority, and have an equal number of votes, then the House of Representatives shall immediately choose by ballot one of them for President; and if no person have a majority, then from the five highest on the list the said House shall in like manner choose the President. But in choosing the President, the votes shall be taken by States, the representation from each State having one vote; a quorum for this purpose shall consist of a member or members from two thirds of the States, and a majority of all the States shall be necessary to a choice. In every case, after the choice of the President, the person having the greatest number of votes of the electors shall be the Vice President. But if there should remain two or more who have equal votes, the Senate shall choose from them by ballot the Vice President.[6]

3. The Congress may determine the time of choosing the electors, and the day on which they shall give their votes; which day shall be the same throughout the United States.

4. No person except a natural born citizen, or a citizen of the United States, at the time of the adoption of this Constitution, shall be eligible to the office of President; neither shall any person be eligible to that office who shall not have attained to the age of thirty-five years, and been fourteen years a resident within the United States.

5. In case of the removal of the President from office, or of his death, resignation, or inability to discharge the powers and duties of the said office, the same shall devolve on the Vice President, and the Con-

---

5 See the Sixteenth Amendment.

6 Superseded by the Twelfth Amendment.

gress may by law provide for the case of removal, death, resignation or inability, both of the President and Vice President, declaring what officer shall then act as President, and such officer shall act accordingly, until the disability be removed, or a President shall be elected.

6. The President shall, at stated times, receive for his services a compensation, which shall neither be increased nor diminished during the period for which he shall have been elected, and he shall not receive within that period any other emolument from the United States, or any of them.

7. Before he enter on the execution of his office, he shall take the following oath or affirmation:—"I do solemnly swear (or affirm) that I will faithfully execute the office of President of the United States, and will to the best of my ability, preserve, protect and defend the Constitution of the United States."

SECTION 2. 1. The President shall be commander in chief of the army and navy of the United States, and of the militia of the several States, when called into the actual service of the United States; he may require the opinion, in writing, of the principal officer in each of the executive departments, upon any subject relating to the duties of their respective offices, and he shall have power to grant reprieves and pardons for offenses against the United States, except in cases of impeachment.

2. He shall have power, by and with the advice and consent of the Senate, to make treaties, provided two thirds of the senators present concur; and he shall nominate, and by and with the advice and consent of the Senate, shall appoint ambassadors, other public ministers and consuls, judges of the Supreme Court, and all other officers of the United States, whose appointments are not herein otherwise provided for, and which shall be established by law: but the Congress may by law vest the appointment of such inferior officers, as they think proper, in the President alone, in the courts of law, or in the heads of departments.

3. The President shall have power to fill up all vacancies that may happen during the recess of the Senate, by granting commissions which shall expire at the end of their next session.

SECTION 3. He shall from time to time give to the Congress information of the state of the Union, and recommend to their consideration such measures as he shall judge necessary and expedient; he may, on extraordinary occasions, convene both Houses, or either of them, and in case of disagreement between them with respect to the time of adjournment, he may adjourn them to such time as he shall think proper; he shall receive ambassadors and other public ministers; he shall take care that the laws be faithfully executed, and shall commission all the officers of the United States.

SECTION 4. The President, Vice President, and all civil officers of the United States, shall be removed from office on impeachment for, and conviction of, treason, bribery, or other high crimes and misdemeanors.

ARTICLE III

SECTION 1. The judicial power of the United States shall be vested in one Supreme Court, and in such inferior courts as the Congress may from time to time ordain and establish. The judges, both of the Supreme and inferior courts, shall hold their offices during good behavior, and shall, at stated times, receive for their services, a compensation, which shall not be diminished during their continuance in office.

SECTION 2. 1. The judicial power shall extend to all cases, in law and equity, arising under this Constitution, the laws of the United States, and treaties made, or which shall be made, under their authority;—to all cases affecting ambassadors, other public ministers and consuls;—to all cases of admiralty and maritime jurisdiction;—to controversies to which the United States shall be a party;7—to controversies between two or more States;—between a State and citizens of another State;—between citizens of different States;—between citizens of the same State claiming lands under grants of different States, and between a State, or the citizens thereof, and foreign States, citizens or subjects.

2. In all cases affecting ambassadors, other public ministers and consuls, and those in which a State shall be party, the Supreme Court shall have original jurisdiction. In all the other cases before mentioned, the Supreme Court shall have appellate jurisdiction, both as to law and fact, with such exceptions, and under such regulations as the Congress shall make.

3. The trial of all crimes, except in cases of impeachment, shall be by jury; and such trial shall be held in the State where the said crimes shall have been committed; but when not committed within any State, the trial shall be at such place or places as the Congress may by law have directed.

SECTION 3. 1. Treason against the United States shall consist only in levying war against them, or in adhering to their enemies, giving them aid and comfort. No person shall be convicted of treason unless on the testimony of two witnesses to the same overt act, or on confession in open court.

2. The Congress shall have power to declare the punishment of treason, but no attainder of treason shall work corruption of blood, or forfeiture except during the life of the person attainted.

ARTICLE IV

SECTION 1. Full faith and credit shall be given in each State to the public acts, records, and judicial proceedings of every other State. And the Congress may by general laws prescribe the manner in which such acts, records and proceedings shall be proved, and the effect thereof.

SECTION 2. 1. The citizens of each State shall be entitled to all privileges and immunities of citizens in the several States.8

7 See the Eleventh Amendment.
8 See the Fourteenth Amendment, Sec. 1.

2. A person charged in any State with treason, felony, or other crime, who shall flee from justice, and be found in another State, shall on demand of the executive authority of the State from which he fled, be delivered up to be removed to the State having jurisdiction of the crime.

3. No person held to service or labor in one State under the laws thereof, escaping into another, shall, in consequence of any law or regulation therein, be discharged from such service or labor, but shall be delivered up on claim of the party to whom such service or labor may be due.[9]

SECTION 3. *1.* New States may be admitted by the Congress into this Union; but no new State shall be formed or erected within the jurisdiction of any other State; nor any State be formed by the junction of two or more States, or parts of States, without the consent of the legislatures of the States concerned as well as of the Congress.

2. The Congress shall have power to dispose of and make all needful rules and regulations respecting the territory or other property belonging to the United States; and nothing in this Constitution shall be so construed as to prejudice any claims of the United States, or of any particular State.

SECTION 4. The United States shall guarantee to every State in this Union a republican form of government, and shall protect each of them against invasion; and on application of the legislature, or of the executive (when the legislature cannot be convened) against domestic violence.

ARTICLE V

The Congress, whenever two thirds of both Houses shall deem it necessary, shall propose amendments to this Constitution, or, on the application of the legislatures of two thirds of the several States, shall call a convention for proposing amendments, which in either case, shall be valid to all intents and purposes, as part of this Constitution, when ratified by the legislatures of three fourths of the several States, or by conventions in three fourths thereof, as the one or the other mode of ratification may be proposed by the Congress; Provided that no amendment which may be made prior to the year one thousand eight hundred and eight shall in any manner affect the first and fourth clauses in the ninth section of the first article; and that no State, without its consent, shall be deprived of its equal suffrage in the Senate.

ARTICLE VI

1. All debts contracted and engagements entered into, before the adoption of this Constitution, shall be as valid against the United States under this Constitution, as under the Confederation.[10]

2. This Constitution, and the laws of the United

States which shall be made in pursuance thereof; and all treaties made, or which shall be made, under the authority of the United States, shall be the supreme law of the land; and the judges in every State shall be bound thereby, any thing in the Constitution or laws of any State to the contrary notwithstanding.

3. The senators and representatives before mentioned, and the members of the several State legislatures, and all executive and judicial officers, both of the United States and of the several States, shall be bound by oath or affirmation to support this Constitution; but no religious test shall ever be required as a qualification to any office or public trust under the United States.

ARTICLE VII

The ratification of the conventions of nine States shall be sufficient for the establishment of this Constitution between the States so ratifying the same.

Done in Convention by the unanimous consent of the States present the seventeenth day of September in the year of our Lord one thousand seven hundred and eighty-seven, and of the independence of the United States of America the twelfth. In witness whereof we have hereunto subscribed our names.

[Names omitted]

• • •

Articles in addition to, and amendment of, the Constitution of the United States of America, proposed by Congress, and ratified by the legislatures of the several States, pursuant to the fifth article of the original Constitution.

AMENDMENT I [FIRST TEN AMENDMENTS RATIFIED DECEMBER 15, 1791]

Congress shall make no law respecting an establishment of religion, or prohibiting the free exercise thereof; or abridging the freedom of speech, or of the press; or the right of the people peaceably to assemble, and to petition the government for a redress of grievances.

AMENDMENT II

A well regulated militial, being necessary to the security of a free State, the right of the people to keep and bear arms, shall not be infringed.

AMENDMENT III

No soldier shall, in time of peace be quartered in any house, without the consent of the owner, nor in time of war, but in a manner to be prescribed by law.

AMENDMENT IV

The right of the people to secure in their persons, houses, papers, and effects, against unreasonable

9 See the Thirteenth Amendment.
10 See the Fourteenth Amendment, Sec. 4.

searches and seizures, shall not be violated, and no warrants shall issue, but upon probable cause, supported by oath or affirmation, and particularly describing the place to be searched, and the persons or things to be seized.

AMENDMENT V

No person shall be held to answer for a capital, or otherwise infamous crime, unless on a presentment or indictment of a grand jury, except in cases arising in the land or naval forces, or in the militia, when in actual service in time of war or public danger; nor shall any person be subject for the same offense to be twice put in jeopardy of life or limb; nor shall be compelled in any criminal case to be a witness against himself, nor be deprived of life, liberty, or property, without due process of law; nor shall private property be taken for public use, without just compensation.

AMENDMENT VI

In all criminal prosecutions, the accused shall enjoy the right to a speedy and public trial, by an impartial jury of the State and district wherein the crime shall have been committed, which district shall have been previously ascertained by law, and to be informed of the nature and cause of the accusation; to be confronted with the witnesses against him; to have compulsory process for obtaining witnesses in his favor, and to have the assistance of counsel for his defense.

AMENDMENT VII

In suits at common law, where the value in controversy shall exceed twenty dollars, the right of trial by jury shall be preserved, and no fact tried by a jury shall be otherwise reëxamined in any court of the United States, than according to the rules of the common law.

AMENDMENT VIII

Excessive bail shall not be required, nor excessive fines imposed, nor cruel and unusual punishments inflicted.

AMENDMENT IX

The enumeration in the Constitution of certain rights shall not be construed to deny or disparage others retained by the people.

AMENDMENT X

The powers not delegated to the United States by the Constitution, nor prohibited by it to the States, are reserved to the States respectively, or to the people.

AMENDMENT XI [JANUARY 8, 1798]

The judicial power of the United States shall not be construed to extend to any suit in law or equity, commenced or prosecuted against one of the United States by citizens of another State, or by citizens or subjects of any foreign State.

AMENDMENT XII [SEPTEMBER 25, 1804]

The electors shall meet in their respective States, and vote by ballot for President and Vice President, one of whom, at least, shall not be an inhabitant of the same State with themselves; they shall name in their ballots the person voted for as President, and in distinct ballots, the person voted for as Vice President, and they shall make distinct lists of all persons voted for as President and of all persons voted for as Vice President, and of the number of votes for each, which lists they shall sign and certify, and transmit sealed to the seat of the government of the United States, directed to the President of the Senate;—The President of the Senate shall, in the presence of the Senate and House of Representatives, open all the certificates and the votes shall then be counted;—The person having the greatest number of votes for President, shall be the President, if such number be a majority of the whole number of electors appointed; and if no person have such majority, then from the persons having the highest numbers not exceeding three on the list of those voted for as President, the House of Representatives shall choose immediately, by ballot, the President. But in choosing the President, the votes shall be taken by States, the representation from each State having one vote; a quorum for this purpose shall consist of a member or members from two thirds of the States, and a majority of all the States shall be necessary to a choice. And if the House of Representatives shall not choose a President whenever the right of choice shall devolve upon them, before the fourth day of March next following, then the Vice President shall act as President, as in the case of the death or other constitutional disability of the President. The person having the greatest number of votes as Vice President shall be the Vice President, if such number be a majority of the whole number of electors appointed, and if no person have a majority, then from the two highest numbers on the list, the Senate shall choose the Vice President; a quorum for the purpose shall consist of two thirds of the whole number of Senators, and a majority of the whole number shall be necessary to a choice. But no person constitutionally ineligible to the office of President shall be eligible to that of Vice President of the United States.

AMENDMENT XIII [DECEMBER 18, 1865]

SECTION 1. Neither slavery nor involuntary servitude, except as a punishment for crime whereof the party shall have been duly convicted, shall exist within the United States, or any place subject to their jurisdiction.

SECTION 2. Congress shall have power to enforce this article by appropriate legislation.

AMENDMENT XIV [JULY 28, 1868]

SECTION 1. All persons born or naturalized in the United States, and subject to the jurisdiction thereof, are citizens of the United States and of the State wherein they reside. No State shall make or enforce any law which shall abridge the privileges or immunities of citizens of the United States; nor shall any State deprive any person of life, liberty, or property, without due process of law; nor deny to any person within its jurisdiction the equal protection of the laws.

SECTION 2. Representatives shall be apportioned among the several States according to their respective numbers, counting the whole number of persons in each State, excluding Indians not taxed. But when the right to vote at any election for the choice of electors for President and Vice President of the United States, representatives in Congress, the executive and judicial officers of a State, or the members of the legislature thereof, is denied to any of the male inhabitants of such State, being twenty-one years of age, and citizens of the United States, or in any way abridged, except for participating in rebellion, or other crime, the basis of representation therein shall be reduced in the proportion which the number of such male citizens shall bear to the whole number of male citizens twenty-one years of age in such State.

SECTION 3. No person shall be a senator or representative in Congress, or elector of President and Vice President, or hold any office, civil or military, under the United States, or under any State, who having previously taken an oath, as a member of Congress, or as an officer of the United States, or as a member of any State legislature, or as an executive or judicial officer of any State, to support the Constitution of the United States, shall have engaged in insurrection or rebellion against the same, or given aid or comfort to the enemies thereof. But Congress may by a vote of two thirds of each House, remove such disability.

SECTION 4. The validity of the public debt of the United States, authorized by law, including debts incurred for payment of pensions and bounties for services in suppressing insurrection or rebellion, shall not be questioned. But neither the United States nor any State shall assume or pay any debt or obligation incurred in aid of insurrection or rebellion against the United States, or any claim for the loss or emancipation of any slave; but all such debts, obligations, and claims shall be held illegal and void.

SECTION 5. The Congress shall have power to enforce, by appropriate legislation, the provisions of this article.

AMENDMENT XV [MARCH 30, 1870]

SECTION 1. The right of citizens of the United States to vote shall not be denied or abridged by the United States or by any State on account of race, color, or previous condition of servitude.

SECTION 2. The Congress shall have power to enforce this article by appropriate legislation.

AMENDMENT XVI [FEBRUARY 25, 1913]

The Congress shall have power to lay and collect taxes on incomes, from whatever source derived, without apportionment among the several States, and without regard to any census or enumeration.

AMENDMENT XVII [MAY 31, 1913]

The Senate of the United States shall be composed of two senators from each State, elected by the people thereof, for six years; and each senator shall have one vote. The electors in each State shall have the qualifications requisite for electors of the most numerous branch of the State legislature.

When vacancies happen in the representation of any State in the Senate, the executive authority of such State shall issue writs of election to fill such vacancies: *Provided,* That the legislature of any State may empower the executive thereof to make temporary appointments until the people fill the vacancies by election as the legislature may direct.

This amendment shall not be so construed as to affect the election or term of any senator chosen before it becomes valid as part of the Constitution.

AMENDMENT XVIII[11] [JANUARY 29, 1919]

After one year from the ratification of this article, the manufacture, sale, or transportation of intoxicating liquors within, the importation thereof into, or the exportation thereof from the United States and all territory subject to the jurisdiction thereof for beverage purposes is thereby prohibited.

The Congress and the several States shall have concurrent power to enforce this article by appropriate legislation.

This article shall be inoperative unless it shall have been ratified as an amendment to the Constitution by the legislatures of the several States, as provided in the Constitution, within seven years from the date of the submission hereof to the States by Congress.

AMENDMENT XIX [AUGUST 26, 1920]

The right of citizens of the United States to vote shall not be denied or abridged by the United States or by any State on account of sex.

Congress shall have the power to enforce this article by appropriate legislation.

AMENDMENT XX [JANUARY 23, 1933]

SECTION 1. The terms of the President and Vice President shall end at noon on the 20th day of January, and the terms of Senators and Representatives at noon on the 3d day of January, of the years in which such terms would have ended if this article had not been ratified; and the terms of their successors shall then begin.

11 Repealed by the Twenty-first Amendment.

SECTION 2. The Congress shall assemble at least once in every year, and such meeting shall begin at noon on the 3d day of January, unless they shall by law appoint a different day.

SECTION 3. If, at the time fixed for the beginning of the term of President, the President-elect shall have died, the Vice President-elect shall become President. If a President shall not have been chosen before the time fixed for the beginning of his term, or if the President-elect shall have failed to qualify, then the Vice President-elect shall act as President until a President shall have qualified; and the Congress may by law provide for the case wherein neither a President-elect nor a Vice President-elect shall have qualified, declaring who shall then act as President, or the manner in which one who is to act shall be selected, and such person shall act accordingly until a President or Vice President shall have qualified.

SECTION 4. The Congress may by law provide for the case of the death of any of the persons from whom the House of Representatives may choose a President whenever the right of choice shall have devolved upon them, and for the case of the death of any of the persons from whom the Senate may choose a Vice President whenever the right of choice shall have devolved upon them.

SECTION 5. Sections 1 and 2 shall take effect on the 15th day of October following the ratification of this article.

SECTION 6. This article shall be inoperative unless it shall have been ratified as an amendment to the Constitution by the legislatures of three-fourths of the several States within seven years from the date of its submission.

AMENDMENT XXI [DECEMBER 5, 1933]

SECTION 1. The Eighteenth Article of amendment to the Constitution of the United States is hereby repealed.

SECTION 2. The transportation or importation into any State, Territory, or possession of the United States for delivery or use therein of intoxicating liquors in violation of the laws thereof, is hereby prohibited.

SECTION 3. This article shall be inoperative unless it shall have been ratified as an amendment to the Constitution by conventions in the several States, as provided in the Constitution, within seven years from the date of the submission thereof to the States by the Congress.

AMENDMENT XXII [MARCH 1, 1951]

No person shall be elected to the office of the President more than twice, and no person who has held the office of President, or acted as President, for more than two years of a term to which some other person was elected President shall be elected to the office of the President more than once.

But this article shall not apply to any person holding the office of President when this article was proposed by the Congress, and shall not prevent any person who may be holding the office of President, or acting as President, during the term within which this article becomes operative from holding the office of President or acting as President during the remainder of such term.

This article shall be inoperative unless it shall have been ratified as an amendment to the Constitution by the legislatures of three-fourths of the several States within seven years from the date of its submission to the States by the Congress.

AMENDMENT XXIII [MARCH 29, 1961]

SECTION 1. The District constituting the seat of Government of the United States shall appoint in such manner as the Congress may direct:

A number of electors of President and Vice President equal to the whole number of Senators and Representatives in Congress to which the District would be entitled if it were a State, but in no event more than the least populous State; they shall be in addition to those appointed by the States, but they shall be considered, for the purposes of the election of President and Vice President, to be electors appointed by a State; and they shall meet in the District and perform such duties as provided by the twelfth article of amendment.

SECTION 2. The Congress shall have power to enforce this article by appropriate legislation.

AMENDMENT XXIV [JANUARY 23, 1964]

SECTION 1. The right of citizens of the United States to vote in any primary or other election for President of Vice President, for electors for President or Vice President, or for Senator or Representative in Congress, shall not be denied or abridged by the United States or any State by reason of failure to pay any poll tax or other tax.

SECTION 2. The Congress shall have power to enforce this article by appropriate legislation.

AMENDMENT XXV [FEBRUARY 10, 1967]

SECTION 1. In case of the removal of the President from office or of his death or resignation, the Vice President shall become President.

SECTION 2. Whenever there is a vacancy in the office of the Vice President, the President shall nominate a Vice President who shall take office upon confirmation by a majority vote of both Houses of Congress.

SECTION 3. Whenever the President transmits to the President pro tempore of the Senate and the Speaker of the House of Representatives his written declaration that he is unable to discharge the powers and duties of his office, and until he transmits to them a written declaration to the contrary, such powers and duties shall be discharged by the Vice President as Acting President.

SECTION 4. Whenever the Vice President and a majority of either the principal officers of the executive departments or of such other body as Congress may by law provide, transmit to the President pro tempore of the Senate and the Speaker of the House of Representatives their written declaration that the President is unable to discharge the powers and duties of his office, the Vice President shall immediately assume the powers and duties of the office as Acting President.

Thereafter, when the President transmits to the President pro tempore of the Senate and the Speaker of the House of Representatives his written declaration that no inability exists, he shall resume the powers and duties of his office unless the Vice President and a majority of either the principal officers of the executive departments or of such other body as Congress may by law provide, transmit within four days to the President pro tempore of the Senate and the Speaker of the House of Representatives their written declaration that the President is unable to discharge the powers and duties of his office. Thereupon Congress shall decide the issue, assembling within forty-eight hours for that purpose if not in session. If the Congress, within twenty-one days after receipt of the latter written declaration, or, if Congress is not in session, within twenty-one days after Congress is required to assemble, determines by two-thirds vote of both Houses that the President is unable to discharge the powers and duties of his office, the Vice President shall continue to discharge the same as Acting President; otherwise, the President shall resume the powers and duties of his office.

AMENDMENT XXVI [JUNE 30, 1971]

SECTION 1. The right of citizens of the United States who are eighteen years of age or older to vote shall not be denied or abridged by the United States or by any State on account of age.

SECTION 2. The Congress shall have power to enforce this article by appropriate legislation.

PRESIDENTS, VICE-PRESIDENTS, AND CABINET MEMBERS, 1789–1881

President		Vice-President		Secretary of State		Secretary of Treasury	
1. George Washington	1789	John Adams	1789	T. Jefferson E. Randolph T. Pickering	1789 1794 1795	Alex. Hamilton Oliver Wolcott	1789 1795
2. John Adams Federalist	1797	Thomas Jefferson Democratic- Republican	1797	T. Pickering Jonh Marshall	1797 1800	Oliver Wolcott Samuel Dexter	1797 1801
3. Thomas Jefferson Democratic- Republican	1801	Aaron Burr Democratic- Republican George Clinton Democratic- Republican	1801 1805	James Madison	1801	Samuel Dexter Albert Gallatin	1801 1801
4. James Madison Democratic- Republican	1809	George Clinton Independent- Republican Elbridge Gerry Democratic- Republican	1809 1813	Robert Smith James Monroe	1809 1811	Albert Gallatin H. W. Campbell A. J. Dallas W. H. Crawford	1809 1814 1814 1816
5. James Monroe Democratic- Republican	1817	D. D. Thompkins Democratic- Republican	1817	J. Q. Adams	1817	W. H. Crawford	1817
6. John Q. Adams *	1825	John C. Calhoun *	1825	Henry Clay	1825	Richard Rush	1825
7. Andrew Jackson Democrat	1829	John C. Calhoun Democrat Martin Van Buren Democrat	1829 1833	E. Van Buren E. Livingston Louis McLane John Forsyth	1829 1831 1833 1834	Sam D. Ingham Louis McLane W. J. Duane Roger B. Taney Levi Woodbury	1829 1831 1833 1833 1834
8. Martin Van Buren Democrat	1837	Richard M. Johnson Democrat	1837	John Forsyth	1837	Levi Woodbury	1837
9. William H. Harrison Whig	1841	John Tyler Whig	1841	Daniel Webster	1841	Thos. Ewing	1841
10. John Tyler Whig and Democrat	1841			Daniel Webster Hugh S. Legare Abel P. Upshur John C. Calhoun	1841 1843 1843 1844	Thos. Ewing Walter Forward John C. Spencer Geo. M. Bibb	1841 1841 1843 1844
11. James K. Polk Democrat	1845	George M. Dallas Democrat	1845	James Buchanan	1845	Robt. J. Walker	1845
12. Zachary Taylor Whig	1849	Millard Fillmore Whig	1849	John M. Clayton	1849	Wm. M. Meredith	1849
13. Millard Fillmore Whig	1850			Daniel Webster Edward Everett	1850 1852	Thomas Corwin	1850
14. Franklin Pierce Democrat	1853	William R. D. King Democrat	1853	W. L. Marcy	1853	James Guthrie	1853
15. James Buchanan Democrat	1857	John C. Breckinridge Democrat	1857	Lewis Cass J. S. Black	1857 1860	Howell Cobb Philip F. Thomas John A. Dix	1857 1860 1861
16. Abraham Lincoln Republican	1861	Hannibal Hamlin Republican Andrew Johnson Unionist	1861 1865	W. H. Seward	1861	Salmon P. Chase W. P. Fessenden Hugh McCulloch	1861 1864 1865
17. Andrew Johnson Unionist	1865			W. H. Seward	1865	Hugh McCulloch	1865
18. Ulysses S. Grant Republican	1869	Schuyler Colfax Republican Henry Wilson Republican	1869 1873	E. B. Washburne Hamilton Fish	1869 1869	Geo. S. Boutwell W. A. Richardson Benj. H. Bristow Lot M. Morrill	1869 1873 1874 1876
19. Rutherford B. Hayes Rebublican	1877	William A. Wheeler Republican	1877	W. M. Evarts	1877	John Sherman	1877

* No distinct party designations.

Secretary of War		Attorney-General		Postmaster-General†		Secretary of Navy		Secretary of Interior	
Henry Knox	1789	E. Randolph	1789	Samuel Osgood	1789	Established		Established	
T. Pickering	1795	Wm. Bradford	1794	Tim. Pickering	1791	April 30, 1798.		March 3, 1849.	
Jas. McHenry	1796	Charles Lee	1795	Jos. Habersham	1795				
Jas. McHenry	1797	Charles Lee	1797	Jos. Habersham	1797	Benj. Stoddert	1798		
John Marshall	1800	Theo. Parsons	1801						
Sam'l Dexter	1800								
R. Griswold	1801								
H. Dearborn	1801	Levi Lincoln	1801	Jos. Habersham	1801	Benj. Stoddert	1801		
		Robert Smith	1805	Gideon Granger	1801	Robert Smith	1801		
		J. Breckinridge	1805			J. Crowninshield	1805		
		C. A. Rodney	1807						
Wm. Eustis	1809	C. A. Rodney	1809	Gideon Granger	1809	Paul Hamilton	1809		
J. Armstrong	1813	Wm. Pinkney	1811	R. J. Meigs, Jr.	1814	William Jones	1813		
James Monroe	1814	Richard Rush	1814			B. W. Crownin-			
W. H. Crawford	1815					shield	1814		
Isaac Shelby	1817	Richard Rush	1817	R. J. Meigs, Jr.	1817	B. W. Crownin-			
Geo. Graham	1817	William Wirt	1817	John McLean	1823	shield	1817		
J. C. Calhoun	1817					Smith Thompson	1818		
						S. L. Southard	1823		
Jas. Barbour	1825	William Wirt	1825	John McLean	1825	S. L. Southard	1825		
Peter B. Porter	1828								
John H. Eaton	1829	John M. Berrien	1829	Wm. T. Barry	1829	John Branch	1829		
Lewis Cass	1831	Roger B. Taney	1831	Amos Kendall	1835	Levi Woodbury	1831		
B. F. Butler	1837	B. F. Butler	1833			Mahlon Dickerson	1834		
Joel R. Poinsett	1837	B. F. Butler	1837	Amos Kendall	1837	Mahlon Dickerson	1837		
		Felix Grundy	1838	John M. Niles	1840	Jas. K. Paulding	1838		
		H. D. Gilpin	1840						
John Bell	1841	J. J. Crittenden	1841	Francis Granger	1841	George E. Badger	1841		
John Bell	1841	J. J. Crittenden	1841	Francis Granger	1841	George E. Badger	1841		
John McLean	1841	Hugh S. Legare	1841	C. A. Wickliffe	1841	Abel P. Upshur	1841		
J. C. Spencer	1841	John Nelson	1843			David Henshaw	1843		
Jas. M. Porter	1843					Thos. W. Gilmer	1844		
Wm. Wilkins	1844					John Y. Mason	1844		
Wm. L. Marcy	1845	John Y. Mason	1845	Cave Johnson	1845	George Bancroft	1845		
		Nathan Clifford	1846			John Y. Mason	1846		
		Isaac Toucey	1848						
G. W. Crawford	1849	Reverdy Johnson	1849	Jacob Collamer	1849	Wm. B. Preston	1849	Thomas Ewing	1849
C. M. Conrad	1850	J. J. Crittenden	1850	Nathan K. Hall	1850	Wm. A. Graham	1850	A. H. Stuart	1850
				Sam D. Hubbard	1852	John P. Kennedy	1852		
Jefferson Davis	1853	Caleb Cushing	1853	James Campbell	1853	James C. Dobbin	1853	Robert McClelland	1853
John B. Floyd	1857	J. S. Black	1857	Aaron V. Brown	1857	Isaac Toucey	1857	Jacob Thompson	1857
Joseph Holt	1861	Edw. M. Stanton	1860	Joseph Holt	1859				
S. Cameron	1861	Edward Bates	1861	Horatio King	1861	Gideon Wells	1861	Caleb B. Smith	1861
E. M. Stanton	1862	Titian J. Coffey	1863	M'tgomery Blair	1861			John P. Usher	1863
		James Speed	1864	Wm. Dennison	1864				
E. M. Stanton	1865	James Speed	1865	Wm. Dennison	1865	Gideon Wells	1865	John P. Usher	1865
U. S. Grant	1867	Henry Stanbery	1866	A. W. Randall	1866			James Harlan	1865
L. Thomas	1868	Wm. M. Evarts	1868					O. H. Browning	1866
J. M. Schofield	1868								
J. A. Rawlins	1869	E. R. Hoar	1869	J. A. J. Creswell	1869	Adolph E. Borie	1869	Jacob D. Cox	1869
W. T. Sherman	1869	A. T. Ackerman	1870	Jas. W. Marshall	1874	Geo. M. Robeson	1869	C. Delano	1870
W. W. Belknap	1869	Geo. H. Williams	1871	Marshall Jewell	1874			Zach. Chandler	1875
Alphonso Taft	1876	Edw. Pierrepont	1875	James N. Tyner	1876				
J. D. Cameron	1876	Alphonso Taft	1876						
G. W. McCrary	1877	Chas. Devens	1877	David M. Key	1877	R. W. Thompson	1877	Carl Schurz	1877
Alex. Ramsey	1879			Horace Maynard	1880	Nathan Goff, Jr.	1881		

† Not in Cabinet until 1829.

PRESIDENTS, VICE-PRESIDENTS, AND CABINET MEMBERS, 1881–1973

President		Vice-President		Secretary of State		Secretary of Treasury		Secretary of War*	
20. J. A. Garfield Republican	1881	C. A. Arthur Republican	1881	James G. Blaine	1881	Wm. Windom	1881	R. T. Lincoln	1881
21. Chester A. Arthur Republican	1881			F. T. Frelinghuysen	1881	Chas. J. Folger W. Q. Gresham Hugh McCulloch	1881 1884 1884	R. T. Lincoln	1881
22. G. Cleveland Democrat	1885	T. A. Hendricks Democrat	1885	Thos. F. Bayard	1885	Daniel Manning Chas. S. Fairchild	1885 1887	W. C. Endicott	1885
23. Benj. Harrison Republican	1889	Levi P. Morton Republican	1889	James G. Blaine John W. Foster	1889 1892	Wm. Windom Charles Foster	1889 1891	R. Proctor S. B. Elkins	1889 1891
24. G. Cleveland Democrat	1893	A. E. Stevenson Democrat	1893	W. Q. Gresham Richard Olney	1893 1895	John G. Carlisle	1893	D. A. Lamont	1893
25. William McKinley Republican	1897	Garret A. Hobart Republican Theo. Roosevelt Republican	1897 1901	John Sherman Wm. R. Day John Hay	1897 1897 1898	Lyman J. Gage	1897	R. A. Alger Elihu Root	1897 1899
26. Theodore Roosevelt Republican	1901	Chas. W. Fairbanks Republican	1905	John Hay Elihu Root Robert Bacon	1901 1905 1909	Lyman J. Gage Leslie M. Shaw G. B. Cortelyou	1901 1902 1907	Elihu Root Wm. H. Taft Luke E. Wright	1901 1904 1908
27. W. H. Taft Republican	1909	J. S. Sherman Republican	1909	P. C. Knox	1909	F. MacVeagh	1909	J. M. Dickinson H. L. Stimson	1909 1911
28. Woodrow Wilson Democrat	1913	Thomas R. Marshall Democrat	1913	Wm. J. Bryan Robert Lansing Bainbridge Colby	1913 1915 1920	W. G. McAdoo Carter Glass D. F. Houston	1913 1918 1920	L. M. Garrison N. D. Baker	1913 1916
29. Warren G. Harding Republican	1921	Calvin Coolidge Republican	1921	Chas. E. Hughes	1921	Andrew W. Mellon	1921	John W. Weeks	1921
30. Calvin Coolidge Republican	1923	Charles G. Dawes Republican	1925	Chas. E. Hughes Frank B. Kellogg	1923 1925	Andrew W. Mellon	1923	John W. Weeks Dwight F. Davis	1923 1925
31. Herbert Hoover Republican	1929	Charles Curtis Republican	1929	Henry L. Stimson	1929	Andrew W. Mellon Ogden L. Mills	1929 1932	James W. Good Pat. J. Hurley	1929 1929
32. Franklin D. Roosevelt Democrat	1933	J. Nance Garner Democrat H. A. Wallace Democrat H. S. Truman Democrat	1933 1941 1945	Cordell Hull E. R. Stettinius, Jr.	1933 1944	Wm. H. Woodin Henry Morgenthau, Jr.	1933 1934	Geo. H. Dern H. A. Woodring H. L. Stimson	1933 1936 1940
33. Harry S. Truman Democrat	1945	Alben W. Barkley Democrat	1949	James F. Byrnes Geo. C. Marshall Dean G. Acheson	1945 1947 1949	Fred M. Vinson John W. Snyder	1945 1946	R. H. Patterson K. C. Royall	1945 1947
34. Dwight D. Eisenhower Republican	1953	Richard M. Nixon Republican	1953	J. Foster Dulles Christian A. Herter	1953 1959	George C. Humphrey Robert B. Anderson	1953 1957	*Sec'y of Defense* Est. July 26, 1947 J. V. Forrestal L. A. Johnson G. C. Marshall	1947 1949 1950
35. John F. Kennedy Democrat	1961	Lyndon B. Johnson Democrat	1961	Dean Rusk	1961	C. Douglas Dillon	1961	R. A. Lovett C. E. Wilson N. H. McElroy T. S. Gates, Jr.	1951 1953 1957 1959
36. Lyndon B. Johnson Democrat	1963	Hubert H. Humphrey Democrat	1963	Dean Rusk	1963	G. Douglas Dillon Henry H. Fowler Joseph W. Barr	1963 1965 1968	R. S. McNamara C. M. Clifford M. R. Laird Elliot Richardson James Schlesinger	1961 1968 1969 1973 1973
37. Richard M. Nixon Republican	1969	Spiro T. Agnew Republican Gerald R. Ford Republican	1969 1973	William P. Rogers Henry A. Kissinger	1969 1973	David M. Kennedy John B. Connally George P. Schultz	1969 1971 1972		

* Lost cabinet status in 1947.

Attorney-General	Postmaster-General	Secretary of Navy†	Secretary of Interior	Secretary of Agriculture‡	Other members
W. MacVeagh 1881	T. L. James 1881	W. H. Hunt 1881	S. J. Kirkwood 1881		**Sec'y of Commerce and Labor** Est. Feb. 14, 1903
B. H. Brewster 1881	T. O. Howe 1881 W. Q. Gresham 1883 Frank Hatton 1884	W. E. Chandler 1881	Henry M. Teller 1881		G. B. Cortelyou 1903 V. H. Metcalf 1904 O. S. Straus 1907 Chas. Nagel 1909
A. H. Garland 1885	Wm. F. Vilas 1885 D. M. Dickinson 1888	W. C. Whitney 1885	L. Q. C. Lamar 1885 Wm. F. Vilas 1888	N. J. Colman 1889	(Dept. divided, 1913)
W. H. H. Miller 1889	J. Wanamaker 1889	Benj. F. Tracy 1889	John W. Noble 1889	J. M. Rusk 1889	**Sec'y of Commerce** Est. March 4, 1913
R. Olney 1893 J. Harmon 1895	W. S. Bissell 1893 W. L. Wilson 1895	Hilary A. Herbert 1893	Hoke Smith 1893 D. R. Francis 1896	J. S. Morton 1893	W. C. Redfield 1913 J. W. Alexander 1919 H. C. Hoover 1921
J. McKenna 1897 J. W. Griggs 1897 P. C. Knox 1901	James A. Gary 1897 Chas. E. Smith 1898	John D. Long 1897	C. N. Bliss 1897 E. A. Hitchcock 1899	James Wilson 1897	H. C. Hoover 1925 W. F. Whiting 1928 R. P. Lamont 1929 R. D. Chapin 1932 D. C. Roper 1933
P. C. Knox 1901 W. H. Moody 1904 C. J. Bonaparte 1907	Chas. E. Smith 1901 Henry C. Payne 1902 Robt. J. Wynne 1904 G. B. Cortelyou 1905 G. von L. Meyer 1907	John D. Long 1901 Wm. H. Moody 1902 Paul Morton 1904 C. J. Bonaparte 1905 V. H. Metcalf 1907 T. H. Newberry 1908	E. A. Hitchcock 1901 J. R. Garfield 1907	James Wilson 1901	H. L. Hopkins 1939 Jesse Jones 1940 Henry A. Wallace 1945 W. A. Harriman 1946 C. W. Sawyer 1948 S. Weeks 1953
G. W. Wickersham 1909	F. H. Hitchcock 1909	G. von L. Meyer 1909	R. A. Ballinger 1909 W. L. Fisher 1911	James Wilson 1909	L. L. Strauss 1958 F. H. Mueller 1959 L. H. Hodges 1961
J. C. McReynolds 1913 Thos. W. Gregory 1914 A. M. Palmer 1919	A. S. Burleson 1913	Josephus Daniels 1913	F. K. Lane 1913 J. B. Payne 1920	D. F. Houston 1913 E. T. Meredith 1920	L. H. Hodges 1963 John T. Conner 1965 A. B. Trowbridge 1967 C. R. Smith 1968
H. M. Daugherty 1921	Will H. Hays 1921 Hubert Work 1922 Harry S. New 1923	Edwin Denby 1921	Albert B. Fall 1921 Hubert Work 1923	H. C. Wallace 1921	M. H. Stans 1969 Peter G. Peterson 1972 Frederick B. Dent 1973
H. M. Daugherty 1923 Harlan F. Stone 1924 John G. Sargent 1925	Harry S. New 1923	Edwin Denby 1923 Curtis W. Wilbur 1924	Hubert Work 1923 Roy O. West 1928	H. M. Gore 1924 W. M. Jardine 1925	**Sec'y of Labor** Est. March 4, 1913 W. B. Wilson 1913 J. J. Davis 1921
Wm. D. Mitchell 1929	Walter F. Brown 1929	Chas. F. Adams 1929	Ray L. Wilbur 1929	Arthur M. Hyde 1929	W. N. Doak 1930 Frances Perkins 1933
H. S. Cummings 1933 Frank Murphy 1939 Robt. H. Jackson 1940 Francis Biddle 1941	James A. Farley 1933 Frank C. Walker 1940	Claude A. Swanson 1933 Chas. Edison 1940 Frank Knox 1940 James V. Forrestal 1944	Harold L. Ickes 1933	H. A. Wallace 1933 C. R. Wickard 1940	L. B. Schwellenbach 1945 M. J. Tobin 1948 M. P. Durkin 1953 J. P. Mitchell 1953 A. J. Goldberg 1961 W. Willard Wirtz 1962
Tom C. Clark 1945 J. H. McGrath 1949 J. P. McGranery 1952	R. E. Hannegan 1945 J. L. Donaldson 1947	James V. Forrestal 1945	H. L. Ickes 1945 Julius A. Krug 1946 O. L. Chapman 1951	C. P. Anderson 1945 C. F. Brannan 1948	G. P. Schultz 1969 J. D. Hodgson 1970 Peter Brennan 1973
Herbert Brownell, Jr. 1953 W. P. Rogers 1957	Arthur E. Summerfield 1953	**Sec'y of Health Educ. & Welfare** Est. April 1, 1953 O. C. Hobby 1953 M. B. Folsom 1955 A. S. Flemming 1958	Douglas McKay 1953 Fred Seaton 1956	Ezra T. Benson 1953	**Sec'y of Housing and Urban Development** Est. Sept. 9, 1965 Robt. C. Weaver 1966 George W. Romney 1969 James T. Lynn 1973
Robt. F. Kennedy 1961	J. Edward Day 1961 John A. Gronouski 1963	Abraham A. Ribicoff 1961 A. Celebrezze 1962	Stewart L. Udall 1961	Orville L. Freeman 1961	**Sec'y of Transportation** Est. Oct. 15, 1966
Robt. F. Kennedy 1963 Nicholas deB. Katzenbach 1965 Ramsey Clark 1967	John A. Gronouski 1963 Lawrence F. O'Brien 1965 Marvin Watson 1968	A. Celebrezze 1963 John W. Gardner 1965 Wilbur J. Cohen 1968	Stewart L. Udall 1963	Orville L. Freeman 1963	Alan S. Boyd 1967 John A. Volpe 1969 Claude S. Brinegar 1973
John N. Mitchell 1969 Richard Kleindienst 1972 Elliot Richardson 1973	Winton M. Blount 1969	Robert H. Finch 1969 Elliot L. Richardson 1970 Casper W. Weinberger 1973	Walter J. Hickel 1969 Rogers C. B. Morton 1971	Clifford M. Hardin 1969 E. L. Butz 1971	

† *Lost cabinet status in 1937.*   ‡ *Cabinet status since 1889.*

PRESIDENTIAL ELECTIONS, 1789–1856

Year	Number of States	Candidates	Party	Popular Vote*	Electoral Vote†	Percentage of Popular Vote
1789	11	George Washington	No party designations		69	
		John Adams			34	
		Other Candidates			35	
1792	15	George Washington	No party designations		132	
		John Adams			77	
		George Clinton			50	
		Other Candidates			5	
1796	16	John Adams	Federalist		71	
		Thomas Jefferson	Democratic-Republican		68	
		Thomas Pinckney	Federalist		59	
		Aaron Burr	Democratic-Republican		30	
		Other Candidates			48	
1800	16	Thomas Jefferson	Democratic-Republican		73	
		Aaron Burr	Democratic-Republican		73	
		John Adams	Federalist		65	
		Charles C. Pinckney	Federalist		64	
		John Jay	Federalist		1	
1804	17	Thomas Jefferson	Democratic-Republican		162	
		Charles C. Pinckney	Federalist		14	
1808	17	James Madison	Democratic-Republican		122	
		Charles C. Pinckney	Federalist		47	
		George Clinton	Democratic-Republican		6	
1812	18	James Madison	Democratic-Republican		128	
		DeWitt Clinton	Federalist		89	
1816	19	James Monroe	Democratic-Republican		183	
		Rufus King	Federalist		34	
1820	24	James Monroe	Democratic-Republican		231	
		John Quincy Adams	Independent Republican		1	
1824	24	John Quincy Adams		108,740	84	30.5
		Andrew Jackson		153,544	99	43.1
		William H. Crawford		46,618	41	13.1
		Henry Clay		47,136	37	13.2
1828	24	Andrew Jackson	Democrat	647,286	178	56.0
		John Quincy Adams	National Republican	508,064	83	44.0
1832	24	Andrew Jackson	Democrat	687,502	219	55.0
		Henry Clay	National Republican	530,189	49	42.4
		William Wirt	Anti-Masonic	33,108	7	2.6
		John Floyd	National Republican		11	
1836	26	Martin Van Buren	Democrat	765,483	170	50.9
		William H. Harrison	Whig		73	
		Hugh L. White	Whig	739,795	26	49.1
		Daniel Webster	Whig		14	
		W. P. Mangum	Whig		11	
1840	26	William H. Harrison	Whig	1,274,624	234	53.1
		Martin Van Buren	Democrat	1,127,781	60	46.9
1844	26	James K. Polk	Democrat	1,338,464	170	49.6
		Henry Clay	Whig	1,300,097	105	48.1
		James G. Birney	Liberty	62,300		2.3
1848	30	Zachary Taylor	Whig	1,360,967	163	47.4
		Lewis Cass	Democrat	1,222,342	127	42.5
		Martin Van Buren	Free Soil	291,263		10.1
1852	31	Franklin Pierce	Democrat	1,601,117	254	50.9
		Winfield Scott	Whig	1,385,453	42	44.1
		John P. Hale	Free Soil	155,825		5.0
1856	31	James Buchanan	Democrat	1,832,955	174	45.3
		John C. Fremont	Republican	1,339,932	114	33.1
		Millard Fillmore	American	871,731	8	21.6

*Percentage of popular vote given for any election year may not total 100 percent because candidates receiving less than 1 percent of the popular vote have been omitted.
†Prior to the passage of the Twelfth Amendment in 1804, the electoral college voted for two presidential candidates; the runner-up became Vice-President. Data from Historical Statistics of the United States, Colonial Times to 1957 (1961), pp. 582–683, and The World Almanac.

PRESIDENTIAL ELECTIONS, 1860–1932

Year	Number of States	Candidates	Party	Popular Vote	Electoral Vote	Percentage of Popular Vote
1860	33	Abraham Lincoln	Republican	1,865,593	180	39.8
		Stephen A. Douglas	Democrat	1,382,713	12	29.5
		John C. Breckinridge	Democrat	848,356	72	18.1
		John Bell	Constitutional Union	592,906	39	12.6
1864	36	Abraham Lincoln	Republican	2,206,938	212	55.0
		George B. McClellan	Democrat	1,803,787	21	45.0
1868	37	Ulysses S. Grant	Republican	3,013,421	214	52.7
		Horatio Seymour	Democrat	2,706,829	80	47.3
1872	37	Ulysses S. Grant	Republican	3,596,745	286	55 6
		Horace Greeley	Democrat	2,843,446	*	43.9
1876	38	Rutherford B. Hayes	Republican	4,036,572	185	48.0
		Samuel J. Tilden	Democrat	4,284,020	184	51.0
1880	38	James A. Garfield	Republican	4,453,295	214	48.5
		Winfield S. Hancock	Democrat	4,414,082	155	48.1
		James B. Weaver	Greenback-Labor	308,578		3.4
1884	38	Grover Cleveland	Democrat	4,879,507	219	48.5
		James G. Blaine	Republican	4,850,293	182	48.2
		Benjamin F. Butler	Greenback-Labor	175,370		1.8
		John P. St. John	Prohibition	150,369		1.5
1888	38	Benjamin Harrison	Republican	5,447,129	233	47.9
		Grover Cleveland	Democrat	5,537,857	168	48.6
		Clinton B. Fisk	Prohibition	249,506		2.2
		Anson J. Streeter	Union Labor	146,935		1.3
1892	44	Grover Cleveland	Democrat	5,555,426	277	46.1
		Benjamin Harrison	Republican	5,182,690	145	43.0
		James B. Weaver	People's	1,029,846	22	8.5
		John Bidwell	Prohibition	264,133		2.2
1896	45	William McKinley	Republican	7,102,246	271	51.1
		William J. Bryan	Democrat	6,492,559	176	47.7
1900	45	William McKinley	Republican	7,218,491	292	51.7
		William J. Bryan	Democrat; Populist	6,356,734	155	45.5
		John C. Woolley	Prohibition	208,914		1.5
1904	45	Theodore Roosevelt	Republican	7,628,461	336	57.4
		Alton B. Parker	Democrat	5,084,223	140	37.6
		Eugene V. Debs	Socialist	402,283		3.0
		Silas C. Swallow	Prohibition	258,536		1.9
1908	46	William H. Taft	Republican	7,675,320	321	51.6
		William J. Bryan	Democrat	6,412,294	162	43.1
		Eugene V. Debs	Socialist	420,793		2.8
		Eugene W. Chafin	Prohibition	253,840		1.7
1912	48	Woodrow Wilson	Democrat	6,296,547	435	41.9
		Theodore Roosevelt	Progressive	4,118,571	88	27.4
		William H. Taft	Republican	3,486,720	8	23.2
		Eugene V. Debs	Socialist	900,672		6.0
		Eugene W. Chafin	Prohibition	206,275		1.4
1916	48	Woodrow Wilson	Democrat	9,127,695	277	49.4
		Charles E. Hughes	Republican	8,533,507	254	46.2
		A. L. Benson	Socialist	585,113		3.2
		J. Frank Hanly	Prohibition	220,506		1.2
1920	48	Warren G. Harding	Republican	16,143,407	404	60.4
		James M. Cox	Democrat	9,130,328	127	34.2
		Eugene V. Debs	Socialist	919,799		3.4
		P. P. Christensen	Farmer-Labor	265,411		1.0
1924	48	Calvin Coolidge	Republican	15,718,211	382	54.0
		John W. Davis	Democrat	8,385,283	136	28.8
		Robert M. La Follette	Progressive	4,821,289	13	16.6
1928	48	Herbert C. Hoover	Republican	21,391,993	444	58.2
		Alfred E. Smith	Democrat	15,016,169	87	40.9
1932	48	Franklin D. Roosevelt	Democrat	22,809,638	472	57.4
		Herbert C. Hoover	Republican	15,758,901	59	39.7
		Norman Thomas	Socialist	881,951		2.2

*Because of the death of Greeley, Democratic electors scattered their votes.

PRESIDENTIAL ELECTIONS, 1936–1972

Year	Number of States	Candidates	Party	Popular Vote*	Electoral Vote†	Percentage of Popular Vote
1936	48	Franklin D. Roosevelt	Democrat	27,752,869	523	60.8
		Alfred M. Landon	Republican	16,674,665	8	36.5
		William Lemke	Union	882,479		1.9
1940	48	Franklin D. Roosevelt	Democrat	27,307,819	449	54.8
		Wendell L. Willkie	Republican	22,321,018	82	44.8
1944	48	Franklin D. Roosevelt	Democrat	25,606,585	432	53.5
		Thomas E. Dewey	Republican	22,014,745	99	46.0
1948	48	Harry S. Truman	Democrat	24,105,812	303	49.5
		Thomas E. Dewey	Republican	21,970,065	189	45.1
		J. Strom Thurmond	States' Rights	1,169,063	39	2.4
		Henry A. Wallace	Progressive	1,157,172		2.4
1952	48	Dwight D. Eisenhower	Republican	33,936,234	442	55.1
		Adlai E. Stevenson	Democrat	27,314,992	89	44.4
1956	48	Dwight D. Eisenhower	Republican	35,590,472	457‡	57.6
		Adlai E. Stevenson	Democrat	26,022,752	73	42.1
1960	50	John F. Kennedy	Democrat	34,227,096	303§	49.9
		Richard M. Nixon	Republican	34,108,546	219	49.6
1964	50	Lyndon B. Johnson	Democrat	42,676,220	486	61.3
		Barry M. Goldwater	Republican	26,860,314	52	38.5
1968	50	Richard M. Nixon	Republican	31,785,480	301	43.4
		Hubert H. Humphrey	Democrat	31,275,165	191	42.7
		George C. Wallace	American Independent	9,906,473	46	13.5
1972	50	Richard M. Nixon	Republican	45,767,218	521	61.0
		George S. McGovern	Democrat	28,357,668	17	38.0

*Percentage of popular vote given for any election year may not total 100 percent because candidates receiving less than 1 percent of the popular vote have been omitted.
†Prior to the passage of the Twelfth Amendment in 1804, the electoral college voted for two presidential candidates; the runner-up became Vice-President. Data from Historical Statistics of the United States, Colonial Times to 1957 (1961), pp. 682–683, and The World Almanac.
‡Walter B. Jones received 1 electoral vote.   §Harry F. Byrd received 15 electoral votes.

JUSTICES OF THE UNITED STATES SUPREME COURT, 1789–1973

Name (Chief Justices in Italics)	Service (Terms)	(Years)	Name (Chief Justices in Italics)	Service (Terms)	(Years)
John Jay (N.Y.)	1789–1795	6	Henry B. Brown (Mich.)	1890–1906	16
John Rutledge (S.C.)	1789–1791	2	George Shiras, Jr. (Pa.)	1892–1903	11
William Cushing (Mass.)	1789–1810	21	Howell E. Jackson (Tenn.)	1893–1895	2
James Wilson (Pa.)	1789–1798	9	Edward D. White (La.)	1894–1910	16
John Blair (Va.)	1789–1796	7	Rufus W. Peckham (N.Y.)	1895–1909	14
James Iredell (N.C.)	1790–1799	9	Joseph McKenna (Calif.)	1898–1925	27
Thomas Johnson (Md.)	1792–1793	½	Oliver W. Holmes (Mass.)	1902–1932	30
William Paterson (N.J.)	1793–1806	13	William R. Day (Ohio)	1903–1922	19
John Rutledge (S.C.)*	1795–1795		William H. Moody (Mass.)	1906–1910	4
Samuel Chase (Md.)	1796–1811	15	Horace H. Lurton (Tenn.)	1910–1914	4
Oliver Ellsworth (Conn.)	1796–1800	4	*Edward D White* (La.)	1910–1921	11
Bushrod Washington (Va.)	1798–1829	31	Charles E. Hughes (N.Y.)	1910–1916	6
Alfred Moore (N.C.)	1800–1804	4	Willis Van Devanter (Wyo.)	1911–1937	26
John Marshall (Va.)	1801–1835	34	Joseph R. Lamar (Ga.)	1911–1916	5
William Johnson (S.C.)	1804–1834	30	Mahlon Pitney (N.J.)	1912–1922	10
Brock. Livingston (N.Y.)	1806–1823	17	James C. McReynolds (Tenn.)	1914–1941	27
Thomas Todd (Ky.)	1807–1826	19	Louis D. Brandeis (Mass.)	1916–1939	23
Joseph Story (Mass.)	1811–1845	34	John H. Clarke (Ohio)	1916–1922	6
Gabriel Duval (Md.)	1811–1835	24	*William H. Taft* (Conn.)	1921–1930	9
Smith Thompson (N.Y.)	1823–1843	20	George Sutherland (Utah)	1922–1938	16
Robert Trimble (Ky.)	1826–1828	2	Pierce Butler (Minn.)	1923–1939	16
John McLean (Ohio)	1829–1861	32	Edward T. Sanford (Tenn.)	1923–1930	7
Henry Bladwin (Pa.)	1830–1844	14	Harlan F. Stone (N.Y.)	1925–1941	16
James M. Wayne (Ga.)	1835–1867	32	*Charles E. Hughes* (N.Y.)	1930–1941	11
Roger B. Taney (Md.)	1836–1864	28	Owen J. Roberts (Pa.)	1930–1945	15
Philip P. Barbour (Va.)	1836–1841	5	Benjamin N. Cardozo (N.Y.)	1932–1938	6
John Catron (Tenn.)	1837–1865	28	Hugo L. Black (Ala.)	1937–1971	34
John McKinley (Ala.)	1837–1852	15	Stanley F. Reed (Ky.)	1938–1957	19
Peter V. Daniel (Va.)	1841–1860	19	Felix Frankfurter (Mass.)	1939–1962	23
Samuel Nelson (N.Y.)	1845–1872	27	William O. Douglas (Conn.)	1939–	
Levi Woodbury (N.H.)	1845–1851	6	Frank Murphy (Mich.)	1940–1949	9
Robert C. Grier (Pa.)	1846–1870	24	*Harlan F. Stone* (N.Y.)	1941–1946	5
Benjamin R. Curtis (Mass.)	1851–1857	6	James F. Byrnes (S.C.)	1941–1942	1
John A. Campbell (Ala.)	1853–1861	8	Robert H. Jackson (N.Y.)	1941–1954	13
Nathan Clifford (Maine)	1858–1881	23	Wiley B. Rutledge (Iowa)	1943–1949	6
Noah H. Swayne (Ohio)	1862–1881	19	Harold H. Burton (Ohio)	1945–1958	13
Samuel F. Miller (Iowa)	1862–1890	28	*Fred M. Vinson* (Ky.)	1946–1953	7
David Davis (Ill.)	1862–1877	15	Tom C. Clark (Tex.)	1949–1967	18
Stephen J. Field (Calif.)	1863–1897	34	Sherman Minton (Ind.)	1949–1956	7
Salmon P. Chase (Ohio)	1864–1873	9	*Earl Warren* (Calif.)	1953–1969	16
William Strong (Pa.)	1870–1880	10	John M. Harlan (N.Y.)	1955–1971	16
Joseph P. Bradley (N.J.)	1870–1892	22	William J. Brennan (N.J.)	1956–	
Ward Hunt (N.Y.)	1872–1882	10	Charles E. Whittaker (Mo.)	1957–1962	5
Morrison R. Waite (Ohio)	1874–1888	14	Potter Stewart (Ohio)	1958–	
John M. Harlan (Ky.)	1877–1911	34	Byron R. White (Colo.)	1962–	
William B. Woods (Ga.)	1880–1887	7	Arthur J. Goldberg (Ill.)	1962–1965	3
Stanley Matthews (Ohio)	1881–1889	8	Abe Fortas (Tenn.)	1965–1969	4
Horace Gray (Mass.)	1881–1902	21	Thurgood Marshall (Md.)	1967–	
Samuel Blatchford (N.Y.)	1882–1893	11	*Warren E. Burger* (Minn.)	1969–	
Lucius Q. Lamar (Miss.)	1888–1893	5	Harry A. Blackmun (Minn.)	1970–	
Melville W. Fuller (Ill.)	1888–1910	22	Lewis F. Powell, Jr. (Va.)	1971–	
David J. Brewer (Kans.)	1889–1910	21	William H. Rehnquist (Ariz.)	1971–	

*Appointed and served one term, but not confirmed by the Senate.

Elizabeth I, 17, 19-20
Ellsburg, Daniel, 655
Emancipation Proclamation (1863), 303, 309, 318, 322
Embargo Act (1807), 176, 181
Emergency Banking Relief Act (1933), 528
Emerson, Ralph Waldo, 244, 282, 291
EPIC campaign, 535-36
Erie Canal, 224
Export-Import Bank, 535

Fair Deal program, 605-6
Fair Employment Practices Commission, 590
Fair Employment Standards Act (1938), 541
Fall, Albert, 489
Farm Credit Administration, 529
Farm Holiday movement, 536
Faubus, Orval, 641
Federal Deposit Insurance Corporation, 529
Federal Farm Loan Act (1916), 454
Federal Reserve Act (1913), 452
Federal Reserve Board, 489, 491, 510, 541, 629, 664
Federal Trade Commission Act (1914), 452, 491
Federalist party, 140, 147, 149, 150, 153, 156-61, 164, 167-68, 170, 174, 177, 181, 192, 194
Fenno, John, 146
Fermi, Enrico, 617
Fifteenth Amendment (1870), 327
Fillmore, Millard, 205, 271, 277
Finney, Charles G., 233, 237, 264
Fire-eaters, 217-18
Fish, Hamilton, 403
Fitzgerald, F. Scott, 236, 476, 503-5
Florida, 147, 197, 208
Foote, Henry, 269
Foraker Act (1900), 418
Forbes, Charles R., 489
Force Act (1833), 218
Ford, Henry, 358, 491
Foster, William Z., 535, 549
Fourier phalanxes, 230
Fourteen Points program, 467, 483, 573
Fourteenth Amendment (1868), 327
Fox sisters, 226-27
France, 9, 15-16, 76, 77, 80, 86, 92, 107, 141, 147, 149, 158, 173-76, 200, 486, 560-62, 570-71, 576, 595, 607, 609, 649-50, 663
Franklin, Benjamin, 63, 66, 71, 77, 85-87, 111, 122, 146, 183
Frazier, E. Franklin, 555
Freedmen's Bureau, 325, 329-30
Freedom riders, 642
Free Soil party, 267-68
Free Speech movement, 658
Fremont, John C., 277-78, 318

French and Indian War, 77, 80, 90, 92, 107
Freneau, Philip, 146
Freudianism, 505-6
Freylinghuysen, Theodore, 74
Friedan, Betty, 661
Fugitive Slave Act (1793), 269
Fugitive Slave Act (1850), 295
Fulbright, J. William, 652
Fuller, Margaret, 247-48
Funding and Assumption, 151-52

Gag rule (1837), 217, 265
Galbraith, John, 510-11, 631
Gallatin, Albert, 224
Garfield, James A., 377, 387, 408
Garner, John Nance, 523
Garrison, William Lloyd, 215, 217, 233, 262, 264-67
Garvey, Marcus, 459, 556
General Strike (1919), 479
Geneva Conference (1955), 626-27
George III, 80, 91-92, 102-3, 106
George, Henry, 371, 377, 394, 429
Georgia, 126, 209; as colony, 44-45
Germany, 482-84, 514-16, 559-60, 562, 571, 573-74, 595, 597, 606, 617; East Germany, 639; West Germany, 606, 609, 626, 663, 666
Gerry, Elbridge, 158
Gilbert, Sir Humphrey, 19-20
Glorious Revolution, 51-53
Goldwater, Barry, 648
Gompers, Samuel, 415, 444, 454
Good Neighbor Policy, 534-35
Gorgas, Josiah, 300
Gould, Jay, 355, 356
Grady, Henry W., 367
Grange Movement, 355
Grant, Ulysses S., 303-4, 309, 330-31, 391, 403
Great Awakening, 38, 74, 76, 91
Great Britain, 119, 144, 147-50, 154, 158, 172, 176-77, 180-84, 198-200, 252-54, 264, 486, 560-62, 570-71, 576, 578-79, 595, 597, 607, 609, 627, 650; investments of, in U.S., 201-2, 221-22; (see also Parliament)
Great Society program, 630, 646, 648, 664
Great White Fleet, 446
Greeley, Horace, 205, 331
Greene, Nathaniel, 136
Grier, Robert C., 278
Grimké sisters, 233, 265
Guam, 415
Guaranteed income plan, 666
Guatemala, 627, 638
Gulf of Tonkin Resolution, 651, 654
Guthrie, Woody, 521-22, 551, 572, 604, 659

Haiti, 460
Half-Way Covenant, 33

Hamilton, Alexander, 118, 122, 135, 140, 146-48, 156, 170; economic policies of, 150-53
Hampton Institute, 370
Hancock, John, 99
Hanna, Mark, 399, 401-2, 441
Hanson, Ole, 479
Harding, Warren G., 486-91, 498
Hardwick, Thomas, 479
Harriman, Averell, 596-97
Harrington, Michael, 631
Harrison, Benjamin, 377, 386, 393, 408, 415
Harrison, William Henry, 177, 206, 252
Hartford Convention, 181
Harvard University, 71, 495, 499
Hat Act (1732), 63
Hawaii, 406-7
Hawthorne, Nathaniel, 232, 236, 244, 246-47
Hay, John, 413, 419-20, 446
Hayes, Rutherford B., 331, 334, 342, 377
Haymarket affair, 360
Hearst, William, 409-10, 523
Hemingway, Ernest, 236, 503, 505
Henry, Patrick, 64, 90, 94
Hicks, Granville, 549
Hill, James J., 351
Hiss, Alger, 611-12, 656
Hitler, Adolf, 559-60, 571
Ho Chi Minh, 609, 650
Hoffa, James, 640
Home Missionary Society, 233
Home Owners Loan Act (1933), 592
Homer, Winslow, 373
Homestead Act (1862), 314
Hooker, Thomas, 31
Hoover, Herbert, 346, 476, 488, 495, 509-17, 523-25, 534, 546, 567, 571, 629; depression policies of, 511-13
Hoover, J. Edgar, 638
Hoover-Stimson Doctrine, 515-16
Hopkins, Harry, 540, 555, 603
Hopkins, Mark, 356
House, Edward, 466
Houston, Sam, 213, 215
Howard University, 330
Howells, William Dean, 373, 443
Hughes, Charles Evans, 486, 488; as Chief Justice, 544-46
Hughes, Langston, 549
Hull, Cordell, 532-35, 574
Hull, William, 180
Humphrey, Hubert H., 615, 656
Hundred Days, 528-32
Huntington, Collis P., 356
Hutchinson, Anne, 31
Hutchinson, Thomas, 56, 94, 95, 100

Ickes, Harold, 528, 555
Immigration, 64-65, 71, 225, 248-49, 436-38; restrictions, 498

700

Imperialism (*see* Overseas Expansion)
Impressment, 176
Indentured servants, 65, 68
Indians: before 1776, 6-11, 22, 34, 44, 48, 76, 77, 92; in national period, 174-75, 177, 182-84, 203, 345-46; and removal policy, 208-9, 212
Indo-China, 597, 609 (*see also* Laos, Cambodia, Vietnam)
Industrial Conference, 480
Industrial education movement, 370, 456
Industrial labor, 359-60, 480, 555; unions, 230, 358-59, 443-44, 489-90, 495-96, 530-31, 542; (*see also* unions listed by name)
Industrial Workers of the World, 470
Insull, Samuel, 510
Internal improvements, 193-94, 197, 224-25
International Bank for Reconstruction and Development, 592
International Ladies Garment Workers Union, 542
International Monetary Fund, 592
Interstate Commerce Act (1887), 355
Interstate Commerce Commission, 355, 443, 445, 491, 642
Intolerable Acts (1773), 103
Iron Act (1750), 63
Irving, Washington, 236
Isolationism, 406, 558-60, 571-72
Italy, 515, 558-59, 561, 595
Ives, Charles, 471

Jackson, Andrew, 184, 189-90, 196-97, 213, 218, 221-22, 224, 388, 391, 447, 452; and Bank War, 190, 220-21; and Democratic party, 204-8; Indian policy of, 209, 212
Jackson, George, 645
Jackson, Thomas "Stonewall," 303, 308
Jacobin Clubs, 148
James II, 42-44, 51, 76
James, Henry, 236, 373
James, William, 434
Jamestown colony, 21-22
Japan, 446, 460, 486, 515-16, 533-34, 558-60, 568, 573-74, 579-83, 595-96, 617, 666; U.S. occupation of, 568
Jay, John, 111, 128, 149, 156
Jazz, 506-7
Jefferson, Thomas, 85, 87, 112-13, 117, 139-40, 144, 146-47, 151, 156, 158, 183, 185-86, 192, 387, 391, 406; and Declaration of Independence, 105-6; and Embargo, 176; and Louisiana Purchase, 172-75; Presidency of, 161, 164-76
Jeffersonian economic theory, 150-53

Jim Crow legislation, 371
Job Corps, 646
Johnson Act (1924), 498
Johnson, Andrew, 309, 325-26, 329
Johnson, Hugh, 530-31
Johnson, James Weldon, 459
Johnson, Lyndon, 634, 636, 640, 646, 648, 650-58
Johnson, Tom, 435
Jones, Leroi, 660
Jones, Samuel M., 435
Joplin, Scott, 471
Joseph, Nez Percé Indians, 339-40
Journal of Negro History, 459
Judiciary Act (1789), 129, 167
Judiciary Act (1801), 164-65

Kansas, 277, 279
Kansas-Nebraska Bill (1854), 274-77
Keating-Owen Act (1916), 454
Kellogg, Frank B., 486
Kenna, "Hinky Dink," 394
Kennedy, John F., 636-42, 645-50, 670
Kennedy, Joseph P., 636
Kennedy, Robert, 639-42, 655
Kent State University affair, 667
Kentucky, 116, 296
Keynes, John Maynard, 547
Khrushchev, Nikita, 626-27, 639
King, Martin Luther, 621-22, 641, 655
King George's War, 77
King Phillip's War, 48
King William's War, 76
Kinsey reports, 471
Kissinger, Henry, 655, 664
Knights of Labor, 359-60
Know-Nothing party, 249, 276-77
Knox, Frank, 571
Korean War, 568, 608-10, 624-26, 629, 650
Krutch, Joseph Wood, 505, 549
Ku Klux Klan, 330, 496-97, 518

La Follette, Robert, 440, 454
Lamar, L. Q. C., 370
Lamont, Thomas P., 534
Land Ordinance (1785), 117
Land speculation, 203, 222, 251-52
Landon, Alfred M., 542-43, 648
Lane, Franklin K., 470
Lane Theoolgical Seminary, 241, 264
Lansing, Robert, 460
Laos, 639, 654
League of Armed Neutrality, 109
League of Nations, 482-86, 514-16, 559
League of Women Voters, 502
Lebanon invasion, 627
Lecompton (Kan.) Constitution, 279, 281
Lee, Mother Ann, 229
Lee, Robert E., 281, 303, 311
Leisler's Rebellion, 51
Lemke, William, 536, 543

Lend-lease program, 572-73, 596
Leopard and *Chesapeake* affair, 176
Lewis and Clark Expedition, 172, 339
Lewis, John L., 542
Lewis, Sinclair, 503-4
Liberty party, 266-67
Liliuokalani, 407
Lincoln, Abraham, 247, 268, 279-81, 283-84, 293-96, 309, 311, 391, 426, 441; and civil liberties, 314, 316-17; in Lincoln-Douglas debates, 279-81, 284; and Reconstruction, 322, 324-25
Lindbergh, Charles, 518, 571
Lippmann, Walter, 490
Livingston, Robert, 173-74
Lloyd, Henry Demarest, 426
Locofocos, 221
Lodge, Henry C., Sr., 446, 483-84
Lodge, Henry C., Jr., 624
London Economic Conference, 532-33
Long, Huey P., 536-37, 543
Longfellow, Henry Wadsworth, 282
Lords of Trade, 49, 52
Louisbourg fort, 77, 80
Louisiana Purchase, 172-75
Lovejoy, Elijah, 217
Low, Seth, 435
Lowden, Frank, 487
Lowell, James Russell, 257
Lundy, Benjamin, 264
Lusitania incident, 463

McAdoo, William G., 487-89, 523
MacArthur, Douglas, 513, 567-69, 580-82, 609-10
McCarran Internal Security Act (1950), 615
McCarthy, Eugene, 655
McCarthy, Joseph R., 610-17, 626, 636
McClellan, George B., 309
McCracken, Paul, 664
McGovern, George, 669
McKinley, William, 398, 409-11, 429, 441, 488
McNamara, Robert, 654
McNary-Haugen Bill (1927), 491
Macon's Bill No. 2 (1810), 177
McReynolds, James, 544
Madison, James, 122-23, 146-48, 152, 160, 167, 177, 192-93
Mahan, Alfred T., 406, 446
Mailer, Norman, 660
Maine, 252-53
Maine incident, 410
Malcolm, Daniel, 99
Malcolm X, 645
Manhattan Project, 617
Mann-Elkins Act (1910), 449
Mann, Horace, 234
March on Washington (1963), 642-45
Marshall, George Catlett, 576, 615

Marshall, John, 158, 164-67, 203, 209, 262
Marshall, Thurgood, 634
Marshall Plan, 597
Maryland, 296; colony, 25-26, 48, 51-52, 58
Mason-Dixon Line, 44
Massachusetts, 121; as colony, 27-33, 48-49, 51-52, 58, 70, 72, 94-95, 100, 103; (see also Revolutionary War)
Mayflower Compact, 27
Medicare program, 648
Mellon, Andrew, 476, 488, 490-91
Melville, Herman, 244-45
Mencken, H. L., 505
Mercantilism, 40, 63, 81-83
Meredith, James, 642
Mexican Americans, 632-34
Mexican War, 254-58
Mexico, 198, 212-15, 254, 460-61, 466, 535; Revolution, 632
Millerites, 227
Minuet, Peter, 42
Missouri Compromise (1820), 194, 215, 268, 274-75, 278, 294-95
Mitchell, John (U.M.W.), 444
Mitchell, John (Attorney General), 669
Molasses Act (1733), 63, 94
Moley, Raymond, 532
Monroe, James, 167, 173, 192-94, 196-97, 199
Monroe Doctrine, 198-201, 483; Roosevelt corollary of, 446
Montgomery bus boycott, 621, 641
Morgan, Arthur, 556
Morgan, J. P., 356, 443, 452, 572
Mormons, 229-30
Morrill Land Grant Act (1862), 314, 379
Morris, Gouverneur, 122-23
Morris, Robert, 118, 122
Morris, Nelson, 356
Mott, Lucretia, 234
Muscle Shoals project, 491
Myrdal, Gunnar, 590-91

Napoleonic Wars, 175-77, 184
Nashville Convention, 269, 271
NAACP, 457, 555-56, 590, 634, 640, 645
NATO (see Treaties)
National Association of Manufacturers, 433
National banks, 153, 180, 190, 193, 201, 203, 206, 253, 313, 387-88; and Bank War, 220-21
National Federation of Women's Clubs, 433
National health insurance plan, 605
National Housing Act (1949), 605
National Industrial Recovery Act (1933), 529-31, 548
National Labor Relations Act (1938), 542

National Organization of Women, 661
National Recovery Administration, 530-31, 539, 545
National Republican party, 205
National Security Council, 608, 664
National Union for Social Justice, 538
Nat Turner's Rebellion, 215-16, 260
Navigation laws, 40, 49, 52, 58, 63
Neibuhr, Reinhold, 606
Netherlands, 76, 114, 119, 141
Neutrality Act (1935), 510, 558-59
Neutrality Act (1937), 562
New Deal, 513-14, 583, 605, 630, 646; general principles of, 527-28, 531, 539, 547-48, 554-57; Supreme Court during, 544-47
New Freedom, 450
New Jersey, 126; as colony, 42, 52
New Left, 657, 661-62
New Nationalism, 449-50
New Negro movement, 459
New York, 118, 128, 147, 167; as colony, 42, 51, 59, 94
Niagara Movement, 456-57
Nicaragua, 448, 460
Nimitz, Chester, 582
Nineteenth Amendment (1920), 502
Nixon, Richard M., 466, 615, 630, 638, 654-57, 663-71
Non-Intercourse Act (1807), 177, 181
Norris, Frank, 434
Norris, George, 449, 491, 528
Northern Securities case, 443
Northwest Ordinance (1787), 117
Noyes, John Humphrey, 232-33, 264
Nye Committee, 559

Office of Price Administration, 585
Office of Scientific Research and Development, 617
Ogelthorpe, James, 45
Ohio Company, 117
Omnibus Bill, 269-70
Oneida community, 232-33
Open Door policy, 419-20, 460, 486, 573
Oppenheimer, J. Robert, 617
Oregon Territory, 197, 199, 202, 254
Otis, James, 90, 94
Overseas Expansion, 406-10, 415, 419
Owen, Robert Dale, 230

Pacifism, 234, 462-63, 652-55, 658
Paine, Thomas, 85-87, 105, 114, 130
Palmer, A. Mitchell, 479-82, 487
Panama Canal, 447
Panama Conference, 200-201
Panay incident, 573
Parker, Alton B., 444
Parks, Rosa, 641
Parliament, 40, 49, 90, 92, 98-99, 102, 105
Paxton Boys, 91

Peace Corps, 640, 646
Peirce, Charles Sanders, 434
Pelley, William Dudley, 535
Pendleton Act (1883), 377
Penn, William, 43-44
Pennsylvania, 116, 118, 141, 153, 167; as colony, 43-44, 52, 57, 59, 71, 91
Pentagon Papers, 654-55
People's party, 378, 392-93, 399, 401
Pequot War, 10
Perkins, Frances, 367
Pershing, John J., 461, 467
Philippines, 412, 418, 533-34, 568, 581-82
Pickering, John, 165
Pierce, Franklin, 247, 274-75, 277, 297
Pilgrims, 27
Pinchot, Gilbert A., 449
Pinckney, Charles C., 158, 161, 170, 177
Pinckney, Thomas, 149, 158
Pingree, Hazen, 439
Plantation Duty Act (1673), 49
Platt Amendment (1901), 418, 534
Plymouth Company, 20-21
Poe, Edgar Allan, 236
Polk, James Knox, 254-58, 268
Pontiac, 92
Popular sovereignty principle, 268, 274, 279
Populists (see People's party)
Port Huron Statement, 657
Portsmouth Conference, 446
Post, Louis F., 482
Powderly, Terence V., 360
Powell, Adam Clayton, Sr. and Jr., 455-56
Powhatan, 9, 22
Princeton University, 71
Proclamation Act (1763), 92
Progressive movement, 430-41, 449, 454-59, 468-69, 490-91
Progressive party (1912), 450
Progressive party (1948), 604
Prohibition, 234, 249, 496-98
Public Law 78 (1951), 634
Public Utilities Holding Companies Act (1935), 541
Public Works Administration, 528, 547, 555
Puerto Rico, 415, 418
Pujo Committee, 452
Pulitzer, Joseph, 372, 409
Pullman, George, 494-95
Pullman strike, 398
Puritanism, 26-33, 37-38, 73, 91

Quakers, 73
Quartering Act (1765), 92
Queen Anne's War, 76

Race riots, 479-80, 590, 645, 648
Railroads, 225, 351, 353, 355; and government aid, 313-14
Randolph, A. Philip, 590

Tariffs (cont.)
Compromise of 1833, 218; Morrill (1861), 313; McKinley (1890), 387; Wilson-Gorman (1894), 396; Payne-Aldrich (1909), 449; Underwood (1913), 452; Fordney-McCumber (1922), 491; Smoot-Hawley (1930), 512; Trade Agreements Act (1934), 533
Taylor, Frederick, 509-10
Taylor, Zachary, 255, 257, 268, 270
Tea Act (1773), 102
Teapot Dome scandal, 489
Tecumseh, 177, 180, 183-84
Teller, Henry M., 399
Temperance movement (see Prohibition)
Tennent brothers, 74
Tennessee Valley Authority, 529, 556, 605, 648
Texas, 198, 212-25, 253-54, 257, 269
Thirteenth Amendment (1865), 322
Thomas, Norman, 571
Thoreau, Henry, 244-45, 257, 266
Thurmond, J. Strom, 604
Tilden, Samuel J., 331, 334
Tillman, Ben, 396
Tocqueville, Alexis de, 235
Tonnage Act (1798), 151
Toombs, Robert, 300
Townsend, Francis, 538, 543
Townshend duties, 98-100
Transcendentalism, 247
Treaties: Adams-Onís (1819), 197-98, 212; Aix-la-Chapelle (1748), 77; Commerce and Navigation (Japan), 574; Convention (1818), 202; Franco-American Alliance (1778), 108, 110-11, 147-50, 158, 161; Guadelupe-Hidalgo (1848), 258; Hay-Pauncefote (1901), 447; Jay's (1794), 149-50; Kellogg-Briand Pact (1928), 486, 514; Lansing-Ishii Agreement (1917), 460; NATO (1949), 607, 624, 626-27; nuclear test ban (1963), 639, 657; Oregon boundary (1846), 254; Paris (1763), 77; Paris (1783), 111, 119; Paris peace talks (1968-73), 654; Peace of Ghent (1814), 181-82; Pinckney's (1795), 149, 172; reciprocal trade agreements (1930s), 533; Rush-Bagot (1817), 202; strategic arms limitation (1972), 663; Versailles (1919), 482-84, 513, 559; Washington agreements (1921), 486, 515, 561; Webster-Ashburton (1842), 253; Indian treaties, 182-84, 212
Trist, Nicholas, 258
Trollope, Frances, 235
Trotter, William Monroe, 455
Truman, Harry S., 568-69, 591, 595-97, 599-611, 615, 617, 626, 641
Truman Doctrine, 597
Tugwell, Rexford G., 556-57, 603

Turner, Frederick Jackson, 367
Turner, Nat, 215-16, 230
Tuskeegee Institute, 370
Twain, Mark, 343, 373
Tweed, William M. "Boss," 364
Tydings-Mc Duffie Act (1934), 534
Tyler, John, 253-54, 294

Underground railroad, 266
Union League clubs, 376
Union party (1936), 543
Unitarianism, 73, 244
United Mine Workers, 444, 542
United Nations, 582, 592, 609, 663-64
U.S. Housing Authority, 541
U.S. Sanitary Commission, 304
United States Steel Corporation, 443, 640
Universal Negro Improvement Association, 459
Urban League, 640

Vallandigham, Clement, 316-17
Van Buren, Martin, 195, 204-6, 217, 254, 268
Vandenburg, Arthur, 608
Van Devanter, Willis, 544-46
Veblen, Thorstein, 373
Venezuela dispute, 408
Vesey, Denmark, 215
Vietnam War, 622, 633, 639, 646, 648, 650, 652, 654-56, 667, 669-70
Virginia, 116, 128, 142, 194, 215, 296; as colony, 21-25, 46, 57-58, 71, 77, 90
Virginia and Kentucky Resolutions (1798), 160
VISTA program, 646
Voting laws (suffrage), 195, 204, 440

Wade-Davis Bill (1864), 324
Wagner, Robert F., 542
Walker, David, 215
Wallace, George, 604, 656, 669
Wallace, Henry, 488, 596-97, 604
War Hawks, 180
War Industries Board, 469
War of 1812, 144, 177, 180-84
War on Poverty, 646, 648
War Trade Board, 469
Warehouse Act (1916), 454
Warren, Earl, 588, 603, 634-36, 656
Warsaw Pact, 626-27
Washington, Booker T., 370, 372, 454-59
Washington, George, 58, 77, 85, 87, 92, 113, 116, 122-23, 128, 140, 146, 156-67, 192; and foreign relations, 148-50; in Revolution, 107-11
Washington Arms Conference, 486, 514
Washington Peace Conference (1861), 294
Watergate scandal, 668-69

Wayne, Anthony, 177
"Wealth Tax" (1935), 541
Webster, Daniel, 206, 220, 253, 268, 270-71
Webster, Noah, 139
Weld, Theodore D., 233, 242, 264-65
Welfare capitalism, 494-95
Whig party, 204-8, 253, 271, 274, 276, 322
Whiskey Rebellion, 153, 156
White, Walter, 555
White, William Allen, 572
White Citizen's Councils, 641
Whitefield, George, 74
Whitman, Walt, 244-47, 291-92
Whitney, Eli, 135-37
Wilkes, John, 100
Willkie, Wendell, 571
Wilson, Henry, 277, 284-85
Wilson, James, 105, 122
Wilson, Woodrow, 144, 317, 428, 450, 455, 480, 559, 562; foreign policy principles of, 459-60, 463-69; and League of Nations, 482-84, 487; Presidency of, to 1916, 451-54
William and Mary, 51-52, 76
William and Mary College, 71
Williams, Roger, 29-30
Wilmot Proviso, 267
Winthrop, John, 28, 58, 68, 144, 466
Wirt, William, 205
Witchcraft trials, 74
Women's rights movement, 234-35, 265, 365; (see also National Organization of Women)
Wood, Leonard, 487
Wood, Robert E., 571
Woodstock festival, 64, 659
Wool Act (1699), 63
Works Progress Administration, 540, 547, 555
World Court, 558
World Disarmament Conference, 559
World War I, 349, 461-66, 469-70, 571, 585-86, 611; U.S. military in, 467; revisionist historians, 559; U.S. loans, 467; (see also Debt Moratorium)
World War II, 570-82, 586, 588-89, 590-91, 595, 626, 629, 634, 650, 660; Japanese-American internment during, 586-88; Normandy invasion in, 579; U.S. economy in, 583-85
Wright, Frank Lloyd, 434

X, Y, Z affair, 158, 161, 175

Yale University, 71
Yalta Conference, 595, 611
Young, Brigham, 230

Zimmerman telegram, 466

704